The Story of God Bible Commentary Series Endorsements

"Getting a story is about more than merely enjoying it. It means hearing it, understanding it, and above all, being impacted by it. This commentary series hopes that its readers not only hear and understand the story, but are impacted by it to live in as Christian a way as possible. The editors and contributors set that table very well and open up the biblical story in ways that move us to act with sensitivity and understanding. That makes hearing the story as these authors tell it well worth the time. Well done."

Darrell L. Bock

Dallas Theological Seminary

"The Story of God Bible Commentary series invites readers to probe how the message of the text relates to our situations today. Engagingly readable, it not only explores the biblical text but offers a range of applications and interesting illustrations."

Craig S. Keener

Asbury Theological Seminary

"I love The Story of God Bible Commentary series. It makes the text sing, and helps us hear the story afresh."

John Ortberg

Senior Pastor of Menlo Park Presbyterian Church

"In this promising new series of commentaries, believing biblical scholars bring not only their expertise but their own commitment to Jesus and insights into today's culture to the Scriptures. The result is a commentary series that is anchored in the text but lives and breathes in the world of today's church with its variegated pattern of socioeconomic, ethnic, and national diversity. Pastors, Bible study leaders, and Christians of all types who are looking for a substantive and practical guide through the Scriptures will find these volumes helpful."

Frank Thielman

Beeson Divinity School

"The Story of God Bible Commentary series is unique in its approach to exploring the Bible. Its easy-to-use format and practical guidance brings God's grand story to modern-day life so anyone can understand how it applies today."

Andy Stanley

North Point Ministries

"I'm a storyteller. Through writing and speaking I talk and teach about understanding the Story of God throughout Scripture and about letting God reveal more of His story as I live it out. Thus I am thrilled to have a commentary series based on the Story of God—a commentary that helps me to Listen to the Story, that Explains the Story, and then encourages me to probe how to Live the Story. A perfect tool for helping every follower of Jesus to walk in the story that God is writing for them."

Judy Douglass

Director of Women's Resources, Cru

"The Bible is the story of God and his dealings with humanity from creation to new creation. The Bible is made up more of stories than of any other literary genre. Even the psalms, proverbs, prophecies, letters, and the Apocalypse make complete sense only when set in the context of the grand narrative of the entire Bible. This commentary series breaks new ground by taking all these observations seriously. It asks commentators to listen to the text, to explain the text, and to live the text. Some of the material in these sections overlaps with introduction, detailed textual analysis, and application, respectively, but only some. The most riveting and valuable part of the commentaries are the stories that can appear in any of these sections, from any part of the globe and any part of church history, illustrating the text in any of these areas. Ideal for preaching and teaching."

Craig L. Blomberg

Denver Seminary

"Pastors and lay people will welcome this new series, which seeks to make the message of the Scriptures clear and to guide readers in appropriating biblical texts for life today."

Daniel I. Block

Wheaton College and Graduate School

"An extremely valuable, and long overdue series that includes comment on the cultural context of the text, careful exegesis, and guidance on reading the whole Bible as a unity that testifies to Christ as our Savior and Lord."

Graeme Goldsworthy

author of *According to Plan*

MATTHEW

The Story of God Bible Commentary

MATTHEW

Rodney Reeves

Tremper Longman III & Scot McKnight
General Editors

ZONDERVAN ACADEMIC

ZONDERVAN ACADEMIC

Matthew

Published by Zondervan, 3950 Sparks Drive SE, Suite 101, Grand Rapids, MI 49546, USA. Zondervan is a registered trademark of The Zondervan Corporation, L.L.C., a wholly owned subsidiary of HarperCollins Christian Publishing, Inc.

Requests for information should be addressed to customercare@harpercollins.com.

Zondervan titles may be purchased in bulk for educational, business, fundraising, or sales promotional use. For information, please email SpecialMarkets@Zondervan.com.

ISBN 978-0-310-32714-1 (hardcover)
ISBN 978-0-310-53779-3 (ebook)

HarperCollins Publishers, Macken House, 39/40 Mayor Street Upper, Dublin 1, D01 C9W8, Ireland (https://www.harpercollins.com)

Cover design: Ron Huizinga
Cover image: iStockphoto®
Interior composition: Kait Lamphere

Printed in the United States of America

26 27 28 29 30 31 32 33 34 35 36 /TRM/ 15 14 13 12 11 10 9 8 7 6 5 4 3 2

Dedicated to
Prof. James A. Brooks,
my father in the academy

and to the memory of
Rev. Thomas M. McClain
(1927–2011),
my father in ministry

Old Testament series

1 ■ Genesis—*Tremper Longman III*
2 ■ Exodus—*Christopher J. H. Wright*
3 ■ Leviticus—*Jerry E. Shepherd*
4 ■ Numbers—*Jay A. Sklar*
5 ■ Deuteronomy—*Myrto Theocharous*
6 ■ Joshua—*Lissa M. Wray Beal*
7 ■ Judges—*Athena E. Gorospe*
8 ■ Ruth/Esther—*Marion Taylor*
9 ■ 1–2 Samuel—*Paul S. Evans*
10 ■ 1–2 Kings—*David T. Lamb*
11 ■ 1–2 Chronicles—*Carol M. Kaminski and Christine Palmer*
12 ■ Ezra/Nehemiah—*Douglas J. Green*
13 ■ Job—*Martin A. Shields*
14 ■ Psalms—*Elizabeth R. Hayes*
15 ■ Proverbs—*Ryan P. O'Dowd*
16 ■ Ecclesiastes/Song of Songs—*George Athas*
17 ■ Isaiah—*Mark J. Boda*
18 ■ Jeremiah/Lamentations—*Andrew G. Shead*
19 ■ Ezekiel—*D. Nathan Phinney*
20 ■ Daniel—*Wendy L. Widder*
21 ■ Minor Prophets I—*Beth M. Stovell*
22 ■ Minor Prophets II—*Beth M. Stovell*

New Testament series

1 ■ Matthew—*Rodney Reeves*
2 ■ Mark—*Timothy G. Gombis*
3 ■ Luke—*Kindalee Pfremmer DeLong*
4 ■ John—*Nicholas Perrin*
5 ■ Acts—*Dean Pinter*
6 ■ Romans—*Michael F. Bird*
7 ■ 1 Corinthians—*Justin K. Hardin*
8 ■ 2 Corinthians—*Judith A. Diehl*
9 ■ Galatians—*Nijay K. Gupta*
10 ■ Ephesians—*Mark D. Roberts*
11 ■ Philippians—*Lynn H. Cohick*
12 ■ Colossians/Philemon—*Todd Wilson*
13 ■ 1, 2 Thessalonians—*John Byron*
14 ■ 1, 2 Timothy, Titus—*Marius Nel*
15 ■ Hebrews—*Radu Gheorghita*
16 ■ James—*Mariam J. Kamell*
17 ■ 1 Peter—*Dennis R. Edwards*
18 ■ 2 Peter, Jude—*C. Rosalee Velloso Ewell*
19 ■ 1, 2, & 3 John—*Constantine R. Campbell*
20 ■ Revelation—*Jonathan A. Moo*
21 ■ Sermon on the Mount—*Scot McKnight*

Contents

Acknowledgments 11
The Story of God Bible Commentary Series 12
Abbreviations 15
Introduction to Matthew 16
Resources for Teaching and Preaching 37
1. Matthew 1:1–17 39
2. Matthew 1:18–2:23 51
3. Matthew 3:1–17 64
4. Matthew 4:1–22 78
5. Matthew 4:23–5:16 95
6. Matthew 5:17–48 109
7. Matthew 6:1–18 123
8. Matthew 6:19–7:12 135
9. Matthew 7:13–8:1 149
10. Matthew 8:2–17 160
11. Matthew 8:18–34 171
12. Matthew 9:1–17 184
13. Matthew 9:18–34 197
14. Matthew 9:35–11:1 208
15. Matthew 11:2–30 222
16. Matthew 12:1–21 238
17. Matthew 12:22–50 249
18. Matthew 13:1–52 261
19. Matthew 13:53–14:21 276

20. Matthew 14:22–36 288
21. Matthew 15:1–20 300
22. Matthew 15:21–39 311
23. Matthew 16:1–20 322
24. Matthew 16:21–17:13 334
25. Matthew 17:14–27 347
26. Matthew 18:1–35 356
27. Matthew 19:1–12 372
28. Matthew 19:13–20:16 380
29. Matthew 20:17–34 394
30. Matthew 21:1–22 404
31. Matthew 21:23–22:14 418
32. Matthew 22:15–46 433
33. Matthew 23:1–39 447
34. Matthew 24:1–25:46 462
35. Matthew 26:1–30 483
36. Matthew 26:31–56 498
37. Matthew 26:57–75 511
38. Matthew 27:1–26 525
39. Matthew 27:27–66 539
40. Matthew 28:1–20 556
Scripture Index 569
Subject Index 597
Author Index 615

Acknowledgments

First and foremost, thanks to Scot McKnight for the invitation to contribute to this important and unique commentary series. To me, Scot embodies the best of Christian scholarship—bridging academic study and service to the church. He is a rare gift, a generous spirit with an erudite mind and a kind heart, and a committed disciple of Jesus Christ. It was a great source of encouragement to have such an outstanding Matthean scholar looking over my shoulder as I worked on this commentary. His perceptive comments, coupled with the insightful, "open-hearted" critique of another superb Matthean scholar, Joel Willitts, were incredibly helpful to me. Truly, they are brothers in Christ, great gifts of the Lord for his church. Thanks also to Katya Covrett (executive editor) and Christopher Beetham (senior production editor) for their expertise, improving the quality of the work beyond measure.

I'm thankful for friends and family who read parts of the manuscript. It dawned on me toward the end of my work that, since this commentary series is written primarily for ministers of the gospel of Jesus Christ, it might be a good idea to get feedback from those who are serving the church today. Thanks to Vernon Burger, Danny Chisolm, Timothy Howe, and Billy Russell for their comments and words of encouragement. Also, thanks to Andrew Reeves for his kind words and permission to use his work. Finally, I am especially grateful to my wife, Sheri, for her generous gift of time in reading the entire manuscript. Sheri has a keen eye for spotting infelicities and vagaries, making helpful suggestions to iron out the wrinkles. And, just as important to me, her words of encouragement often came at the moment I needed them the most. It meant the world to me when, having read a section, she would say, "This is my favorite part."

To God be the glory.

The Story of God Bible Commentary Series

The word of God may not change, but culture does. Think of what we have seen in the last twenty years: we now communicate predominantly through the internet and email; we read our news on iPads and computers; we can talk on the phone to our friends while we are driving, while we are playing golf, while we are taking long walks; and we can get in touch with others from the middle of nowhere. We carry in our hands small devices that connect us to the world and to a myriad of sources of information. Churches have changed; the "Nones" are rising in numbers and volume, and atheists are bold to assert their views in public forums. The days of home Bible studies are waning; there is a marked rise in activist missional groups in churches, and pastors are more and more preaching topical sermons, some of which are not directly connected to the Bible. Divorce rates are not going down, marriages are more stressed, rearing children is more demanding, and civil unions and same-sex marriages are knocking at the door of the church.

Progress can be found in many directions. While church attendance numbers are waning in Europe and North America, churches are growing in the South and the East. More and more women are finding a voice in churches; the plea of the former generation of leaders that Christians be concerned not just with evangelism but with justice is being answered today in new and vigorous ways. Resources for studying the Bible are more available today than ever before, and preachers and pastors are meeting the challenge of speaking a sure word of God into shifting cultures.

Readers of the Bible change, too. These cultural shifts, our own personal developments, the progress in intellectual questions, as well as growth in biblical studies and theology and discoveries of new texts and new paradigms for understanding the contexts of the Bible—each of these elements works on an interpreter so that the person who reads the Bible today asks different questions from different angles.

Culture shifts, but the word of God remains. That is why we as editors of The Story of God Bible Commentary series, a commentary based on the New International Version 2011 (NIV 2011), are excited to participate in this new series of commentaries on the Bible. This series is designed to address this generation with the same word of God. We are asking the authors to explain what the Bible says to the sorts of readers who pick up commentaries so they can understand not only what Scripture says but what it means for today. The Bible does not change, but relating it to our culture changes constantly and in differing ways in different contexts.

When we, the New Testament editors, sat down in prayer and discussion to choose authors for this series, we realized we had found fertile ground. Our list of potential authors staggered in length and quality. We wanted the authors to be exceptional scholars, faithful Christians, committed evangelicals, and theologically diverse, and we wanted this series to represent the changing face of both American and world evangelicalism: ethnic and gender diversity. I believe this series has a wider diversity of authors than any commentary series in evangelical history.

The title of this series, emphasizing as it does the "Story" of the Bible, reveals the intent of the series. We want to explain each passage of the Bible in light of the Bible's grand Story. The Bible's grand Story, of course, connects this series to the classic expression *regula fidei*, the "rule of faith," which was the Bible's story coming to fulfillment in Jesus as the Messiah, Lord, and Savior of all. In brief, we see the narrative built around the following biblical themes: creation and fall, covenant and redemption, law and prophets, and especially God's charge to humans as his image-bearers to rule under God. The theme of God as King and God's kingdom guides us to see the importance of Israel's kings as they come to fulfillment in Jesus, Lord and King over all, and the direction of history toward the new heavens and new earth, where God will be all in all. With these guiding themes, each passage is examined from three angles.

Listen to the Story. We believe that if the Bible is God speaking, then the most important posture of the Christian before the Bible is to listen. So our first section cites the text of Scripture and lists a selection of important biblical and sometimes noncanonical parallels; then each author introduces that passage. The introductions to the passages sometimes open up discussion to the theme of the passage while other times they tie this passage to its context in the specific book. But since the focus of this series is the Story of God in the Bible, the introduction leads the reader into reading this text in light of the Bible's Story.

Explain the Story. The authors follow up listening to the text by explaining each passage in light of the Bible's grand Story. This is not an academic series, so the footnotes are limited to the kinds of texts typical Bible readers and preachers readily will have on hand. Authors are given the freedom to explain the text as they read it, though you should not be surprised to find occasional listings of other options for reading the text. Authors explore biblical backgrounds, historical context, cultural codes, and theological interpretations. Authors engage in word studies and interpret unique phrases and clauses as they attempt to build a sound and living reading of the text in light of the Story of God in the Bible.

Authors will not shy away from problems in the texts. Whether one is examining the meaning of "perfect" in Matthew 5:48, the problems with Christology in the hymn of Philippians 2:6–11, the challenge of understanding Paul in light of the swirling debates about the old, new, and post-new perspectives, the endless debates about eschatology, or the vagaries of atonement theories, the authors will dive in, discuss evidence, and do their best to sort out a reasonable and living reading of those issues for the church today.

Live the Story. Reading the Bible is not just about discovering what it meant back then; the intent of The Story of God Bible Commentary series is to probe how this text might be lived out today as that story continues to march on in the life of the church. At times our authors will tell stories about what this looks like; at other times they may offer some suggestions for living it out; but always you will discover the struggle involved as we seek to live out the Bible's grand Story in our world.

We are not offering suggestions for "application" so much as digging deeper; we are concerned in this section with seeking out how this text, in light of the Story of God in the Bible, compels us to live in our world so that our own story lines up with the Bible's Story.

Scot McKnight, general editor New Testament
Lynn Cohick, Joel Willitts, and Michael Bird, editors

Abbreviations

1 En.	1 Enoch
2 En.	2 Enoch
ABRL	Anchor Bible Reference Library
ACCS	Ancient Christian Commentary on Scripture
BDAG	Danker, Frederick W., Walter Bauer, William F. Arndt, and F. Wilbur Gingrich. *Greek-English Lexicon of the New Testament and Other Early Christian Literature*. 3rd ed. Chicago: University of Chicago Press, 2000.
BECNT	Baker Exegetical Commentary on the New Testament
DJG	Green, Joel B., Jeannine K. Brown, and Nicholas Perrin, eds. *Dictionary of Jesus and the Gospels*. 2nd ed. Downers Grove, IL: InterVarsity Press, 2013.
ICC	International Critical Commentary
Jub.	Jubilees
JSNTSup	Journal for the Study of the New Testament Supplement Series
JTS	*Journal of Theological Studies*
LAE	Life of Adam and Eve
LNTS	The Library of New Testament Studies
LXX	The Greek Old Testament (Septuagint)
m.	Mishnah
NAC	New American Commentary
NASB	New American Standard Bible
NCBC	New Cambridge Bible Commentary
NICNT	New International Commentary on the New Testament
NIGTC	New International Greek Testament Commentary
NRSV	New Revised Standard Version
NSBT	New Studies in Biblical Theology
NTS	*New Testament Studies*
SGBC	The Story of God Bible Commentary
Sir	Sirach
SNTSMS	Society for New Testament Studies Monograph Series
TNIV	Today's New International Version
T. Sol.	Testament of Solomon
WBC	Word Biblical Commentary
Wis	Wisdom of Solomon
ZECNT	Zondervan Exegetical Commentary on the New Testament

Introduction

In his commentary on Matthew, R. T. France accuses scholars of focusing on the introductory, critical matters of the work while ignoring the lengthier, expositional part of the commentary.[1] I wonder if the inverse is true for ministers and teachers. When I was a pastor, facing the weekly demands of preaching and teaching the Bible, I don't think I ever read a commentary from the beginning. Rather, I would skip over the critical issues that scholars love to discuss in the introduction and go straight to the exposition of the text. Teasing out the implications of the sources Matthew used for a particular episode, determining the authenticity of a particular saying of Jesus, or sorting out the arguments of Matthew's historical readers had little to no impact on the meaning of the text. In other words, the things that scholars say students are supposed to care about had nothing to do with what I, the preacher, cared about when it came to standing before a congregation to declare, "Thus saith the Lord."

But then again, shouldn't some of these questions matter to the preacher? For example, on the most basic level Jesus doesn't say the exact same thing when we compare his sayings in Matthew with the other Gospels. (None of us appreciate being misquoted or mistranslated.) The same event can show up in different places in the Gospels, each writer setting forth a different chronology from the other. (Getting the facts right is crucial to determining what happened.) And, in light of these differences, why do we have four Gospels? Was it really necessary? Wouldn't the church have been better off not having to deal with these differences, instead having one Gospel that covered it all? Evidently the early church didn't think so, for after the first Gospel was written (Mark?) other writers decided to offer their accounts of Christ too. So, why did Matthew write his Gospel? Did he believe Mark's was inadequate? And if that was the case, why did he use Mark as a source for his Gospel (especially since Mark *wasn't* a disciple of Jesus, and Matthew *was* one of the Twelve)? Was Matthew writing for a different kind of reader, one that Mark's Gospel didn't relate to? ("I can't get into Mark's version, but I really like Matthew's Gospel.") Don't we all do that, preferring one Gospel over the other three (most evangelical lay people I meet love John)? So, what makes Matthew's Gospel unique? And, shouldn't we appreciate Matthew's version on its own terms, even though some of us may prefer the Gospel according to John?

1. R. T. France, *The Gospel of Matthew*, NICNT (Grand Rapids: Eerdmans, 2007), 1.

All of these questions matter to the preacher and teacher. Even though we may teach or preach from a particular passage in Matthew's Gospel, we know we can't make sense of the part without the whole. And since we have three other Gospels with which to compare and contrast it, we can't help but ask, "Why did Matthew tell the story like *that*?" and "Why did Matthew put that episode *there*?" and "Why did Matthew include *that bit of information* when no other Gospel writer did?" In fact, without Mark, Luke, and John we wouldn't ask many of these questions. And yet, even if we had only Matthew's Gospel, there are certain questions any reader would ask about any piece of literature: Who? What? When? Where? Why? How? Since we are reading more than a literary work—we believe we are reading the word of God—then answers to these questions are even more relevant. For the Gospel of Matthew isn't just a story to be believed or discounted, to entertain or inspire, or to hear or perhaps admire. Rather, Matthew presents what he thinks is a "hold-on-this-changes-everything-because-it's-a-real-life" account about a flesh-and-blood person, Jesus the Christ—a man who lived at a particular time, in a particular place, of a particular people, who did some amazing things and taught some peculiar ideas, who was rejected by religious leaders and executed by governing officials, who was raised from the dead, and who inspired several men and women to carry on with his mission. In other words, Jesus was more than a man. According to Matthew, Jesus is the very Son of God, predestined to make good on every promise God made to his people, Israel, for the sake of the whole world. And, since all of these things happened in this world and for our world, answering the basic questions of life (who, what, when, where, why, and how) are especially *apropos*—not only for the first book of the New Testament but also for the entire word of God.

Who? Author and Audience

Unlike John's Gospel (John 21:24–25), there is no reference to the author of the first Gospel. And, unlike Luke (1:1–4), the author of our Gospel makes no reference to the recipient of his work and gives no explicit reason as to why he wrote it. But that doesn't mean the Gospel according to Matthew is odd. Of the four Gospels, not a single author identifies himself by name. And, even though Luke wrote his Gospel for a certain "Theophilus," some think he isn't the recipient of the Gospel. Rather, Theophilus was more than likely the patron who provided the funds to publish Luke's two-volume work.[2]

2. David E. Garland, *Luke*, ZECNT (Grand Rapids: Zondervan, 2011), 56.

So, since the first Gospel is technically anonymous and his intended audience isn't identified, how do we go about answering the first question, "Who?"

Regarding authorship, we could rely on church tradition, which assigned the first book of the New Testament to Matthew fairly early—at least by the end of the first century.[3] That's why the earliest extant manuscripts of the Greek New Testament ascribe the Gospel to Matthew. But scholars over the last two hundred years have questioned church tradition, especially when it comes to the authorship of certain books like Matthew's Gospel. Since apostolic reputation was key to books being accepted as Scripture by the early church, some wonder whether anonymous works ascribed to famous followers of Christ were actually penned by them. Looking more carefully at the Gospel according to Matthew, scholars question whether a Galilean disciple of Jesus could have (would have?) written his Gospel in Greek. There was a very early tradition among the church fathers that Matthew actually produced a collection of the teachings of Jesus in Aramaic.[4] But there is little evidence that what lies behind the Greek version of Matthew is an Aramaic Gospel.[5] A few scholars have suggested that we've misunderstood the tradition: it is not that Matthew wrote his sayings source in the Hebrew dialect (Aramaic) but that he arranged his Gospel in a Hebraic way[6]; for example, his fondness for arranging the material in twos, threes, and sevens.[7] But, even if that were the case, why would Matthew (an eyewitness of the life and times of Jesus of Nazareth) rely upon Mark's Gospel as a source (as most scholars infer) for his "Jewish" arrangement of the material? Mark wasn't an apostle, so why did Matthew use Mark?

Some think that is the wrong inference. A few scholars argue it's the other way around: Mark used Matthew. But that raises other problems. Why would Mark cut out important material (like the infancy narrative, the Sermon on the Mount, and perhaps the resurrection appearances) in order to have enough room to add unnecessary details to the same stories? (The length of our Gospels is the maximum size for a document written on a papyrus roll.) Scholars who recognize Marcan priority and defend Matthean authorship point to another church tradition that may explain why Matthew used Mark. The same church father who claimed that Matthew wrote the sayings of Jesus in the Hebrew dialect also goes to great lengths to explain how Peter was the

3. See W. D. Davies and Dale C. Allison Jr., *The Gospel according to Saint Matthew*, 3 vols., ICC (London: T&T Clark, 1988–97), 1:7–8.

4. Craig A. Evans, *Matthew*, NCBC (New York: Cambridge University Press, 2012), 1–3.

5. Craig S. Keener, *A Commentary on the Gospel of Matthew* (Grand Rapids: Eerdmans, 1999), 38–39; Craig L. Blomberg, *Matthew*, NAC (Nashville: Broadman & Holman, 1992), 40.

6. Evans, *Matthew*, 2–3.

7. For a lengthy list of examples, see Davies and Allison, *Matthew*, 1:85–87.

actual "author" of Mark's Gospel. Serving as his secretary, Mark wrote down Peter's recollections and didn't arrange the material as deliberately as Matthew. So, in light of Peter's important role in the early church—something Matthew highlights in his Gospel—it would make sense that Matthew would use Mark's Gospel, especially since Matthew didn't become a disciple of Jesus until much later (Matt 9:9).[8] And, I can't help but wonder if some of our modern sensibilities about ownership of intellectual property, the reservations we have about derivative work, and the taboos associated with plagiarism jaundice our view of what we consider credible authorship. In a world that prized honor and community identity, perhaps it would add credibility to Matthew's work that he didn't rely upon himself to author the most important story ever written. Besides, if the early church simply pulled an apostolic name out of the hat in order to add credibility to this Gospel, why didn't they ascribe it to a bigger name, like James, Andrew, Philip, or any of the top six names listed in Matthew 10:2–3 (Matthew comes in eighth)?[9]

So, who wrote the Gospel according to Matthew? If we believe church tradition, the "eighth" disciple of Jesus did. If we don't accept church tradition, then we have no idea. And the truth of the matter is that no argument carries the day, whether for or against Matthean authorship.[10] I lean toward accepting church tradition on this matter. Nevertheless, whether we believe Matthew wrote it or not, there's still more to learn about who wrote the first canonical Gospel from the "implied author." The implied author (whom we will call "Matthew") is derived from information we glean about him[11] when reading his work, whether from his literary style or even the content he chose to include or ignore. Of course, what helps us see the distinctiveness of his work is when we compare Matthew to the other three Gospels. And, although he follows the same general chronology as the other synoptic Gospels, Matthew's preferences are revealed by his arrangement of the material (sometimes he breaks from the synoptic order) and the way he tells the story—what he chooses to emphasize. Consider, for example, the beginning of his Gospel. Who starts a narrative like that except a man who finds the genealogy of Jesus incredibly important to the claims he makes about his subject from the start (Matt 1:1)? And, why all the talk about fulfilled prophecy unless the Hebrew Scriptures were vitally important to the story of Jesus "the Messiah"? We've already mentioned Matthew's fondness for numbers

8. Blomberg, *Matthew*, 43–44.

9. Evans, *Matthew*, 3–4.

10. See Scot McKnight, *The Sermon on the Mount*, SGBC (Grand Rapids: Zondervan, 2013), 15–17.

11. Assuming a male author due to the male-dominant, first-century Mediterranean world.

(gematria), arranging material in groups of two, three, five, and seven—numbers with great symbolic meaning for Jewish people. Matthew also loves comparing Jesus to the heroes of Israel (typology), especially the giver of the law, Moses. The Pharisees play a heightened role as Jesus's primary antagonists. Jesus sends his disciples on their first "mission trip" to recover the lost sheep of Israel—no gentiles or Samaritans wanted (Matt 10:56). Our writer cares very much about Jewish matters: how the law is to be rightly interpreted (5:27–48; 19:3–9), obedience to those who sit in Moses's seat (23:2–3), hoping Judeans don't have to travel on the Sabbath when Jerusalem is judged by God (24:20), paying the temple tax (17:24–27), and what will happen to the unrepentant Galilean cities (11:20–24). Add it all up, and most scholars come to the conclusion that the implied author is a Jewish Christian who is out to prove that Jesus is the Messiah of God for whom Israel has been waiting a long, long time.[12]

But who would want (or need) to hear a story like that? Sorting out the historical readers of Matthew's Gospel proves to be more difficult than identifying the author. Church tradition gives us no clue (except location, which we'll discuss below). So, scholars are prone to pick out golden nuggets about the implied reader embedded in the Gospel in order to fashion the makeup of Matthew's community. It is a fairly speculative enterprise since we don't know Matthew's target reader, the exact audience Matthew was aiming at (the same is true for the other three Gospels). However, we know some things about the history of the early church (not only from Acts but other sources, especially the church fathers)—in particular that Jewish Christianity had a hard time maintaining its influence and identity in a sea of swelling numbers of gentile converts whipped about by a storm of controversy in the synagogues about Jesus. And so, putting it all together—a composite of the implied reader derived from a close reading of Matthew's Gospel situated within the historical context of early Christianity that was evolving from a Jewish movement to a worldwide gentile religion—scholars come up with this: Matthew's readers were probably Jewish Christians who were either recently driven out of the synagogue or were still worshiping God with kinsmen who didn't appreciate their brand of messianic Judaism because it revolved around Jesus. That explains why Matthew's implied readers seem to hold Jewish interests: they 1) knew the Hebrew Scriptures well, 2) wanted to see how Jesus fulfilled prophecy, 3) obeyed the law and, perhaps, respected the Pharisees, 4) followed Jewish customs yet were willing to criticize them, 4) supported the temple but were suspicious of its leadership, 5) were informed by Jewish eschatology

12. See the summary of the internal evidence in Davies and Allison, *Matthew*, 1:72–96.

(they especially anticipated the imminent day of the Lord), and 6) perhaps had some concerns about the gospel mission to the gentiles.[13] In other words, as Luz colorfully describes the assumptions Matthew made about his reader, "he has a Jewish 'encylopedia.'"[14] Thus, from author to reader Matthew is a very Jewish Gospel—probably written by a Jew for Jews.

What? Story and Sermon

The answer to this question should be simple enough. What is the book of Matthew? It's a Gospel. But what does the word "gospel" mean? Ask people, "What is the gospel?" and very few would say, "Matthew." (When I occasionally poll my students, who primarily come from evangelical churches, most often they say something like "the plan of salvation" or "the good news that Jesus paid the price for our sins." They rarely think of the entire literary work we call the Gospel according to Matthew.) Technically, Matthew is a narrative about the life and times of Jesus of Nazareth. Therefore, the first book of the New Testament could be called a *story* about Jesus according to Matthew. But some of us think the word "story" implies fiction. And yet we all know that Matthew is doing more than providing a history of Jesus. His work is an interpretation (some might even say, "biased interpretation") of the significance of Jesus. This isn't just about what Jesus did and said, but why it matters. So, is that the reason "Gospel" was applied to the first four books of the New Testament? It was a handy term that Mark used to introduce his work to the literary world (Mark 1:1), a title that seems to have been subsequently affixed to the other three "Gospels" as well.[15]

Of course, we see the problem right away. There is supposed to be only one gospel; Paul makes that very plain (Gal 1:6–9). And yet, we have *four* Gospels about Jesus, not to mention other perspectives on Christ that show up throughout the New Testament.[16] Evidently, in the parlance of the early church, the term "gospel" came to mean two things at once: the past details of Jesus's life and the present significance of his person and work (what

13. For a brief list of characteristics of the implied reader, see Ulrich Luz, *Matthew: A Commentary*, trans. James E. Crouch, 3 vols., Hermeneia (Minneapolis: Fortress, 2001–7), 1:15–16. For a helpful summary of the issues surrounding the identity of Matthew's community, see J. K. Brown, "Matthew," *DJG* 575–76.

14. Luz, *Matthew*, 1:16.

15. See Scot McKnight, "Matthew as 'Gospel,'" in *Jesus, Matthew's Gospel and Early Christianity: Studies in Memory of Graham N. Stanton*, ed. Daniel M. Gurtner, Joel Willitts, and Richard A. Burridge, LNTS 435 (London: T&T Clark International, 2011), 68.

16. See David B. Capes, Rodney Reeves, and E. Randolph Richards, *Rediscovering Jesus: An Introduction to Biblical, Religious and Cultural Perspectives on Christ* (Downers Grove, IL: IVP Academic, 2015).

theologians call "Christology").[17] So, the gospel is both a narrative and a message, a person and a theology, a source of faith and a way of life. Therefore, fittingly, the first four books of the New Testament came to be called "Gospels" because they serve a twofold purpose simultaneously: they are stories that preach,[18] narratives that work like sermons, accounts of the life of Jesus that inspire faith and discipleship. And, the way Matthew tells his story says as much about his view of Jesus as the effect he hopes his Gospel will have on his readers. According to Matthew, Jesus is God's Son who initiated the kingdom of heaven on earth. For readers who have eyes to see and auditors who have ears to hear, that means Jesus is the *last* king of Israel—the one who makes every promise of God come true. Therefore, those who see and hear will follow the king into his kingdom, the true reign of God that lasts forever. To say the least, this is not your average "life story."

So, is this type of work—that which came to be called "Gospel"—unique to the literary world? Some scholars think so because of the way the Gospels came to be. At first, there were individual stories about Jesus circulating among Christians in oral form; some intended to inspire faith in unbelievers, other material (especially the sayings of Jesus) meant to teach the church how to live as disciples of Jesus. Whatever their origin or purpose, early evangelists discovered that these gospel stories preach. Each episode is a unit that works by itself—a mini story with an introduction, setting, conflict, and resolution (we commonly call them "passages of Scripture"; scholars refer to them as pericopae). When the apostles started dying, someone decided these gospel stories needed to be written down. Thus, the literary "Gospel" was born. This wasn't an attempt to get on paper a biography of Jesus. In fact, some scholars say the Gospels do not rise to the level of the traditional Greco-Roman biography. Rather, the literary origin of the Gospel owes more to the evangelistic and catechetical needs of the early church. Therefore, some think "the Gospel" belongs to a brand new category of genre.[19] If a first-century custodian of the library in Alexandria, Egypt were to come across a copy of the Gospel according to Matthew, he would have to shelve it by itself.

In the last few decades, however, a scholarly consensus has formed around the conclusion that in fact the four Gospels do classify as ancient biography. They are very similar in form, style, and content to Greco-Roman biographies written about the same time.[20] These ancient *bioi* ("lives") may not conform

---

17. Graham N. Stanton, *The Gospels and Jesus* (Oxford: Oxford University Press, 1989), 6.

18. John Nolland, *The Gospel of Matthew: A Commentary on the Greek Text*, NIGTC (Grand Rapids: Eerdmans, 2005), 20.

19. See Stanton, *Gospels and Jesus*, 15–30.

20. See the article by R. A. Burridge, "Gospel: Genre," *DJG*, 337–41.

to our standards of modern biography (including a presupposed "distance" between the author and subject to preserve an attempt at objectivity),[21] but like our literary Gospels they share several generic features common to Greco-Roman biography.[22] Of course, that the Jews did not produce biographies about their famous rabbis means that Jesus would have been the first Jewish subject to be featured in this way—which makes perfect sense, since the absence of rabbinic *bioi* may prove that such a work would have been at odds with the primacy of the Torah as *the* subject of study. Since Jesus, according to Matthew, made himself the final interpretation of the law ("follow me!"), then it would follow that his disciples would write a story that featured him as the focal point of study. Indeed, according to Matthew it was Jesus's life and work that defined righteousness. To obey him in word and deed is to follow him: the fulfillment of the law and the prophets. And, this may reveal a unique feature of the Gospels compared to standard ancient biographies. The story of Jesus is also a sermon; he is not only a subject to study but a life to imitate. Therefore, since the early church considered the life and times of Jesus of Nazareth the most important message the world would ever hear, it's no wonder they wanted more than one Gospel.

When?

Even though Matthew teases us with a vague reference to his time—a rumor about the empty tomb that was "widely circulated among the Jews *to this very day*" (Matt 28:15, emphasis added)—he never tells his readers exactly when he wrote his Gospel. According to scholarly opinion, though, Matthew's Gospel must have been written sometime between AD 40–100.[23] Since Ignatius of Antioch quoted Matthew (ca. AD 107), then the first Gospel couldn't "have seen the light of day much later than A.D. 100."[24] And, if Matthew used Mark's Gospel, then the earliest it could have been written was sometime after Mark's Gospel was published. If church tradition is reliable, some scholars believe that Peter's imprisonment was the motivation behind Mark getting down on paper the gospel according to the apostle. Since according to church tradition Peter was martyred during the Neronian persecution (AD 64–68), then Matthew's Gospel would have been written after that.

21. "For Greek and Roman historians, the ideal eyewitness was not the dispassionate observer but one who, as a participant, had been closest to the events and whose direct experience enabled him to understand and interpret the significance of what he had seen" (Richard Bauckham, *Jesus and the Eyewitnesses: The Gospels as Eyewitness Testimony* [Grand Rapids: Eerdmans, 2006], 9).

22. Keener, *Matthew*, 16–24.

23. Davies and Allison, *Matthew*, 1:127–28.

24. Ibid., 130.

Of course, if Matthew was the first Gospel written, then it was obviously published sometime after the resurrection of Jesus (AD 30 or 33), with enough time—ten years?—for a church of mixed ethnicity to have been established in Antioch (perhaps the location of Matthew's community). But since the majority of scholars hold to Marcan priority, then the earliest date for Matthew is usually posited sometime in the mid-to-late 60s.[25]

Like the implied author and reader, scholars look for historical details in Matthew's work that may indicate more precisely when the Gospel was written—hints about the implied date. For example, since the temple in Jerusalem was destroyed by the Romans in AD 70—a cataclysmic event predicted by Jesus (Matt 24:1–2)—then references to an operating temple or to certain details about its destruction may betray Matthew's time of writing. That is why some scholars date Matthew in the 60s; they think the Gospel must have been written before AD 70 in light of Jesus's instructions about proper devotion to God in his temple. For example, Jesus taught his disciples that they should leave their gift at the altar and be reconciled to their Jewish brothers before returning to the temple to complete their offering (Matt 5:23–24). The point would be irrelevant to Matthew's readers if the temple were already destroyed. Furthermore, why include a story about paying the temple tax, an episode unique to Matthew's Gospel (17:24–27), if the temple lay in ruins during Matthew's time of writing? That would be another moot point, wouldn't it?

Some scholars think the time of the temple's destruction is determinative for dating Matthew's Gospel, but for different reasons. They argue that Matthew must have been written after AD 70 because of the way he allows certain details about the event to creep into Jesus's teaching. For example, they think Matthew's version of the parable of the wedding banquet (Matt 22:1–14) betrays an *ex post facto* point of view. In particular, when Jesus refers to the mistreated king who sent his army to destroy the obstinate city—burning it to the ground (v. 7)—it sounds like the very thing that happened to Jerusalem when the Roman general Titus sacked the city in AD 70.[26] Therefore, Matthew must have written his Gospel after the event since he colored the parable of Jesus in ways that are absent from Luke's version (Luke 14:16–24). But if Matthew was sculpting Jesus's teaching to fit the details of the destruction of the temple, wouldn't it have served his purposes better to include such information when Jesus predicted the catastrophe (Matt 24:15–21)?[27] Therefore, some scholars find other reasons to date Matthew's Gospel after AD 70—for

25. See Keener, *Matthew*, 42–44; Evans, *Matthew*, 4–5; France, *Matthew*, 19.

26. Davies and Allison, *Matthew*, 1:131–32.

27. Nolland, *Matthew*, 16–17; Davies and Allison, *Matthew*, 1:131.

example, the more prominent role the Pharisees played in opposing Jesus. After the temple was destroyed, the only Jewish sect that survived the catastrophe was the Pharisees. The Sadducees (the custodians of the temple), the Herodians (who needs them? Rome is in charge), and the Zealots (the rebels who died fighting the Romans) all perished. Consequently, the Pharisees inherited the power of leading the Jewish people in the aftermath, establishing their interpretation of the law as the guide for all Israel. That is why Matthew highlights the contest between Jesus and the Pharisees over the proper interpretation of the Scriptures (Matt 5–8; 23). It reflects the hostilities that existed between Matthew's community and the synagogue after the destruction of the temple.[28]

There is one more factor that should be considered: if Matthew the disciple was the author of the first Gospel, then knowing when he died would set the latest possible date for his work. But church tradition is vague about the details of Matthew's death. So the range of possible dates for Matthew's Gospel from AD 40–100 is still applicable. Little more can be said with much certainty. Nevertheless, in light of the probability that Matthew used Mark, I think the more compelling arguments concerning the implied date place Matthew sometime shortly after the destruction of the temple in the mid to late 70s.

Where?

There is no church tradition that locates Matthew's audience specifically. We know that Matthew's Gospel was first popular in Syria; the earliest references to the Gospel appear in the letters of Ignatius (bishop of Antioch) and perhaps the Didache (an early Jewish-Christian work possibly originating from Syria).[29] That bit of information, coupled with the unusual reference to Syria as the place where Jesus's fame spread pretty quickly (Matt 4:24),[30] has led several scholars to suggest that Matthew wrote his Gospel for Christians in Antioch or Damascus—two well-known cities beyond Palestine where early (Jewish) Christianity flourished among Greek speakers. Others suggest a Galilean or Judean provenance or even contiguous regions surrounding Palestine (like Egypt, Phoenicia, or the Transjordan). But all of these are only suggestions, built on the assumption that Matthew wrote his Gospel for a particular community of a certain location at a particular time.[31]

---

28. See Davies and Allison, *Matthew*, 1:133–38.
29. Keener, *Matthew*, 41.
30. Evans suggests that "the reference to 'Syria' sticks out like a sore thumb" (*Matthew*, 5).
31. For all the possibilities, see Davies and Allison, *Matthew*, 1:138–47.

Other scholars have questioned the idea of a "Matthean community"—that Matthew's Gospel was written to address certain needs of a specific church in a particular location. Rather, they argue that Matthew published his Gospel for a general readership.[32] That is not to say that the implied reader doesn't exist in Matthew's Gospel, as if it were a mere fabrication. Certainly Matthew wrote his account of the life and times of Jesus of Nazareth with a certain reader in mind. We can see the Jewish emphases of Matthew's version of the significance of Jesus when compared to Mark's Gospel. Yet to assume that the implied reader somehow shines a light on the intended recipients of Matthew's Gospel as if it were a letter sent to certain readers is incredibly presumptuous. Just because Matthew's Gospel seems to have been especially popular among Syrian churches with a strong Jewish-Christian identity doesn't necessarily mean that Matthew wrote his Gospel only for those Christians—as if other kinds of Christians (whether Jewish, gentile, or even God-fearers in Egypt, Asia Minor, or Rome) who found the first Gospel useful would be seen as a bonus to Matthew ("Wow. Gentiles in Rome love my work? I never saw that coming"). We may see how Matthew's work would have encouraged Jewish Christians facing difficulties in Syria or Palestine, but that doesn't prove they were Matthew's target audience.

Furthermore, *bioi* were never written for a specific, ethnic, geographical audience. Rather, works like these were published for mass consumption,[33] which would have been especially true of our literary Gospels, consumed by all Christians scattered all over the Mediterranean world. The fact that the four Gospels were so quickly copied and distributed widely attests to their common appeal. Indeed, even though Matthew's Gospel reveals Jewish interests, his literary work was never ghettoized, as if it were intended only for insiders. Besides, to say Matthew wrote his Gospel only for Jewish Christians in Antioch because they needed instructions directly from the mouth of Christ to address certain ecclesiological crises shifts the focus of the narrative away from the obvious subject of the Gospel.[34] *Jesus* is the centerpiece of Matthew's narrative, not the fabricated needs of a hypothetical congregation that supposedly compelled our writer to craft words that would come directly from the mouth of Jesus. *Who Jesus is* (more than what his readers wanted him to be) was the driving force behind Matthew's Gospel.

---

32. See Richard Bauckham, "For Whom Were the Gospels Written?," in *The Gospels for All Christians: Rethinking the Gospel Audiences*, ed. Richard Bauckham (Grand Rapids: Eerdmans, 1998), 9–48.

33. Richard A. Burridge, "About People, by People, for People: Gospel Genre and Audiences," in Bauckham, *Gospels for All Christians*, 131–44.

34. Ibid., 123–24.

Why?

The purpose of Matthew's Gospel comes into clearer focus when we compare his work to the other three Gospels. Certainly all four evangelists wrote their stories to convince their readers of the significance of Jesus of Nazareth. But when we contrast the way they tell their version of events, it becomes quite apparent that each writer gave his own slant on the story, especially when we take into account all the unique material. For example, as we mentioned before, we can't help but wonder why Matthew started his Gospel with the genealogy of Jesus. Moreover, why is his version so different from Luke's? Why did Matthew group together this huge body of teaching material that we call "the Sermon on the Mount," even placing it before the reader as the first, public, momentous thing Jesus did? And what's the mission to the "lost sheep of Israel" all about (Matt 10:6; 15:24)? No other Gospel has Jesus sending his disciples first to the Jews, purposefully ignoring Samaritans and gentiles. Does that imply Jesus was reluctant to expand his ministry to those outside of Israel? Doesn't that explain why Jesus spurned the Canaanite woman (Matt 15:21–24)? Or, why did Matthew make a big deal about Peter's confession—something that inspired Jesus to hand over the keys of the kingdom to him? In Mark's Gospel, Jesus rebuked Peter for what he said (Mark 8:29–30). Why did Matthew spend an entire chapter explaining how Jesus publicly put the Pharisees on notice for their hypocrisy (Matt 23:1–36)? Shouldn't all the skirmishes between Jesus and the Pharisees over the law have sufficed to reveal the differences between them (the other Gospel writers thought so)? Furthermore, why did Matthew feel obliged to add several parables after Jesus's famous Olivet Discourse? Mark has a simple warning from Jesus, "Be on guard! Be alert! You do not know when that time will come," followed by a brief version of the parable of the absentee master (Mark 13:33–37). Matthew tells a much longer version of the story (Matt 24:45–51) and adds three more parables to hammer home the point: be faithful while the master/bride groom tarries (25:1–46). So why did Matthew include all of this unique material? Scholars think it may have something to do with Matthew's purpose; they are literary additions that not only set his Gospel apart from the other three but also may reveal why he wrote it.

The trick is finding a literary or theological thread that holds the fabric of Matthew's Gospel together—not only the unique material but also his version of episodes shared by the other Gospels.[35] For example, some scholars think

35. For a helpful survey of the material unique to Matthew and how it may reveal his purpose, see James D. G. Dunn, *Neither Jew nor Greek: A Contested Identity*, Christianity in the Making 3 (Grand Rapids: Eerdmans, 2015), 249–76.

Matthew wrote his Gospel to present Jesus as the new Moses appointed by God to lead Israel out of exile.[36] They point to the way Matthew purposely arranged the lineage of Jesus so that the last fourteen generations bring the story of Israel's exile to an end because the Messiah has come (Matt 1:17). That also explains why the first thing Jesus does is to ascend a mountain and deliver his version of the law of righteousness—as if he were a new Moses. The imagery of a Shepherd King travelling about Galilee to reclaim the lost sheep of Israel as if Jesus were all of Israel's heroes rolled up into one (prophet, priest, and king) serves Matthew's typological purpose. That is why Matthew keeps pointing out all the Scripture that has been fulfilled with the advent of Jesus as the Christ. Jesus is everything Israel had been waiting for, the embodiment of every promise God made to Israel, and the people see it. Like a herd of sheep they follow him *everywhere*—even into the desert—knowing the Great Shepherd will take care of them, feeding them in the wilderness, performing signs much greater than anything Moses could do with a rod and staff. Only this new Moses will not only lead them out of slavery and through the desert but also into the promised land. The cross and resurrection proved it. Therefore, the culminating effect, the undeniable inference, the force of Matthew's purpose is this: the exile is over; the meek will inherit the land; the kingdom of heaven has come to earth because the true Son of God has ascended to David's throne forever.

Other scholars think Matthew was trying to negotiate a difficult problem that developed between Jewish Christians (including perhaps kinsmen who rejected Jesus as the Christ if the "Matthean community" was still part of the synagogue) and the influx of gentile Christians into the church.[37] Did Jesus intend from the beginning to include gentile converts in his mission to reclaim Israel? Some say no, since "the mission commandment of the risen Lord is set in antithesis to the command of the earthly Jesus (28:19–20; 10:5–6)."[38] Within a few decades of early Christianity the majority of Israel had rejected the gospel, and gentiles were responding favorably to it. Therefore, Jesus's mission to reclaim the lost sheep of Israel had to be refashioned in light of the early church's experience. So Matthew supposedly wrote his Gospel to redirect the predominantly Jewish-Christian community to embrace their new mission. In order to help them give up on reclaiming Israel and restoring the land, Matthew highlights the Jewish leadership's rejection of Jesus (both in the synagogue and the temple) and shows how, from the very beginning, it was God's plan to include gentiles for salvation. That's why Matthew lists gentiles in the genealogy of Jesus. That's why he tells the story of magi showing up

36. See the relevant passages discussed in the commentary below, 97–98.

37. See the discussion in Luz, *Matthew*, 1:50–56.

38. Ibid., 1:50.

for the birth of the Christ. That's why Jesus praises the Roman centurion for having a faith greater than any Jew.[39] Matthew includes these subtle hints throughout his Gospel ("Yes, Jesus really did embrace gentile believers") in order to prepare his readers for the expanded, worldwide mission that shows up at the end of the story. To be sure, Jesus's first priority was the reclamation of Israel and the land. But, just like the prophets before him, Jesus was rejected by his own people—especially Jerusalem. None of this took Jesus (or God) by surprise. All of this was by divine design, and Matthew's Gospel shows his readers how and why it happened.

Since it is difficult to figure out in Matthew's Gospel whether the kingdom of heaven has come to earth or not, some scholars think Matthew was trying to answer a different eschatological problem. Jesus proclaimed, "Repent, for the kingdom of heaven has come near" (Matt 4:17). At times it appears as though the heavenly kingdom has invaded earth—the miracles seem proof enough. For example, Jesus said that his ability to cast out demons proved that "the kingdom of God has come upon you" (12:28). He even talked about the kingdom of heaven being present among them, like seed growing or yeast leavening (13:31–33), that it already belonged to those who were poor in spirit and persecuted for righteousness (5:3, 10). But the presence of the kingdom of heaven on earth wasn't obvious to everyone. It was hidden, mysterious, small, and barely noticeable. People needed the right kind of eyes to see and ears to hear it. But one day the kingdom would come with such ostentatious display—in dramatic fashion with undeniable power—that everyone would see it, both the damned and the faithful (24:29–31). The will of God will be evident on earth as it is in heaven. The day of reckoning is coming. Jesus will reign as the king of Israel and, therefore, over the whole world. The question was what would be the sign of his coming (24:3)? Had he already given it? Was it the "sign of Jonah" (16:4)? Or was it something else, like the destruction of the temple (23:38–24:2, 15–21) or some cosmic portent that signaled the end of the world (24:29–30)? The fact that Matthew leaves the question open leads some scholars to conclude that the first Gospel was written to encourage Christ believers to remain faithful in light of the imminent coming of Christ.

This is why the date of Matthew's Gospel is crucial to some scholars. If his Gospel was written before the destruction of the temple, then Matthew was encouraging his readers to see the "signs of the times"—not only the events in Palestine that signaled the end of the temple (just as Jesus predicted), the end of the world, and therefore the second coming of Christ, but also to have eyes to see the kingdom's mysterious presence in the ever-expanding mission of the

39. In all of these instances, see the discussion below, 46–48, 53, 57–58, 166–68.

church.[40] On the other hand, some scholars think Matthew wrote his Gospel after AD 70—a disaster that created a crisis in the early church. Since Jesus seemed to tie his second coming to the destruction of the temple, then there must have been some sort of delay in the *parousia* of Christ. And so, with the temple in ruins and no obvious sign of Christ's imminent return, Matthew wrote his Gospel to hold out hope to the faithful: "Yes, Jesus is still coming—perhaps even soon—but ours is not to know when. Rather, we're supposed to remain faithful while the master is away."[41] Whether before the temple was destroyed or in light of it, Matthew's expanded version of the Olivet Discourse may be key to understanding the ambiguity of the already/not yet kingdom of heaven coming to earth—a teaching that Luke revises according to his purposes (Luke 21:5–36; Acts 1:6–7) and John seems to have given up on (there is no Olivet Discourse in the fourth Gospel).

There are several odd references in Matthew's Gospel that may point to another purpose. When Jesus sends the Twelve to recover the lost sheep of Israel, he gives them instructions that appear to be more relevant for a much later time.[42] He warns them that they "will be brought before governors and kings as witnesses to them and to the Gentiles" (Matt 10:18)—a situation more indicative of the early church than the experience of the Twelve. He talks about welcoming prophets, emphasizing the importance of showing proper hospitality to itinerant disciples (vv. 40–42), advice that really wouldn't apply to the Twelve since they were the ones travelling. And so these instructions sound like they were intended for the early church—Christians scattered all over the Mediterranean world, connected by their common gospel purpose of receiving and sending missionaries. Jesus also gives advice to the church, assuming his absence—in particular, how to deal with an unrepentant sinner (18:15–20). He warns them to be ready for his return, even though he hasn't left (24:42; 25:13). Finally, as he gives a worldwide mission to the eleven who followed him to the mountain, he commands them to make other disciples by teaching them to keep his commandments—something he emphasized from the beginning (7:24; 28:20). Indeed, more than any other Gospel, Matthew emphasizes that disciples are made when they are taught to keep the commandments of Christ. Therefore, in light of these emphases, some scholars argue that Matthew wrote his Gospel as a kind of manual for discipleship—a careful recounting of the words and works of Jesus so that the early church would know how to carry on his mission in his absence.[43] By seeing how Jesus

---

40. Nolland, *Matthew*, 14–17.

41. Keener, *Matthew*, 42–44.

42. See the commentary below, 211–18.

43. See Dunn, *Neither Jew nor Greek*, 260–65.

made disciples, second, third, fourth, and following generations of Christians would know how to make disciples of all nations.

Some scholars prefer locating the purpose of Matthew's Gospel in the person of Jesus rather than the supposed needs of his readers. For example, not persuaded by the arguments for seeing Jesus as the "new Moses," scholars think Matthew was trying to present Jesus as the embodiment of the Torah, of Wisdom, or of Yahweh himself.[44] In other words, Matthew wrote his Gospel to present his Christology, his theological view of the significance of the person and work of Jesus. Some of the peculiarities of his gospel story may indicate an attempt to address some minor issues within the early church. But the main point—the motivating purpose—of Matthew's Gospel was to present Jesus as the king of Israel for the sake of the whole world. Therefore, it shouldn't surprise us that perhaps all of these distinctive features (fulfillment of Scripture, new Moses, new temple, son of David, way of righteousness, reclamation of Israel, mission to the gentiles) would appear in Matthew's Gospel. For he was convinced that Jesus was the Christ, the Savior, the Immanuel, the Son of God. And he would use every argument, promise, prophecy, typology, and commandment to prove it.

How?

Matthew's Gospel reveals significant intentionality. His literary work didn't result from some haphazard arrangement of stories. Rather, like a careful craftsman Matthew fashioned his work in ways that reveal his purpose, a literary design intended to have a rhetorical effect on his readers. After all, from the start Matthew makes the claim that Jesus is "the Messiah the son of David, the son of Abraham" (Matt 1:1), and what follows is a persuasive argument meant to back up his claim. But it's how he goes about proving the point—a narrative that weaves the story of Israel and Jesus into one fabric—that inspires readers to take notice of his literary genius. Matthew's Gospel is brilliant, taking his audience on a journey that not only recounts certain events in the life of Jesus and his disciples but shows us why every episode, every teaching, every ironic twist and turn of the plot, every character, every conflict, and every bit of dialogue matters. It's not just that Jesus shows great intention in everything he says and does; Matthew does too. There's strategic symmetry in what he writes, clever literary devices to help readers connect the dots, significant structure to the narrative that makes you want to sit up and take notice. He wastes no words, often trimming away unnecessary details

44. See the brief description in Brown, "Matthew," 580–81.

found in Mark's account. There is no filler, no throwaway line, no empty scene intended only to carry the plot along its predestined path. Rather, a turn of phrase here and an ironic pun there, an echo of Israel's past and a sign of things to come, a story coming full circle and a new narrative breaking through—in Matthew's literary world promise and fulfillment are fused together to inspire readers to see things they've never seen before. The delight of discovery, the hope of recovered meaning, loose ends tied up, all things becoming new—Matthew inspires us to see and hear the kingdom Jesus lived and proclaimed in ways that were barely imaginable before we picked up the first Gospel. Indeed, the more you read and the more you hear, the more you want to lean in and watch *everything* that happened, not wanting to miss a single moment. For we know this story matters more every time we read it—the brilliant work of a Spirit-inspired literary artist who helps us *truly* see his subject, *Jesus*, the one who *saves* the whole world.

A painter with words, Matthew captures his subject with broad brushes, sweeping colors, and fine techniques intended to inspire his readers to get the big picture as well as pay careful attention to the details. Scholars have noticed an overall literary structure to Matthew's Gospel, perhaps even complementing his theological purpose. For example, the teaching of Jesus appears to come in five blocks of material (Matt 5–7; 10; 13; 18; 24–25) reminiscent of the five books of the Torah. At the same time, the first two words of the first Gospel, *biblos geneseōs* (lit., "book of generation/genealogy," Matt 1:1), sends the reader back to the first book of the Torah, Genesis, with its repeating refrain literally rendered, "This is the book of the generations of. . ." (Gen 2:4; 5:1; etc.).[45] This isn't a happy coincidence; both in its macrostructure and microsemantics, the literary design of Matthew's Gospel signals to the observant reader how the story of Israel has been fulfilled in the story of Jesus. Matthew has made these connections, and he expects his readers to see the same significance. Of course, the fact that from the beginning Matthew holds his readers by the hand to help them correlate prophecy and fulfillment (Matt 2:5, 17, 23; 3:3; etc.) doesn't diminish the more subtle approach he takes at times. Indeed, Matthew appears to have written for a variety of readers on several levels of familiarity with the Scriptures. Some need to be shown; others will see what is hidden—just like the kingdom of heaven. In other words, perhaps Matthew has learned well from his teacher; his literary technique mirrors the way Jesus taught his disciples and the crowds about the kingdom of God. Sometimes the gospel is proclaimed plainly; at other times it is only understood by those who have eyes to see it.

45. See below, 42–43.

There are other ways that Matthew has stitched his Gospel together to reveal a literary pattern of meaning. Some scholars have noticed another macrostructure in the first Gospel where the transitional phrase "from that time on Jesus began to. . ." (Matt 4:17; 16:21) marks the two most important pivotal points in the unfolding plot. Consequently, we can see how Matthew develops the story according to a three-part outline: "(I) The Presentation of Jesus Messiah (1:1–4:16); (II) The Ministry of Jesus Messiah to Israel and Israel's Repudiation of Jesus (4:17–16:20); (III) The Journey of Jesus the Messiah to Jerusalem and His Suffering, Death, and Resurrection (16:21–28:20)."[46] Some have seen a geographical pattern to the story of the Christ, perhaps even intended to mirror the story of Israel: from Jerusalem, to Egyptian exile, back to the promised land to reconstitute Israel, from the northern kingdom (Galilee) to the southern kingdom (Judea).[47] Others say the structure of Matthew's Gospel simply derives from Mark's chronology. There is nothing peculiar about Matthew's overall arrangement of the narrative; he has simply enhanced Mark's version of the gospel story.[48] So, which is it? Did Matthew inherit Mark's outline, or did our writer organize the story of Jesus according to another discernible pattern? To be sure, in certain places there are significant differences in the chronologies of Mark and Matthew, making Matthew's Gospel even more difficult to outline. There are many different ways we could arrange the story according to a particular literary grid. Perhaps that's the key: Matthew's narrative is so complex, we shouldn't be surprised to discover several literary maps embedded in the Gospel—a set of coordinates that help the reader determine where the story came from and where it's going geographically, theologically, politically, and scripturally. Indeed, while reading the Gospel according to Matthew, readers well travelled in the narratives of Israel's story often find themselves saying, "This reminds me of the time when Jacob . . . or Moses . . . or David or. . . ." This is a *big* story where several plotlines of the narrative of God and his people intersect at one, precipitous moment.

Matthew's ability to draw his readers into the narrative world, helping us not only to see the kingdom of heaven coming to earth in the ministry of Jesus but also to experience it, moves us from being visitors to the gospel story to becoming participants in it. The transformation is subliminal. One minute, we're reading about how Jesus fell asleep in the boat during an awful storm. Convinced they're going to drown, fear overcomes the disciples as they try to roust the Lord. And, before we know it, we're in the boat with them,

46. Jack Dean Kingsbury, *Matthew as Story*, 2nd ed. (Philadelphia: Fortress, 1988), 40.
47. France, *Matthew*, 3–7.
48. For further discussion, see Nolland, *Matthew*, 4–9, 23–29.

wondering why Jesus could sleep at a time like this, only to hear his words as if he were speaking directly to us, "You of little faith, why are you so afraid?" (Matt 8:26).[49] Or, when Jesus teaches his disciples, "Love your enemies and pray for those who persecute you" (5:44), we realize, of course, that he was referring to the Romans.[50] And yet, having joined the crowd on the mountain, listening to his compelling sermon, before long we take his words to heart as if he were discipling us. There are even times when Jesus seems to lift his eyes past the Twelve and take notice of us standing on the margins of the narrative. All of the sudden he appears to look directly at us to give comforting words for our time, our situation, and the challenges we face: "For where two or three gather in my name, there am I with them" (18:20).[51] This happens all the time. Even though we know Jesus gave specific instructions to the Twelve to reclaim the lost sheep of Israel, we act like his advice applies to us gentiles. Certainly we know he gathered the eleven to the mountain to give *them* authority to make disciples of all nations, but we accept the Great Commission as if it were our responsibility too. Indeed, Matthew sucks us into the narrative, telling his version of events like an eyewitness—a story so compelling we can't help but be transported back in time, watching the miracles of Jesus, hearing the teaching of our Lord, acting like we are eyewitnesses too.[52] That's the literary effect of Matthew's Gospel. As Jesus makes disciples of the Twelve, he ends up making disciples of us too because we have ears to hear and eyes to read the Gospel according to Matthew.

Matthew writes a very inclusive story, inviting his readers to find their place in the gospel.[53] But he doesn't just accomplish his purpose by telling engaging stories. He expands the temporal boundaries of the narrative to include events that will occur beyond the end of the Gospel (Matt 28:20), things that will happen in the reader's future. For example, the open-endedness of the *parousia* of Christ points the reader to a future that includes not only the twelve disciples but also Matthew's readers. "Because implied readers find themselves in a world that shares the same temporal boundaries as the narrative world of the Gospel (i.e., the time prior to the coming of the Son of Man), they can be said to be included in the narrative."[54] Readers get the sense of a divine ordering of time in the ministry of Jesus as the Christ—not only in prophecies fulfilled and promises realized in his person and work but also

49. See below, 173–77.

50. See below, 117–19.

51. See below, 363–67.

52. Bauckham, *Jesus and the Eyewitnesses*, 164.

53. Luz, *Matthew*, 1:11–12; 3:640.

54. David B. Howell, *Matthew's Inclusive Story: A Study in the Narrative Rhetoric of the First Gospel*, JSNTSup 42 (Sheffield: JSOT Press, 1990), 159.

in the certainty of a future predicted by the one who fulfills all righteousness. In other words, because Matthew helps us see how Jesus finishes what the God of Israel started—the covenant with all of its blessings and curses—then readers can't help but believe that those who follow Jesus will enter into the fulfillment of that everlasting covenant: the kingdom of heaven coming to earth. That's why we read the Great Commission as if it were our own. Making disciples of all nations and teaching them to obey the commandments of Jesus—this fulfills all righteousness and therefore continues the mission of Jesus Christ to the end of the world when he returns and reigns on earth as he does in heaven.[55] We are a part of the kingdom work of God that started with Abraham, was realized through Jesus Christ, and extends through those who follow him—even those who come after us. This is God's doing. Therefore, we get the clear sense in Matthew's Gospel that everything happens for a reason, even the unlikely death and resurrection of the Messiah, because the divine ordering of time reveals the sacred hand of God. And so as we read Matthew's Gospel and follow Jesus, we realize we are living in that sacred time too.

That's one of the reasons why, I think, Matthew loves to frame episodes with what scholars call an *inclusio*. It's a way to bracket material, where the author marks the beginning and end of things in order to bring the reader along to see how God is at work. Matthew's narrative world is an orderly world where God starts something and then finishes it, and Jesus is the incarnation of that divine work. And so, for example, scholars point to the clever way Matthew frames his entire Gospel with the idea of divine presence—that "God is with us" from the beginning to the end. In particular, the story begins with the angel's promise that Jesus will "save his people from their sins" (Matt 1:21), bringing back the long-desired presence of God (vv. 22–23).[56] Then the entire gospel story reveals how that happens in the ministry of Jesus; the kingdom of heaven invades the earth. Therefore, it comes as no surprise to the reader when Jesus promises his disciple-making followers that "surely I am with you always, to the very end of the age" (Matt 28:20). Jesus is Immanuel from start to finish.

There are other places where Matthew frames the narrative to help the reader see a divine ordering of things.[57] One of my favorite examples of *inclusio* is when Jesus sends the Pharisees away with some homework. They need to learn a lesson from Hosea (Hos 6:6): "Go and learn what this means: 'I desire mercy, not sacrifice.' For I have not come to call the righteous, but sinners" (Matt 9:13). The problem was that Jesus had shared table with Matthew and

55. See below, 564–68.
56. See below, 55–56.
57. For several examples, see Brown, "Matthew," 573.

his notorious friends ("tax collectors and sinners," vv. 10–11). Of course, that such a teaching came from a prophet who was commanded by God to take back his adulterous wife as a lesson for Israel's unfaithfulness must have left a bad taste in the mouths of these righteous teachers of the law. How could one keep the righteous requirements of the law and yet claim to follow the teaching of the great prophet Hosea? Well, the following episodes in Matthew's narrative reveal how it can be done (9:14–12:6): true righteousness is revealed by mercy (questions about genuine repentance, touched by an unclean woman and touching a dead girl, healing the blind and mute who beg "have mercy on us," reclaiming the lost sheep of Israel, the martyrdom of John the Baptizer, the invitation to unrepentant Galileans to come to Jesus, the disciples eating grain on the Sabbath). Consequently, when the Pharisees attack Jesus's disciples for violating the Sabbath, he's not surprised. They hadn't done their homework, hadn't learned the lesson: "If you had known what these words mean, 'I desire mercy, not sacrifice,' you would not have condemned the innocent" (12:7).[58]

Jesus knows what he's doing. It's because he knows who he is and, therefore, what he came to do. And, Matthew shows us why we should believe him. Jesus lives up to his name. He is the embodiment of "Yahweh saves." By his death and resurrection, the fortunes of humanity were changed forever. Jesus is Immanuel, "God with us." Wherever he goes, so goes the reign of God, pushing back malevolent forces, healing the sick, raising the dead, reclaiming the lost, overcoming evil with good, and bringing light to those who sat in darkness for a very long time. In Matthew's Gospel, Jesus even lives up to what the people claim about him. He is the Son of David, the Messiah, the prophet with great authority, a friend of tax collectors and sinners. Matthew enables us to see all these things clearly. And yet, at the same time, we realize that we have much to learn. That Jesus gave the Twelve the nickname "little faith" is enough to give us pause. Would we fare any better? Having eyes to see and ears to hear Matthew's Gospel, we might offer the proper confession, "You are the Messiah, the Son of the living God" (Matt 16:16). But like Peter, we may be just as offended by the cross when it's time to pick it up and follow our Lord. It's one thing to listen to him reverently when he says to us, "Whoever wants to be my disciple must deny themselves and take up their cross and follow me. For whoever wants to save their life will lose it, but whoever loses their life for me will find it" (vv. 24–25). It's quite something else to do it (7:24–27).[59] Matthew shows us not only why we should, but how. For he was a man who also knew what he was talking about since he left everything to follow Jesus (9:9).

58. See below, 242–43.
59. See below, 154–56.

Resources for Teaching and Preaching

If we were to think of the Scriptures as the soil of God's word, then here are a few resources that I have found particularly helpful for surveying the land, working the field, digging deep, and cultivating the ground for sermons and lessons from the Gospel according to Matthew.

Surveying the Land (Brief Overview):

Brown, Jeannine K. "Matthew, Gospel of." Pages 570–84 in *Dictionary of Jesus and the Gospels*. Rev. ed. Edited by Joel B. Green, Jeannine K. Brown, and Nicholas Perrin. Downers Grove, IL: IVP Academic, 2013.

Hays, Richard B. "The Gospel of Matthew." Pages 105–90 in *Echoes of Scripture in the Gospels*. Waco: Baylor University Press, 2016.

Kingsbury, Jack Dean. *Matthew as Story*. 2nd ed. Philadelphia: Fortress, 1988.

Working the Field (Brief Commentaries That Cover the Ground Well):

Blomberg, Craig L. *Matthew*. NAC 22. Nashville: Broadman & Holman, 1992.

Garland, David E. *Reading Matthew: A Literary and Theological Commentary*. Macon, GA: Smyth & Helwys, 2001.

Digging Deep (Critical Commentaries That Unearth Rich Resources):

Davies, W. D., and Dale C. Allison. *The Gospel according to Saint Matthew*. 3 vols. ICC. Edinburgh: T&T Clark, 1988–97.

Luz, Ulrich. *Matthew 1–7, Matthew 8–20, Matthew 21–28*. 3 vols. Translated by James E. Crouch. Hermeneia. Minneapolis: Fortress, 2001–7.

Cultivating the Ground (Commentaries Conducive for Sermon Preparation):

France, R. T. *The Gospel of Matthew*. NICNT. Grand Rapids: Eerdmans, 2007.

Keener, Craig S. *A Commentary on the Gospel of Matthew*. Grand Rapids: Eerdmans, 1999.

CHAPTER 1

Matthew 1:1–17

LISTEN to the Story

1This is the genealogy of Jesus the Messiah the son of David, the son of Abraham:

2Abraham was the father of Isaac,
Isaac the father of Jacob,
Jacob the father of Judah and his brothers,
3Judah the father of Perez and Zerah, whose mother was Tamar,
Perez the father of Hezron,
Hezron the father of Ram,
4Ram the father of Amminadab,
Amminadab the father of Nahshon,
Nahshon the father of Salmon,
5Salmon the father of Boaz, whose mother was Rahab,
Boaz the father of Obed, whose mother was Ruth,
Obed the father of Jesse,
6and Jesse the father of King David.
David was the father of Solomon, whose mother had been Uriah's wife,
7Solomon the father of Rehoboam,
Rehoboam the father of Abijah,
Abijah the father of Asa,
8Asa the father of Jehoshaphat,
Jehoshaphat the father of Jehoram,
Jehoram the father of Uzziah,
9Uzziah the father of Jotham,
Jotham the father of Ahaz,
Ahaz the father of Hezekiah,
10Hezekiah the father of Manasseh,
Manasseh the father of Amon,

Amon the father of Josiah,
[11]and Josiah the father of Jeconiah and his brothers at the time of the exile to Babylon.
[12]After the exile to Babylon:
Jeconiah was the father of Shealtiel,
Shealtiel the father of Zerubbabel,
[13]Zerubbabel the father of Abihud,
Abihud the father of Eliakim,
Eliakim the father of Azor,
[14]Azor the father of Zadok,
Zadok the father of Akim,
Akim the father of Elihud,
[15]Elihud the father of Eleazar,
Eleazar the father of Matthan,
Matthan the father of Jacob,
[16]and Jacob the father of Joseph, the husband of Mary, and Mary was the mother of Jesus who is called the Messiah.

[17]Thus there were fourteen generations in all from Abraham to David, fourteen from David to the exile to Babylon, and fourteen from the exile to the Messiah.

Listening to the Text in the Story: Genesis 1:1–5:2; 12:1–3; 15:1–6; 17:1–19; 38:6–26; 49:9–12; Joshua 2:1–21; 6:22–25; Ruth 1:22–4:22; 1 Samuel 16:1–13; 2 Samuel 2:1–4; 5:1–5; 7:1–16; 11:2–12:25; 23:1–7; 2 Kings 24:10–25:26; 1 Chronicles 1:34; 2:1–15; 3:1–19.

The story of Jesus the Messiah didn't begin with his birth—as fantastic as it was. Rather, Matthew believed the only way his readers would be able to make sense of the life of Jesus, from his birth to his resurrection, was to go back to the beginning of Israel's story. Of course, to tell a condensed version of the entire story of Israel in prose—no matter how brief—would take several pages of precious papyri. Besides, it wouldn't be necessary; Matthew assumes his readers know the macrostory embedded in the genealogy of Jesus. Reciting a revised version of Jesus's ancestry from Abraham to Joseph would sound like a roll call that echoed the promises of God.[1] That's because God made promises

1. "The history of Israel passes before their eyes in concentrated form" (Luz, *Matthew*, 1:82).

to certain individuals for the sake of all his people. The covenant between God and Israel was always mediated through one man. God promised Abraham that he would be the father of many descendants who would inherit the earth. God promised one of Jacob's sons, Judah, that a king would come from his tribe. God promised King David that one of his great-great-great-(how many great?)-grandsons would bring justice to Israel forever. Israel's hope started with one man ("the father of a multitude") and would end with another (the Messiah, "the anointed one"). Indeed, what Matthew claims from the beginning is that one man—that one hope—the Messiah of Israel, has come in the person of Jesus. In him all the promises of God come true.

That would be quite a lofty claim for several reasons, but especially because over the centuries God made *many* promises to Israel that had not come true. In fact, that is what made the God of Israel rather unique: he is the kind of God that makes promises and then leaves, expecting his people to trust him in the meantime. God promised the seventy-five-year-old Abraham that he would be the father of millions of descendants, as many as the stars of the heavens and the grains of sand on the earth, and that they would inherit a land of their own. The problem, of course, was that Abraham was a nomad, had no children, and time was running out; he was already an old man and his wife was persistently barren (considered at that time as the curse of God). I can imagine "father" Abraham staring into the night sky and muttering to himself, "Really? That many descendants? To dream of such things is all well and good, but it would be nice to have one." Nearly twenty-five years later, God finally shows up and delivers the good news to the more-than-patient couple. The old man and his elderly wife will finally get a start on seeing the lofty vision come true: they will have a son, Isaac, and God will get the last laugh. Israel eventually multiplies like rabbits in the fertile land of Egypt. Yet the question remained: Would they ever inherit the earth?

The same thing happened to David. God promised David that his kingdom would be so stable that it would last forever. And yet, even though David managed to unite the divided tribal confederacy under his reign, he didn't seem capable of ruling his own divided house. A rebel son who forced his father to abdicate the throne temporarily, another son's incestuous rape of his sister, the murder of one son by another, the death of the infant son born of David's adulterous relationship with Bathsheba, the rebel son assassinated by the king's captain—how could anyone claim (especially David) that God's promise was coming true? If anything, David's kingdom appeared destined for self-destruction, for everyone knows that a house divided against itself cannot stand. And even though Solomon's reign brought unrivaled peace and prosperity, after David's son died a civil war broke out between the north and the south—a civil war that was never resolved—and eventually ripped apart the indivisible kingdom. It was just a matter of time before a foreign power, a stronger king, would show up and finish off the crippled kingdom. Babylonian captivity seemed to dispel any notion that David's house would stand forever. So, even though Israel didn't find the strength to "sing the songs of the LORD while in a foreign land" (Ps 137:4), they still wanted to know: When will God make good on the promises he made to David, to Abraham, to all Israel? Where is the son of David who will bring the reign of God's justice? How will the children of Abraham—scattered like nomads—ever inherit the promised land? When will their captivity end?

Matthew thinks he has the answer.

EXPLAIN the Story

The first line of Matthew's Gospel reads like a title; literally, "A book [*biblos*] of genesis [*geneseōs*] of Jesus Christ, son of David, son of Abraham." Is Matthew 1:1 the title of the entire Gospel? It could be because Mark did the same thing, stringing together several nouns without a verb, "The beginning of the good news about Jesus the Messiah, the Son of God" (Mark 1:1). Moreover, the books of the Law took their titles from the first word or phrase of each; for example, Genesis is designated as *bere'shith* ("in the beginning"), and Exodus is known by the title *we'elleh shemoth* ("and these are the names"). English titles of the Old Testament books, however, derive from the Septuagint (LXX), the Greek translation of the Hebrew Scriptures; for example, Genesis (*genesis*) comes from 2:4; literally, "This is the book [*biblos*] of genesis [*geneseōs*] of heaven and earth." Therefore, some suggest that Matthew intended his readers to hear an echo of the first book of the Bible in the title of his Gospel, as if he were writing the story of a new Genesis, a new beginning through Jesus Christ.[2] As appealing as that may sound to our ears, the problem is that the word *genesis* appears several places in Genesis (2:4; 5:1; 6:9; 10:1, 32; 11:10, 27; 25:12, 19; 36:1; 37:2) as the heading of a series of stories (often including a genealogy) that trace the lineage or "generations" of a particular patriarch. Furthermore, Matthew uses *genesis* to introduce the story of the birth of Jesus; literally, "the genesis [*genesis*] of Jesus Christ was like this" (1:18). So it is more likely that Matthew 1:1 is not a title for the entire Gospel but a heading for both the genealogy of Jesus, "This is the genealogy [*geneseōs*] of Jesus the

2. See Davies and Allison, *Matthew*, 1:153, who translate v. 1, "Book of the New Genesis wrought by Jesus Christ, son of David, son of Abraham"; Luz, *Matthew*, 1:69, prefers the simpler phrase, "Book of the Genesis of Jesus Christ," because he believes that Matthew wasn't claiming a "new creation" theology at work in Jesus since he is a part of creation.

Messiah the son of David, the son of Abraham," and the birth narrative, "This is how the birth [*genesis*] of Jesus the Messiah came about" (1:18).

Jesus's Family Tree

We may be drawn to the names Matthew singles out in verse one: Abraham, David, Jesus. Indeed, the genealogical table—by its very structure—highlights these three as the MVPs of Israel's story. It starts with Abraham, peaks with David, and ends with Jesus—the trinity of salvation history. Curiosity might draw our eyes to the four women listed, three by name and one by association, leading us to infer that the point of the genealogy is to give voice to the marginalized, to include outsiders, to privilege the scandalous. Others might delight in the threefold schema built around a rhythmic pattern of fourteen names that signal the turning points of Israel's story embedded in Abraham's family tree. Time marches to the beat of an unalterable destiny. Finally, the type A bean counters among us might trip over the mathematical problem of adding up fourteen generations when only thirteen names are listed in the third group. Crunching the numbers while comparing Matthew's genealogy with other lists forces us to tease out the implications of why certain names appear and why others are completely ignored. Certainly Matthew could count (he was a tax collector, after all), so why the gaps? Are we supposed to read between the lines and discover a subliminal message—certain names have been "blotted out" from the sacred record—intended for those who have eyes to see and ears to hear? To be sure, Matthew's unique genealogical list invites intrigue. Yet we shouldn't miss the main point of the genealogy, the "silent" partner who is easily overlooked because his assumed presence goes without saying. The major figure of Jesus's family tree is God.[3]

It is easy to get lost in the genealogy, assuming a biological momentum to the perpetual force of life. Of course we know that "Abraham was the father of Isaac," and that "Isaac was the father of Jacob," and so on. But that's not the whole story, as if becoming a father is naturally to be expected. Rather, Matthew assumes we know the story behind the "begats," the theological presumption within the story of Israel. Israel didn't come into existence by "natural processes." Abraham didn't wake up one day and say to himself, "I think I'll start a nation today." Rather, God created Israel. God chose a Chaldean and brought life to his dead loins. God chose a dead womb to bring laughter to the world. If it weren't for God, Israel wouldn't exist at all. Therefore, like all of creation—every living thing!—Israel belongs to God.

3. "Thus, the genealogy is not a record of man's biological productivity but a demonstration of God's providence" (Raymond E. Brown, *The Birth of the Messiah: A Commentary on the Infancy Narrative in the Gospels of Matthew and Luke*, new updated ed., ABRL [New York: Doubleday, 1993], 68).

That's why he kept making promises to Israel. They are his children; he is their father. And like any good father would intend, his children were meant to be blessed. So every name that appears in the genealogy represents both blessing and promise; every son of the covenant embodies both the fulfillment and hope of God's promise.

And yet, the way Matthew sees it, the story of God's covenant with Israel can't be reduced to a list of names revealing a direct line of descent, tracing the proper lineage of kingship. For if that were the case, one would simply show how Jesus has the proper messianic pedigree, listing his lineage from David to Joseph. Rather, Matthew believes Israel's story and Jesus's family history turn on two significant events, two pivotal persons: the kingdom finally arriving with David, and the Babylonian exile beginning with Jeconiah. Indeed, the ordering of the generations into three groups of fourteen leads the reader to mark the turning point of God's dealings with Israel during these two decisive transitions. David bridges the first two groups, Jeconiah the last two. David represents the high-water mark of God's blessing (the kingdom has come!), while Jeconiah's reign marks the beginning of the end (the kingdom is gone?). In other words, Jesus's genealogy not only reveals Israel's ascent to kingship but also Israel's descent into exile. But to simplify the graph of God's blessing as a straight line peaking with David only to drop off precipitously like a downward vector marking the stock-market crash is misleading. There have been bumps and bruises, ups and downs along the way of God's covenant blessing. Names like Tamar and Judah, David and Uriah, Hezekiah and Manasseh remind the reader that the high points and low points of Israel's story are mingled together. Even during the exile, one should not infer that Israel was abandoned by God, as if there were no bright spots shining in the darkness. God was still blessing Israel by begetting sons of David in Babylon. It was one of those born in exile who led the expedition back home to rebuild the temple: Zerubbabel. It's not like the genealogical record goes silent without a king on the throne. The sons of David keep coming. Indeed, if any inference is to be made it is this: it's time. The exile is over because the Messiah has been born, and he will establish the throne of David forever.[4]

Jesus's Family Issues

Even though the story of Israel can be easily inferred from Jesus's genealogy, Matthew's version still invites curiosity. Why did he include women, especially these four? Why did he leave out several names in order to arrange the genealogy in three groups of fourteen? Furthermore, why does the last section,

4. Davies and Allison, *Matthew*, 1:180.

tracing the descendants from Babylonian exile to the Messiah, contain only thirteen names? And finally, since one man can't have two genealogies, why is Luke's version different from Matthew's?[5]

Starting with the last question, it's a bit unfair to ask why Matthew's genealogy of Jesus is different from Luke's. If he were alive today, Matthew might say, "Go ask Luke!" The Gospel writers certainly didn't see their work as part of a fourfold series on the life of Jesus; they had no idea they were writing Scripture for a collection that we would eventually call "The New Testament." But because we have four Gospels in our canon, we cannot help but wonder, "Why the difference?" In fact, that question comes up often when comparing the four Gospels because there are significant differences between them in chronology, in the actual words of Jesus, in the names of the twelve disciples, and in details pertaining to the same episodes. In other words, throughout this commentary we could spend much time trying to answer the question, "Why is Matthew's version different from . . . ?" Some scholars try to answer the question based on critical opinions about which Gospel was written first, determining who used whom, and tracing the theological motivations of each writer in order to explain the differences. But such an approach is risky. What if we are wrong about literary dependence? To point out deviation implies a standard. Which Gospel is the standard? Even if we could be convinced that one Gospel writer used another, is it possible to infer theological reasons for differences based more on what we're looking for than what the Gospel writers implied? Who can tell? Besides, meaning isn't necessarily located in uniqueness. The material that is shared by the Gospel writers is just as important to serving the purposes of the overall story as the differences between them.

So, for the purposes of this study, we will notice the differences between Matthew and the other three Gospels. But, like many other scholars, we want to locate the significance of the episode in the context of Matthew's story. Rather than try to explain why Matthew's version is different, even trying to harmonize his Gospel with the other three, I want to keep our focus on the narrative world in Matthew, looking for internal evidence within each passage to arrive at the coherent meaning of the Gospel. So, for example, to return to the genealogy of Jesus according to Matthew and Luke, the obvious differences show up in the order, placement, and the list of names for each. Most of us don't seem to have a problem with the differences in order (Matthew descending, Luke ascending) or placement of the genealogical table (Matthew at the beginning, Luke between the baptism and temptation of Jesus). It's in

5. For a comparison between the two, see Brown, *Birth of the Messiah*, 84–94.

the variance of names where the trouble lies. Between Abraham and David, both Gospels agree nearly verbatim. The problem, of course, is the different names listed between David and Zerubbabel, and between Zerubbabel and Joseph. How could this be? Some suggest Matthew's version is Joseph's lineage and Luke's is Mary's. Yet that wouldn't explain why the family lines merge at Shealtiel and Zerubbabel only to diverge again after Zerubbabel. Some argue that the practice of levirate marriage (or even adoption) could explain the different descendants of Zerubbabel, but that doesn't account for the differences after David. Obviously, Matthew traces royal lineage through Solomon, and Luke follows David's descendants through his third son, Nathan (Luke 3:31), but why? In other words, when it comes to explaining the differences between the genealogies we can suggest possibilities—this could have happened—but we are unable to offer reasons. Therefore, it might be more beneficial to ask, "Why is Jesus's genealogy arranged the way it is in Matthew's Gospel?" (A question we would ask even if we didn't have Luke's version.)

It is quite apparent that Matthew's threefold schema of fourteen generations is contrived, especially when we compare it to the genealogies preserved in 1 Chronicles. Sometimes Matthew follows direct lines of descent; for example, fourteen names between Abraham and David. Other times he skips over several names; for example, four names between Jehoram and Jotham (1 Chr 3:11–12) are reduced to one (Jehoram, Uzziah, Jotham; Matt 1:8–9). In other words, it was more important to Matthew that the genealogy of Jesus conform to a fourteen-generation schema than to list every ancestor. Why? Jews believed in divine timing. That is to say, since God is at work in history, the timing of events must bear a divine stamp. In particular, the numerical length of days, months, or years reveal a divine pattern, symbolized by certain "perfect" numbers: three, four, five, seven, ten, twelve (or any combination).[6] Therefore, Matthew deliberately ordered Jesus's genealogy in three groups of fourteen to reflect the imprint of David's royal lineage. David's name in Hebrew consists of three consonants (*dwd*), and since each Hebrew letter also represents an alphabetically ordered number (gematria; *d*=4, *w*=6), then the sum of David's name equals fourteen. And since David's name appears as the fourteenth name in the genealogy, then the divine timing of David's heir is evident in the royal rhythm of three fourteens, which also happens to mark the major turning points in Israel's history.[7]

---

6. According to Augustine, since there are *forty* generations between Abraham and Christ, the genealogy echoes the wilderness wanderings of Israel and foreshadows the number of days of Christ's temptation in the desert (Manlio Simonetti, ed., *Matthew 1–13*, ACCS 1A [Downers Grove, IL: InterVarsity Press, 2001], 10).

7. See Davies and Allison, *Matthew*, 1:163–65.

But that still doesn't answer the question: Why does Matthew list only thirteen names from Jeconiah to Jesus? It could be that Matthew is counting David twice (v. 6), or that one of Jeconiah's unnamed "brothers" rounds out the middle list of fourteen (v. 11).[8] Others have suggested that perhaps Mary was to be counted among the last group of fourteen names (but that still doesn't account for why the previous four women listed were not counted).[9] All of this gets pretty messy for us because Matthew seems to be making many assumptions: these names can be omitted, while these names can be assumed. And yet, the Israelite tradition preserved in the Hebrew Scriptures is notorious for approximating numbers that don't match up (anyone who has compared Chronicles with Samuel and Kings is familiar with the "problem"). So I can imagine Matthew saying to us, "So, there are some names that don't appear here or there. What's the difference as long as God is at work? The God of Israel is making good on his promises, yes? Then there are three groups of fourteen—end of discussion."

Finally, why did Matthew include these four women—Tamar, Rahab, Ruth, and Uriah's wife—in Jesus's genealogy? Although family lineages are traced through fathers, it wasn't unusual to include women in genealogies: concubines (1 Chr 1:32; 2:46, 48), sisters (1:39; 2:16), daughters and daughters-in-law (2:4, 21, 35, 49), wives (1:50; 2:26), and mothers (2:3, 18, 19, 24, 29). So we may be making too much of the fact that women were included in Jesus's family tree. And yet one cannot help but wonder: Why *these* four? Some think the back story of each woman sets up the story of Mary. The reason Matthew listed these women is that they share a similar, scandalous history: Tamar acted like a prostitute to become pregnant by her father-in-law; Rahab was a prostitute; Ruth approached a man to sleep with him; Uriah's wife, Bathsheba, committed adultery with David. In other words, David's royal lineage is tainted by women of questionable behavior, which makes Mary's circumstances—a virgin giving birth to a son—seem rather tame. Or, another way of looking at it, despite (or perhaps even through) their scandalous behavior these women became heroes of Israel's faith because they preserved the line of David, just like Mary.

And yet, even though the circumstances surrounding these women were suspicious, the Bible goes to great lengths to absolve them of any wrongdoing due to the questionable behavior of the men (Judah and David), or due to their own virtuous character (Ruth and Mary), or faithful behavior (Rahab). In other words, the "sex-scandal" theme is an imposition, forced onto these five stories with different contexts. This is why interpreters look

8. See Donald A. Hagner, *Matthew 1–13*, WBC 33A (Waco, TX: Word, 1993), 6.

9. See Brown, *Birth of the Messiah*, 83.

for another common denominator (one that has nothing to do with Mary): all four women were gentiles.[10] Even though the ethnic identity of only one of the women is stated explicitly (Ruth, the Moabite), the non-Israelite status of the other three is inferred (not only from the biblical narratives—Tamar is neither a sister nor a cousin, Rahab is from Jericho, and Bathsheba was married to a Hittite—but also due to the fact that "rabbis felt compelled to defend vigorously this blemish in David's bloodline"[11]). Since the Lord himself commanded Moses to kill all the Israelite men who married Moabite women (Ruth's ancestors; Num 25:1–5), and Ezra advised the men of Judah to divorce their foreign wives (Ezra 10:9–12), then having a royal line "polluted" by the impurity of gentile women makes the story of the Messiah's pedigree even more intriguing. Indeed, according to Matthew, Jesus has all kinds of blood running through his veins—just like King David. And therefore perhaps the hope of David's kingdom was supposed to include all kinds of people, because Jesus is the Messiah born for Israel and the whole world.

LIVE the Story

Every genealogy tells a story. In fact, ask someone about their family tree and see if they don't start telling stories about their "faithful great grandmother" or "crazy great-great uncle" or "mischievous second cousin, the black sheep of the family." It shouldn't surprise me, but whenever I hear about their family, it often sounds like we're related. It seems that all of us have our fair share of larger-than-life personalities, notorious rebels, and wallflowers in our family tree. But what especially comes up nearly every time is that many of us have a well-known person in our genealogy. Go back far enough, and nearly all of us are related to someone famous. People love to bring up that part of their family history. It's as if descending from someone special makes us feel important, validating our existence. We all love to point out the bright spots—the stars—in our family stories.

Recently, I discovered that I'm a descendant of Daniel Boone and his son Nathan. I had never really cared much about tracing my genealogical roots until the local dentist, Don Jump, told me that we were related: "Your great-great grandfather Rentfrow married my grandfather John Henry Jump's sister, Jemima, who were both great-grandchildren of Nathan Boone. That means your great-great-great-great-great-great-grandfather was Daniel Boone." Then he showed me a picture of "our" family circa 1884, posing in

10. Keener, *Matthew*, 78–81.

11. David E. Garland, *Reading Matthew: A Literary and Theological Commentary* (Macon: Smyth & Helwys, 2001), 19.

their Sunday-go-to-meeting clothes in front of an old barn in Polk County, Missouri. What struck me about the picture was how plain they looked, how ordinary they appeared to be. As I tried to take in the significance of the snapshot, I kept thinking to myself, "*These* people are the direct descendants of the great American folk hero, Daniel Boone." Staring at one of the little boys in the picture (a seven-year-old version of my great grandfather), I couldn't help but imagine boastful claims he might have made among his childhood friends: "Look at these muscles! I'm so strong I could wrestle a bear, just like my great-great-great grandfather, Daniel Boone." And, in this imaginary dialogue I could also hear his buddies retort, "Ah shut up, boy. You may think you are Daniel Boone, but we all know you're just little John."

Learning that you're a descendant of Daniel Boone causes all kinds of strange thoughts to run through your head. Knowing that I carry his DNA makes me wonder, "Is that why I love the outdoors? Maybe I was meant to be a frontiersman too. The idea of 'roughing it,' heading to the lake with nothing more than a backpack and a fishing pole, has always appealed to me (even though I've never tried it!). Is my drive to be someone special biological? Is it because I carry the genes of Daniel Boone that I feel a kinship with Native Americans? Am I the living embodiment of the mythology that is Daniel Boone?" Of course, when I think about the other side of Boone's legacy—his weaknesses, his foibles, his failures—the idea that I am living a predestined life due to my genealogy no longer sounds appealing. Boone was plagued by financial trouble throughout his life due to his poor judgment in land speculation and political alliances. He was an opportunist who sided with enemies whenever it was in his best interests. He seemed bent on creating a larger-than-life legend, built on self-promotion, which led to fictional tales of his so-called "heroic" life published in dime-store novels—something he resented in his final years. Even Boone became contemptuous of the legend that he created, knowing he was much less of a man than the myth of the folk hero celebrated by all.[12] Indeed, how could any of us ever live up to the ideal past of our family history when all of us know we carry within ourselves the good, the bad, and the ugly?

That's what I appreciate about Matthew's version of Jesus's genealogy. Matthew didn't offer a sanitized account of Jesus's pedigree. He relates the story of Israel's hope, the royal line of David, warts and all.[13] Indeed, Jesus's

---

12. See the biography by Michael A. Lofaro, *Daniel Boone: An American Life* (Lexington: The University Press of Kentucky, 2003), especially 133–83.

13. "Yea, it was for this cause He came, not to escape our disgraces, but to bear them away. . . . He vouchsafed to have also such kinsfolk, being in no respect ashamed of our evils. And this He was proclaiming from the very beginnings of his birth, that He is ashamed of none of those things that belong to us" (John Chrysostom, *Homilies on the Gospel of St. Matthew*, vol. 10 of *The Nicene and Post-Nicene Fathers*, series one, ed. Philip Schaff, 14 vols. [Repr., Grand Rapids: Eerdmans, 1991], 15–16).

genealogical roots sink deep into the dirt of humanity. No doubt, Israel's tree was nourished by a rich soil that produced massive limbs of great strength and beauty. David's kingdom was so magnificent that all other kings would be compared to him. Talk about living up to an ideal family history! Did Jesus ever wonder about the implications of his family history? "Is that why I think about the kingdom all the time? Because I'm a son of David?" Others recognized his potential: "Lord, Son of David, have mercy on us!" and "Hosanna to the Son of David!" (Matt 20:30; 21:9). And yet, Jesus never claimed such a lofty title, preferring to refer to himself as the "Son of Man"—a man who knew about the temptation of lust, anxiety about the future, the troubles of the day, and the loneliness of sorrow (5:28–30; 6:25, 34; 26:38). When he warned the crowd about the drastic measures needed to overcome the power of lust, did he think about his ancestral father, King David? When he tried to encourage us not to worry about the future, was he pondering his own destiny in light of the story of Judah? When a woman prepared him for burial even though he was still very much alive, inciting his disciples to mock her foolish gesture, did he think of all the women in his family tree who were faithful to the Lord despite being falsely accused and dismissed by men (26:6–13)? When he cried out, "My God, my God, why have you forsaken me?" (27:46), did it feel like he was reliving the story of Israel's exile in Babylon? Did Jesus know he was the living embodiment, the genuine incarnation of his genealogy, with all the hopes and disappointments, joys and sorrows, strengths and weaknesses, ups and downs, kings and despots, heroes and villains, promise and fulfillment of Israel's story, the momentum and destiny of our story? Did Jesus realize he was not only *the* Son of David but also *our* Son of Man?

Matthew implies he must have known, for the *genesis* of Jesus the Messiah is where the gospel story of his life begins (Matt 1:1). Yes, Jesus was born to be king. This was God's doing. But that didn't mean he would drop out of heaven like some alien from another world. Matthew wants to make it plain: Jesus didn't "become" one of us. He *is* one of us—all of us—the good, the bad, and the ugly. His genealogy proves it.

CHAPTER 2

Matthew 1:18–2:23

LISTEN to the Story

[18]This is how the birth of Jesus the Messiah came about: His mother Mary was pledged to be married to Joseph, but before they came together, she was found to be pregnant through the Holy Spirit. [19]Because Joseph her husband was faithful to the law, and yet did not want to expose her to public disgrace, he had in mind to divorce her quietly.

[20]But after he had considered this, an angel of the Lord appeared to him in a dream and said, "Joseph son of David, do not be afraid to take Mary home as your wife, because what is conceived in her is from the Holy Spirit. [21]She will give birth to a son, and you are to give him the name Jesus, because he will save his people from their sins."

[22]All this took place to fulfill what the Lord had said through the prophet: [23]"The virgin will conceive and give birth to a son, and they will call him Immanuel" (which means "God with us").

[24]When Joseph woke up, he did what the angel of the Lord had commanded him and took Mary home as his wife. [25]But he did not consummate their marriage until she gave birth to a son. And he gave him the name Jesus.

[2:1]After Jesus was born in Bethlehem in Judea, during the time of King Herod, Magi from the east came to Jerusalem [2]and asked, "Where is the one who has been born king of the Jews? We saw his star when it rose and have come to worship him."

[3]When King Herod heard this he was disturbed, and all Jerusalem with him. [4]When he had called together all the people's chief priests and teachers of the law, he asked them where the Messiah was to be born. [5]"In Bethlehem in Judea," they replied, "for this is what the prophet has written:

> [6]'But you, Bethlehem, in the land of Judah,
> are by no means least among the rulers of Judah;

> for out of you will come a ruler
> who will shepherd my people Israel.'"

7Then Herod called the Magi secretly and found out from them the exact time the star had appeared. 8He sent them to Bethlehem and said, "Go and search carefully for the child. As soon as you find him, report to me, so that I too may go and worship him."

9After they had heard the king, they went on their way, and the star they had seen when it rose went ahead of them until it stopped over the place where the child was. 10When they saw the star, they were overjoyed. 11On coming to the house, they saw the child with his mother Mary, and they bowed down and worshiped him. Then they opened their treasures and presented him with gifts of gold, frankincense and myrrh. 12And having been warned in a dream not to go back to Herod, they returned to their country by another route.

13When they had gone, an angel of the Lord appeared to Joseph in a dream. "Get up," he said, "take the child and his mother and escape to Egypt. Stay there until I tell you, for Herod is going to search for the child to kill him."

14So he got up, took the child and his mother during the night and left for Egypt, 15where he stayed until the death of Herod. And so was fulfilled what the Lord had said through the prophet: "Out of Egypt I called my son."

16When Herod realized that he had been outwitted by the Magi, he was furious, and he gave orders to kill all the boys in Bethlehem and its vicinity who were two years old and under, in accordance with the time he had learned from the Magi. 17Then what was said through the prophet Jeremiah was fulfilled:

> 18"A voice is heard in Ramah,
> weeping and great mourning,
> Rachel weeping for her children
> and refusing to be comforted,
> because they are no more."

19After Herod died, an angel of the Lord appeared in a dream to Joseph in Egypt 20and said, "Get up, take the child and his mother and go to the land of Israel, for those who were trying to take the child's life are dead."

21So he got up, took the child and his mother and went to the land of Israel. 22But when he heard that Archelaus was reigning in Judea in place of his father Herod, he was afraid to go there. Having been warned in a dream, he withdrew to the district of Galilee, [23]and he went and lived in a town called Nazareth. So was fulfilled what was said through the prophets, that he would be called a Nazarene.

Listening to the Text in the Story: Genesis 25:21–34; 26:34–27:41; Exodus 1:15–2:10; Numbers 20:14–21; 24:17–19; Deuteronomy 22:13–21, 23–27; 24:1; 2 Samuel 8:11–14; Psalm 137:7; Isaiah 7:10–15; 8:8–10; 9:6–7; 11:1–5; 60:1–7; Jeremiah 49:7–22; Lamentations 4:20–22; Obadiah 1–7, 10–18; Malachi 1:2–5; 1 Maccabees 5:3.

When foreign magi wandered into Herod's Jerusalem palace asking, "Where is the one who has been born king of the Jews?" they had no idea they walked into the middle of a controversy. What may have sounded to them like an innocuous request—after all, if a new king had been born, where else would they expect to find him except in the home of the current king?—was in reality a centuries-old question, loaded with all kinds of political baggage. It was a question that had been asked thousands of times by the children of Israel, especially during the days of Herod's kingdom. That's because Herod was an illegitimate king. Everyone knew who was actually "running the place." It may have looked like Herod was king of Israel—with all the pageantry and administrative industry indicative of client kingdoms—but Rome was the power behind the throne. Herodian officials excised taxes, but everyone knew most of the money went to Caesar: "Herod made the show; Caesar got the dough." In the minds of his subjects, therefore, Herod was nothing more than a puppet-king with Rome pulling the strings. But, even more than that, Herod was not the legitimate ruler of Israel because he wasn't "born" king of the Jews. He acquired the throne via power politics, that is, through shrewd maneuvers by his father (a friend of Caesar) and by his own cutthroat tactics to remove every possible rival. Herod was a ruthless tyrant, killing and imprisoning every potential enemy (even his own wife and sons!) in order to hold onto his crown. Indeed, such a power grab was the *only* way he could have become "king of the Jews." Herod was born an Idumaean (Edomite), which made him a descendant of Esau (the son of Isaac and the brother of Jacob).

Knowing the story of Esau and Jacob makes Herod's rule over Israel appear even more out of place. When Rebekah inquired of the Lord as to why her twins were fighting *in utero*, she heard the prophecy:

> Two nations are in your womb,
> and two peoples from within you will be separated;
> one people will be stronger than the other,
> and the older will serve the younger. (Gen 25:23)

As the story goes, the fate of Esau's subservience is sealed after he sells his birthright to Jacob, and then he eventually loses his father's blessing to the conniving ways of his mother and brother. That was the way it happened; that was the way it was supposed to be. By divine ordination and human manipulation, the sons of Jacob (Israelites) were to rule over the sons of Esau (Edomites): "A star will come out of Jacob; a scepter will rise out of Israel. He will crush the foreheads of Moab. . . . Edom will be conquered" (Num 24:17–18a). And, most of the time that seemed to be the case, especially during David's reign (2 Sam 8:13–14). Edom is often a marginal note in the covenant story of Israel; the sons of Esau are portrayed as embittered cousins, jealous of Jacob's seed. Never strong enough to challenge Judah in war, the Edomites were notorious for marauding the border villages of their neighbors (Obad 1–7). They were the ones cheering on Nebuchadnezzar when his army destroyed Jerusalem (Ps 137:7; Obad 10–13). Eventually displaced to Idumaea, they were forced to convert to Judaism by the Hasmonean king, John Hyrcanus.[1] A thoroughly subjugated people, imagine how much they would have relished the irony of one of their own, Herod, as king of Israel. "Forget the prophecy," they would say, "for who can deny that Esau rules over Jacob when Jesus was born?"

EXPLAIN the Story

Herod and Joseph are the two main characters in the story of Jesus's birth. The actual birth of Jesus doesn't get much press in Matthew's Gospel. Unlike Luke's version, there are no details of manger scenes and shepherd routines. Not here. Matthew would rather tell the stories surrounding the birth of the Messiah, the prior circumstances and aftereffects of such a prophetic advent. In other words, it's what's going on behind the scenes that intrigues Matthew more. That's because the story of Jesus's birth is more than a narrative of Israel's covenant story coming true. It's about two kingdoms colliding, two irrepressible forces clashing. The kingdom of heaven invading earth. The reign of God versus the rule of men. Herod against Joseph. It may look like a simple story about a boy born to Jewish parents, a son of David who would

1. Josephus, *Ant.* 13.9.1.

excite the messianic hopes of his people. But even Herod knew it is more than that. This is about who is running the show, who has the power to make it happen, who will win in the end, who is the legitimate king of Israel. In other words, as we read Matthew's Gospel, we will discover that the answer to the magi's provocative question, "Where is the one who has been born king of the Jews?" slowly unfolds before the reader—not only in the mysterious events surrounding his birth but eventually in the ironic placard affixed on the cross of his death: "This is Jesus, the King of the Jews" (Matt 27:37).

The Messiah Is Immanuel

The prophets longed for the day when the king of Israel ruled with such righteous judgment and justice that it would seem as though God himself were sitting on David's throne (sometimes it's difficult to tell whether the psalmist is writing about God or the king or both; e.g., Pss 45 and 47). That's the way the prophets saw it: if justice flowed like a river down to the lowest of the low—the defenseless and the helpless, widows and orphans—then God was present among his people (Amos 5:14–24). If the poorest of the poor were not experiencing the justice of God, then God was not there (Isa 1:21–23; 3:13–15; Jer 7:3–15; Mic 6:8). These sirens of social justice didn't believe in trickle-down economics, which is why the prophets would often point to the widows and orphans as the litmus test of God's reign. They were totally dependent upon God. If justice came to those who could not defend themselves, then God was the one who did it. So, the way the prophets saw it, widows and orphans were warning signs—canaries in the gold mine of Israel's fortune. If they were dying, watch out! It's just a matter of time until the whole thing blows up. The prophets, therefore, anticipated a day when the Lord would visit his people and take care of business. His presence would mean justice for all—bad news for those in power, good news for those who needed God's help. In other words, Immanuel ("God with us") would either be a welcomed relief or a feared punishment, depending upon who you were (Isa 7:14–25; 8:7–15).

Even though they had been looking for God's messiah for many years, the way he came into the world surprised everyone, from top to bottom. In fact, by the time they realized what was going on—both Joseph and Herod—God had already been at work, setting up the dominoes that would fall by divine design. Mary was already pregnant before Joseph was clued in by the angel. ("Why didn't God give him a 'heads up'"?) The star appeared two years before the magi knocked on Herod's door. Rather than set up a grand entrance for Immanuel, with invitations (and warnings!) sent out by a proud, expectant father, God appears to have smuggled his son through the backdoor without fanfare. Of course, how each man plays his part is nearly predictable. Herod, the illegitimate king and son of Esau, will do everything within his power to stop Immanuel. Joseph, the righteous, unsuspecting husband and son of David, will do everything without any power to protect him. And yet, it is God who will move heaven and earth to make this one thing, this one promise, finally come true. "This is how the birth of Jesus the Messiah came about" (Matt 1:18). A virgin shall conceive and bring forth a son. This was God's doing. "Do not be afraid to take Mary home as your wife, because what is conceived in her is from the Holy Spirit" (Matt 1:20). So, this is what happens when God visits his people. This is how the reign of God comes to earth. This is the day that the Lord has made, when Immanuel comes to save his people from their sins. The exile is over. The salvation of the Lord is here.

That's another surprising part of the story—that Israel needed someone to save them from their sins. God had set up the temple and the whole Levitical system to take care of such matters. The prescribed sacrifices offered to God took care of everything, whether sins of deception or sins of ignorance (Lev 5:14–6:7). The problem according to the prophets (like Isaiah) was that, even when God's house was full of worshipers bringing their bloody sacrifices, God was not pleased (Isa 1:10–25). To obey is better than sacrifice. Seeking justice trumps burnt offerings. "See how the faithful city has become a prostitute!" (v. 21). Israel needed a savior, the "anointed one" to help God's people get their house and his in order. Malachi anticipated what the day of divine deliverance would bring: a messenger (prophet!) to prepare the way of the Lord, God coming "suddenly" to his temple, priests purified by the fiery presence of the Lord, righteous men bringing acceptable sacrifices (Mal 3:1–4). All of this would eventually happen according to Matthew's version of the prophecies fulfilled in his Gospel story: the prophetic messenger, justice for the defenseless, the cleansing of the temple, the acceptable sacrifice—Jesus proves he is Immanuel. And it all started when a righteous man obeyed God and named his virgin-born son "Jesus" (Yahweh saves).[2]

A Man Had Two Sons

The ironic juxtaposition of Joseph's obedience and Herod's insolence serves well Matthew's purpose of defining true righteousness (a theme Jesus picks up from the very beginning during his famous Sermon on the Mount). Of course, the law defines what is right. But, who is truly obeying what God requires? Joseph was "truly faithful to the law," but he ends up disregarding the

---

2. By naming the child, the father claims the son legally; see Charles H. Talbert, *Matthew*, Paideia Commentaries on the New Testament (Grand Rapids: Baker Academic, 2010), 33. Garland (*Reading Matthew*, 22) refers to the "dual paternity of Jesus" (Son of David/Joseph; Son of God).

punishment required by the law for Mary's circumstances (Deut 22:13–21). To follow the letter of the law would result in Mary being put to death by stoning so as to "purge the evil from among you" (v. 21). There was an escape clause for those who didn't want to take such drastic measures. Since betrothal was as binding as marriage, Joseph could have divorced Mary quietly by issuing a bill of divorce and sending her away from his house (Deut 24:1)—the very thing he decided to do (Matt 1:19).[3] But then an angel from God convinced Joseph in a dream not to follow the law. Rather, he was not only supposed to stay betrothed to Mary but was commanded to take her "home as his wife" (Matt 1:24)—something the Judeans were known to do during the betrothal period, but not the Galileans.[4] In so many respects, then, Joseph appeared to be a lawbreaker: he took his pregnant fiancée home to live with him. But to those who knew the inside story (Joseph, Mary, and God!), Joseph was a righteous man—doing exactly what God required, even waiting to consummate the marriage until after the baby was born. Joseph did what was right despite how it looked.

Herod was the photographic negative of Joseph. He wanted to appear as though he intended to do the right thing, but the evil desires of his heart would be eventually exposed. He wants to know what the law says about the Messiah's birth, but it becomes apparent that he thinks such information is inadequate when he calls the magi "secretly" to get additional details about the mysterious star (Matt 2:7). One minute he's consulting God's word, the next he's cuddling up to pagan astrologers. (Forgive the analogy, but the offense may be compared to a state governor in the Bible Belt driving away from church services—hoping to hear "God's will" in the Sunday sermon—then deciding to stop by the local palm reader on the way home.) His duplicity becomes ever more apparent when he relies upon the magi to find this potential rival to the throne. He sends *them* (not the chief priests and scribes; they would have seen through Herod's ruse) to Bethlehem to look for the Christ-child; the current "king of the Jews" feigns sincere interest, hoping to hoodwink these ignorant outsiders: "Go and search carefully for the child. As soon as you find him, report to me, so that I too may go and worship him" (v. 8). Even the casual reader, perhaps having never heard of the notorious Herod and his sinister ways, knows this is suspect. Kings do not bow down to children; the only person Herod would bow down to is Caesar.

Righteousness is hard to spot sometimes. You would think that wouldn't be the case since the law is *the* standard for right behavior. Shouldn't it be readily apparent who is obeying the law and who isn't? And, to make matters

3. It was dishonorable for a man not to divorce his unfaithful fiancée (Keener, *Matthew*, 91).
4. Davies and Allison, *Matthew*, 1:199–200.

even more complex, what about those who don't even acknowledge the law? By definition, ignorant outsiders shouldn't be considered "righteous," for how could they do the right thing if they don't know what is right? And yet, here come the magi. Without knowing it, these outsiders blurred the lines of righteousness according to the law. Consider how "wrong" these foreigners are: 1) they don't belong to God's elect, 2) they act like they know what the God of Israel is up to simply because they can "read" the stars,[5] 3) they show up at the wrong place looking for the Messiah, awakening the jealous rage of a crazed ruler, 4) they give away their treasures to a complete stranger without confirming his identity (perhaps putting the little family at risk—gold attracts thieves), and 5) they went straight home (because of a dream!) and never returned to check on their investment.[6] Even in the best light (of a star, no less), these so-called "wise guys" come off looking like simpletons. Fools. Yet in their rather naive and simple way, the magi end up contrasting what right behavior looks like in the company of a king and his entourage who should know better. While the insiders are fumbling through the sacred wisdom of God's word, the outsiders end up finding the Messiah because they follow a star.[7] Matthew wants to make this plain: the magi didn't go to Bethlehem because of what the prophet Micah predicted, looking for the ruler who will "shepherd" Israel.[8] They headed for the city of David's birth only because the star reappeared to show them the way (Matt 2:9–10). Like children easily attracted to bright lights, they were "overjoyed with exceeding great joy"[9] when the star led them directly to the house.[10] Once they arrived, "they bowed down and worshiped him," presented their gifts and left (v. 11). Not knowing any better, the magi did the right thing. They offered proper acts of obeisance to the king of the Jews—something Herod must have expected for himself.

---

5. Stars and especially comets were interpreted by pagans as omens marking the birth of powerful rulers (Davies and Allison, *Matthew*, 1:233–35). For Jews, astral signs signaled the end of the world (Isa 34:4; Ezek 32:7–8; Joel 2:30–31).

6. One wonders what the magi would think, returning to Jerusalem about thirty-three years later, only to find a man hanging on a cross with the sign above his head, "This is Jesus, the King of the Jews."

7. Bailey finds a reference to the star "rising" in Isaiah 60:1–7, a messianic text that Matthew "de-Zionized," identifying these Arab magi as "your sons [who] come from afar, and your daughters [who] are carried on the hip," who are also the "nations" and "kings" who bring their treasures on camels (Kenneth E. Bailey, *Jesus through Middle Eastern Eyes: Cultural Studies in the Gospels* [Downers Grove, IL: IVP Academic, 2008], 53–54).

8. Contra Keener, *Matthew*, 99–100.

9. Matthew's wording in the Greek text is emphatic.

10. Some commentators try to make sense of the star in astronomical terms, tracking certain alignments of planets that created the illusion of a "new star" appearing around the birth of Jesus (see Brown, *Birth of the Messiah*, 171–73). But such efforts are unnecessary, for how does one explain that a massive, fiery ball of gas (like our sun) hovered directly above a one-room house in Bethlehem? Obviously, this was no ordinary "star."

It's no wonder, then, that after the magi showed up looking for the one "born" king of the Jews, Herod "was disturbed, and all Jerusalem with him" (v. 3). Given his track record, Jerusalem knew what this meant. An unbalanced tyrant is easily provoked; a paranoid man with great power must be placated at all costs. That dignitaries came to Herod's palace bearing expensive gifts, only to leave unexpectedly without saying goodbye, pushed him over the edge. By the time Herod "realized that he had been outwitted by the Magi," it was too late (v. 16). The child had been smuggled out of Bethlehem. But Herod didn't know that. The only thing he knew was that he had been tricked by the magi, which must have convinced him they were up to no good. "Did they travel to Bethlehem? Did they find the child? Were the locals in cahoots with these foreigners? Were they scheming some coup d'état?" Whatever the wicked king inferred, he took his frustration out on the people in and around Bethlehem. (Did Jerusalem breathe a sigh of relief?) By having all the boys in the region slaughtered, two years of age and younger, Herod took drastic measures to make sure no "Messiah" would oppose him.[11] Since infanticide was the ultimate revenge against one's enemies (2 Kgs 8:12; Ps 137:9; Isa 13:16; Hos 13:16), Bethlehem knew where they stood with their king.

The Refugee Returns Home (Sort Of)

The reason Israel hoped for God to come like a shepherd and gather the "lost sheep" is because they had been disappointed by their rulers so many times—both priests and kings. The royal histories (the books of Samuel and Kings) and the prophets tell the same story, over and over again: when the king did what was evil in the sight of the Lord, the people suffered the consequences. At the same time, the people were not completely innocent in the matter; their complicity in rebelling against God was cannon fodder for the prophets: they were getting what they deserved (Isa 63:10). And yet it is not as if God left them to their misery, consigning Israel to the inevitable consequences of their sin. The people would cry out to God for relief. God would send a "Moses" to deliver his people from the despotic king and to shepherd them to the land of God's blessing (Isa 63:11–12). And the journey always involved time in the wilderness, when Israel needed to learn how to "live in tents again" and obey God (Hos 12:9; cf. 2:14). Then the faithful remnant—the sheep of God's pasture—would return to graze in the promised land of the covenant until another wicked king led the people astray (8:4; 13:9–11; Jer 23:1–4).

---

11. Although it is possible to exaggerate the number of victims (given the demographics at the time, scholars estimate no more than twelve to twenty children were murdered; see Brown, *Birth of the Messiah*, 204–5), the atrocity of a king destroying his own subjects (the very people he was supposed to protect) in such a callous, heinous way cannot be overstated.

This is why prophets like Hosea and Jeremiah warned their generations that it was time to go back to "Egypt" (Hos 11:1–11; Jer 16:10–15; 23:7–12). The way they saw it, God would repeat the cycle until Israel learned the lesson and God raises up a "righteous Branch, a King who will reign wisely and do what is just and right in the land" (Jer 23:5).

The last turn of the wheel of Israel's history, the cycle finally broken according to Matthew, happened when Joseph took his family to Egypt to flee the wrath of the wicked king Herod. And, once again, as in the days of Moses the path of deliverance would take a circuitous route, this time from Judea to Egypt to Galilee. Even though Micah predicted the Messiah would be a mighty Shepherd-King like David, at this point Jesus looks more like a helpless lamb trying to escape slaughter. But then again, that fits the story of Israel's redemption.[12] In desperate times, God shows up to lead his flock away from danger and into the protection of his covenant blessing. One cannot help but wonder: Why doesn't the Almighty dispose of his opponents? If Herod is the problem, why not remove the threat immediately? Instead, it looks like Joseph (and God?) is forced to wait around in exile until Herod dies. And, even after the angel tells Joseph it's safe to return "to the land of Israel," it took a dream to warn him not to go back home to Bethlehem (Matt 2:19–23; remember, in Matthew's story the trip to Nazareth isn't a homecoming). Since Herod's son took his father's place in Judea—the son of a tyrant is most likely a tyrant—Joseph moves his family to a little village in Galilee, perhaps hoping to live in obscurity. But Matthew sees a higher purpose in this convoluted drama. The Passover-like, nighttime escape from Bethlehem, the return to exile in Egypt, only to wind up in Nazareth (of all places!)—all of it was by divine design.[13] It may have appeared that Joseph and his family were pawns in the hands of a wicked king, victims of the volatile times of a transition of royal power that forced them to leave home. Instead, every twist and turn of the story fulfilled what the prophets had predicted: "He would be called a Nazarene" (v. 23).

It is hard to tell whether Matthew had Isaiah 11:1, Jeremiah 23:5, or some other passage in mind when he referred to the fulfilled prophecy.[14] The Isaiah connection depends upon a wordplay that can only be seen in Hebrew (*netser*, "branch," sounds like *Nazaret*, "Nazareth"). When Isaiah spoke of a "branch" that would shoot out of the stump of Israel, he was playing off the imagery of

12. "Whereas we prefer to think of a single specific fulfillment of a prophet's prediction, Matthew's typological interest leads him rather to find patterns which will recur repeatedly throughout God's dealings with his people" (France, *Matthew*, 57).

13. "We may say, then, that while Jesus culminates Israel's history in chapter 1, in chapter 2 he repeats it" (Davies and Allison, *Matthew*, 1:282).

14. See the discussion in Davies and Allison, *Matthew*, 1:276–81.

a felled tree—a sign of God's judgment against his people (Isa 6:13)—whose root system didn't die but produced a branch of hope (11:1). Later, it seems "the branch" became the go-to image in messianic prophecy (Jer 23:5; 33:15; Zech 3:8; 6:12), which may explain why Matthew claims that several "prophets" predicted that "he would be called a Nazarene" (Matt 2:23). So it is quite apparent that the exact reference was not important to Matthew. It's the fact that Jesus winds up in Galilee that matters the most. Indeed, Matthew expects his readers to recognize the pattern, the divine illocution of the story of Israel's hope—Jesus as the embodiment of Israel will have come full circle to redeem *all* of God's people: from Judah, through Egypt, to Israel (Ephraim). If this shepherd, predicted long ago, is to gather the lost sheep of Israel, he must not only reclaim the throne of David in Jerusalem but also reconstitute the lost tribes of the northern kingdom, Israel.[15] What was lost after king David—a divided kingdom—will be reunited in new life that springs from the holy stump: "In those days and at that time I will make a righteous Branch sprout from David's line; he will do what is just and right in the land" (Jer 33:15).

The way Matthews sees it, then, this is the last time Rachel will weep for her children (Jer 31:15–18).

LIVE the Story

This is the Christmas story? Matthew's version of our favorite holiday is hardly recognizable except for the star and the wise men. Joseph nearly divorcing Mary, Herod's diabolical ploy, the slaughter of the innocents, the flight to Egypt, waiting for a wicked king to die—none of these things make the cover of Christmas cards. We prefer idyllic pastoral scenes of shepherds tending their flock by night, winged angels hovering in radiant splendor, the customary Christmas crèche featuring parents attending the newborn, the quiet shelter of a wooden stable with barn animals reverentially witnessing the miracle. In other words, we feature Luke's story over Matthew's. But even Luke's account has been sanitized so as not to offend our holiday sensibilities of good cheer and great joy. (Whenever I read Luke's account, I cannot help but hear the voice of Linus, Charlie Brown's trusted friend, as the narrator. "Lights please.") Yet Luke's nativity story has its dark moments too—with poll taxes and displaced imperial subjects. Even the manger scene was not as comfy as we try to make it out to be. (One wonders what a "scratch and sniff" Bible would do to bring us down to reality: [scratch, scratch] "Whew! *That* doesn't

15. See Joel Willitts, *Matthew's Messianic Shepherd-King in Search of 'the Lost Sheep of The House of Israel'* (Berlin: de Gruyter, 2007), 58–67.

smell like Christmas!") Even in our world that prizes so-called "reality TV," we don't want the real Christmas story.

There's a reason why such scenes, especially from Matthew's nativity story, never appear on our Christmas cards. No one would buy them because no one wants to see it. Can you imagine staging the "slaughter of the innocents" during the Christmas play? Herodian soldiers enter stage right, bearing swords, murdering all the two-year-olds on the Bethlehem stage. Parents shriek in horror, covering the eyes of their children, "Don't look, Johnny! I don't know what they're trying to do up there. Must have their holidays confused. Hey, this isn't Halloween!" Yet there it is in Matthew's story. In all of its glory. And, we turn our eyes away from the tragedy because everyone knows Christmas is about warm feelings, nostalgic recollections, and finding serenity in the midst of our chaotic lives.

So we center on the only part of Matthew's story that works for us: the gift-giving wise men. Rather than play down the episode, we go to the other extreme and exaggerate the significance of what happened. Indeed, this may be the worst case of contrived justification bound up in all Christian holidays. (We don't even *try* to justify the Easter bunny on Resurrection Sunday.) Once my children learned the truth about Santa Claus, they asked, "Why do we get gifts on Jesus's birthday? Shouldn't we give him a gift?" As I tried to justify the custom, appealing to the behavior of the wise men only made things worse. We all know why gift-giving has become the generating center of the holiday; the commercialization of Christmas is built on the foundation of greed. We always want more. Some families try to counteract our selfish inclinations stoked by holiday shopping with serving food to the homeless on December 25th. Others have launched a "war on Christmas," trying to reclaim the religious significance of Advent, focusing our attention with the worn-out cliché "the reason for the season" and offering strangers the defiant greeting, "Merry Christmas." Why do we try so hard? Perhaps it's because Christians presume Christmas is *our* holiday, a holy observance that must be defended against the pagan influences of our corrupt society.

But Matthew would remind us—especially through the story of the wise men—that Jesus doesn't belong to us. He was born for the whole world. That's why the magi showed up in the first place, with their gaudy gifts and pagan astrology. In their own, flawed way, they recognized the significance of his birth. I think about that part of Matthew's version of Christmas when I walk through shopping malls during the holiday season, taking in the irony of hearing "O, Come All Ye Faithful" as background music to the economic boon of the retail industry. "Even unbelievers know this matters," I mutter to myself. There's something strangely appealing to me about seeing all kinds of people—even the "wrong kind of people" in their pagan ways—celebrating Christmas. Jesus belongs to everyone, whether we like it or not. And as Matthew's story reminds us, not everyone will like it—especially the powerful, the insiders, those who think they're appointed to rule the world. Submit to King Jesus? Hardly. They have an empire to run, a kingdom of this world to rule, and they will do everything in their power—even shed innocent blood—to protect it. Oh, they may pay lip service to Jesus, promising to worship him. But we all know that you can't take some politicians at their word. Feigning sincerity is their craft; power politics is their game. And they'll destroy anyone who dares to oppose them. There's no way on earth (perhaps in hell one day? Phil 2:10–11) they will bend their knee to another. Indeed, those who try to rule the world *always* reject the King. *That's* what Christmas is all about, too.

So, despite the popularity of our sanitized versions of Luke's account, I'm drawn to Matthew's story—all of it—the parts we like and especially the parts we ignore. It's not because I want to shore up the economic welfare of our country. It's not because I have some peculiar desire for dwelling on the macabre realities of life. It's not because American politics always leaves a bad taste in my mouth. No; somehow I find hope knowing that even when Jesus was born, there were outsiders bearing gifts, politicians trying to hold onto power, and people in Bethlehem screaming, "Where is God?" Rachel mourning for her children. Mary probably grieved over the news down in Egypt, living off of the gold provided by the magi. After all, the Bethlehem women were a part of their little community—friends who shared resources, stories, and daily chores. They did life together. Their children played together. Such news may have even compelled Mary to ask the same question in the face of such human suffering, "God, where are you?"

He's a vulnerable baby, hiding out in Egypt due to the generosity of pagans, waiting for a wicked king to die.

For some reason, I love that part of the story nobody tells during Christmas.

CHAPTER 3

Matthew 3:1–17

LISTEN to the Story

1 In those days John the Baptist came, preaching in the wilderness of
Judea 2 and saying, "Repent, for the kingdom of heaven has come near."
3 This is he who was spoken of through the prophet Isaiah:

> "A voice of one calling in the wilderness,
> 'Prepare the way for the Lord,
> make straight paths for him.'"

4 John's clothes were made of camel's hair, and he had a leather belt
around his waist. His food was locusts and wild honey. 5 People went out
to him from Jerusalem and all Judea and the whole region of the Jordan.
6 Confessing their sins, they were baptized by him in the Jordan River.

7 But when he saw many of the Pharisees and Sadducees coming to
where he was baptizing, he said to them: "You brood of vipers! Who
warned you to flee from the coming wrath? 8 Produce fruit in keeping
with repentance. 9 And do not think you can say to yourselves, 'We have
Abraham as our father.' I tell you that out of these stones God can raise
up children for Abraham. 10 The ax is already at the root of the trees, and
every tree that does not produce good fruit will be cut down and thrown
into the fire.

11 "I baptize you with water for repentance. But after me comes one
who is more powerful than I, whose sandals I am not worthy to carry. He
will baptize you with the Holy Spirit and fire. 12 His winnowing fork is in
his hand, and he will clear his threshing floor, gathering his wheat into the
barn and burning up the chaff with unquenchable fire."

13 Then Jesus came from Galilee to the Jordan to be baptized by John.
14 But John tried to deter him, saying, "I need to be baptized by you, and
do you come to me?"

15 Jesus replied, "Let it be so now; it is proper for us to do this to fulfill
all righteousness." Then John consented.

[16]As soon as Jesus was baptized, he went up out of the water. At that moment heaven was opened, and he saw the Spirit of God descending like a dove and alighting on him. [17]And a voice from heaven said, "This is my Son, whom I love; with him I am well pleased."

Listening to the Text in the Story: 1 Kings 17:1–6; 2 Kings 1:3–10; Psalm 2; Isaiah 40:1–14; 42:1–4; Joel 2:25–32; Malachi 3:1–5; 4:1–6.

God warned Israel that he would suddenly return to his people in full power and glory. That day would be a day of judgment and blessing, a day of darkness and light, a day of fire and purification. Both a great *and* terrible day of the Lord. Yet he promised his people that the day wouldn't catch them "flat footed." God would warn Israel ahead of time, just before he showed up, to prepare them for his marvelous appearance. What were the warning signs? There were several, but one in particular caught the imagination of the people. The prophet who mysteriously left earth in a chariot of fire would return from heaven to deliver his last sermon. Right before the day of the Lord, Elijah would come back to turn the hearts of Israel back to God (Mal 4:5–6). Elijah's return would be the taletell sign that the end of the world was near. So, to say the least, everyone was looking for Elijah, for then Israel would know what time it was.

How did John know it was time for the kingdom of heaven to come to earth? Did God tell him, "John, it's time"? Was it because he knew about the unusual circumstances of Jesus's birth, that the Messiah had been born? And, even if he did, why now? ("Let's see. Jesus would be about thirty years old. That's a good age to start a messianic movement.") Did John infer it was time because of the political and social circumstances of his day—like the prophets of old, who considered a profane temple and a corrupt monarchy operating in the shadow of a looming, foreign power a sign of God's imminent judgment? Or did he simply wake up one morning, put on a prophet's costume, head for the Judean desert, and preach repentance to the rocks to see if anyone would show up? Furthermore, where did he get the idea to baptize the repentant? No prophet before him did anything like it. Baptism in the Jordan River was never prophesied as an end-of-the-world sign. Why did he do it? What did it mean? And finally, why did the Judeans flock to John? What persuaded them that he was a legitimate prophet? Even though he dressed like Elijah (2 Kgs 1:8), he performed no miracle like the great prophet. Even though John preached the same old, well-known (some might say, "worn-out") prophetic message of repentance, many false prophets appeared who didn't attract such a dramatic following.[1] In fact, Zechariah warned his generation that many Elijah wannabes would show up, trying to deceive the people into thinking the time had come since the appearance of Elijah was supposed to be *the* sign. But Zechariah knew the Judeans wouldn't be fooled; he anticipated that they would kill the imposters as a warning to any false prophet who would dare to make such an audacious claim (Zech 13:2–6). And yet, here comes John, for no "apparent" reason, looking like Elijah, preaching in the Judean desert, declaring the fateful day of the Lord has come, and just about everyone acts like he's the real deal. Why?

Matthew answers none of these questions. John appears in Matthew's narrative as mysteriously as he appeared in the Judean desert: without introduction and little explanation (same was true for Elijah,[2] 1 Kgs 17:1). Matthew doesn't even feel obliged to provide any historical context except to write that "in those days John the Baptist came" (Matt 3:1). It's as if Matthew knows John needs no introduction. He simply identifies John "the Baptist" (who gave him this title?) as "the voice of one calling in the wilderness" (3:3) and assumes all of his readers will know who he is. That's how famous the Baptizer was; long after his death John's baptism still mattered (Acts 19:3–4). In fact, John's authority as a prophet was so unquestionable, even Jesus decided to appeal to John's clout to get out of trouble with the temple authorities (Matt 21:23–27). The Jewish people were convinced John was a prophet from God. In certain respects, then, it appears John knew it was time because the people were ready for Elijah to return, just as Malachi prophesied he would, to prepare Israel "before that great and dreadful day of the Lord comes" (Mal 4:5). But it wasn't just that sinners showed up in the middle of the desert looking for repentance—John knew it was time for the Messiah because the people needed more than what he could give them to get ready for God. It's one thing to find cleansing in the river. It's quite something else to be purified by the fiery presence of God's Spirit. John knew this as well as anyone: his baptism would be inadequate. The kingdom of heaven coming to earth would require more than water. This is why he predicted the coming of another one "more powerful than I" (Matt 3:11)—but each in his own order. First water, then fire. First the desert, then the Spirit. John would come first, but Jesus would be preeminent; one can only give what one has.

1. Josephus, *Ant.* 20.8.6; *J.W.* 2.13.4–5.

2. France, *Matthew*, 100.

EXPLAIN the Story

The desert is a strange place for anyone to expect to meet God. After all, since God is life, and death reigns in the wilderness, one should look for God in a place called "paradise." But, of course, the story of Israel's life was seeking God in the desert because the curse of sin turned paradise into a wilderness. Israel found God in the desert when Moses led his people to the edge of the promised land. The prophets knew that the wilderness was the very place where God always seemed to get the attention of his people (Hos 2:14–23). Isaiah predicted a prophet would need to show up in the wilderness to prepare the way for God to come and lead Israel out of exile so that she might return to the land of his promise—a "new exodus" (Isa 40:1–11). It makes perfect sense: the only way to inhabit the uninhabitable is if God shows up and gives life. The desert seemed to be the *one* place where Israel proved they were children of God because they had to trust him to provide. A cursed ground does not yield good fruit. And nowhere is it more evident that the ground is cursed than the place where death reigns. Indeed, if God is going to reverse the curse of sin and death, the first place he needs to show up is in the desert. That's why John lived in the desert. That's why people "from Jerusalem and all Judea and the whole region of the Jordan" (Matt 3:5) trekked out in the middle of nowhere to be baptized by him. The desert is the very place where the repentant are led to meet the God of Israel. It's the meek who will inherit the land. That's the way the story goes.

People Get Ready, Jesus Is Coming

John's message was fairly simple: repent because God's reign is coming to earth. Matthew prefers the expression "the kingdom of heaven" over the Markan/Lukan phrase "the kingdom of God" to emphasize that God's reign coming to earth will require divine agency.[3] Israel longed for the day when God's heavenly reign would invade earth—not just Israel's land but the whole earth ("Oh, that you would rend the heavens and come down"; Isa 64:1). So when John preached that "the kingdom of heaven has come near," he was speaking spatially and temporally (Matt 3:2). That is, John believed the kingdom of heaven was descending to earth at that time. More than that, he claimed it was already happening, that the "ax is already at the root of the trees" (v. 10).

3. See Robert Foster, "Why on Earth Use 'Kingdom of Heaven'? Matthew's Terminology Revisited," *NTS* 48 (2002): 487–99. Jonathan T. Pennington argues that the phrase "the kingdom of heaven [plural]," refers to the invisible, divine realm of God's rule, while reference to "heaven [singular]" indicates the visible, earthly realm of God's reign (*Heaven and Earth in the Gospel of Matthew* [Leiden: Brill, 2007], 136–42).

That's why Israel needed to repent. But, the way John saw it, experiencing the reign of God did not depend upon the repentant. It wasn't a matter of "if we don't repent we'll miss out" or "look, the kingdom is bending low; we better repent so God's reign will come." Rather, John believed *everyone* would witness the kingdom of heaven coming to earth. Those who refused to repent would experience God's judgment, while those who heeded his message and produced "fruit in keeping with repentance" would avoid the wrath of God (v. 8). This is not a "feel good" message of deliverance. To put it bluntly, John wasn't preaching "good news."[4] Indeed, the Baptist seems to offer very little hope to Israel other than the fact that he was convinced a stronger man would follow him and finish the job he started, gathering the harvest and burning up the chaff (v. 12).

So John's project was eschatological: an emphasis on changed behavior due to the imminent "end of the world."[5] And since the Baptizer was preparing all Israel for the day of divine visitation, did John's message apply to him? Did John require of himself the "fruit of repentance"? Perhaps so, for that would explain his austere life in the desert, which was probably a recent change of residence for him—not to mention his peculiar diet and clothing.[6] Yet the fact that he dressed like Elijah and appeared in the Judean desert by the Jordan river (just like Elijah, 1 Kgs 17:5) made it evident that John was acting like a prophet, and the people certainly saw it that way. Furthermore, since prophets were known for their peculiar behavior—prophetic acts that symbolized their message (like Jeremiah's broken pot or Isaiah's exposed backside)—then John's baptism and weird diet may have revealed his eschatological purpose. But why locusts and wild honey? Most attribute John's food to an act of piety, living only on what the land provided (2 Macc 5:27). Even today grasshoppers and locusts are a staple for Bedouin shepherds—the realities of life in the desert.[7] Moreover, locusts in John's day were among the creepy-crawlies that were edible because they weren't unclean (Lev 11:20–23). But why would the Gospel writers specifically mention *locusts* and wild honey? That wasn't the *only* "clean" wilderness fare available to him. Besides, such a diet was expected of desert dwellers—of course John was going to live off the land. What other

4. Davies and Allison, *Matthew*, 1:290.

5. "John's message is characterized as having two aspects: (1) an ethical imperative [repent] . . . based on (2) an eschatological reality [the kingdom of heaven has come near]" (David L. Turner, *Matthew*, BECNT [Grand Rapids: Baker Academic, 2008], 106).

6. "John's clothing and diet model the message he preaches" (Turner, *Matthew*, 109). For a discussion of John's peculiar lifestyle, see Keener, *Matthew*, 116–19. A few scholars have suggested that John had already adopted desert life due to his association with the Qumran community—an opinion that hasn't yielded much support (see Davies and Allison, *Matthew*, 1:290–91).

7. Davies and Allison, *Matthew*, 1:296.

options would he have? The wilderness isn't farmable. In other words, perhaps John's diet was a symbolic act embodying more than pious self-deprivation.

Joel predicted that, before the day of the Lord—the day when God would "pour out my Spirit on all people" (Joel 2:28)—God would repay Israel for what the locust robbed from the land. "I will repay you for the years the locusts have eaten. . . . You will have plenty to eat, until you are full. . . . Then you will know that I am in Israel, that I am the LORD your God" (vv. 25–27). The prophet consoled the Judeans, "Do not be afraid, land of Judah, . . . for the pastures of the wilderness are becoming green. The trees are bearing their fruit . . . the threshing floors will be filled with grain" (vv. 21, 22, 24). All of these images show up in Matthew's story about John: locusts, barren land of Judea, fruit-bearing trees, threshing floor filled with grain, and baptism of the Spirit. To be sure, what appears as reasons for hope in Joel's oracle sounds like judgment in John's message. Yet perhaps John's ministry wasn't all gloom and doom, that eating locust wasn't a sign of self-denial. After all, the Gospels emphasize he ate locusts and honey. Since the promised land was supposed to be a place flowing with milk and honey, perhaps John ate locust as a prophetic act declaring that Joel's vision was coming true.[8] John was making a dramatic claim that the eschatological hour had arrived. He ate locusts *and* wild honey because the time had come to devour the devourer (locusts), for God's promises to come true, and for the barren land to produce a bountiful harvest. His desert diet was a prophetic sign of hope mingled with dire warnings about the approaching judgment of God. It's quite a picture to imagine: a wilderness man announcing the coming wrath of God, bits of locusts dangling from his lips, his camel-hair shirt matted with honey, offering water baptism to the repentant. It's no wonder, then, that all the Gospels describe John the same way.[9] Like the prophets of old, what the Baptizer *did* was the message as much as what he *said*—which leads to the even more puzzling question: Why did he baptize?

Drastic Times Call for Drastic Measures

It's quite apparent that John's baptism was something new. After all, the reason he earned the nickname "the Baptist" wasn't because John took a business-as-usual approach to Israel's circumstances. There was something unique about this water ritual that led the people to identify John as "the Baptizer." That's why comparisons with Jewish water rituals at that time don't match up with John's baptism. (Of course, it would be anachronistic to compare

8. I owe this insight to David Capes (personal communication).

9. Strangely enough, the Gospel writers never give a physical description of Jesus nor describe explicitly what he wore or ate even though he is the main character of their story.

John's baptism to Christian baptism. Even though it might be easy for us to project Christian imagery on this Jewish ritual, John certainly wasn't baptizing candidates—arms folded and leaning back into the water-like burial—with the pronouncement: "Buried in the likeness of his burial; raised in the likeness of his resurrection." Obviously, John's baptism wasn't a Christian baptism.) The Pharisees emphasized the importance of ongoing rituals of purification to maintain holiness. Contact with unclean things made one impure. And since purity is a requirement of holiness, then the Jewish people who followed the teaching of the Pharisees baptized themselves often, either completely immersing themselves in water collected in a carved-out-of-stone bath called a *mikvah* or by washing themselves with water stored in large purification pots (which would look to us like they were "washing up for supper").[10] But, the differences between John's baptism and the ritual washings required for purification make it evident that the Baptist wasn't offering the same thing: 1) John's baptism was a one-time washing vs. the necessity of repeated purification; 2) John's baptism was an act of repentance that followed a confession of sin vs. ritual cleansing that often had nothing to do with sin; for example, impurity due to the birth of a child, marital sex, menstruation (Lev 12:1–5; 15:16–33); and 3) John baptized the penitent vs. self-baptism of the ritually unclean.[11]

Proselyte baptism comes closer to John's baptism. Gentile converts to Judaism experienced a one-time cleansing as part of the ritual (which included circumcision and a sacrifice) that was necessary for purification and to mark a change in status. That idea appears to show up a few places in the Qumran literature where these Jewish sectarians required novitiates to submit to baptism as an entry rite of purification as well as daily washing rituals of all members. Yet scholars question whether both practices (proselyte and novitiate baptism) existed in John's day. Besides, John's baptism differed from this Jewish ritual as well: he was the one who administered the rite (one wonders what that looked like—did he "dunk" them or pour water on their heads?), and his baptism was a *one-time act only* required of *Jews* (not gentiles) who repented of sin. So John's baptism seems to be unique compared to Jewish rites of purification. Therefore, we still don't know why he did it, other than the fact that John believed his baptism was necessary to prepare Israel for the day of God's visitation. In fact, the way the Baptist saw it, Jews who refused to repent of their sin and be baptized were relying upon their ethnicity to avert the wrath

10. See Jodi Magness, *Stone and Dung, Oil and Spit: Jewish Daily Life in the Time of Jesus* (Grand Rapids: Eerdmans, 2011), 16–21.

11. For further discussion, see the definitive work by Everett Ferguson, *Baptism in the Early Church: History, Theology, and Liturgy in the First Five Centuries* (Grand Rapids: Eerdmans, 2009), 60–96.

of God—something John believed was a foolish mistake: "Do not think you can say to yourselves, 'We have Abraham as our father.' I tell you that out of these stones God can raise up children for Abraham" (Matt 3:9).

That idea—that John so easily dismissed ethnic identity as evidence of covenant membership—wasn't new. It's the reason the Qumran community withdrew from "the world" and predicted God's judgment on the rest of Israel (1QS 8:13–14). It's what Paul claimed ("For not all who are descended from Israel are Israel. Nor because they are his descendants are they all Abraham's children"; Rom 9:6–7), building his argument of gentile inclusion on Isaiah's remnant theology (vv. 27–29; Isa 10:22–23). By requiring baptism, then, "John was treating his fellow Jews as if they were spiritually gentiles."[12] Those who refused to repent and submit to baptism revealed, according to John, that they were not true descendants of Abraham. This is why the Baptist emphasized the importance of bringing "fruit in keeping with repentance" to the river. John didn't stand ready to baptize everyone. Indeed, he refused to baptize—"winnowing" the chaff from the wheat—those who were unworthy to be called "children of Abraham" because they did not truly repent.[13]

Yet how did John know they weren't ready to repent, dismissing them out of hand as a "brood of vipers"? It's because they were Pharisees and Sadducees (Matt 3:7), which makes their first appearance in Matthew's Gospel function as an ominous sign for the rest of the story. These people are the bad guys (16:1–12; 22:15–23:36). Matthew doesn't feel obliged to explain why the Baptizer was suspicious of these two influential groups of Jewish leaders—sects that were rarely paired together because they were often at odds with each other, theologically and politically (Acts 23:6–10; Josephus, *Ant.* 13.10.6). Since they probably came from Jerusalem, maybe this was the familiar "city slickers"-versus-the-"country bumpkin" showdown that seems to happen regardless of cultural context. Or, perhaps as members of the Sanhedrin, these official Jewish leaders were on surveillance, suspicious of the rogue prophet and his radical ways infecting the ignorant masses. To them, John's message—no Jew is acceptable to God unless he or she is baptized by him—must have sounded like an outrageously arrogant claim as well as a biting critique of their leadership. So the distrust probably worked both ways. It had been a long time since a prophet had attracted as much attention as John: "He was a sensation."[14] And yet, unbeknownst to them, John's appearance in the desert was only the beginning of things to come—just as the Baptist predicted.

12. Keener, *Matthew*, 121.
13. Turner, *Matthew*, 109, 112–13.
14. Davies and Allison, *Matthew*, 1:298.

The Messiah Is Anointed

Every king of Israel needed a prophet, not only to anoint him but also to keep him accountable to God. Saul had Samuel, David had Nathan, Hezekiah had Isaiah. In fact, Psalm 2 reads like a script for the installation of the new king of Israel where both the heir to the throne *and* the prophet recite lines during the anointing (Ps 2:1–7). So when Jesus comes to the Jordan to be "anointed" by John the prophet, it seems that the stage is set for the installation of the new king of Israel. But there are problems. John objects to playing his part in anointing Jesus, and with good reason: John's baptism was a sign of repentance marking all of the true children of Abraham—not the Messiah (Matt 3:14). Besides, the prophet had announced that the "coming one" would be so empowered by the Holy Spirit that John wouldn't be worthy to carry the man's sandals (v. 11), much less baptize him. Jesus didn't need John's baptism of repentance. Rather, the Baptist stated the obvious: John is the one who must be baptized because he needed what only Jesus can give—the baptism of the Holy Spirit and fire.[15]

For some reason Jesus insisted on being baptized by John, and the Baptist relented (v. 15). Why? Some commentators key on the first part of Jesus's reply, "Let it be so for now," implying that submitting to John's baptism was only a temporary necessity—it wasn't quite time for the baptism of the Spirit.[16] Others find the reason for Jesus's baptism in that he believed it would "fulfill all righteousness," either 1) to satisfy expectations regarding how the Messiah was to be revealed by "Elijah," or 2) to identify with the righteous remnant of Israel, or 3) to model humility by being baptized with sinners, or 4) to identify with the Servant of the Lord (Isa 42:1–7; 52:13–53:12).[17] It's difficult to figure out what Jesus meant by his rather enigmatic response to John; all of these reasons make a lot of sense. Besides, Matthew is quick to point out that Jesus was a righteous man—especially when he defied the standards of righteousness according to the Pharisees (Matt 5:17–20; 6:1–18; 8:10–17; 12:1–21; 15:1–20; 21:28–46; 23:1–36). Therefore, the fact Jesus was "anointed by God" right after he was "anointed by the prophet" confirms, in their very first "contest," that Jesus was right and the Pharisees were wrong. Was God about to visit Israel, and was John's ministry a sign of the times? Obviously, the Pharisees didn't think so. Jesus, on the other hand, was convinced it was time to "fulfill all righteousness." And, because of what happened that day—heaven split opened, the Spirit of God anointed Jesus, the heavenly voice confirmed the new king of Israel—it's quite apparent that God *openly* sided with

15. "[John] is not asking for the reversal of roles at the Jordan. His point is that his own baptism is by its very nature provisional and anticipatory" (Nolland, *Matthew*, 153).

16. "The implication is that the baptism of the Spirit is not yet. For now, John has been commissioned by God to prepare Israel by making it pass through the waters" (Garland, *Reading Matthew*, 37).

17. See the discussion in Davies and Allison, *Matthew*, 1:321–23.

John and Jesus. Indeed, to punctuate the matter, this is one of the few times in Matthew's Gospel when God actually speaks for himself. And, ironically, when God speaks, he's quoting what the prophets said they heard him say.

The heavenly acclamation (Matt 3:17) sounds like a conflation of Psalm 2:7, "you are my son," and Isaiah 42:1, "my chosen one in whom I delight"—a combination of references to a newly enthroned king and a king to come.[18] According to Matthew, Jesus fit the bill from the beginning, not only because of his royal pedigree and birth but especially due to the fact that Isaiah 42 reads like a summary of Jesus's ministry (Matt 12:15–21). In other words, to put it bluntly, God knew what he was doing when he "spoke up" at Jesus's baptism, delivering this "mash-up" of lines taken from both royal coronation and prophetic proclamation, kingdom present and kingdom come. Anointed by God's Spirit (the Messiah of the Lord!), Jesus was not only installed as the long-awaited king of Israel, but he was empowered to make good on every promise God ever made—not only to Israel but to the whole world.[19] This is why several commentators hear echoes of "new creation" in the dove-like appearance of the Holy Spirit (Gen 1:2; 8:8–12).[20] The baptism of Jesus is, therefore, a pivotal event in Matthew's story, chock-full of theological potential. Indeed, in this one event we see the beginning and the end, the promise and the fulfillment, prophet and king, heaven and earth, water and Spirit, Father and Son.

Jesus is the beloved one because he fulfills all righteousness. God said as much to anyone who had ears to hear: "This is my Son" (Matt 3:17).[21] And, according to Matthew the second time God speaks up, he will say *exactly* the same thing but add a warning: "Listen to him!" (Matt 17:5). Even God has to say things twice. Why wouldn't they hear it the first time?

It's almost as if Matthew was saying: "Get ready, Israel; watch out, world. You'd better pay attention. John was right. It's time."

LIVE the Story

Does God still send prophets to his people today? Do we need these "eschatological alarm clocks" to wake us up? Are there prophets among us, like John

18. For discussion of whether the "servant" passages in Isaiah refer to a king or a prophet, see John Goldingay, "Servant of Yahweh," in *Dictionary of the Old Testament Prophets*, ed. Mark J. Boda and J. Gordon McConville (Downers Grove, IL: IVP Academic, 2012), 701–6.

19. Keener calls it "a proleptic enthronement fulfilled after the resurrection" (Keener, *Matthew*, 135).

20. The dove could symbolize many things; see Davies and Allison, *Matthew*, 1:331–34.

21. In Mark and Luke, the heavenly voice addresses Jesus, "You are my Son, whom I love; with you I am well pleased" (Mark 1:11; Luke 3:22). But, in Matthew's version the Father doesn't address Jesus but speaks to others about Jesus (the Baptizer, those gathered at the Jordan, even those reading Matthew's Gospel): "This is my Son, whom I love; with him I am well pleased" (Matt 3:17).

the Baptizer, trying to get our attention through their bizarre behavior and Chicken Little message, "The sky is falling! The sky is falling!"? And, even if there were, how could we tell the difference between the true prophets of God and the homeless men on the street corner, holding their cardboard signs, railing against the masses for our worldly ways—men who are easily passed over as mentally ill. Indeed, if "Elijah" were to show up today, wouldn't most of us ignore him because we're hardened to the spectacle? Been there, seen that.

Like painters, prophets are more easily recognized as legitimate once they're dead and gone (Isa 53:3–12). Looking back in history, we have this uncanny ability to spot true prophets who shook up the church at that time: Antony of Egypt, Francis of Assisi, Teresa of Avila, Martin Luther, John Wesley, William Seymour, Martin Luther King Jr.—to name only a few. Of course, what they did to their generation was revolutionary. Moreover, many of them attracted a following. But for the most part, their ideas (and especially their way of life) were a great source of irritation to their contemporaries. Odd. Peculiar. Bizarre. These prophets have left an indelible mark on the memory of the church. We admire them from the safe distance that history affords us, knowing we probably would have dismissed these oddballs as eccentric madmen and hysterical women. Who among us would have joined them in their madness?

Antony sold his possessions and lived in the desert for years. Francis gave away his fortune too, but preferred living in the forest to commune with nature and talk to birds. Teresa spent hours praying to Christ, beating her body into submission in order to see him. Luther empowered commoners to worship God in their native tongue and gave up the frock for married life. Wesley and his odd "methods" of sanctification, Seymour and the radically diverse congregation who gathered on Azusa Street, King's peaceful revolution of civil rights for all—these are the prophets who suddenly appeared "from nowhere" and told the church: "It's time." Time for renewal. Time for God. Time for justice. Time for *that day*—the day we've all been waiting for—when God shows up, his kingdom comes, and all is well. The problem, of course, is that when prophets show up, it certainly doesn't appear that "all will be well." Rather, like massive stones thrown into peaceful waters, these hard-headed rebels seem determined to make a splash. Which is why prophets are never welcomed by their own people (Matt 13:57). Those who know them best are able to recognize strange behavior when they see it. "Did you hear that Francis renounced his father's wealth, lives like a beggar, and calls the moon his sister and the sun his brother? Poor man's lost his mind." We are able to admire Francis because strangers make better prophets. Today we might even listen more attentively to alarming messages delivered by social sirens who are unfamiliar to us. But God tends to send prophets to their own kind for their time. So how can we tell the difference between a true prophet of God and the great pretender? If God still sends "Elijahs" to warn his people that "the time is near," doesn't that mean we'll always have to contend with "Elijah" wannabes?

Some might say we don't need Elijah anymore since John fulfilled the prophecy (Matt 17:11–12) and the end of the age has come through Jesus Christ. We know the time is always near because at any moment God could say, "It is done" (Rev 16:17; 21:6). But Jesus warned of false prophets during the last days (Matt 24:11), and Paul gave his converts the difficult advice of testing a prophetic word without being contemptuous of it (1 Thess 5:20–21). In fact, the apostle counted on prophets to build up the church, encouraging them to be eager to prophesy (1 Cor 14:1)—something Jesus anticipated as well (Matt 10:41). So even though we may not think of prophets as God's gift to his people, the early church accepted them as much as any other ministry, knowing they had to negotiate the difference between true and false prophets. In fact, the Didache ("the teaching," a late first-, early-second-century manual of instruction) gives evidence of this, where an entire chapter is devoted to helping Christians identify true itinerant prophets: 1) they stay for only a day, two days max; 2) they accept only bread for the next day's journey; 3) they never ask for money; 4) they never order a meal for themselves; 5) they only speak "in the Spirit"; 6) they practice what they preach; 7) they don't encourage others to imitate their bizarre behavior; and 8) they only talk of money when it is to be given to other people in need (Did. 11:3–12).[22] Such advice would be enough, even for today, to help the church avoid hucksters. But perhaps the best person to help us sort out the difference between true prophets and Elijah wannabes is the man who broke the Elijah mold: John the Baptist.

True prophets preach repentance and the reign of God. True prophets help us confess our sins. True prophets call people to the desert to meet God. True prophets are satisfied with nothing less than good deeds of justice. True prophets don't care about fancy clothes. True prophets are suspicious of politicians and religious elites. True prophets warn people about the wrath of God. True prophets don't talk about themselves. True prophets know they are unworthy slaves. True prophets always point to Jesus as the mightier one. True prophets say things like, "He must increase and I must decrease." And, finally, true prophets know they have nothing to give except what has been given to them. Come to think of it, true prophets never claim too much or too little.

---

22. The Didache also recognizes the possibility that a genuine prophet might want "to settle among you" (13:1). In that case, he is to receive the firstfruits of the harvest because he, "like the worker, is worthy of his food" (v. 2).

Indeed, because of this, true prophets know when it is time to head for the wilderness and get serious about God.

When I think about the prophetic voice today—especially in my little evangelical world—one of the most deserted places where we might find a prophet crying in the wilderness of our religious life is in the arts. Like most congregations, the only art that is celebrated in my church (beside public speaking) is music. Song and sermon reign supreme as coregents in the art of worship. No other artist is welcome—no writer, no painter, no sculptor, no dancer, no cinematographer. For the most part (and it pains me to admit it), evangelical Christians don't read or write, don't paint or carve, don't visit galleries or attend dance festivals. You couldn't find a more deserted place in the life of most evangelicals than the arts. Therefore, it comes as no surprise that creativity and artistic expression are discouraged in most churches—even seen as dangerous. We may encourage children to finger paint during Sunday school, but expressionism has no place among the adults. We may sing about "dancing before the Lord," but only children are allowed to make "creative movements" during their songs. So when our daughter Emma, who makes a living as a professional dancer and instructor, tried to offer one of her pieces during a worship service a few years ago, most of the congregants watched respectfully and offered a kind word ("that's nice"). But no one else has dared to try to "dance before the Lord." No matter how good we are, we'll sing. No matter our level of interest, we'll recite. But that's it. Creative expression of our devotion to God is somewhat nil in the church—which is why I think that's the perfect place for a prophet to show up these days, in the wilderness of art.

We were taking a hike in the desert-like environs that surround one of my favorite places on earth: the Laity Lodge situated by the Frio River (northwest of San Antonio, Texas). Even though I don't remember her name, I'll never forget the conversation we had that day as we walked along the path leading up to one of the favorite destinations of guests who enjoy an afternoon hike: the scenic Circle Bluff overlooking the canyon and the river. She had been invited to the Lodge to play her violin as a member of a chamber quartet. I was there to hear a famous speaker, a theologian I admire. But this wasn't happenstance. The purpose of Laity Lodge is to bring theologians and artists together to explore our common confession—an unusual confab that often leads to fascinating conversations. As we hiked up the hill with other creation lovers, we talked about our families. And, as it often happens with parents of young-adult children, we swapped stories about the challenges of our new "advisory" role—no longer telling our sons and daughters what they're supposed to do with their lives. She talked about her son, a twenty-something musician, who seemed perfectly satisfied with the unpredictable wages earned by his talent. He was living on his own, content with scraping by at a subsistence level—even resorting to dumpster diving, grazing on the meals he found in the food-desert world of urban life. Her husband was embarrassed, and she was pained by the hobo lifestyle of their talented son. Whenever they approached him about their concerns, he would launch into a railing attack against corporate greed and the wasteful habits of our culture.

The conversation grew silent for a moment as we made our way around flowering cactus and tumbleweeds, edging closer to the bluff. Then she said, "I just want to know, 'Why?' Why is he doing this?"

"Maybe he's a prophet," I said, at which point she stopped in her tracks, made an abrupt about face, walked up to me with a stone-cold look of concern, and said accusingly, "What did you say? You think he's a prophet?"

"Well, perhaps I'm being a little presumptuous. I don't know your son, and it's easy for me to offer this snap judgment. Is he a prophet? I don't know. But he's certainly acting like one."

Soft lines returned to the edges of her face, her eyes falling to the ground, taking in the desert around us. Then she looked back at me and said softly, "I need to share this with my husband. I don't think you're right. But, it never occurred to me that. . . ." Her voice trailed off. "A prophet, huh?" Then we walked to the edge of the bluff overlooking the Frio River, taking in the site of a desert canyon carved by the cold, blue waters of a crystal clear stream. I couldn't help but think about John the Baptizer.

"Lord, please keep sending your prophets to us, even though we may not have eyes to see or ears to hear their warning. It's time. No more snooze button. No more slumber. No more lazy repose. Time to wake up. Time to get up. Time to get ready. Time to do the right thing. Time to believe. Time to hear our God say, 'This is my beloved Son.' Help us listen to him! Gather your people as wheat. And may we be baptized in the fiery Spirit of the Anointed One."

Listen. Do you hear it? A voice is crying in the wilderness of our contentment.

CHAPTER 4

Matthew 4:1–22

LISTEN to the Story

1Then Jesus was led by the Spirit into the wilderness to be tempted by the devil. 2After fasting forty days and forty nights, he was hungry. 3The tempter came to him and said, "If you are the Son of God, tell these stones to become bread."

4Jesus answered, "It is written: 'Man shall not live on bread alone, but on every word that comes from the mouth of God.'"

5Then the devil took him to the holy city and had him stand on the highest point of the temple. 6"If you are the Son of God," he said, "throw yourself down. For it is written:

> 'He will command his angels concerning you,
> and they will lift you up in their hands,
> so that you will not strike your foot against a stone.'"

7Jesus answered him, "It is also written: 'Do not put the Lord your God to the test.'"

8Again, the devil took him to a very high mountain and showed him all the kingdoms of the world and their splendor. 9"All this I will give you," he said, "if you will bow down and worship me."

10Jesus said to him, "Away from me, Satan! For it is written: 'Worship the Lord your God, and serve him only.'"

11Then the devil left him, and angels came and attended him.

12When Jesus heard that John had been put in prison, he withdrew to Galilee. 13Leaving Nazareth, he went and lived in Capernaum, which was by the lake in the area of Zebulun and Naphtali—14to fulfill what was said through the prophet Isaiah:

> 15"Land of Zebulun and land of Naphtali,
> the Way of the Sea, beyond the Jordan,
> Galilee of the gentiles—
> 16the people living in darkness

> have seen a great light;
> on those living in the land of the shadow of death
> a light has dawned."

[17]From that time on Jesus began to preach, "Repent, for the kingdom of heaven has come near."

[18]As Jesus was walking beside the Sea of Galilee, he saw two brothers, Simon called Peter and his brother Andrew. They were casting a net into the lake, for they were fishermen. [19]"Come, follow me," Jesus said, "and I will send you out to fish for people." [20]At once they left their nets and followed him.

[21]Going on from there, he saw two other brothers, James son of Zebedee and his brother John. They were in a boat with their father Zebedee, preparing their nets. Jesus called them, [22]and immediately they left the boat and their father and followed him.

Listening to the Text in the Story: Exodus 16:1–17:7; 32:1–33:4; 34:27–28; Deuteronomy 6:1–8:20; 9:7–25; 1 Kings 19:1–8, 19–21; Job 1:6–2:10; Psalm 91; Isaiah 9:1–7; Ezekiel 20:33–44; Hosea 2:14–23.

The first line of this story sounds like a contradiction to our ears. God's Spirit led Jesus into the desert to be tempted by the devil? That seems wrong on so many levels. Why would he do that? The desert is such a hostile place. Furthermore, why would God set up a confrontation between Jesus and the devil—especially when Jesus is so vulnerable, having fasted for forty days? It looks like God is aiding and abetting Satan in his dirty work. That doesn't seem right at all, especially since Jesus taught his disciples to pray for the opposite: "Lead us *not* into temptation but deliver us from the evil one" (Matt 6:13). Is that why Jesus added that line to the Lord's Prayer? Was he essentially teaching his disciples to pray, "Lord, please don't do to us what you did to Jesus"? Besides, everyone knows that God doesn't tempt his children (Jas 1:13). So why did the temptation of Jesus have to happen? Doesn't it make better sense for Jesus to head straight for Jerusalem to claim David's throne? After all, he is the Spirit-anointed Messiah of God, fully empowered to take back what rightfully belongs to God's Son. Israel had been waiting long enough. Satan had caused enough trouble. Wasn't it time for the kingdom of heaven to come crashing into earth with such an irrepressible force that everyone would know that the day of the Lord had finally arrived? Jerusalem should have been the Messiah's first stop—not some wasteland—knowing the story must start and end there. It's the Messiah's destiny to rule the whole world from the city of shalom. Indeed, this whole scenario—retreating to the desert to face the devil—seems like the story is going backward, not forward.

Well, in certain respects Jesus has to go back to go forward because Matthew sees Jesus as the guarantor of Israel's hope. To put it bluntly, before Jesus can save the whole world, he must save Israel. That's the way God set it up. The Lord made promises to Abraham that must come true—that he would not only be the father of a nation (Israel) but that he would also be the father of a multitude of nations (Gen 12:2; 17:5–6). Of course, all the covenant blessings (especially the land!) were dependent upon Israel's obedience, something the prophets kept reminding the people over and over again. That's why God's people repeatedly found themselves in the desert, in exile. Until they learned the lesson of faithfulness, Israel wouldn't see all the promises of God come true. Indeed, the way Hosea saw it, God's torturous relationship with his people looked more like a marriage gone wrong: Boy sees girl. Boy wins girl. Boy takes girl home. Boy loses girl. Boy is angry with girl. Boy tries to woo girl back again. And, according to the divine script of God's love affair with Israel, the only place his people seemed to learn to trust him was in the wilderness (Hos 2:14–15). God must "allure her" and "speak tenderly to her" in the desert. This is what the prophets knew better than anyone: covenant romance between God and his people happens to be rekindled in the wilderness (Ezek 20:33–44).

But the desert is a dangerous place. Even though God shows up there in miraculous ways—how else does one survive?—the wilderness is also where the unfaithful die (Num 14:26–35). The desert was the perfect training ground for Israel's faith. Those who were tempted to disobey God suffered the consequences; they died in the desert because they failed the test. The faithful few, on the other hand, made it out alive because they trusted God's word. That's why the wilderness ended up being the place where God turned slaves into children, where the Father of Israel tested the secrets of the hearts of his people—at least, that's the way Moses saw it (Deut 8:1–3). The wilderness was the very place where the test of faithfulness could turn into temptation to sin. In fact, how one responded in the desert would reveal the difference: the faithful would come out of the desert tested; the faithless would fall in the wilderness of temptation. What makes this double-edged sword of test/temptation even more intriguing is that both meanings are carried by the same Greek word: *peirazō*. When Moses claimed that God led Israel for forty years in the desert to *test* them (according to the LXX), or when Matthew describes how Jesus was led by the Spirit into the wilderness to be *tempted* by the devil, in both cases it's the same root word. The implication is unmistakable: in the covenant story of Israel's relationship with God, tests were always occasions for temptation, and every temptation was a test. The pressure of desert life would either bring out the best or the worst in people. That's the lesson Israel was supposed to learn. Trusting God in the wilderness is how the meek inherit the earth. And, therefore, that's why Jesus had to go into the wilderness to be tested/tempted—to reveal the best of Israel, the faithful child of God, the hope of the whole world.

Cue the accuser. Enter the dragon. Let the test/temptation begin.

EXPLAIN the Story

There is a sense that God has left Jesus alone in the desert to be tempted by the devil. His Spirit may have led Jesus there, but it's the devil who greets him after forty days. God's absence is evident, not only during the forty days but throughout the story. It is deserted, after all; an inhospitable place—the desolation that some believed was the haunt of demons.[1] But more than that, the fact that Jesus has nothing to eat for forty days indicates the lack of providential care. God provided manna in the wilderness for Israel. Jesus, on the other hand, goes hungry because God hasn't done for him what he did for Israel. Of course, the children of God had to complain about their dire circumstances before God did anything about it. (Then again, they didn't give him much of a chance to provide; as soon as they crossed the Red Sea, they whined and fussed about their plight!) Now it's quite obvious Jesus didn't complain about his situation, which is why he hungered for *forty* days—echoing the forty years that Israel lived on manna in the desert. This is Matthew's emphasis: Jesus fasted for forty days *and nights* (oh, the hunger pangs that especially show up at night!) *because he was hungry* (Matt 4:2). Not because he was modeling some pious deprivation. Not because he sought some higher spiritual wisdom. For forty days and nights Jesus was starving for food because God didn't provide. *Then* the devil showed up (not God or his Spirit or his angels). By this time, Jesus had already been tested by his circumstances. Now, the test (the lack of divine provision) will provide opportunity for temptation. Where is God when you need him the most? The absence of God is the hardest test of all—desperate in a desolate place, the beginning of temptation.

"Let There Be Bread"

The first temptation is the key to the rest of the story. Setting. Timing. Dialogue. What transpires between Jesus and the devil in their first encounter

1. Davies and Allison, *Matthew*, 1:354.

depends upon our ability to connect the dots between Israel's failure in the desert and the threefold temptation of the Messiah. The fact that Jesus keeps quoting from Deuteronomy 6–8 in his repartee is telling (Matt 4:4/Deut 8:3; Matt 4:7/Deut 6:16; Matt 4:10/Deut 6:13). God led Israel into the desert "in order to train it like a son."[2] They were supposed to learn that "man does not live by bread alone but on every word that comes from the mouth of the LORD" (Deut 8:3). God tried to teach the same lesson—under similar conditions—to Moses and Elijah (Exod 34:28; 1 Kgs 19:8). Therefore, the timing of Satan's appearance after forty days and nights to tempt Jesus to turn desert stones into bread because God hasn't provided food (like he did for Israel, Moses, and Elijah) reveals that even the accuser knows the drill. Desert. Forty days. Time for temptation. Israel complained. Moses eventually disobeyed. Elijah needed angel-food bread to make it to Horeb. What will Jesus do?

"Let's see. Where have I seen this before? Oh, yes, yes, yes. A child of God hungry in the wilderness, alone. He keeps doing this, doesn't he? Over and over again. And the number forty keeps coming up too. What a delicious irony. God leads you here and leaves. Now, here I am to welcome you to this God-forsaken place to play my part. And what is that? To accuse, to tempt, to help you discover your destiny—to fail like the rest of them. Come. Let's read our lines, rehearse the same old story. I will say, 'See! God has failed you. He's brought you here to die.' Fear will overwhelm you. You'll figure out quick that God won't save you now. You'll cry out in anguish. You'll question God. You'll disobey him. Then you'll take your medicine and learn the lesson like the rest. Your God fails you when you need him the most, and here I am to help you see it. Open your eyes, Jesus. All you see is death. Dirt, stones, no food. Was John right? Is it time for God to restore the land, to turn the desert into paradise? Where is it? Let's see it. Here. Now. You're hungry, aren't you? If God can turn these stones into children of Abraham, like the Baptist claimed, then certainly his Son could turn them into bread. Isn't that what God does? He speaks and it is so? 'Let there be light!' Okay, Son of God, say it. Prove it. Speak, and it will be so. Time for paradise. Turn these stones to bread."

With this imaginary version of Satan's ploy, we see the variety of scholarly opinions about the purpose of the temptation story compressed into one. What is the point of it all?[3] Some see the temptation narrative as rehearsal, a recapitulation of Israel's story.[4] If Jesus is the embodiment of Israel, then he

---

2. Luz, *Matthew*, 1:152.

3. Keener summarizes three interpretations: the salvation-historical (recapitulation of Israel's story), christological/messianic, and parenetic (model of discipleship) (*Matthew*, 137).

4. Theodore of Mopsuestia wrote, "For since Adam met with luxury in paradise and, through deception, deteriorated to what is worse, it was necessary that [the Spirit] lead Christ into the

must relive Israel's quest and succeed where God's people failed.[5] Others think Satan's purpose was to get Jesus to alter his God-given mission,[6] to test his messianic mission,[7] or to take a shortcut to messiahship by avoiding suffering.[8] Finally, some read the story as a model for overcoming temptation—that Jesus teaches through his example how we can defeat the devil—by quoting Scripture and trusting God.[9] The problem, of course, is that one can see all three purposes in the temptation story; it depends on where you look. Certainly, the momentum of Matthew's narrative to this point has been to set up Jesus as the fulfillment of Israel's story. Echoes of Israel's past (as well as explicit fulfillment of Old Testament prophecies) bounce around loudly during the first four chapters of Matthew's Gospel. And yet, if we keep reading, we will hear echoes of the temptation narrative throughout the rest of the Gospel. For example, the Lord's Prayer sounds like a prayer guide based on "lessons learned in the desert," with requests for daily bread, protection from temptation, and petition for the kingdom to come to earth.[10] Later, Jesus will miraculously provide bread in the desert—twice (Matt 14:13–21; 15:29–38).[11] Later, Jesus will enter the temple and "throw himself down" before the authorities, challenging them as God's Son (his provocation must have looked like a death wish to many; 21:12–46).[12] Later, Jesus will receive all authority to rule over *every* kingdom and all their glory, sending his disciples to carry on the mission (28:18–20).[13] In other words, the temptation of Jesus is an eschatological event, a looking-back and summing-up of Israel's history while, at the same time, a proleptically embodied, discipleship-modeled victory over Satan, sin, and death. Once again, we've arrived at a pivotal moment in Matthew's narrative where the past and the future are rolled up into one.

---

wilderness in order to enfeeble the devil's force by someone greater in strength" (Simonetti, *Matthew 1–13*, 56; see also Garland, *Reading Matthew*, 39).

5. France, *Matthew*, 127–28.

6. Matt Woodley, *The Gospel of Matthew: God with Us*, Resonate Series (Downers Grove, IL: IVP Books, 2011), 47.

7. So Keener, *Matthew*, 139–41 (even though he holds out the possibility that all three interpretations are served by the text): "Jesus was not a magician"; "Jesus was not a deluded visionary"; "Jesus was not a political revolutionary."

8. Nolland writes, "The devil suggests that sonship is privilege to be exploited, that Jesus should use his opportunities to see to his own needs" (*Matthew*, 163).

9. So Luz; Matthew is "a Gospel that unfolds from the beginning what obedience to God means. It thus anticipates, as it were, *in nuce* the way the Son of God has gone before his disciples in the entire Gospel—the way that finally leads to resurrection and to authority over heaven and earth" (*Matthew*, 1:155). According to Gregory the Great, Jesus modeled the way to overcome gluttony, vain ambition, and greed, (Simonetti, *Matthew 1–13*, 62–63).

10. Luz, *Matthew*, 1:152.

11. Ibid., 1:152–53.

12. Davies and Allison, *Matthew*, 1:367.

13. Talbert, *Matthew*, 62.

Indeed, Matthew is claiming that because Jesus is God's promised Son, the desert will bloom, the land will be restored, and the meek will inherit the earth. It's just a matter of time.

It's quite evident, then, that much was at stake when Satan tempted Jesus to speak like God and turn desert stones into bread. When Jesus quoted Moses's warning that Israel should have learned the lesson that the only thing in life that really matters is, ironically, God's word—not only commandments but also promises—he knew it was the only way to live in the desert. After all, God gave his word (Torah) in the wilderness. That's where Israel was supposed to discover life, not only by obeying God's commandments but also by trusting his promises, like a son obeying his father because he trusts him. So it is significant that Jesus quoted a promise of God in the desert. In response to the second and third temptations, Jesus recites commandments. But here, in the wilderness, believing the promises of God—contrary to all appearances—is what brings life. In fact, trusting God's promise of provision in the desert is the essence of faith. "I'm going to live even though death is all around me!" Why? *Because God is on my side*. This is the believer's claim. Especially in the wilderness God's child says, "The LORD is my refuge." And so the Father replies, "Because he loves me . . . I will rescue him; I will protect him. . . . He will call on me, and I will answer him; I will be with him in trouble, I will deliver and honor him. With long life I will satisfy him and show him my salvation" (Ps 91:14–16). This is why Jesus quoted God's word. It is life in the desert. Furthermore, this is how God's Son, God's word, Jesus ("Yahweh Saves"), will reveal that he is salvation, even in the wilderness.

"Is the Lord among Us or Not?"

There are different settings for the last two temptations. Even though it was the Spirit who led Jesus into the wilderness, Satan decides he needs a change in scenery. That's because Jesus has already proven himself in the desert. Now, it's the devil's turn to call the shots, to challenge Jesus on another level. In fact, Matthew sees a topographical progression in the order of the temptations as they increase in intensity. The first stop, the most basic of all appetites (hunger) is tested in the desert. Then, in order to appeal to Jesus's pride—the height of arrogance—the second temptation takes place on the pinnacle of the temple (which would have been the highest point in Jerusalem since the temple was situated on the peak of Mt. Zion). Finally, the highest mountain is where the ultimate temptation must take place: worship reveals everyone's top priority. And yet, even though Satan is leading Jesus to different places, the Messiah keeps returning to the story of Israel in the desert for guidance, quoting passages from Deuteronomy 6.

Taking Jesus to the temple was a shrewd move. It's one thing to question whether God will provide in the desert. It's quite something else to question whether God will provide at his holy temple. After all, the temple earned the nickname "The Lord Will Provide" because of what God did for Abraham when he nearly sacrificed his covenant son, Isaac: "And to this day [during the days of the temple?] it is said, 'On the mountain of the Lord it will be provided'" (Gen 22:13–14). God didn't provide bread in the wilderness. But surely he would provide protection in God's house, the very place where the psalmist boasts that "God is our refuge and strength, an ever-present help in trouble" (Ps 46:1). So Satan knows what he's doing, quoting a portion of Psalm 91, where God promises that if you say "the Lord is my refuge," then God will say "I will protect him, for he acknowledges my name" (Ps 91:9, 14). In fact, the psalmist even spells out how the Lord would do it: "He will command his angels concerning you, and they will lift you up in their hands, so that you will not strike your foot against a stone" (Matt 4:6; Ps 91:11–12). "Throw yourself down," then, becomes the second test as to whether God will do what he promised.

When Jesus quoted the commandment, "Do not put the Lord your God to the test" (Deut 6:16), he was not only rebutting Satan's "scriptural" suggestion, he was also giving another reason for Israel's failure in the desert. Jesus didn't quote the last part of the verse, "as you did at Massah," which tells the rest of the story, embedded in a pun that is hard to see in English. The word *Massah* means "test." If we could hear it in Hebrew, we would recognize that Jesus was cleverly quoting a bit from Moses's farewell speech, "Don't Massah the Lord your God as you did at Massah." These children of Israel, who had *survived* the desert, who were about to enter the land of promise, knew exactly what Moses was talking about. All he had to say was, "Remember Massah," and they would be flooded with memories of how God provided water in the desert. Israel had just witnessed the miraculous appearance of manna. Now they were thirsty. "So they quarreled with Moses and said, 'Give us water to drink.'" Moses's response is telling: "Why do you quarrel with me? Why do you put the Lord to the test [Massah]?" (Exod 17:2). After Moses complained to God (and feared for his life), the Lord made water flow from the rock when Moses struck it with his famous staff (vv. 5–6). Moses named the place "Massah" and "Meribah" (which means "quarrel"), *apropos* to the desert where tests often lead to quarreling. But the incident really spells out something more significant. Israel may have complained to Moses about the lack of water, convinced their leader had brought them out to the desert to "die of thirst" (v. 3). But their beef was really with God: "They tested the Lord saying, 'Is the Lord among us or not?'" (v. 7). The test revealed the secrets of their hearts. This wasn't just about being thirsty in the desert. Israel's dire circumstances made them question the very presence of God. When they complained to Moses, they were essentially saying, "Is God here?"

That's what the accuser was doing. He was tempting Jesus to question the presence of God—a dastardly and wily tactic when God's absence seems undeniable. "Are you the Son of God? Is this not God's temple, where 'the presence of the Lord' is invoked through sacrifice? Isn't it true that the 'Lord Provides'—here of all places? Isn't this the very location where God saved the covenant son, Isaac? Will he not protect you? He promised he would. You've already said you live only by God's word. Doesn't God's word say that he will command angels to protect you? So, you won't turn stones to bread. Let's see if God will protect you from stones. 'You will not strike your foot against a stone.' Isn't that what God has said? It's one thing to *say* you trust God's word. Practice what you preach, right Jesus? God has already tested you—forty days without food. Now it's time to test God. Throw yourself down. Let's see if God will do what he promised. Is the Lord among us or not?"

It is curious to me how Satan's appeal to a promise of God (something Jesus relied upon in the desert) is now being used against Jesus at the temple. One minute God's promises are true and reliable—a single line of defense against temptation. The next minute the promises of God can be used as weapons of temptation. Of course, the fact that Satan is trying to use Scripture to make his point makes the whole scenario suspect. The evil one has only evil intent. He wants those who are tested to turn the tables on God and test him for a change! Some might rightly point to the classical hermeneutical problem of taking a passage out of context, which certainly leads to abuse. Nowhere in Psalm 91 is the faithful child of God led to test the surety of God's word by presuming upon his protection. Satan is surely committing the cardinal sin of twisting God's word to fit his purposes—something even the most pious can be guilty of. Jesus, of course, would have easily seen through Satan's ruse on both counts. And, therefore, his response should have been different: either dismissive of the tempter ("consider the source") or offering a lesson in hermeneutics ("that's not what the Bible means"). But he does neither. I would have expected Jesus to ignore the accuser with silence or at least to offer the same barb as he did to the Sadducees: "You are in error because you do not know the Scriptures or the power of God" (Matt 22:29). Now that's a great comeback! Instead, Jesus seems to have "lowered himself" and played the Scripture-quoting game that most theological arguments degenerate to: "God says this." "Oh yeah? Well, God says that!" (Ad infinitum ad nauseum.) So, why did he do it?

I think the key to understanding this war of words between Jesus and Satan is the setting. Led by the Spirit to the desert, Jesus was tempted to command.

Brought to the temple by Satan, Jesus was tempted to act. In the desert, Jesus overcame temptation by relying upon God's promise. At the temple, Jesus rebuffed Satan's prodding by quoting God's commandment. Promises in the desert; commandments at the temple. Led by the Spirit; brought by Satan. Context matters. The Spirit may lead to the wilderness where it's tempting to make things happen—let there be bread!—rather than to rely on the promises of God. The accuser may show up even at the holiest of places where it's tempting to test God by presuming upon his promises because people say, "The LORD will provide," and others question him in the desert, "Is the LORD among us or not?" Those who survive the desert may even feel privileged to make demands upon God at his temple.[14] This is the lesson Israel should have learned: trust God (promise) when the Spirit leads you to the desert; don't test God (command) when tempted to question his presence. To confuse the two—promise and command—is to miss the difference between God's test and Satan's temptation.

Deal with the Devil

The last temptation is less confusing because Satan makes a straightforward proposal: worship in exchange for favors. The encounter takes place on a "very high mountain," where people believed they could get closest to God. But seeking high places to worship God can also be occasions for idolatry.[15] Ironically, there's a lot of God-talk that goes on here: ruling the world, the glory of kingdom, bowing down, worship. But it's all pretense. Satan's offer is based on the presumption that this is the way God works: worship me, and I'll give you stuff. Some might question whether "all the kingdoms of the world and their splendor" were Satan's to give.[16] Others hear an implicit critique of the Roman Empire's goal of world domination.[17] But all commentators recognize that the crux of the matter is false worship, a violation of the first commandment. This is the ultimate temptation because whom we worship is whom we will

---

14. "The devil's 'if' is not an expression of doubt. . . . Rather, it is on the basis of the possibilities that are his as Son that Jesus is being encouraged to act . . . the devil suggests that sonship is a privilege to be exploited" (Nolland, *Matthew*, 163).

15. Davies and Allison, *Matthew*, 1:370.

16. The Jewish view of world power was that every kingdom had its own "angel" governing the nation, an intermediary agent of God's rule. Some were benevolent and some were malevolent, but God had delegated his power to them. Michael protected Israel, and God's archenemy (known by several names: Azazel, Beelzebul, the devil, Satan) ruled Babylon (1 En. 8:1–4; 9:6; 10:4–8; 13:1–2; 40:9; 61:10; 2 En. 20:1–4; Jub. 15:31–32; LAE 9:1–15:3; Dan 10:13, 20–23). So, "despite the devil's claims (cf. Lk 4:6), God not Satan had *ultimate* authority over the world's kingdoms" (Keener, *Matthew*, 142 [emphasis his]).

17. See Warren Carter, *Matthew and Empire: Initial Explorations* (Harrisburg, PA: Trinity Press International, 2001), 169–79.

serve. Israel worshiped a golden calf in the desert and died in the wilderness. They learned the hard way that all that glitters isn't gold. Besides, what good is a gold god in the desert? The Lord is no fertility god; he doesn't operate on a quid-pro-quo basis. He doesn't demand worship in exchange for his services. That's Satan's ploy. Rather, God is the one to be served because he is worthy of worship. God commands worship; Satan tries to buy it. For this and many other reasons, Jesus refused to bow down and worship Satan. The splendor of the kingdoms of this world pale in comparison to the glorious kingdom of God—a kingdom Jesus came to establish on earth as it is in heaven. God's Son would give his life for nothing less: "What good will it be for someone to gain the whole world, yet forfeit their soul?" (Matt 16:26).[18]

Finally, Jesus issued a command: "Away from me, Satan!" (Matt 4:10); so the devil left him (Jesus does have the power of God's word!). What Jesus refused to demand in the desert and command from the height of the temple, God eventually provided: angels came to take care of him (v. 11).[19] Because Jesus passed the test, he is now ready to leave the desert and take back the land Satan has stolen, to plunder the "strong man's house and carry off his possessions" (12:29).[20] And yet, again, we find Jesus's next move to be rather unexpected. Instead of going to Jerusalem, Jesus returns to his home turf, Galilee. Matthew seems to give two reasons for this: 1) John's imprisonment (4:12), and 2) to fulfill prophecy (vv. 13–17). The first reason is a little puzzling. Did Jesus "withdraw" to Galilee to avoid the same fate as John? The region had already proven to be a safe haven for him when he was a child, tucked away from the evil gaze of the wicked sons of Herod. But retreating to Galilee to hide from Herod doesn't make sense here, for at this time Herod Antipas ruled Galilee. Is this evidence that Jesus looked to John once again to discern the divine timing of his own destiny?[21] Perhaps. But that doesn't explain why he started his ministry in Galilee. Whatever the reason for mentioning John's imprisonment, it is quite evident to Matthew that Jesus began preaching in Galilee—especially Capernaum—the same message as the Baptizer, "Repent, for the kingdom of heaven has come near," to fulfill prophecy (vv. 14–17).

One of Isaiah's lasting visions is that God would gather all his people—not only the exiles of Israel but also gentiles who love him—to his temple (Isa 56:1–8). How? God would show up in such a powerful way that the people "walking in darkness," and "living in the land of deep darkness" would

---

18. Nolland, *Matthew*, 167.

19. "[Angels] occupy the place the devil has left" (Luz, *Matthew*, 1:155).

20. Keener, *Matthew*, 144.

21. "What happens to the eschatological Elijah makes known to the Messiah what to do next" (Davies and Allison, *Matthew*, 1:376).

see "a great light" and be drawn to him (Isa 9:2; Matt 4:16). And where is this dark land where the light of God's presence must shine? "The land of Zebulun and the land of Naphtali . . . Galilee of the nations, by the Way of the Sea, beyond the Jordan" (Isa 9:1; Matt 4:15). Of course, "beyond the Jordan" depends upon a person's location, whether inside Israel or among the diaspora.[22] Both Naphtali and Zebulun were the first tribes displaced during the Assyrian conquest, so tribal boundaries were no longer operative (or even identifiable) in Jesus's day. Furthermore, according to recent scholarly opinion Galilee was populated by Jews (perhaps even from Judea) more than gentiles.[23] So most scholars think Matthew wasn't trying to use Isaiah to pinpoint the exact location of the beginning of Jesus's ministry or to offer a demographic assessment of the region. These four vague geographical descriptions—the border between two northern tribes, the way of the sea, beyond the Jordan, gentile Galilee—shouldn't be taken literally. Rather, Matthew was making a theological claim regarding the significance of Isaiah's prophecy and Jesus's first ministry in Galilee. Jerome saw the same thing: Jesus launched his kingdom work in the region around Capernaum as a sign that he was taking back what was first lost to the Assyrians over seven hundred years before.[24] In other words, Matthew believed that the people in Galilee were sitting in darkness, waiting for the light of God's presence, because the prophecy hadn't been fulfilled—not because the region was overrun by gentiles or that Galilee was a place of "spiritual darkness" and lived under the oppressive "shadow of death" more than Judea. The way Matthew has set it up implies not only that Jesus is the light of God's presence predicted by Isaiah but also that the first evidence of the messianic kingdom had dawned on Israel *in Galilee*.

We don't know how long Jesus preached in Galilee (Matt 4:17) before he decided to take a more direct approach to finding disciples (vv. 18–22). Up to this point in the narrative, Jesus has been a passive character, dependent on parents, John, and the Spirit. Now, for the first time Jesus takes the initiative and makes things happen.[25] The way he gathered disciples broke from rabbinical tradition where it was customary for students to seek the master.[26]

22. See the interesting discussions in Davies and Allison, *Matthew*, 1:382–83; Luz, *Matthew*, 1:158; and France, *Matthew*, 141–43, where the significance of one's perspective is informed by geography; that is, is "beyond the Jordan" reflective of a Palestinian resident or an exile in Assyria?

23. See Jonathan L. Reed, *Archaeology and the Galilean Jesus: A Re-examination of the Evidence* (Harrisburg, PA: Trinity Press International, 2000), 23–61; James D. G. Dunn, *Jesus Remembered*, Christianity in the Making 1 (Grand Rapids: Eerdmans, 2003), 293–97; Davies and Allison, *Matthew*, 1:383–85.

24. See Davies and Allison, *Matthew*, 1:381–83; Luz, *Matthew*, 1:159.

25. France, *Matthew*, 143.

26. Martin Hengel, *The Charismatic Leader and His Followers*, trans. James C. G. Greig, Studies of the New Testament and Its World (Edinburgh: T&T Clark, 1981), 50–51.

Also, Jesus didn't invite them to study Torah, a noble goal.[27] Instead, he commanded them—like one of the prophets of old (Elijah/Elisha)—to "follow me."[28] This unconventional "rabbi" called disciples to study *him*, to learn how to "fish for people" for the kingdom of heaven (v. 19). "Jesus does not offer abstract principles or simply his version of the Torah for a new society. Instead, he offers himself to his disciples."[29] The fact that he first called Galilean fishermen to help him is significant. One might think scribes in Judea would make for better students. Yet, throughout the story Jesus will find the "least and the last" as ideal candidates for his kingdom. That they "immediately" leave their businesses, families, and homes to follow Jesus (vv. 20, 22)—a man unknown to them, a man who simply calls them to come—proves they have "seen the light."[30]

LIVE the Story

Jesus must have told his disciples about his victory over Satan.[31] But why? And when? Did it come up in conversation with the first disciples? "Where have you been?" "I just came from the desert." "The desert? What were you doing there?" "Well, after I was baptized by John and the Spirit, I felt like I needed to go there. You know, to learn the lessons of our forefathers. Then, after forty days the devil showed up. . . ." The purpose of the temptation would be the same reason Jesus told his disciples about the encounter. If Jesus defeated the devil on our behalf—something only he had the power to do—then Jesus would have related the story to the Twelve as proof of his messiahship. But, as everyone knows, most war heroes are reticent to discuss their victories in battle. Besides, the miracles Jesus performed, the authority of his teaching, and especially the resurrection was more than enough to convince the disciples that Jesus was the Christ. Jesus may have told his disciples about the threefold temptation as a way of illustrating the purpose of his kingdom, to distinguish common messianic expectations from his agenda. Despite the miracle of multiplying bread and fish, he didn't come to feed people in the desert like Moses. Jesus came to teach them to feed on God's word (the point of John's version of the "sign"; John 6:1–69). He wasn't "testing God" to protect him

27. Keener, *Matthew*, 153.

28. France, *Matthew*, 147.

29. McKnight, *Sermon on the Mount*, 14.

30. Gregory the Great said, "The kingdom of heaven has no price tag on it: It is worth as much as you have" (Simonetti, *Matthew 1–13*, 73).

31. Of course, critical scholarship infers that the temptation narrative was probably invented by the early church or by the evangelist, perhaps deriving from a midrash of Deuteronomy 6–8. See Davies and Allison, *Matthew*, 1:350–53; Luz, *Matthew*, 1:148–51, 153–55.

when he confronted the temple authorities. He knew he would die on a cross. Jesus didn't instigate a revolutionary war to overthrow the kingdoms of men. Rather, he relinquished his power on earth to gain a heavenly kingdom that comes through sacrifice. But Jesus didn't need to recount the temptation narrative to teach these lessons to the Twelve. His entire life's work was a moving picture—a 24–7 tutorial—about the kingdom of God.

Perhaps Jesus told the story to teach his disciples how to overcome temptation. That seems to be the most obvious reason. Everyone experiences temptation—even God's children, even Jesus. Everyone experiences times of testing—even the faithful, even the Son of God. This is what the Father does: he leads his children into the desert to teach them to obey him, to trust him. Indeed, God tests believers to reveal their faithfulness. He especially loves to test his children soon after he's given them good gifts. Adam was given paradise, and God said, "Don't eat from this tree." Abraham and Sarah welcomed their long-awaited son, and God said, "Take Isaac to Moriah to sacrifice him." Israel was delivered from the Egyptian army, and the Lord tested them in the desert. Even Satan knew the sequence of God's modus operandi: "You've given Job everything. Now it's time to test him." This is the divine pattern. *This is what always happens.* Consequently, having received the Holy Spirit, Jesus knew it was time to go to the desert to be tested. And so this is why disciples of Jesus follow him into the desert. We know we must be tested because Christ overcame Satan, sin, and death (our enemies!) for us. Indeed, because of Christ we have been given much. Therefore, to whom much is given, much is tested—not only to reveal that we are God's children, not only to prove that we trust him no matter what, not only to follow our Lord into the desert, but also to learn how to overcome our common enemy and follow Jesus out of the wilderness to inherit the land of God's promises in Christ. None of us want to live as slaves in the wilderness of our own appetites. Jesus taught us: there *must* be more to life than bread. All of us wonder at times—especially in the desert—is God here? Jesus promised us: the *meek* shall inherit the land. Idolatry is everywhere; we are wired to serve what we worship. Jesus reminded us: we *will* serve the one, true God because we worship him. This is Adam's story. This is Israel's story. This is Jesus's story. Therefore, the "first" temptation of the Christ is *our* story—a very *human* reality for every single one of us.

We all know what it's like to go through dry times—surviving "the troughs" as C. S. Lewis put it—when the core of our humanity, the essence of what we are, is tested and revealed.[32] Religious or not, we all talk about overcoming "temptation." Which is why Lewis, the fellow of Magdalen College

32. C. S. Lewis, *The Screwtape Letters* (New York: Macmillan, 1943), 46.

at Oxford, professor of Medieval English literature at Cambridge, became a household name after the surprising success of his infamous *The Screwtape Letters*. An imaginary correspondence between a senior devil, Screwtape, and his young apprentice, Wormwood, published during World War II created the perfect storm of intrigue and opinion offered as a social commentary on the question of theodicy—all under the guise of fiction. Lewis's keen eye "to see through human failings, his capacity to analyse other people's annoyingness, his rich sense of comedy and satire" was on full display in *Screwtape*, aiding its success.[33] But it's the idea that we all know what it feels like to be tempted, wondering how the great human drama is played out on a day-by-day basis, that makes this silly scenario—one devil writing to another—seem so real. The material first appeared in England as articles in a magazine called the *Guardian*. The public response was so overwhelming, Lewis insisted on warning his readers in the preface of the book that "the devil is a liar. Not everything that Screwtape says should be assumed to be true even from his own angle."[34] When the articles first appeared in the *Guardian*, Lewis explained that "a country clergyman wrote to the editor, withdrawing his subscription on the ground that 'much of the advice given in these letters seemed to him not only erroneous but positively diabolical.'"[35] Some people mistakenly take satire seriously, which is easy to do when dealing with the devil and temptation. Lewis covers nearly all the vices in the voice of Screwtape, who instructs Wormwood on how to exploit the baser appetites of humanity and when to goad human pride (the basis of the first two temptations of Christ). Tellingly, the third temptation of Christ—a frontal assault on true worship—never shows up in *The Screwtape Letters*. Nevertheless, the context of the temptation narrative, the desert, is front and center. In fact, it could be said that Screwtape builds most of his "tempting" advice on the presence/absence of God.

> And that is where the troughs come in. You must have often wondered why the Enemy [God] does not make more use of His power to be sensibly present to human souls in any degree He chooses and at any moment. . . . Merely to over-ride a human will (as His felt presence in any but the faintest and most mitigated degree would certainly do) would be for Him useless. He cannot ravish. He can only woo. For His ignoble ideas is to eat the cake and have it; the creatures are to be one with Him, but yet themselves; merely to cancel them, or assimilate them, will not serve. He is prepared to do a little over-riding at the beginning. He will

33. A. N. Wilson, *C. S. Lewis: A Biography* (New York: HarperCollins, 1990), 177.
34. Lewis, *Screwtape Letters*, 9.
35. C. S. Lewis, *The Screwtape Letters and Screwtape Proposes a Toast* (New York: Macmillan, 1962), v.

> set them off with communications of His presence which, though faint, seem great to them, with emotional sweetness, and easy conquest over temptation. But He never allows this state of affairs to last long. Sooner or later He withdraws, if not in fact, at least from their conscious experience, all those supports and incentives. He leaves the creature to stand up on its own legs—to carry out from the will alone duties which have lost all relish. It is during such trough periods, much more than during the peak periods, that it is growing into the sort of creature He wants it to be. Hence the prayers offered in the state of dryness are those which please Him best. . . . He wants them to learn to walk and must therefore take away His hand; and if only the will to walk is really there He is pleased even with their stumbles. Do not be deceived, Wormwood. Our cause is never more in danger than when a human, no longer desiring, but still intending, to do our Enemy's will, looks around upon a universe from which every trace of Him seems to have vanished, and asks why he has been forsaken, and still obeys.[36]

That is the crux of the matter. None of us want to be alone, even though it's easy for us to believe that we are all alone in temptation. "Nobody knows what I'm going through right now." Whether tempted or tested, it very much feels like we are facing the desert by ourselves, that God is no longer with us. Of course, what makes the temptation story of Jesus so ironic is that Christ is Immanuel, "God with us." Furthermore, this "Immanuel" will cry out on the cross of his death, "My God, My God, why have you forsaken me?" (Matt 27:46). Of all people, Jesus knows what it feels like to face tests/temptations alone: "Couldn't you men keep watch with me for one hour? . . . Watch and pray so that you will not fall into temptation" (26:40–41). Watch and pray—two bits of advice that sum up well the lessons Jesus learned in the desert and passed onto his disciples. Watch Jesus. See how he overcame temptation, defeated the devil, and came out of the desert a stronger man—strong enough to bind the enemy and plunder his house. Also, pray. Pray as he taught us to pray, "Lead us not into temptation, but deliver us from the evil one." For our enemy always stands at the ready—when we are the most vulnerable—to tempt us to believe that God is no longer present, that we are no longer his children, that the Lord is no longer on our side, that we are all alone. That is a lie. We all face the same temptations. We all go through dry times in the desert. Yet the one who is called "Immanuel," the Son of God, the Messiah, the God who saves, the man who came out of the desert very much alive, has promised that he will never leave us or forsake us (28:20).

36. Lewis, *Screwtape Letters* (1943 ed.), 46–47.

He has called us to follow him through the desert, to the mountain, beyond the Jordan, into Jerusalem, to the cross, out of the grave, even to the end of the world. And, because we are *his* disciples, we know that we are never alone.

> No temptation has overtaken you except what is common to mankind. And God is faithful; he will not let you be tempted beyond what you can bear. But when you are tempted, *he will also provide a way out* so that you can endure it. (1 Cor 10:13, emphasis added)

Indeed, the way is Jesus Christ, our Immanuel.

CHAPTER 5

Matthew 4:23–5:16

LISTEN to the Story

23Jesus went throughout Galilee, teaching in their synagogues, pro-
claiming the good news of the kingdom, and healing every disease and
sickness among the people. 24News about him spread all over Syria, and
people brought to him all who were ill with various diseases, those suffer-
ing severe pain, the demon-possessed, those having seizures, and the para-
lyzed; and he healed them. 25Large crowds from Galilee, the Decapolis,
Jerusalem, Judea and the region across the Jordan followed him.

5:1Now when Jesus saw the crowds, he went up on a mountainside and
sat down. His disciples came to him, 2and he began to teach them.

He said:

3"Blessed are the poor in spirit,
  for theirs is the kingdom of heaven.
4Blessed are those who mourn,
  for they will be comforted.
5Blessed are the meek,
  for they will inherit the earth.
6Blessed are those who hunger and thirst for righteousness,
  for they will be filled.
7Blessed are the merciful,
  for they will be shown mercy.
8Blessed are the pure in heart,
  for they will see God.
9Blessed are the peacemakers,
  for they will be called children of God.
10Blessed are those who are persecuted because of righteousness,
  for theirs is the kingdom of heaven.

11"Blessed are you when people insult you, persecute you and falsely
say all kinds of evil against you because of me. 12Rejoice and be glad,

because great is your reward in heaven, for in the same way they persecuted the prophets who were before you.

[13]"You are the salt of the earth. But if the salt loses its saltiness, how can it be made salty again? It is no longer good for anything, except to be thrown out and trampled underfoot.

[14]"You are the light of the world. A town built on a hill cannot be hidden. [15]Neither do people light a lamp and put it under a bowl. Instead they put it on its stand, and it gives light to everyone in the house. [16]In the same way, let your light shine before others, that they may see your good deeds and glorify your Father in heaven.

Listening to the Text in the Story: Exodus 19:3–6; 24:12–13; Deuteronomy 11:26–28; 18:15–19; 30:1–20; 2 Chronicles 36:15–16; Psalms 24:3–6; 37:7–11, 22–34, 37–40; 120:7; 126:1–6; Proverbs 11:17; Isaiah 9:1–7; 42:5–9; 51:1–8; 55:1–3; 60:1–4, 15–22; 61:1–11; Hosea 2:21–23.

When Jesus found his first disciples, fishermen, they were casting and mending their nets. Galilean fishermen used circular nets anchored around the edges and a rope tied to the middle so that after throwing the net in the water, the fishermen would simply pull on the rope, causing the weights to draw the net together at the bottom and capture the fish. With the stone weights clanging against each other during the drawing process, the cords of the net getting tangled, fish thrashing about in the trap, the nets would tear causing large gaps for the fish to escape. Untangling ropes and sewing up holes were the constant chores of lake fishermen. One wonders what was going through the minds of Peter and Andrew, James and John, when Jesus told them he would teach them how to fish for people. Did they constantly draw comparisons between their trade and this new enterprise? What nets would they use to capture people? Would stuff get all twisted up when they fished for disciples? And, probably the question any Galilean fisherman wanted answered, would they still have to spend all those hours mending their nets?

Matthew makes it plain that Jesus drew huge crowds—fishing for men and women—when he performed miracles. In almost a matter-of-fact way, Matthew summarizes the early ministry of Jesus as teaching, preaching, and healing (Matt 4:23). Even though he doesn't explain at this point what Jesus taught in the synagogues or describe Jesus's sermons about the kingdom of heaven (both will come later in full course), our Gospel writer does offer a few lines—rather nonchalantly—about the incredible success of Jesus's healing work (vv. 24–25). Jesus cast a big net over the country when he started healing people—and not just any people, but especially the ones considered "hopeless" because doctors couldn't help them: the demonized, paralyzed, and lunatics.[1] Truly these were the people "living in darkness . . . in the land of the shadow of death" (Matt 4:16), overpowered by the evil one. We tend to take for granted the powers of medicine, the privilege of going to hospitals where perfect strangers—experts in their field—take care of us. Sure, healthcare is big business in our country. It's big business because we demand the best healthcare. Can you imagine living in New Testament times, when these luxuries didn't exist? There were no emergency rooms, no surgical options, no FDA-approved drugs. Many physicians were slaves, "medicine men," who practiced what would look to us like a cross between homeopathic medicine and voodoo. Getting sick would mean you had just as much a chance of dying as getting better. Diseased people throughout the Roman Empire flocked to temples where Asclepius (the god of healing) offered the last hope of remedy to those willing to pay. It's no wonder, then, that crowds schooled like fish to see Jesus, not only from the four corners of Israel but also from neighboring gentile territories like Syria.[2] He was healing people—the worst kind of diseased people—for free. Evil was defeated for a change; Satan was losing his grip. What makes it even more astonishing is that Matthew doesn't act like it's a big deal. "Yeah. Jesus caught a bunch of people by healing them. But, it's what he said that matters more."

Teaching, preaching, healing. Even the order of the list reveals Matthew's priorities when summing up the significance of Jesus. Primarily, Jesus came to teach, and the famously entitled "Sermon on the Mount" stands as a tremendous monument to his didactic purpose. The motivation for the Sermon according to Matthew was the sight of so many people: "Now when Jesus saw the crowds, he went up on a mountainside and sat down" (the posture of rabbis taking the seat of Moses to teach; Matt 5:1; 23:2). Jesus drew the net when he healed. Now it was time to catch the fish, and the way he would "make disciples" of all who followed him (Matt 4:25) was to teach them his commandments—the same method of instruction he passed on to his disciples (Matt 28:20).[3] Because of the Sermon's setting and the direct references Jesus made to the law, many scholars hear echoes of Moses's ascent to

1. Garland, *Reading Matthew*, 49–50. The word used to describe epileptics (*selēniazomenous*) means something like "moonstruck," similar to our "lunatic." The Romans believed uncontrolled seizures had something to do with the moon's effect on certain people; Jews attributed the malady to demonic oppression. See France, *Matthew*, 659–60n10.

2. Garland, *Reading Matthew*, 50.

3. Luz, *Matthew*, 1:176–77.

Mt. Sinai to receive God's word (Exod 19:3–4).[4] In other words, what we have here is another attempt by Matthew to present Jesus as the "new Moses," the prophet who was supposed to come to Israel and speak the very words of God (Deut 18:15–19).[5] That Matthew places Jesus's teaching front and center, adding stories of healing and preaching afterward (Matt 8:1–9:34), concluding the section with the same summary statement (9:35) that begins the entire unit (4:23–9:35), makes it quite evident that the Sermon on the Mount takes priority as the opening salvo of Jesus's kingdom initiative.[6] Indeed, in no uncertain terms Jesus challenges his listeners—and comes out swinging against the scribes and Pharisees—on what righteousness should look like in the kingdom of God.[7]

EXPLAIN the Story

Before we launch into the beginning of the Sermon, there are two observations that are important to interpreting Jesus's teaching. First, when we read the Sermon (especially in Greek), it is evident that Jesus is describing the kind of people who will make up the kingdom of heaven. Plural pronouns appear throughout the Sermon. He's not describing a particular individual, setting up only a personal ethic of behavior. Rather, he's purposely characterizing the righteousness of a people group.[8] When we read, "Blessed are the poor in spirit" or "You are the light of the world," it's easy to interpret these sayings individualistically—that Jesus is describing the person who is spiritually poor, the individual who is supposed to be the "light of the world." In fact, we teach our children to sing, "This little light of *mine*, I'm going to let it shine." But the pronoun is plural, "*You all* are the light of the world." Jesus was talking about a group of people who shine like a city on a hill, a people group who recognize

4. For the fullest explanation of the Moses typology, see Dale C. Allison Jr., *The New Moses: A Matthean Typology* (Philadelphia: Fortress, 1993), 137–270.

5. McKnight, *Sermon on the Mount*, 21–24.

6. Many scholars see the Sermon as a collection of Jesus's teaching, delivered at different times and under various circumstances. That Luke has a different version of the Sermon (Luke 6:20–49), with some of the sayings sprinkled through his Gospel at different times (11:2–4, 9–13, 33–36; 12:22–34; 13:23–30; 14:34–35; 16:13) is evidence that Jesus repeated his teachings many times and in many places. The implication, then, is that the Sermon on the Mount reflects Matthew's emphases (by gathering, arranging, structuring the Sermon) as much as what Jesus taught in one setting. See Hans Dieter Betz, *The Sermon on the Mount: A Commentary on the Sermon on the Mount including the Sermon on the Plain (Matthew 5:3–7:27 and Luke 6:20–49)*, Hermeneia (Minneapolis: Augsburg Fortress, 1995), 1–5, 44–66, 88.

7. "Righteousness is a prominent theme (5:10, 20; 6:1, 33)" (Davies and Allison, *Matthew*, 1:452).

8. So also McKnight: "These blessings of Jesus are not directed at ethical attributes . . . nor is this a virtue list by which to measure our moral progress. Instead, these blessings are heaped on *people groups* who are otherwise rejected by society" (*Sermon on the Mount*, 33 [emphasis his]).

their spiritual poverty. So what we should be teaching our children to sing is: "This little light of ours, we're going to let it shine" (which doesn't rhyme, but the little ditty would be truer to what Jesus taught). Throughout the Sermon, I'll keep returning to this significant feature of Jesus's teaching, reminding us to consider what the corporate reality of our discipleship means for the kingdom. We often emphasize having a personal relationship with Jesus—and rightfully so—but we don't talk much about our corporate relationship with him.

The second observation is this: Scot McKnight is right to emphasize the end of the Sermon as the beginning point of our study.[9] To see where Jesus ended up, calling his disciples to do what he said, is key to making sense of the punch of the Sermon. Of course, we have the advantage as readers. Rather than having to wait and wonder where the speaker is going (how many times does that question cross your mind while listening to a sermon?), we can skip to the end and see what Jesus was up to, the "call for a decision," the nub of the matter at hand. In fact, like any superb persuasive speaker, Jesus puts before his listeners a binary choice—mutually exclusive—characterized as two gates, two paths, two kinds of prophets, two kinds of trees, two kinds of builders (Matt 7:13–27). The question left in the minds of the listeners is this: Which gate are we going to enter; which path are we going to take; what kind of prophet, tree, or builder are we going to be? Jesus's or the other guy's? Now, at this point, we all know which gate, path, prophet, tree, and builder belongs to Jesus. His is the "straight and narrow," the true prophet, the good fruit, the wise builder. But whose gate, path, prophet, tree, and builder is the other choice, the opposite of Jesus, the way we shouldn't take? If Jesus was essentially standing before the crowd saying, "Follow me, don't follow them," then who are "them," the false prophets, the bad fruit, the way that is broad and leads to destruction? It's the scribes and the Pharisees. Jesus made it plain from the beginning: "Unless your righteousness surpasses that of the Pharisees and the teachers of the law, you will certainly not enter the kingdom of heaven" (Matt 5:20). The foil of Jesus's Sermon, the contrasting way of his kingdom, is the very people who were supposed to know righteousness best—a crucial observation to make as we have ears to hear the majestic Sermon on the Mount.

Blessed Are the Cursed

Given the makeup of the crowd around Jesus—the poor, the oppressed, the marginalized, the sick and lame—the first words out of Jesus's mouth should have been, "Cursed are you." That's because everyone knew—and the

9. McKnight, *Sermon on the Mount*, 19–21.

Pharisees were the teachers who reminded the people—that those who disobey God's law are cursed with diseases, famine, exile, and foreign oppressors, while those who obey are blessed with health and abundance in the land (Deut 28:20–52, 58–68; 30:1–20). The logic of working backward, from effect to cause, revealed that Israel in general and the diseased, displaced, and impoverished in particular were cursed by God because they violated his commandments. That's one of the reasons why the Pharisees emphasized complete obedience to God's law. Righteousness was not optional. If Israel would ever see God's kingdom come—throwing out the Romans, gathering the elect, healing the diseased, restoring the land—the people would need to learn the lesson spelled out so well in Deuteronomy. It was their choice: obey God and be blessed; disobey God and be punished. It must have been apparent to nearly everyone that the cursed who gathered around Jesus that day were spiritually impoverished rebels.

These people—the poor, the mourners, the meek, the hungry, the persecuted—must have been shocked to hear Jesus pronounce them "blessed." The evidence of their blessing, according to Jesus, was the arrival of the kingdom of heaven, the promise of a better future. Now, those who had just been healed or exorcized could have shouted a hearty "amen!" to Jesus's claim. But to most, the Beatitudes must have sounded like a pipe dream. The hungry will be filled? The lamenters won't mourn anymore? The poor will be rich in the kingdom?[10] The meek will inherit the land? That wasn't true of their world (the rich, strong, healthy, and powerful made sure of that). Besides, Jesus never explains *how* these things will come true. To climb a mountain and claim all of these blessings have come true must have sounded presumptuous, even delusional ("he acts like he's Moses!"). But, hold on. Jesus wasn't making this stuff up. As any good cross-reference Bible will reveal, practically all the Beatitudes come from the Old Testament (in order of the eight sayings: Isa 61:1; Isa 61:2; Ps 37:11; Isa 55:1–2; Prov 11:17; Ps 24:4–5; Ps 34:14; there is no Old Testament promise of blessing for the persecuted[11]). And it's especially

10. Commentators (esp. patristics and Reformation) see Jesus's qualification of the poor in Matthew's version, that is, poor "in spirit," as pertaining only to spiritual matters; see Luz, *Matthew*, 1:190–93; Nolland, *Matthew*, 198–200. But in Jesus's world, to separate economic reality from spiritual problems would be considered nonsense. The fact that Israel was suffering under "exilic" conditions undeniably proved the absence of God's blessing, that is, spiritual poverty. When God is present, there is justice. When he is "absent," when the poor are not experiencing the justice of God, the entire nation is spiritually impoverished, especially the wealthy (even though they refused to admit it—see the prophets, e.g., Amos 4:1–3). The poor had no doubts about their poverty. So also Nolland: "The poor in spirit will be those who sense the burden of their present (impoverished) state, and see it in terms of the absence of God; who patiently bear that state, but long for God to act on their behalf and decisively claim them again as his people" (*Matthew*, 200–201).

11. Davies and Allison, *Matthew*, 1:459.

the passage from Isaiah 61 that seems to have inspired Jesus's Sermon—timing as well as content. Having just been fully immersed by the "Spirit of the Lord," Jesus came to bring relief, "good news to the poor," and "release from darkness for the prisoners" just as Isaiah predicted he would (61:1). So when Jesus pronounced these people "blessed," he was simply claiming the promises of God.[12]

Yet what was "the blessing"?[13] Was Jesus speaking like a Jewish philosopher, finding blessing in the virtues themselves, much like what was taught in Wisdom literature (Sir 19:20; cf. Jas 1:25)? In other words, was Jesus teaching his disciples they should find blessing in recognizing their spiritual poverty, their need for humility, and their hunger for righteousness?[14] Or should the emphasis of the Beatitudes fall on the blessings that will be realized in the future? So Jesus wasn't saying, "You're poor. Deal with it. Can't you find the good in poverty?" Rather, the blessings are to be found in the promises that will come true on the last day: inheriting the land, being comforted, being filled, and seeing the kingdom of heaven come to earth. If that's the case, Jesus was talking like an apocalyptic prophet: "It's bad now. But one day it will get better, very soon. So hold on."[15] Or is the truth somewhere in the middle? On this reading, Jesus was laying down what it takes for Israel to *begin* to realize the kingdom of God. In other words, the Beatitudes are ethical requirements for entering the kingdom, disguised as blessings—a sort of halfway house between apocalyptic hope and pearls of wisdom.[16] It would be as if Jesus were saying, "Those who humble themselves—truly repent—will inherit kingdom blessings now and then."[17]

The reason it's difficult to decide what Jesus was claiming in the Beatitudes is that some of them sound like wise sayings extolling the virtues of the righteous: "Blessed are the pure in heart, for they will see God" (Matt 5:8). "Blessed are those who hunger and thirst for righteousness, for they will be filled" (v. 6). "Blessed are the merciful, for they will be shown mercy" (v. 7). Other beatitudes sound like predictions of eschatological reversal: "Blessed are the

12. Luke does the same thing, but in his Gospel Jesus makes the correlation more explicit, appealing directly to Isa 61:1–2 (Luke 4:16–21), which got him in big trouble with his own people (see vv. 28–30).

13. The word (*makarios*) is notoriously difficult to translate; it means more than "happy," yet it was also used to describe favorable circumstances (most often due to divine approval). See the discussion in Davies and Allison, *Matthew*, 1:431–34.

14. Turner writes: "These character traits are gracious gifts indicating God's approval, not requirements for works that merit God's approval" (*Matthew*, 147).

15. See Luz, *Matthew*, 1:189–90, who sees the eschatological emphasis *apropos* to the *Sitz im Leben* ("situation in life") of Jesus.

16. Garland, *Reading Matthew*, 53–55; according to Luz this is the *Sitz im Leben* of Matthew's readers, that is, how the Evangelist has interpreted Jesus's teaching (*Matthew*, 1:187–88).

17. See Keener, *Matthew*, 165–67.

meek, for they will inherit the earth" (v. 5). "Blessed are those who mourn, for they will be comforted" (v. 4). "Blessed are the poor in spirit, for theirs is the kingdom of heaven" (v. 3). And finally, some sound like a blending of both, the realization of blessings dependent upon a probable future: "Blessed are those who are persecuted because of righteousness, for theirs is the kingdom of heaven" (v. 10)—especially if we see v. 11 as further explanation (Jesus's disciples certainly hadn't experienced such persecution). "Blessed are the peacemakers, for they will be called children of God" (v. 9)—like persecution, peacemaking hasn't happened yet. It's no wonder, then, that many scholars either choose one approach and try to shoehorn the other beatitudes into the glass slipper,[18] or they organize the eight beatitudes around other categories: vertical relationship/disposition toward God/humility (vv. 3–6), horizontal relationship/demeanor toward others/justice (vv. 7–10).[19] Of course, regardless of their approach scholars stress the importance of interpreting the Beatitudes in light of the entire Sermon. Taken out of context, the Beatitudes can mean just about anything. So we need to figure out why Jesus opened the Sermon with these beatitudes. Oftentimes introductions are explained by conclusions.

Blessed Are the Ones Who Follow Jesus

The way Jesus ended the Sermon reveals his intent; he was trying to make disciples of the crowd:[20] "Enter through the narrow gate" (Matt 7:13). The cursed were drawn to him because of the miracles he performed. It's one thing to talk about the reign of God as "blessings"; it's quite something else to make it happen: "Blessed are you." But, it's not just what Jesus can do for you that matters: "Man shall not live on bread alone, but on every word that comes from the mouth of God" (4:4). Jesus was looking for disciples—those who had ears to hear God's word—to join him in bringing the kingdom of heaven to earth, to "do to others what you would have them do to you" (7:12). They were to hear from him and see in him what the kingdom of heaven should

18. For example, Turner, *Matthew*, 146–47, places the Beatitudes on the horns of the dilemma, grace vs. works, and concludes that all the Beatitudes must be read together as eschatological blessings (grace). I've been tempted to re-arrange the beatitudes, especially vv. 8–9. Wouldn't it make better sense if Jesus had said, "Blessed are the pure in heart, for they will be called children of God" (only God sees our hearts), and "Blessed are the peacemakers, for they will see God" (when peace comes, it certainly looks like heaven on earth!).

19. See, for example, Talbert, *Matthew*, 75–78; Garland, *Reading Matthew*, 55–59. The problem, of course, is v. 8 belongs to the first category, and v. 6 (depending on the meaning of "righteousness," i.e., social justice) could belong to the second category. McKnight offers three categories: humility, righteousness/justice, peace (*Sermon on the Mount*, 37–49).

20. Contra France, who believes the Sermon was intended only for the disciples (see Matt 5:1): "The focus of these chapters is not then the wider proclamation of the 'good news of the kingdom' (4:23), but the instruction of those who have already responded to that proclamation" (France, *Matthew*, 153).

look like on earth. To follow Jesus, then, was to fulfill the hope of Israel to see the righteousness of God. But why him and not someone else? Wouldn't the Pharisees—standard-bearers of righteousness—have just as much claim to direct Israel in the way they should go? Well, according to Jesus they know what is right; they just don't do it (23:3). Jesus, on the other hand, practices what he preaches because he is the embodiment of Israel, the anointed one, the righteousness of God. Therefore, the entire Sermon—from introduction, exposition of Scripture, illustrations, to conclusion—is an invitation to follow Jesus because of *the way* he sees the kingdom of heaven coming to earth. It's as much about him as what's expected of his disciples because following him (the king) is the way of righteousness (the kingdom).

That's why scholars see a christological focus to the Sermon.[21] When Jesus stood before the crowd and began to bless the cursed, he did so knowing he was the eschatological fulfillment of God's promise to Israel. So, the Beatitudes picture "eschatology in the process of realization,"[22] the vision of Jesus for the kingdom, the embodiment of God's righteousness dawning on Israel—the light shining in the darkness. And yet, for all Matthew has done to set up this moment, to present Jesus as the one who will make it all happen, here's the shocker: Jesus knew he couldn't do it by himself. This is why he preached the Sermon; from the beginning Jesus intended to extend his messianic work *through* his disciples. Even though we see the attributes of Christ throughout the Sermon—not only in the introduction (meek, righteous, pure in heart, merciful) but especially in the heart of the Sermon (don't hate, turn other cheek, love enemies, don't judge)—Jesus was also describing the kind of people who make up the kingdom, the ones who follow him: the poor in spirit, the ones who hunger and thirst for righteousness, the children of God who make peace, the ones who are persecuted because of Jesus.[23] The very last beatitude—the add-on in vv. 11–12—is the most revealing reason why Jesus opened the Sermon with these sayings. The kind of people who are drawn to him (the cursed) are the very ones who *are* blessed and *will be* blessed when they follow him. These are the ideal candidates for his kingdom, the kind of people he's looking for to help him do God's will on earth as it is in heaven. And what is the final evidence of their discipleship, that they are truly doing the work of the kingdom? They will be persecuted because of Jesus, which means they will be persecuted just like the prophets before them.

---

21. "The implicit Christology of the beatitudes is remarkable" (Davies and Allison, *Matthew*, 1:438; so also Garland, *Reading Matthew*, 59; McKnight, *Sermon on the Mount*, 13–14, 25–26).

22. Davies and Allison, *Matthew*, 1:439.

23. Chrysostom wrote: "In pronouncing them blessed, who are persecuted, and chased, and suffer all intolerable things; not for them only, but also for all who arrive at the same excellency, He weaves His crown" (*Homilies*, 91–92).

Since Jesus put his disciples in the same category as the prophets of Israel, now the beatitudes come into clearer focus. Prophets were often considered by their contemporaries as the bane of Israel, the cursed of God, only appreciated in retrospect. Think of Jeremiah or Hosea. Both were laughingstocks, ridiculed and maligned by the people. Once their message came true, however, Israel realized their mistake (but it takes a prophet to give voice to their horror):

> He was despised and rejected by mankind,
> a man of suffering, and familiar with pain.
> Like one from whom people hide their faces
> he was despised, and we held him in low esteem.
> Surely he took up our pain
> and bore our suffering,
> yet we considered him punished by God,
> stricken by him, and afflicted. (Isa 53:3–4)

Jesus saw his kingdom operating under the same prophetic conditions.[24] Like God, Jesus sends his disciples as "blessed" messengers because they do God's will. And like the prophets before them, Jesus predicted Israel would not take it well. Instead, these "Jesus prophets" will be maligned by the people and considered cursed by God (the poor in spirit, those who mourn, the meek, the hungry). Nevertheless, Jesus preached that the "cursed" ones are blessed in what they are doing—righteousness/following Jesus—and will be blessed with heavenly rewards. Knowing that in advance, Jesus tells his disciples that they should "rejoice and be glad" (Matt 5:12). In fact, later when Jesus sends the Twelve to recover the lost sheep of Israel, he promises rewards to any who show his "prophets" hospitality because "anyone who welcomes you welcomes me, and anyone who welcomes me welcomes the one who sent me. Whoever welcomes a prophet as a prophet will receive a prophet's reward, and whoever welcomes a righteous person as a righteous person will receive a righteous person's reward" (Matt 10:40–41).

The people described in the Beatitudes, the disciples of Jesus, are the salt of the earth (v. 13). Since salt has so many uses, one would expect Jesus to explain what he meant by the analogy.[25] But he doesn't. Instead, he only entertains the downside of salt losing its effect, literally, "becoming moronic" (*mōranthē*). Since salt can't be salted (the attempt is just as foolish as trying to make water wet), then "unsalty salt" is good for nothing, thrown out with the trash. It's one thing to be persecuted for righteousness on account of Jesus. It's quite something else to be treated like a doormat for nothing. Jesus

24. So also France, *Matthew*, 173.

25. See Davies and Allison for a complete list of possibilities (*Matthew*, 1:472–73).

knew his disciples would be rejected. But he wouldn't accept the idea that his followers were worthless. Rather, he claimed his disciples were the salt of the earth—their essence is their purpose; who they are is what they do. Salt salts. Disciples disciple. Salt doesn't exist for any other purpose, and neither do disciples. That's the point of the metaphor, which is more clearly seen in the next analogy: those who follow Jesus are the light of the world (v. 14).

Light exists for one purpose: to light up the darkness. So too, his disciples are like a city shining on a hill (which could be a slam against Jerusalem[26]—imagine the laughter running through the crowd when Jesus made that claim: "You think the Pharisees and Sadducees, the scribes and the priests are righteous before God? That they are the true Israel? The 'covenant for the people, and a light to the gentiles' [Isa 42:6]? No! It's people like you—the poor, the meek, the persecuted. You are blessed. You are the covenant. You are the city of God. You are the light of the world."[27]) Gathered on a mountain, *together* these disciples shine so bright they cannot be hidden. That's what light does. It can't help but light up its environs. Therefore, like a lamp lighting up a dark room, Jesus's disciples deserve to be placed on a lampstand (Matt 5:15). They may be treated like the prophets before them, rejected by Israel, thrown out like worthless salt. But they are the salt of the land, the light of the world. They are meant to shine, to light up the darkness (echoing 4:16?[28]). They aren't "lit up" only to be hidden. How foolish. Jesus's disciples must light up the world with their righteousness/their "good deeds"/following Jesus.[29] Then, Jesus claims, eventually the world will see their work for what it is—*good* deeds/the kingdom of *heaven* on earth—and will glorify God, "your Father in heaven" (v. 16). Indeed, even though they will be persecuted, peacemakers will be called children of God . . . one day.

LIVE the Story

If you ask the average person, "Are you blessed?" most would say, "Yes," and then list the typical evidence: health, family, job, home. Even individuals who are sick, experiencing family problems, or have lost their jobs or homes often point to one of the other "blessings" to maintain their claim. How often do we

26. Garland, *Reading Matthew*, 60. For the pros and cons of this interpretation, see Davies and Allison, *Matthew*, 1:475.

27. So also McKnight, *Sermon on the Mount*, 56–57, who sees the two metaphors applied, respectively, to Israel (salt of the land) and the world (light to the nations).

28. Luz, *Matthew*, 1:207: "Thus the task given the disciples corresponds to the mission of Christ himself."

29. "That to which the Matthean Jesus calls is neither private nor to be ghettoized in the Christian community" (Nolland, *Matthew*, 215).

hear victims of tornadoes, standing in front of the wreckage they once called "home," say, "At least we have our health and each other." To be sure, these taken-for-granted evidences of God's grace are blessings—especially appreciated when they are lost. What is interesting to me, however, is that none of these things make Jesus's list of what it means to be "blessed" in the kingdom. Apparently, we don't think like Jesus on the matter because we see "blessings" as basic requirements for *our* happiness. Of course, happiness depends upon favorable circumstances. When things go wrong, we are not happy about it. We want things to change. So we pursue happiness—to make our circumstances better—and when things get better, we claim we are blessed. In other words, we often operate with the presumption that blessings are meant for our happiness. But Jesus didn't see it that way at all; blessings are more important than that.[30]

For the May 30, 1991 issue of *Rolling Stone* magazine, Mikal Gilmore interviewed Bob Dylan. The article, "Bob Dylan at Fifty," had for its byline the teaser: "Happiness is not on my list of priorities. Anyone can be happy." Toward the end of the article, Gilmore reveals what Dylan meant:

> I asked him, Did he think he was a happier man these days than twenty years earlier?
>
> "Oh, man, I've never even thought about that," Dylan said, laughing. "Happiness is not on my list of priorities. I just deal with day-to-day things. If I'm happy, I'm happy—and if I'm not, I don't know the difference." He fell silent for a few moments and stared at his hands. "You know," he said, "these are yuppie words, happiness and unhappiness. It's not happiness or unhappiness, it's either blessed or unblessed. As the Bible says, 'Blessed is the man who walketh not in the counsel of the ungodly.' Now, that must be a happy man. Knowing that you are the person you were put on this earth to be—that's much more important than just being happy.
>
> "Anyway, happiness is just a balloon—it's just temporary stuff. Anybody can be happy, and if you're not happy, they got a lot of drugs that can make you happy. But trust me: Life is not a bowl of cherries."[31]

Of course, the privileged life of a rock star isn't a compelling place to sort out the difference between "happiness or unhappiness . . . blessed or

30. Which is why translating the Beatitudes, "happy is the one who . . ." misses the point and misleads the reader. Jesus wasn't talking about *happenstance* (from the old English word "hap," from which we get the word "happy").

31. Mikal Gilmore, "Bob Dylan at Fifty," *Rolling Stone*, May 30, 1991, www.rollingstone.com/music/news/bob-dylan-at-fifty-19910530?page=3. I heard about this interview through the backstory to the song, "Happy is a Yuppie Word," written by Jon Foreman (Switchfoot), who was inspired by Dylan's prophetic observation.

unblessed." What does Dylan have to complain about? (For that matter, what do I have to complain about?) Nevertheless, his astute observation stands. He gets it. For all our "pursuit of happiness," life can be incredibly vapid without a higher purpose, without "knowing that you are the person you were put on this earth to be." And, according to Jesus the only purpose, the only way to "be blessed," is to follow him, to be a blessing, to live for the kingdom of God. That's why Jesus believed people needed to repent, to change their minds about what it means to be blessed, to see the kingdom of heaven come to earth through those who are considered "cursed"—people who are surely "unhappy" according to our standards.

I've often wondered what the Beatitudes would be according to the Pharisees. Of course, it would be easy to create the list of beatitudes according to the priorities of our culture. Think of whom we champion as our heroes: "Blessed are the rich. Blessed are the famous. Blessed are the powerful. Blessed are the beautiful." We Christians scoff at such vanities; we know the ways of the world leave you empty. Yet Jesus didn't offer the Beatitudes as a critique of the pagan world. Rather, he was challenging the conventional wisdom of his own people.[32] So, what would the Pharisees—the epitome of righteousness—list as quintessential to receiving the blessings of God? Moreover, in light of what Christians prize as God's blessing, would we find their beatitudes more appealing than Jesus's list? Indeed, if we were to agree with the Pharisees, this is what Jesus should have said:

> Blessed are the rich in spirit, for theirs is the favor of God (Matt 23:2, 6–7).
> Blessed are those who grieve over their sin, for they shall be forgiven (9:2–3).
> Blessed are those who fast for righteousness's sake, for they shall be approved (9:14).
> Blessed are the zealous, for they stand up for what is right (12:1–2).
> Blessed are the pure, for they will avoid God's wrath (22:15–17).
> Blessed are those who judge rightly, for they shall be judged righteous (9:10–11).
> Blessed are the guardians of tradition, for they shall be called the defenders of God (15:1–2).
> Blessed are those who are persecuted because of holiness, for theirs is the favor of God (15:12–14).

"Happy" may be a yuppie word, but "blessed" is the language of the righteous. And Jesus's beatitudes should make us all reconsider—to rethink, to repent, to change our minds about—who is truly blessed by God.

---

32. "Instead of congratulating the Torah observant or the rigorously faithful or heroic, he blesses the marginalized who stick with God through injustice" (McKnight, *Sermon on the Mount*, 31).

The Beatitudes describe a group of people—those who follow Jesus—who know we need each other to be blessed. None of us can be blessed by ourselves. We all need to be comforted. We all need to be filled. We trust that the meek will inherit the earth *together*. We believe the persecuted will realize the kingdom *together*. We must show mercy to others. We must seek peace for others. No man is a city. No woman is the light. I can't follow Jesus by myself. It takes every single one of us together to realize the blessings of God, to be the salt of the earth, to light up the whole world, to see the kingdom of heaven come to earth through Jesus Christ.

CHAPTER 6

Matthew 5:17–48

LISTEN to the Story

17“Do not think that I have come to abolish the Law or the Prophets;
I have not come to abolish them but to fulfill them. 18For truly I tell
you, until heaven and earth disappear, not the smallest letter, not the
least stroke of a pen, will by any means disappear from the Law until
everything is accomplished. 19Therefore anyone who sets aside one of the
least of these commands and teaches others accordingly will be called least
in the kingdom of heaven, but whoever practices and teaches these com-
mands will be called great in the kingdom of heaven. 20For I tell you that
unless your righteousness surpasses that of the Pharisees and the teachers
of the law, you will certainly not enter the kingdom of heaven.

21“You have heard that it was said to the people long ago, ‘You shall
not murder, and anyone who murders will be subject to judgment.’ 22But I
tell you that anyone who is angry with a brother or sister will be subject to
judgment. Again, anyone who says to a brother or sister, ‘Raca,’ is answer-
able to the court. And anyone who says, ‘You fool!’ will be in danger of
the fire of hell.

23“Therefore, if you are offering your gift at the altar and there remem-
ber that your brother or sister has something against you, 24leave your gift
there in front of the altar. First go and be reconciled to them; then come
and offer your gift.

25“Settle matters quickly with your adversary who is taking you to
court. Do it while you are still together on the way, or your adversary
may hand you over to the judge, and the judge may hand you over to the
officer, and you may be thrown into prison. 26Truly I tell you, you will not
get out until you have paid the last penny.

27“You have heard that it was said, ‘You shall not commit adultery.’
28But I tell you that anyone who looks at a woman lustfully has already
committed adultery with her in his heart. 29If your right eye causes you
to stumble, gouge it out and throw it away. It is better for you to lose one

part of your body than for your whole body to be thrown into hell. 30And if your right hand causes you to stumble, cut it off and throw it away. It is better for you to lose one part of your body than for your whole body to go into hell.

31"It has been said, 'Anyone who divorces his wife must give her a certificate of divorce.' 32But I tell you that anyone who divorces his wife, except for sexual immorality, makes her the victim of adultery, and anyone who marries a divorced woman commits adultery.

33"Again, you have heard that it was said to the people long ago, 'Do not break your oath, but fulfill to the Lord the vows you have made.' 34But I tell you, do not swear an oath at all: either by heaven, for it is God's throne; 35or by the earth, for it is his footstool; or by Jerusalem, for it is the city of the Great King. 36And do not swear by your head, for you cannot make even one hair white or black. 37All you need to say is simply 'Yes' or 'No'; anything beyond this comes from the evil one.

38"You have heard that it was said, 'Eye for eye, and tooth for tooth.' 39But I tell you, do not resist an evil person. If anyone slaps you on the right cheek, turn to them the other cheek also. 40And if anyone wants to sue you and take your shirt, hand over your coat as well. 41If anyone forces you to go one mile, go with them two miles. 42Give to the one who asks you, and do not turn away from the one who wants to borrow from you.

43"You have heard that it was said, 'Love your neighbor and hate your enemy.' 44But I tell you, love your enemies and pray for those who persecute you, 45that you may be children of your Father in heaven. He causes his sun to rise on the evil and the good, and sends rain on the righteous and the unrighteous. 46If you love those who love you, what reward will you get? Are not even the tax collectors doing that? 47And if you greet only your own people, what are you doing more than others? Do not even pagans do that? 48Be perfect, therefore, as your heavenly Father is perfect.

Listening to the Text in the Story: Genesis 4:3–24; 9:6; Exodus 20:7, 13–17; 21:23–25; 22:25–27; Leviticus 18:1–30; 19:2–34; 20:10–26; 24:17–23; Numbers 30:2–16; 35:16–34; Deuteronomy 15:7–11; 19:4–20:18; 24:1–18; Job 31:1; Psalms 19:7–14; 119; 137:8–9; Proverbs 3:27–28; 20:14; Song of Solomon 4:1–9; Isaiah 50:1, 6–9; Jeremiah 3:6–8; 31:31–34.

This is the hard part—and with good reason. More hard sayings of Jesus show up here, concentrated in these few verses, than anywhere else. Remarkably, this is the only place in Matthew's Gospel where we get to hear Jesus preach an entire sermon, to see how he interpreted the Hebrew Scriptures. In other words, what seems to have inspired Jesus to lay down so many difficult sayings was when he talked like a preacher: "This is what the Bible means." In fact, his narrow-minded interpretation of the law leads some scholars to refer to this part of his sermon as "unrealistic," "naive," "impractical," and "idealistic."[1] You don't read comments like that about the rest of the Sermon on the Mount. No one calls the Lord's Prayer "impractical." Interpreters don't refer to his teaching against false piety as "idealistic," nor do they dismiss his ideas about overcoming anxiety as "naive."[2] Rather, most of us tend to be inspired by the other parts of the Sermon. But these verses? This is where we find it most difficult to take Jesus at his word. Ironic, isn't it? It's the "expositional" part of Jesus's sermon that makes Bible interpreters squirm in our seats. So, this is where we try to smooth out the rough parts. Hard sayings go down hard.

Figuring out what Jesus meant in these verses about being more righteous than the scribes and Pharisees is challenging. The wide variety of opinions among scholars is proof enough (not to mention the difficulty of actually doing what Jesus said). Yet it has as much to do with what Jesus assumed as what he said. First, Jesus acts like he's the final word when it comes to interpreting the Law and the Prophets. (Really? No one else has a valuable opinion?) "You have heard it said. . . . But I say to you" doesn't really leave much room for discussion. Second, to illustrate his point he uses everyday examples that are lost on us (swearing oaths on everything from Jerusalem to your head—what's up with that?). Finally, Jesus speaks more bluntly here than most places, not leaving much wiggle room for "application."[3] To say simply, "Love your enemies," would have left things rather open-ended. We could justify all kinds of ways we truly "love" our enemies, even though to them it would still feel like hatred. But Jesus won't leave it to us. Loving people who already speak our insider "love language" isn't enough (Matt 5:46–47). We must treat our enemies like God treats all of us—the righteous and unrighteous—by taking it on the chin, showering them with good gifts, and helping them even though we disagree (vv. 39–45). No wonder we try to domesticate Jesus's teaching, making this part of the Sermon more reasonable,

1. See the discussion in McKnight, *Sermon on the Mount*, 1–14.

2. And yet, Luz quotes those (Weiss, Montefiore, Bloch) who find Jesus's words "extremely simpleminded," revealing an "economic naivete that has characterized Christianity" (*Matthew*, 1:341).

3. His parables, on the other hand, are just the opposite: obscure and wide open to interpretation.

bringing him down to our level. It's because he's trying to bring us up to his: "Be perfect, therefore, as your heavenly Father is perfect" (v. 48).

EXPLAIN the Story

When Jesus said, "Do not think that I have come to abolish the Law or the Prophets" (v. 17), it sounds like a bit of staging to prepare his audience for the shocking (and therefore easily misinterpreted) claims he's going to make about God's word. But the Beatitudes have already done that; the subversive ideas embedded in his introductory remarks would have caused just about anyone (especially the Pharisees) to question Jesus's fidelity to the law. If the law says you are cursed, then cursed are you. But, as we've already learned, Jesus claimed the opposite: "Blessed are the poor. . . ." So it's no wonder Jesus transitioned from the reversals of the Beatitudes to his radical teaching about what God meant in the law with a warning flare to light up their imaginations: "I know it sounds like I'm questioning the law, but it's about to get worse. But don't take it that way." Of course, the worse part doesn't show up at first. When Jesus upheld the veracity of every "jot and tittle" of the law, he sounded like any other Jew who knew that covenant obedience was the prerequisite of covenant blessing (v. 18). And, to claim every bit of God's word—even the least of the commandments[4]—would be fulfilled before the end of the world was nothing new (vv. 17–19). It wasn't until he dropped the bomb, "unless your righteousness surpasses that of the Pharisees and the teachers of the law, you will certainly not enter the kingdom of heaven" (v. 20), that Jesus must have sounded like he was taking things too far—especially when he claimed he would be the one to fulfill all the Law and the Prophets (v. 17).

To our ears to exceed the righteousness of the Pharisees is simple. All you have to do is avoid hypocrisy. In fact, because of the effectiveness of Jesus's Sermon (as well as the rest of his teaching exposing the shortcomings of the Pharisees—especially the lengthy invective in Matt 23), we use the term *Pharisee* as a synonym for hypocrite. But no one in Jesus's day thought that way. To the Jewish people the Pharisees were more devoted to God's word than anyone else. They were the lay leaders of Israel, dedicated to study the Scriptures (without pay!) and to teach the people what it takes to maintain covenant obedience. Today we would compare them to Sunday school teachers or Bible study leaders—laity who spend hours reading the Bible, attending Bible study seminars to learn from great Bible teachers (at their own expense!)

4. According to Chrysostom, for Jesus to set aside the "least" of the commandments would violate his kingdom agenda to enfranchise the "least" of humanity (*Homilies*, 106).

because they take their faith seriously. In other words, the Pharisees were not "paid professionals" like the priests, although some of them (the scribes) did earn a living from "printing" (transcribing) the Hebrew Scriptures. They knew the Law and the Prophets like the back of their hand; they could "chapter and verse" any biblical quote. They were walking concordances. Because of that, the people looked to the Pharisees to help them understand God's word—especially since the Bible (even the Law) is hard to understand at times. What does it mean to "remember the Sabbath and keep it holy" by avoiding work (Exod 20:8–11)? What qualifies as work? Baking? Washing? Walking? If God expects his people to obey his commandments to be blessed, how would they know if they were truly keeping the requirements of the covenant? The Pharisees told them so.

So when Jesus challenged the righteousness of the scribes and Pharisees—that his disciples must be *more* obedient to God—he was essentially questioning their interpretation of the law.[5] In fact, throughout the entire Sermon on the Mount, Jesus is claiming that the Pharisees are not reading the Scriptures rightly. If they did, then their lives would look like the kingdom of heaven on earth. But they don't, and his criticism of their shortcomings is more easily seen in Matthew 6 where Jesus targets the false piety of the "hypocrites" (6:1–6, 16–18). It seems quite apparent that he's calling out the Pharisees there (see also 23:5–7, 27–28); but Jesus was also targeting the teachers of the law when he compared their voice, "You have heard it said," to his, "But I tell you" (5:21–22, 27–28, 31–32, 33–34, 38–39, 43–44).[6] Since the law must be interpreted to be obeyed (not even the Ten Commandments are self-explanatory),[7] then it takes an authoritative voice to say, "This is what God meant." That is exactly what Jesus was claiming when he interpreted the commandments: do not murder, do not commit adultery, give a bill of divorce, keep your vows to God, eye for eye and tooth for tooth, and love your neighbor. When it comes to the intent of the law, he acts like he knows the

---

5. Martin Pickup, "Matthew's and Mark's Pharisees," in *In Quest of the Historical Pharisees*, ed. Jacob Neusner and Bruce D. Chilton (Waco, TX: Baylor University Press, 2007), 99–102.

6. The vast majority of the Jewish people of Jesus's day didn't own a copy of the Law and the Prophets; the only copies were located at the temple and the synagogues. To hear the Scriptures, the Jewish people had to go to these places. Consequently, much of the time the words of God were recited in Pharisaical tones—literally.

7. Of course, the later, rabbinic Mishnah and the Midrashim catalog myriads of interpretive possibilities. But think about how this is true—on a more basic level—for gentile Christians (then and now) interpreting the Decalogue: #1—Does "before" mean other gods exist? #2—Are the seraphim on the ark of the covenant graven images? #3—What does "vain" mean? #4—Does this apply to Sunday? #5—Does this apply to adult children? #6—Does this apply to war? #7—Does this apply to singles? #8—Are the spoils of war theft? #9—What about your enemy? #10—Is ambition a kind of coveting? See Christian Smith, *The Bible Made Impossible* (Grand Rapids: Brazos, 2011), 29–30, 70–72.

mind of God—a more audacious claim than even the Pharisees would make, for they only spoke for Moses (23:2).

Loving Your Neighbor

Jesus's commentary on the law seems to be organized around two triads of commandments: vv. 21–32 and vv. 33–48. Each triad is introduced by the phrase "to the people long ago" (vv. 21, 33), with the first three commandments coming from Deuteronomy (Deut 5:17, 18; 24:1) and the last three from Leviticus (Lev 19:12, 18; 24:19–20).[8] There seems to be no apparent reason as to why Jesus chose these commandments—or even the significance of their arrangement in groups of three—to indicate what he means by having a righteousness that exceeds the scribes and the Pharisees. In other words, there was nothing distinctive about the Pharisaical tradition regarding these commandments compared to the rest of the law. And yet, in each case Jesus's teaching goes beyond what the law requires—something for which the Pharisees were also known.[9] Indeed, some have suggested that's the bone of contention between Jesus and the Pharisees.[10] They built a hedge around the law, a tradition formed by centuries of interpretation to protect covenant keepers from breaking the law. Jesus aimed to tear down the hedge and replace it with his own interpretation, an approach that doesn't rely upon tradition but rather a pure heart: don't hate, don't lust, don't vow. But this would mean Jesus was more concerned about attitudes than actions, when the thrust of his teaching had as much to do with behavior. For example, don't hate really means be reconciled to your brother; don't lust really means stay married to your wife no matter what.[11] Following Jesus, then, didn't just mean to have a pure heart but also pure actions: "Do to others what you would have them do to you" (Matt 7:12).

Others claim that Jesus's beef was with the adequacy of the law, not its interpreters.[12] Since the law didn't go far enough in requiring what was right, Jesus had to set the record straight, directly challenging the law.[13] In this case, Jesus offered his teaching in antithesis to the law. "The law said this, but I say the opposite." That approach seems to show up in his criticism of vows

8. Davies and Allison, *Matthew*, 1:504.

9. Neusner thinks the Pharisees adopted the purity rites for priests, extending ritual purity beyond the temple (Jacob Neusner, "The Pharisaic Agenda: Laws Attributed in the Mishnah and the Tosefta to Pre-70 Pharisees," in Neusner and Chilton, *Quest of the Historical Pharisees*, 315–23.

10. France, *Matthew*, 188–99.

11. Glen H. Stassen and David P. Gushie, *Kingdom Ethics: Following Jesus in Contemporary Context* (Downers Grove, IL: IVP Academic, 2003), 132–43.

12. See Luz, *Matthew*, 1:228–31.

13. Robert A. Guelich, *The Sermon on the Mount: A Foundation for Understanding* (Waco, TX: Word, 1982), 29.

(5:33–37). The law not only allowed vows and oaths (Num 30:1–15), but it even required them at times (Num 5:19–22; 6:2–12). But Jesus says, "Do not swear an oath at all" (Matt 5:34), as if his teaching stood in opposition to the law. Yet if Jesus were truly opposing the law, he would have encouraged his listeners to *break* their vows—these things don't matter. Indeed, the opposite of "don't murder" would be "go ahead and kill people." Furthermore, giving reasons why it's acceptable to commit adultery would stand in opposition to the seventh commandment.[14] Consequently, Jesus wasn't standing against the law. Rather, he was claiming proof that his interpretation of the law was right because it would lead to righteousness:[15] loving neighbors (5:21–32) *and* enemies (5:33–48). It's as if Jesus were saying, "Look. The teachers of the law aren't getting it right. If they did, they would teach you to do these things. But, they don't. Why? It's because they don't understand what true righteousness is. But, I do. I fulfill the law because of the way I read the law. I know what God meant. So, you better listen to me." Simply put, to do what Jesus said (and did) is to obey God.[16] Jesus defined righteousness for all—even Pharisees.

One wonders how Jesus would have read the entire Torah, not just these few verses. That would make quite a hefty volume, a "Messianic Midrashim"—probably something devout "Jesus followers" would require all of us to memorize. But that wasn't necessary. Apparently, Jesus acts like his interpretation of a handful of verses would be enough to help his disciples begin to understand what he meant by the "more important matters of the law—justice, mercy and faithfulness" (23:23). Indeed, the way he reads these six commandments is a brilliant revelation of what justice, mercy, and faithfulness look like when the kingdom of heaven comes to earth. Take, for example, the first triad. Every Jew knew that, *at the very least*, his kinsmen were his neighbors—the people he is supposed to love. And, the law prescribed what was required to "love your neighbor as yourself." But what happens when the law is used to justify treating kinsmen like enemies? In fact, enmity between neighbors is the assumed context for Jesus's interpretation of what God meant by "don't murder," "don't commit adultery," and "give a certificate of divorce." It's especially evident when Jesus puts calling someone a "fool" on the same level as murder: both words and deeds are liable to judgment—if by a human court how much more by God (5:22)? Yet human courts are unreliable when it comes

14. Contra Luz, *Matthew*, 1:230: "Jesus contrasts the will of God with the Torah itself."

15. So also Keener, *Matthew*, 175–79; Turner, *Matthew*, 165–68; Garland, *Reading Matthew*, 62–65.

16. "For Christ's commandment is not contrary to the law but broader than the law. Christ's commandment contains the law, but the law does not contain Christ's commandment. Therefore, whoever fulfills the commandments of Christ implicitly fulfills the commandments of the law" (Simonetti, *Matthew 1–13*, 101).

to meting justice. "The judge may hand you over to the officer, and you may be thrown in prison" (v. 25)—without mercy: "Truly I tell you, you will not get out until you have paid the last penny" (v. 26). So, what should you do? Rather than treat your neighbor like an enemy—an adversary heading for court—settle the matter as you walk with him or her on the road. Then they are no longer your adversary. In fact, Jesus claims you can't even worship God until you are reconciled to "your brother or sister [who] has something against you" (vv. 23–24). Why? *Because as long as you treat your brother or sister as an adversary, you have God for an adversary* (see also 6:14–15). No sacrifice will make a difference. You can't love God and hate your brother. Remember Cain (Gen 4:3–16).

Enmity against your neighbor doesn't show up as clearly to us in the following verses because we don't have arranged marriages like they did in Jesus's day. Marriages secured economic and social resources between kinsmen. Adultery was theft, stealing the honor of another man by sleeping with his wife.[17] The injured party—the spurned husband—had to divorce his wife to save face, which led to social and economic problems for both families. Was it lawful for the husband to regain the bride price he paid to enter the marriage—money that usually went to the father? Did the wife retain the dowry after divorce, or were her possessions considered damages? What if the husband divorced her for other reasons? Was there any legal recourse available to her family to keep the bride price and take the dowry? Or did the bill of divorce cover these contingencies, determined by a prenuptial agreement called a *ketubah*? Could a Jewish woman initiate a divorce, or was the dissolution of marriage something only a man could do? Scholars debate these questions because documents for the terms of marriage and divorce are sparse.[18] We may not be certain about all the details of arranged marriages, but one thing is evident: the sanctity of marriage was in trouble. Jesus seems to put the blame squarely on the shoulders of men—not surprising given the male-dominant world of his day.[19] The way Jesus saw it, adultery happens because men lust for women, and the only legitimate reason for divorce is adultery. So if men didn't treat women like sexual objects, then the seventh commandment wouldn't be broken, and women wouldn't be victims of divorce. But didn't the bill of divorce (Deut 24:1–4) protect women so that they could remarry (Matt 5:31)? Not according to Jesus. Remarriage after divorce only made

---

17. Bruce J. Malina and Richard L. Rohrbaugh, *Social-Science Commentary on the Synoptic Gospels* (Minneapolis: Fortress, 1992), 53.

18. See David W. Chapman, "Marriage and Family in Second Temple Judaism," in *Marriage and Family in the Biblical World*, ed. Ken M. Campbell (Downers Grove, IL: InterVarsity Press, 2003), especially 184–205, 219–23, 227–31.

19. Jewish writers (men!) blamed women for men's lust; see Keener, *Matthew*, 186–89.

things worse, producing repeat offenders (v. 32).[20] Therefore, men need to take extreme measures—even removing the instruments of lust[21]—to keep the law and avoid the wrath of God (vv. 29–30).

Of course, all of this was a matter of interpretation, not only what constitutes "adultery" but especially the legitimate reason(s) for divorce—what Moses meant by the phrase "becomes displeasing to him *because he finds something indecent about her*" (Deut 24:1, emphasis added). That's fairly vague and very much open to interpretation, which is why even the Pharisees were divided over the proper interpretation of "finds something indecent about her" (Matt 19:3). At the time, one school of teachers (Shammai) limited the indecency to adultery (past or present); the other school (Hillel) left it to the husband to decide what was "indecent," which would be spelled out in the bill of divorce.[22] Obviously, Hillel's interpretation was more popular among the people, for when Jesus restated his position on divorce and remarriage, his disciples mused, "If this is the situation between a husband and a wife, it is better not to marry" (v. 10). But Jesus didn't go to that extreme—being single isn't for everyone (vv. 11–12). He assumes men and women will marry. Rather, the question for him was this: "How far will you go to protect your marriage from adultery and divorce, to keep God's law?" As far as he was concerned, the habits of a lustful heart coupled with the "easy" bill of divorce sabotaged marriage. Indeed, coveting another man's wife violated the law,[23] the opposite of "loving your neighbor."

Loving Your Enemies

Evil is the problem. Jesus identifies evil as the menace that messes up the works when it comes to making vows, exacting revenge, and dealing with enemies. It's the evil one that tempts people to validate empty promises with oaths (Matt 5:37). Evil persons are the ones who abuse others (v. 39). Therefore, it's easy to infer that enemies are evil. And since righteous people hate evil, then it makes perfect sense for righteous people to hate evil people/enemies (cf. Ps 139:19–22). Yet God loves evil people (Matt 5:45). So what are we to do? How should Jesus's disciples overcome evil, especially when

20. "The whole point of the [bill of divorce] was to avoid the charge of adultery on anyone's part when the wife remarries. Jesus's pronouncement, however, assumes that no action a husband might take against his wife can ever sunder the marriage relationship in the eyes of God" (Garland, *Reading Matthew*, 68).

21. Dietrich Bonhoeffer, *Discipleship*, Dietrich Bonhoeffer Works 4 (Minneapolis: Fortress, 2001), 126.

22. The husband's shortcomings could only be inferred by what he found objectionable. Did women wish to spell out their complaints in a bill of divorcement?

23. Yet Jesus *didn't* quote the tenth commandment to back up his teaching (unlike the teachers of the law); see Garland, *Matthew*, 64.

conventional wisdom teaches us to deceive enemies, resist enemies, even hate enemies? Jesus believes the only way to overcome evil is to love our enemies (v. 44). And, when that happens, the kingdom of heaven comes to earth. Why? Because that's when God's children are truly behaving like our heavenly Father (v. 48). Of course, enemies come in all shapes and sizes—from your opponent in the market place, to a man who challenges your honor by slapping your face, or more obviously the Roman soldier who conscripts military service against your will. These are the situations Jesus calls to the memory of his listeners as he sorts out what it means to "love your enemies and pray for those who persecute you" (v. 44).

Evil is easy to spot in others, whether in the mundane affairs of life or the notorious acts of injustice. Take, for example, the daily necessity of making promises. In a world of limited goods, buyers and sellers assumed an adversarial role against each other. Promises of goods delivered or money paid were often backed up by sacred oaths. Jews were reticent to swear an oath to God for fear of breaking the third commandment, taking the Lord's name in vain. Certain circumlocutions were deemed permissible (some more binding than others, depending upon which teacher you consulted) to convince your opponent you meant what you said (vv. 34–36). Now, whether your opponent kept his promise was another matter (this was the problem that the teachers of the law tried to correct by warning: sacred *oaths* to men were the same as *vows* to God that *must* be kept; v. 33).[24] The issue was whether you could refuse the terms of the agreement—a meeting of the minds—when your opponent swore by what was holy.[25] To turn your back on him was the same as turning your back on God. *Even if you suspected he was lying*, sacred oaths made it difficult to discern the truth. Jesus, on the other hand, offered a simple solution: "Do not swear an oath at all" (v. 34). Rather, "all you need to say is simply 'Yes' or 'No'; anything beyond this comes from the evil one" (v. 37). In the ordinary affairs of daily life, loving your enemy means telling the truth.[26]

Evil people leverage any power available to them to take advantage of their enemies, especially when they feel justified in doing it. Jesus identified three sources of power people used to pursue their notions of justice: honor, the court, and military force. The law of retaliation (Lev 24:19–20) was *supposed* to curb the escalation of violence that typically happens between opponents

24. See the discussion in Garland, *Reading Matthew*, 70–72.

25. "Those oaths became the source for scaling honesty in words" (McKnight, *Sermon on the Mount*, 112; see also Keener, *Matthew*, 193–94). We may laugh at such antiquated ideas of swearing oaths to mask intent, but legal contracts serve the same purpose for us. Isn't the first question we ask (regardless of our intent in signing the contract), "Am I bound by law to do it, or is there a loophole?"

26. But what about "extraordinary" situations? See McKnight for an excellent discussion (*Sermon on the Mount*, 115–20).

looking for justice. Evil people, of course, don't keep the law. So what recourse does the victim have in seeking reparation when the enemy slaps your face, takes you to court, or imposes their superior military will? Even the law of retaliation would justify returning the insult, fighting for your rights in court, or attacking enemy soldiers. Jesus, on the other hand, commands his disciples to "not resist an evil person," the one who "slaps you on the right cheek," "wants to sue you and take your shirt," and "forces you to go one mile" (vv. 39–41). Without giving any rationale (as he does in every other case, "if you hate or lust you'll go to hell,"[27] "remarriage is adultery," "swearing oaths is evil," "love your enemies because God does"), Jesus tells his disciples they should turn the other cheek, give up their shirt *and* coat,[28] and go the second mile (vv. 39–41). We try to find reasons embedded in his directives that explain why he gave such "impractical" advice: turning the other cheek is an act of defiance preserving the dignity of the offended, handing over the coat exposes the ruthless greed of the opponent, going the second mile may soften the heart of soldiers calloused by the atrocities of war. These strategies for breaking the vicious cycle of violence may encourage Jesus's disciples to follow his teaching.[29] But Jesus didn't believe any rationale was necessary to do what he said regarding revenge; he had already promised the meek will inherit the earth.[30] Rather than making a fist, Jesus's disciples should be known for always having an open hand (v. 42).

It all comes down to this: love your enemies (vv. 43–44). Of course, everyone loves their own kind. Even enemies love each other (vv. 46–47). But what sets Jesus's disciples apart is that we seek a heavenly reward—the kingdom of heaven coming to earth. And the only way that will happen—God reigning on earth—is when we follow the words and deeds of our king, Jesus. Since God loves his enemies, and Jesus is the ultimate proof of that, then we must love our enemies too (v. 45).[31] No minced words, no complicated explanations. It's fairly straightforward. When we love enemies like God does, then we become like him: perfect in love (v. 48). And, of all people, disciples should know what perfect love looks like; he's the one we follow.

---

27. Which goes far beyond the penalty imposed by the law—death (France, *Matthew*, 199); "no human court is able to impose" the sentence to hell (Nolland, *Matthew*, 231).

28. To take the debtor's coat violated the law (Exod 22:26–27; Deut 24:12–13); see Davies and Allison, *Matthew*, 1:544–46.

29. Dallas Willard, *The Divine Conspiracy: Rediscovering Our Hidden Life in God* (New York: HarperCollins, 1998), 175–84.

30. Richard B. Hays, *The Moral Vision of the New Testament: Community, Cross, New Creation* (New York: HarperCollins, 1996), 338–39.

31. "Love is not being required because it will set the world right. Instead one's motivation to love arises out of a desire to be like God. . . . This means the energy for love will not be exhausted if the conversion of the wicked does not result" (Davies and Allison, *Matthew* 1:556).

LIVE the Story

Most of what Jesus said sounded reasonable, probably even to the Pharisees. Who could argue with the importance of being reconciled to your brother, staying married, or not swearing an oath if you can't keep it? But when Jesus started talking about cutting off your hand or turning the other cheek, he sounded completely *unreasonable*. Every time he explained the intent of God's law, Jesus gave a ridiculous scenario to reveal what he meant. For a Galilean to leave his gift at the temple and return home to be reconciled to his brother (at least two-days' travel), then head back to Jerusalem to finish what he started (another two days), must have sounded absurd.[32] No one was plucking out their eyes or cutting off their hands to keep from lusting (one wonders why Jesus didn't suggest castration). To commit adultery by remarrying a divorced woman, to refuse to defend yourself, to love your enemy—Jesus took everything to the extreme. Imagine how foolish it must have sounded to Jewish subjects of the Roman Empire to voluntarily go "the second mile." Roman law allowed soldiers to force subjects to carry their stuff one mile. To refuse would mean punishment, even death. But to carry the load a second mile, to help the enemy occupy the promised land, was treason. Only traitors supported Rome. But the way Jesus saw it, the kingdom of heaven coming to the whole earth—even to the Romans—required the kind of righteousness that takes love to the extreme.

Extreme is a popular adjective these days. Extreme sports, extreme vacations, extreme workout, extreme diet. It must be desirable to enjoy leisurely activities in extreme measures. But what about the weightier matters of life? How many of us would say we want an extreme marriage or an extreme religion? No thanks. In fact, most would say extreme religion is the source of most of the trouble in the world. An extreme marriage sounds scary, the result of an unhealthy relationship. Serious matters should not be taken to the extreme. So some would say, "We need to be reasonable when it comes to living out our faith." It's no wonder, then, that some see Jesus's teaching as ridiculous: leaving the gift at the altar, plucking out eyes and cutting off hands, remarriage as adultery, turning the other cheek. That's just going too far. Yet when it comes to making the world a better place, few of us would question whether we should take love to the extreme.

But here's the problem: *love* is one of the most profaned words in the English language. It's a word everyone uses for a variety of things that aren't

---

32. Davies and Allison, *Matthew*, 1:518.

love. Just ask the abused wife, the foster child, or the betrayed boyfriend. We know love should be divine; poets write about it all the time. There are *thousands* of songs about heavenly love. And yet none of us seems to have found it because we persist in defining *love* according to our preferences. But for those who follow Jesus, that isn't an option. We can't make love out to be what we want it to be, pining away for true love. We already know what love—perfect love—looks like. It's refusing to take revenge. It's staying married when divorce makes it easy for enemies to part. It's always doing what we promise. It's taking a loss rather than going to court. It's admitting we have enemies and then loving them, even helping them so much that righteous people could accuse us of treason (pick a political issue, love your enemy, and see what happens—"righteous" people will crucify you for it). It's loving others the way God loves us. If we do these things, then we are approaching the full measure of what Jesus was talking about when he said we must have a righteousness that goes beyond the most righteous people in the world. No doubt, when Jesus healed a Roman soldier's servant, it looked like treason. When he refused to defend himself when he was on trial for his life, it looked like resignation. But we know better. This is perfect love—and it's just like God to love everyone completely and perfectly in holiness. So when we see God shower good gifts on "evil people," we shouldn't wonder why. It's because he loves his enemies. Indeed, of all people, disciples of Jesus should know why: "For if, while we were God's enemies, we were reconciled to him through the death of his Son, how much more, having been reconciled, shall we be saved through his life!" (Rom 5:10). Indeed, we shall be saved by his life because he took love to the extreme by loving his enemies. And so should we.

* * *

"I don't want that nigger taking care of me." When an African-American woman shared her story with us—a room full of mostly white people gathered to consider the issue of race and reconciliation—I couldn't help but feel a profound sense of shame. Several musicians had joined Buddy Greene and me to lead a retreat at Laity Lodge to study Paul's letter to the Ephesians through the lens of race relations and the church. They not only led us in song but also taught us the history of gospel music—especially the rich heritage of the so-called "negro spirituals," songs of praise and lamentation offered as worship to God and in defiance of white masters. During one of the sessions when we encouraged everyone to share their stories of overcoming racial prejudice, one of the musicians reluctantly talked about a difficult situation she faced several years ago when she worked as a nurse in a hospital. One of her patients was an elderly lady who didn't want a black woman to take care of her. At first, the woman was rude to her, refusing to do what the nurse asked. Then the patient became belligerent, spewing hateful words at her nurse, treating her like a slave. Undeterred, she continued to take care of the elderly woman, returning kindness to all the indignities she suffered. At one point the old woman became so angry, she shouted her objections to one of the aids, "I don't want that nigger taking care of me!"

The racist slur cut through our room like a knife. All of us were horrified by the woman's hateful words. Here is a dignified, kind, soft-spoken woman, calmly describing what happened to her. She spoke about the whole affair very deliberately, very carefully, very honestly. I sat there feeling utterly ashamed. "We white people can be so hateful," I thought to myself. Anger welled up within me as I put myself in my sister's shoes, wondering how I would have reacted to such evil. Just as I was about to condemn the foolish old woman to hell, the nurse talked about what happened to her. At that moment, with the woman's vile words ringing in her ears, she said the love of Christ overwhelmed her. She saw the woman not as a wicked, spiteful soul but as the one for whom Christ died. And, much to her surprise, the love of Christ welled up in her heart so much that she began to devote herself even more to the old woman's care—often showing up after hours to check on her (the second mile!). Eventually, her kindness melted the heart of the racist, so much so that she began to ask for the nurse in the darkness when night terrors would overwhelm her. Then, summing up the lesson, our sister in Christ said something like, "And so, we see that the love of Christ conquers all; his love covers all our transgressions." Indeed, sister—even the sins of our enemies.

CHAPTER 7

Matthew 6:1–18

LISTEN to the Story

1"Be careful not to practice your righteousness in front of others to
be seen by them. If you do, you will have no reward from your Father in
heaven.
2"So when you give to the needy, do not announce it with trumpets, as
the hypocrites do in the synagogues and on the streets, to be honored by
others. Truly I tell you, they have received their reward in full. 3But when
you give to the needy, do not let your left hand know what your right
hand is doing, 4so that your giving may be in secret. Then your Father,
who sees what is done in secret, will reward you.
5"And when you pray, do not be like the hypocrites, for they love to
pray standing in the synagogues and on the street corners to be seen by
others. Truly I tell you, they have received their reward in full. 6But when
you pray, go into your room, close the door and pray to your Father, who
is unseen. Then your Father, who sees what is done in secret, will reward
you. 7And when you pray, do not keep on babbling like pagans, for they
think they will be heard because of their many words. 8Do not be like
them, for your Father knows what you need before you ask him.
9"This, then, is how you should pray:

'Our Father in heaven,
hallowed be your name,
10your kingdom come,
your will be done,
  on earth as it is in heaven.
11Give us today our daily bread.
12And forgive us our debts,
  as we also have forgiven our debtors.
13And lead us not into temptation,
  but deliver us from the evil one.'

[14]For if you forgive other people when they sin against you, your heavenly Father will also forgive you. [15]But if you do not forgive others their sins, your Father will not forgive your sins.

[16]"When you fast, do not look somber as the hypocrites do, for they disfigure their faces to show others they are fasting. Truly I tell you, they have received their reward in full. [17]But when you fast, put oil on your head and wash your face, [18]so that it will not be obvious to others that you are fasting, but only to your Father, who is unseen; and your Father, who sees what is done in secret, will reward you.

Listening to the Text in the Story: Deuteronomy 6:3–9; 11:13–21; 15:7–11; 2 Samuel 12:16–23; 1 Kings 18:26–29; Psalms 32:1–7; 35:12–14; 51:1–13; 69:16–19; 139:1–18, 23–24; Isaiah 26:16, 20; 29:13–15; 58:2–12; Jeremiah 17:9–10; Sirach 28:1–4.

The Pharisees were the fashion models of righteousness. The way they dressed. The way they prayed. The way they helped others. Few doubted their devotion to God. Therefore, the people looked to them as role models, exemplars of obedience to God. Moreover, since God's covenant blessings depended upon the covenant obedience of his people, the Pharisaical task of modeling holiness was essential to guiding Israel in the way they should go. To be a member of the Pharisees, to have the honorable distinction of belonging to this pious group, was more desirable than we can imagine. That's because the social approval of your group—honor—was the ultimate goal of everyone in the first-century Mediterranean world (everyone, that is, except the shameless miscreants who spat in the face of honor).[1] Honor defined success; therefore, pursuing honor was an unquestionable good. In other words, to get people to admire you for your honorable behavior was a social good recognized by nearly everyone. Consequently, the quest for honor inspired a never-ending contest for "top honors," with challengers always contending for the applause of the crowd. So when it came to the "top honor" of obeying the law, the Pharisees were crowned the winners *by the people*.[2] That's what we tend to

1. See Bruce J. Malina, *The New Testament World: Insights from Cultural Anthropology* (Louisville: Westminster John Knox, 1981), 25–50.

2. The Pharisees were not the only Jewish sect that emphasized obedience to the law. The Sadducees and Essenes had their own approach, the former known for strict adherence (without relying on an interpretive tradition) and the latter known for withdrawing from the world (to avoid contact with the unclean), which may explain why the people favored the Pharisees, who were considered more lenient than the Sadducees and more accessible than the Essenes. For a balanced discussion

forget. The Pharisees didn't foist themselves upon an unsuspecting public; they didn't "govern" the people, forcing reluctant commoners to follow their lead. The people honored the Pharisees as favored teachers of the law, models of piety.[3]

So when Jesus comes along and states in effect, "The Pharisees are not as righteous as you think," he was not only challenging the piety of the Pharisees but also the entire honor game, questioning the value of social approval—especially when it comes to religious activities. Since religious devotion was supposed to be directed toward God, then acts of piety performed for the sake of public approval were misguided and shortsighted. They were misguided because God can see what is secret; shortsighted because public acclaim cancels out divine rewards. Jesus keeps hitting this same point repeatedly as he talks about helping the poor, prayer to God, and fasting from food and drink. If you "practice your righteousness in front of others to be seen by them," then you lose your heavenly reward because God treasures pious acts performed in secret (Matt 6:1–2, 4, 6, 18). Of course, Jesus's criticism of hypocrites is based on a presumption that he knows their motives. But how could that be when God is the only one who knows the secrets of the heart? (See Ps 139:1–18, 23–24.) Once again, then, we hear the authoritative voice of God in the teaching of Jesus when he explained what it meant to have a righteousness that exceeds that of the scribes and Pharisees.

EXPLAIN the Story

It's no coincidence that on the heels of talking about being perfect "as your heavenly Father is perfect" (Matt 5:48), Jesus quickly picks up the problem of false piety. Pursuit of piety nearly always seems to lead to self-righteousness. (Why is that so?) Jesus's warning about righteousness as theatre (6:1) sounds like a contradiction of his earlier word of encouragement: "Let your light shine before others, that they may see your good deeds and glorify your Father in heaven" (5:16). But the difference between the two has to do with motive and result: the good works of Jesus's disciples are for the glory of God. The people will praise *God* for the light. The hypocrites, on the other hand, do the right things for the wrong reasons: pious deeds like helping the poor are done for their own glory (6:2). Therefore, when the people praise *them*, they get the desired result. Consequently, according to Jesus they are paid "in full" for their

---

of the popularity of the Pharisees, see E. P. Sanders, *Judaism: Practice and Belief, 63 BCE–66 CE* (Philadelphia: Trinity Press International, 1992), 399–404.

3. "While the Sadducees are able to persuade none but the rich . . . the Pharisees have the multitude on their side" (Josephus, *Ant.* 13.10.6; see also *Life* 38).

pious deeds (v. 2). "Giving to the needy in order to receive publicity is not giving at all—it is paying for human approval, and it forfeits divine approval."[4]

Jesus puts the reward of social approval at odds with the rewards God will give one day—which doesn't sound like much of a threat to us because many Christians downplay the significance of seeking divine rewards for right behavior. In fact, we operate with the assumption that doing what is right in order to be rewarded by God is an inferior motive. To our way of thinking, what Jesus should have said was, "Don't be like the hypocrites who seek recognition for their good deeds. Instead, you should give to the poor with no thought of yourself. Give for their advantage, not yours. This is about them, not you. Then your heavenly Father will be pleased because you did the right thing for the right reason."[5] But it's quite apparent that Jesus didn't base his teaching about helping the poor, praying, or fasting on the necessity of "pure motives."[6] For Jesus, it was more about not jeopardizing our heavenly rewards, even though he never spells out what kind of rewards God will give or when he will give them.

Actors Crave Applause

To be a hypocrite is to seek public approval for piety. (Later, Jesus will define hypocrisy as duplicity; see Matt 23:3). Notice how Jesus always places the hypocrites in public places when they give alms, pray, and fast. He mentions not only synagogues but also streets as the desired location for these pious performances (6:2, 5). Obviously, one cannot receive accolades without a crowd. Jesus was being clever when he used the term *hypocrite* to describe playing to the audience. The word comes from the world of theatre. To be a hypocrite is to be an actor, one who "wears a mask" (think of the theatrical symbols often used today: two masks, one smiling and the other frowning, representing comedy and tragedy). Eventually, *hypocrite* was used in a pejorative sense (in Greek and especially Jewish literature) to describe a person who feigns sincerity.[7] The theatrics of the hypocrites are evident because they perform their religious acts "in front of others *to be seen*" (*theathēnai*; Matt 6:1), from which we get the word *theatre*. All the elements for a great performance were present: stage, actor, audience. Public piety had become great theatre for both the performers and those who watched the spectacle. One wonders how the adoring crowd showed their approval; Jesus said only that the hypocrites were looking to be "honored by others" (v. 2), which could mean any

4. Turner, *Matthew*, 181.
5. See McKnight for discussion about altruism and rewards (*Sermon on the Mount*, 154–58).
6. Garland, *Reading Matthew*, 78.
7. See Richard B. Vinson, "Hypocrite," *DJG* 394–95.

number of things—from boasting to nonverbal acts of approval. Whatever the "applause," Jesus said these actors received their reward "in full" (6:2, 5, 16).

Perhaps the reason Jesus is so harsh in his caricature of the Pharisees is that other "bit actors" have been pushed to the margins in this staging of pious theatre: the invisible poor and the unseen God. In fact, the needy barely show up at all, hidden by the phrase "alms giving" (*eleēmosunē*; lit., "showing mercy"; 6:2, 3). Like the temple, synagogues collected and distributed alms for the poor.[8] But that didn't stop beggars from showing up in the streets hoping for more. Yet their neediness isn't the point; the stage is set for the main actors and the crowd of onlookers. And to ensure that a good crowd shows up, the hypocrites draw attention to themselves by announcing their generosity with a trumpet blast (v. 2). Whether literal (the shofar blown in Jerusalem calling for alms) or figurative (some ostentatious display by the hypocrites),[9] this pious show isn't for the poor. The hypocrites could care less whether the needy acknowledged their gift. Why? Because the poor have no honor to give—they were considered shameful because of their circumstances (the poor were often considered cursed). Who needs a trumpet when the poor are sitting right there, seeing your every move? No, this show was for the larger, adoring public.

Same situation when the hypocrites pray or fast except the actor pushed to the side this time is God—the one who plays a "minor part" in theatrical righteousness. Of course, he's necessary (just like the poor are for alms). One prays to and fasts for an invisible God. But the way Jesus sees it, hypocritical prayers and fasts are not offered for a divine audience. Rather, the hypocrites pray "to be seen by others" (not "*heard* by others"?; v. 5). They "disfigure their faces to show others they are fasting" (v. 16). In other words, this is all about visibility—what is seen and who is there to see it. To pray on street corners wasn't unusual since many Jews recognized the tradition of praying three times a day: morning, midday, evening.[10] When the time comes, you don't have to rush to a synagogue or the temple—you pray wherever you are. And there was probably nothing unusual about the way the hypocrites prayed, whether posture or content. Standing to pray was common, and the typical Jewish prayers were the *Kaddish* (similar in content to the Lord's Prayer) or the *Tefillah* (the "Eighteen Benedictions"), used regularly in synagogue services.[11] What Jesus found objectionable is that the hypocrites "*love* to pray" in public (v. 5, emphasis added). They must have found it very rewarding, approved by honorable people. But what about God?

8. Craig L. Bloomberg, *Neither Poverty nor Riches: A Biblical Theology of Possessions*, NSBT 7 (Downers Grove, IL: InterVarsity Press, 1999), 102.

9. Davies and Allison, *Matthew*, 1:579–80.

10. Ibid., 1:584.

11. For examples of Jewish prayers, see France, *Matthew*, 243–44; Davies and Allison, *Matthew*, 1:595; McKnight, *Sermon on the Mount*, 173.

Fasting was a public demonstration of grief over sin, impending doom, or death.[12] Acts of lamentation included not only abstaining from food and drink but also ignoring rituals of purification and daily hygiene. Sometimes the mourner would tear his clothes or put on tattered garments, and sit in ashes. Disheveled hair and gloomy appearance finished the look of a person overcome with grief. Seeing someone in sackcloth and ashes, it was difficult to know whether he was grieving over sin or troubles (2 Sam 12:15–23; Job 1:20–22; 2:8–13). But since the Pharisees were known to fast twice a week (Luke 18:12), the people must have interpreted their regimen as pious acts of grief over Israel's sin. And to make sure the people knew it, the hypocrites "disfigure their faces" (Matt 6:16). To "disfigure" your face meant to "hide" your normal appearance (*aphanizō*)—"you don't look like yourself." And yet, ironically, these hypocritical fasters "hid" their appearance *in order to be seen* (*phainō*)—a contradiction in purpose revealing false motives.[13] Sometimes self-denial wears the ugly mask of self-promotion. Since prayer needs no human audience, and fasting is supposed to reveal a grieving heart, the hypocrites missed the point of piety: to find favor with an invisible God, who sees what isn't visible to us.

The solution to the problem of false piety is fairly simple: seek and hide. To seek the reward of God, the pious man or woman must hide their religious acts from public view. Hide in your closet when you pray (Matt 6:6); most modest homes had an inner room where they hid their valuables. Hide your face when you fast (vv. 17–18); most people routinely washed their faces and anointed their heads with oil. Hide your benevolence when you help the poor (vv. 3–4); apparently not letting "your left hand know what your right hand is doing" was another way of saying "give alms discreetly."[14] In other words, Jesus calls for privacy when it comes to seeking God's favor. Why? Because God is the only one who sees what is done in secret (which is also true when it comes to sin). The invisible God sees what isn't visible to humanity. Therefore, if we desire to please only him, our pious deeds must be done "for his eyes only." That way, we share a secret with God—a secret that will be revealed one day when God rewards his faithful children who practice true righteousness.

A Good Jewish Prayer

For some reason Jesus (or Matthew?) throws in the standard Jewish critique of pagan prayers in the middle of his critical remarks about false piety. Up to

---

12. Malina and Rohrbaugh, *Synoptic Gospels*, 64.

13. Davies and Allison, *Matthew*, 1:618.

14. The origin of the saying, which sounds like an aphorism, is unknown, perhaps even invented by Jesus (see Betz, *Sermon on the Mount*, 358–59).

this point, his target has been Jewish hypocrites. But here Jesus makes fun of the babbling prayers of pagans to set up the proper content for prayers offered in secret (Matt 6:7–15). He's criticizing the theology behind their prayers as much as the mindless repetition that distinguished pagan prayers. Jewish people prayed to a God of lovingkindness. They prayed knowing God already knew what they needed and—more than that—wanted to hear from his children (v. 8). Pagans didn't share the same view of god. To them, the gods were aloof, far removed from the daily grind of life. Before you could get the gods to hear your request, you had to get their attention—especially since so many other people were begging the gods for help too. So pagan prayers sounded like a child nagging their parents, repeating the same phrases over and over again (implied by the verb *battalogeō*, translated "babbling" in v. 7).[15] Some pagans employed the strategy of flattery, heaping praise upon praise, extolling the attributes of their god.[16] The longer the list, the better your chances of "buttering up" the god to get what you want. Either way, pagan prayers were apparently *very long*: "They think they will be heard because of their many words" (v. 7). Jesus's disciples shouldn't sound like pagans when they pray. Rather, their prayers should look like this, the so-called "Lord's Prayer" (vv. 9–13).[17]

Here's the surprise: there's nothing uniquely "Christian" about the Lord's Prayer. In fact, it's a very Jewish prayer, similar to the typical prayers offered in the temple and synagogues of the day. For a while, some scholars argued that Jesus's reference to God as "Father" was unique to Israel's experience; therefore, calling God "Abba" (an Aramaic term of endearment) was an early "Christian" form of address (cf. Gal 4:6).[18] Calling the Lord "Abba" in prayer may have been distinctive to Jesus and his disciples, but it wasn't unique—Jews as well as pagans referred to God as Father.[19] To reverence the name of the Lord as holy, to pray for his will to be done on earth, for God to reign over all people, for food and forgiveness of sins, and to be preserved through trials—all of these were common topics of Jewish prayer (the Psalms are filled with similar requests).[20] Some have suggested that the Christian/messianic spin intended

15. BDAG 172. Nolland notes that "more reflective voices [among the Greeks and Romans] were critical of the desire to badger the gods into granting their favors" (*Matthew*, 284).

16. McKnight, *Sermon on the Mount*, 171–72.

17. The last phrase of v. 13, "for yours is the kingdom and the power and the glory forever. Amen," was probably added by Christian scribes much later. See Bruce M. Metzger, *A Textual Commentary on the Greek New Testament*, 2nd ed. (Stuttgart: German Bible Society, 1994), 13–14.

18. Joachim Jeremias, *The Prayers of Jesus* (Philadelphia: Fortress, 1967), 54–65.

19. Keener, *Matthew*, 217–18.

20. For Jewish parallels, see Luz, *Matthew*, 1:317; Davies and Allison, *Matthew*, 595–96; Oscar Cullmann, *Prayer in the New Testament*, Overtures to Biblical Theology (Minneapolis: Augsburg Fortress, 1994), 43–67.

by Jesus can be seen when we consider the eschatological implications of "kingdom come," "daily bread," and "lead us not into temptation/tests."[21] To be sure, the entire Sermon on the Mount reveals that Jesus's ideas about the kingdom of God differed from Jewish expectations. However, some push the requests for daily bread and deliverance from temptation and the evil one into the *eschaton*. In other words, these petitions have to do with the challenges of living during the last days, known as the period of the "messianic woes" (cf. Matt 24:6–13). According to this approach, the Lord's Prayer is really a "Christian" prayer for the end of the world—for the *parousia* ("your kingdom come"), for the eschatological banquet ("tomorrow's bread"—one possible meaning of the peculiar word *epiousios*),[22] for the ultimate victory over the evil one (deliverance from the great tribulation). The problem is that parts of the Lord's Prayer don't sound eschatological, like praying for forgiveness or asking for "daily" bread (a better translation in light of the following verses where Jesus encourages his listeners not to worry about daily provisions; 6:25–26). Like the typical Jewish prayer, then, the Lord's Prayer was a daily prayer for today, "for tomorrow will worry about itself. Each day has enough trouble of its own" (v. 34). Besides, throughout the Sermon, Jesus has been teaching his disciples how to live *presently* for what they pray: the kingdom of heaven coming to earth.

There is one line in the Lord's Prayer, however, that doesn't sound "Christian" at all—especially in light of Jesus's explanation. "Forgive us our debts, as we have forgiven our debtors" means "if you forgive other people when they sin against you, your heavenly Father will also forgive you. But if you do not forgive others their sins, your Father will not forgive your sins" (vv. 12, 14–15). Is Jesus really saying that God's forgiveness of my sins is contingent upon my forgiveness of others, as if God were dependent upon me for my salvation from sin? Once again, we need to pay attention to the plural form of the pronouns, which are evident in the Prayer ("our debts") but hard to see in Jesus's warning ("your sins")—in fact, the entire Prayer is a corporate prayer, employing plural pronouns. We tend to individualize sin, as if my sin is my problem and your sin is your problem. Therefore, Jesus should have taught us to pray, "Forgive my debts as I forgive my debtors"—which would make more sense since this is the prayer I'm supposed to pray in my closet, all by myself. But Jesus would have us pray a corporate prayer even in

---

21. See the discussion in Davies and Allison, *Matthew*, 1:593–94; McKnight, *Sermon on the Mount*, 178–82, 186–87. To sort out the implications of whether *peirasmos* means "test" or "temptation," see France, *Matthew*, 251–52.

22. Davies and Allison think the reference is to manna, "bread for tomorrow," that is, for the *eschaton* (*Matthew*, 1:609).

our closet. We pray to "*our* Father" (he belongs to everyone). We pray for "*our* daily bread" (it takes a *village* to provide bread: farmers, millers, bakers).[23] We pray, "lead *us* not into temptation" (when one suffers, we all suffer). Indeed, the Lord's Prayer is as much a prayer for others as it is for me.

Consider the implications, then, of the corporate reality of sin—a common conviction in Jesus's day. What the Jewish people recognized as a given we tend to ignore: sin is a debt to God and to others.[24] To pretend like my sin affects no one else but me is the height of arrogance and foolishness. Therefore, since my sin affects other people (and their sins affect me), it would be equally arrogant and foolish to pretend as if God is the only one who needs to forgive me (it would be like saying I can hate my brother and still have a right relationship with God; Jesus thinks that's impossible: Matt 5:22–26). Debts, sins, forgiveness—these are social realities that cannot be reduced to individual experience. Therefore, when I pray to God, "Forgive us *our* debts," I'm not only asking him to forgive my *debts* but also to forgive *my* debtor. And if God has heard my prayer and forgiven both him and me, who am I to withhold forgiveness? (Later, Jesus told a parable making the same point in 18:21–35.) To go to God and ask him to "forgive our debts"—all of them, not just mine but the entire community—assumes I've already forgiven my debtors since I'm asking God to forgive them. So, the way Jesus set up the Lord's Prayer, we cannot pray the first part, "Forgive us our debts" without intending the last part, "as *we also have forgiven* our debtors."[25] To hold a grudge against my debtor implies I didn't mean what I prayed—the duplicity of a hypocrite.[26] Jesus made it plain that God doesn't listen to hypocritical prayers. He won't play the role of a "bit actor," especially when it comes to prayer and fasting.

LIVE the Story

False piety is a huge problem today. The reason I know that's the case is because fame is an unquestioned social good in our culture—even in the "Christian" world. Even though Jesus taught that social approval subverts genuine piety, we act like fame and religious devotion are fraternal twins of Christian success. A powerful public image is indispensible to creating a platform of influence built on adoration. And so the people get what they want.

23. Nolland (citing E. Yamauchi) hears here the "daily rhythm of making and consuming bread" (*Matthew*, 290).

24. Keener, *Matthew*, 222–23.

25. So also Augustine (Simonetti, *Matthew 1–13*, 136–37).

26. See Sirach 28:1–5.

Whether we are talking about TV preachers who strut like peacocks before large audiences, Christian celebrities who are celebrated as champions of the gospel, or musicians pursuing rock-star status in the industry, we have created a circus of righteousness for consumers looking for a good show. But Jesus would bring the whole house down with this one, simple observation: fame and piety don't mix. According to him, fame is a huge problem for pious people. Since righteous deeds cannot be seen in the spotlight, genuine piety makes for a terrible photo op. It gets worse: public approval is the dangerous slippery slope to hypocrisy for all of us—famous or not. The more people applaud your efforts, the more likely you will act like a hypocrite and seek their applause. Social media makes it easier for everyone to be famous. Facebook, Twitter, Instagram, YouTube—whatever your drug of choice—instant visibility makes everyone susceptible to the addiction of public approval. So, what do we do? How do we stop the parade of self-recognition that keeps marching to the beat of "fame is good, fame is good, fame is good"? Jesus states the matter plainly: the only way to make sure you're not a hypocrite is to keep your good deeds a secret—a terrible blow to maintaining the image we've carefully created. Whether we like it or not, instant recognition is the casualty of genuine righteousness.

I'm rather pessimistic about the prospects of Christians giving up the pursuit of fame. Seeking immediate social approval is just too easy. "Liking" the right films, the right causes, the right political party, even the right restaurants (really? Has it come to this? What if I don't like chicken sandwiches?), creates the same scenario when Jesus called out the false piety of the Pharisees. And, as he did before, I think Jesus would criticize not only the hypocrites but also the entire honor game that fosters the same problem. Consider the stage: a social issue with religious implications arises; everyone's waiting for the big gun to tweet his or her response. The Christian celebrity weighs in, the Twitterverse lights up with "attaboy" or "attagirl," and the self-righteous bathe in the light of social approval. Like a few others, I've grown weary of the entire circus. One wonders if it will ever reach a critical mass of devastating implosion. Will we ever get sick of seeing ourselves striking a righteous pose? I doubt it. Narcissus had nothing on us. Yet it's the other reason Jesus gives for curbing our appetite for public approval that should make us even more concerned about false piety run amok. He believed we are in danger of losing our heavenly rewards when we act like hypocrites.

The end of the world will be filled with many surprises—at least that's what Jesus emphasized. Whenever he talked about the last day, Jesus envisions the same situation where people will be surprised as to who makes it and who doesn't, who is rewarded by God and who is punished (Matt 7:21–23;

25:31–46). He gives different reasons as to why many will be shocked on judgment day, but they all have one thing in common: they didn't see it coming. They lived with a presumption of arrogant righteousness. Interestingly, Jesus never describes the obvious judgment-day scenario: the pagan protesting eternal damnation. It's always the insider, the "righteous" one, the person making all kinds of religious claims whom Jesus pictures standing slack-jawed in complete and utter shock on the last day. So, it *is* true: "Pride goes before destruction" (Prov 16:18). That should be enough to inspire all of us to seek the humility that is necessary to inheriting the kingdom of God. Throughout the Sermon on the Mount, Jesus has taught specifically and forcefully what humility looks like: the Beatitudes, loving your neighbor, loving your enemy. Yet just when you think he couldn't be more plain in explaining genuine righteousness, the perfect definition of true humility, he says in effect: "You want to know what it takes? Want to be sure you don't act like a hypocrite? Want to ensure your heavenly reward? When you help the poor, don't tell anyone. When you pray, don't let anyone hear you. When you fast (what? We're supposed to fast?), don't show anyone. If people don't know, they can't shower you with praise. Then you won't be tempted to believe the accolades. Then you won't care what people think. Then you will know that what you did was for God's eyes alone. Then you'll only care what God thinks, you'll only seek heavenly rewards, and you'll long for the day when your heavenly Father says to you, 'Well done, good and faithful servant. Here's your reward.'"

To keep our reward secure in heaven and to keep from acting like hypocrites, here are a few challenges I would like to issue to every Christ follower:

1. The next time something good happens to you—especially if it is seen as the evidence of your success—don't post it on social media. Rather than use "blessings" as a way to boast about yourself, promote the success of others.
2. The next time you happen to be in the company of a celebrity, don't take a selfie. Instead of deriving your sense of self-worth from others, find your identity in Christ.
3. The next time a political fight breaks out among Christians, don't advertise which side you're on. Rather than try to prove to everyone how righteous you are, quietly help the victims of political injustice.
4. The next time you attend a Christian conference (or especially if you're invited to speak at that conference), don't tell anyone about it.
5. The next time you help someone financially, do it anonymously.
6. The next time you're asked to pray, keep it short.
7. The next time someone owes you money, forgive the debt.

Of course, I don't expect us to follow these suggestions all the time. But I cannot help but wonder: if we took Jesus's teaching to heart and actually practiced what he preached, we might find a heavenly reward worth much more on the last day than the social approval of our peers this day. Besides, like Jesus said, our God who sees what is done in secret today will bring *everything* to light on the last day—which is more of a promise than a threat for those who follow Jesus.

What a day that will be, when all good deeds are revealed, God is glorified, and everyone is surprised.

CHAPTER 8

Matthew 6:19–7:12

LISTEN to the Story

19"Do not store up for yourselves treasures on earth, where moths and
vermin destroy, and where thieves break in and steal. 20But store up for
yourselves treasures in heaven, where moths and vermin do not destroy,
and where thieves do not break in and steal. 21For where your treasure is,
there your heart will be also.

22"The eye is the lamp of the body. If your eyes are healthy, your whole
body will be full of light. 23But if your eyes are unhealthy, your whole body
will be full of darkness. If then the light within you is darkness, how great
is that darkness!

24"No one can serve two masters. Either you will hate the one and love
the other, or you will be devoted to the one and despise the other. You
cannot serve both God and money.

25"Therefore I tell you, do not worry about your life, what you will
eat or drink; or about your body, what you will wear. Is not life more than
food, and the body more than clothes? 26Look at the birds of the air; they
do not sow or reap or store away in barns, and yet your heavenly Father
feeds them. Are you not much more valuable than they? 27Can any one of
you by worrying add a single hour to your life?

28"And why do you worry about clothes? See how the flowers of the
field grow. They do not labor or spin. 29Yet I tell you that not even Solo-
mon in all his splendor was dressed like one of these. 30If that is how God
clothes the grass of the field, which is here today and tomorrow is thrown
into the fire, will he not much more clothe you—you of little faith? 31So
do not worry, saying, 'What shall we eat?' or 'What shall we drink?' or
'What shall we wear?' 32For the pagans run after all these things, and your
heavenly Father knows that you need them. 33But seek first his kingdom
and his righteousness, and all these things will be given to you as well.
34Therefore do not worry about tomorrow, for tomorrow will worry about
itself. Each day has enough trouble of its own.

7:1"Do not judge, or you too will be judged. 2For in the same way you
judge others, you will be judged, and with the measure you use, it will be
measured to you.
3"Why do you look at the speck of sawdust in your brother's eye and
pay no attention to the plank in your own eye? 4How can you say to your
brother, 'Let me take the speck out of your eye,' when all the time there is
a plank in your own eye? 5You hypocrite, first take the plank out of your
own eye, and then you will see clearly to remove the speck from your
brother's eye.
6"Do not give dogs what is sacred; do not throw your pearls to pigs.
If you do, they may trample them under their feet, and turn and tear you
to pieces.
7"Ask and it will be given to you; seek and you will find; knock and
the door will be opened to you. 8For everyone who asks receives; the one
who seeks finds; and to the one who knocks, the door will be opened.
9"Which of you, if your son asks for bread, will give him a stone?
10Or if he asks for a fish, will give him a snake? 11If you, then, though you
are evil, know how to give good gifts to your children, how much more
will your Father in heaven give good gifts to those who ask him! 12So in
everything, do to others what you would have them do to you, for this
sums up the Law and the Prophets.

Listening to the Text in the Story: Genesis 1:29; Exodus 15:27–16:36; 18:14–26; Leviticus 11:7; 17:1–26:46; 2 Samuel 12:1–5; 1 Kings 10:4–29; 18:21; Psalms 37; 39:5; 84:11–12; 104:27–28; Proverbs 3:5–8; 12:25; 23:4–5; Jeremiah 29:12–14; Sirach 29:11.

Imagine the disciple of Jesus who takes her master's advice. She's heard Jesus say she's supposed to enter her closet to pray. So, that very night during evening prayers, she walks into the inner room of her house and closes the door behind her. Perhaps she's taken a little lamp into the dark, small, cramped space. She can barely see the treasures of her family, locked away from public view and potential thieves. Her husband's tools, her dowry, a small bag of coins, perhaps even some jewelry and pearls wrapped up in a cloth are all hidden in the shadows, keeping her company as she prays "your kingdom come" and "give us today our daily bread" and "as we forgive our debtors." Then the last line of her new prayer echoes in the darkness, "but deliver us from the evil one"—a haunting refrain that makes her wonder how all these things fit together in the kingdom that Jesus so passionately talked about that day on the mountain. Consider the cognitive dissonance of praying to God about debtors and daily provisions while staring at your treasures. For some of us, it would be like going to the bank, entering the vault that housed our valuables, pulling out the secret contents of our safety deposit box, then praying to God about the needs of the world. A corporate prayer offered in the solitary confinement of a treasure room brings to light what is valuable and what is hidden in the dark. "And your Father, who sees what is done in secret, will reward you."

It is telling that Jesus so quickly moved from talking about the necessity of forgiving debtors to the importance of storing up treasures in heaven (Matt 6:14–15, 19–21). Forgiveness is a costly thing. We play down the price of forgiveness, acting like only emotions are involved when it comes to "forgive and forget." Yet as important as our emotional health can be, Jesus taught that sin is more damaging than hurt feelings and emotional scars. He knew that forgiving our debtors would require sacrifice built upon an absolute trust in a generous God. Indeed, to tell a debtor, "You don't owe me anything" (especially when that's not the case—his foolishness cost you a hundred dollars!), is based on the presumption that divine rewards are better than human repayment. Why? Because the treasures of this earth don't last. But heavenly treasures? God's rewards last forever because the kingdom of heaven is eternal. So Jesus will say things like, "Do not store up for yourselves treasures on earth" and "you cannot serve God and money" and "do not worry about your life, what you will eat or drink; or about your body, what you will wear" and "seek first his kingdom" and "with the measure you use, it will be measured to you" and "do not throw your pearls to pigs" and "ask and it will be given to you" and "how much more will your Father in heaven give good gifts" (Matt 6:19, 24, 25, 33; 7:2, 6, 7, 11). In fact, it could be said that this entire passage (6:19–7:12) sums up what it looks like "on the ground" when we offer the heavenly prayer: "Forgive us our debts, as we also have forgiven our debtors" (6:12).

EXPLAIN the Story

Most scholars see this part of the Sermon on the Mount as a random collection of sayings of Jesus. It's difficult to determine how these verses fit together; the transitions from one passage to the next are rough. In fact, this is where Jesus sounds like he's emptying both barrels of his "shotgun sermon." Don't treasure earthly things. Boom. Watch what you watch. Boom. Don't worship money. Boom. Don't worry. Boom. Don't judge, don't help pigs, ask God for anything, and remember the "Golden Rule." Boom, boom, boom, boom. With his rapid-fire warnings (and a respite of encouraging words thrown in every now and then—reloading!), Jesus seems to be shooting at anything that moves against the purposes of God. But Davies and Allison see symmetry in the shot pattern of Jesus's target:[1]

Instruction

Exhortation (6:19–21)	Exhortation (7:1–2)
Parable on the eye (6:22–23)	Parable on the eye (7:3–5)
Second parable (6:24)	Second parable (7:6)

Encouragement

The heavenly Father's care (6:25–34) (argument from minor to major)	The heavenly Father's care (7:7–11) (argument from minor to major)

The Golden Rule (7:12)

To be sure, Jesus moves from one topic to the next with lightning speed, expecting his listeners to keep up with him. Yet one can *see* a method to his madness—indeed, to see clearly is key—linking these two sections of the Sermon with two parables about how we see things, one for each eye. First, loving your neighbor as yourself cannot be reduced to "spiritual things" as disciples seek heavenly rewards. Rather, to seek *first the kingdom of God and his righteousness*—singular vision that is "healthy"—affects even the most mundane realities of life: food and clothing, money and pearls. The kingdom of heaven coming to earth invades every corner of daily living, even the closet (and what's inside!). Second, how we see others reveals how we see ourselves. There's a reciprocity to judgment that some people can't see, which is why they need the corrective vision of the Golden Rule: "Do to others what you would have them to do you" (7:12). It not only sums up the Law and the Prophets but is the essence of the Sermon. Therefore, to see clearly both ourselves and others (instruction, 6:19–24; 7:1–6) is crucial to the kingdom, for it ultimately reveals how we see God (encouragement, 6:25–34; 7:7–11).

But we have a problem: when it comes to making sense of each parable for each eye, we are blind. We can't quite figure out what Jesus meant in the first parable, that we should avoid "the evil eye" because the eye is "the lamp of the body." Jesus sounds very serious when he warned about the effects of bad eyesight: "If your eye [*ophthalmos*] is evil [*ponēros*], your whole body will be filled with darkness. If then the light within you is darkness, how

1. Davies and Allison, *Matthew*, 1:626.

great is that darkness (Matt 6:23)."[2] But his concern is lost on us because we know eyes don't bring light into the "whole body," and we don't believe in the power of "the evil eye." Besides, how can "light" within us be "darkness"? Moreover, regarding the other parable, the ludicrous picture of a man walking around with a plank in his eye is so absurd that the logic breaks down (7:3–5). Of course, exaggeration for effect is often built upon a *non sequitur*. Yet in this case the grotesque imagery is so ridiculous, it obscures the point: not only is it hard for us to *see* someone with a beam protruding from his eye, to suggest that he can "see clearly" once the beam is removed is unimaginable. The man would lose his eye! There's no way he could see the speck in his brother's eye, much less anything else. Is that the point Jesus is making, the absurdity of a "plankless" hypocrite still trying to "judge" another? Indeed, it's hard to see what Jesus meant. One moment he's saying, "Don't judge," and the next he's talking about removing "the speck from your brother's eye," even calling certain people pigs and dogs—certainly very judgmental comments.

So we need to spend some time hearing the parables on Jesus's terms, because the "eyes" are key to seeing the rest of what he's saying. In fact, if Davies and Allison are right, these two parables of the eye are a lens through which we see how all of these "random" sayings about treasures, masters, anxiety, judgment, pigs, dogs, and good gifts a father gives to his son are linked together—twin passages that work like a pair of spectacles improving our vision of the kingdom of God.[3]

How to Overcome the Evil Eye (6:19–34)

I want to start with the end of this passage (encouragement, 6:25–34) and work backward to see why Jesus warned his disciples about the evil eye. As far as Jesus was concerned, if you are convinced that God is on your side—that there is no reason to be anxious about whether you have enough to make it in this life—then why would you look upon the world with the evil eye? Rather, we should look at creation with a "single" eye (*haplous*, NIV: "healthy"; 6:22) and learn the lesson that God takes care of his own. Jesus said, "*Look* at the birds of the air," and "*See* how the flowers of the field grow," inviting his disciples to have "kingdom" eyes (vv. 26, 28).[4] God reigns over his creation.

---

2. My translation. Notice how the NIV turns the analogy into a medical warning, changing "eye" to a plural noun and translating *ponēros* as "unhealthy" and *haplous* as "healthy" (6:22).

3. Luz, *Matthew*, 1:328, reads these two pericopae together (6:19–34 and 7:1–11) as "Guidance for the Community," pointing out catchwords that link them: each section introduced by a prohibition with *mē* ("not"; 6:19, 25; 7:1, 6), with *aphanizō* ("make invisible") and *ophthalmos* ("eye") forming a bridge between the two passages (6:22–23 and 7:3–5).

4. The verbs are *emblepō* and *katamanthanō*, implying not only visual sight but a reflective ability to learn by observation.

If he takes care of birds that don't store up treasures on earth, then certainly the Lord will take care of Jesus's disciples—especially since they "seek first his kingdom," a singular focus of storing up treasures in heaven (vv. 20, 33). If Jesus's disciples will live for the kingdom, then God will take care of everything else—not only food and drink but also clothes and even the length of their days on earth (vv. 25–31). In other words, Jesus works from the presumption that God will take care of our business if we take care of his: to love our neighbor as ourselves.

This is where the evil eye comes in. First-century people believed that eyes were not only—as we say—a "window into the soul" (the belief that we are able to see the spirit of a person in their eyes) but also a lamp for the body, releasing the light from within.[5] If the light within is darkness, then the person has an evil eye, intending harm to others. It's almost like the hypnotist who says, "Look deeply into my eyes," believing he can release his (malevolent?) will on his subject. Of course, if the interior light of the body is bright, then the good-intentioned soul has "bright eyes," bringing favor to others. In Jesus's day, then, to give someone "the evil eye" was an attempt to bring ruin upon an enemy, releasing the power of ill intent. Furthermore, to accuse someone of having "the evil eye" was the same as saying they were greedy, jealous (not wanting others to have), and envious of others (wanting what they have, Matt 20:15). Jesus, on the other hand, wanted his disciples to be generous, to love enemies, and to light up the world because God is generous, he loves his enemies, and he *is* the light of the world. So rather than look upon neighbors as competitors for the limited resources of the world,[6] giving them the evil eye of envy and jealousy, Jesus encouraged his disciples to seek God's righteous kingdom first (the singular eye of loving others), knowing that God is on their side. Besides, to pursue selfishly the necessities of life on earth as the top priority—"If I don't take care of me, who will?" (little faith!)—makes the God of Israel appear as one of the pagan gods, whose devotees know they have to "run after these things, and [yet] your heavenly Father knows you need them" (6:32).

The harried life of "running after these things" is slavery (v. 24). Who wants to devote their numbered days on this earth to serve a master who can't take care of you? "Mammon," a code word for material possessions, is a fickle god. One day you have enough. The next day you're worried whether you will be able to provide for you and your family. Even if you stockpile enough goods in your closet to last a while, other threats "eat away" at your future—not to mention thieves (evil eye!) who act upon their envious greed

5. See the discussions in Davies and Allison, *Matthew*, 1:635–39; McKnight, *Sermon on the Mount*, 207–8.

6. For first-century perceptions of scarce resources, see Malina, *New Testament World*, 71–93.

(vv. 19–20). It's as if there is no safe place on earth for providence. But Jesus would have his disciples locate providence in heaven, not on earth, to serve God and not mammon, to look upon this world with a "kingdom" eye rather than the evil eye.[7] God is the one who's running this place. And since the kingdom of heaven is coming to earth through his son, Jesus Christ, then storing heavenly, secret, invisible treasures—vouchsafed for the future (v. 20)—is the best way to live visibly on earth. God sees it all—the secrets of your heart, the treasures of your life, the light within your body. Indeed, "where your treasure is, there your heart will be also"; therefore, you can be confident that "your Father, who sees what is done in secret, will reward you" (vv. 18, 21). So why borrow tomorrow's grief when the relentless arrival of each day brings its own trouble on earth (v. 34)? Praying "give us today our daily bread" is all we need, because all we can do is seek the kingdom of God *today*: loving our neighbor as ourselves.

Okay. Let's think this through. If God supplies everything we need to live on earth, if our number one priority is to live for his kingdom—to love others, even our enemies—then sharing our treasures on earth is the surest way to store up treasures in heaven.[8] If we refuse to bend our knee to mammon, where fears of scarcity create anxiety about our future, and look upon God's creation with kingdom eyes—see how God takes care of birds and grass?—then we will see the eternal resources of heaven's kingdom on earth. If God takes care of tomorrow, and all we have is today, then what we do after we pray in our closet, "Your kingdom come, your will be done, on earth as it is in heaven," will reveal what we treasure. We may hide our valuables under lock and key—there are thieves—but the question is: Are we loving our neighbors as ourselves? Yet how we love our neighbors with our treasures is difficult; using our pearls to help others is a daunting task. What if they don't deserve it because they've created their own economic mess? What if we've already forgiven their debts—what they owed us—and they still need more? What if they waste the gift on their own foolish, selfish desires? It would be like throwing our pearls to pigs. Surely God doesn't want us to take what is holy—God's good gifts to his children—and give it to people who have gone "to the dogs," does he?

How to Treat Plank Eye (7:1–12)

The end game of Jesus's advice about judging brothers and giving to others has to do with the welfare of his disciples. He's most concerned about what

7. See Talbert, *Matthew*, 97–98, who emphasizes the importance of "seeing" as it relates to character formation—the main purpose of the Sermon according to Talbert.

8. So also McKnight, *Sermon on the Mount*, 206–8, 221–25.

will happen to them if they are not wise in following his instructions. For example, throughout the Sermon Jesus has been teaching his disciples the way of mercy in their pursuit of righteousness: loving enemies, forgiving debtors, trusting God. And built into the kingdom of God is a reward: those who show mercy will receive mercy (5:7), those who forgive will be forgiven (6:14), those who trust God will be entrusted with the riches of the kingdom (v. 33). But just as mercy is reciprocal, so also is judgment (7:2). Therefore, the best advice Jesus could give is this: "Do not judge" (v. 1). But if you don't take his advice and you judge others, then don't be surprised when you are judged in return because judgment (the opposite of mercy, Jas 2:13) begets judgment. In fact, judgment is merciless: it requires *exactly* what is measured out against others. No one wants that kind of judgment (our desire for revenge proves it). Besides, Jesus has already challenged the justice of the lex talionis ("eye for eye") because it fosters abuse by evil people (Matt 5:38–41). Instead, the way Jesus's disciples "do justice" (righteousness!) in his kingdom is to show mercy, always ready to "give to the one who asks you, and do not turn away from the one who wants to borrow from you" (v. 42). "But what about pigs and dogs? If you try to give pigs your pearls, they'll spoil them, and if you try to give what is sacred to dogs, they'll attack you (7:6). See? Even Jesus encouraged us to be judgmental at times." Well, before we accuse Jesus of being judgmental or even inconsistent at this point,[9] we need to understand what he meant by pigs and dogs.

Dogs were wild animals, undesirable scavengers, a menace to all people—gentiles as well as Jews. Pigs, on the other hand, were considered unclean by the Jews (Lev 11:7).[10] To Jewish ears, then, Jesus was stating the obvious: pigs have no use for pearls; people don't feed dogs, especially "sacred" food. To give pigs your pearls or to feed dogs holy food is foolish. The reasons are obvious: pigs don't wear pearls, and dogs have no regard for what is holy and what isn't. So, pearls are wasted on pigs, and wild dogs will bite the hands that feed them. Yet it's obvious Jesus wasn't giving lessons on animal care. In the context of his teaching about judging and the parable of the eye (7:1–5), "pigs" and "dogs" represent certain kinds of people. But who? Certainly, these terms can't be Jewish code words for *all* gentiles because Jesus has already referred to them in benign terms (although the NIV translates *ethnikoi* and *ethnē* in 6:7, 32 as "pagans," it means "peoples"—a Jewish term for everyone

9. Luz goes so far as to say that this verse (Matt 7:6) is so antithetical to everything Jesus taught that it comes from neither Jesus nor Matthew—it was added to the Gospel much later. Therefore, Luz refuses to comment on its meaning (*Matthew*, 1:356).

10. Nolland emphasizes the contrast between scavenger and domesticated animal; dogs were never fed, but pigs were fed to be fattened for the market (*Matthew*, 322–23).

else), and almost as soon as he gave it, he would be violating his own advice (8:5–13). Some think Jesus was relying on common slurs to warn his disciples about undesirable people regardless of ethnicity—the worst of the worst.[11] But how does that square with the unequivocal teaching, "love your enemies," of which there are certainly "dogs" and "pigs"? Others claim we cannot define "dogs" and "pigs" until we identify what is sacred and what are pearls. Jesus was speaking metaphorically about people in relation to the gospel, the pearls of the kingdom (message?) and the sacred food of God (Eucharist?).[12] Either Jesus was warning his disciples that they can't force the gospel on people,[13] or pointing out those who aren't ready for it—like the gentiles. Accordingly, Jesus's advice was timely but not timeless: don't share the gospel with gentiles *now* (pigs/dogs). The gentile mission comes later.[14]

Once again, we find ourselves struggling to make sense of what Jesus meant because his teaching is so enigmatic. Identifying who are dogs and pigs, what is sacred and what are pearls—all of this is in the eye of the beholder. How we see others determines how we will treat them. Of course, if we have something obscuring our vision—a plank in our eye—then we might end up treating our brothers like pigs and our enemies like dogs.[15] "Seeing clearly" is what Jesus is most concerned about here. For if we don't see clearly (explained by the second parable of the eye, 7:3–5), we will judge others and be judged as hypocrites with "plank eye." Then the people we see as "pigs" will despise our pearls, and the ones we've dismissed as "dogs" will turn on us and tear us to pieces (v. 6). In other words, I think Jesus's second parable on the eye deconstructs not only the way we judge one another[16] but also the way we treat "outsiders." The presumption he is challenging is whether *any of us* "see clearly." Notice, in Jesus's parable, *everyone* has something in their eye, whether a beam or a speck. But judgment works from the presumption of infallibility—that we see things clearly. Yet we *all* have a problem (whether we admit it or not).[17] The "infallible" judge has a beam obscuring his vision, and everyone else sees it but him. Notice also that, according to Jesus, no one can help a hypocrite remove the beam from his eye (he must do it himself). But he can't see it because he can't see. Indeed, the only way a hypocrite will see

11. Davies and Allison, *Matthew*, 1:675–77.

12. Turner, *Matthew*, 206–7.

13. Keener, *Matthew*, 242–44.

14. McKnight, *Sermon on the Mount*, 237–38, is one example of this interpretation.

15. Turner, *Matthew*, 207.

16. McKnight, *Sermon on the Mount*, 229: "Since no human lives up to his or her own standard, that standard deconstructs a human's attempt to play God with others."

17. "When I judge, I am blind to my own evil and to the grace granted the other person" (Bonhoeffer, *Discipleship*, 172).

clearly is to admit he *can't see things clearly.* (Any chance of that happening?) What about the person with a speck in their eye? Well, Jesus assumes they will need someone to help them remove the speck because everyone knows you need a clear eye to see it. But the speck-eyed person can't see it because the instrument by which he or she sees is the problem! (What are they going to do? Are they going to pluck out the one good eye with their hand, hold it some distance away from the other eye so they can "see" the speck to remove it and clear up their vision?) They need someone else to see the speck to remove it. So to whom do they turn for help? The only one who can, the hypocrite who admits their own hypocrisy. The humility required to see our hypocrisy helps us see things clearly.

LIVE the Story

The irony of Jesus's strategy, relying upon our ability to "see" ourselves in the parody of his parable, is genius. Consider the implications of having something stuck in our eyes. "Plank eye" can't see that he needs help, but he is trying to help others *who haven't asked for it*, and "speck eye" knows he needs help and asks others to see the speck *because he asked for it*. This makes complete sense. I wouldn't know a person has a speck in his eye *unless he comes to me looking for help*. Why? Because the only person who knows they have the speck in their eye is the one who has it but can't "see" it. I've never walked up to a person, saw a foreign substance in their eye, and said, "Hey. Do you need help with that?" Never. But several times my children and my wife have approached me saying, "Help me. I've got something in my eye." Then I look carefully trying to find the speck, and sometimes I see it, sometimes I don't. It's only when I don't see it that my family member gets upset. "Well, there's got to be something in there. I know it!" Then I look again as my speck-eyed loved one hopes desperately that I can see it—because they can't!—and remove it so they can see. In other words, when dealing with planks and specks, Jesus knew that *we need each other* to see clearly. Only hypocrites think they can see things by themselves, and that invariably leads to judgment (and a lot of damage).[18]

So, when it comes to spotting pigs and dogs, I can't see them by myself. It takes a bunch of "clear-eyed" people—hypocrites who recognize their hypocrisy (humility!)—to help me not waste my pearls on pigs or try to feed dogs the sacred food I treasure. Yes, there are certain kinds of people who act like pigs and dogs—those who don't value your pearls and will devour your

18. "Superiority is masquerading as care and generosity" (Nolland, *Matthew*, 320).

food and try to devour you. Jesus knew this better than anyone. He didn't look at the world with a starry-eyed optimism: "Everyone's good and we're all going to make it!" No, he kept trying to get his disciples to see the world with kingdom eyes; not only admitting that our enemies are evil (Matt 5:39) but also that evil runs through every single one of us—even disciples: "If you, then, though you are evil, know how to give good gifts. . ." (7:11). Yet we're still supposed to love our enemies and our neighbors, giving to *everyone who asks* (5:42). Does that mean pigs too? Well, yes, except Jesus assumed we would know that pigs *don't ask for pearls*. Dogs *don't recognize what is sacred*. Why? Because they are slaves of mammon. I think that's the implication of the symmetry of these two passages (6:19–34 and 7:1–12), twin teachings that run on parallel tracks.[19] In other words, Jesus has already identified pigs and dogs for us. They hoard treasures on earth because nothing is heavenly (materialists say nothing is sacred). They are slaves of mammon because there is no god to serve (nihilists can't see the beauty of pearls). They "eagerly run after" earthly things because they worry about tomorrow (pragmatists seek first their kingdom). To give them our pearls—something they didn't ask for—would be a waste; they don't value them because they don't need them. Jesus's disciples, on the other hand, value pearls and eat sacred food because we serve a God who knows how to give good gifts to his children (7:9–11). How do we know that? Because we ask, "Give us this day our daily bread," and we receive. We seek first his righteous kingdom, and we find endless grace. We knock on heaven's door, and God opens his treasury: all debts are forgiven (7:7–8). Therefore, freely as we receive, freely we give to others—even our pearls!—especially to those who ask. This is the Law and the Prophets (v. 12). This is the righteousness that exceeds all others. This is what it means to be "blessed." This is the kingdom of heaven on earth, and it's ours (5:3, 10).

So, why worry? Worry doesn't work. It doesn't change a thing. Fretting over what will happen doesn't affect the future. You've heard the well-known saying, "Worry is like a rocking chair. It gives you something to do, but it doesn't get you anywhere." Even worse, the stress of rocking back and forth in your mind, playing the mental game of working through a hundred scenarios (and most of them aren't good), is harmful. Anxiety only makes us miserable in the present. Even though we know these things, we will persist in our habit of worry—some of us more than others—to the detriment of ourselves and other people. Of course, worry is seated in fear. We only fret over what could hurt us. (I never worry while I anticipate good things. "Oh no. I hope

19. Don't store treasures on earth and don't judge; having a single eye is to see clearly; pigs and dogs are enslaved to mammon; don't worry because God's children receive good gifts when they ask him; seeking first the kingdom is loving your neighbor as yourself.

the great bonus in pay won't ruin me." Hardly.) Moreover, since bad things happen to everyone, we wonder when evil will come knocking on our door, bringing the bad news everyone dreads: the phone call in the middle of the night, the lab results confirming the diagnosis, the somber look on your boss's face when he calls you into his office. Our bodies uncontrollably respond to the horror: the mind goes blank, peripheral vision is lost, weakness invades muscles, nausea erupts as waves of despair wash over you. Then, as you return to the reality of your distress, a second sickness kicks in as you think about your family, your life, your future. What can be done? How will my family take the news? Is this the end? The fact that I'm okay *at the moment* doesn't bring any comfort. All I can think about is what hasn't happened yet, as if the future is some unknown misery that will slap me in the face, sobering me to the hopeless reality that *there's nothing I can do about it*. Advice to "take it like a man" doesn't help. What I want is to go back to the way things were when I lived in the ignorant bliss that everything is okay, when I believed that God was on my side. But now, I can't help but wonder: Where is God when I need him the most? Why did he let this happen to me? What are we going to do? If God didn't stop the evil then, how can I count on him now? Indeed, worrying about what happens next turns us all into practical atheists. And the one thing atheists need, as far as Jesus was concerned, is a lot of talk about God and a reminder that we're not alone.

Jesus kept bringing up God as he gave two reasons why we shouldn't worry: 1) since God takes care of what he's made, he will take care of us, and 2) we are wasting our God-given life worrying about things we can't change. But that's not the end of it, as if all we need to overcome anxiety is a lot of God talk about creation. Rather, his "theological" argument is built upon the realities of the human condition. Jesus started with this assumption: we worry about what we treasure, we treasure what we are devoted to, and we are devoted to what makes life better *for us*. Everyone knows that earthly treasures make life better. So at this point we would have expected Jesus to talk about sacrificing for the kingdom. "You worry about things that don't matter. Set your affection on spiritual things, and you won't care about the necessities of life." But that's not his argument. Instead, Jesus admitted that earthly treasures make life better: not only the basics (food, drink, and shelter) but also beautiful things like clothes and pearls. Not only that, but God cares about these things too. The problem, according to Jesus, is that earthly treasures don't last; therefore, a person better use them wisely. Yet people foolishly strive after *more* earthly treasures, devoted to them like a slave to his master rather than to God and his kingdom. In other words, these slaves tend to look at the world with an "evil eye"; they don't have a good eye on the kingdom, to see that loving your neighbor is far more valuable than loving things. To invest in people—not things—is the wisdom of the kingdom of God. Indeed, out of everything that has been created by humanity (bread and clothes) and by God (birds and fields), we are the most important treasures on earth—especially to God—which is why we shouldn't worry. It's because people are more important than things.

The husband of a former student of mine told me a story many years ago about a lesson he learned from a man who lived in one of the nations in southern Africa (I can't remember which one). This Western, white family was living and serving with other African, black Christians trying to live for the kingdom of God on earth as it is in heaven. Their standard of living was much less than what he experienced in America, and yet things were not as important to the locals as to the typical American—which is why what happened confused the white missionary. One of his good friends had been saving for *many years* for a little handheld radio. When he finally bought it and brought it home, he showed everyone the clever, little device. The whole town was amazed by the simple gadget. His friend listened to his radio practically all night long, celebrating his treasure. The next day, a neighbor came to see the radio, asking if he could take it home to show his family. The man agreed without hesitation. After several days, the missionary noticed that his friend didn't have his radio. The neighbor had kept the thing for a long time, but that didn't seem to bother his friend. Eventually, after nearly a month the neighbor brought the radio back to its rightful owner, but the radio was broken, obviously neglected and abused. As the missionary watched his friend turn the radio on and off, on and off, realizing it didn't work anymore, he expected an angry showdown. Instead, his friend took the radio to his house and never said a word. Confused, the missionary pointed out the obvious: "Why don't you confront your neighbor? He ruined your radio, something you've saved for years to buy!" His friend, astonished by the missionary's complaint, said simply, "My neighbor is more important than this little radio."

It seems the "plank" in the missionary's eye obscured his vision, especially when he tried to remove the "speck" from the eye of his African brother. The missionary said with tears in his eyes, "I went to southern Africa to share the good news of the kingdom. But what really happened was they taught me what Jesus emphasized: people are more important than things." Then he went on to speculate about how he would have handled the situation—like any other American. How we would get angry. How we would make judgments about the irresponsibility of our brother. How we would try to teach them a lesson about the value of other people's property. To be sure, we would straighten them out, fixing them, forcing them to realize the error of their ways. In fact, that's what we typically do; we turn people into projects and call it the work of God. But that's not what Jesus taught us to do. We are supposed to give to those who ask. We are supposed to forgive our debtors as God has forgiven us. We are supposed to remove the plank from our eyes so that we can see each other with kingdom eyes. Then we will ask God for what we *all* need, and we will receive it because God gives good gifts to *all of his children*. We will seek the kingdom of loving our neighbor as ourselves, and we will find the work of God in *all of us*—our neighbor and ourselves. We will knock on heaven's door, and God will open up the treasures of his mercy for *every single one of us* because we forgive as we are forgiven. This is what it means to be blessed in the kingdom of God, storing up treasures in heaven because we treasure one another on earth.

CHAPTER 9

Matthew 7:13–8:1

LISTEN to the Story

13“Enter through the narrow gate. For wide is the gate and broad is
the road that leads to destruction, and many enter through it. 14But small
is the gate and narrow the road that leads to life, and only a few find it.

15“Watch out for false prophets. They come to you in sheep’s clothing,
but inwardly they are ferocious wolves. 16By their fruit you will recognize
them. Do people pick grapes from thornbushes, or figs from thistles?
17Likewise, every good tree bears good fruit, but a bad tree bears bad fruit.
18A good tree cannot bear bad fruit, and a bad tree cannot bear good fruit.
19Every tree that does not bear good fruit is cut down and thrown into the
fire. 20Thus, by their fruit you will recognize them.

21“Not everyone who says to me, ‘Lord, Lord,’ will enter the king-
dom of heaven, but only the one who does the will of my Father who
is in heaven. 22Many will say to me on that day, ‘Lord, Lord, did we not
prophesy in your name and in your name drive out demons and in your
name perform many miracles?’ 23Then I will tell them plainly, ‘I never
knew you. Away from me, you evildoers!’

24“Therefore everyone who hears these words of mine and puts them
into practice is like a wise man who built his house on the rock. 25The
rain came down, the streams rose, and the winds blew and beat against
that house; yet it did not fall, because it had its foundation on the rock.
26But everyone who hears these words of mine and does not put them into
practice is like a foolish man who built his house on sand. 27The rain came
down, the streams rose, and the winds blew and beat against that house,
and it fell with a great crash.”

28When Jesus had finished saying these things, the crowds were amazed
at his teaching, 29because he taught as one who had authority, and not as
their teachers of the law.

8:1When Jesus came down from the mountainside, large crowds fol-
lowed him.

Listening to the Text in the Story: Deuteronomy 13:1–5; 18:15–22; 30:11–31:2; Joshua 24:2–28; Nehemiah 9:5–10:39; Psalms 1; 18:2–36; 119:29–35; Ezekiel 13:9–17; 22:23–29; Zechariah 13:2–5; Wisdom of Solomon 5:6–7; Sirach 15:11–17.

When Moses stood before the Israelites and offered his final goodbye—a *very* long farewell (Deut 5:1–28:68)—he kept placing the future before the people with the tagline, "when you enter the land." Curiously, he didn't say, "When *we* enter the land," for the prophet knew he wouldn't be there to see it all come to pass. Indeed, the absence of Moses is the pretext for these final warnings, offered to Israel as a "last-ditch effort" before they left the prophet and crossed over to the other side. The future depended on them and whether they would remember Moses's last sermon. So, the prophet tried to nail it down, calling them one last time to the moment of decision: "I have set before you life and death, blessings and curses. Now choose life, so that you and your children may live" (30:19).

Jesus ended his famous Sermon on the Mount much the same way.[1] He not only places before the crowd the same choice—life and death, blessings and curses—he also sounds like he won't be present to lead his disciples through the narrow gate. Indeed, the absence of Jesus is the assumed context for their future—just like it was for Moses and the children of Israel. Thus, Jesus encourages them to *find* the small gate in order to follow the narrow path (Matt 7:13–14). One would think it should be as easy as following Jesus wherever he goes—that's got to be the "straight and narrow." Yet, even though the crowd would follow him down the mountain once the Sermon is over (8:1), Jesus talks at the end of the Sermon like he's not going to be with them when false prophets "come to you in sheep's clothing" (7:15). At that time (sometime in the future?), they won't be able to rely on Jesus to help them figure out who are the false prophets and who are not. Rather, Jesus assumes *they* will have to discern which prophets are "doing" good fruit and which are "doing" bad fruit (no middle ground?).[2] In other words, Jesus ended his sermon with a significant assumption: it's going to be up to his listeners whether they "choose life" or destruction, to be wise rather than foolish builders. The *only* thing they'll have is what Jesus taught them: "Everyone who hears these words of mine and puts them into practice" (7:24). In other words, as it was in the days of Moses and the children of Israel, to do God's will means hearing (remembering?) and doing what was taught—the Sermon on the Mount.

1. Allison, *New Moses*, 190–94.

2. Most translations appropriately translate the verb *poieō* as "bears," but it does obscure the major emphasis of "doing" (a form of the verb appears nine times in this passage); see McKnight, *Sermon on the Mount*, 267–68.

EXPLAIN the Story

When Jesus put before the crowd a binary world, requiring them to make a choice between two options, he sounded like the prophets before him. Everything was black and white to them because God wasn't ambivalent about anything. God either loved or he hated (Mal 1:2–3), he blessed or he cursed (Deut 11:26–28), he rewarded or he punished (1 Kings 9:3–9). Therefore, according to the prophets a person was either obedient or rebellious, wise or foolish, holy or unclean. There was no in between. So when Jesus reduced all life decisions to two gates, characterized all leaders as two kinds of prophets, trees, and fruit, and spoke only of two kinds of builders preparing for the judgment day, he wasn't being arrogant or unreasonable. (Don't we all get a little suspicious of speakers who reduce complex realities to the simplistic claim, "The world consists of two kinds of people"?) Rather, Jesus was relying upon a "two-ways" tradition that was indicative of the prophets, as well as wisdom and other Jewish literature at the time.[3] In fact, the tradition of speaking of life as a choice between two roads, two ways, two destinations was adopted by the earliest Christians to distinguish their faith from all others. Paul claimed we are either "slaves to sin" leading to death or "slaves of God" resulting in life (Rom 6:19–23). The Didache opens with the line: "There are two ways, one of life and one of death, and there is a great difference between these two ways" (1:1).[4] In our world today, many operate with the assumption that there are many paths to God. But the way the Jews and early Christians saw it, there's only one way to God. All other ways/religions are really one path leading to the same destination: destruction.

But even within their own ranks, both Jews and early Christians distinguished among themselves those who were truly devoted to God and those who were as bad as pagans. For example, the Dead Sea Scrolls are filled with characterizations of the true Israel as "children of light" while all other Jews (and the rest of the world) are labeled "children of darkness" (e.g., 1QS 3:13–4:26). Paul warned his converts about those who preach a "different gospel," masquerading as angels of light (like Satan!) but who are really false apostles (2 Cor 11:4–15). In the Epistle of Barnabas, the writer describes "two ways of teaching and power, one of light and one of darkness," consigning those of the darkness to Satan, the "ruler of the present era of lawlessness" (Barn. 18:1–2; the way of light, 19:1–12; the way of darkness,

3. See the list of references in Turner, *Matthew*, 213–14.

4. Michael W. Holmes, ed., *The Apostolic Fathers: Greek Texts and English Translations*, 3rd ed. (Grand Rapids: Baker Academic, 2007), 345.

20:1–2).[5] In the same way, throughout the Sermon Jesus contrasted his way of righteousness to the pseudo-righteousness of the hypocrites—the scribes and the Pharisees (Matt 5:20). They say, "Don't murder"; he says, "Don't hate." They say, "Don't commit adultery"; he says, "Don't lust." They say, "Permit divorce"; he says, "Don't divorce." They say, "Keep your vows"; he says, "Don't make vows." They say, "Love your neighbor"; he says, "Love your enemies." They give, pray, and fast in public; Jesus says to do these things in private. They are judged as "plank-eyed" hypocrites because they judge. Jesus, on the other hand, teaches the reciprocity of mercy and forgiveness. So it shouldn't surprise us that Jesus ends his sermon with a familiar challenge, setting before the crowd a choice between two gates, two paths, the way of the hypocrites and the way of Jesus. The way of hypocrisy is broad and well populated. The way of Jesus is narrow and "only a few find it" (7:14). The gate is as small as one commandment: "Do to others what you would have them do to you" (v. 12). All people are traveling on one of two paths, and the end is either life or death. (You can't travel down two paths any more than you can serve two masters.) So, which way will you choose? No decision could be more serious, for we all are given only one life to live, and two paths are set before us: the way of judgment that ends in destruction and the way of mercy that leads to life.[6]

The Deceivers and the Deceived[7]

The choice seems obvious. Who wouldn't prefer mercy over judgment, righteousness over hypocrisy, life over death? Sounds easy. "Do unto others," right? I want people to show me mercy; so, I will extend mercy to others. (It's certainly better than receiving judgment because I've judged others!) Well, Jesus makes it plain that the small gate—his way of righteousness—opens to a "troubled" path. The word for "straight" or "narrow" (*thlibō*) is more often translated "distressed," "persecuted," or "troubled" in other places (2 Cor 1:6; 1 Thess 3:4; 2 Thess 1:7). That's why many scholars suggest we should speak of "the Jesus way" as passing through a small gate that leads to a path of affliction—which certainly would be in keeping with the warnings Jesus offered throughout his teaching, especially at the beginning of the Sermon (5:10–12).[8] Those who judge will bring judgment upon themselves, but it is the merciful, the meek, and the forgiving who will be persecuted. It also may

5. Holmes, *Apostolic Fathers*, 433, 435.

6. In light of Matt 7:23, Turner thinks the two ways are Jesus versus antinomianism (*Matthew*, 217, 220).

7. McKnight, *Sermon on the Mount*, 266–68.

8. Davies and Allison, *Matthew*, 1:700; Luz, *Matthew*, 1:372; Nolland, *Matthew*, 333–34.

explain why Jesus goes immediately from talking about the troubled path (7:14) to the threat of false prophets (vv. 15–20). These "wolves in sheep's clothing" may *talk about* the importance of entering the small gate (following Jesus) and staying on the difficult path (doing his teachings), but the fruit of their lives say otherwise. They profess the way of Jesus, but they don't live it.[9] Indeed, they do not practice what they preach—a sure sign of hypocrisy. Yet these false prophets aren't deceived. They know they are wolves masquerading as sheep, dressed up in "sheep's clothing"—perhaps a reference to the prophet's garb, like Elijah (John the Baptizer!). Therefore, they will share the same fate John pronounced upon the Pharisees and Sadducees: like worthless trees that produce only bad fruit, they will be cut down and thrown into the fire (Matt 3:10; 7:19). Although the people may go to them, looking for grapes and figs (nourishment for the journey), their prickly facade (thorns and thistles of false piety and judgment) and the rotten fruit of their lives (hating their brothers, divorcing their wives, taking revenge against their enemies) should make these false prophets *easily* recognizable to Jesus's disciples (7:16–18). They neither look like a good source of food, nor do they offer anything that is good for you. Jesus was confident that his disciples would know them by their fruit (vv. 16, 20). So why the warning?

False prophets were a problem for Israel, especially since true prophets were often rejected, abused, and scorned by the people because their messages were offensive, sometimes appearing to border on heresy, like the temple sermon of Jeremiah (Jer 7:1–15). In light of God's promise to Solomon—the Lord said he would put his name on the temple "forever" (1 Kgs 9:3)—Jeremiah's prediction of the impending destruction of the temple must have sounded like false prophecy (Jer 7:14). Since God warned Israel that false prophets make predictions that don't come true (Deut 18:21–22), or they make predictions that come true but their message sounds heretical (Deut 13:1–5), men like Jeremiah didn't have a chance of being recognized as God's prophet. In other words, the pattern of discerning prophets typically went like this: Israel listened to false prophets because their message was appealing (Jer 23:16–21) and rejected true prophets because they didn't like what they heard, regardless of signs performed. But Jeremiah said Israel should have known better. False prophets are easy to spot: their lawless behavior led Israel astray (Jer 23:9–15, 22).[10] Jesus claimed the same thing: people may prophesy in his name—and even perform wondrous signs—but the lawless deeds of false

---

9. Did Jesus envision the Pharisees masquerading as "true prophets" among his disciples, or was he warning his followers of their own potential for hypocrisy? See Keener, *Matthew*, 251–52; Luz, *Matthew*, 1:376–78. Nolland thinks Matthew targeted both groups (*Matthew*, 336–37).

10. France, *Matthew*, 289–91.

prophets should make it evident that they are bad trees (Matt 7:22–23). Only those who do the will of God (v. 21), who enter the small gate and walk the difficult path of following Jesus, are good trees that produce good fruit. Yet what does good fruit from a good tree look like? They look like merciful, peaceful, forgiving, loving, compassionate, righteous, faithful followers of the Jesus way—those who hear and do what Jesus taught. Consequently, what Jesus said about bad trees is true of good trees: "By their fruit you will recognize them."

Live a lie long enough, and you'll begin to believe it. That's the presumption behind the judgment-day scenario Jesus envisioned for false prophets.[11] At first, the deception of the wolves dressed up like sheep was obvious to everyone: the wolf knows he's pretending, and the sheep recognize the lie by his behavior. By the time of the end of the world, however, these false prophets stand self-deceived before Judge Jesus (a role typically assigned to God). Of course, Jesus was never fooled by the deception of the deceivers. They may call him "Lord," prophesy in his name, even perform many signs, but he knew all along that they didn't belong to him (vv. 21–22). They were not his sheep. Ironically, in the end the only ones deceived by the deception were the false prophets themselves. Say things long enough, and you'll eventually believe the words that come from your mouth. This is the danger of living a lie: self-deception. What makes self-deception so scary is wondering how the deceived are awakened to the reality of their lie—especially since they're convinced they're right. The deceived rely upon their words for their reality. Even on the last day, standing before Jesus, the deceived will still try to argue their way into the kingdom. It's not until Jesus has the last word, "Then I will tell them *plainly*, 'I never knew you. Away from me, you evil doers'" (v. 23), that the lie of their lives will catch up with them. Tragically, it's too late for them *to do* anything about it; they had their chance to hear the words of Jesus *and do them* long before judgment day. Indeed, the surest way not to be self-deceived is to hear and do what Jesus said and did. Such a person is wise and follows Jesus to the end.

Finding a Firm Foundation

Jesus ended the Sermon with a parable. He had used several little parables before—simple analogies (city shining on a hill, salt losing its saltiness, eye as lamp of the body, plank eye and speck eye, dogs and pigs, small gates versus

11. France, *Matthew*, 286, is convinced these are two different groups of people: the deceivers (vv. 15–20) and the deceived (vv. 21–23). Others see the entire passage (vv. 15–23) directed against false prophets (Davies and Allison, *Matthew*, 1:701–2; Luz, *Matthew*, 1:374–77; McKnight, *Sermon on the Mount*, 264–68).

broad paths, wolves in sheep's clothing, good fruit and bad trees). But this parable is a little more involved because it has several elements to it: wise and foolish builders, rock versus sand foundations, houses built, rain coming down, streams rising, winds beating against the house, houses that stand and houses that collapse (Matt 7:24–27). The previous parables of Jesus were a bit enigmatic—especially to us. But the meaning of this parable seems plain enough: building your life upon the Sermon on the Mount makes you a wise person, who is able to weather the storms of life. Some commentators wonder whether the bad weather has to do with everyday trials or the messianic woes that come just before the end of the world. In other words, is this a wisdom saying to guide our lives "in the meantime" or an eschatological warning preparing the faithful for the last days? (Recall that we faced the same question regarding the Beatitudes.) If this is sage advice, Jesus was reminding his disciples that they won't "fall apart" when bad things happen to them because they're prepared for the difficulties in life—they expect persecution.[12] If Jesus was issuing a final warning about preparing for the end of the world, then he was basically saying, "The only way you'll make it during the last days is to do what I have taught you." (This would then be similar to the saying, "the one who stands firm to the end of the world will be saved"; Matt 24:13).[13] Either way, the point is the same: the wise person "hears these words of mine and puts them into practice" (Matt 7:24); the foolish person doesn't, and the results will be devastating (vv. 26–27).[14]

The imagery of homes devastated by floodwaters is familiar to all people through the ages. As long as people persist in building homes by rivers, there will be repeated scenes of floods destroying property. Those of us who live in the safety of the hill country (who needs flood insurance?) can't help but wonder, "Why do the river people keep inviting such misery? Come join us on the mountain, and you'll never have to fear the floods again." But the river people say, "What's a little cleanup every now and then? Our house is still standing. The concrete foundation didn't crack. Besides, it was about time to renovate the old homestead anyway." And therein lies the difference between Jesus's day and ours. We can put houses just about anywhere we want because of the way foundations are laid. Footings are dug and concrete is poured to create the necessary foundation for homes built on the mountain or by the river. Dig deep enough, and massive condos can be built right on

12. Augustine, *Sermon on the Mount* 2.24.87.

13. Davies and Allison, *Matthew*, 1:722; Luz, *Matthew* 1:380; Keener, *Matthew*, 255.

14. France, *Matthew*, 297, and Nolland, *Matthew*, 344, take a both/and approach. Nolland writes, "The wisdom perspective . . . is here applied by means of storm imagery to the period of stress and disturbance which ushers in the eschaton."

the sandy beach, as close to the water as you want. But in Jesus's day, you couldn't put your house anywhere you wanted. Rather, one had to look for a rock upon which to build the house.[15] In lower Galilee, basaltic formations of large boulders—the hazard of farmers (Matt 13:5)—could be found hiding under the shallow ground, especially up the mountain. But to build a house on sand near a wadi (dry-bed creeks that would swell with water during the rainy season) was shortsighted foolishness. To ignore the years of wisdom of your neighbors who built their houses on rock foundations was the height of arrogance. It was only a matter of time until everyone would see the house on beachfront property come crashing down (Matt 7:27).

Situated on a mountain, Jesus encouraged the crowds to build their lives on his rock-solid words. No need to look anywhere else for a foundation. If they did what he said, choosing to live in the shelter of his words, then no persecution, no flood, no affliction, no trouble would overwhelm them. Even during the last days, when the earth groans under the weight of messianic woes unleashed on a troubled world, Jesus predicted his disciples would weather the storm because they chose to follow him to the end. It's no wonder, then, that the crowds marveled at his teaching and followed him down the mountain (7:28; 8:1). No one spoke like this. Even their experts—the scribes—didn't speak with such confidence (7:29). Jesus knew what he was talking about: to have a righteousness that exceeds that of the scribes and Pharisees, to live with the confidence that you are blessed by God because you follow Jesus, to enter the kingdom of heaven now, to pray for God's will on earth as it is in heaven, to look upon all creation with kingdom eyes, to love your neighbor as yourself, to love even your enemies. This is the only way to live—to enter the narrow gate leading down a difficult path that ends with great rewards for the wise. Only a fool would think otherwise. Yet it will take the rest of the story to see the difference.[16]

LIVE the Story

The way of mercy is difficult; it requires humility, forgiveness, and sacrifice. The way of judgment is easy; only words are required to condemn others. And it's quite apparent that words are not difficult to come by when we judge others. All you need to do is read the comment section of any online news story or blog to see the vitriolic spew of arrogant judges. When we speak our minds, the underbelly of humanity is easily exposed. Snap judgments and

15. See Bailey, *Jesus through Middle Eastern Eyes*, 322–24.
16. Garland, *Reading Matthew*, 89.

knee-jerk reactions to what others say and do are almost always hateful and abusive. What bothers me is that I see the same tendency on so-called "Christian" blogs and online magazines. One should expect kindhearted, gentle, and yet pointed dialogue among those of differing opinions in the Christian blogosphere. Nothing could be further from the truth. At times I can't tell the difference between the comment section on a story at cnn.com or christianitytoday.com. Only those who "scream" the loudest, using unmercifully cruel "zingers," get noticed. Ad hominem attacks and arrogant non sequiturs abound in the Christian world of crusaders defending the faith. The way of judgment is broad, and many people find it. It's enough to make the pure in heart wonder how anyone could see God on this path of destruction. Indeed, the comment section is no place for the meek; the humble are wise not to build their house there. Come to think of it, I've never read a single comment beginning with the line, "I could be wrong but. . . ." Judges don't talk like that.

Yet, to judge judges for their judgmental words is easy to do. Everyone recognizes the bad fruit, the destructive words of hypocrites who can't see the plank in their eye. We who love words and reverence their power—especially those of us who make a living by using words—should be the first to recognize the dangerous satisfaction that comes with condemning the hypocrisy of judges.[17] (The irony is hard to miss, like when I preach a sermon about how faith that relies upon words is useless according to James. Shouldn't it be the shortest sermon I ever preach, knowing that we'd all rather see a sermon than hear one?) Jesus knew that too, which is why he made it clear that offering a sermon on a mountain or merely hearing a sermon wouldn't be enough. He had to come down from the mountain and show us all what mercy looks like, and he expected his disciples—true prophets—to follow him all the way to the end. Merely repeating what Jesus said is never enough. To see the red letters animated in living color (incarnation!), in ourselves and in others, is to see the kingdom of God.

* * *

He was the best Christian I've ever known. Words fail me as I try to describe why. Of course, he would have hated it that I put it in print. In fact, he was surprised that I singled him out as the one Christian I have admired the most. When I was his pastor, I always felt better about the kingdom knowing he was

17. See the devastating critique by McKnight, based on the observations of Mark Powell, who noticed that preachers tend to identify with Jesus trying to straighten out the hypocrites (the laity). McKnight says of all people, preachers should be the first to see themselves as potential "false prophets" (*Sermon on the Mount*, 269–70).

around. He was a gentle man. Never heard him say a bad thing about anyone. He was a Sunday-school teacher and a well-respected surgeon. He was a family man, devoted to his wife and children. He loved to hunt deer and ducks. He died of cancer a few years ago, and I still don't understand why the Lord took him. He did so much for the kingdom. In his own quiet way, he inspired so many. I know it's not right to say this, but it felt like the enemy gained a huge advantage when Buck Rusher died. Here's why.

He led his Sunday-school class to start a Bible study on the "wrong side of the tracks" in Jonesboro, Arkansas. The poor people who showed up not only heard about the mercy of God, they experienced it. In His Steps ministry, started many years ago, continues to this day. But that wasn't enough. Buck and his wife, Pam, made several trips to the continent of Africa to help the poor and sick, to spread the good news of God's reign on earth. Then they took their efforts to Mongolia. But making several trips a year wasn't enough. Shutting down his practice temporarily, Buck and Pam moved to Mongolia, where he introduced laparoscopy to the local surgeons. He would make several trips back home to gather more equipment and supplies, returning to Mongolia to continue to teach and spread the gospel of Jesus Christ. The Mongolian government gave him the highest honor, recognizing him for training physicians and giving his equipment to the hospitals where he worked. And even though his first three-year stay in Mongolia was successful, he knew his work wasn't done. Only a few health-care professionals had shown any interest in the gospel. So, after returning home to the States for a few years, he and Pam returned to Mongolia, training more physicians and telling others about King Jesus. By this time, I had left his hometown church to join the faculty where I teach. Buck would send questions to me via email, wanting biblical answers to the challenges he faced in spreading the gospel. Never discouraged by the lack of results, Buck and Pam kept sowing the seed and watering the ground.

Then it happened. For some reason known only to the Holy Spirit, there was a breakthrough. A Mongolian physician, one of Buck's close friends, became a Christian. Then, a few more health-care professionals committed to Christ. About the same time, a few ladies Pam had befriended believed in Jesus. Soon, more than fifty new believers were baptized in the bathtub of Buck and Pam's apartment—in the dead of winter! He was so excited. I'll never forget the email he sent with many pictures attached. All the work, all the love, all the mercy extended, all the prayers, all the patient care—Buck and Pam saw the kingdom of God explode in that very cold part of the world, and they couldn't have been more overjoyed. Even though the Lord had blessed them with grandchildren by this time, they were just as excited to share pictures of new believers as of the sweet grandson that was born in the States while they were away.

Then the bad news. Returning to the States after their second term in Mongolia, Buck began to experience horrible headaches. The diagnosis: a brain tumor that would require risky surgery. Buck knew the odds were slim, but he and Pam were confident the Lord would do what was best. We all prayed. The doctors and nurses did their best. The Lord did not heal him. I called him just a few days before he died. He couldn't hear very well; the radiation and the disease had so ravaged his body that there wasn't much of him left. Fighting back the tears, I tried to comfort him. Practically shouting into the phone, I said, "Buck, I never told you this but you're the best Christian I've ever known." After a long pause, he said with a whisper of a voice, "Well, I don't know about that. But I sure have been a blessed man. Pam is here, she's taking care of me." By this time, I was crying my eyes out. "You have many people who love you. We've all prayed for you. You're almost there, Buck." Then he said with a strong voice, "Not yet. I've got a long ways to go."

I'll never forget that. This dying man—the surest evidence to me of the kingdom of God—declared humbly on his deathbed: "Not yet. I've got a long ways to go."

When I think of Buck's life, the teachings of Jesus in the Sermon on the Mount, and lessons that should be learned, I can't help but wonder if every disciple of Christ shouldn't say the same thing. Entering the small gate, walking the difficult path to the end, some of us (especially the judges) might be tempted to say, "You're almost there." But the meek who inherit the earth, the merciful who receive mercy, the humble in spirit who are pure in heart will say, "Not yet. I've got a long ways to go."

I miss you, Buck.

CHAPTER 10

Matthew 8:2–17

LISTEN to the Story

2A man with leprosy came and knelt before him and said, "Lord, if you
are willing, you can make me clean."

3Jesus reached out his hand and touched the man. "I am willing," he
said. "Be clean!" Immediately he was cleansed of his leprosy. 4Then Jesus
said to him, "See that you don't tell anyone. But go, show yourself to the
priest and offer the gift Moses commanded, as a testimony to them."

5When Jesus had entered Capernaum, a centurion came to him, ask-
ing for help. 6"Lord," he said, "my servant lies at home paralyzed, suffering
terribly."

7Jesus said to him, "Shall I come and heal him?"

8The centurion replied, "Lord, I do not deserve to have you come
under my roof. But just say the word, and my servant will be healed. 9For
I myself am a man under authority, with soldiers under me. I tell this
one, 'Go,' and he goes; and that one, 'Come,' and he comes. I say to my
servant, 'Do this,' and he does it."

10When Jesus heard this, he was amazed and said to those following
him, "Truly I tell you, I have not found anyone in Israel with such great
faith. 11I say to you that many will come from the east and the west, and
will take their places at the feast with Abraham, Isaac and Jacob in the
kingdom of heaven. 12But the subjects of the kingdom will be thrown out-
side, into the darkness, where there will be weeping and gnashing of teeth."

13Then Jesus said to the centurion, "Go! Let it be done just as you
believed it would." And his servant was healed at that moment.

14When Jesus came into Peter's house, he saw Peter's mother-in-law
lying in bed with a fever. 15He touched her hand and the fever left her, and
she got up and began to wait on him.

16When evening came, many who were demon-possessed were brought
to him, and he drove out the spirits with a word and healed all the sick.
17This was to fulfill what was spoken through the prophet Isaiah:

"He took up our infirmities
and bore our diseases."

Listening to the Text in the Story: Leviticus 13:1–14:32; Deuteronomy 30:2–10; 2 Kings 5:1–27; Psalm 107; Isaiah 19:18–25; 25:4–9; 43:5–13; 49:1–25; 53:4; 56:3–8; Malachi 1:11.

It's easy to talk about mercy on a mountain, away from the mundane realities of a fallen world. God shows up on mountains. Sacred space is carved out on a mountain, a temple enshrining the holy presence of God. God's people travel to a mountain to worship him. God's word is delivered on a mountain. Everyone is conversant in holy talk on the mountain. Muddled thoughts seem to vanish in the crisp, clear mountain air. On the mountain, all things come into focus. Our vision clear, one can see for miles. Indeed, from such a lofty vantage point, it's easy to look down upon our world with wistful hopefulness, believing the entire earth is sacred. But, come down from the mountain, and the harsh realities of a profaned world will slap you in the face, awakening you from your heavenly dream. The clarity—that singular moment on the mountain when we knew we saw the world as it should be—is lost in the valley. Words that seemed so solid, so reliable in the heights, sound like empty promises scattered on the cursed ground. Lofty goals and high ideals, dragged through the mud of everyday life, become soiled burdens that are too easily discarded. God's presence may be undeniable on the mountain, but his absence in the valley causes even the faithful to wonder whether the glory of God extends to the ends of the earth, all the way down to the very bottom of our world.

I can't help but wonder if several Galileans, listening to Jesus's words, questioned what they heard that day on the mountain. It reminds me of one of my favorite scenes from the irreverent movie *The Life of Brian*, a satirical look at the life of Jesus and his followers. Jesus is off camera, delivering the Sermon. A large crowd has already gathered around him on the mountain. Near the edge of the crowd, an old man is having a hard time listening to the famous preacher. Craning his neck to hear the barely audible words, the old man turns in frustration to another bystander and asks incredulously, "Did *he* say, 'Blessed are the *cheesemakers*'?" In my mind's eye, I see the same thing happening when Jesus said in effect things like, "Blessed are the poor in spirit," and "Pluck out your eyes, cut off your hands," and "Turn the other cheek," and "Love your enemies," and "Don't judge." We typically picture the crowd listening attentively, even reverently to Jesus. After all, this is the Son of God. But there must have been some people in the crowd—especially the Pharisees (if there were any there[1])—who had a hard time swallowing what Jesus was feeding them that day. "Did he say, '*Love* your *enemies*'? Does he *really* believe the *meek* will inherit the land? How in Gehenna is that going to happen? 'Don't judge.' Really? Don't judge? We live in a profaned world, filled with unclean people. How are we supposed to do what God commanded—to remain pure and holy—without judging who is clean and who isn't? Mercy rather than judgment, huh? Easy to say. Come down from the mountain and show us what that looks like. And, while you're at it, why don't you demonstrate how loving the Romans will convince them to leave the land God promised to us." Yet, according to Matthew that's exactly what Jesus did. He walked through the valley of the shadow of death and revealed that God is with us, especially the least of these. The mercy of God's glorious kingdom shall reach the ends of the earth, even to the very bottom of the world. The cursed are blessed. Enemies are loved. "Yes, you heard him right," Matthew would reply. "The miracles of mercy in the following chapters of my Gospel [see 8:2–9:34][2] prove that Jesus meant what he said on the mountain."[3]

EXPLAIN the Story

The Pharisees could be rather fanatical—rightfully so—about maintaining holiness through purity. They were the descendants of a group that called themselves the *Hasidim* ("faithful ones").[4] Cleanness was a big deal to the Pharisees because God commanded Israel to avoid unclean things (food, people, clothing, homes). He, being a holy God, required a holy people. So, Leviticus (the handbook for priests) is filled with warnings about what not to touch as well as instructions regarding purification (Lev 11:1–15:33). But there's one kind of uncleanliness that gets more press than the rest, requiring even more extreme measures to avoid contamination: leprosy. Apparently, all kinds of skin diseases fell into this broad category. Everything from boils to psoriasis to the dreaded Hansen's disease[5] (what we call "leprosy" today) was

1. Scholars question whether the Pharisees would be seen often outside of Jerusalem where they lived; see Sanders, *Judaism: Practice and Belief*, 388–402; Dunn, *Jesus Remembered*, 306–8.

2. "Perhaps [Matthew] wished his readers to relate to the individual incidents in the light of the Sermon on the Mount" (Nolland, *Matthew*, 348).

3. According to France, half the miracles of Jesus in Matthew's Gospel appear in chapters 8–9 (*Matthew*, 300).

4. For a brief summary of the discussion regarding the origin of the Pharisees, see Lynn Cohick, "Pharisees," *DJG* 673, 676–79.

5. Some scholars question whether anyone at the time suffered from Hansen's disease (Davies and Allison, *Matthew*, 2:10–11).

treated the same. Although contamination could occur from contact with other kinds of impurity—menstruating woman, mold, corpses—people with skin diseases were considered the most dangerous. Rather than hide their appearance (don't we all try to cover up imperfections in our complexion?), they were required to magnify their pitiful state: disheveled hair, dressed in torn rags, they had to live alone, a safe distance from the clean. At all times, "lepers" were to look like the disease they carried. They were the embodiment of uncleanness, the quintessential "untouchables," dead people walking.[6] Yet, keeping up appearances of impurity wasn't enough; whenever lepers ventured into villages of pure people, they had to announce their arrival by shouting, "Unclean, unclean!" (Lev 13:45–46). Is it any wonder that lepers were treated as the ultimate rejects of society? Ostracized by the pure, skin-diseased persons were thought to be condemned by God. After all, God was the one who was essentially saying through the law of Moses, "Stay away from these people!"[7] To maintain holiness, the pure had to be protected from the unclean.

Those afflicted with various skin diseases were not the only unclean people moving about in a profaned world. Those who buried the dead were unclean (Lev 21:1–4). Mothers, after giving birth, were unclean (12:1–8). Married people, after copulation, were unclean (15:16–18). The difference, of course, was that these people could become clean again by submitting to purification rites. Lepers, on the other hand, could only be purified once the disease was gone, which had to be confirmed by the priest (14:3–32). In the meantime, anyone who touched the unclean was rendered unclean. Even coming in contact with something the unclean person touched, like their bed, chair, or clay pot, would make the clean unclean (15:1–12). That's why one Jewish group, the Essenes, took matters into their own hands to avoid defilement. They withdrew from the world, living together in their own settlements, tucked away from a profaned world filled with unclean people and things.[8] The Pharisees, on the other hand, believed such drastic measures were unnecessary. They took their campaign of holiness to the people, encouraging the pure to avoid defilement and the unclean to submit to purification rites.[9] Evidently, Jesus had other ideas about how to negotiate a world of unclean people: neither withdrawing from the world nor avoiding the unclean was the way of holiness in the kingdom of God. Instead, he believed the merciful touch of a holy man made the unholy clean again.

6. Indeed, curing leprosy was put on the same level as raising the dead (France, *Matthew*, 306).

7. Keener, *Matthew*, 261.

8. Josephus, *War* 2.8.4–5. The Essenes were also known to share all things in common, generously sharing their possessions with one another (Josephus, *War* 2.8.3–4).

9. Sanders, *Judaism: Practice and Belief*, 440–43, 48–50.

Loving Your Neighbor

It is no coincidence, according to Matthew, that the first person Jesus encountered when he came down from the mountain was a leper. Here we have the perfect test case for Jesus's teaching to see how the poor in spirit are blessed, how mercy triumphs over judgment. Leprosy was the visible definition of uncleanness, and a leper was the epitome of defilement. Therefore, the wisdom of holy judgment would compel any law-abiding Jew to avoid contact with this man.[10] Indeed, the leper probably approached Jesus shouting, "Unclean! Unclean!" as the sea of humanity parted, making room for the walking corpse.[11] After the leprous man knelt before Jesus, he made a very presumptuous statement. Notice, the leper didn't *ask*, "Please, heal me, if you are able," or "I beg of you, have mercy on me." Rather, he stated matter-of-factly, "Lord, if you are willing, you can make me *clean*" (Matt 8:2, emphasis added). No request. No begging. He simply affirmed what was true: Jesus had the power to make him clean. The only question was whether Jesus was willing to extend mercy to someone like him.

If we think of the purity scale as a ladder reaching to heaven, then the priests and the Pharisees would be on the top rungs, and the sick and diseased would be dangling at the bottom of the ladder. With little hope of being restored, lepers couldn't even climb the ladder of holiness; they were the dirt upon which the ladder stood. (You can't make dirt clean.) So when the leper approached Jesus, he knew that Jesus could heal him, but was Jesus willing to make him clean? It's one thing for Jesus to heal the sick and lame. But a leper? He was completely unclean, perpetually unholy, cursed by God because he had obviously disobeyed the law. How low would Jesus go to restore humanity? How long was the reach of his mercy? Jesus knew what was at stake, which explains why he touched the man before he pronounced him clean (v. 3). He didn't have to do it. Jesus could have healed the man with the words, "Be clean!" and left it at that. Or, he could have let his words carry the message of his mercy: "I am willing." But neither was enough. The simple gesture of touching the leper would speak louder than his words or even the miracle of making him clean. I imagine the crowd gasping in horror when Jesus did the unthinkable. I see with my mind's eye the surprised look on the disfigured face of the leper when Jesus touched him. (I even let my imagination run wild, seeing Jesus give the poor man a big bear hug, but of course that would be truer of our culture than his.) Jesus knew what he was doing. The lesson is undeniable. Jesus reversed the polarity of holiness when he touched

---

10. Jesus ignored the purity "map" of the Pharisees, refusing to recognize the boundaries of clean and unclean (Malina and Rohrbaugh, *Synoptic Gospels*, 72–73).

11. According to Josephus, lepers were the same as dead persons (Josephus, *Ant.* 3.264).

the leper and made him clean. Before, touching the wrong thing made a man unclean. Before, the unclean polluted the world with their impurity. Before, holy people avoided the unclean. But now, in the merciful kingdom of God the clean can make the unclean clean. Now, "holiness, not uncleanness, was understood to be contagious."[12] Now, holy people embrace the impure. Indeed, Jesus redefined what it meant to "be holy as God is holy": show mercy.

The leper was a Jew, evident by the reminder Jesus gave to the healed man to obey the Mosaic law. Before, he was just "a man with leprosy" (v. 2). Now, his identity restored, he must have the priest confirm his cleanness so that he can be reintroduced to the world that was once dead to him—a process that took eight days (Lev 14:2–32).[13] Why did Jesus tell this Jewish man to go to the temple first before he told anyone else (Matt 8:4)? For whose benefit? Jesus's? The priest's? The leper's? We might find an ulterior motive in Jesus's directive. Perhaps he's trying to prove to the religious establishment that his way is better than theirs when it comes to keeping the law, spreading his fame to Jerusalem before he gets there. Or, he's affirming the role of the priest—his beef wasn't with them but the scribes and the Pharisees. Or, Jesus knew the only way the onetime leper would be restored to public life was to have him confirmed clean by the priest. All these reasons make sense, especially since Jesus said the man's appearance in the temple would serve "as a testimony to them" (v. 4).[14] At the same time, one cannot help but wonder: Why *wouldn't* Jesus remind the man to go to the priest? God gave the law to Israel. Both Jesus and the cleansed leper were Jews. Of course there would be benefits to keeping the law, for Jesus, for the priest, and for the former leper. It's why God gave the law to his people in the first place, teaching them to love their neighbors as themselves.

At the end of a long day (miracles, sermon, more miracles), Jesus finally went "home" to Capernaum, perhaps looking for a little rest (Matthew saw Peter's house as Jesus's home during his Galilean ministry; 9:1). But the day wasn't over. Peter's mother-in-law was sick with fever (8:14). Without a word or a request Jesus took the initiative, "touched her hand and the fever left her" (v. 15). In turn, the restored woman got up to "wait on him" and restore him. That Jesus touched her, another Jew, but didn't touch the sick servant of the Roman soldier in the previous story (vv. 5–13, see below), was telling for Matthew. These two "touching" miracles (the leper and the feverish woman) form an *inclusio*, framing the way Jesus restored his own people. Indeed, the scene of many demonized and sick people showing up that night (v. 16) led

12. Marcus J. Borg, *Conflict, Holiness, and Politics in the Teachings of Jesus* (Harrisburg, PA: Trinity Press International, 1998), 147.

13. France, *Matthew*, 308–9.

14. Davies and Allison, *Matthew*, 2:16.

Matthew to claim that Isaiah's prophecy concerning Israel's healing was coming true: "He took up *our* infirmities and bore *our* diseases" (v. 17, emphasis added; see Isa 53:4).[15] Notice, in his vision of how the Suffering Servant would take on the sins of his people, Isaiah used insider language: "He was pierced for *our* transgressions. . . . We all, like *sheep*, have gone astray" (Isa 53:5–6, emphasis added). This redemptive work was for Israel. According to Matthew, all along Jesus was out to reclaim the lost sheep of Israel (Matt 10:5–6), not only healing a leper but also a woman sick with fever, his Jewish neighbors. That more Jews showed up at his door looking for help (8:16) was to be expected because of Isaiah's prophecy. Yet, sandwiched between these miracles of Israel's restoration is the story of God's redemptive work extended through Israel to the gentiles as well (vv. 5–13)—something Isaiah also envisioned (Isa 19:18–25; 25:6–9; 56:6–8). It's one thing to love your neighbor; it's quite another when your neighbor happens to be your enemy: "When Jesus had entered Capernaum [Jesus's hometown!], a centurion came to him" (Matt 8:5). According to Matthew's arrangement, then, *all* of Isaiah's prophecies were coming true because Jesus not only loved his Jewish neighbors but loved his enemies too. By weaving these stories together, Matthew's claim is unmistakable: "He took up *our* infirmities" was not only a reference to Israel but to *all* humanity.

Loving Your Enemy

Once again, it is curious to me that neither the leper nor the centurion actually made a request of Jesus. In fact, if Matthew hadn't set up the episode with the introductory participle (*parakalōn*, "asking"), one might get the impression—simply from his words—that the Roman soldier was barking an order at Jesus: "My servant lies at home paralyzed, suffering terribly" (Matt 8:5–6). That doesn't sound like a request at all. Accustomed to bossing people around (v. 9), it would make sense that a centurion responsible for nearly a hundred soldiers[16] would expect an "inferior" subject of the Roman Empire to take care of the matter by simply calling attention to the problem. Even Jesus seemed to tease out the implications of this peculiar situation, making the inference, "Shall I come and heal him?" (v. 7).[17] It's almost as if Jesus were saying, "What does *your* problem have to do with *me*?" (see Luke 12:14 for a

15. "In Matthew, it is not the demons who first identify Jesus as the Holy One of God . . . but the authoritative Scripture" (Garland, *Reading Matthew*, 97).

16. Most scholars think that the centurion was under the charge of Herod Antipas since there is no record of a Roman legion occupying Palestine at this time. For further discussion, see Keener, *Matthew*, 263–65; France, *Matthew*, 311–12.

17. Some translate the phrase as a declarative, "I will go and heal him." The Greek construction isn't definitive, although most see the emphatic *egō* indicating an interrogative future; see Davies and Allison, *Matthew*, 2:22.

similar tone).[18] Yet it's quite apparent that the Roman soldier didn't approach Jesus based on the cultural script of Rome's domination of Palestine. It's true. He never asked Jesus to do anything. But the reason he never asked Jesus for help is because he knew he wasn't worthy of it (Matt 8:8). More than that, he knew that Jesus didn't need to come to his house and lay hands on his servant (touch!) to heal him (v. 9). Like a soldier talking to another soldier, the centurion counted on Jesus recognizing what they had in common. The blunt tone, commands given; this is the way soldiers talk. Yes, the centurion was making huge assumptions, but it had nothing to do with Roman privilege or Jewish subservience. He was bolder than that! He not only presumed upon the mercy of Jesus—that he would be willing to help him—but especially the power of Jesus's command. "Just say the word, and my servant will be healed" (v. 8). When a powerful soldier issues commands, things get done.

At this point, Jesus no longer saw a centurion, a powerful soldier, an enemy of Israel. Instead, standing before him was a man who had a faith greater than any Jew (including his disciples, v. 10). This surprised him. Jesus expected to find great faith among Abraham's children. But a gentile, and a Roman soldier to boot? Overwhelmed by the man's faith, Jesus applied Jewish talk about the gathering of the diaspora on the last day to this man and other gentiles who would join in the messianic feast reserved for Israel (vv. 11–12). To be sure, Isaiah made predictions of gentile inclusion, that Assyrians and Egyptians would show up in Jerusalem to worship the Lord (Isa 19:18–25). But the language of gathering the sheep of Israel from the far reaches of the earth—from the east to the west—bringing them back to the promised land to enjoy the justice of God's reign on earth expressed a particularly *Jewish* hope (Isa 43:5–13; 49:1–25).[19] Jesus, however, expanded the ethnic borders of the vision to include gentiles like this Roman soldier.[20]

It's quite a daring move when you think about it. No longer an enemy of Israel destined for the wrath of God, Jesus claims a Roman soldier will sit down with the great heroes of Israel's faith (Abraham, Isaac, and Jacob) and dine at the heavenly banquet on earth because he had faith in the Messiah. The ultimate outsider becomes the ultimate insider. Even more, Jesus predicted that some of the insiders—"sons of the kingdom,"[21] his Jewish kinsmen?[22]—will

18. "An outsider who would entreat his favor must first acknowledge the privilege of Israel" (Keener, *Matthew*, 267).

19. So also Davies and Allison, *Matthew*, 2:27–28.

20. According to Keener, Jesus may have intended the association, but Matthew is the one who applied the eschatological gathering of the diaspora to the gentiles (*Matthew*, 269–70).

21. The NIV at 8:12 translates *huioi* as "subjects," which may unnecessarily imply imperial overtones, i.e., the "subjects" of the kingdom would be the Romans.

22. Luz, *Matthew*, 2:9. Could the "sons of the kingdom" refer to Herod's government?

be "thrown outside, into the darkness" on the last day (Matt 8:12). Therefore, the way Jesus saw it, gentile inclusion will mean Jewish exclusion, an idea Paul relied upon to explain the mysterious eschatology at work when God saves all nations (Rom 11:7–36). This isn't "replacement" eschatology where gentiles occupy the place of Israel in the kingdom. Rather, much like John the Baptist and the prophets before him (Matt 3:9; Isa 10:22–23; Hos 2:23), Jesus was warning his people that "not all who are descended from Israel are Israel" (to use Paul's phrase; Rom 9:6). Indeed, when it comes to the kingdom of heaven, Jesus believed God was prepared to reward faith wherever he found it, whether Jew or Roman. That's exactly what he did, telling the soldier, "Let it be done just as you believed it would." Then Matthew expectedly adds, "And his servant was healed at that moment" (Matt 8:13). Great faith, merciful reward. Powerful command, expected result. Enemy loved, kingdom come.

LIVE the Story

One of the purposes of this commentary series is to get us to see the power of narrative, trying to live the Gospel story as if it were the story of our lives (because it is!).[23] There are several ways to accomplish this purpose. We can transport ourselves back to New Testament times, making the quantum leap by projecting ourselves into the Gospel narrative, identifying with one of the characters. Or, we can try to bring the narrative wrapped in first-century clothes into the twenty-first century—a thought experiment where we imagine what the Gospel story would look like today. Sometimes these "road trips" into the biblical world are round trips, going back in time, packing our bags with the "souvenirs" we found wearing first-century spectacles—trying to live the story on their terms—then coming back to the reality of our world by unpacking what we learned and changing the way we live (what Dodd called "the bold and even perilous attempt to translate the whole into contemporary terms").[24] This approach may sound a little foreign to us since most Bible studies depend upon a more propositional approach. Read the narrative. Extract the moral of the story. Apply the principle to our lives. Yet immersing

23. Referring to the following pericope (8:23–27), Luz claims: "We can, indeed we must, put our own *experiences* in our story [the stilling of the storm] and be understood anew 'in' it. Only those who themselves are 'in the ship' can understand it correctly" (*Matthew*, 2:22 [emphasis his]).

24. C. H. Dodd, *The Present Task in New Testament Studies: An Inaugural Lecture Delivered in the Divinity School on Tuesday 2 June 1936* (Cambridge: Cambridge University Press, 1936), 40. "The ideal interpreter would be one who has entered into that strange first-century world, has felt its whole strangeness, has sojourned in it until he has lived himself into it, thinking and feeling as one of those to whom the Gospel first came; and who will then return into our world, and give the truth he has discerned a body out of the stuff of our own thought" (ibid., 40–41).

ourselves into the narrative world of a story we're reading (or watching) is a rather common experience. Think of what happens when we go to the movies. At first we're aware of our surroundings, perhaps even taking inventory of the crowd. ("Sure hope those children settle down when the film starts!") Once the lights go down and the flickering images appear on the screen, we are quickly transported to another time and place, living in the narrative world of the film, trying to find our place in the script, identifying with certain characters. We so embody the story that our palms get sweaty, our hearts fall in our chests, and we even jump out of our seats as if our emotions are somehow tied to the unfolding drama of the movie. Once the film is over, we carry the story with us, constantly thinking about why certain characters stay with us, why this or that plot twist continues to puzzle us, wondering what we would do given the same situation. That's the power of narrative. It should happen every time we read the Bible, especially the Gospels, because it is the story of our lives.

When I think about these three episodes in Matthew's Gospel—the leper, the centurion, and Peter's mother-in-law—I can't help but see myself and the people I love in the Gospel story. For example, my son has a mild, recurring skin problem, something he's had to deal with ever since college. Then I read the story of the leper, and it dawns on me, "My goodness. If we were living in New Testament times, Andrew would be banished from society, sent away from even his family, because of a mild rash that won't go away." Then I think of the separation, the pain of seeing someone you love treated like they are cursed by God, known only by the "disease" they carry, and my heart falls to the ground in despair. Today, certain people are treated like lepers, cursed by God, and I think about the pain of such rejection. Gays. Muslims. The mentally ill. The righteous may dismiss them as "unclean" to be avoided at all costs, but I can't help but think they are somebody's son or daughter. "Love your neighbor as yourself" takes on new meaning when I remember that my children are somebody's neighbors. I realize this is a touchy subject. I'm certainly not suggesting that gays are leprous or that Muslims will come to us asking to be made clean or that the mentally ill must be "healed" before they can serve the Lord. (Hardly.) Yet sometimes we treat them like they're infectious, as if the only right thing for holy people to do is keep them away from us. But that's not the Jesus way. Mercy is supposed to trump judgment when we love our neighbors. The holiness of love is supposed to be contagious in the kingdom of God. Jesus proved it when he touched the man.

I also see my wife in the story of the women healed of fever. The episode doesn't get much attention in Matthew's Gospel, and Peter's mother-in-law probably would have wanted it that way. She's the kind of person who stands in the background, out of the limelight, not wanting to bother anyone. She didn't even ask Jesus for help. But Jesus sees. He knows. He recognizes those who would rather serve than be served. So I see Jesus, slight grin spreading across his face, taking in the sight of the woman who jumps at the chance to serve her Lord, and that's when I think about my sweet wife, Sheri. Throughout our entire life together, countless times I've seen her jump at the chance to join in the behind-the-scenes work that's required to serve others. She can't stand the limelight. She hates it when anyone tries to recognize her. But her gratitude to the Lord is easily seen when she loves her neighbor as herself.

I see reflections of our two daughters, Emma and Grace, in other Gospel stories as well. But the hardest part is to see myself in the Gospel story. One doesn't want to be pretentious and identify with Jesus or to be associated with his opponents, the Pharisees. Yet there are times when I catch a glimpse of my story in light of the Gospel. For example, like most white men I identify with the privileged position of the Roman centurion. Especially in Baptist life where men still run everything, there's a seductive power in believing you've been given a divine birthright of authority. Indeed, some of us might even act like the Lord is there to serve us, to maintain our powerful positions. That's why I'm particularly drawn to the part of the story when the soldier said, "Lord, I do not deserve to have you come under my roof" (Matt 8:8). No doubt, this Roman soldier was a man who had blood on his hands. Yet he knows the only one who can help him is this man of mercy—a man who will have blood on his hands because of people like him, Roman soldiers, and people like me. Thinking about my past, even though I've never drawn a sword to kill my enemy, I realize I have blood on my hands too: hateful words, spiteful revenge, shameful derision, cutting sarcasm. So, inspired by the faith of a Roman centurion, I come to Jesus, talking like a soldier, needy like a leper: "I'm not worthy for you to come to my house. I don't deserve anything you've done for me. All I know is that whenever you give the word, I am whole again. Say the word, Lord. I know you are willing. Make me clean."

And he does.

Thank God for the mercy of Christ that heals a leprous heart and restores a murderous soul like mine.

Now, Lord, let us follow you down the mountain, loving our neighbors *and* our enemies just as you loved us: a leper, a woman, and a Roman soldier.

CHAPTER 11

Matthew 8:18–34

LISTEN to the Story

[18]When Jesus saw the crowd around him, he gave orders to cross to the
other side of the lake. [19]Then a teacher of the law came to him and said,
"Teacher, I will follow you wherever you go."

[20]Jesus replied, "Foxes have dens and birds have nests, but the Son of
Man has no place to lay his head."

[21]Another disciple said to him, "Lord, first let me go and bury my
father."

[22]But Jesus told him, "Follow me, and let the dead bury their own dead."

[23]Then he got into the boat and his disciples followed him. [24]Suddenly
a furious storm came up on the lake, so that the waves swept over the boat.
But Jesus was sleeping. [25]The disciples went and woke him, saying, "Lord,
save us! We're going to drown!"

[26]He replied, "You of little faith, why are you so afraid?" Then he got
up and rebuked the winds and the waves, and it was completely calm.

[27]The men were amazed and asked, "What kind of man is this? Even
the winds and the waves obey him!"

[28]When he arrived at the other side in the region of the Gadarenes,
two demon-possessed men coming from the tombs met him. They were
so violent that no one could pass that way. [29]"What do you want with us,
Son of God?" they shouted. "Have you come here to torture us before the
appointed time?"

[30]Some distance from them a large herd of pigs was feeding. [31]The
demons begged Jesus, "If you drive us out, send us into the herd of pigs."

[32]He said to them, "Go!" So they came out and went into the pigs,
and the whole herd rushed down the steep bank into the lake and died
in the water. [33]Those tending the pigs ran off, went into the town and
reported all this, including what had happened to the demon-possessed
men. [34]Then the whole town went out to meet Jesus. And when they saw
him, they pleaded with him to leave their region.

Listening to the Text in the Story: Exodus 20:12; Leviticus 21:1–4, 11–12; 1 Kings 19:19–21; Job 26:10–12; 38:8–11; Psalms 65:5–8; 89:9–10; 107:23–30; Proverbs 1:20–33; Isaiah 51:9–11, 15; Jeremiah 16:5–7; Ezekiel 24:15–24; Jonah 1:4–16.

The first time Jesus saw the crowds, he ascended a mountain and delivered his famous sermon (5:1). This time he wanted to get away from them, so he "gave orders to cross to the other side of the lake" (8:18). Had the large mass of people become a nuisance, keeping him and his disciples awake all night (v. 16)? Or, did it have more to do with getting the disciples alone so he could teach them? Getting in a boat to cross the Sea of Galilee would accomplish both purposes, but perhaps his reason for traveling to the other side of the lake had more to do with the destination. This may have been the second time Jesus left Israel and traveled to gentile territory (Matt 2:14; 8:28).[1] Inspired by the crowds, did Jesus decide to take his "show on the road," to reach out to gentiles in order to extend his messianic mission "to all the nations" (Isa 49:6)?[2] Whatever the reason, Matthew puts together a sequence of stories[3] that teach two lessons: the authority of Jesus and the cost of discipleship.[4]

EXPLAIN the Story

Ever since Günther Bornkamm's study of the stilling of the storm,[5] scholars have argued that Matthew's primary purpose in placing this story so early in his Gospel (compared to Mark and Luke) was to remind the church about the cost of discipleship.[6] The conversation between Jesus and two potential disciples (Matt 8:18–22) sets up the episode as a lesson in faith—what it means to follow Jesus into the boat, a prophetic image "of the little ship of the

1. That Jesus traveled to *gentile* territory is more evident in Mark's version (Mark 5:1, 20).

2. Bruce Chilton, *Rabbi Jesus: An Intimate Biography* (New York: Doubleday, 2000), 168–73. Chilton thinks Jesus was inspired by the centurion to cast about gentile territory to find support for his kingdom that would oppose Herod Antipas.

3. The episodes of stilling the storm and healing the Gadarene demoniac(s) (as well as the account of the wanna-be disciples in Luke) appear much later in Mark (4:35–5:20) and Luke (8:22–39; 9:57–60), one of two places where Matthew deviates from Synoptic chronology and rearranges the material to tell his own story (see also Matt 9:18–11:30).

4. France, *Matthew*, 334–35.

5. Günther Bornkamm, Gerhard Barth, Heinz Joachim Held, *Tradition and Interpretation in Matthew*, trans. Percy Scott (London: SCM, 1963), 52–57. Tertullian was the first to read this story ecclesiologically (*Baptism* 12), referenced by Davies and Allison, *Matthew*, 2:69. See also Luz for a brief history of interpretation (*Matthew*, 2:21).

6. Luz, *Matthew*, 2:21–22.

Church."[7] The sequence of events according to Matthew's version is especially revealing. Where Mark and Luke have Jesus still the storm *before* he gives the lesson on faith (Mark 4:39–40; Luke 8:24–25), Matthew pictures Jesus reprimanding his disciples for their "little faith" while the storm rages (Matt 8:26). It's as if Jesus were speaking directly to Matthew's persecuted community, asking them, "Why are you so afraid?" even as they cry out in prayer, "Lord, save us!"—when they should have known that Jesus would bring them safely through the storm to the other side. As long as Jesus is in the boat with them, everything will be alright.

Some scholars think Bornkamm's reading goes too far because he treats the miracle like an allegory, making the disciples the center of the story. Instead, the focus of Matthew's narrative is christological.[8] The function of these miracle stories was to confirm the identity of Jesus. Only God has authority over the wind and the sea (Job 26:10–12; 38:8–11; Ps 65:5–8; 89:9–10; 107:23–30). Therefore, Jesus's power over nature reveals his authority as God, something Matthew has claimed from the beginning with his narration of Christ's miraculous birth, his heavenly baptism and the approving divine voice, and his authoritative teaching. Once the storm is over, the disciples ask, "What kind of man is this?"—a question they will answer for themselves the next time they are in a boat fighting the wind and the waves (14:22–33): "Truly you are the Son of God." The purpose of these two boat stories, therefore, was to reveal the identity of the Christ, the Son of God. Even the exorcism of the Gadarene demoniac—especially when compared to Mark's version (Mark 5:1–20)—moves the attention of the reader away from the beneficiary to the wonder-working power of Jesus the Messiah (Matt 8:28–34; notice how the fate of the formerly demon-possessed men is ignored in Matthew's version). These stories are about Jesus: who he is and what he came to do.

Yet, one can see how this sequence (would-be disciples, stilling of the storm, exorcism of the Gadarene demoniacs) in Matthew's Gospel serves both purposes: a lesson on discipleship and the revealing of the divine authority of Jesus. In fact, these two miracles (stilling of the storm and casting out demons) may illustrate what Jesus meant when he said, "The Son of Man has no place to lay his head" (v. 20), and, "Let the dead bury their own dead" (v. 22). Jesus was asleep in the boat before he calmed the storm (v. 24). And, the Gadarene demoniacs lived with dead people (v. 28). In other words, although we see the authority of Jesus when he calmed the storm, sacrificing for the kingdom

7. Bornkamm, *Tradition and Interpretation in Matthew*, 55.

8. Blomberg, *Matthew*, 145, 150; Keener, *Matthew*, 279.

is also emphasized. Even Jesus, the great "Son of Man" (Dan 7:13–14),[9] was unable to grab a little shut-eye while crossing the lake. Then, when they arrived on the other side, two demoniacs who lived in a cemetery tried to block Jesus and his entourage from traveling down the road. Once Jesus disposed of the menaces (v. 32), rather than welcoming him with gratitude the locals shooed him away (v. 34). So, Jesus left (9:1), which may explain what he meant by the saying, "let the dead bury their own dead." Therefore, what we have here is the creative genius of Matthew's narrative technique, pairing sayings of Jesus with stories that flesh out his teaching—a device other Gospel writers used as well.[10] Indeed, these stories belong together[11] because our discipleship (ecclesiology) depends upon his lordship (Christology).

The Scribe Who Wanted to Follow Jesus

We're so used to this story, we're no longer surprised by it—but we should be. For a teacher of the law to say he wants to be a disciple is amazing, given what Jesus said about scribes during the Sermon on the Mount. As far as Jesus was concerned, the scribes weren't even close to entering the kingdom of heaven, which would be the opposite of what most people would think. After all, a scribe was a man who not only made a living at producing the Scriptures—a holy occupation—but he was considered an expert because he spent so much time studying them. So, for a scribe to come to Jesus and say, "I will follow you wherever you go" (Matt 8:19), was a tremendous act of humility. Essentially, he agreed with Jesus. Even as a scribe, he knew the only way he could participate in the heaven-coming-to-earth kingdom was to follow Jesus. That should make him the ideal disciple, humble and willing to go wherever Jesus goes, which makes Jesus's response even more astonishing. To our way of thinking, Jesus should have said, "Fantastic! I've been looking for men like you, the meek who are ready to inherit the land by following me. Welcome him, my brothers. This is a man after God's heart." But rather than encourage the scribe, Jesus appears to offer a warning: "Do you really know what you're getting into? Following me will mean many sleepless nights. You better count the cost before you get into the boat." Jesus seems to temper the man's zeal with a reality check:[12] even

---

9. The significance of Jesus's self-designation, "Son of Man," continues to inspire debate. For a helpful summary of the issues, see Darrell L. Bock, "Son of Man," *DJG* 894–900.

10. For example, notice how Luke fleshes out the two characters of Jesus's parable, the Pharisee and the tax collector (Luke 18:9–14) in the following episodes of the rich ruler (vv. 18–24) and Zacchaeus (19:1–10); see Rodney Reeves, *A Genuine Faith: How to Follow Jesus Today* (Grand Rapids: Baker, 2005), 140–44.

11. Garland, *Reading Matthew*, 98.

12. Most commentators find fault with the scribe, either for taking the wrong approach (calling Jesus "teacher" and trying to become his disciple when Jesus is the one who chooses his disciples [Davies and Allison, *Matthew*, 2:41; Luz, *Matthew*, 2:17]) or for having a flawed character (being

the Son of Man has no place to call home.[13] We even hear Jesus offer the discouraging word in somber tones, picturing a grim look on his face when he says, "Foxes have dens and birds have nests, but the Son of Man has no place to lay his head" (v. 20). Then, in our mind's eye we see the smile wiped off the face of this naive, overly enthusiastic scribe as he walks away, unwilling to commit to a life of sacrifice.

Yet nowhere in the story are we told whether the scribe ended up following Jesus. Matthew leaves it open-ended. *We* assume he didn't follow Jesus, which may say more about us than it does about the scribe. For example, why would we think that Jesus had a serious look on his face, as if he were issuing a grim warning: "Foxes have holes, birds have nests. . . ." What if Jesus had a big smile on his face because he was offering a declaration of *freedom*, as if following him would mean you'll never be anxious about anything—especially where you bed down for the night (Matt 6:25–34)?[14] Since each day has enough trouble of its own, counting on the hospitality of God might be the best way to live in a world that is heaven sent but hell possessed. Indeed, the fact that Jesus found rest in a boat during a storm proves that faith in a Father who knows how to give good gifts to his children is all that a disciple needs. If God takes care of foxes and birds, how much more will he take of Jesus and his disciples, even those of *little* faith? Of course, those of us who have *much* have a lot to lose, which is why we hear a somber tone in Jesus's words and believe the scribe didn't follow Jesus. It also may explain why we think that the main point of the stilling of the storm—what it costs us to follow Jesus—is obvious. It's no wonder, then, as we join the disciples and follow Jesus, that we carry his words into the boat like a prison sentence: "Foxes have holes, birds have nests. . . ." Once the storm kicks up, and our life is in peril ("who can sleep at a time like this?"), we can't help but look around at our shipmates and wonder, "Where's the scribe?" Maybe we need a mirror to see him.

Isn't it a little aggravating to be roused from a restful sleep, especially when people wake you up at the *wrong time* for no good reason? That's why I hear a little frustration—perhaps even anger?—in Jesus's voice when he said, "You of little faith, why are you so afraid?" (8:26). Really, that translation calms it down a bit. What Jesus said (according to Matthew's Greek translation of Jesus's Aramaic words) was, "Why are you acting like *cowards*, 'Littlefaith'?"

---

overly ambitious; "Eagerness that cloaks ambition is no virtue in disciples" [Garland, *Reading Matthew*, 99]). Yet neither explanation squares with Matthew's Gospel; for example, Jesus seems to invite all comers (11:28–30), and Peter's impetuous behavior didn't disqualify him (14:28–31).

13. Some scholars hear an allusion to Wisdom wandering the earth, trying to find a home among God's people (Prov 1:20–33).

14. This would make his disciples even more dependent upon others than the Levites (Keener, *Matthew*, 274).

Like a big brother scolding his little brothers, Jesus called them out, using the nickname he gave them—one word in Greek—*oligopistoi*, "little faith." (Isn't that what all big brothers do? "Hey squirt, get over here"). One cannot help but wonder, were the disciples confused when Jesus scolded them? What if the disciples had never awakened Jesus? Would the storm have passed without Jesus doing anything about it? Or, were they supposed to find the "Jonah" among them ("Where is that scribe?") and throw him overboard (Jonah 1:4–16)? Why did they wake Jesus up? What did they expect him to do about it? It wasn't to calm the storm; that took them by surprise (Matt 8:27). Several of them were fishermen. They had experienced weather like this many times. The topography of the lake—situated several feet below sea level, with mountains and deep valleys surrounding it, creating natural wind tunnels that would wreak havoc—made boaters vulnerable to sudden storms.[15] They knew what to do (drop sails, steer the vessel into the wind); surely they'd weathered storms like this before. So, perhaps it wasn't the fierce winds or the vicious waves that alarmed them. Perhaps what really bothered them in the middle of this terrible storm was that Jesus acted as if he were completely oblivious to their plight. "Look at him. He's sleeping like he doesn't have a care in the world."

What did Jesus expect of his disciples? To ride out the storm and let him sleep? Why did he chastise them for their cowardice, for living up to their moniker, "Littlefaith"? Surely he didn't expect them to join him, did he? Imagine the absurdity of that scenario. Peter, taking in the site of the waves and Jesus fast asleep, turns to his shipmates and says, "We're supposed to be his followers, right? Apparently, it's time to take a nap. I think I'll curl up over there and catch a few zzzzzz's." Hardly. Everyone knows it's nearly impossible to sleep when you fear for your life. I think Jesus's agitation had more to do with what they said. Roused from a sound sleep, the first thing he heard was: "Lord. Save! We are *perishing* [*apollumetha*]" (a more literal translation of v. 25). That was an exaggeration. They weren't dying. In trouble? Yes. Needing help? Apparently so, especially if this was one of the worst storms they had ever seen. Coupled with the fact that the waters were the primordial abode of malevolent powers, like Leviathan (Job 3:8; Ps 104:25–26), whom only the Lord could tame (Job 41:1; Isa 27:1), and it's no wonder these fishermen quickly turned into cowards: "When it [Leviathan] rises up, the mighty are terrified; they retreat before its thrashing" (Job 41:25).[16] But if you're in a boat while Leviathan is thrashing about, there is no retreat. To the disciples, then, the malevolent powers attacking them while Jesus slept spelled certain doom.

15. Keener, *Matthew*, 278.

16. Davies and Allison, *Matthew*, 2:74–75; Keener, *Matthew*, 279–80.

But in Matthew 7:13 Jesus had already told them that his way wasn't the path that leads to "destruction" (*apōleia*, the noun form of the verb *apollymi* from which comes *apollumetha* in 8:25). Therefore, to say "we are perishing" was the same as saying "the way of Jesus leads to destruction." That couldn't be right because Jesus had promised them that, despite entering the "troubled" gate, his way would lead to life (7:14). This is why Jesus was frustrated by their "little faith."[17] They should have known better. They're following a man who can "rebuke" the demonized wind and sea (*epitimaō*; the same word is used when Jesus "rebukes" the demon possessing a boy; see 17:18). But, only *God* can tame Leviathan (Job 41:1–42:2). So, "What kind of *man* is this?" (Matt 8:27, emphasis added). Indeed. They hadn't figured it out yet, but they will—especially the next time they get into a boat and there's tough sailing (see 14:22–33).

The Disciple Who Wanted to Obey the Law

One of the "top ten" commandments was, "Honor your father and your mother, so that you may live long in the land the Lord your God is giving you" (Exod 20:12)—a commandment Jesus cited when he challenged the hypocrisy of the scribes and the Pharisees (Matt 15:3–9). One of the most important ways a son would honor his father was to ensure his father received a proper burial when he died. Unlike the Romans who marked graves with memorials to honor the deceased, the Jews took other measures to honor their loved ones. Since graves were unclean, to have a memorial stone erected at the place of interment inviting people to visit the deceased would be dishonorable to the Jewish people. Instead, they focused on the funeral itself. The length of mourning and the number of lamenters would reveal the level of honor of the deceased *and his family*. In other words, where the size of the monument revealed the importance of the family of the deceased in Roman society, the size of the funeral reflected the honorable standing of the Jewish family burying their dead. The longer the period of mourning (most families grieved the dead for a week by refusing food, not bathing, and occasionally visiting the burial site; kings were mourned for a month) and the greater number of professional lamenters and members of the community mourning the dead, the more the family was honored. Typically, the deceased would be cleaned, anointed with spices, wrapped in cloth, and then laid in the house for at least a day. Then, professional mourners (according to the Mishnah the poor were

17. Clement of Alexandria wrote, "The exclamation 'save us' is commendable, since it shows faith. But to say 'we are perishing' brings a charge of littleness of faith against those who were in deep distress" (Simonetti, *Matthew 1–13*, 169).

to have at least two flute players and one wailing woman)[18] would lead the family, those carrying the bier, and the long line of mourners to the burial site. Wealthier families used rock-hewn rooms to house the corpse until the flesh rotted off the skeleton. Then the bones of the deceased would be collected, placed in a bone box (ossuary), and interred in the family tomb. Those of modest means either buried the body in the ground or interred the corpse in caves.[19] To be sure, burial practices revealed the honorable reputation of the family as much as the deceased.

Consequently, when one of the disciples asked for permission to bury his father before they crossed the lake (Matt 8:21; How long will they be gone? Who knows?), Jesus offered a startling reply, "Follow me, and let the dead bury their own dead" (v. 22). We don't know the circumstances prompting the son's request. Had his father just died? Or, was his family still in the process of grieving the death of his father? Or, perhaps the time had come to move his father's bones to the family tomb. Some question whether the father was dead; perhaps he was deathly ill. Yet if that were the case, one would have to wonder: What was the son doing out on the road, some distance away from his home, while his father was near death? (The same question could be asked even if his father had recently died.) That's why some commentators suggest the man's father was very much alive. In other words, the disciple was asking Jesus for a temporary reprieve from following him, sanctioned by his responsibility to ensure the honor of his father, burying him properly when the time came, perhaps many years later. Yet if that were the case, this disciple would be making a rather audacious request, for the same obligation would have applied to several of Jesus's disciples whose fathers were still alive—like James and John (4:21). The circumstances surrounding the son's request determine how we read Jesus's response. Either Jesus was indifferent to the grief of one of his disciples, thereby making his demand "follow me" even more scandalous. Or this disciple was trying to weasel his way out of following Jesus across the lake—to unknown territory—by using the law as an excuse.

As it was with the scribe, so it is with this disciple. We know neither the motives of the son nor the result of his encounter with Jesus. Once again, Matthew leaves it to the reader to puzzle over Jesus's words. What did Jesus mean, "let the dead bury their own dead"? Those who think the father was already dead try to find reasons why Jesus would make such a calloused, insensitive demand of a disciple who simply wanted to honor his father just as the law required. For example, perhaps Jesus was following the precedent

18. See m. Ketubbot 4:4.

19. See Magness, *Stone*, 145–80, for discussion of first-century Jewish burial practices of lower classes compared to the elite.

established by the prophets Elijah (1 Kgs 19:19–21), Jeremiah (Jer 16:5–7), or Ezekiel (Ezek 24:15–24). Elisha asked permission to say goodbye to his family when Elijah called him to be his disciple. When Elijah consented, Elisha went home and "burned his bridges": he torched his farming equipment, slaughtered his team of oxen, gave away all the meat, and followed after Elijah. So, if someone greater than Elijah is here, then Jesus was expecting his disciple to do more—not only to turn his back on his work but even on his family (see Matt 12:46–50). Following Jesus takes precedence over everything. Yet what about the law's requirement to honor your father? Perhaps Jesus took a lesson from Jeremiah when God told him, "Do not enter a house where there is a funeral meal; do not go to mourn or show sympathy, because I have withdrawn my blessing, my love and my pity from this people" (Jer 16:5). If Jesus came to reverse the curse and restore God's blessing, then Jeremiah's prophetic word would be especially relevant in light of the son's request. Or perhaps Jesus was calling up the example of Ezekiel, who was told by God not to grieve over his soon-to-be-dead wife to teach a lesson to Israel, who refused to grieve over their sin (Ezek 24:15–27). In this case, Ezekiel's situation would parallel the circumstances of the son whose father hadn't died but was near death due to age or sickness. Maybe Jesus was implying that his disciples were the new priests (Lev 21:11) or a new kind of Nazirite (Num 6:6).[20] Whatever the case, Jesus was talking like a prophet when he said, "Let the dead bury their own dead," essentially claiming that the gravity of the moment—the kingdom is here!—trumped all other obligations, including the family.[21] Of course, if the disciple simply didn't want to leave the area (the very opposite of the scribe's willingness to follow Jesus wherever he went) and was using the law to justify his decision, then Jesus saw through the ruse. In that case, we wouldn't find Jesus's demand the least bit offensive, for every disciple must "count the cost" of following him.

But that still doesn't explain the enigmatic phrase, "let the *dead* bury their own dead." Who are "the dead"? Those who don't follow Jesus? If so, does that mean those who refuse to follow Jesus are already "spiritually" dead, that their relationship with the God of Israel is null and void? Or, was Jesus claiming that those who don't follow him have a death wish, that they are destined to die without hope, without honor, without reward? They may be still breathing, but in the eschatological scheme of things, they're already dead like the corpses they prepare for burial. In other words, was Jesus making a spiritual or theological claim, offering a commentary on their devotion or destiny? According to Matthew, the following story about the Gadarene

20. Davies and Allison, *Matthew*, 2:55–58.

21. Hengel, *Charismatic Leader*, 8–15.

demoniacs (Matt 8:28–34) should help us identify the "the dead" who "bury their own dead."

"Is it time yet?" That's what the demonized men wanted to know when they ran out of the tombs and blocked Jesus from coming any further (v. 29). This is where we need to be careful and not allow Mark's version of the same story to color our interpretation—a tall order because Mark's story (Mark 5:1–20) is certainly more colorful than Matthew's account. The location, the number of demoniacs, the self-mutilation, the nakedness, the superhuman strength, the "legion" of demons, the man restored, clothed, and "in his right mind," his desire to follow Jesus, the report of his witness throughout the Decapolis—these details reveal a different emphasis for each Gospel. Whether Gadara or Gerasa, both Matthew and Mark have Jesus and his disciples coming to gentile territory on the southeast side of the Sea of Galilee. In Mark's version, the salvation of the demonized man means that Jesus's first attempt to spread the gospel beyond the borders of Israel was successful. But unlike Mark, Matthew's account "is not a story about mission but about power."[22] In Matthew's version, we don't get to see the formerly demonized men sitting fully clothed, in their right mind, begging to follow Jesus. Instead, Matthew focuses our attention on the battle between Jesus and the evil powers, provoking the question: Is it time for God's end-of-the-world power to be unleashed on the devil and his minions?

Our answer depends on how we interpret the scenario of Jesus granting the request of the demons to enter the pigs, resulting in their destruction (Matt 8:30–33). Notice that it wasn't Jesus's idea to make "deviled ham" that day. *They* came up with the plan. Therefore, when Jesus commanded them, "Go!" was he giving them a reprieve, sparing their destruction because it wasn't time yet?[23] Or, was Jesus allowing them to choose their own form of "torture" (to be cast into swine) before they were destroyed (drowned in the lake) because the time had come for their judgment?[24] Whether we can sort out the fate of the demons after the pigs died doesn't really matter to Matthew. For him the point of the story is this: it's time. Time for the kingdom of heaven to invade earth. Time for evil to relinquish its death grip on God's creation. Time for disciples to follow Jesus to the ends of the earth, to the gates of hell, to the end of the world: "If it is by the Spirit of God that I drive out demons, then the kingdom of God has come upon you" (12:28). Indeed, what Matthew has done is provide a commentary for his readers, explaining what Jesus meant, that it was time: "Follow me, let the dead bury their own dead" (8:22). However, the

22. France, *Matthew*, 343.
23. Turner, *Matthew*, 246–47.
24. Luz, *Matthew*, 2:25.

episode of his encounter with the Gadarene demoniacs ends with a chilling indictment of those who can't tell time: "Then the whole town went out to meet Jesus. And when they saw him, they pleaded with him to leave their region" (v. 34). So, he did (9:1). Why did they send him away? Were they angry with him for killing their swine? "No surprise that a Jewish man would kill our pigs." Or, did his power scare them? Persons acquainted with the demonic were easily dismissed as weirdos.[25] Yet didn't they realize that they sent away the only man who could give them life, essentially writing their own death sentence? How sad is that? Just as sad as a disciple who decides to leave Jesus and join a burial society, a people whose only purpose is their dead-end destiny: to bury the dead, marking time until they all die.

LIVE the Story

"And they all lived happily ever after." We are a people who love closure, especially stories that end well. We know life goes on and that troubles will come our way, but when the stories we read or the films we watch *end* with the loose *ends* tied up, it makes us feel better about the future. Even if the narrative takes a dark turn and "they don't live happily ever after," as long as we know what happened in the end we are satisfied. Sure, there can be a few questions that linger, the trajectory of a plotline that is hard to predict with certainty. (No wonder we gather for coffee afterwards, each one playing the prophet, enjoying the banter of sorting out "what happens next.") But stories that leave us hanging on the most important questions, "Did she survive? Did he return? Did they ever find what they were looking for? Was that really the end of the world?"—in essence, "What's the point?"—well, most of us walk away from those stories shaking our heads, frustrated by the open-endedness of that world. The postfilm chorus, "What was that?" or "I don't get it," compels many of us to return to the predictable world of blockbuster films where everything is tidied up for viewers who crave safe and sound. If we can't find meaning in the meantime, we'd better find it in the end.

If Matthew's Gospel were a film, it would probably be a blockbuster. In the end, we know what happens to the main characters; the "villains" lose, the hero overcomes the catastrophe, and the plot finds resolution. There's even a mountaintop scene to finish the film: the resurrected Messiah passes the torch of his work to his faithful followers, predicting their success that they will teach "everything I have commanded you," even promising he would be with them "to the very end of the age" (Matt 28:16–20). Music swells.

25. Malina and Rohrbaugh, *Synoptic Gospels*, 80.

Camera takes video from the heavens, giving a bird's-eye view of Jesus and the disciples. Screen goes black. "The End." Credits roll. As they file out of the auditorium, the only question left for the audience to figure out would be, "When will Jesus come back?" The postfilm discussion would reveal that practically all of the loose ends were gathered up, woven into a comfortable quilt with an impressive pattern. Everyone can see the point of this film. Even some of the questions that surfaced for those who read the book would have been answered. What was the expression on Jesus's face when he said, "Foxes have holes, birds have nests. . ."? What was his tone of voice when he said, "Follow me, and let the dead bury their own dead"? The director would have sorted out most of the details for us. We would know whether the scribe followed Jesus. ("Was he in the boat scene?") We would understand the circumstances surrounding the son's request to bury his father. The director may have even identified the anonymous disciple for us: "Wasn't that James or John who asked Jesus if they could go home and bury Zebedee? It sure looked like one of them. Remember, they both had those funky beards." The places where Matthew left episodes open-ended would be tidied up, leaving little to our imaginations.

But, I must say, I typically don't enjoy blockbuster films. Instead, I prefer movies that make you puzzle over *everything*, like the significance of *all* characters (not just the lead actors), the purpose of a tortured plot, trying to make sense of the vagaries of an unresolved narrative (like Terrence Malick's *The Tree of Life* or Richard Linklater's *Boyhood*). These films don't try to answer every question or solve every problem. Closure isn't their purpose. Instead, they leave many loose and frayed ends lying around for you to figure out, just like life. So, when I come into Matthew's narrative world and find a loose end here and there, I relish the moment—a gift from this brilliant Gospel writer—as if it were an invitation to ponder things unsettled, just like life. Perhaps we're not supposed to know whether the scribe followed Jesus.[26] There are people in my life who I want to believe are following him, but I don't know for certain. Are they in the boat with us? And what about me? I made a vow to follow Jesus wherever he would take me, and yet I have a place to lay my head at night—just like a fox. Is that why I can't find any sleep when the storms of life pound away at my houseboat, when waves of despair threaten to wash over me? I'll admit it: sometimes I am a coward. I fear worst-case scenarios, perhaps even exaggerating the peril of the moment. I know I'll feel much better once the storm passes. Throughout the sleepless night, I keep repeating to myself, "As long as Jesus is in the boat with me, everything will be alright." But what

26. I marvel over how nearly every commentator feels obliged to settle the issue; most think neither the scribe nor the disciple ended up following Jesus.

about those I love? Are we in the same boat? Are we all going to make it safely to the other side? I need to know. But Jesus says, "Follow me, and let the dead bury their own dead." That sounds rather harsh. I'm not sure I can do that. Does it have to be that way? "Lord, I don't think I can walk away from them. But I still want to follow you."

Tell me, Matthew. Am I that scribe? Does Jesus call me "Littlefaith"? Am I following him?

Sometimes I wish there was a director who would cast the film of Matthew's Gospel so that I wouldn't have to wonder about the part I play in the life story of Jesus the Messiah. Then again, for those of us who prefer the book anyway—relishing the open-endedness of life despite all the uncertainty—maybe we're supposed to puzzle over these things. I realize, of course, that most of the time many of us search the Scriptures, looking for answers to life's most important questions: Who am I? Why am I here? What am I supposed to do? Certainly, when we read the Bible—especially the Gospels—we find the answer to all three questions: we are disciples of Jesus Christ. But the longer I follow him, the more I question what it means to be his disciple, especially when he leads us into the ship of faith to battle the storms of doubt.

It wasn't like that in the beginning, when I found certainty in the simplicity of the gospel: believe in Jesus and you will be saved. I used to sing with naive gusto: "Wherever he leads I'll go." And when I first followed him into the lifeboat, it seemed like we were headed for smooth sailing—so calm even Jesus could take a nap. Then the first storm hit, and I wondered why it had to be so hard. I kept expecting the Lord of the storm to make things better. But it only got worse. It was my first pastorate, and several members hated me from the start. In the middle of the tempest, as the waves of doubt washed over me, I questioned God. "Why have you led me here? What did I do to deserve this?" No relief. The storm continued to rage. I dropped sails and started to row, trying to win over the people who despised me so. That only made things worse. "What's going on here? Why are you letting this happen? I followed you to this place, and this is what I get?" Finally, in desperation I found myself constantly repeating (for weeks!) the disciples' prayer: "Lord, save me! I'm dying." And all I got from him was, "Little faith, why are you so afraid?"

My reply was, "I'm afraid you've forgotten about me. I'm afraid it will never get better. I'm afraid I made a mistake. I'm afraid despair will overwhelm me. I'm afraid I won't make it to the other side." Then it dawned on me in the middle of the storm, with the oppressive waves beating against the ship of my faith: at least I know I'm in the boat. How else could I explain the stormy sea? And, if I'm here, then he's here too—even though at times it seems like he's asleep.

CHAPTER 12

Matthew 9:1–17

LISTEN to the Story

1Jesus stepped into a boat, crossed over and came to his own town.
2Some men brought to him a paralyzed man, lying on a mat. When Jesus
saw their faith, he said to the man, "Take heart, son; your sins are forgiven."
3At this, some of the teachers of the law said to themselves, "This
fellow is blaspheming!"
4Knowing their thoughts, Jesus said, "Why do you entertain evil
thoughts in your hearts? 5Which is easier: to say, 'Your sins are forgiven,'
or to say, 'Get up and walk'? 6But I want you to know that the Son of
Man has authority on earth to forgive sins." So he said to the paralyzed
man, "Get up, take your mat and go home." 7Then the man got up and
went home. 8When the crowd saw this, they were filled with awe; and they
praised God, who had given such authority to man.
9As Jesus went on from there, he saw a man named Matthew sitting
at the tax collector's booth. "Follow me," he told him, and Matthew got
up and followed him.
10While Jesus was having dinner at Matthew's house, many tax col-
lectors and sinners came and ate with him and his disciples. 11When the
Pharisees saw this, they asked his disciples, "Why does your teacher eat
with tax collectors and sinners?"
12On hearing this, Jesus said, "It is not the healthy who need a doctor,
but the sick. 13But go and learn what this means: 'I desire mercy, not
sacrifice.' For I have not come to call the righteous, but sinners."
14Then John's disciples came and asked him, "How is it that we and
the Pharisees fast often, but your disciples do not fast?"
15Jesus answered, "How can the guests of the bridegroom mourn while
he is with them? The time will come when the bridegroom will be taken
from them; then they will fast.
16"No one sews a patch of unshrunk cloth on an old garment, for the
patch will pull away from the garment, making the tear worse. 17Neither

do people pour new wine into old wineskins. If they do, the skins will burst; the wine will run out and the wineskins will be ruined. No, they pour new wine into new wineskins, and both are preserved."

Listening to the Text in the Story: Leviticus 26:14–33; Deuteronomy 28:15–68; 2 Samuel 12:11–23; 2 Chronicles 21:12–19; Psalm 26:4–6; Isaiah 1:4–18; 43:25; 58:3–7; 62:4–5; Daniel 7:13–14; Hosea 6:1–6; Amos 5:21–27; Micah 6:6–8.

Sin is a serious problem. Murder. Hatred. Violence. Envy. Jealousy. Strife. Bigotry. Idolatry. Adultery. Lust. Theft. Deceit. Abuse. Coveting. Apathy. Complacency. Arrogance. Conceit. Greed. Extortion. Bribery. Slander. Rape. Laziness. Drunkenness. Promiscuity. Fornication. Selfishness. Sin is pervasive, a violation of everything that is sacred. Therefore, sin has a devastating effect on everyone. (Think of all the destruction we endure in the world every day and imagine how much of it would be gone if there were no human sin.) So, God gave the Torah to Israel to deal with the problem of sin and fulfill his intentions for all creation. In addition to the covenant promises he made to Israel, God gave commandments to guide his people—laws not only telling them what to do to avoid sin but also what to do in response to sin. In other words, the law wasn't just a list of commandments to keep Israel from sinning; embedded in the law was a complex Levitical system to deal with the aftermath of sin—not only requiring sacrifices offered to God in the tabernacle/temple to restore holiness but also acts of restitution to one another to effect justice. The law was God's gift to his people, sacred countermeasures to enable Israel to overcome sin, establish justice, and realize the Lord's purpose for them and the whole world.

When you read the Torah—especially Leviticus, the handbook for Levites—you can't help but get the impression that God was thorough about what it takes to deal with the problem of sin. There are lots of details; one must follow the rules carefully. Priests (sons of Aaron, no less) bring coals from the wrong fire, and boom, they're killed by God (Lev 10:1–2). When it comes to seeking God's forgiveness, you better do things right. Moreover, God seems to cover every contingency; different sins require different sacrifices and acts of restitution. For example, if a man commits adultery, then both he and his neighbor's wife must be "cut off" from Israel (18:20, 29). But if a man commits adultery with a betrothed slave, then he can be restored to the community by offering a sacrificial ram (19:20–22). Furthermore, there were not only sacrifices for intentional sins but also sins of ignorance—a just-in-case-I-violated-a-commandment-and-didn't-realize-it-until-now sacrifice (4:1–5:19). It took countless sacrificial animals, significant amounts of effort, a multitude of priests, and many commandments to take care of the problem of sin. Indeed, any and every sin had to be dealt with; no one could afford to be ambivalent or presumptuous when it came to dealing with such a serious matter. Therefore, temple traffic was supposed to indicate Israel's obedience to God. When God's house was full, Israel was taking care of their sin problem.

Yet, the prophets weren't satisfied when the temple was filled with worshipers seeking forgiveness through sacrifice. Like Samuel they preached, "To obey is better than sacrifice" (1 Sam 15:22), challenging the presumption of always finding forgiveness as long as the appropriate animal was brought to the temple. In fact, Isaiah claimed the site of hundreds of worshipers crammed into the temple—all bringing their sacrifices—made God angry (Isa 1:10–15). Why? Because they didn't come with the right attitude: "These people come near to me with their mouth and honor me with their lips, but their hearts are far from me. Their worship of me is based on merely human rules they have been taught" (29:13)—something Jesus claimed was true of his generation as well (Matt 15:7–9). Isaiah rebuked God's people for believing that sacrifices alone would cover a multitude of sins. Like the prophets before him and those who followed, Isaiah claimed God's wrath wasn't consumed by their offerings. Animals weren't enough to placate an angry God. Israel needed to correct the injustices—their unrighteous deeds against each other—that made so many temple sacrifices necessary. Temple traffic alone didn't reveal that God's people were taking their sin seriously. Israel needed to repent, change their ways, be reconciled to each other to find forgiveness in the temple (Jesus taught the same; Matt 5:23–24). Therefore, according to the prophets the Lord would discipline his people until they learned the lesson, "To obey is better than sacrifice."

EXPLAIN the Story

There must have been a problem, then, with Israel's obedience in Jesus's day. Since the Romans occupied the promised land, it was apparent to everyone that God was still punishing his people for their disobedience. Who were these rebels dragging down the rest of Israel? The Essenes thought the priests were the problem—as in the days of Malachi when the temple needed purification (Mal 2:1–9; 3:1–4). The priests could have quoted Malachi as well, placing the blame on the people for offering inferior sacrifices (1:8, 12–14).

The Sadducees promoted devotion to the temple. The Pharisees thought the problem was impurity. John preached repentance and baptized those who confessed their sins (Matt 3:2–6). Competing voices tried to steer Israel in the way they should go. So, when Jesus entered the scene—forgiving sins without sacrifices, accepting tax collectors without repentance, eating with sinners rather than fasting—his cavalier attitude cut against the grain of the necessary sobriety associated with taking sin seriously. Rather than grieve over sin, Jesus acted like it was time to party, and the sinners loved him for it. Predictably, the righteous people didn't like it at all, so they called him out on it. Although Jesus had taken several swings at the scribes and the Pharisees, jabbing them for their pseudo-righteousness, this is the first time they punched back—a fight that would go several rounds before another adversary would enter the ring and take him down. Until then, Jesus danced around like a prizefighter, avoiding the wild swings of his opponents, counterpunching his way into the hearts of the people. In the fight over how God forgives sinners, the people began to root for Jesus. But they had no idea where Jesus's campaign of forgiveness would eventually take him. When that day came, they would grieve and fast (9:15). But as long as the "bridegroom" was with them, it was time to celebrate the "new wine" of God's mercy.

The Hardest Thing to Say

Evidently, Jesus did something a little different when he healed the paralytic brought to him at Capernaum (9:2–8). He had healed many paralytics before (4:24), but this time Jesus decided to make an extraordinary claim, offering a theological commentary on his healing ministry. As I mentioned before,[1] sickness and sin were paired together in the minds of the people because of the Law and the Prophets (Lev 26:14–33; Deut 28:15–68; 2 Chr 21:12–19; Amos 4:4–13). If the people disobeyed God, then sickness and disease, famine and death would follow—an undeniable sign of God's curse. So, the *only* way to reverse the curse (easily inferred from the Law and the Prophets) was for the people to return to God by obeying him so that he would heal his people and restore their land. That's the standard line you read in the Law and the Prophets. But what does it mean when a miracle worker shows up and starts healing people and restoring the land *first*, before the people repent and obey? Isn't that backward, perhaps even a bit subversive? That's what the Pharisees said (Matt 9:34), an accusation they will throw at Jesus again a few chapters later (12:22–24). They questioned the legitimacy of his miracles, claiming Jesus performed them not by the hand of God but by the power of "Beelzebul,

1. See above, 98–100. See also Davies and Allison, *Matthew*, 2:89–90; Luz, *Matthew*, 2:27.

the prince of demons" (v. 24). Of course, Jesus exposed the fallacy of their inference: doing good wouldn't serve Satan's purposes at all (vv. 25–29), which is why the Pharisees were always on the lookout, trying to catch Jesus doing something *wrong* (12:2, 10; 15:1–2; 19:3; 22:15–17, 34–36). They were convinced that he wasn't an agent of God because he didn't do things the right way.

But the people didn't care. As long as Jesus delivered the goods, reversed the curse, they would sing his praises and glorify God (9:8). Some even began to call him the "Son of David," the long-awaited king who would restore the monarchy and bring justice to Israel and the whole world (v. 27). Indeed, Jesus's ability to heal *every single* person brought to him—especially the demonized—caused the people to exclaim, "Nothing like this has ever been seen in Israel" (v. 33). Yet, it wasn't just jealousy over Jesus's fame that compelled the Pharisees and the scribes to question Jesus's legitimacy. It was the way he healed people (12:10–14), and especially it was the claims he made about the healings that convinced them that Jesus was a blasphemer (9:3; 12:28). In the case of the healed paralytic, Jesus used the occasion to prove that God had forgiven the man's sin—a very audacious claim since no sacrifice had been offered.[2] Simply by the authority of his word, Jesus pronounced the paralytic's sins forgiven (9:2, 6). Since disease was supposed to be the result of sin, the evidence of forgiveness would be seen when God restored the man to health.[3] That put the onus on Jesus—exactly where he wanted it. So, before he healed the man, Jesus provoked the Pharisees with a riddle to drive home the point: "Which is easier: to say, 'Your sins are forgiven,' or to say, 'Get up and walk'?" (v. 5). Before they had a chance to answer (there's no scene of them discussing among themselves, "What do we say? If we say this, then he'll say that"; cf. 21:25–27), Jesus proved he had "authority on earth to forgive sins" by healing the man (9:6–7). In other words, to everyone that day the answer to the riddle was obvious: it was much easier to say, "Your sins are forgiven" since who can tell if it's true? But to say, "Get up, take your mat and go home"—that's much harder because if it didn't happen, then Jesus would be exposed as a false prophet (Deut 18:21–22).[4]

But I'm not so sure that solves the riddle. Since Jesus never gave an answer, maybe he assumed that we would puzzle over the riddle, or perhaps we're supposed to wonder, "Which was easier for him to say?"[5] Or, to flip the question around given our vantage point, perhaps we should ask, "What was harder for

2. Keener, *Matthew*, 289; Garland, *Reading Matthew*, 102.

3. Graham H. Twelftree, *Jesus the Miracle Worker* (Downers Grove, IL: InterVarsity Press, 1999), 116.

4. Davies and Allison, *Matthew*, 2:92–93.

5. See Twelftree, *Jesus the Miracle Worker*, 116–17.

Jesus to say that day, 'Your sins are forgiven,' or 'Get up and go home'"? For readers who know the whole story, even the narrative to this point, it's obvious that it wasn't hard for Jesus to heal people. Matthew has made that plain enough. I think the riddle also explains why Jesus teased the crowd (including the Pharisees) by doing something different with this paralytic. Healing the diseased wasn't difficult for him. Getting all Israel to believe that the kingdom of heaven had come through him? Now that was far more challenging. Of course, everyone in the narrative world of Matthew's Gospel knew why the people brought the paralytic to Jesus when he returned home (9:1–2). So when Jesus said, "Take heart, son; your sins are forgiven," it must have been a *huge* let down, especially to the paralytic! This wasn't the time for religious mumbo jumbo about sin and forgiveness. They didn't come to him for a lesson about redemption. They wanted to *see* redemption. Besides, if God had truly forgiven the man's sins, shouldn't the paralytic get up and walk home immediately upon hearing Jesus's pronouncement? Since the people thought that unforgiven sin was the cause of sickness and disease, saying, "Get up" wouldn't be necessary, would it? But that's not the way it happened. Instead, Jesus drove a wedge between "your sins are forgiven" and "get up" by inserting a riddle, creating space between the two acts of redemption, forgiveness and restoration. I can't help but wonder why, especially for the sake of the man lying on a pallet, paralyzed.

The question "which was harder for Jesus to say?" takes on new meaning when we puzzle over the riddle in light of the entire story of God's redemption. I think it was harder for Jesus to say, "Your sins are forgiven," knowing what it would take for that to be true. When Jesus pronounced the sins of the paralytic forgiven, he made a promise to him that he would carry his sins (and the whole world!) to the cross of his death. Of course, no one in the crowd that day knew the plan of redemption, that Jesus "did not come to be served, but to serve, and to give his life a ransom for many" (20:28). But they would eventually find out, even fasting for grief when he was taken away from them (9:15). In the meantime, however, Jesus expected the people to celebrate because God's mercy had come to those who needed it the most—the cursed, the wounded, the broken, the paralyzed. No act of repentance, no fasting required.[6] The man didn't even ask for his sins to be forgiven. Jesus simply did it. And the proof that Jesus meant it was not only seen when he raised this man from his mat, but especially when he "offered his life a ransom for many" and God raised him from the dead.

6. Garland, *Reading Matthew*, 103. See Sanders, who emphasizes that Jesus didn't require the usual acts of repentance for forgiveness (sacrifice, restitution, fasting), which is what got him in trouble with the religious authorities (*Jesus and Judaism* [Philadelphia: Fortress, 1985], 204–8).

In light of everything Jesus endured to bring about our forgiveness, it must have been much harder for him to say that day, "Your sins are forgiven." But that's not what the crowd was celebrating. When Matthew pointed out that they praised God, "who had given such authority to man" (v. 8), they were talking about his authority to heal—something the paralytic surely celebrated. But I can't help but wonder whether the paralytic eventually celebrated the other kind of authority Jesus demonstrated that day. Home alone that night, having crawled into bed by his own power, did he offer a prayer of thanks? "Adonai, thank you for healing me. Even though I don't deserve it—didn't even ask for it—thank you for forgiving my sins." Indeed, the Son of Man did have authority on earth to forgive sins, just as the angel predicted: "You are to give him the name Jesus, because he will save his people from their sins" (1:21). The paralytic was just the beginning.

Eating at the Wrong Time with the Wrong People

It's easy to see a correlation between the healing of the paralytic and the calling of Matthew (Matt 9:9–13). Neither man asked for Jesus to do what he did. The paralytic had his sins forgiven, and the tax collector became a disciple of Jesus. Furthermore, both men apparently popped up quickly in response to Jesus's word: the paralytic "got up and went home," and the tax collector "got up and followed him" (v. 9). We might even be tempted to merge their stories together, seeing Matthew just as paralyzed by corruption as the paralytic was paralyzed by disease. "It is not the healthy who need a doctor, but the sick," Jesus would say about Matthew and his friends (v. 12), almost leading the reader to hear echoes between these two stories. In both cases the Pharisees and scribes objected to Jesus's behavior regarding sin and sinners. Is that why Matthew put his own story here, so that we would see him and the paralytic as fraternal twins of God's mercy? That's certainly the lesson the scribes and Pharisees were supposed to learn. Having just seen Jesus forgive the paralytic's sins by healing him, they were forced to stand and watch Jesus dine with a bunch of tax collectors and sinners (vv. 10–11). It was too much to take in for one day. "Why does your teacher eat with tax collectors and sinners?" they asked the disciples. The answer should have been apparent—at least that's what Jesus thought. Sick people need a doctor, right (v. 12)? That seems obvious. Sinners need God, right? Still don't understand, huh? Time for a little homework: "Go and learn what this means, 'I desire mercy, not sacrifice'" (v. 13). Boy, are they going to learn a lesson they'll never forget.

The issue between Jesus, the Pharisees, and even John's disciples had to do with this question: *How* can we restore sinners to God? Of course, the question rests on two presumptions: those doing the restoring are righteous and those who need restoration are the sinners. Everyone should know the difference between the two groups. And just in case anyone was unclear about the distinction, the righteous people were the first to point out who was righteous and who wasn't. The righteous are the ones who are serious about sin. Even though the Pharisees and the Baptizer had very different ideas about how to deal with the problem of Israel's sin, they agreed on one thing: fasting was necessary for repentance. It's easy to see why. Of the six festivals Israel observed to commemorate God's salvation, there was only one that required fasting: Yom Kippur, the "Day of Atonement." Forgiveness and fasting went together like feasting and Passover. Evidently, both the Pharisees and the Baptizer (11:18) extended the practice of fasting beyond the once-a-year ritual. In fact, the Pharisees were known to fast twice per week, Mondays and Thursdays. But Jesus defied the tradition, choosing to *eat* with sinners rather than join the righteous in fasting.[7] This was the way he would restore sinners to God (9:13). That's a completely different approach, feasting when you should be fasting. Yet it wasn't the Pharisees who raised the objection this time. Instead, John's disciples were the ones who wanted to know, "How is it that we and the Pharisees fast often, but your disciples do not fast?" (9:14). In their minds, the man who preached repentance (4:17) should lead sinners to perform the proper acts of repentance.[8]

Jesus knew his methods were unconventional. He had already decided it was time for something new, something radical—an approach to sin that would change everything. It was time for the mercy of God. His approach, however, wasn't completely brand new. Hosea had already predicted long ago that God would prefer mercy over sacrifice once he had disciplined Israel for their sin (Hos 6:1–6). As far as Jesus was concerned, it was time to show sinners the mercy of God; it was the only way to recover them, to lead them to the kingdom. Nevertheless, eating with sinners to deal with Israel's sin problem seemed completely backward, out of place, and upside down to the righteous. Feasting was the last thing sinners needed to do to get serious about their sin. But Jesus acted like times had changed. The bridegroom is here! Mourning at a time like this would be completely out of place (Matt 9:15).[9] Besides, to go back to the old ways of repentance would be like sowing a new patch on an old piece of clothing or trying to put new wine in an old container (vv. 16–17). It would just make things worse. That's what mercy does; it destroys the old ways of dealing with sin. You can't pour mercy into the wineskin of judgment. You can't cover the hole in your worn-out jeans of sin management with the

7. Evans, *Matthew*, 204–5.
8. Davies and Allison, *Matthew*, 2:107; Luz, *Matthew*, 2:34–35.
9. France, *Matthew*, 356.

fresh patch of God's forgiveness. It was time for new wineskins to hold God's mercy, a new way to get serious about sin. It was time to eat with sinners.[10] Of course, those of us who gather around the Lord's Table know exactly why that is true, as we eat and drink our way into the kingdom of God.

LIVE the Story

There's one more reason why the Pharisees objected to Jesus's approach to dealing with sinners that we haven't mentioned. It has to do with table fellowship. In Jesus's day, the company you kept revealed your social worth. So honorable people would be careful to associate only with honorable people. Moreover, one of the clearest signals of your sense of social worth—a statement of self-importance—was to invite honorable people to your table to eat with you (Matt 22:1–14). While we can't tell whether the house Jesus entered was Matthew's, Peter's, or belonged to someone else in Capernaum (Who's the host?),[11] it's quite apparent that Jesus made a risky decision to eat with "many tax collectors and sinners" (9:10) because guilt by association ruled the honor game. By eating with them, Jesus identified with them. He was basically saying to everyone watching the spectacle, "These are my kind of people," unafraid of the social consequences of associating with them.[12] In the minds of the righteous, Jesus's table company confirmed their suspicions about him. He was a blasphemer (v. 3), which is why he ate with other notorious sinners. Birds of a feather flock together. Therefore, when the Pharisees asked his disciples, "Why is he doing this?" they were pointing out the obvious: righteous people don't associate with the worst sinners. By refusing to join the party, they were "standing up for what was right." Indeed, from where they were standing, the Pharisees proved they were righteous. Yet from where Jesus was sitting, he was out to prove something else: it was time to party because the mercy of God changes everything. Here's why.

If everyone needs God's mercy, then we can no longer speak of a division between the righteous and the sinners. Even the righteous make mistakes.

---

10. Peter Chrysologus, bishop of Ravenna from AD 433 until his death in 450, wrote: "Jesus's sitting at table has more significance for Matthew than just dining. Jesus will be feasting not on food but on the return of sinners. He will call them back through feasting, collegiality and human affection, enjoying himself with their pleasant conversation while reclining at table. He knew that if they recognized him as a powerful judge they would be shattered by the terror of his majesty and overwhelmed by the sheer presence of God unveiled" (Simonetti, *Matthew 1–13*, 178).

11. Matthew wrote literally, "the house," leaving it to his readers to infer whose house. Luke identifies the house as belonging to Matthew (Luke 5:29).

12. "Mercy involves the crossing of boundaries erected by society at large" (Davies and Allison, *Matthew*, 2:116).

Even those who "stand up for what is right" don't always do what is right (Matt 23:2–3). Therefore, everyone depends upon God's mercy to be righteous. Indeed, the way Jesus saw it, no sinner can be righteous without God's merciful forgiveness. That's how all sinners are restored. So, since "being right" depends upon the unlimited mercy of God, then why not be a people who give away God's mercy no matter what, to everyone without limit, as he has done for us? We didn't earn this mercy. (If we did, it would cease to be mercy!) It's not ours to own or distribute as we see fit, ensuring that the right people get it because they've done the right thing. That's what the Pharisees believed. Instead, Jesus taught his disciples to live by his party line: "Freely you have received; freely give" (Matt 10:8).

What does that look like? It looks like telling a paralytic, "Your sins are forgiven," even though he didn't ask for it. "Hey, don't go around telling people God forgives them when they haven't said the sinner's prayer. That's blasphemous." To Jesus, showing God's mercy also means eating with the wrong kind of people, knowing the righteous will judge you for it. "You know, all you're doing is encouraging bad behavior. These sinners need to repent." Yes, indeed. Freely give away God's mercy and see what happens. Those who think they've earned it won't like it at all. They think God's mercy is wasted on bad people who never learn their lesson. In fact, that's how I know when I'm sharing the limitless mercy of God: when it looks to righteous people like I'm encouraging bad behavior—like feasting with a bunch of sinners when they should be fasting, making them get serious about their sin.

Isn't that the way it goes? We aren't surprised when God shows us mercy; in fact, we expect it because we've said the right prayer or offered the proper acts of repentance. Yet when the righteous see the mercy of God extended to sinners who don't deserve it—they're not serious about their sin!—it looks like we're ignoring their bad behavior. "They'll never learn their lesson," we mutter to ourselves, "as long as we keep coddling them." So, mercy for us is grace, but mercy for them is foolishness. Yet Jesus won't let us get away with the us-versus-them view of the world. All of us are sick. All of us need a doctor. All of us are sinners. All of us need the mercy of God. Those who don't—the righteous and the healthy—will never see the kingdom of God because they don't recognize the King who says, "Go and learn what this means, 'I desire mercy, not sacrifice.' For I have not come to call the righteous, but sinners" (9:13). It won't be evident that the righteous and healthy have learned their lesson until they join the party—the table where a bunch of sinners gather to eat and drink the mercy of God. Ironically, it's the only way to get serious about *our sin*.

In his magnificent book *Exclusion and Embrace*, Miroslav Volf plumbs the depths of Jesus's uniquely brilliant approach to repentance, forgiveness, and reconciliation. There's so much in this book to talk about. It is an amazing exploration into the hard, long, patient work of seeking justice through God's work of redemption through Christ. Volf describes what he calls "the drama of embrace." Act one: opening the arms, a gesture of invitation also seen in the crucifixion of Jesus. Act two: waiting, the patient work of creating space for "the other." Act three: closing the arms, the necessary act of reciprocity; "it takes *two* pairs of arms for *one* embrace."[13] Act four: opening the arms again, the end of embrace that confirms our need for negotiating differences.[14] Put in more pedestrian terms, hugging doesn't solve our problems, but it's a good start. The covenant of embrace is no pretentious claim to settling all our differences. Instead, it affirms our common struggle "for *a nonfinal reconciliation based on a vision of reconciliation that cannot be undone*" because of the cross and resurrection of Christ.[15] Exclusion, Volf argues, can only happen at the hands of those unwilling to join the embrace. The gospel of reconciliation is no recipe for religious manipulation or pious coercion. Envy and enmity—twin themes prompting Jesus's call for repentance—are the main causes of exclusion, perpetuating the nasty cycle of revengeful violence. To break the cycle, *everyone* must repent—we and they, friends and enemies—which is "one of the most difficult acts for a person, let alone a community, to perform."[16] So, how do we do it?

Jesus knew what he was doing when he ate with sinners. Requiring sinners to perform proper acts of repentance appeals only to the righteous because they feel justified in their demand. This is especially true of victims of injustice. Ironically, they are empowered by their righteous indignation because they see themselves as powerless victims of oppression. So, their repentance—their forgiveness of sins—ends up being dependent upon the confession of their unrepentant oppressors. In fact, "resistance to repentance will be even greater if we see ourselves as disprivileged and powerless victims."[17] That explains why Jesus joined the table of tax collectors and sinners. Rather than treat them like "disprivileged and powerless victims" of righteous judgment ("those sinners aren't fasting!"), Jesus empowered them by joining the feast, treating them like *all* children of Abraham who need God's redemption. That's why he talked openly of (and they probably reveled in) the sick needing a doctor. Jesus came for all sinners.[18] Of all people, tax collectors knew they were sinners in need

---

13. Miroslav Volf, *Exclusion and Embrace: A Theological Exploration of Identity, Otherness, and Reconciliation* (Nashville: Abingdon, 1996), 143 (emphasis his).
14. Ibid., 140–47.
15. Ibid., 110 (emphasis his).
16. Ibid., 119.
17. Ibid., 119.
18. Davies and Allison, *Matthew*, 2:100–101.

of repentance.[19] All they needed was his warm embrace, an open invitation to join the party of God's endless mercy at the table of his forgiveness. One of their own, Matthew, proved Jesus would take all comers (Matt 9:9).[20]

A group of people calling themselves Equality Riders and belonging to an organization named Soulforce visited our campus a few years ago. Their mission was to visit several Christian colleges and universities to challenge policies that discriminate against gays and lesbians. When we found out they were coming, some in our ranks wanted to prevent them from coming to our college, thinking we should hire local police to guard the entrance to our campus. Most of us, however, wanted to welcome them as guests, to use their visit as an opportunity for us to have a campus-wide discussion on human sexuality according to the Scriptures. By the time Soulforce arrived, we had spent several months studying the Scriptures, praying, and fasting. We had a great time. Our students enjoyed interacting with our visitors. Several times during the day, we politely engaged one another in meaningful discussions. There seemed to be a sense of mutual respect between us, even though we disagreed with one another. Our differences were especially evident during an open forum where some of the Equality Riders and members of the college community explored a Christian view of human sexuality. Everything seemed to be going well when, all of the sudden, the tone of our discussion turned hostile. One of the members of Soulforce began to rail against anyone who held to a traditional view of human sexuality, accusing those who disagreed with her of hate speech. Incredulous, one of our students asked, "So, you're saying that I can't have a different opinion? That if I express my belief that God is not glorified by same-sex couples, it's hate speech?" "Yes," the woman said defiantly, and continued her vitriolic attack. Quickly other Equality Riders jumped in and made an attempt to tone down the rhetoric, telling personal stories of how they had been wounded by homophobic slurs and cruel jokes. The sin of hateful Christians weighed heavy on our hearts.

At that point, I invited all of us to confess our sins—especially those of us who were guilty of hurting gays and lesbians with our words. "Since Christian confession of sin is one of the distinctive marks of our faith, then perhaps we might find some agreement in that. All of us have sinned and fallen short of the glory of the Lord." But the idea wasn't received very well by our guests,

19. Hated by their kinsmen, tax collectors like Matthew worked for the Herodian government, a client kingdom of Rome required to pay duties on produce to Caesar. Most of these "tax farmers" collected tolls from traveling merchants as well as local farmers and fishermen, benefiting Herod and his administration as much as Roman interests (see Keener, *Matthew*, 292–93).

20. "The earliest church considered the tax collector's sudden obedience to Jesus's call to be one of the 'miracles' in our chapter of miracles" (Frederick Dale Bruner, *Matthew: A Commentary*, rev. ed., 2 vols. [Grand Rapids: Eerdmans, 2004], 1:419.

insisting that they were not the ones who had something to confess. At that moment, one of our faculty tried to lead the way. He talked about how easy it was for him to deceive himself, that he tends to justify his sin, that he needed to confess his sins to others, that he needed to be forgiven. To which the outspoken woman replied, "I have nothing to be forgiven of. I have done nothing wrong. I am proud of who I am. I have no sin to confess." The room fell silent. The contrast couldn't have been more evident. Some of us were there to confess our sins; others were there to judge.

After the meeting, a member of Soulforce took one of our students aside and confessed, "We've never experienced the kind of reception that we received here. You all have been so gracious and kind and respectful." Then she began to apologize for the brash behavior of her outspoken colleague. "You need to understand. It's been a long trip, and we're very tired." Our senior student then offered to pray for her and her companions, that they would have the strength to finish their journey. After their brief prayer meeting, the young lady boarded the bus and left. For several days, these two young women exchanged emails, continuing their conversation about gays, human sexuality, and Christianity. Then, one day, our senior student came to me with some exciting news. Her friend had decided to leave the tour and reconsider human sexuality according to the Scriptures. She said it was because of the way Soulforce was welcomed by our campus. They were expecting judgment but received mercy, and that had made all the difference in the world to her. "So, I guess it wasn't hate speech after all, was it?" I said. "No," she smiled, "I guess not."

No wonder Jesus acted like it was time to party when he joined a group of sinners. God forgives all of us, even a paralytic and a tax collector, a college student and a freedom rider. Hallelujah! *Every single one of us*. Jesus will bear a cross to prove that God forgives all of us—it is the opened-arm invitation to everlasting mercy, a divine embrace that lasts forever.

Come to the table and eat. He has dealt with our sin.

CHAPTER 13

Matthew 9:18–34

LISTEN to the Story

[18]While he was saying this, a synagogue leader came and knelt before
him and said, "My daughter has just died. But come and put your hand
on her, and she will live." [19]Jesus got up and went with him, and so did
his disciples.

[20]Just then a woman who had been subject to bleeding for twelve
years came up behind him and touched the edge of his cloak. [21]She said
to herself, "If I only touch his cloak, I will be healed."

[22]Jesus turned and saw her. "Take heart, daughter," he said, "your faith
has healed you." And the woman was healed at that moment.

[23]When Jesus entered the synagogue leader's house and saw the noisy
crowd and people playing pipes, [24]he said, "Go away. The girl is not dead
but asleep." But they laughed at him. [25]After the crowd had been put
outside, he went in and took the girl by the hand, and she got up. [26]News
of this spread through all that region.

[27]As Jesus went on from there, two blind men followed him, calling
out, "Have mercy on us, Son of David!"

[28]When he had gone indoors, the blind men came to him, and he
asked them, "Do you believe that I am able to do this?"

"Yes, Lord," they replied.

[29]Then he touched their eyes and said, "According to your faith let it
be done to you"; [30]and their sight was restored. Jesus warned them sternly,
"See that no one knows about this." [31]But they went out and spread the
news about him all over that region.

[32]While they were going out, a man who was demon-possessed and
could not talk was brought to Jesus. [33]And when the demon was driven
out, the man who had been mute spoke. The crowd was amazed and said,
"Nothing like this has ever been seen in Israel."

[34]But the Pharisees said, "It is by the prince of demons that he drives
out demons."

Listening to the Text in the Story: Leviticus 15:19–31; Numbers 15:38–41; 19:11–22; Deuteronomy 22:12; 1 Kings 17:17–24; 2 Chronicles 35:25; Isaiah 35:3–6, 10; 42:1–2, 6–9, 16; Jeremiah 9:17–21; Ezekiel 24:17; Amos 5:2, 16–17.

Jesus made people either mad or glad. There seemed to be no in between with him. To say he was a polarizing figure is merely stating the obvious—an observation that makes some of us uncomfortable. After all, as disciples of Jesus we want everyone to admire him, like him, follow him. But that's not the case now, and it certainly wasn't the situation back then. We may want to blame those hostile to Jesus for their own stubbornness, ignorance, or blind foolishness. They must be the ones who have the problem. For, if the truth is believable, everyone should trust in Christ—especially those who were eyewitnesses of everything he said and did. Why didn't they see who Jesus was, especially since he was supposed to be the embodiment of every hero Israel ever hoped for? Shouldn't it have been obvious? Not necessarily. Jesus did some things that were completely unexpected and downright offensive, like declaring forgiveness of sins without the necessary temple sacrifices or feasting with sinners when they should have been fasting. Furthermore, Jesus didn't treat everyone the same. For some people, Jesus dropped everything to do what they wanted, giving them the "royal treatment"—whether a Jewish paralytic or Roman soldier, a synagogue leader or cursed leper, a demon-possessed boy or a Canaanite woman. Other people he ignored, not only Sadducees and Pharisees but also blind men and adoring crowds, rubbing many of them the wrong way. Jesus provoked a variety of different responses from many different kinds of people, depending as much upon what he was trying to do as what they were expecting from him. In many ways, Jesus was predictably unpredictable—something even Christians today are reticent to admit. To put it in modern terms, if Jesus had used a public-relations department, they would have been continuously frustrated with their client.

EXPLAIN the Story

I love the way Matthew set up the next series of stories with the phrase "while he was saying this" (Matt 9:18). That one little phrase bridges two groups of people—the sinners and the righteous—heightening the dramatic moment of Jesus's "unpredictable" behavior.[1] He had been talking to his disciples and the

1. Nolland, *Matthew*, 394.

rest of the sinners dining with him about new wine requiring new wineskins when, at that very moment, a "leader of the synagogue" burst into the house and interrupted him with some terrible news: "My daughter has just died" (v. 18). Picture the scene. The Pharisees are standing outside, watching Jesus eating with these notorious sinners when they should have been fasting; the party is in full swing, everyone inside eating, drinking, laughing, storytelling; Jesus is adding a story of his own about wine and wineskins, expecting his dinner companions to make the connection. Then, all of the sudden, a well-respected leader of the synagogue blows past the crowd of Pharisees, falls at Jesus's feet, and interrupts the teacher with his desperate plea and audacious request: "My daughter has just died. But come and put your hand on her, and she will live" (v. 18). Now, what do you suppose was going through the minds of both groups, the outsiders and the insiders? Would the Pharisees outside muse to themselves about the foolish behavior of a desperate man who falls on his face before a blasphemer? Would Matthew and his friends inside marvel over the humility of the synagogue leader, or would they laugh at the ironic site of such an important man begging for Jesus's help? Moreover, what would they expect Jesus's response to be? Would Jesus ignore the man because he only helps sinners? Would he make an example of him, making a "righteous" man grovel over his pitiful condition? Did the Pharisees scoff with a loud "harrumph"? Did Matthew turn to his friends, relishing the reversal of roles, and say, "This ought to be rich! Look who's the outsider now? Finally, he's going to know what rejection feels like"? Or, did Jesus's newest disciple pity the broken-hearted father who's made such a ridiculous request, knowing that death is irreversible?

We'll never know what any of the spectators thought that day. Yet one thing is certain: everyone was in for a surprise. And, once again, there would be all kinds of responses to what Jesus said and did: some glad, some mad.

Reverence and Humility

Like Mark and Luke, Matthew tells the following two episodes as one story: healing the bloody woman and raising the dead girl (Matt 9:18–26; Mark 5:22–43; Luke 8:41–56). Both episodes are linked by three factors: both beneficiaries were female, both were unclean, and both needed Jesus's touch—one reaching out to touch the edge of his cloak, the other grasped by the hand of Jesus. At the same time, the main characters of the story—the synagogue leader and the menstruating woman[2]—couldn't be more different, especially when it came to their social status. The leader of the synagogue was

2. Matthew used the same term as the LXX (Lev 15:33) for menstruating women (see Nolland, *Matthew*, 395).

greatly respected because he played a significant role in the religious life of Capernaum. He was responsible for overseeing Sabbath services, organizing community events hosted by the synagogue, and probably secured resources needed for its operation, like procuring Torah scrolls, furniture, and maintenance of the building (if the synagogue had its own "prayer hall").[3] In other words, this was a high-profile man, accustomed to being treated with honor. So the actions he took to get Jesus to help him make perfect sense. When he found Jesus in the house, he didn't wait around outside, hoping to get Jesus's attention once the party was over (12:46). He didn't send a messenger to Jesus, trying to broker an arrangement to get the healer to come to his house (Luke 7:3–5). No, this man took matters into his own hands, barged into the house, went straight to Jesus, interrupted his teaching, and asked for the impossible: to bring his little girl back from the dead. And yet, for all his boldness and his nothing-is-going-to-stop-me approach, there was the undeniable display of his reverent humility that made his appeal even more dramatic. This honorable man fell on his face before a rogue prophet and stated the matter plainly. No begging. No flattery. He simply stated the facts. His dead daughter would live again if Jesus touched her.

Obviously, the "woman who had been subject to bleeding for twelve years" didn't take the same bold approach (Matt 9:20). She had been waiting outside the house for Jesus to come out, at least that's the implication of Matthew's version. Jesus and his disciples had no sooner left the house to follow the synagogue leader when "just then" the woman "came up behind him and touched the edge of his cloak" (v. 20). The fact that she had been hiding in the crowd of onlookers and snuck up from behind as soon as Jesus left, hoping to touch the hem of his robe without being noticed, says as much about her as it does about Jesus. She didn't barge into the house and confront him with her need. Imagine how strange that would have been. An unclean woman pushes through the Pharisees, defiling them with her impurity (Lev 15:19–27), enters the house, and interrupts the meal with an inappropriate comment and impertinent demand: "I've been menstruating for twelve years. No man will have me. I've had enough! Heal me, Jesus." Instead, she took a more clandestine approach, knowing that her uncleanness was shameful and contagious. "If I only touch his cloak, I will be healed" (Matt 9:21). She probably wanted to pull off the secret stunt for Jesus's sake as much as hers, trying to avoid the embarrassment of asking for help when Jesus appeared to be in such a hurry. The Galilean prophet had already proven that he could reverse the polarity of holiness, making the unclean clean with the touch of his hand (recall the

---

3. See Anders Runesson, "Synagogue," *DJG* 904–6, who distinguishes between "public synagogues" (open to all) and "association synagogues" (established by certain groups, like the Pharisees).

leper). Since Jesus wore the garments of a holy man, tassels hanging from the four corners of his robe (Num 15:38–39), the unclean woman must have figured that grabbing his holy tassels would do the trick. No bother. No delay. No one would know. But Jesus wouldn't let her get away with it (Matt 9:22).

The way Matthew relates this story, the reasons Jesus outed the woman seem rather apparent. First, he wanted to make it plain that a woman like her—one of the "untouchables"—was a person of great faith. No more hiding in the shadows of her shame, she would become a living memorial to the healing power of faith. Jesus emphasized that it was her faith in him that "saved" her.[4] Private faith became public knowledge, a lesson for everyone. Also, by calling attention to the fact that he was aware of her intent ("she said to herself"), Jesus revealed his miraculous knowledge of the secret of her heart. Finally, Matthew claimed that "the woman was healed at that moment"—the moment when Jesus said, "Your faith has healed you." In other words, she wasn't healed when she grabbed the tassels of his garment, as if they had magical powers (see, however, Matt 14:36). It was the affirmation of her faith by the power of his word that brought about her healing. Notice how many times Jesus points out the crucial role of faith when he heals people (see 8:10; 9:2, 22, 28–29; 15:28). For Matthew, then, faith in Jesus is the point of the story, the essence of our salvation. Of course, the synagogue leader had already demonstrated great faith by asking for the impossible. To stop a woman from bleeding to death saves a life; everyone knows that. But to save a girl who cannot bleed—death's insignia—was unheard of, which is why the funeral was in full swing by the time Jesus and his disciples arrived at the synagogue leader's home (9:23).

Contempt and Flattery

The mourners must have noticed when the father left his house soon after his daughter died. Israel had professional mourners (typically women), who were not only responsible for helping the family grieve over the deceased by wailing and playing laments on reed instruments, but they also determined when it was time to prepare the body for burial—essentially serving as experts in establishing the time of death (Jer 9:17–20).[5] So, when Jesus shows up and says, "Go away. The girl is not dead but asleep" (9:24), it must have sounded to the mourners as if Jesus were accusing them of incompetence. Without even assessing the girl's condition (it was the sight of the mourners whipping up a noisy crowd and playing pipes that provoked Jesus), the newcomer

4. Where the NIV translates "your faith has *healed* you," Matthew literally wrote, "your faith has *saved* you."

5. Keener, *Matthew*, 304–5.

took over and cleared the house: "Get out of here, you bumblebees! You've started the funeral prematurely!" It's no wonder that "they laughed at him," contemptuous of his bold claim. They knew death's pallor when they saw it: no breath, ashen face, clammy skin. Yet, they didn't protest when Jesus threw them outside. Why would they? It was just a matter of time until the pretense of Jesus's claim would soon be exposed as foolish nonsense. Within a few hours, they would be called in to finish what they started. Corpses don't "wake up" from death. Yet that's exactly what happened. Giving little detail, Matthew says that Jesus "took the girl by the hand, and she got up" (v. 25), which must have left everyone puzzling over the obvious question—the elephant in the room, as it were. Who was right, the mourners or Jesus? Was the girl dead or just sleeping? Ask the father. He knew she was dead; he had said so to Jesus. Yet whether it was Jesus or the experts who were right, it probably didn't matter to the father. His daughter was alive! No wonder "news of this spread through all that region" (v. 26)—word that probably reached two blind men, who wouldn't have been able to see it to believe it.

Isaiah anticipated the day when the blind would see the kingdom of God (Isa 35:3–6; 42:6–7, 16). To Isaiah it was another sign of God's righteous reign on earth. So, when two blind men tried to get Jesus's attention when he left the synagogue leader's house, it appears as though Matthew has set up another fulfillment of prophecy—something he loved to do. However, Jesus ignored them, kept on walking, and didn't bother to stop for a moment, which is a little surprising since up to this point Jesus seemed willing to heal everyone who came to him. It's almost if he didn't hear them cry out, "Have mercy on us, Son of David!" (Matt 9:27). That certainly should have gotten his attention. These blind men could "see" who Jesus was, the true "Son of David,"[6] the same messianic title that Matthew used to begin his Gospel: "This is the genealogy of Jesus the Messiah the son of David" (1:1). In fact, by calling out to him as "the Son of David," they (of all people!) are the first characters in Matthew's narrative world to recognize Jesus as "the Messiah."[7] They got it right! They know who Jesus is. Yet, Jesus wasn't impressed by their perceptiveness. Their acclamation didn't influence him one bit. Jesus appears ambivalent when he should have celebrated their messianic praise. Indeed, according to the way Matthew has set up this story—even his entire Gospel—Jesus should have stopped, turned around, walked up to these blind men who were following him, and used the opportunity to confirm their

6. Some scholars think that the blind men were referring to Jesus as "Solomon," relying upon a legend that the "son of David" was given a magical ring to defeat demons (T.Sol. 1:5–7); see Luz, *Matthew*, 2:47–48; Keener, however, thinks not (*Matthew*, 306).

7. Bruner, *Matthew*, 1:434.

messianic claims by healing them in front of the crowd (which is *exactly* what happened later; see 20:29–34). Instead, to get what they wanted, the blind men had to pursue Jesus, following him until he stopped at someone's house (9:28). Why?[8]

Flattery was a nuisance to those who constantly received it. But flattery was the only tool available to those who needed help from the rich and powerful. In the honor game the wealthy, the powerful, and the honorable were constantly approached by people who needed favors. Since honor was the most desirable commodity in the first-century world, the rich and the powerful were accustomed to receiving the praise of the people. This is the way the honor game worked: those who had honor wanted more of it, and those who needed help honored the rich and powerful—a social arrangement of need and desire. So, wherever the "haves" went, the "have-nots" were always jockeying for attention, trying to schmooze the rich and powerful with accolades. And, occasionally, it worked. Accepting the honorific praise, the rich would bestow "gifts" upon the needy, who would then be indebted to their patron and thereby willing to perform many tasks and duties at the beck and call of their "lord." Of course, the farther down the social ladder, the less chance a person was of receiving any favors from the rich and powerful. The higher-ups had to be careful, doling out their gifts sparingly, not wanting to become "attached" to just anyone. That made the lowlife try even harder, heaping over-the-top praise upon the rich and powerful patrons, all the while knowing they had a slim chance of manipulating the honor game to their advantage.

So, when these two blind men tried to get Jesus's attention by shouting out, "Have mercy on us, *Son of David*"—the most honorific title given to any Jewish man—Jesus ignored their attempt at flattery. He seemed to see through their intentions of manipulating the honor game even though the title was appropriate. Indeed, as the rest of the story reveals, Jesus assessed the situation accurately. These men were opportunists, relentless in their pursuit of getting what they wanted. They followed Jesus all the way into the house, boldly approaching him with the same chutzpah as the synagogue leader. Suspicious of their sincerity Jesus asked them, "Do you believe that I am able to do this?" to which they appropriately replied, "Yes, Lord" (9:28). Therefore, because of their faith Jesus healed them, but he also "warned them sternly, 'See that no one knows about this'" (v. 30). But they didn't obey their new "lord."[9] Instead, they broadcast the miracle "all over that region" (v. 31). Why did Jesus demand that his new clients keep the favor a secret? I think it's

8. For several other possibilities, see ibid., 1:438–39.

9. "First-hand observation or experience of the supernatural scarcely guarantees faithful discipleship" (Davies and Allison, *Matthew*, 2:138).

because he refused to play the honor game, knowing that the newly sighted blind men would be compelled to boast about their patron—not only for his sake but also for theirs. After all, now they were "somebody," beneficiaries of the most powerful man, the Messiah, the Son of David. In other words, they disobeyed Jesus because they wanted to take advantage of the situation—the same motivation that compelled them to flatter Jesus in the first place.

LIVE the Story

Matthew rounds out these episodes with a brief account that sets in sharp relief a contrast between the responses of the people and the Pharisees to Jesus's healing ability (Matt 9:32–34). Just as the newly sighted blind men were exiting the house, a demon-possessed man was brought in to see Jesus. After Jesus cast out the demon, the man was able to talk, which caused the crowd (standing outside the house?) to respond with complete and utter amazement: "Nothing like this has ever been seen in Israel" (v. 33). Imagine what it must have felt like to be there, standing outside the house where Jesus was staying. To our eyes the scene would have reminded us of a new health clinic set up in the rough side of town, with sick people streaming through the doors looking for relief. Blind men enter the house; they come out seeing! Mute man enters the house; he comes out speaking! No one had ever seen anything like it. Who wouldn't stand around all day and gawk at the spectacle, even celebrating the "good news"? Well, the Pharisees didn't join in the praise. They had already dismissed Jesus as a blasphemer. It must have been unnerving for them to see him pull off miracle after miracle. Since they loved to stand around and offer commentary on what they saw, what could they say to rebut the people's observation? So the Pharisees said, "It is by the prince of demons that he drives out demons" (v. 34). Some people are so stubborn! Once they make up their minds about a person or a situation, there's no going back, no admitting, "I could have been wrong." No. They'll ride the horse of their infallible opinion off a cliff just to prove that there's no going back. Their mind is made up. In their righteous judgment, the Pharisees were convinced Jesus was a blasphemer. Nothing, *not even the work of God*, would change their minds.

I've often wondered how I would have responded to the miracles of Jesus. Would I have joined the Pharisees, keeping a safe distance from the mania, refusing to be swept up in the euphoria, trying to maintain some sense of objectivity? "Simple minds are easily swayed," I would remind myself. "Some people are willing to believe anything." Of course, my reluctance to believe the miraculous would have more to do with our presumption in the West that things like this don't happen today. The Pharisees knew these miracles occurred. They simply dismissed them as inauthentic because, to their minds, Jesus had deceived the masses by using the wrong kind of power, giving the appearance of a divine work. We, on the other hand, dismiss the miraculous because "faith healers" make false claims to divine power. We've seen too many hucksters prey on desperate folks who are willing to play along with the charade of pseudohealings and gifts of clairvoyance. Conveniently, only those afflicted with hidden ailments like back pain, heart conditions, or cancer are staged for the audience. But secret cameras and hidden microphones used by investigative journalists have unmasked the sham of these religious salesmen, who play on the emotions of the crowd, tricking them into believing that "something happened." The cold eye of the camera doesn't lie. What looks like a miracle is really a sleight-of-hand stunt. No wonder we don't see faith healers traveling across the country anymore, setting up tents to attract the masses to their healing shows. Television programs like *20/20* and Internet sites like snopes.com have shut down the circus of faith healings. Instead, we watch reality shows where trackers search for visual evidence of Sasquatch, and ghost hunters record paranormal activity by taking readings with their scientific equipment.

It says a lot about us that a New Testament scholar like Craig Keener has written the massive, two-volume work *Miracles*, numbering 884 pages, trying to convince readers that miracles still happen today.[10] In addition to his own expertise, Keener has read *thousands* of articles and books of several academic disciplines—history, philosophy, psychology, anthropology—and catalogued hundreds of eyewitness accounts to consider one question: Do miracles happen?[11] The rigor of his work, the sheer volume of his copious footnotes, the painstaking manner in which he leaves no stone (even pebble!) unturned is impressive beyond words. To sneak a peak into *Miracles*, hoping to make a quick assessment of his argument, is like trying to take a sip of water from a fire hydrant. There's just too much to swallow. Yet, for all his hard work and patient erudition that produced such a remarkable study, I cannot help but wonder: Why did he write it? Obviously, we want it—especially scholars who love to read magnificent works like this (anything that challenges the status quo of New Testament scholarship will certainly attract

10. Craig S. Keener, *Miracles: The Credibility of the New Testament Accounts*, 2 vols. (Grand Rapids: Baker Academic, 2011). Keener uses the argument of analogy to justify the credibility of New Testament accounts of miracles (inverting the typical Pentecostal approach to vindicating the miraculous): since miracles happen today, then they must have happened back then.

11. The bibliography runs from page 885 to page 1050 (small font, double column).

attention). Furthermore, it would be foolish to underestimate the value of such a thorough study. Keener has a mind like a steel trap, and his work will appeal to others who have the same mental prowess, even those who disagree with his conclusions. And that's the point. Equally gifted minds will not agree with him because arguments can only take you so far—something Keener knows all too well. In fact, Keener admits that the reason he's convinced miracles happen today is because he's seen them, especially in developing countries.[12] And therein lies the rub. In places where medical help is scarce, miracles are reported.[13] Where faith is required, the miraculous happens—but it's still something that needs to be proven to people like us.

Like the two blind men Jesus met going home, I've never seen a miracle. I've heard many claim that God healed them, sometimes even recounting medical evidence to prove it, like before and after x-rays or c-scans. I've prayed for many people—especially when I was a pastor—that God would perform a miracle and heal the man who was in his final hours, dying of cancer, or the young lady who was brain dead due to a horrible automobile accident. But the miracle never happened. That's when I would earn my salary, consoling family members who couldn't understand why God didn't heal their loved one when he had healed others. For them, it wasn't difficult to believe in miracles; the hard part was holding on to their faith in God when the miraculous didn't happen. Afterward, alone in my office, I wondered what it would have been like to witness a miracle that day, marveling over seeing a brain-dead girl rise from her bed or watching physicians puzzle over tests that confirmed that a man's cancer was completely gone. Then I would think about what happened in Jesus's day, the excitement of the crowds as they witnessed dozens of miracles, declaring, "Nothing like this has ever been seen in Israel" (Matt 9:33). "Been seen." "Wait a minute," I say to myself, "the crowds didn't actually *see* miracles. They saw the *results*, like formerly blind men walking out of the house or a man speaking after the exorcism." Certainly, on rare occasions Jesus performed miracles in public, even for skeptical eyes (like the healing of the paralytic). Yet, in most cases only a few people saw the miracle, typically the afflicted and the disciples. The gathered crowd may have seen the results (once removed), but everyone else relied upon reports (twice removed): "News of this spread through all that region" (v. 26), including from those who received the miracle: "But they went out and spread the news about him

---

12. Ibid., 733.

13. This observation shows up several times throughout his work; for example: "Thus, a number of Westerners who began successfully praying for others to be healed first learned the practice in the Majority World, quite often in regions where many lacked access to adequate medical technology" (ibid., 229–30).

all over that region" (v. 31). Interestingly, the same thing happens today: only a few of us have witnessed miracles (firsthand and once removed); the rest of us rely upon reports.

I had mixed emotions reading through pages and pages of eyewitness accounts in Keener's *Miracles*. Sometimes I felt like a Pharisee, questioning the legitimacy of the account: "A shaman makes a girl who had been dead for days get up and play the drums. Really?"[14] Most of the time, however, I kept repeating the monosyllabic exclamation, "Wow!" as I tried to wrap my mind around the wondrous stories of miracles that have been reported from all over the world. Keener is no fool, and neither are the ones who have witnessed these things, some of whom are even the hard-nosed, academic types that I run around with—reluctant witnesses to things scholars dismiss as fiction. (For scholars, the worst sin is to accept what is unreasonable.) Yet, witnesses can't help but say what they saw. To deny the miraculous would be worse than fiction—a lie. At the same time, I can't help it that I've never seen a miracle. Nevertheless, even though at times I find myself siding with the Pharisees in their skepticism, I want to join the crowd in amazement when believers report the miraculous. It's because I believe God performs miracles today. Jesus was right; it takes faith to see miracles: "According to your faith let it be done to you" (v. 29).

"Have mercy on me, Son of David. I want to see."

14. Ibid., 540 (Keener expresses skepticism too).

CHAPTER 14

Matthew 9:35–11:1

LISTEN to the Story

[35]Jesus went through all the towns and villages, teaching in their synagogues, proclaiming the good news of the kingdom and healing every disease and sickness. [36]When he saw the crowds, he had compassion on them, because they were harassed and helpless, like sheep without a shepherd. [37]Then he said to his disciples, "The harvest is plentiful but the workers are few. [38]Ask the Lord of the harvest, therefore, to send out workers into his harvest field."

[10:1]Jesus called his twelve disciples to him and gave them authority to drive out impure spirits and to heal every disease and sickness.

[2]These are the names of the twelve apostles: first, Simon (who is called Peter) and his brother Andrew; James son of Zebedee, and his brother John; [3]Philip and Bartholomew; Thomas and Matthew the tax collector; James son of Alphaeus, and Thaddaeus; [4]Simon the Zealot and Judas Iscariot, who betrayed him.

[5]These twelve Jesus sent out with the following instructions: "Do not go among the Gentiles or enter any town of the Samaritans. [6]Go rather to the lost sheep of Israel. [7]As you go, proclaim this message: 'The kingdom of heaven has come near.' [8]Heal the sick, raise the dead, cleanse those who have leprosy, drive out demons. Freely you have received; freely give.

[9]"Do not get any gold or silver or copper to take with you in your belts—[10]no bag for the journey or extra shirt or sandals or a staff, for the worker is worth his keep. [11]Whatever town or village you enter, search there for some worthy person and stay at their house until you leave. [12]As you enter the home, give it your greeting. [13]If the home is deserving, let your peace rest on it; if it is not, let your peace return to you. [14]If anyone will not welcome you or listen to your words, leave that home or town and shake the dust off your feet. [15]Truly I tell you, it will be more bearable for Sodom and Gomorrah on the day of judgment than for that town.

[16]"I am sending you out like sheep among wolves. Therefore be as shrewd as snakes and as innocent as doves. [17]Be on your guard; you will be

handed over to the local councils and be flogged in the synagogues. [18]On
my account you will be brought before governors and kings as witnesses
to them and to the Gentiles. [19]But when they arrest you, do not worry
about what to say or how to say it. At that time you will be given what to
say, [20]for it will not be you speaking, but the Spirit of your Father speaking
through you.

[21]"Brother will betray brother to death, and a father his child; children
will rebel against their parents and have them put to death. [22]You will be
hated by everyone because of me, but the one who stands firm to the end
will be saved. [23]When you are persecuted in one place, flee to another.
Truly I tell you, you will not finish going through the towns of Israel
before the Son of Man comes.

[24]"The student is not above the teacher, nor a servant above his master.
[25]It is enough for students to be like their teachers, and servants like their
masters. If the head of the house has been called Beelzebul, how much
more the members of his household!

[26]"So do not be afraid of them, for there is nothing concealed that will
not be disclosed, or hidden that will not be made known. [27]What I tell you
in the dark, speak in the daylight; what is whispered in your ear, proclaim
from the roofs. [28]Do not be afraid of those who kill the body but cannot
kill the soul. Rather, be afraid of the One who can destroy both soul and
body in hell. [29]Are not two sparrows sold for a penny? Yet not one of them
will fall to the ground outside your Father's care. [30]And even the very hairs
of your head are all numbered. [31]So don't be afraid; you are worth more
than many sparrows.

[32]"Whoever acknowledges me before others, I will also acknowledge
before my Father in heaven. [33]But whoever disowns me before others,
I will disown before my Father in heaven.

[34]"Do not suppose that I have come to bring peace to the earth. I did
not come to bring peace, but a sword. [35]For I have come to turn

'a man against his father,
  a daughter against her mother,
a daughter-in-law against her mother-in-law—
  [36]a man's enemies will be the members of his own household.'

[37]"Anyone who loves their father or mother more than me is not wor-
thy of me; anyone who loves their son or daughter more than me is not
worthy of me. [38]Whoever does not take up their cross and follow me is

not worthy of me. [39]Whoever finds their life will lose it, and whoever loses their life for my sake will find it.

[40]"Anyone who welcomes you welcomes me, and anyone who welcomes me welcomes the one who sent me. [41]Whoever welcomes a prophet as a prophet will receive a prophet's reward, and whoever welcomes a righteous person as a righteous person will receive a righteous person's reward. [42]And if anyone gives even a cup of cold water to one of these little ones who is my disciple, truly I tell you, that person will certainly not lose their reward."

[11:1]After Jesus had finished instructing his twelve disciples, he went on from there to teach and preach in the towns of Galilee.

Listening to the Text in the Story: Genesis 19:1–29; Numbers 27:15–17; 1 Samuel 14:45; 1 Kings 22:17; Nehemiah 5:13; Psalm 122:7–9; Isaiah 49:5–6; Jeremiah 23:1–8; 50:6; Ezekiel 16:49–50; 34:1–24; 37:24–28; Joel 2:18–24; Micah 7:1–7; Zechariah 10:2–3; 1 Enoch 90:1–36; Testament of Solomon 3:1–4:3; 6:1–11.

The last time Jesus saw the crowds coming to him looking for a miracle, it inspired him to preach the Sermon on the Mount (Matt 4:24–5:2), taking his cause directly to the people. This time the site of so many helpless people—like sheep without a shepherd—made him realize he needed help. So he decided to recruit twelve disciples to extend the reach of his kingdom to places he hadn't visited yet. Even though Matthew says Jesus "went through all the towns and villages" teaching, preaching, and healing (the essence of his mission; see 4:23), evidently there was more work to be done. The huge crowds that showed up looking for relief proved it. These "harassed and helpless" sheep flocked to Jesus as if he were the Great Shepherd whom the prophets predicted would come to restore Israel (Isa 49:5–6; Jer 3:14–15; 23:3–6; Ezek 34:11–16; 37:24–28). The pitiful site moved Jesus to have "compassion on them" and to ask God for help (Matt 9:36). Turning to his disciples to join him in prayer, Jesus shifts metaphors. We might have expected him to say, "Pray to the Lord to send more shepherds into the fields to gather the flock of Israel." Instead, Jesus told his disciples to pray for more farmers to reap the fields because "the harvest is plentiful but the workers are few" (v. 37). His assessment of the situation was both an acknowledgement and an indictment—an acknowledgement that they were seeing the results of God's work through him, the Baptizer, and the prophets before him. Yet it was also an indictment of the religious leadership; they were abusive shepherds who weren't taking care of God's flock (Jer 23:1–2; Ezek 34:1–10; Zech 10:2–3). It also may explain why Jesus switched to the harvest metaphor, an image of both eschatological reward (Joel 2:18–19, 24) and judgment (see comments on Matt 3:12).

EXPLAIN the Story

The crisis of scattered sheep or plentiful harvest still doesn't explain why Jesus believed it was necessary to recruit additional workers for the kingdom. Couldn't he do it by himself? Sure, it might take several decades to gather all the lost sheep of Israel, but he had plenty of time, right? Not necessarily. As readers, we know he doesn't have all the time in the world; eleven chapters later Jesus will enter Jerusalem and be crucified. Yet Jesus acts like he's crunched for time for other reasons. The desperate condition of the "lost sheep of Israel" requires immediate action to "heal the sick, raise the dead, cleanse those who have leprosy, drive out demons" (Matt 10:8). The urgent mission of the Twelve may also be evident in the instructions he gave as he sent them away: don't waste time by going to the gentiles or Samaritans; rather, go straight to the "lost sheep of Israel" (vv. 5–6). The itinerant missionaries don't have enough time to secure necessary provisions for the trip, even extra sandals or shirts (v. 10). They don't even have time to prepare sermons or rebuttals in the face of their accusers (vv. 19–20).[1] Why? Because Jesus sounds like he believes the end of the world is near: "Truly I tell you, you will not finish going through the towns of Israel before the Son of Man comes" (v. 23). Also, the harvest metaphor implies expediency: the time had come, and if we don't get into the fields now the grain will be lost. Jesus even anticipated that his disciples would experience the "messianic woes" that were to come upon Israel just before judgment day, reminding them that "the one who stands firm to the end will be saved" (vv. 21–23, 28, 34–39). The message seems obvious: there's so little time, and so much work to be done before it all hits the apocalyptic fan. This is why Jesus pressed his followers into immediate service. He saw the "signs of the times" and determined he had to recruit twelve disciples to restore the twelve tribes of Israel before it was too late.

Sometimes, however, Jesus sounds like the kingdom coming to earth is still a long way off. He presumes his disciples will stay a while in every receptive town (v. 11), only leaving when they are rejected or run out of town (vv. 14, 23). He predicts that his disciples eventually will be brought before

1. Like Moses (Exod 4:12)? See Davies and Allison, *Matthew*, 2:185.

foreign governors and kings (v. 18). He even looks past the immediate situation of the Twelve and gives instructions to hosts somewhere in the future (to whom is he talking?), friends who will welcome "these little ones" as if they were Jesus himself (vv. 40–42). Indeed, most Christians take these instructions to heart, as if Jesus were not only giving specific directions to the Twelve but also general advice to the church. In fact, we tend to pick and choose the parts that applied only to the Twelve (don't take money or extra clothing, being beaten in synagogues, shaking the dust off one's feet) and separate them from the instructions that have timeless appeal, the places where Jesus seems to lift his eyes above the Twelve and speak directly to us (families divided, not denying Christ before other people, not fearing those who "kill the body," finding life and losing it). Indeed, it's his last piece of instruction about traveling prophets and righteous people, promising those who take them into their homes that they will receive "a prophet's reward" or "a righteous person's reward" (vv. 41–42), that reflects the life of the church much later—a situation addressed by the Didache as well (Did. 11:3–13:7). In other words, Jesus's instructions for the Twelve sound like timeless instructions for the mission of the church. If that's the case, then Jesus wasn't in a hurry when he sent the Twelve to restore Israel. Their austere lifestyle was supposed to reflect the cost of discipleship—the gift of the poor to the poor—and not the shortness of time.[2] So the purpose of the training mission was to prepare the Twelve for the future when they would carry on the work of the kingdom after Jesus ascended to heaven (Matt 10:32–33).

Once again, we find ourselves having to sort out whether we should interpret Jesus's teaching eschatologically or existentially, just as we encountered with the Sermon on the Mount. In this case, however, we have the enigmatic phrase "before the Son of Man comes" (v. 23) that makes it even more challenging to decide whether Jesus was giving advice for the "last days" or for the unforeseeable distant future.[3] What did he mean by the coming of the Son of Man? Was Jesus talking about his first coming or second coming? That is to say, when he predicts that the Twelve won't visit all the towns of Galilee before the "Son of Man" comes, was Jesus expecting some sort of divine intervention witnessed by the Twelve, a mysterious display of the kingdom of God coming to earth, like the cross, or the temple veil ripped in two, or the resurrection (both his as well as the "saints"; Matt 27:45–28:7)? Or was Jesus looking way down the road, past the last verse of Matthew's Gospel, to his second coming that will happen much later (Matt 24:26–31)? Was Jesus giving instructions

2. Davies and Allison, *Matthew*, 2:171; Luz, *Matthew*, 2:77–78; Garland also hears an allusion to Elijah, who went about naked and barefoot (*Reading Matthew*, 112–13).

3. For a good, brief survey of different interpretations, see Turner, *Matthew*, 277.

only to the Twelve[4] (the end of the world is near, so hurry up), or was he talking to us too (as long as "the Lord tarries"; we've got a lot of work to do, so be faithful)? Indeed, the "already/not yet" dilemma confronts us again.

Gathering the Lost Sheep of Israel

Half of what Jesus said to the twelve disciples seems to apply to their immediate situation because most of his instructions are very detailed and provincial (Matt 10:1–23). For example, the specific names of the twelve "missionaries" are given (vv. 2–4). They are told not to travel down any road that leads to gentile or Samaritan territory (vv. 5–6; in other words, they are to stay in Galilee). They are told what to say and what to do (vv. 7–8). Jesus even gives specific details regarding money, clothing, and any other provisions for their trip (vv. 9–10). He tells them how to seek hospitality, where to stay and where not to stay, and what they're supposed to do when their message is received or rejected (vv. 12–15). He even tells them what to do when they are arrested and brought before *local* councils and *foreign* officials (vv. 17–20). Then he sets a provincial benchmark, a timetable of sorts: they won't "finish going through the towns of Israel" (much less the whole world) "before the Son of Man comes" (v. 23). In other words, in vv. 1–23 Jesus gave instructions to the Twelve about how to recover *only* the lost sheep of Israel in Galilee—a work for that time and that place.[5] As readers, we may find analogies between our context and their charge, but we obviously don't (and can't!) take these verses literally. The so-called "Great Commission," Matthew 28:19–20, makes it obvious why: Jesus eventually instructed his disciples to "make disciples of *all nations*"—not just Israel—another place where we read Jesus teaching his disciples as if he were speaking to us too.

After Matthew 10:23, the rest of Jesus's instructions to the Twelve are rather vague, having no geographical, historical, or temporal referents. There's only one line that is chained to the first-century context: the part about "two sparrows sold for a *penny*" (*assarion*) (v. 29).[6] The rest of the passage (vv. 26–42) could apply to any time and any place. Commentators spend a lot of time explaining what Jesus meant in the first half of his instructions to the Twelve (vv. 5–23) due to all the historical, social, economic, geographical, and political allusions. Who are the Samaritans? What is the belt? Why not a staff? What does it mean to "shake the dust off your feet"? Who are the governors

---

4. Or even to Matthew's readers? (See Luz, *Matthew*, 2:73–81).

5. Scot McKnight, *A New Vision for Israel: The Teachings of Jesus in National Context* (Grand Rapids: Eerdmans, 1999), 133–35.

6. The *assarion* was a Roman copper coin worth about 1/16 of a denarius (a day's wage); see Davies and Allison, *Matthew*, 2:207.

and kings? Why only the towns of Israel? Yet there's very little explaining to do when it comes to vv. 26–42 because nearly everything Jesus said makes sense in the twenty-first century as much as the first century. In other words, the last half of Jesus's instructions for missionaries has more of an aphoristic quality to it, like parts of the Sermon on the Mount. In fact, much of vv. 26–42 is similar to what Jesus said during the monumental Sermon: reasons not to worry; disciples are more important than birds; acknowledgement before God in heaven; warnings about persecution; disciples are like prophets; and rewards gained and lost. Why the similarities? Like any good sermon, some things bear repeating because they are timeless.

So does this mean we can ignore the first part of Matthew 10 since Jesus's instructions to the Twelve have to do with circumstances surrounding the mission to reclaim the lost tribes of Israel, and we can concentrate only on the last half? That's what some scholars contend because they argue the mission to Israel has been replaced by the gospel mission to the gentiles. Some even see a clear line of demarcation in Matthew's Gospel: at first, Jesus tried to gather the lost sheep of Israel, but they refused. So he shifted his focus and decided to bring gentiles into the kingdom instead (Matt 21:43). According to this reading, then, the "Great Commission" should be translated, "Go and make disciples of all *gentiles* [*ethnē*]" (28:19).[7] There are several problems with this approach, beginning with the assumption that "lost sheep" = all Israel. That can't be the case because Jesus gave geographical restrictions to his disciples. The Twelve weren't to reclaim the lost sheep in gentile territory, that is, the Jews of the diaspora (or perhaps even Judea?).[8] Furthermore, up to this point Matthew has been deliberate in establishing the kind of people Jesus came to recover: the poor, the broken, the powerless, the marginalized.[9] They were the ones drawn to him like "sheep without a shepherd" (9:36). Besides, Jesus didn't expect to find "lost sheep" among the Jewish leadership (the "wolves" in Galilee [10:16–17] and the leaders in Jerusalem [20:18]), who were certainly part of Israel. In fact, some suggest Jesus restricted his mission effort to *Galilee* to signal the end-time recovery of the ten lost tribes of the northern kingdom, beginning the restoration of the twelve tribes with twelve disciples.[10] Isaiah believed the restoration of Israel would begin with a holy remnant. Before Israel could be a "light to the gentiles,"[11] God had to "restore the tribes of

7. See Luz, *Matthew*, 2:72–75.

8. "Jesus's orders address *geography* more than ethnicity" (Keener, *Matthew*, 315 [emphasis his]).

9. So also Bruner, *Matthew*, 1:461.

10. See Willitts, *Matthew's Messianic Shepherd-King*, 189–200; also Sanders, *Jesus and Judaism*, 98: "The expectation of the reassembly of Israel was so widespread, and the memory of the twelve tribes remained so acute, that *'twelve' would necessarily mean 'restoration'*" (emphasis his).

11. Garland, *Reading Matthew*, 112.

Jacob and bring back *those of Israel I have kept*" (Isa 49:6, emphasis added), which explains the priority of Jesus's mission to recover the "lost sheep of Israel" first (Matt 10:6). This is the eschatological order of things, the restoration of Israel for the sake of the world (so also Paul; see Rom 1:16; 2:9; 9:4–7, 23–29; 11:1–5, 11–12, 25–29). So, the "found sheep" (disciples of Jesus; Matt 10:16) were sent to recover the "lost sheep" (those who would receive them; vv. 11–13), leaving the rest to be condemned along with Sodom and Gomorrah (vv. 14–15)—just as Isaiah predicted (Isa 1:9; 10:20–23).[12]

Where does that leave us? Here's the long and the short of it: much of the advice Jesus gave to the Twelve that day had to do with their immediate mission. With the eschatological clock winding down, they had to visit as much of Galilee as they could to make disciples for the kingdom. They knew "the coming of the Son of Man" was near—when Daniel's vision would come true (Dan 7:13–14)—but they had no idea what it would look like when Jesus was "given authority, glory and sovereign power; [and] all nations and peoples of every language worshiped him" (v. 14). In the unfolding drama of the rest of Matthew's Gospel, we see how it happened and was even confirmed by the resurrected Jesus: "*All authority* in heaven and on earth has been given to me" (Matt 28:18, emphasis added). In the meantime, their mission to recover the "lost sheep of Israel" was crucial to the restoration of Israel and therefore the whole world (Matt 28:19–20). Indeed, their participation in expanding the reach of Jesus's kingdom throughout Galilee *contributed* to "the coming of the Son of Man." It was the beginning of *their* effort to bring the kingdom of heaven to earth, which is why the church has rightly read Jesus's instructions to the Twelve as if they were our marching orders as well. It's because we have the same mission to extend the reach of Jesus's heavenly kingdom to the ends of the earth—not only Israel but "to all nations and peoples of every language" (Dan 7:14). That's why the "already/not yet" tension in Jesus's teaching shows up here as well; his timely advice ("already") proves to be timeless ("not yet"). Indeed, instructions to the Twelve that seem expeditious ("Get out there as quick as you can; the harvest is ripe!") may not *always* apply to *every* situation today, but they still *could* apply. Sometimes disciples don't have time to make provisions for the journey, needing instead to rely upon the hospitality of the people they've come to serve (Matt 10:9–14).[13] At the same time, Jesus didn't intend for *all* his disciples to *always* be shoeless and penniless (see Matt 25:34–40). Sometimes we find ourselves penned in hostile territory, like sheep among wolves, brought before the rulers of the world, and arrested

12. For other references in Jewish literature to the Sodom-and-Gomorrah trope, see Evans, *Matthew*, 221.

13. France, *Matthew*, 383–86.

for our faith (10:16–20). At other times it's best to run for our lives (v. 23). As the eschatological clock winds down, there seem to be different time zones to the "kingdom of heaven has come near" (v. 7). Yet, regardless of the time, we know that "the one who stands firm to the end will be saved" (v. 22). "There is always pleasure in the beginning, but the end is the time of testing."[14]

Reaping a Difficult Harvest

As they go into the fields of harvest, Jesus is convinced that his disciples will be treated the same as he (Matt 10:24–25). Part of the reason has to do with their mission: like Jesus, they were to preach the same message and perform the same ministry (vv. 7–8). Therefore, Jesus anticipated that they would receive the same chilly reception: they will be called "Beelzebul." They will be rejected by family, persecuted, and run out of town (vv. 21–23). Like Jesus, they won't bring peace but division (vv. 34–37). Like Jesus, they must carry a cross (v. 38). Like Jesus, they must lose their lives (v. 39). Therefore, to welcome his disciples would be the same as receiving Jesus (v. 40). Yet Jesus hadn't experienced any of these things except being called "Beelzebul" (though even that's not *exactly* what the Pharisees said: "It is by the prince of demons that he drives out demons" [9:34]; they didn't call him "Beelzebul" until later [12:24]). Up to this point, Jesus has been incredibly popular, drawing only the ire of a few (the scribes and Pharisees). In fact, despite the opinion of the Pharisees the crowds celebrated his words and deeds with great praise (7:28–29; 9:8, 33). Things had been going rather well for Jesus, so why wouldn't he expect the same for his disciples? Well, as readers we know the rest of the story: eventually the wheels will come off. It won't go well for him or them. In other words, Jesus's prediction regarding the Twelve only makes sense in light of what eventually happened to him (Matt 26:14–27:50) and them. Yet we're never told what happened to the Twelve; in Matthew's Gospel the apostles never returned to Jesus with a report about their "harvesting" efforts (cf. Mark 6:12–13, 30). Instead, they simply show up later without fanfare or explanation, ironically harvesting actual "heads of grain" because they were hungry (Matt 12:1).

So why was Jesus so glum about the upcoming missionary effort of the Twelve? Moreover, why didn't Matthew report both the successes and failures of the Twelve when they returned to Jesus? Are we to infer that the mission to recover the lost sheep of Israel was a complete bust, especially in light of Jesus's prophetic denouncement of three Galilean towns—Chorazin, Bethsaida, Capernaum—in 11:20–24? If that were the case, it might explain why Jesus's

14. Simonetti, *Matthew 1–13*, 202 (anonymous).

instructions to the Twelve—especially the last half of the mission discourse (10:26–42)—sound so generic, as if these verses were meant for Matthew's readers more than the Twelve.

Certainly in Matthew's narrative world, the Twelve never experienced what Jesus predicted. In fact, Jesus's warnings about the future seem more relevant to the challenges faced by the early church after Matthew 28:20 (read Acts!). Nevertheless, this isn't the first time Jesus anticipated that his disciples would be persecuted like the prophets (Matt 5:10–12, 38–48). Furthermore, Jesus saw himself as a prophet (13:57), who sent his disciples as prophets (23:34), and he predicted both for himself and for them the same destiny as the prophets of old: they would be rejected and killed by their own people (vv. 34–36).[15] But that didn't mean failure;[16] to be treated like the prophets was a sure sign that they were God's emissaries. Notice that Jesus didn't predict whether their campaign to gather the lost sheep of Israel would be successful. Rather, he seems to be more concerned about the welfare of his disciples (much like in the Sermon on the Mount), knowing that "suffering foreseen . . . is more easily endured."[17] Indeed, practically all of his advice in the last half of the mission discourse has to do with how to handle being treated like God's prophets: "Do not be afraid of those who kill the body but cannot kill the soul" (10:28); "Whoever acknowledges me before others, I will also acknowledge before my Father in heaven" (v. 32); "I did not come to bring peace, but a sword" (v. 34); "Anyone who loves their father or mother more than me is not worthy of me" (v. 37); "Whoever loses their life for my sake will find it" (v. 39). Since God was the one who sent prophets to Israel, Jesus assured his disciples of the same authority: "Anyone who welcomes you welcomes me, and anyone who welcomes me welcomes him who sent me" (v. 40). Faithfulness to God in the face of a difficult harvest is what mattered most to Jesus.

Therefore, even though the mission discourse is filled with several warnings—not only the certainty of being persecuted but also the dire consequences of not being faithful to the end—Jesus encouraged the apostles (and future generations of disciples) to remember several things. They have nothing to be ashamed of because they have nothing to hide (vv. 26–27). They have nothing to fear because God is on their side (vv. 28–31). If they die, Jesus will be their advocate in heaven (v. 32). If their family abandons them, they will be welcomed into Jesus's household (vv. 35–37, 40–42). Whatever they lose for Jesus's sake will be restored in the end (v. 39). Whoever follows Jesus must carry a cross all the way to the end (v. 38). In the end, both these prophets

15. Keener, *Matthew*, 313–15.

16. Bruner, *Matthew*, 1:469.

17. Davies and Allison, *Matthew*, 2:230.

and those who help them will receive a prophet's reward (v. 41). These are the righteous ones: those who ask the Lord of the harvest to send farmers into the fields and then become the answer to their own prayers because they freely give what they freely received (9:38; 10:8). Indeed, anyone who gives so much as a cup of cold water to these farmers harvesting such a difficult crop "will certainly not lose their reward" either (10:42).

LIVE the Story

There are so many unanswered questions—details we would love to know—concerning Jesus's instructions to the Twelve. For example, why these twelve men? We have some details about a few of them, but what about the rest? Where were they from? Why did he choose them? When Jesus "gave them authority to drive out impure spirits and to heal every disease and sickness" (Matt 10:1), how did he do it? Did he lay hands on them? Did they know it when it happened? ("Wow. I feel powerful now!") Was their only message, "The kingdom of heaven has come near" (v. 7)? That's a short sermon. Or did they repeat what they heard from Jesus? In other words, when Jesus told them to preach that "the kingdom of heaven has come near," was that shorthand for the entire Sermon on the Mount? How did they heal people? Did they do it "in the name of Jesus"? Were there times when they were unable to heal the sick or cast out demons (17:16), and if so, why? And why did Jesus encourage the Twelve to "pass the peace" to their hosts when he said he didn't come to bring peace (10:12–13)? Is this the same thing we do during Eucharist? I can't help but wonder why none of these details were given, especially if the mission of the Twelve to recover the lost sheep of Israel is supposed to be prescriptive for Matthew's readers. In other words, if these instructions were intended to guide future Christians in our evangelistic endeavors, why is it that we're given no details when it comes to how to do it?

Perhaps it is because these details don't matter. Remember, Jesus seems ambivalent about the success of the Twelve, whether they will get results. The only thing he cares about is whether the Twelve will keep the faith as they gather the lost sheep and reap a difficult harvest. Besides, I don't think Jesus's instructions to the Twelve should be taken as guidelines for missionaries today. In fact, I think we misread these verses when we try to apply them to the Christian mission of bringing the message to unbelievers. Jesus didn't send his disciples to the gentiles, hoping to bring them to faith in the God of Israel. This was a mission to reclaim people who already believe—the sheep of God's pasture. So, making the link between his context and ours, we shouldn't take Jesus's words to the Twelve as instructions on how to win unbelievers to Christ. Rather, for us these verses have to do with restoring Christians to the fold, believers who have lost their way because of abusive shepherds. The first mission effort launched by Jesus wasn't to convert pagans. No. The first thing he did to establish the reign of God on earth was to restore his own people—the ones broken by their own religion. Now, that changes things, doesn't it?

Jesus thought like a pastor, as one who tends the flock of God. His compassion for the "harassed and helpless, like sheep without a shepherd" (Matt 9:36) compelled him to recruit the Twelve to help him recover them all. And how would they do it? First, they would *talk* about the reign of God on earth, and then they would *do* something about it: healing, raising, cleansing, and exorcising. Notice, Jesus didn't give his apostles little sermons to preach on how to get lost sheep to return to God. Indeed, the *last* thing wounded sheep need to hear is another sermon—especially one that is meant to set them straight. Imagine what that would sound like, Jesus giving advice on how to recover a lost sheep with a sermon: "Okay. Here's how you get our brothers and sisters to come back to synagogue. First, tell them that they've sinned against God by dropping out. They know they've done wrong. It's time for them to repent of their waywardness. Next, help them remember why it's important to attend Sabbath services and worship God. Tell stories about the good times we have in worship. Say, 'this is how we show the world that we're different.' Then ask them, 'Who can claim to be God's children if they don't show up on the Sabbath to praise Him?' If they start complaining about their bad experiences when they attended, listen politely and then give them the zinger, 'Well, none of us are perfect. So, you'll fit right in.' They've been in the world so long, they've forgotten what it means to be holy." Sounds ridiculous, doesn't it? Perhaps it's because I've gone too far. There certainly is no evidence that these "lost sheep" had left the synagogue. Yet it was the site of the sick and diseased—those who were considered "cursed by God"—that prompted Jesus to send his disciples into the fields of harvest. That's why I see a correlation; it's because many of the "lost-sheep" Christians that I've met quit coming to church because of bad things that happened in their lives.

In the Baptist tradition, we have need of interim preachers to bridge the gap between the outgoing and incoming pastor. Since we have no hierarchy within the denomination—every church has local autonomy to hire and fire their ministers—the transition between ministers can be a troubling time. I have served as an interim preacher for more than thirty churches in Arkansas and Missouri. Of course, every church is different; every congregation has its own history and personality. Yet almost all of them have one thing in common: when their pastor leaves (most often under bad circumstances), members start fighting with one another. Sometimes the skirmishes are minor. But often it's a pretty ugly scene with several groups jockeying for power. As the newcomer, members would favor me with stories about past injustices and new battle lines, old wounds and potential troubles. Lost in the fray were members caught in the crossfire, the casualties of church wars fought by laity and leadership. Some of them were hurt by abusive pastors; others were tired of fighting with their church family, refusing to take a side. So, they quit coming to church. I had made it my mission to visit many of these "lost sheep" during one of my interim assignments. Some had moved on to join other congregations. But most of them had dropped out of church for one simple reason: they had enough trouble in their own lives, and they didn't want to go to church to add any more. I often didn't know what else to say except "I'm sorry."

Driving home one night, I thought about the mission of the Twelve to reclaim Israel and began to wonder: What if we took a more "Jesus" approach to restoring the "lost sheep" of the church? What would that look like?[18]

After welcoming us into their homes, we would tell them: "Our God still reigns. Life was never meant to be hell on earth. No. Heaven has come near to you today." Then, we would try to help them overcome the bad things that have happened to them. Instead of condemning the sheep for losing their way,[19] what if we healed the sick, raised the dead, restored the ostracized, and expelled evil? Well, we might find that some would welcome the relief. But Jesus also warned that some won't like it at all. "Who do you think you are coming into my house and acting like you bring heaven with you?" In fact, they might be offended, insulted, or simply angry with us that we even tried. That's why I think Christians give up on each other. We expect everyone to welcome us with open arms, especially those within our family of faith. But that's not what always happens. Jesus knew that better than anyone, which is why he warned his disciples that they would be treated like prophets—at times rejected, abused, and even run out of town. Rather than give up on one another because of "hurt feelings," perhaps we should expect the same. If we're going to join Jesus in the work of recovering lost sheep, we need to

18. Shouldn't it also include a mission to reclaim the lost sheep of Israel today—not as pagans but as God's people? Stuart Dauermann writes: "This is what it means to make Jewish disciples of Yeshua: not disciples of Yeshua who happen to be Jewish, but Jewish disciples who follow Yeshua in the context of a renewed vision of Jewish community, covenant, and consummation" ("Messianic Jewish Outreach," in *Introduction to Messianic Judaism: Its Ecclesial Context and Biblical Foundations*, ed. David Rudolph and Joel Willitts [Grand Rapids: Zondervan, 2013], 95).

19. Chrysostom wrote: "And he bids them have not only gentleness as sheep, but also the harmlessness of the dove. . . . Let us then be ashamed, who do the contrary, who set like wolves upon our enemies. For as long as we are sheep, we conquer" (*Homilies*, 220).

take him at his word: we're going to be treated like prophets. Wolves will be ready to devour us (Matt 10:16). Rulers will be threatened by us (vv. 18–19). They may even call us names because they hate us (vv. 22, 25). Our own family may turn against us (vv. 34–36). This is hard work, a difficult harvest. But we need to remember that God never gives up on anyone—especially his children. So, when we look around and see so many wounded souls, so many broken lives, so many sheep "harassed" by abusive shepherds and disheartened by difficult circumstances, shouldn't we all turn to one another and say, "The harvest is plentiful but the workers are few. Ask the Lord of the harvest, therefore, to send out workers into his harvest field" (Matt 9:37–38)? If we did, who knows? We might even become the answer to our own prayers.

Even when we recover "lost sheep," we're still making disciples.

CHAPTER 15

Matthew 11:2–30

LISTEN to the Story

2When John, who was in prison, heard about the deeds of the Messiah, he sent his disciples 3to ask him, "Are you the one who is to come, or should we expect someone else?"

4Jesus replied, "Go back and report to John what you hear and see: 5The blind receive sight, the lame walk, those who have leprosy are cleansed, the deaf hear, the dead are raised, and the good news is proclaimed to the poor. 6Blessed is anyone who does not stumble on account of me."

7As John's disciples were leaving, Jesus began to speak to the crowd about John: "What did you go out into the wilderness to see? A reed swayed by the wind? 8If not, what did you go out to see? A man dressed in fine clothes? No, those who wear fine clothes are in kings' palaces. 9Then what did you go out to see? A prophet? Yes, I tell you, and more than a prophet. 10This is the one about whom it is written:

> 'I will send my messenger ahead of you,
> who will prepare your way before you.'

11Truly I tell you, among those born of women there has not risen anyone greater than John the Baptist; yet whoever is least in the kingdom of heaven is greater than he. 12From the days of John the Baptist until now, the kingdom of heaven has been subjected to violence, and violent people have been raiding it. 13For all the Prophets and the Law prophesied until John. 14And if you are willing to accept it, he is the Elijah who was to come. 15Whoever has ears, let them hear.

16"To what can I compare this generation? They are like children sitting in the marketplaces and calling out to others:

> 17'We played the pipe for you,
> and you did not dance;
> we sang a dirge,
> and you did not mourn.'

[18]For John came neither eating nor drinking, and they say, 'He has a
demon.' [19]The Son of Man came eating and drinking, and they say, 'Here
is a glutton and a drunkard, a friend of tax collectors and sinners.' But
wisdom is proved right by her deeds."

[20]Then Jesus began to denounce the towns in which most of his
miracles had been performed, because they did not repent. [21]"Woe to you,
Chorazin! Woe to you, Bethsaida! For if the miracles that were performed
in you had been performed in Tyre and Sidon, they would have repented
long ago in sackcloth and ashes. [22]But I tell you, it will be more bearable
for Tyre and Sidon on the day of judgment than for you. [23]And you,
Capernaum, will you be lifted to the heavens? No, you will go down to
Hades. For if the miracles that were performed in you had been performed
in Sodom, it would have remained to this day. [24]But I tell you that it will
be more bearable for Sodom on the day of judgment than for you."

[25]At that time Jesus said, "I praise you, Father, Lord of heaven and
earth, because you have hidden these things from the wise and learned,
and revealed them to little children. [26]Yes, Father, for this is what you were
pleased to do.

[27]"All things have been committed to me by my Father. No one knows
the Son except the Father, and no one knows the Father except the Son
and those to whom the Son chooses to reveal him.

[28]"Come to me, all you who are weary and burdened, and I will give
you rest. [29]Take my yoke upon you and learn from me, for I am gentle
and humble in heart, and you will find rest for your souls. [30]For my yoke
is easy and my burden is light."

Listening to the Text in the Story: Genesis 18:16–19:29; Deuteronomy 21:18–23; Job 28:12–28; Psalm 8:2; Proverbs 1:20–33; 8:1–21, 32–36; Isaiah 14:13–15; 23:1–18; 29:14; 35:1–10; 42:1–7; 61:1–3; Jeremiah 6:16; Lamentations 5:4–5; Ezekiel 26:2–28:24; Malachi 3:1–5; 4:1–6; Sirach 51:23–30; Wisdom of Solomon 9:1–18.

What do you do when faithfulness to the Lord doesn't pay off? You've done everything right, and yet you don't get the desired result. What happens next? This is a chapter about unrequited desire and the frustration that so easily comes when things don't work out like they should.

John the Baptist did his job. God sent him to Israel to warn them that the day of the Lord had dawned on them. That meant judgment, just as the prophets of old had predicted.[1] Like Isaiah, the Baptizer compared the upcoming judgment of God to someone taking an ax to the roots of a tree (Matt 3:10; Isa 6:13). But John didn't think he was strong enough to wield the ax. The great oak of Israel would be felled by someone "more powerful than I" (Matt 3:11), the prophet of God who was supposed to come to baptize the people in the consuming fire of God's Spirit, gathering the harvest before "burning up the chaff with unquenchable fire" (v. 12). It's not that God was finished with Israel. As Job said, "At least there is hope for a tree: If it is cut down, it will sprout again, and its new shoots will not fail" (Job 14:7). Isaiah believed the same: "A shoot will come up from the stump of Jesse; from his roots a Branch will bear fruit. The Spirit of the Lord will rest on him—the Spirit of wisdom and understanding" (Isa 11:1–2). To make that happen, the only thing John could do was preach repentance, offer water baptism, and wait for God. So when Jesus showed up in the wilderness, looking to be baptized by the prophet who wore the garments of Elijah, John knew he wouldn't have to wait any longer for the coming one. In fact, John hoped that Jesus would start with him, baptizing him with the consuming fire of God's Spirit, since judgment begins with the house of God (Matt 3:14). But John still had to play his part. He baptized Jesus in water, God baptized Jesus with his Spirit, and the heavenly voice confirmed the event: God was "well pleased" with his beloved Son (v. 17). John should have thought the same about himself. God must certainly have been pleased with him because he did his job, and this should have been a comforting thought to a prophet who was thrown in prison because he obeyed God (4:12).

But God's judgment didn't come. Instead, Jesus seemed bent on showing the mercy of God. Rather than fast like John's disciples, Jesus joined the party. Instead of withdrawing to the desert, Jesus went to town. After a while, it became obvious to everyone that John and Jesus took very different approaches to preparing for the imminent day of the Lord. "John came neither eating nor drinking," while the Son of Man did the opposite (Matt 11:18–19). In fact, you couldn't find two prophets who devoted their lives to God more differently than John and Jesus. Yet they were supposed to be working *together* to bring Israel back to God. Of course, we've seen this before; we find a synergistic method to their madness: the ol' "bad cop, good cop" routine. But that's not the way the prophets of old worked the system. To them, no trickery was necessary, especially when it came to obeying God. Israel needed to get right or get left—kings as well as commoners. That's the way John saw it too. There was no time for playing games. Tell it to the people

1. James D. G. Dunn, *Jesus and the Spirit* (Grand Rapids: Eerdmans, 1997), 59.

straight. This was a matter of life and death. Indeed, John knew that better than anyone, waiting in Herod's prison for judgment day.

EXPLAIN the Story

Is it any wonder that John sent a few of his disciples to Jesus because he wanted to know, "Are you the one who is to come, or should we expect someone else?" (Matt 11:3)? When you're about to die for a cause—especially *because* of a cause—there should be no doubts. John's entire life led to this moment. Everything he worked for, everything he said would only matter if Jesus did what he was supposed to do and say. The significance of John's life depended on Jesus. If Jesus let him down, if he didn't turn out to be "the one," then John must have wondered: "Am I about to die for the wrong man? Is there someone else? Is there enough time? Will I live to see the day—the day I predicted had come? Isn't it time for Malachi 3–4 to come true? Am I the messenger? Is Jesus the 'coming one'? Or, am I wrong? Did I miss something?" Then again, I'm probably presuming too much here, projecting onto John the typical "identity crisis" of twenty-first-century Westerners. Yet there must have been some concern, some question in John's mind, for why else would he send his disciples to ask Jesus, "Are you the one?"[2] Notice, however, it wasn't John's identity that mattered here. The issue was the identity of Jesus—a question that hangs over the entire narrative of Matthew's Gospel—because who Jesus is determines not only the significance of John but also Matthew, the rest of the Twelve, and anyone who has eyes to read or ears to hear the Gospel. "Blessed is anyone who does not stumble on account of me" (Matt 11:6).

Having Ears to Hear Prophecy

Jesus was in a difficult spot. John was the first to "believe" in Jesus. The Baptizer announced his arrival. He prepared the way for the Messiah. Yet now Jesus has to respond to John's doubts while a crowd eavesdrops on their long-distance conversation. Evidently, it was "the deeds of the Messiah" that troubled Herod's prisoner—deeds that up to this point had inspired the crowds to *celebrate* the work of God (Matt 9:8, 33). It seems, however, that John didn't like what he was hearing. What was Jesus supposed to do? Perhaps he should set the record straight for the benefit of the crowd, blasting John for his impertinence: "How dare he question my authority?" Yet a rift between the two might be troublesome. In light of the well-known eschatological timetable

2. Chrysostom suggests that John sent his disciples to inquire of Jesus for their benefit not his; they needed to learn for themselves the identity of Jesus (*Homilies*, 239–40).

(17:10–13), what would it say about Jesus if he implied that John *wasn't* the forerunner of the Messiah? Furthermore, casting doubt on John's identity would be risky; the people were convinced that the Baptizer was a prophet of God (21:26). So, was John right or not? At the same time, shoring up John's reputation would be beneficial to Jesus's mission. If Jesus took advantage of the opportunity and worked to convince the crowd that John was "Elijah" (and therefore, by implication, that he himself was the Messiah), it might settle the issue in the minds of the people. That kind of approach, however, doesn't sound like Jesus at all; he never tried to coax the people into approving of him. Jesus knew who he was (and certainly he knew who John was: "He is the Elijah who was to come" [11:14]). Jesus had no doubts about John, but John—the one who was supposed to identify the Messiah—had doubts about Jesus. To say the least, John's question placed Jesus on the horns of a dilemma. Reprimand John or build him up? Assure John's disciples or persuade the crowd?

Most of what Jesus said that day was directed to the crowd (vv. 7–30). He gave a rather brief response to John's question, never answering it directly (vv. 4–5). John's disciples were to report everything they had seen and heard from Jesus. That's it. He didn't say, "Go tell John not to worry. I am the one." Instead, he left it to the Baptizer to figure it out. Indeed, it's the way Jesus paraphrased his mission that reveals his presumption: John should recognize the prophecies of Isaiah coming true through Jesus (see Isa 26:19; 35:1–10; 42:1–7; 61:1–3). Listing his deeds—blind see, lame walk, lepers are cleansed, deaf hear, dead are raised, poor get good news—was all that needed to be said because prophets recognize prophecy. Jesus counted on John to hear the voice of Scripture when the disciples reported what they heard and saw. At the same time, Jesus issued a veiled warning in the form of a beatitude—not only for John and his disciples but for the crowd as well: "Blessed is anyone who does not stumble on account of me" (Matt 11:6). Jesus knew he would offend many. He certainly wasn't what John, his disciples, or anyone else expected. Yet Jesus didn't seem to be too concerned about John getting it right; he left it to the Baptizer to infer that he was "the one who is to come." It was the *crowd* that needed to be straightened out about several things, not only about prophecies fulfilled but also about the nasty rumors circulating among the people concerning John and Jesus (vv. 7–19).

After John's disciples left, Jesus turned his attention to the crowd and began to scold them for their imperceptiveness (vv. 7–14). He questioned their motives for trekking out to the desert (approximately a two-day trip for most Galileans) to see the phenomenon called "the Baptizer." They didn't go to hear prophecy. They went to see a prophet, which is why Jesus belittled them for their sightseeing adventure. "What did you expect to see, huh? You didn't go all the way to the Jordan to see reeds bending in the desert winds, did you? Looking for a prophet fit for a palace, like one of Herod's advisors?[3] Hardly. You wanted to see a *real* prophet, dressed like Elijah. Well, guess what. You can tell everyone you saw *him*—not just any prophet but the *one who was prophesied* to prepare the way for God.[4] Yet this is what really matters: it's not what you saw; it's what you heard. Did you hear him? He's the greatest prophet that ever lived, so you better listen to him! For, if you did, you would know that all Scripture has pointed to this moment. God's reign has come near to you. But it doesn't come through violence. That's what Herod[5] or the Zealots would have you think. The kingdom of heaven isn't for those who wield swords. No. The kingdom of heaven is for those who have ears to hear the Prophets as well as the Law because everything they predicted is coming true. Don't you see? This means the weakest, most insignificant person in the kingdom—God's kingdom—is greater than the greatest prophet who ever lived. Anybody got ears? You better use them. Since John was Elijah, what does that say about you?"

That's my paraphrase of Jesus's compact retort—a reading that depends upon several interpretive decisions. For example, what did Jesus mean by the phrase "a reed swayed by the wind" (11:7)? Was he speaking literally (as I have it), or was Jesus referring metaphorically to spineless prophets? Why did Jesus say, "From the days of John the Baptist until now, the kingdom of heaven has been subjected to violence, and violent people have been raiding it" (v. 12)? Does "from the days of John the Baptist" refer to John's birthday or the beginning of his ministry? In other words, was Jesus talking about the violence of Herod the Great or of his son, Herod Antipas? There's even some question about the translation "has been subjected to violence." The verb could also be translated as an intensive middle, "is coming forcefully," which could refer to the power of Jesus's ministry. If that were the case, then Jesus would be claiming that ever since John's baptism, the kingdom of heaven has been invading earth through the power of his miraculous deeds (healing the sick, raising the dead, etc.), while at the same time there are also "violent men" (Herod or the Zealots) who were trying to take it by force.[6] Finally, what's the implication of Jesus's claim that "all the Prophets and the Law prophesied until John" (v. 13)? Was Jesus drawing a clear eschatological line in the sand, relegating the Baptizer to the old age, separated from the new age of his messianic kingdom?

---

3. Keener, *Matthew*, 337.
4. Bruner, *Matthew*, 1:510.
5. Keener writes: "Jesus here reprimands those who laid claim to the kingdom but without just, legal claim" (*Matthew*, 339).
6. For a good discussion of the options, see Turner, *Matthew*, 294–96.

Moreover, what about the Law? Does this mean that Jesus set up an expiration date? Had the Law and the Prophets done their job so that it was time to set them aside since the new age of the kingdom had come?[7] Or, is it more likely that Jesus is claiming what Matthew has been showing all along: that the fulfillment of Scripture is a sure indication that this was a unique time in Israel's history—that all of God's promises were coming true in Jesus?

However we answer these questions, one thing is evident: as Jesus was making claims about John, Matthew was making claims about Jesus, tying together the significance of their tandem ministry.[8] The way Matthew saw it, whoever had ears to hear "Elijah" would recognize the Messiah. Consequently, those who dismissed one would dismiss the other—something Jesus noticed about "this generation" (Matt 11:16–19). These people had ears to hear, all right. But they were listening to the scuttlebutt *about* John and Jesus rather than listening *to them*. Certainly, John and Jesus were the odd couple: the ascetic and the feaster—two extremes at opposite ends. Therefore, one would think that people would be attracted to one instead of the other. Yet that wasn't the case. Evidently, some (many? most?) people dismissed *both* of them. The only people who really liked Jesus were tax collectors and sinners. John may have baptized many, but he had only a few disciples—John was little more than a curiosity to the masses (vv. 7–9). So even though the Baptizer was a phenomenon, the people began to attribute John's odd behavior to a demon. They thought that only a malevolent power would drive a man to take fasting to such extremes, punishing his body. And what about Jesus and his carousing? Well, the same group dismissed him as a rebellious son, nothing more than a "glutton and a drunkard" (v. 19).[9] They must have thought, "No wonder the man loves hanging out with people who can't control themselves. Only sinners welcome sinners." Whether saint or sinner, the crowd couldn't be pleased.

According to Jesus, what the people thought about him and John said more about them than it did about him and the Baptizer. But it's difficult to tell if Jesus was criticizing "this generation" for their apathy or for being fickle (v. 16). It depends on identifying the voices of the children reciting the rhyme, "We played the pipe for you, and you did not dance; we sang a dirge, and you did not mourn" (v. 17). If Jesus saw himself and John as "we," then Jesus was making fun of the apathetic attitude of the crowds.[10] Jesus "played the pipe" trying to get the people to celebrate the arrival of the kingdom of heaven, while John "sang a dirge" in order to get the crowds to mourn over

7. See the Davies and Allison, *Matthew*, 2:257.
8. Bruner, *Matthew*, 1:510.
9. See Deut 21:20 (Keener, *Matthew*, 342; Evans, *Matthew*, 241).
10. So Chrysostom (*Homilies*, 246).

Israel's sin, and the people didn't care either way.[11] On the other hand, if the children reciting the rhyme were the people of "this generation," then the one refusing to dance is John and the one refusing to mourn is Jesus.[12] In other words, by placing the rhyme on the lips of the crowds, Jesus was criticizing them for their fickle responses to both John's and his ministry. The people were mocking John for his morose approach to life. ("Quit acting so glum, chum. Get up and dance!") Yet they were troubled by the fact that Jesus didn't know when it was time to quit partying. ("Hey, this isn't the time to dance. It's a funeral, for goodness sake!") Both approaches make sense, but I think the former fits the context better. Jesus had just criticized the crowd for their lack of response to John (vv. 4–15) and was about to rebuke them for ignoring the significance of his own ministry among them (vv. 20–24). Furthermore, vv. 17–19 follow a chiastic form:[13]

A. "We [Jesus] played the pipe for you"
B. "We [John] sang a dirge"
B. "John came neither eating nor drinking"
A. "The Son of Man came eating and drinking"

Besides, the last line of v. 19—the perfect segue to Jesus's indictment of the Galilean villages—clinches it for me: "But wisdom is proved right by her deeds." "This generation" may have dismissed John and Jesus for their bizarre behavior and extreme approaches to getting right with God. But Jesus was convinced that the wisdom of their tandem ministry would be vindicated by God—something Matthew was out to prove in the rest of his Gospel. In other words, as far as Matthew was concerned, the wisdom revealed in chapters 1–10 (John is the forerunner, Jesus is the coming one) will be "proved right" by chapters 12–28.[14] Ironically, then, the jester of the crowd ("he is a glutton and a drunkard!") will be killed as the rebellious son in Jerusalem: "You must purge the evil from among you" (Deut 21:18–21). The only question left to the reader is whether anyone will have ears to hear the prophecy and eyes to see the kingdom of God.

Having Eyes to See Wisdom

Since Jesus didn't prescribe the customary approach to repentance via fasting, how did he expect Israel to return to God? If people lamenting over their sin

11. This is what France calls "the traditional interpretation" (*Matthew*, 434).

12. Davies and Allison, *Matthew*, 2:261–62.

13. Turner, *Matthew*, 296.

14. Davies and Allison describe Matthew 1–11 as "the offer" and 12–27 as "the refusal" (*Matthew*, 2:294–97).

by taking up the wearing of sackcloth and sitting in ashes wasn't necessary, what *would* provoke God's people to repent of their sin? A prophet wearing camel hair, living in the desert, observing a wild-honey-and-locust diet didn't do it: "He's demon possessed!" A rebel defying the "repentance" tradition by eating and drinking with notorious sinners when he should have been fasting seemed to make things worse: "He's a lousy drunk!" No. As far as Jesus was concerned, the one thing that should have compelled the Galileans to fall on their faces before God and repent of their sin was the undeniable sign of God's presence: miracles. Jesus thought the miracles he and his disciples performed would not only draw lost sheep into the fold but would also convince Israel to repent of their sin (Matt 11:20–24). The kingdom of heaven had come to earth. Yet despite all the miracles, nothing happened. No repentance. No sackcloth and ashes. This made no sense to Jesus. It's one thing to dismiss John as a crazy man and Jesus as a party animal. But to ignore the miraculous? That was incomprehensible. Sure, sometimes the crowd gave glory to God for what they saw (9:8). But Jesus expected the people to respond to the glory of God like Isaiah did, confessing that they were a people of "unclean lips" because they recognized that they were in the presence of "the King" (Isa 6:5). Evidently, the Galileans began to take all these miracles for granted, which enraged Jesus: "Woe to you, Chorazin! Woe to you, Bethsaida! For if the miracles that were performed in you had been performed in Tyre and Sidon, they would have repented long ago in sackcloth and ashes" (Matt 11:21). Pagans—and not just any pagans but *very bad* pagans (Ezek 26:2–28:24)—would have responded more appropriately to God's work than Jesus's own people. Sodom receiving a better verdict on judgment day than Capernaum (Matt 11:23–24)? Really? Wow. Jesus was *really* angry.

At this point (even though we know better), one might expect Jesus to say, "Let them all go to hell." After all, they missed their chance. They were acting like children who couldn't be pleased no matter what they saw. Jesus had already done so much to reveal what heaven on earth looks like. (It is a beautiful picture, isn't it? The sick restored. The broken healed. Evil defeated. Laughter and eating and drinking around the table of God's mercy. The relief that comes knowing God is on our side. Things made right. Forgiveness. Good times.) Yet, he didn't leave the Galileans to the misery of their foolishness, banishing them to eternal damnation. He didn't stomp off in total frustration to find a more receptive audience, "lost sheep" who grazed other pastures of Israel's land. ("So, you don't want to hear it anymore, huh? Don't like what you see? Reject me? Fine. I'll take my show on the road and find people who will appreciate me, you bunch of thick-headed, hardhearted buffoons!") Rather than sulk over the poor results of his kingdom effort to this point, Jesus *praised*

God for what was happening. Yes, Jesus was angry. But he still saw his Father at work in his reclamation project. In fact, simple "children" who needed God the most—not the "wise and learned"—saw it too. The mysterious presence of the kingdom (the Messiah is here!) was hidden from the eyes of those who think they see everything (Matt 11:25). But the eyes of "little children" see things that "wise and learned" people don't see. Indeed, the way Jesus saw it, this was just the way the God of Israel worked: exalting the lowly, finding the lost, restoring the broken, revealing himself to the least of these. Nothing pleases him more than when children recognize the wisdom of God (v. 26).

Throughout Proverbs, Wisdom appears as a woman who calls out to the masses to see if anyone would recognize her and listen to her words. She goes to the public square. She lifts her voice on top of the wall. Wisdom cries out to the people gathered at the city gate, preaching her sermons against the foolish ways of those who mock God (Prov 1:20–22). What if they don't listen and continue in their foolishness? Well, after calamity comes (and disaster is certain when fools refuse to follow sage advice), Wisdom says she will "laugh when disaster strikes you" (v. 26). In the midst of their miserable condition the people will finally turn to her for help, but by then it will be too late: "Then they will call to me but I will not answer; they will look for me but will not find me, since they hated knowledge and did not choose to fear the Lord" (vv. 28–29). Good advice doesn't help fools suffering the consequences of their stupidity. Wisdom is the first to say, "I told you so." Since fools mock Wisdom, she decides to return the favor: "You wouldn't listen to me because you didn't recognize me. Now you want my help? Okay, here's a little advice: 'Learn your lesson. You made your bed; now lie in it'" (the gist of vv. 30–33).

At times, Jesus sounds like Wisdom, berating the masses for their foolish inability to hear and see what is set plainly before them (Matt 11:20–24). He acts like he's the embodiment of Wisdom, even going so far as to say, "Nobody understands me. Nobody gets it. I'm the only one who knows God. And, God is the only one who recognizes me" (v. 27).[15] Yet, even in the face of such disappointment and the crushing loss that comes to those who "don't get it," Jesus strikes a different tone than Wisdom. All is not lost. Time hasn't expired; there's no "I told you so" in Jesus's voice. It's because he believes God has revealed himself to some people—to "little children" (v. 25). Furthermore, Jesus believes that, as long as God's Son is still present, he's able to reveal the Father to whomever he "chooses to reveal him" (v. 27).[16]

15. Luz hears here echoes of Jesus as "Immanuel" (*Matthew*, 2:169–70); Davies and Allison see allusions to Moses (Exodus 33:12f.; see *Matthew*, 2:282–87).

16. "If revelation is accessible to 'babes,' then it is accessible to all" (Garland, *Reading Matthew*, 133).

So, rather than withdraw from the foolish masses who don't have ears to hear or eyes to see Wisdom—leaving them to the miserable result of their bad choices—Jesus takes her message to the streets once again: "Come to me, all you who are weary and burdened, and I will give you rest" (v. 28). Thank God! Jesus believes in second chances, even for fools. And, here's why: wisdom will become the fool for fools who can't see wisdom. The Son *will reveal* the Father's will to them—this is the way of wisdom!—because he chooses to become one of them.

I think that idea—the incarnation of "foolish" wisdom—is embedded in the imagery of Jesus's call to "take my yoke upon you and learn from me, for I am gentle and humble in heart, and you will find rest for your souls. For my yoke is easy and my burden is light" (vv. 29–30). The yoke imagery has a double meaning. First, Jewish rabbis referred to the yoke of the law as a necessary burden that leads to a wise life.[17] In fact, Jesus sounds a lot like Ben Sira summoning students to learn the wisdom of obedience from him:

> Draw near to me, you who are uneducated,
>   and lodge in the house of instruction.
> Why do you say you are lacking in these things,
>   and why do you endure such great thirst? . . .
> Put your neck under her yoke,
>   and let your soul receive instruction;
>   it is to be found close by.
> See with your own eyes that I have labored but little
>   and found for myself much serenity. (Sir 51:23–27 NRSV)

The difference is that Jesus invited future disciples not only to learn from him but to "take *my yoke* upon you," as if the yoke belonged to him.[18] Rabbis would speak of placing the yoke of *the law* on their students, a heavy burden that required training, not only to carry but to get used to it—a rather uncomfortable fit. Jesus invited disciples to place *his* yoke on their shoulders because it "fits well" (a better translation of *chrēstos* than "easy"), and the burden of his yoke is "light" (Matt 11:30).[19]

Most commentators think the yoke refers to part of the tackle required to pair up two oxen to pull heavy objects, like a cart or a plow.[20] (On this reading, Jesus claims his yoke is "easier" because he pairs up with his disciples to pull the heavy load of the law.) But France finds a better fit for the analogy.

---

17. Keener, *Matthew*, 348–49.
18. Davies and Allison, *Matthew*, 2:289–90.
19. France, *Matthew*, 450: "A comfortably fitting yoke and a light burden is the ideal combination."
20. See Nolland, *Matthew*, 476–77.

He thinks Jesus was referring to a human yoke, a piece of wood "worn by a single person to distribute the weight of a load across the shoulders."[21] The imagery takes your breath away. Yes, Jesus was referring to the yoke of the law, just like the rabbis. Moreover, as commentators rightly point out, unlike the rabbis Jesus talked about the yoke as if it were *his*. But what does this mean? I think the yoke is his cross.[22] He's talking about a yoke for humans, not animals. In my mind's eye, then, I see Jesus picking up a beam, placing it on his shoulders and wrapping his arms around it—like a man carrying the crossbeam to his own crucifixion—and in effect saying, "Come to me, all you who are weary and burdened, and I will give you *Shabbat*.[23] Take my yoke upon you and *become my disciple* [*mathete*] because I *am a lowly man* [*praus . . . kai tapeinos tē kardia*]. Here, you will find *Shabbat* for your soul.[24] For my yoke fits you well; the burden of my law is light." No wonder Jesus believed everyone—even fools!—would get another chance to see wisdom. In his humiliation, Jesus would reveal the folly of God's wisdom to all who have eyes to see (1 Cor 1:18–2:16).

LIVE the Story

Most of us can identify with this story in several ways. Consider John. How many times have you found yourself suffering difficult circumstances because you did the right thing? It's one thing to live with the regret of your mistakes—like some of the people of Chorazin, Bethsaida, or Capernaum must have felt long after the death and resurrection of Jesus. Did they think back to the day, remembering how they "missed" their Messiah? "He was right here. He did so many marvelous things. The rascals in Jerusalem crucified him. But now we hear he's been raised from the dead! Who could have seen that coming? He must be God's Messiah! And we didn't see it." But John didn't have the advantage of post-Easter contemplation. He was murdered before he knew the rest of the story. Of course, prophets are supposed to see what others don't, peering into the future in light of prophecies past. They are able to see the handwriting on the wall and make sense of what is to be. They know God's

---

21. France, *Matthew*, 449. See also Keener, *Matthew*, 348; Garland, *Reading Matthew*, 134; and especially Talbert, *Matthew*, 150, who also hears echoes of Lam 5:5.

22. Referring to the execution of Jesus, Brown notes: "Often it [the crossbeam] was carried behind the nape of the neck *like a yoke*, with the condemned's arms pulled back and hooked over it" (Raymond E. Brown, *The Death of the Messiah: From Gethsemane to the Grave*, 2 vols., ABRL [New York: Doubleday, 1994], 2:913 [emphasis mine]).

23. Davies and Allison, *Matthew*, 2:287, quotes Augustine: "Christ is the true Sabbath."

24. The eschatological age was often described in sabbatical terms (Davies and Allison, *Matthew*, 2:288–89).

promises *must* come true because his word is infallible. Yet what happens when God lets you down, when his promises don't come true for *you*? It's hard to join in the praise of the people who are getting their miracles—the blind see, the lame walk, lepers are healed, the deaf hear, the dead are raised—when you are about to die in prison. Doesn't God see your faithfulness? Has he forgotten you? Do you shake your fist at God and say, "What about me, God? What about me? I'm going to die, and you're not doing anything about it." That's a heavy load to carry—when things don't turn out like we think they should. Then again, perhaps this is the time to pick up his yoke and shoulder the cross, only to discover that his burden is light because it fits *you* so well. Who could have seen that coming? Only prophets who learn from their master, wear his yoke, and find rest for their soul because they know the rest of the story.

Corrie ten Boom, author of the bestseller *The Hiding Place*, tells the story of being awakened in the middle of the night by her sister while they slept with several hundred other women in a German concentration camp during World War II. Both she and her sister had been arrested by the Gestapo for hiding Jewish refugees in their home in the Netherlands.

> Bep, my sister, awakened me and repeated to me in a whisper what God had told her about the work that would be waiting for us after our release.
>
> "We must open a home for people who have suffered so much here and in other places where life has been completely disrupted by war. But the most important part of our task will be to tell everyone who will listen that Jesus is the only answer to the problems that are disturbing the hearts of men and of nations. We shall have the right to speak because we can tell from our experience that His light is more powerful than the deepest darkness. Surely, nothing could be darker than our experiences here. I keep telling myself, 'Things cannot possibly grow worse,' but every day we see that our misery only deepens. How wonderful that the reality of His presence is greater than the reality of the hell about us! We shall have to do a lot of traveling, but we must never spend our energies in collecting funds. God will provide everything we need: money, health, wisdom, and the necessary languages. All of our efforts must go into bringing the gospel, for we shall have many opportunities."
>
> Bep's eyes did not see the dirty throng around us. She was gazing into the future, and a glow of happiness brightened her emaciated face.
>
> Three days later she passed away, and ten days later, just one week before all women of my age were killed, I was released from the concentration camp.[25]

25. Corrie ten Boom, *Amazing Love: True Stories of the Power of Forgiveness* (Grand Rapids: Fleming H. Revell, 1953), 9–10.

See? It's true. The poor do get good news—even in prison—because they know the rest of the story.[26]

Perhaps we can also see ourselves in the faces of the imperceptive people. How often does God show up in our midst, and we miss him? Even worse, we begin to take miracles for granted because God is so reliable. When things turn out like they should—according to our expectations—we take it as business as usual. It's hardly a time to repent of our sin like Jesus expected. Isn't that odd? We tend to think of our need to repent when things go wrong, when Wisdom is mocking us for our foolish decisions, when we're having to live with the consequences of our stupidity. "Oh God! I'm so sorry. Please get me out of this mess and I'll serve you." But heaven is silent. Wisdom doesn't answer. And Sodom bears witness to the judgment of God. Perhaps it's time to repent of our sin when things are going well, when we see the miraculous glory of God's care every day. Rather than act like we deserve his blessing, we should say, "We're not worthy." Indeed, after witnessing the glory of God, maybe we need a few "Isaiahs" to show up and remind us it's time to confess our sins.

I had heard about the dramatic change that occurred in his life, how he used to be completely disinterested in spiritual things, would sit in the corner with a catatonic look on his face during Bible study, never saying a word. His conversion had occurred just before I became his pastor. When I met him, Bill Panneck was one of the most refreshing, energetic, committed, kind, engaged members at Central Baptist Church in Jonesboro, Arkansas. An exceptional dentist, he often joined mission work in underdeveloped countries to provide dental care and share the gospel. He taught a Sunday-school class of thirty-somethings, was the chairman of deacons, and also chaired the committee that had recently taken on the massive project of relocating the church facilities. You couldn't find a more endearing, dedicated, loving couple than he and his wife, Patti. In the best sense of the expression, when it came to building up the body of Christ and advancing the kingdom of God, they were "all in." After hearing one of his friends talk about how much Bill had changed, the next time I saw him I found out why he made such an about-face in his life. Since it happened during a five-week-long revival meeting at the church, I expected to hear the usual when-I-came-to-the-end-of-my-rope-I-found-Christ testimony. But that's not his story.

Bill said things were going well in his life. Good business. Comfortable home. Great friends. Of course, there were a few personal problems—issues at home between he and his wife—but nothing out of the ordinary. During one

---

26. Which Bruner thinks is the climax of the series of messianic deeds (*Matthew*, 1:508–9). See Dunn, *Jesus and the Spirit*, 60–61.

of the revival services he began to think: "There has to be more to life than this." Sure, God had been good to him. He really had nothing to complain about. But he felt like he was missing something. He went to church. He paid his tithe. God had blessed him with so much. Indeed, the more he thought about the blessings of God, the more gratitude welled up in his heart. "Then it hit me," he said with the usual twinkle in his eye and thick southern accent, "God has been so good to me. I wanted to give all that I am for him."

"That's it?" I said quizzically.

"Yep. That's it. I can't explain it, but all of the sudden it's like God's Spirit zapped me, and I knew right then and there I was going to change. I would live for Christ and Christ alone."

Since our conversation that day, I've thought about Bill's testimony quite a bit and wondered why we don't hear that story more often. But then again, in light of what Jesus discovered in Galilee perhaps we know why. Perhaps it's because many of us need to repent of our sin of presumption.

Finally, some of us—especially preachers—tend to identify with Jesus's frustration over the lack of response to his ministry. When I was a pastor, I often wondered what it would take to replicate Jesus's ability to do "power and glory." Want to draw a crowd? Make sure God shows up, and people will flock to see it. Jesus performed miracles—undeniable signs of the power and glory of God's presence—and the masses were drawn to the spectacle like moths to a flame. Of course, we didn't perform miracles on Sunday—it took a lot of hard work and preparation to make things happen during worship services. Although some churches tried to compensate for the lack of the miraculous, creating sensational worship experiences that appealed to all five senses, I hoped that people would appreciate our usual efforts on any given Sunday. Music. Readings. Prayers. Preaching. The whole routine made it easy for all of us to fall into the pattern of hitting our mark with the people responding in kind. Did God "show up"? Well, we weren't sure, so sometimes we would do special things—out of the ordinary events—hoping to capture the awe of divine presence. Every once in a while I wondered, "What if we could do 'power and glory' like Jesus did? What if we could perform miracles? That would work. After witnessing the miraculous, certainly the people would know that we've been visited by God!" Then I would think of Jesus—especially this passage—and remember that *even he* couldn't inspire people to see the presence of God. No one did "power and glory" better than Jesus (not only miracles but *amazing* sermons),[27] and look where it got him? A cross—the very place where "power and glory" would show up best. Indeed,

27. "*Not merely in [Jesus's] exorcisms and healings, but chiefly in his preaching, is God's eschatological reign visible and present*" (Dunn, *Jesus and the Spirit*, 61 [emphasis his]).

the yoke of Jesus is where disciples find rest and burdens become light because the cross fits us so well.

> I did not come with eloquence or human wisdom as I proclaimed to you the testimony about God. For I resolved to know nothing while I was with you except Jesus Christ and him crucified. I came to you in weakness with great fear and trembling. My message and my preaching were not with wise and persuasive words, but with a demonstration of the Spirit's power, so that your faith might not rest on human wisdom, but on God's power. (1 Cor 2:1–5)

This is the power of a crucified life.

So, like Paul, perhaps the best way to do "power and glory" is to preach the cross of Jesus Christ and wear his yoke well.

CHAPTER 16

Matthew 12:1–21

LISTEN to the Story

[1]At that time Jesus went through the grainfields on the Sabbath. His
disciples were hungry and began to pick some heads of grain and eat them.
[2]When the Pharisees saw this, they said to him, "Look! Your disciples are
doing what is unlawful on the Sabbath."

[3]He answered, "Haven't you read what David did when he and his
companions were hungry? [4]He entered the house of God, and he and his
companions ate the consecrated bread—which was not lawful for them to
do, but only for the priests. [5]Or haven't you read in the Law that the priests
on Sabbath duty in the temple desecrate the Sabbath and yet are innocent?
[6]I tell you that something greater than the temple is here. [7]If you had known
what these words mean, 'I desire mercy, not sacrifice,' you would not have
condemned the innocent. [8]For the Son of Man is Lord of the Sabbath."

[9]Going on from that place, he went into their synagogue, [10]and a man
with a shriveled hand was there. Looking for a reason to bring charges
against Jesus, they asked him, "Is it lawful to heal on the Sabbath?"

[11]He said to them, "If any of you has a sheep and it falls into a pit on the
Sabbath, will you not take hold of it and lift it out? [12]How much more valu-
able is a person than a sheep! Therefore it is lawful to do good on the Sabbath."

[13]Then he said to the man, "Stretch out your hand." So he stretched
it out and it was completely restored, just as sound as the other. [14]But the
Pharisees went out and plotted how they might kill Jesus.

[15]Aware of this, Jesus withdrew from that place. A large crowd followed
him, and he healed all who were ill. [16]He warned them not to tell others
about him. [17]This was to fulfill what was spoken through the prophet Isaiah:

> [18]"Here is my servant whom I have chosen,
>   the one I love, in whom I delight;
> I will put my Spirit on him,
>   and he will proclaim justice to the nations.
> [19]He will not quarrel or cry out;

no one will hear his voice in the streets.
[20]A bruised reed he will not break,
and a smoldering wick he will not snuff out,
till he has brought justice through to victory.
[21]In his name the nations will put their hope."

Listening to the Text in the Story: Genesis 2:2–3; Exodus 16:22–30; 20:8–11; 21:33–34; 31:13–17; Leviticus 19:9–10; 24:5–9; Numbers 15:32–36; Deuteronomy 22:4; 23:24–25; Ruth 2:2–3; 1 Samuel 21:1–6; 1 Kings 13:1–6; 2 Chronicles 6:18–21; Nehemiah 13:15–22; Isaiah 42:1–4; 66:1–2; Hosea 6:6; Micah 6:6–8; 1 Maccabees 2:32–41.

The last time we saw the disciples, Jesus had sent them into the fields to bring in the harvest of the kingdom of heaven, warning them to expect persecution (Matt 9:37–10:42). Now we see them harvesting actual fields of grain because they were hungry, and they get in trouble for it (12:1). Even though it looks like petty theft to us—grazing while shopping at the grocery store is still stealing—the disciples weren't doing anything wrong when they grabbed handfuls of grain to eat as they walked through the fields. The law made provisions for the poor to glean fields after the harvesters had done their work (Lev 19:9–10; Deut 23:24–25; Ruth 2:2–3). Of course, one could catch them on a technicality: it appears that the twelve were grazing *before* the harvest, probably around the end of April or the beginning of May.[1] But that wasn't what provoked the Pharisees to call Jesus on the carpet for the illegal behavior of his disciples (Matt 12:2). The problem was that they were harvesting handfuls of grain on the Sabbath day. Since work was strictly forbidden on the seventh day, harvesting even a few heads of grain would be in violation of the law (Gen 2:2–3; Exod 16:22–30; 20:8–11; 31:13–17; 34:21; 35:2; Num 15:32–36; Neh 13:15–22). At least, that's what the Pharisees thought. Jesus, however, didn't see a problem[2] (Matt 12:3–8), and his rebuttal—once again—reveals why he and the Pharisees didn't see eye to eye when it came to obeying the law.

The crux of the matter was interpretation. Jesus didn't read the law like the Pharisees: "Haven't you *read* what David did . . . ? Or haven't you *read* in the Law?" (vv. 3, 5, emphases added). Since the Scriptures couldn't be read without interpretation—no one takes the Scriptures objectively, for then there would be no arguments over what they mean—then what we're seeing here is

1. Davies and Allison, *Matthew*, 2:306, situates the early harvesting between April and June, which would be too late—long after the festival of firstfruits.

2. "Here we see the disciples operating under the yoke of Jesus" (Nolland, *Matthew*, 480).

a battle over authority. Who is reading the Scriptures rightly, and who isn't? Who is obeying the law, and who isn't? Of course, just before this episode Jesus had made the claim that his way of obeying God—his yoke—was "easy and my burden is light" (11:30). In fact, he went so far as to say that his followers would find rest (Sabbath!) if they wore his yoke—the implication being that the yoke of the Pharisees was burdensome, something Jesus would accuse them of later, recalling the yoke imagery: "They tie up heavy, cumbersome loads and put them on other people's shoulders, but they themselves are not willing to lift a finger to move them" (23:4). The heavy load of carrying the Pharisaical interpretation of the law was especially evident when it came to obeying the fourth commandment. To keep the Sabbath holy, all Israel, foreigners living in the land, and even animals were not supposed to work. But that provokes a question of interpretation: What is work? One would expect to find a list of prohibited activities embedded in the law, or at least several rulings by Moses and the elders to help God's people obey the commandment. Yet, that's not the case. Only two kinds of work are clearly prohibited in the law: gathering sticks and starting a fire (Exod 35:3; Num 15:32–36).[3] Beyond that, Nehemiah had the gates of Jerusalem closed to ensure no merchants carried their loads through the holy city on the Sabbath (Neh 13:19). But that's it. When it came to keeping the Sabbath holy by not working, no other "biblical" advice is given.

This is where the Pharisees come into the picture. For about four-hundred years (starting with Ezra), the scribes had issued rulings to define what was not lawful on the Sabbath. But not all the teachers agreed on every rule. In fact, by the time of Jesus there were two schools of interpretation of the law: one led by the rabbi Hillel (a more liberal approach) and the other by Shammai (the conservative approach). There are dozens of places where these two schools disagreed as to what constituted work on the Sabbath Day. For example:

A. The House of Shammai say, "They do not sell [anything] to a gentile or bear a burden with him,
B. "and they do not lift up a burden on his back,
C. "unless there is sufficient time for him to reach a nearby place [while it is still day]."
D. And the House of Hillel permit.[4]

But there are *many* places where they all agreed as to what kind of work violated the Sabbath: sewing, plowing, reaping, threshing, grinding, etc.[5]

3. Davies and Allison, *Matthew*, 2:311.

4. See m. Shabbat 1:7 (*The Mishnah: A New Translation*, ed. Jacob Neusner [New Haven: Yale University Press, 1988]).

5. See m. Shabbat 7:2.

The Pharisees kept these traditions alive, not only by observing them but by memorizing them and passing them down to future generations. Eventually, all the rabbinical teachings were written down, preserved in a book called "the Mishnah"—categorized according to six divisions, dealing with issues of interpretation regarding Sabbath and other appointed times, as well as agriculture, women, damages, holy things, and purity. To our gentile eyes, these rules appear excessive, even obsessive. But to a people who desired more than anything to obey God, expert advice on how to keep the law—especially when the commandments are vague—was valued by most and cherished by many.

EXPLAIN the Story

When Jesus's disciples were caught harvesting grain on the Sabbath (Matt 12:1), they were in clear violation of the law according to expert opinion. When the Pharisees pointed out their illegal behavior to Jesus (v. 2, evidently Jesus *wasn't* participating in their rebel ways), they must have expected Jesus to correct his entourage: "Okay guys. That's enough." Teachers were responsible for making sure their disciples obeyed God. But he didn't make them stop. Instead, much to the chagrin of the Pharisees, Jesus defended the behavior of his disciples by appealing to the Scriptures as well as his authority as the "Son of Man" (versus their expert tradition) to define what is lawful on the Sabbath (vv. 12:3–8).[6] Up to this point, the Pharisees had been lobbing accusations at Jesus from a distance. Now, for the first time they decided to get in his face and force a showdown over who was right and who was wrong when it came to obeying God's law—a crucial matter for the kingdom of heaven. For, how can God reign *on earth* outside the rule of law he's already given? If harvesting is permitted on the Sabbath, then why not sowing, plowing, and grinding? What does it mean to "remember the Sabbath and keep it holy"? Who's to say? Before long, everyone will do what is right in their own eyes (Judg 21:25)—an ominous sign of rebellion against the King of Israel, the One who makes the rules and judges those who disobey him (Neh 13:15–18).

"Mercy Triumphs over Judgment"[7]

The Pharisees hadn't done their homework. When they objected to Jesus's table company several chapters ago (Matt 9:11), rather than argue with them Jesus told them to "go and learn what this means" and then quoted part of

6. According to Chrysostom, Jesus broke the Sabbath law to bring it to an end (*Homilies*, 255).

7. "Speak and act as those who are going to be judged by the law that gives freedom, because judgment without mercy will be shown to anyone who has not been merciful. *Mercy triumphs over judgment*" (Jas 2:12–13, emphasis added).

Hosea 6:6, "I desire mercy, not sacrifice" (Matt 9:13). Then, in the following episodes Jesus gave several "lessons" on what that should look like: feasting instead of fasting, touching an unclean woman and dead girl, healing the blind and mute, sending the Twelve to recover the lost sheep of Israel, defending the Baptizer, and giving Galileans a second chance (9:14–11:30). That should have been enough to help the Pharisees see what Hosea meant. Mercy runs knee-deep through every episode. But the Pharisees didn't get it, which is why they accused Jesus's disciples of desecrating the Sabbath. To them, grabbing a handful of grain on the Sabbath was just as bad as harvesting the entire field. But to Jesus, helping the hungry trumped the sacrifices that were necessary to observe the Sabbath, like preparing food before the holy day. How could the poor do that when they had no food to prepare?[8] Besides, according to the Scriptures feeding the hungry was more important than observing the law (Matt 12:3–4). Case in point: when David ate God's bread (1 Sam 21:1–6). Here was a clear example of God preferring mercy over sacrifice—something the priest Ahimelek recognized. Every Friday, priests made twelve loaves of bread and gave them to God on the Sabbath (Lev 24:5–9). Commonly referred to as the *showbread*, these loaves were then consumed by the priests because they were the only ones holy enough to dine at God's table. When David showed up at the tabernacle, asking for food for him and his companions, the priest gave him several loaves of the showbread to satisfy their hunger, which Jesus pointed out "was not lawful for them to do" (Matt 12:4). Therefore, the argument goes that human need superseded the requirements of the law.

But the Pharisees could have replied, "What did that episode have to do with the Sabbath? Sure, an exception was made for David to eat priestly fare (a man who would become the greatest king of Israel!), but your disciples would hardly compare. Besides, David didn't violate the Sabbath when he ate the showbread." Jesus, anticipating any attempt to poke holes in his argument, therefore appealed to the oxymoron of priests having to break the Sabbath to serve God on the Sabbath (Matt 12:5; see Num 28:9–10). If priests are innocent when they violated the Sabbath by working on the holy day, how much more were Jesus's disciples innocent because "something greater than the temple is here" (Matt 12:6)? In other words, if service to God by offering sacrifices in his temple was more important than Sabbath law, then service to God when "something greater than the temple is here" would supersede the Pharisees' teachings about the kind of work that violates the Sabbath.[9] The

8. Luz emphasizes the "social" benefit of the Sabbath: "As in Deut. 5:14–15, the Sabbath exists for the poor, the hungry, or the slaves" (*Matthew*, 2:184). See also Nolland, *Matthew*, 482.

9. Davies and Allison, *Matthew*, 2:314.

implication of Jesus's argument, then, is incredibly ironic: like priests who serve God, sometimes you have to "work" on the Sabbath to keep it holy. God's mercy demands it.[10]

"Something Greater Than the Temple Is Here"

It's all well and good to argue over proper interpretation of the Scriptures—all Jews did that, whether Pharisees, Essenes, or Sadducees. But when Jesus pulled rank on the Pharisees by claiming authority beyond the Scriptures,[11] well, that went too far. It's one thing to claim your work is more important than the priests who serve God in his temple—a debatable topic (one wonders if some of the Pharisees thought the same about themselves). It's quite something else to imply you are that special "something" that is greater than the temple (Matt 12:6). Who says things like that? And if that weren't enough, to go on and make the outlandish claim that you have the authority to break the Sabbath because "the Son of Man is Lord of the Sabbath" (v. 8)—what does a Pharisee say to that? There's no arguing with a man like that. When a fool talks like he's God, when a pretender goes around acting like he's the boss, the only thing left to do is help him realize his foolish end. Play along with the theater of the absurd. Make sport of the idiot. Set him up for failure. Bait him with trick questions. Help him paint himself into a corner. Then, when the whole show comes crashing down on him, everyone will see what should have been obvious all along. There is *nothing* greater than the temple except God himself.

When Jesus entered "*their* synagogue," it could have been one that was associated with the Pharisees (Matt 12:9, emphasis added).[12] That would make the showdown between Jesus and the Pharisees even more intriguing because it happened on their home turf. Unlike the Synoptic parallels,[13] Matthew has the Pharisees instigating the Sabbath controversy, prodding Jesus with the question: "Is it lawful to heal on the Sabbath?" (Matt 12:10). On that day, there just happened to be a man with a "shriveled hand"—either planted by the Pharisees or providing a serendipitous moment. (Since there was no joyful celebration after the man was healed—which is what typically happened—one might infer that the whole scenario was carefully staged by the Pharisees. They knew Jesus would heal the man; that was the point, to catch him in impropriety.) Either way, the Pharisees goaded Jesus into healing

10. Luz thinks the "something greater" is mercy (*Matthew*, 2:181–82).

11. France, *Matthew*, 457.

12. A. Runesson, "Synagogue," *DJG* 905–6. Most scholars think otherwise; "their" means "Jewish"; see Luz, *Matthew*, 2:187. France suggests "their" refers to Capernaum (*Matthew*, 463).

13. In Mark (3:4) and Luke (6:9), Jesus is the one who asks the question.

the man on the Sabbath day. But, before he restored the man's hand, Jesus appealed to the crowd, counting on conventional wisdom to define what is lawful on the Sabbath. After all, experts in the law can talk all day about what is theoretically permitted. Yet it's the practice of the people that determines what is lawful, especially when it comes to gray areas of Sabbath observance (even the Pharisees didn't agree on everything). So, if it were to be expected that a man would rescue his sheep that had fallen into a pit (perhaps a trap for wolves[14]) on the Sabbath, then "how much more valuable is a person than a sheep!" (v. 12). Therefore, by the common practice of the people, "it is lawful to do good on the Sabbath" (v. 12). In other words, the people had already decided the issue. There should be no Sabbath controversy because everyone knew that Israel, the sheep of God's pasture, was more important than sheep. To make the point even more dramatic, Jesus didn't even need to "take hold" of this sheep—work!—to restore his hand. He simply gave the word, "Stretch out your hand" (*exactly* what God said to Moses when he delivered his sheep from the "pit" of Egypt; Exod 14:16), and the man was healed. Indeed, this man, Jesus, talked like God—especially on the Sabbath day.

The Pharisees got what they wanted: proof that Jesus would violate the Sabbath by doing his healing work. Sure, the man had a withered hand. But there was no emergency here. Jesus could have waited until the next day to heal the man.[15] So, the way the Pharisees saw it, they were justified when they "plotted how they might kill Jesus" (Matt 12:14) because Sabbath violators deserved death (Num 15:32–36). The irony is rich: because Jesus was goaded into "doing good" on the Sabbath, the Pharisees were provoked to "do evil" on the Sabbath, *working* on the holy day to hatch a plot to get rid of him. No more casting aspersion from the sidelines. From now on, the Pharisees would hound Jesus until he was dead. Fully aware of their evil intentions, Jesus withdrew from the area (Matt 12:15). But that didn't stop the crowds from following him. The sheep of God's pasture recognized their shepherd because he healed them, even on a Sabbath day. Jesus wasn't looking for a fight. He didn't heal the people for notoriety. In fact, he tried to keep the whole thing quiet, warning the masses *not* "to tell others about him" (v. 16), which is incredibly counterintuitive to those who get good news. Yet, according to Matthew this is exactly what Isaiah predicted would happen (Isa 42:1–4; Matt 12:18–21).[16] God's chosen servant won't quarrel with the people. He won't call attention to himself, crying out in the streets of the city. Instead, he will

14. Keener, *Matthew*, 358.

15. Davies and Allison, *Matthew*, 2:318.

16. This scriptural citation, which Garland notices is the longest in Matthew's Gospel, summarizes the ministry of Jesus to this point in the narrative (*Reading Matthew*, 139–40).

bring justice[17] to the whole world, even to those the rest of the world has given up on—like limp measuring sticks that are good for nothing (a man with a useless hand), or smoldering wicks that give no light but only smoke up the place (hungry disciples who create a scene). God's Servant won't stop until there is justice for all. When that happens, it will be so good that even the gentiles "will put their hope" in his name (Matt 12:21).

LIVE the Story

It's easy to take potshots at the Pharisees. More than anyone else, they were the ones who gave Jesus problems throughout his ministry. They constantly appear in Matthew's narrative world as killjoys trying to ruin the party, cloying legalists obsessing over the picky details, flies that needed to be swatted away during a picnic. Pesky pests. Yet, despite the constant drip of their annoying presence, it wasn't the Pharisees that got Jesus killed. Even though they were the first to decide that Jesus needed to be done away with, it was the Sanhedrin (led by the high priest and the Sadducees) who would turn him over to the Romans for execution. To be sure, talk about being "greater than the temple" will get righteous Jewish people riled up. On the other hand, going to the temple and acting like you're more important than the priests who run the place—well, that will get you killed (Matt 21:12–46). The question, "By what authority are you doing these things? . . . And who gave you this authority?" (v. 23), was the issue. The only answer that would justify Jesus's behavior was "God"—whether cleansing the temple or working on the Sabbath. However, Jesus didn't come out and say, "I'm God," preferring to refer to himself as "something greater than the temple" and the "Son of Man," who is "Lord of the Sabbath" (Matt 12:6, 8), which was more than enough to confirm the suspicions of the Pharisees (and eventually the Sadducees). Jesus made *everything*—not only the law but also the temple—about himself. When the Pharisees questioned him about the law, Jesus talked about himself (vv. 6, 8). When the priests challenged him for his behavior in the temple, he told a parable about himself (Matt 21:33–39). It's no wonder they thought Jesus was a dangerous man who needed to be killed. He acted like devotion to God should be centered on him.

It's hard to think like a first-century Jew when you are a twenty-first-century gentile. We don't see a problem when Jesus claimed authority over the Sabbath. He's the Lord. What he says goes. Why couldn't the Pharisees

17. Yet, Luz notes that *krisis* in secular Greek literature never means "justice" (*Matthew*, 2:194; see, however, Davies and Allison, *Matthew*, 2:327; Nolland, *Matthew*, 493; Bruner, *Matthew*, 1:558).

see that? Besides, who keeps the Sabbath anyway? Gentiles certainly don't![18] Indeed, that is the point. For hundreds and hundreds of years, Sabbath observance is what marked out Israel from the rest of humanity. To violate the Sabbath, therefore, would be the same as forsaking your identity as God's people—a people who are to be holy because God is holy.[19] The Creator of all things not only marked out sacred space (the temple) but also sacred time (Sabbath) for his sacred people. But since most Christians (typically gentiles) recognize neither sacred space nor time, we really don't understand why the Pharisees got all bent out of shape over what Jesus said about the temple and the Sabbath. Yet, since God sanctified both, perhaps we should be concerned—especially since we believe Jesus was right to claim that he is "greater than the temple" and "Lord of the Sabbath."

Jacob Neusner has done gentile Christians a great service by recreating what his issue with Jesus would have been if he were living in the first century. Neusner is a twenty-first-century Jewish scholar and rabbi who imagines how he would have responded to Jesus's words and deeds. It is when Jesus linked Sabbath observance to the temple to make claims about himself that both intrigued and disturbed this twenty-first-century Jewish time traveler:

> When, therefore, Jesus says that something greater than the Temple is here, he can only mean that he and his disciples may do on the Sabbath what they do because they stand in the place of the priests in the Temple: the holy place has shifted, now being formed by the circle made up of the master and his disciples.
>
> What troubles me, therefore, is not that the disciples do not obey one of the rules of the Sabbath. That is trivial and beside the point. What captures my attention is Jesus's statement that at stake in their actions is not the Sabbath but the Temple, a truly fresh formulation of matters. His claim, then, concerns not whether or not the Sabbath is to be sanctified, but where and what is the Temple, the place where things are done on the Sabbath that elsewhere are not to be done at all. . . .
>
> So why should anyone not have concurred that the intent of these several statements in sequence—"Come to me, all who labor and are heavy-laden, and I will give you rest"; "you will find rest for your souls; for my yoke is easy and my burden is light"; "it is lawful to do good on the Sabbath"—is wholly captured in the simple and necessary conclusion: "For the son of man is lord of the Sabbath." That, and that alone, is what is at stake in the master's teachings concerning the one of the Ten Commandments that concerns the Sabbath day. . . .

18. Seventh Day Adventists try.

19. Garland compares violating the Sabbath to desecrating the American flag (*Reading Matthew*, 136).

And why wonder whether or not Jesus realized that, in these teachings of his about the Sabbath, he surely appeared not to fulfill but to abolish the Sabbath? Of course he knew perfectly well what the Sabbath meant in the Torah's presentation of it, and obviously he realized how surprising was his decision on the proper conduct of his disciples on the Sabbath. So, it seems to me self-evident, what we face is an irreconcilable conflict. Either "Remember the Sabbath Day to keep it holy" or "The son of man is the Lord of the Sabbath"—but not both.[20]

Neusner sees what's at stake. He recognizes what Jesus was doing: Jesus made the law and the temple about him. The implication is undeniable: "In the end the master, Jesus, makes a demand that only God makes."[21] It's either Jesus or the Torah. And so Neusner sees himself walking away from Jesus as he leaves Galilee for Jerusalem, explaining to Jesus in an imaginary conversation why he can't follow him to the holy city:

> I really don't see how your teachings and the Torah's teachings come together. That isn't because things you say don't appeal to the Torah; some of them do. It's because most of what you say and most of what the Torah says scarcely intersect.
>
> To put it simply: You talk about the kingdom of heaven. To me, that means living under the rule of God. The Torah gives us the rules that form the rule of God. And *about most of these rules you have very little to say.*[22]

For Neusner, then, one has to decide to follow Jesus or follow the rules. You can't do both. And, I think he's right.

It is astounding to me how many Christians think our faith is about keeping rules. Of course, outsiders might be prone to caricature Christians as uptight legalists who love to judge others. But when a group of adolescents raised in church talk about our faith as if it was "Moralistic Therapeutic Deism,"[23] then it's time to ask the question: What Jesus are we following? Certainly not the one identified by Neusner. The Jesus he encountered in Matthew's Gospel wasn't about keeping all the rules. Instead, Jesus defied the rules because he was convinced the rule of God was about him, the King. Thus, quite naturally, following him would be the same as living according to the rule of God. The kingdom of heaven on earth isn't about rules; it is about

---

20. Jacob Neusner, *A Rabbi Talks with Jesus*, rev. ed. (Montreal: McGill-Queen's University Press, 2000), 82–84.

21. Ibid., 68.

22. Ibid., 152 (emphasis mine).

23. Christian Smith, with Melinda Lundquist Denton, *Soul Searching: The Religious and Spiritual Lives of American Teenagers* (New York: Oxford University Press, 2005), 162–71.

a relationship revealed by obedience *to him*—something frustrating for rule keepers. For, if holiness depended upon keeping a list of rules, nothing would be left to chance. We would all know who's "holy" and who isn't.

I grew up in a Southern Baptist church, hearing sermons about "keeping the Sabbath holy." That meant not working on *Sundays*—not only refusing to work at your job but also abstaining from doing housework or yardwork. Moreover, if you were really serious about keeping "the Sabbath" holy, you wouldn't go out to eat after worship services because "forcing" others to work on Sunday was just as bad as doing it yourself. There were many other rules that we were supposed to keep to show the world what it meant to be a Christian: not drinking alcohol, not smoking cigarettes, not dancing, not watching R-rated movies, not using curse words (not even cleaned-up versions, like "dadgummit" or "shoot"), girls not wearing miniskirts, guys not wearing long hair, not listening to rock music, not running in the sanctuary (we had a fellowship hall for that), not reading books that referred to magic or that took the Lord's name in vain or used vulgar language or had steamy love scenes, and (above all else) no inappropriate sexual behavior (no French kissing, no heavy "petting," no public displays of affection). I realize, of course, that most of these rules were directed toward us teenagers who came of age in the raucous times of the 60s and 70s (it was especially evident when we saw deacons lighting up in the parking lot before and after worship services). Furthermore, our Baptist legalism was a far cry from the teachings of the Pharisees—a hedge built around the law to keep it holy. Besides, given the promiscuity of our world today, many of these old-fashioned rules sound laughable. But, if Christian Smith's study is any indication of what teenagers believe about the essence of our faith, Christianity is still seen as a religion of rules—not just for young people but also adults. If you don't believe me, try violating one of the many unwritten (unbiblical) rules in church today and see what happens. (Be careful, *we all have rules.*) You may find that following Christ isn't enough to be a Christian. Yet we claim to follow the Lord of the Sabbath, the one who defied tradition and invited us to find Sabbath rest *in him*. So, it seems the moralists among us have a serious decision to make: either bear the burden of trying to keep all the rules or follow Jesus. You can't do both. Two rabbis said so, and one claimed to be greater than the temple.

Lay down your burden. Lay it down. It's just a list of rules. Besides, like the other rabbi said, about most of these rules Jesus has very little to say.

CHAPTER 17

Matthew 12:22–50

LISTEN to the Story

22Then they brought him a demon-possessed man who was blind and
mute, and Jesus healed him, so that he could both talk and see. 23All the
people were astonished and said, "Could this be the Son of David?"

24But when the Pharisees heard this, they said, "It is only by Beelzebul,
the prince of demons, that this fellow drives out demons."

25Jesus knew their thoughts and said to them, "Every kingdom divided
against itself will be ruined, and every city or household divided against
itself will not stand. 26If Satan drives out Satan, he is divided against him-
self. How then can his kingdom stand? 27And if I drive out demons by
Beelzebul, by whom do your people drive them out? So then, they will
be your judges. 28But if it is by the Spirit of God that I drive out demons,
then the kingdom of God has come upon you.

29"Or again, how can anyone enter a strong man's house and carry off
his possessions unless he first ties up the strong man? Then he can plunder
his house.

30"Whoever is not with me is against me, and whoever does not gather
with me scatters. 31And so I tell you, every kind of sin and slander can be
forgiven, but blasphemy against the Spirit will not be forgiven. 32Anyone
who speaks a word against the Son of Man will be forgiven, but anyone
who speaks against the Holy Spirit will not be forgiven, either in this age
or in the age to come.

33"Make a tree good and its fruit will be good, or make a tree bad and
its fruit will be bad, for a tree is recognized by its fruit. 34You brood of
vipers, how can you who are evil say anything good? For the mouth speaks
what the heart is full of. 35A good man brings good things out of the good
stored up in him, and an evil man brings evil things out of the evil stored
up in him. 36But I tell you that everyone will have to give account on the
day of judgment for every empty word they have spoken. 37For by your
words you will be acquitted, and by your words you will be condemned."

[38]Then some of the Pharisees and teachers of the law said to him, "Teacher, we want to see a sign from you."

[39]He answered, "A wicked and adulterous generation asks for a sign! But none will be given it except the sign of the prophet Jonah. [40]For as Jonah was three days and three nights in the belly of a huge fish, so the Son of Man will be three days and three nights in the heart of the earth. [41]The men of Nineveh will stand up at the judgment with this generation and condemn it; for they repented at the preaching of Jonah, and now something greater than Jonah is here. [42]The Queen of the South will rise at the judgment with this generation and condemn it; for she came from the ends of the earth to listen to Solomon's wisdom, and now something greater than Solomon is here.

[43]"When an impure spirit comes out of a person, it goes through arid places seeking rest and does not find it. [44]Then it says, 'I will return to the house I left.' When it arrives, it finds the house unoccupied, swept clean and put in order. [45]Then it goes and takes with it seven other spirits more wicked than itself, and they go in and live there. And the final condition of that person is worse than the first. That is how it will be with this wicked generation."

[46]While Jesus was still talking to the crowd, his mother and brothers stood outside, wanting to speak to him. [47]Someone told him, "Your mother and brothers are standing outside, wanting to speak to you."

[48]He replied to him, "Who is my mother, and who are my brothers?" [49]Pointing to his disciples, he said, "Here are my mother and my brothers. [50]For whoever does the will of my Father in heaven is my brother and sister and mother."

Listening to the Text in the Story: Exodus 4:1–9, 29–31; Deuteronomy 13:1–5; 1 Kings 10:1–13; Proverbs 10:18–21; Isaiah 32:6–7; 40:11; 57:3; 61:1; Ezekiel 23:1–49; 34:11–16; Hosea 1:2–4:1; 5:3–4; Jonah 1:12–3:10; Zechariah 13:7–9.

Although we aren't privy to the secret meeting of the Pharisees when they "plotted how they might kill Jesus" (Matt 12:14), the fruit of their labor is readily evident in these episodes. They faced a formidable challenge when it came to figuring out how to destroy Jesus. He was gaining in popularity, especially at their expense. They had to get rid of him for their own sakes as much as for the people of Israel, who were being led astray by this false prophet. They couldn't hire a hit man or arrange for Jesus to die as the result of a strange accident; that would be murder, and the Pharisees were bent on keeping the law. Besides, it wouldn't help them in restoring their honor in the eyes of the people. In their bout with Jesus, the Nazarene had thrown several punches, dealing a few severe blows to the Pharisees' social standing—the last punch being the worst: healing a cursed man on the Sabbath in one of their synagogues (vv. 11–13). That situation was supposed to mark the beginning of Jesus's downfall, revealing to the people why he was a dangerous man. Anyone who blatantly disregarded the Sabbath was worthy of death. Yet their attempt to entrap Jesus backfired when he appealed to the common practice of the people: anyone would save a sheep trapped in a pit on the Sabbath day. Why should a man be put to death for doing good on the Sabbath, especially since the welfare of Israel is supposed to be more important than sheep? To make matters worse in the eyes of the Pharisees, Jesus didn't even have to touch this man to restore him. He simply gave the word, and the man's hand was "completely restored, just as sound as the other" (v. 13). How do you stop a crafty man like that?

The only way to have Jesus killed was to get the people on their side. The law prescribed for false prophets to be put to death to "purge the evil from among you" (Deut 13:5). Rebellious sons had to be killed, but it would be up to the people to "stone them to death, because they tried to turn you away from the LORD your God" (v. 10). For example, it was the Synagogue of the Freedmen who "stirred up the people and the elders and the teachers of the law" to gain broad support to have Stephen stoned as a blasphemer (Acts 6:9–7:58).[1] Likewise, the Pharisees would need to mount a campaign against Jesus to sway the people, the elders, and the teachers of the law to their side. The teachers of the law had already accused Jesus of blasphemy (Matt 9:3). Later on, Jesus would provoke the elders with his "temple tantrum"—the *coup de grace* leading to his arrest (21:12, 45–46). In the meantime, the Pharisees would need to take up the difficult task of convincing the masses that Jesus was a false prophet who should be stoned to death, especially when "all the people" were saying things like, "Could this be the Son of David?" (12:23).[2] At this point, Jesus was winning the war of public relations. Why wouldn't he? He healed people. He cast out demons. He welcomed outcasts. He even

---

1. Whether Jewish leaders in Jerusalem had the power to enforce capital punishment is debated among scholars. Since the Roman Empire controlled Judea as an imperial province, governing it directly by procurators, it's unlikely the Romans would have given capital jurisdiction to the civil authorities. Thus, the martyrdom of Stephen looks more like a lynch mob. On the other hand, Herod Antipas, tetrarch of Galilee and Perea, had the power to execute "criminals" (Matt 14:9–10).

2. Garland, *Reading Matthew*, 141, notes that David had success in driving away evil spirits from Saul (1 Sam 16:14–23).

loosened Sabbath regulations so that a poor man could glean a handful of grain and eat it. How could *anyone* reverse public opinion of such a do-gooder—a man of the people and for the people?

EXPLAIN the Story

Prophets tend to alienate the people. They do strange things. They deliver provocative messages. In a word, they drive people mad, both royalty and commoners, which is why most of the time prophets meet an untimely end. Even though Jesus had increased in popularity and amassed a huge following due to his miraculous deeds and inspiring messages, he also said several things that must have offended most people. He mocked the Galileans for acting like children who must be entertained (Matt 11:7–19). Jesus condemned *entire* villages to hell—Chorazin, Bethsaida, and Capernaum—for not repenting of their sin (11:21–24). He referred to the people of his time as "a wicked and adulterous generation" (12:39). To be sure, Jesus not only acted like a prophet, but he talked like one too. One would think that such offensive behavior would be enough to ensure his ruin. In other words, the Pharisees could have counted on the inevitable. Prophets invariably take their cause to Jerusalem where they seemed destined to meet their fate (23:37). Jesus would eventually self-destruct—that's what prophets do. Yet rather than wait on the inevitable, the Pharisees decided to take matters into their own hands. They were determined to expose Jesus as a false prophet and take responsibility for his death: "But the Pharisees went out and plotted how *they might kill Jesus*" (12:14, emphasis added). All they needed was the support of the people to pull it off.

Tactic #1: Smear Campaign

The Pharisees couldn't deny that Jesus performed miracles. The beneficiaries of Jesus's healing work wouldn't keep it quiet; they spread his fame all over the region whether Jesus liked it or not (Matt 9:29–31). With all of these once-cursed-but-now-blessed people walking around, there was no denying that Jesus had the power to heal everyone who came to him. They were walking advertisements of Jesus's ministry, which must have encouraged others to seek out Jesus for help—some even bringing their worst cases to him—like a blind *and* mute, demon-possessed man (12:22). The more Jesus healed, the more they came; the diseased, disabled, and demon-possessed flocked to him like sheep to a shepherd. When Jesus saw the crowd gather, he would often tell them what he thought about the kingdom of heaven, contrasting his ideas with the Pharisees, pointing out how wrong they were about righteousness according to the law and about holiness without mercy. In response, the Pharisees tried to confront Jesus, challenging him to his face about his Sabbath behavior (vv. 1–13). But that didn't work. So they shifted their strategy, hanging around the edges of the crowd, trying to plant doubts in the minds of the people about Jesus. Just as the crowd was marveling over Jesus's latest miracle, wondering whether he was the long-awaited Messiah, the Pharisees picked up their old refrain, "It is only by Beelzebul, the prince of demons, that this fellow drives out demons" (12:24; cf. 9:34). Obviously out of earshot of their slanderous charge, Jesus saw the Pharisees talking to some people and surmised that they were up to no good because he "knew their thoughts" (12:25). Last time he ignored their ridiculous accusation. This time he couldn't let it pass.

The Pharisees crossed a line when they accused Jesus of being in league with the devil, the ruler of demons known by many names: Satan, Belial, Mastema, Azazel, and Beelzebul ("Lord of the house"; one of the names of the ancient Canaanite god, Baal).[3] In essence, the Pharisees explained away Jesus's power over demons because he was the "Lord of their house." These demons were merely obeying their dark lord, who had given Jesus his irrepressible power. Such an accusation reveals two inferences. First, Jesus must have had a unique authority over evil spirits, because other Pharisees were known to exorcize demons too (v. 27). In other words, if Jesus had merely performed exorcisms just like the Pharisees (or as infrequently as the Pharisees), then he wouldn't have posed such a serious threat. Either the huge number of exorcisms performed by Jesus or the simplicity of his approach—he simply commanded them to leave, unlike other Jewish "magicians" who had to use all kinds of special incantations and prayers—forced the Pharisees to account for Jesus's unusual ability.[4]

Second, the Pharisees were convinced that Jesus's healing power didn't come from God.[5] In a binary world of either good or evil powers (there are no neutral powers), that meant Jesus's power had to come from the devil, God's adversary—which made no sense to Jesus. Would Satan *ever* do God's work, cleaning up Israel's house by driving out unclean spirits? Kings don't go to war against their own army. Divided cities and families self-destruct (vv. 25–26). Satan may be evil, but he isn't stupid. If Satan wasn't using Jesus as his tool to destroy his own kingdom, then Jesus's power must be attributed to God.

3. France, *Matthew*, 478.

4. If the world was under the control of Satan, then the implication of the Pharisees' charge is: "Why is there no resistance to Jesus by Satan?" (Nolland, *Matthew*, 502).

5. "Historically it is the first of a long series of Jewish testimonies that reject Jesus because of magic" (Luz, *Matthew*, 2:203). This is the point of no return according to Luz: "Now no more bridges can be built" (ibid).

According to the logic of Jesus's argument, then, his ability to cast out demons was the undeniable sign of the reign of God on earth (v. 28). God was taking back what rightfully belongs to him—Israel! Indeed, the only way to explain Jesus's victory over Satan was that he was stronger than the devil, able to tie him up and rob his house (v. 29).[6] The only person more powerful than the devil is God. Therefore, ipso facto, Jesus was doing the work of God when he cast out demons.[7]

In their campaign to smear Jesus, the Pharisees were playing a dangerous game. It's one thing to launch an ad hominem attack—that's what desperate people do when they're losing the argument. (Don't have superior logic to challenge the merits of someone's position? Employ a diversionary tactic: attack the character of your opponent; then listeners might be distracted by the fact that you were actually losing the argument.) But to attribute to Satan the work of God, that's unforgiveable.[8] It's the kind of blasphemy that has eternal consequences (vv. 31–32). To call the work of the Spirit the work of the devil was "blasphemy against the Spirit [that] will not be forgiven" (v. 31). Yet Jesus claimed that blasphemy against him—the ad hominem attacks—was forgivable. Why? Well, Jesus knew that his identity was "hidden" to certain people (11:25–27);[9] the work he did to bring the kingdom of heaven to earth was hard for some to see (he will tell several parables in the following chapter that make the point; see 13:1–46). However, if a person is so blind that they think the Spirit's power is the devil's power, then how will they ever be convinced otherwise when it's the Spirit who convicts people of their sinful deceit? If they can't recognize the Spirit of God—the only power that is true—how will they ever be convinced that they're wrong? Indeed, whenever the Holy Spirit moves to convict them of self-deceit, they will think it's the devil trying to deceive them. Therefore, the perpetual motion of their sin of self-deceit will last forever.[10] I think that's what Jesus meant when he said blaspheming the Holy Spirit is unforgivable (see John 16:7–13).[11]

How wrong could the Pharisees be? Jesus was born of the Holy Spirit (Matt 1:18, 20). He baptized others with the Holy Spirit (3:11). His entire life was directed by the Holy Spirit (4:1; 12:18–21). He gave his disciples

---

6. Keener thinks the "binding of the strong man" happened when Jesus defeated Satan at the temptation (*Matthew*, 365).

7. Davies and Allison, *Matthew*, 2:337–38.

8. One wonders about the converse: Is calling the work of Satan the work of God just as blasphemous, resulting in eternal damnation?

9. Nolland, *Matthew*, 506.

10. The Scriptures are filled with warnings of self-deceit; see especially Jas 1:22–27.

11. So also Keener, *Matthew*, 365–66; for other possibilities, see Turner, *Matthew*, 323–24; Luz, *Matthew*, 2:206–9.

the Holy Spirit (10:1, 20; 28:19). He performed miracles by the Holy Spirit (12:28). He died when he surrendered his Spirit (27:50). From start to finish, Jesus was the embodiment of God's Holy Spirit. Why couldn't they see it? According to Jesus, the Pharisees didn't recognize the Holy Spirit in him because they were evil. Evil trees only produce evil fruit. Evil men only store evil treasures. Evil words reveal an evil heart (12:33–35). And that's a dangerous habit—running your mouth when you have an evil heart. That is because, according to Jesus, the judgment will not only be a day of reckoning for evil deeds but also reckless words (v. 36). It's a scary thing to ponder. Jesus claimed, "By your words you will be condemned" (v. 37). No wonder the Scriptures warn readers constantly about the devastating and deceiving power of the tongue. Our mouths can get us into big trouble—not only with people but especially with God.

Tactic #2: Entrapment

It looks like an innocent request when the Pharisees and teachers of the law asked Jesus to give them a sign (Matt 12:38). Prophets were expected to perform miraculous signs to verify their divine calling. Moses performed signs to prove to both Israel and Pharaoh that he was God's servant (Exod 4:1–9, 29–31; 7:8–13). Elijah did the same, vindicated by God in the presence of his enemies (1 Kgs 18:16–40).[12] So, by Jesus's day it was reasonable to expect would-be prophets and messiahs to perform signs to convince the people that God was on their side.[13] But Jesus didn't accept their challenge. The fact that they even asked for a sign proved to him that they were "a wicked and adulterous generation" (Matt 12:39). But how could that be the case in light of the biblical precedent of prophets like Moses and Elijah performing signs? The reason Jesus didn't submit to their request is embedded in his enigmatic answer (vv. 40–45). It had to do with their lack of response to the miracles he had already performed—a response that should have led to repentance, especially since "something greater than Jonah" and "something greater than Solomon is here" (vv. 41–42). Besides, Jesus had already put the Galileans on notice for their lack of repentance. He previously warned those who didn't have "eyes to see and ears to hear" the significance of his miracles that evil cities like Tyre, Sidon, and Sodom would have a better time of it on judgment day than they (11:20–24). Evidently, the point needed to be repeated. Because the people of Nineveh "repented at the preaching of Jonah, and now something greater than Jonah is here," the Ninevites "will stand up at the judgment with this generation and condemn it" (12:41). Even the Queen of Sheba

12. France, *Matthew*, 488–89.

13. Ibid., 489.

recognized God's wisdom when she heard it. Therefore, since "something greater than Solomon is here," she will also "rise at the judgment with this generation and condemn it" (v. 42). In other words, the Pharisees shouldn't have to ask for a sign.[14] So many had already been given, and they proved that they missed them by asking for another—something even the Ninevites or the Queen of Sheba didn't do.

Yet there seems to be more to it than that. Jesus wasn't just referring to signs that had already happened. He talked about the sign of Jonah as something that would take place in the future, and that it would be the *only* sign given to this "wicked and adulterous generation" (v. 39). However, if miracles were signs and Jesus was still to perform several more miracles, then what could he mean that "none will be given it except the sign of the prophet Jonah"? What was the "sign of the prophet Jonah" that was still to come?

We know what the sign of Jonah is because we know the rest of the story. When Jesus said, "For as Jonah was three days and three nights in the belly of a huge fish, so the Son of Man will be three days and three nights in the heart of the earth" (v. 40),[15] we recognize the sign: Jesus was predicting his death, burial, and resurrection—the only sign that will prove that "something greater than Jonah" is here (v. 41). But why is this the *only* sign that will be given to them? It's because they themselves—the religious leaders—will play their part in making the sign come true.[16] That's why Jesus found affinity in the Jonah story, calling it the only sign that will be given to the Pharisees and their "wicked and adulterous generation." Like Jonah, Jesus was rocking the boat of their world. As the story goes, the passengers had determined (with Jonah's help!) that the prophet was the problem—that as soon as they threw him overboard, the storm would pass, the seas would be calmed, and Jonah's fate would be left to God (Jonah 1:4–17). The way Jesus saw it, the Pharisees were in the same boat. They had already determined (with Jesus's help!) that the Galilean prophet needed to be thrown overboard—killed—to calm the storm of their religious world. That's why they asked him for a sign, hoping to prove that Jesus was a false prophet according to Deuteronomy 13:1–4.

The Pharisees were already convinced that Jesus was leading the people to revere other gods: Beelzebul! The Galileans were following Jesus, not the Lord. They were obeying him, not the commandments. So the Pharisees put Jesus to the test to see if he would fall into their trap (see also Matt 16:1) and

14. According to Garland, the request for a sign was evil because Satan did the same thing during the temptation of Christ (*Matthew*, 142).

15. The problem of three days/nights not matching the chronology of Jesus's death, burial, and resurrection is a modern one; time was reckoned inclusively in Jesus's day (1 Kgs 20:29; Esther 4:16–5:1); see Turner, *Matthew*, 327.

16. Luz, *Matthew*, 2:218–19.

perform the sign, thereby proving that he was a false prophet who needed to be killed. But Jesus saw through their ruse and decided to subvert their challenge, turning their plans to have him killed into a vindication of his ministry: a sign would be performed that proved "something greater than Jonah is here." Ironically, *they would be the very ones* who played a significant part in ensuring the sign came true.[17] Moreover, here's the kicker: the Pharisees thought they would make things better by having Jesus killed. Yet, according to Jesus things would only get worse. Having swept Israel's house clean of demons, with no superior occupant to take up residence (the King of Israel!), seven demons would move back in and wreck the place.[18] As a result, "the final condition of that person is worse than the first. That is how it will be with this wicked generation" (Matt 12:43–45). Indeed, when that happens, it *really* will look like Beelzebul is "Lord of the house." But with Jesus out of the way, the Pharisees will have nobody to blame but themselves.

LIVE the Story

Jesus didn't make it easy on us. He put the matter plainly: "Whoever is not with me is against me, and whoever does not gather with me scatters" (Matt 12:30). No one can be ambivalent about him. Jesus left no room for compromise. Either you belong to him or you don't. Either you're for him or you're not. Since there was no middle ground with him, we can't help but look at others and ask: Is he with Jesus? Is she gathering sheep? Because, if he's not for Jesus, then he must be against him. If she's not gathering sheep with us, she must be working against the purposes of God—scattering sheep. Of course, all of us "insiders" tend to work with a presumption of certainty about ourselves. We know we are with Jesus. We're certain we are gathering sheep into the fold of God. This sense of infallibility—what some would prefer to call an "unshakeable faith"—compels us to identify those who aren't with us. That is because if they aren't with us, then they aren't with Jesus. If they aren't gathering sheep with us, they aren't doing the work of God. They are the blasphemers; every word they say must be scrutinized because everyone knows the mouth is the trapdoor of the heart. They are the bad trees. As infallible judges, it's up to us to inspect the fruit of their lives and prove that these outsiders are rotten to the core. We do this so that when we show up at Jesus's house to report that we're doing everything we can to protect his "family," we're certain he will reward us with a pat on the back for our faithfulness. But then we find him hanging

17. Luz, *Matthew*, 2:218.
18. Turner, *Matthew*, 327.

out with people we don't recognize—hey, they aren't part of the family, are they?—so we send word of our presence:

> Someone told him, "Your mother and brothers are standing outside, wanting to speak to you."
>
> He replied to him, "Who is my mother, and who are my brothers? Pointing to his disciples, he said, "Here are my mother and my brothers. For *whoever does the will of my Father in heaven* is my brother and sister and mother. (Matt 12:47–50, emphasis added)

I grew up in a church where we were taught to be suspicious of Catholics and charismatics. Those who belonged to the Catholic Church were not family. Charismatics were outsiders trying to infiltrate our ranks and destroy our fellowship. Catholic doctrine led the deceived to pray to Mary, bow to idols, and earn their way to heaven. Charismatic practices of speaking in tongues and anointing with oil were divisive ploys to tear apart churches that once knew the sweet bonds of unity. Catholics pushed for one church that would rule the world through the pope—the antichrist in disguise—an apocalyptic sign of the last days. Charismatics claimed they were spreading the anointing of the Spirit, but we were told their senseless babblings proved they were demonic. That's when I would get a little nervous, hearing my pastor attribute the charismatic "blessing" of speaking in tongues to the work of the devil. You better be sure you know what you're talking about when you do that. Because Jesus said in effect, "You can talk bad about me. That will always be forgiven. But when you talk bad about the Holy Spirit, you're on dangerous ground." In fact, Jesus said it was unforgivable.

So, I would walk away from these sermons armed with warnings about these dangerous "outsiders," always a little suspicious of people who *say* they are Christians. Then I met a Catholic girl who loved Jesus more than I did. She beamed when she talked about him, incessantly boasting about the Lord. She sounded more like a religious fanatic than anyone I had ever met at youth camp. But more than that, she cared about people my church practically ignored. She shared her stuff with the homeless. She worked during the holidays at the soup kitchen downtown. She talked a lot about world hunger and the mentally ill and drug addicts, as if these were problems I should care about. But more than anything else, she was especially concerned about people who didn't know Jesus. She was a Jesus freak, the first "Catholic Christian" I had ever met. The power of her life meant more to me than any sermon laced with anti-Catholic rhetoric.

I've never spoken in tongues. But I've had other experiences that fit more in the Pentecostal tradition than my Baptist upbringing would allow.

I don't talk about what happened to me, partly because I wonder what others would think but mostly because the Lord intended them for my ears and eyes only. Besides, Jesus warned everyone who had ears to hear about speaking casually about such important things as the work of the Holy Spirit: "For by your words you will be acquitted, and by your words you will be condemned" (v. 37). It should make a man or woman think twice about speaking in a tongue that condemns others to the work of Satan. If you've ever been on the receiving end of such an attack, then you know why such empty words can be so dangerous: it's because hateful words can do so much damage. Which is why I marvel over Jesus's response when he was attacked. I admire his confidence, convinced that he was not only doing the work of God ("Sure, go ahead and say bad things about me") but was also empowered by the Holy Spirit ("Can't you see the good fruit?"). No wonder he compared his opponents to vipers. Their poisonous tongues revealed their wicked hearts (v. 34).

Perhaps that's a clue to negotiating the difficult world of criticism. There are snakes in the grass, and their bite is always poisonous. If you've ever been put in a position of leadership in the church, you know there will always be critics to point out your weaknesses, failures, botched efforts, and flawed tendencies. The temptation, of course, is to dismiss every criticism as "satanic." But there are times when wise counsel ends up being helpful—even though it hurts to hear it. The work of the Spirit involves correction as well as encouragement. He will use all kinds of people to conform us to the image of God's Son. Yet, to be open to all criticism, to take every harsh word to heart, to be porous to every poisonous word will destroy you. So, how can we tell the difference between the correction of the Spirit and the venomous bite of the Serpent? Based on lessons learned from the Scriptures and from experience—mine and others—here's some advice:

1. Consider the source. The Pharisees *always* criticized Jesus, never had a kind word for him. A person who only has harsh things to say to you should probably be ignored. All they want to do is tear down rather than build up. Evil people only have evil things to say.
2. Is it logical? This is the hardest thing to do because we'd rather not see the issue from the perspective of our critics. And yet that's what Jesus did when he considered the inference that he exorcized demons by the power of Satan. When your enemy claims, "You're trying to destroy this church," consider how illogical that would be; church demolition is self-destruction. If you are destroying the church, you are destroying yourself.

3. Forgive slander. Even Jesus had people say bad things about him. He expected it, knowing he would forgive them for it. Since we follow Christ, we should forgive slander too—not only against him but against us.
4. Always defend the Holy Spirit. Your enemies will attack you. Unbelievers may slander Jesus. But when someone dares to curse the Spirit's work—not only in us but even in our critics—that's when we cannot remain silent. Where there is healing, restoration, justice, peace, hope, humility, and what Paul listed as the "fruit of the Spirit" (Gal 5:22–23), then the Spirit is at work. Satan cannot do any of these things. He seeks only to steal, kill, and destroy the work of God (John 10:10). Whenever you hear anyone speak against the Holy Spirit, warn them once—perhaps twice. "After that, have nothing to do with them" (Titus 3:10). God will judge them for their reckless words.

Indeed, "*everyone* will have to give account on the day of judgment for every empty word they have spoken" (Matt 12:36, emphasis added).

Perhaps, then, we need a different version of the quaint little children's song to help us take Jesus's warning to heart:

So, be careful little mouths what you say.
Be careful little mouths what you say.
For, the Father up above *will squash you like a bug.*
So, be careful little mouths what you say.

CHAPTER 18

Matthew 13:1–52

LISTEN to the Story

1That same day Jesus went out of the house and sat by the lake. 2Such large crowds gathered around him that he got into a boat and sat in it, while all the people stood on the shore. 3Then he told them many things in parables, saying: "A farmer went out to sow his seed. 4As he was scattering the seed, some fell along the path, and the birds came and ate it up. 5Some fell on rocky places, where it did not have much soil. It sprang up quickly, because the soil was shallow. 6But when the sun came up, the plants were scorched, and they withered because they had no root. 7Other seed fell among thorns, which grew up and choked the plants. 8Still other seed fell on good soil, where it produced a crop—a hundred, sixty or thirty times what was sown. 9Whoever has ears, let them hear."

10The disciples came to him and asked, "Why do you speak to the people in parables?"

11He replied, "Because the knowledge of the secrets of the kingdom of heaven has been given to you, but not to them. 12Whoever has will be given more, and they will have an abundance. Whoever does not have, even what they have will be taken from them. 13This is why I speak to them in parables:

> "Though seeing, they do not see;
> though hearing, they do not hear or understand.

14In them is fulfilled the prophecy of Isaiah:

> 'You will be ever hearing but never understanding;
> you will be ever seeing but never perceiving.
> 15For this people's heart has become calloused;
> they hardly hear with their ears,
> and they have closed their eyes.
> Otherwise they might see with their eyes,
> hear with their ears,

understand with their hearts
and turn, and I would heal them.'

16But blessed are your eyes because they see, and your ears because they hear. 17For truly I tell you, many prophets and righteous people longed to see what you see but did not see it, and to hear what you hear but did not hear it.

18"Listen then to what the parable of the sower means: 19When anyone hears the message about the kingdom and does not understand it, the evil one comes and snatches away what was sown in their heart. This is the seed sown along the path. 20The seed falling on rocky ground refers to someone who hears the word and at once receives it with joy. 21But since they have no root, they last only a short time. When trouble or persecution comes because of the word, they quickly fall away. 22The seed falling among the thorns refers to someone who hears the word, but the worries of this life and the deceitfulness of wealth choke the word, making it unfruitful. 23But the seed falling on good soil refers to someone who hears the word and understands it. This is the one who produces a crop, yielding a hundred, sixty or thirty times what was sown."

24Jesus told them another parable: "The kingdom of heaven is like a man who sowed good seed in his field. 25But while everyone was sleeping, his enemy came and sowed weeds among the wheat, and went away. 26When the wheat sprouted and formed heads, then the weeds also appeared.

27"The owner's servants came to him and said, 'Sir, didn't you sow good seed in your field? Where then did the weeds come from?'

28'An enemy did this,' he replied.

"The servants asked him, 'Do you want us to go and pull them up?'

29'No,' he answered, 'because while you are pulling the weeds, you may uproot the wheat with them. 30Let both grow together until the harvest. At that time I will tell the harvesters: First collect the weeds and tie them in bundles to be burned; then gather the wheat and bring it into my barn.'"

31He told them another parable: "The kingdom of heaven is like a mustard seed, which a man took and planted in his field. 32Though it is the smallest of all seeds, yet when it grows, it is the largest of garden plants and becomes a tree, so that the birds come and perch in its branches."

33He told them still another parable: "The kingdom of heaven is like yeast that a woman took and mixed into about sixty pounds of flour until it worked all through the dough."

34Jesus spoke all these things to the crowd in parables; he did not say
anything to them without using a parable. 35So was fulfilled what was
spoken through the prophet:

"I will open my mouth in parables,
I will utter things hidden since the creation of the world."

36Then he left the crowd and went into the house. His disciples came
to him and said, "Explain to us the parable of the weeds in the field."
37He answered, "The one who sowed the good seed is the Son of Man.
38The field is the world, and the good seed stands for the people of the
kingdom. The weeds are the people of the evil one, 39and the enemy who
sows them is the devil. The harvest is the end of the age, and the harvesters
are angels.
40"As the weeds are pulled up and burned in the fire, so it will be at
the end of the age. 41The Son of Man will send out his angels, and they
will weed out of his kingdom everything that causes sin and all who do
evil. 42They will throw them into the blazing furnace, where there will be
weeping and gnashing of teeth. 43Then the righteous will shine like the
sun in the kingdom of their Father. Whoever has ears, let them hear.
44"The kingdom of heaven is like treasure hidden in a field. When a
man found it, he hid it again, and then in his joy went and sold all he had
and bought that field.
45"Again, the kingdom of heaven is like a merchant looking for fine
pearls. 46When he found one of great value, he went away and sold every-
thing he had and bought it.
47"Once again, the kingdom of heaven is like a net that was let down
into the lake and caught all kinds of fish. 48When it was full, the fishermen
pulled it up on the shore. Then they sat down and collected the good fish
in baskets, but threw the bad away. 49This is how it will be at the end of
the age. The angels will come and separate the wicked from the righteous
50and throw them into the blazing furnace, where there will be weeping
and gnashing of teeth.
51"Have you understood all these things?" Jesus asked.
"Yes," they replied.
52He said to them, "Therefore every teacher of the law who has
become a disciple in the kingdom of heaven is like the owner of a house
who brings out of his storeroom new treasures as well as old."

Listening to the Text in the Story: Genesis 26:12; Exodus 12:15–20; Leviticus 11:9–12; Deuteronomy 29:2–4; 2 Samuel 12:1–14; Psalm 78:1–8; Proverbs 2:1–5; 3:13–18; Isaiah 6:8–13; 42:18–20; 55:10–11; Ezekiel 12:1–6; 17:22–23; 31:2–14; Zephaniah 1:2–6; Zechariah 7:11–14.

It's hard to change people's minds about God. Once they make up their mind about him—especially how God works—there's little you can do to change their thinking. Most of us are pretty stubborn about our views of God. Someone might drag out the Scriptures to show what it says in God's word, but that usually leads to an argument. Haggling over the meaning of Scripture rarely works (and it's usually an ugly site to behold). Helping people won't redirect their affections either, especially when they're mad at God. They may appreciate your efforts, but they won't thank God for it. So, what should you do? Well, perhaps we should take a lesson from Jesus. The first time he saw the crowd, he preached a sermon, taking his case directly to the people (Matt 5:1–2). Even though the people marveled over his teaching as a new sensation (7:28–29), Jesus didn't make many new disciples (9:9). His second strategy was to send his disciples to the people to minister to their needs (9:36–10:8). But that didn't seem to work either; the people didn't repent of their sin like Jesus thought they should (11:20–24). These are the same two strategies we employ today: preach sermons, help people. That should be enough to change people's ideas about God and join the kingdom, right? Yet, it wasn't enough for Jesus, so why should we think it should be sufficient today? Which is why we need to consider his third strategy: tell stories. Jesus told parables to change people's minds about God and his kingdom.

It was such a bold move, the disciples puzzled over Jesus's new strategy: "Why do you speak to the people in parables?" (13:10). His reasons seem just as puzzling. Reason #1: "Because the knowledge of the secrets of the kingdom of heaven has been given to you, but not to them" (v. 11). Reason #2: "Whoever has will be given more, and they will have an abundance. Whoever does not have, even what they have will be taken from them" (v. 12). Reason #3: "In them is fulfilled the prophecy of Isaiah" (vv. 14–15). In other words, Jesus told parables because the crowds were already damned to ignorance. The parables were intended to hide the king and his kingdom from those who had already shut their eyes and stopped up their ears due to their hard hearts. They had their chance and blew it; the crowds had already proven that they didn't have eyes to see Jesus's miracles or ears to hear Jesus's teaching. Their inability to understand the parables was expected, sealing their fate, doomed to God's judgment because of their ignorance. And yet Jesus had to explain the meaning of the parables to his twelve disciples because they didn't understand them either (vv. 18–23, 36–43, 49–50). It seems the disciples couldn't "see" what Jesus meant because they didn't have ears to hear the parable without Jesus's explanation. Nevertheless, Jesus continued to give parables to *them* as well as to the crowds. So, obviously, the parables weren't intended to obscure the meaning of his kingdom; Jesus told the parables to insiders too (vv. 36–50).[1] Besides, Jesus summoned the crowd with invitations to "see" at the beginning (in v. 3 the story begins with "see" or "behold," which isn't translated in the NIV) and to "have ears to hear" at the end of his parables (v. 9). What's up with that? If Jesus never intended for the crowds to understand him, should we infer that he was merely taunting them when he invited them to "see" and "hear"? (Picture the "insiders" in the boat with Jesus, giggling among themselves as they make sport of the ignorant masses: "Look at them. They don't have a clue! They're so stupid they have no idea what he's saying." Then Jesus, egging them on, flashes a grin and offers several strange stories in rapid fire, "Listen to this! . . . And this. . . . And this. . . ." All the while, the crowd stands on the seashore dumbfounded, blank stares on their faces, as everyone cracks up in the boat. "Dumb sheep.")

Why did Jesus teach in parables? Scholars have spent a lot of time (with varied results) trying to answer the disciples' question. It's not that the parables were a brand new form of teaching; there are several examples of *mashal* (the Hebrew word for "parable") in the Old Testament (Judg 9:7–15; 2 Sam 12:1–4; 14:1–20; 2 Kgs 14:9–10; Isa 5:1–7). But Jesus relied on parables more than any other teacher; the sheer volume of parables in the Gospels attests to his fondness for the medium. So, why did he favor them so much? We can infer several reasons (memorable, witty, accessible, creative, timeless appeal, etc.), but Jesus's three-part answer in Matthew 13:11–17 really boils down to one reason: parables both conceal and reveal the kingdom of heaven—all at the same time. They not only conceal/reveal the meaning of the kingdom but also the identity of the hearer. In other words, the parables have a reflected quality: how we read them reveals who we are. That is to say, parables "read" us as we read them. Parables work on us as we work on them. This mirror effect is clearly seen in Nathan's famous parable of the poor man, the rich man, and the little lamb (2 Sam 12:1–4). Without realizing it, David saw himself in the mirror of Nathan's parable. But he didn't see his reflection in the story until the prophet said, "You are the man!" (v. 7). The double effect of the parable revealed both the king's blindness (his inability to "see"—the

1. Davies and Allison, *Matthew*, 2:382; Nolland, *Matthew*, 537.

parable's concealing effect) and his reflection (his ability to "see"—the parable's revealing effect). Jesus counted on the same double effect in his own parables: to reveal those who are blind to their reflection (Matt 13:14–15). Unlike Nathan, however, Jesus never pointed out to his listeners where they show up in his parables. ("You are the shallow soil!") He left it to his listeners to figure it out, and, ironically, only those who had ears to hear would be able to see their reflection in the mirror of Jesus's parables (vv. 16–17).[2] Read and be read. Indeed, those who see *understand* the parables (vv. 11, 23, 51). Those who don't understand are blind. The parables reveal the difference.

All of this almost makes you want to look away from the mirror for fear of what you might see (or worse, might *not* see). And there's the rub. Those who have been given the "knowledge of the secrets of the kingdom of heaven" (v. 11) can't help but try to see what Jesus was saying through his parables: "Explain to us the parable of the weeds in the field" (v. 36). Understanding not only depends upon Jesus's teaching (vv. 18–23, 37–43) but our participation (seeking the treasure, vv. 44–46; revealing the treasure, v. 52). That's why the parables can't be understood by "simply reading off the meaning from the words."[3] Rather, as France rightly suggests, to understand a parable means "entering into an interactive process to which the hearer must contribute if true understanding is to result."[4] This is why Jesus preferred parables. They cannot be received passively. Parables invite interpretation. And because they are so open ended, different people will respond differently to the same story. What we bring to the story will reveal who we are because we contribute to the meaning of the parable to understand it. And "in a situation where some are open to truth and some are not, parables, as imaginative challenge rather than simple proposition, are an appropriate way to communicate new ideas."[5] Jesus knew what he was doing. If the people couldn't see the kingdom in his sermons or his miracles, it was time to hold up a mirror to the people and say, "What do you see?" If they saw themselves, they might just catch a glimpse of the kingdom of heaven on earth.[6]

At the same time, Jesus was doing more than revealing and concealing the identity of his listeners. His parables were windows into the world of God's reign on earth as it is in heaven. This is why he prefaced several parables

---

2. Nolland, *Matthew*, 530–31.

3. France, *Matthew*, 502. Luz, *Matthew*, 2:298, writes: "*One cannot understand the parables of the kingdom of heaven by exegesis alone*" (emphasis his).

4. France, *Matthew*, 502.

5. Ibid., 509–10.

6. See Scot McKnight, *Kingdom Conspiracy: Returning to the Radical Mission of the Local Church* (Grand Rapids: Brazos, 2014), 65–79, where he emphasizes that the kingdom primarily consists of people: "That's the kingdom vision of Jesus: a people ruled by God who appoints Jesus as King" (77). Luz, *Matthew*, 2:250, writes: "The disciples must understand that they *themselves* are the issue" (emphasis his).

with "the kingdom of heaven is like . . ." (vv. 24, 31, 33, 44, 45, 47). He was essentially saying: "This is how the heavenly kingdom works on earth. Look at it like this." Of course, the reason his kingdom vision was so hard to see was because the way God rules the earth is quite different from the way humanity tries to rule the world. The priorities of human rule are different (sometimes the complete opposite) from God's. Jesus told stories to get people to see what is valuable, what is effective, what is eternal. More than that, he reordered the world of everyday life—constructing an imaginative world built on kingdom priorities—and invited his listeners not only to live in it but also to build it.[7] These parables were intended to be more than "cautionary tales," warning people about the unseen world of evil sowers and end-time angelic reapers (judgment). Jesus used earthy parables to teach his disciples what to treasure on earth. "It is performative language that tries to deconstruct the auditors' old world and open them up to a new way of seeing."[8] Jesus told stories and invited people to inhabit them—his word, his world.[9]

EXPLAIN the Story

We might be led to think that Matthew bunched up several parables here (seven or eight, depending on whether you count v. 52) like he did with the Sermon on the Mount, stringing together Jesus's teaching in one place like pearls. But Mark did the same thing, though with fewer parables (four in Mark 4:1–34); Luke spreads them out a bit (two in Luke 8:4–18; two in 13:18–21). The impression given is that Matthew (more than Mark and Luke) wants to pile it on, as if Jesus were sowing the seed of the kingdom all at once. It's a lot to take in, sorting out the meaning of parables built on farming, baking, commerce, and fishing. Of course, first-century listeners would understand the word pictures drawn from everyday life far better than we do. Yet to compare these things to the kingdom of heaven? What a mystery! Indeed, most of Jesus's listeners would have been as confused as the twelve disciples, wondering among themselves, "What was that?" We certainly don't see the crowds celebrating Jesus's teaching like they did after the Sermon on the Mount (Matt 7:28–29). There, Jesus spoke plainly. Here, he seems to conceal as much as reveal. Therefore, perhaps Matthew has done us a favor by stringing together

7. "*A parable is an extended metaphor* and as such it is *not a delivery system for an idea* but a house in which the reader/listener is invited to take up residence" (Bailey, *Jesus through Middle Eastern Eyes*, 280 [emphasis his]).

8. Talbert, *Matthew*, 167.

9. For helpful guidelines to interpreting the parables of Jesus, see Klyne R. Snodgrass, *Stories with Intent: A Comprehensive Guide to the Parables of Jesus* (Grand Rapids: Eerdmans, 2008), 24–31.

these pearls, for scholars find meaning in their symmetrical arrangement.[10] One pearl isn't enough to see the beauty of the kingdom of heaven. Put them together, and a pattern of meaning becomes more evident. So, Matthew's purpose is clear: these parables need to be read together to be understood.[11]

The Kingdom Is Hard to See at First, but One Day . . .

If God is going to do something, it's got to be big, right? One would expect God Almighty to be loud and proud, orchestrating an ostentatious display that no one can miss, making waves, calling down fire, lighting up the sky, great theater, show time. But Jesus kept emphasizing over and again that the kingdom of heaven on earth starts out small, barely noticeable, hidden from our eyes. Sown seeds are hidden in the ground (Matt 13:3–8, 24–26, 31). Leaven is hidden in dough (v. 33). A found treasure was hidden in a field (v. 44). A fishing net is submerged in the lake, catching all kinds of fish (v. 47). A householder's treasure is kept in his storeroom (v. 52). Notice also how Jesus emphasizes the small size of these things: small seed becomes a big shrub (v. 32), a little yeast leavens sixty pounds of flour (v. 33), and a single pearl is of great value (vv. 45–46). Indeed, small things are hard to see.

Yet why would Jesus insist that God's reign on earth starts out so small, barely visible, hidden from our eyes? In light of what we've read in Matthew's Gospel to this point, one could infer the opposite is true. When the kingdom of heaven invades earth, amazing things happen: fantastic birth, fulfilled prophecies, mesmerizing sermons, astonishing miracles—light finally overpowering darkness, evil defeated by good.[12] Yet the people of Israel didn't see it.[13] What should have been obvious was hidden from their eyes. Even though Jesus was spreading the gospel seed everywhere he went, on all kinds of soil, the fruit of his labor had yet to be seen. Yes, the people were drawn to him. They even gathered to hear him speak. But the crowd standing by the seashore looked more like the soils of the beaten path, the shallow ground, and weed-infested fields than the "good earth" (13:1–15).[14] Even Jesus was frustrated by

---

10. Most scholars see either a threefold or twofold structure to Matthew's arrangement. For the triadic argument (vv. 1–23, 24–43, 44–52) see Davies and Allison, *Matthew*, 2:371–72; for the chiastic (vv. 1–35, 36–52) see Turner, *Matthew*, 332–33.

11. Some scholars, however, take the opposite approach: each parable must be stripped of its literary context to understand Jesus's original intention. See, for example, Charles W. Hedrick, *Many Things in Parables: Jesus and His Modern Critics* (Louisville: Westminister John Knox, 2004), 11–14; Amy-Jill Levine, *Short Stories by Jesus: The Enigmatic Parables of a Controversial Rabbi* (San Francisco: HarperOne, 2014), 16–17.

12. "With Matthew the parables become 'commentaries' on the story of Jesus" (Luz, *Matthew*, 2:292).

13. Israel was scandalized by their hard hearts, the wiles of Satan, and the humble presence of the kingdom (Garland, *Reading Matthew*, 146).

14. Turner, *Matthew*, 335.

the fact that he hadn't made many disciples (11:7–24). Despite all his labor, God was more pleased to have "hidden these things from the wise and the learned, and revealed them to little children" (v. 25). Isaiah had predicted the same (Isa 6:9–10; Matt 13:11–15). The secrets of the kingdom would be lost on many people, hidden from their eyes—but not for long.

Jesus was convinced that one day all would be revealed. The kingdom that started out so small would end up undeniably magnificent. Seeds that fell on the good soil would yield a bumper crop (Matt 13:8; cf. Gen 26:12). The mustard seed would grow to a plant large enough to shelter birds (Matt 13:32). A little yeast would eventually permeate every inch of sixty pounds of dough, producing enough bread to feed a village (v. 33). One day, the kingdom of God would be big, very big. It was only a matter of time. Indeed, Jesus believed time was on his side. He never doubted that his kingdom effort—even though it started out so small—would eventually take over the whole world. The question was: Did his disciples see it now? Therefore, embedded in his parables were not only an optimistic claim but also an ominous challenge. Are you perceptive enough to see it now when the kingdom is barely evident (in parables and in life)? Because, if you are, then you will reap the rewards of the kingdom when it comes in full force, when *everyone* will see it. However, if you don't see it till then—when it is undeniably present—it will be too late. Like weeds thrown to the fire or bad fish thrown away, those who don't have eyes to see the kingdom now will be damned in the end (vv. 30, 40–42, 48–50). Makes you want to keep studying the parables, doesn't it? Like one of those old 3-D pictures trapped in a two-dimensional world of mysterious patterns, we'll keep staring at the parable until it comes into full view. Where there is depth, there is meaning.

The Kingdom Is Counterintuitive, but Once You See It . . .

In nearly every parable he told, Jesus always included a little surprise—some unexpected twist in the story. As a matter of fact, that's why we have so many books on the parables of Jesus. Scholars not only want to know why Jesus created so many parables (is this an effective form of communication?), but they want to get to the bottom of things: What do these stories mean? The problem lies in the part that doesn't make sense. Everyone can see the trouble. It's where the story breaks down, is a little obscure, a glitch in the narrative that's hard to figure out. That is where scholarly opinion divides. The wrinkle in the stories is where we find so many possible meanings. It's the puzzling part of the parable that makes us puzzle over its meaning. For example, is the farmer of the parable of the soils competent or foolish (Matt 13:3–9)? It depends on how we read the role of the three unproductive soils and the significance of the yield from the good soil. Why would the farmer waste good seed on bad soil? When the good soil produces "a hundred, sixty or thirty times what was sown" (v. 8), was that a typical yield for Galilean farmers? Some commentators argue that competent farmers knew their fields and would sow their seed before plowing, knowing where to spread more seed on the fertile ground.[15] Other commentators claim only a foolish or inexperienced farmer would waste seed on all kinds of soil,[16] plowing his field after sowing in hopes of making even a footpath productive.[17] Most scholars say we don't know (or that it doesn't matter[18]): the parable doesn't indicate when the farmer plowed the field.[19] His competency isn't the issue. The focus of the parable is on the four kinds of soil, prompting the listener to wonder: What kind of soil am I? Once the listeners see themselves in the story, then the parable does its work. Bad-soil people will be challenged to change their ways (watch out for Satan, don't be so shallow, get rid of the weeds); people of the good earth will be encouraged (God will produce a good crop in us).[20]

Yet Jesus doesn't imply that the soils can "change their ways." Their fatal flaws seem permanent; the success of the gospel is predetermined by the quality of the soil. So, was Jesus teaching there will be more failure than success when it comes to sowing the gospel seed because only a fourth of the field is good soil? Well, that depends on how we interpret the yield of the good soil. If Jesus was referring to the amount of grain per stalk, then the yield of the harvest (for barley or wheat) was fairly typical: one hundred grains in each head would have been at the top end, but not miraculous.[21] According to this way of figuring the yield, the farmer was successful; there is no hint of failure. Jesus simply mentioned the bad soils to acknowledge the typical risk all Galilean farmers face. Yet Jesus didn't consider the *greater* risks associated with crop failure: rainfall, pestilence, even war. Besides, yields were more often figured by determining the ratio of seed sown per grain harvested (especially for production taxes).[22] In that case, a tenfold harvest was fairly standard for farming regions like Galilee. That would mean, then, that Jesus was

---

15. Keener, *Matthew*, 376–77. France presumes a competent farmer: "Unless this is an extraordinarily incompetent farmer, the majority of the seed falls into good ground and produces a crop" (*Matthew*, 505).

16. Nolland, *Matthew*, 526.

17. K. D. White, "The Parable of the Sower," *JTS* 15 (1964): 300–307.

18. Blomberg cleverly calls it a "fruitless debate" (Craig L. Blomberg, *Interpreting the Parables* [Downers Grove, IL: InterVarsity Press, 1990], 228); see also Turner, *Matthew*, 338.

19. See the discussion in Bernard Brandon Scott, *Hear Then the Parable: A Commentary on the Parables of Jesus* (Minneapolis: Augsburg Fortress, 1989), 353.

20. Bruner, *Matthew*, 2:16–25.

21. Davies and Allison, *Matthew*, 2:385.

22. Keener, *Matthew*, 377.

predicting a superabundant harvest—"a hundred, sixty or thirty times *what was sown*"—for all of his kingdom work. That is to say, despite all the opposition he faced to this point (bad soil everywhere!), Jesus's kingdom effort would yield a nearly miraculous harvest of disciples. In light of this, is this parable about a competent farmer who counts on a typical yield in light of usual circumstances or a foolish farmer who counts on God to produce an abundant harvest despite significant opposition?

Before we can answer the question, there's one more wrinkle in the parable that needs to be ironed out. (See? These parables are frustratingly obscure.) *When* did the farmer sow his seed? Most commentators assume Jesus was referring to the customary practice of sowing a grain harvest at the beginning of the rainy season: late autumn. Then, after the necessary "late rains" in early spring would bring the crops to maturation (Deut 11:14; Joel 2:23), workers would harvest the fields in early May—offering their firstfruits as a sacrifice during the Jewish festival called Pentecost. We tend to associate harvest with fall, but Galilean farmers celebrated their harvest in spring. Therefore, one wonders whether Jesus's fictitious farmer had followed the calendar of conventional wisdom, deciding instead to put in a second crop during the dry season when patchy rainfall made crop failure a near certainty.[23] How do we know this? Notice the threat of the scorching heat of the sun that causes the plants to wither because "they had no root" due to the shallow soil (Matt 13:6). Such scorching heat would have to happen in January, when the seedlings first appeared. Although a January heat wave isn't impossible, it is far more likely that Jesus was talking about the scorching heat of the summer sun.[24] In other words, the surprising twist of the story—what his Galilean listeners would have inferred immediately—was that Jesus compared his kingdom work to the risky "second" crop sown by a Galilean farmer who counted on God to bring a miraculous harvest in the end. Therefore, Jesus hasn't ignored the most common risk in farming lower Galilee: rainfall. God is the one who makes it rain, and Jesus counted on God to make it rain even though most Galileans (three out of four kinds of soil) would reveal that his farming efforts were fruitless. Who sows a crop like this? Only a farmer who believes he will find good soil for his gospel seed despite such a risky crop because God is on his side.

Such counterintuitive moves show up in the other parables as well. The servants ask to remove the weeds from the wheat fields per conventional wisdom (v. 28).

---

23. See Scott, *Hear Then the Parable*, 353, although he mistakenly refers to winter wheat (the primary crop) as the "second planting."

24. When trying to date the feeding of the five thousand (Matt 14:19), Keener notices that Jesus directed the multitude to sit on the grass, thereby concluding the miracle must have occurred at springtime "before the summer heat had withered the grass . . . when the previous year's grain stores would be running low" (*Matthew*, 404)—an observation Keener could have applied to the parable of the soils.

Due to their narrow leaves, tares were distinguishable from wheat before maturation.[25] Leaving the weeds would certainly spoil the crop; pulling them made better sense ("Why does God allow evil to persist?"). But the landowner argues it isn't worth the risk of pulling up the wheat along with the tares (v. 29). He will let them grow side by side until the harvest. Nevertheless, in the end the landowner believes there will still be enough wheat to gather "into my barn" (v. 30). Regarding the other parables, mustard plants (a small amount serves their purpose) can grow so big they'll take over a garden (v. 32), even harboring birds that are a nuisance to farmers (cf. v. 4). A woman may try to "hide" a little yeast (the Jewish symbol for sin)[26] in the corner of a lump of dough, but it will eventually leaven the entire batch (v. 33). A man who sells all that he has to buy a field with a buried treasure would surely raise the suspicions of the locals, especially the owner (v. 44). (How's he going to farm the field without any resources?)[27] A merchant who sells all his possessions to buy one pearl hasn't managed his risk at all, making his investment more vulnerable to loss or theft (v. 46). (He's eventually going to need to sell it!) In every parable except one (the parable of the fishnet), the main figures of Jesus's stories tend to defy conventional wisdom, leading listeners to infer that the way the kingdom of heaven comes to earth is counterintuitive. How is God's will "done on earth as it is in heaven"? It's not what you think.[28]

LIVE the Story

The parables provoke many other questions that deserve our attention, sorting out details that help us understand them. For example, Jesus pointed out that the field in the parable of the wheat and tares "is the world" (Matt 13:38). It would be a mistake, therefore, to interpret the parable as a commentary on the composition of the church—that every church has true believers and false.[29] Rather, since the field is the world (and Israel knew this better than we do), there are unbelievers among us who benefit from the same gifts of God as we do: it rains on the just and the unjust. So even though it looks as if evil thrives at the expense of God's generosity, sons and daughters of the kingdom must learn to be patient knowing that, one day, God "will weed out of his kingdom everything that causes sin and all who do evil" (v. 41). Justice is coming. On another

25. According to Luz, there are several "unusual" farming practices in this parable (*Matthew*, 2:254–55).

26. Garland, *Reading Matthew*, 151–52.

27. This story provokes several moral and legal problems; see Luz, *Matthew*, 2:276.

28. "Can something so *contemptible* be representative of the work of God?" (Garland, *Reading Matthew*, 152, emphasis original).

29. Luz, *Matthew*, 2:269–70; contra Bruner, *Matthew*, 2:28.

note, why would Jesus compare his disciples who "understand all these things" to *scribes* when the scribes are the very ones who continually opposed Jesus (vv. 51–52)? Was Jesus anticipating that there would be scribes in his kingdom, teaching others his law and his way? (Someone like Matthew!)[30] And what is the significance of the "old" and "new treasures" (v. 52)? Was Jesus referring to the Torah (old) and his interpretation of it (new), or something else?[31] So many questions. Indeed, these stories tend to conceal as much as they reveal. What are we to make of them? How are we supposed to live out these stories—to inhabit the world Jesus envisioned—when we are still puzzling over their meaning?

We may not settle on every detail, but when read together these parables teach a few lessons (among many!) about this mysterious kingdom that must be revealed to be understood and obeyed.[32]

The kingdom of heaven is subversive. In these stories, Jesus turns the world "right-side up." Of course, if we see things according to the wisdom of this world, it will appear as though Jesus turned the world upside down. For example, in a world of limited resources, the threat of scarcity compels the wise to be efficient with what they have. But when it comes to sowing the gospel seed, Jesus teaches that we should be foolishly generous—sowing a risky crop on all kinds of soil—because God is the one who will bring about a superabundant harvest.[33] The kingdom of heaven doesn't depend on efficiency to be effective. In fact, since the gospel seed is in endless supply (eternal!), no one can waste it—even those who share the good news at the wrong time with the wrong people. Sow the seed and let God take care of the results.

The kingdom of heaven is irrepressible. Like a mustard plant that can take over a garden, like yeast that leavens the entire lump of dough, the kingdom of heaven is invading our world, and it won't stop until it reaches every corner of the earth. We tend to think of evil as unstoppable; everywhere we look we see weeds spoiling our fields. In the face of overwhelming injustice, sometimes our efforts for the justice of God's kingdom seem so small, barely noticeable, and dwarfed by the madness of evil people. Yet what is small on earth is big in heaven—it's just a matter of time until earth catches up with heaven's purpose. The least will become the greatest. The last will be first. One day, God will weed out the devil's work from his beautiful garden (vv. 41–42). One day, the righteous will "shine like the sun" regardless of the season (v. 43). One day, this "little" kingdom of heaven brought to earth by *one* man will become so

30. See the discussion in Davies and Allison, *Matthew*, 2:444–46.

31. Ibid., 447–48.

32. "For Matthew 'parables' are publicly spoken stories that without interpretation from Jesus remain secretive and without obedience remain 'unfruitful'" (Luz, *Matthew*, 2:289).

33. Also Nolland, *Matthew*, 529.

big it will take angels to gather the harvest of disciples into the barn of God's salvation, to pull the net full of fish to the shore and divide the good from the bad (vv. 30, 49–50). God will finish what he started, and it will be big.

The kingdom of heaven is invaluable. The problem is this: what we value on earth isn't the same as what is important to God. According to Jesus there is *nothing on earth* more important than the kingdom of heaven. Once you see it, you'll desire it more than anything. Like a merchant who finds the greatest pearl or a man who discovers a buried treasure, you'll sell everything to get it because you recognize what is eternally valuable—storing "treasures in heaven" (6:20)—something a rich, young man wouldn't do (19:21–30).[34]

The kingdom of heaven is mysterious. To our Western minds, a mystery is a puzzle to solve. Once we figure it out, we move on to other problems. But to Eastern minds, a mystery is a wonder to behold.[35] The fact that we are unable to figure it out proves that it's divine. Indeed, Jesus taught that the kingdom of heaven coming to earth is a mystery, something that is hidden from the "wise and the learned and revealed to little children" (11:25). No wonder Jesus preferred parables, stories that *conceal and reveal* the mystery of the kingdom of heaven. Parables make us discover meaning, search for the greatest pearl, find the buried treasure, inhabit another world. The medium is the message. Therefore, as we move into the house of Jesus's story world, puzzling over the way he has rearranged the mental furniture, we begin to see a new way to live. When that happens, we cannot help but wonder, "Why haven't we seen this before?"—especially since these mysteries have been around since the beginning of time: "I will open my mouth in parables, I will utter things hidden since the creation of the world" (Matt 13:35; Ps 78:2). The kingdom of heaven coming to earth is a story of God restoring all creation to his purpose, from beginning to end, the old and the new. Yet only those who have ears to hear the parables can see the story of the kingdom and their place in it.

When I think about the distinctive features of the kingdom of heaven on earth—subversive, irrepressible, invaluable, mysterious—and look at the world with "kingdom eyes" to see what Jesus was driving at, considering the effect his stories have on us, it begins to dawn on me what he was talking about: love. Love turns everything right-side up. Love cannot be stopped and never runs out. Love is the most desirable thing on earth; most people will do anything to get it. Love is wonderful, astonishing, and indescribable. Love is truly a mystery.

---

34. Luz, *Matthew*, 2:278–79.

35. Andrew Louth, *Introducing Eastern Orthodox Theology* (Downers Grove, IL: IVP Academic, 2013), 4–5, 21, 142; see also Smith, *Bible Made Impossible*, 45–48; E. Randolph Richards and Brandon J. O'Brien, *Misreading Scripture with Western Eyes: Removing Cultural Blinders to Better Understand the Bible* (Downers Grove, IL: InterVarsity Press, 2012), 33–35, 212–13.

Jesus was trying to get his disciples to see how God rules the world—a king and his kingdom on earth—through love. Not just any love, but the love of God revealed in and through the Messiah and his disciples. That's why he told stories, envisioning what the world would look like if we loved one another with such a heavenly love. Where the apostle Paul took a more descriptive approach—using lofty terms—to elevate love as that which is absolutely indispensable to our faith (1 Cor 12:31–13:13), Jesus made up earthy stories to envision a kingdom of heaven grounded in love. Indeed, that is the good news of the kingdom: like good seed, the love of Christ has been sown in the world, and those who are good soil will not only receive it but bear the fruit of it—a bumper crop in the end. It is the love of Christ that opposes evil, that leavens the whole world. It is a priceless pearl, a hidden treasure, the net that gathers the disciples of Jesus.

So, when it comes to determining whether we are doing the work of the kingdom, here is the only thing we need to know: Do we see the love of Christ—objectively and subjectively? That is, do our efforts promote devotion to Christ? Do our efforts reflect Christ's love? If both are true, then the king is advancing his kingdom on earth as it is in heaven. If the love of Christ is not evident, it's not the work of the kingdom.

I wish I would have understood that more clearly when I was a pastor. Too many times we tended to evaluate the success of ministry according to the wisdom of the world. Is this program efficient? Is the ministry sustainable? Are we producing quantifiable results? Are we hitting our intended target? Are the people satisfied? And finally, do we want to do it again? If so, then it was steady as she goes—no more questions. As I think about it now in light of the parables of Jesus, I wonder how provocative it would have been to ask: Are we *foolishly wasteful* with the love of Christ? Are we *overcoming evil* with good? Are we *risking everything* for Christ and his kingdom? Are we *compelled by the love of Christ*, disciples drawn into a net like fish, to do ministry together? Do we celebrate it when, sometimes, we *don't understand* what's happening? If so, then we are seeing the parables of Christ and his kingdom come true—stories that are lived as well as heard.

Jesus was a genius. We're still inspired by his parables.

Kind of makes you want to tell stories about the King and his kingdom, doesn't it?[36]

36. As an example of the power of story, Luz claims the legendary story of a suffering Chinese mother, written by the Christian theologian Choan-Seng Song, "is more powerful than an entire work of dogmatics or a multivolume New Testament commentary" (*Matthew*, 2:298n15).

CHAPTER 19

Matthew 13:53–14:21

LISTEN to the Story

53When Jesus had finished these parables, he moved on from there.
54Coming to his hometown, he began teaching the people in their syna-
gogue, and they were amazed. "Where did this man get this wisdom and
these miraculous powers?" they asked. 55"Isn't this the carpenter's son? Isn't
his mother's name Mary, and aren't his brothers James, Joseph, Simon and
Judas? 56Aren't all his sisters with us? Where then did this man get all these
things?" 57And they took offense at him.

But Jesus said to them, "A prophet is not without honor except in his own town and in his own home."

58And he did not do many miracles there because of their lack of faith.

14:1At that time Herod the tetrarch heard the reports about Jesus, 2and
he said to his attendants, "This is John the Baptist; he has risen from the
dead! That is why miraculous powers are at work in him."

3Now Herod had arrested John and bound him and put him in prison
because of Herodias, his brother Philip's wife, 4for John had been saying
to him: "It is not lawful for you to have her." 5Herod wanted to kill John,
but he was afraid of the people, because they considered John a prophet.

6On Herod's birthday the daughter of Herodias danced for the guests
and pleased Herod so much 7that he promised with an oath to give her
whatever she asked. 8Prompted by her mother, she said, "Give me here on a
platter the head of John the Baptist." 9The king was distressed, but because
of his oaths and his dinner guests, he ordered that her request be granted
10and had John beheaded in the prison. 11His head was brought in on a
platter and given to the girl, who carried it to her mother. 12John's disciples
came and took his body and buried it. Then they went and told Jesus.

13When Jesus heard what had happened, he withdrew by boat pri-
vately to a solitary place. Hearing of this, the crowds followed him on
foot from the towns. 14When Jesus landed and saw a large crowd, he had
compassion on them and healed their sick.

[15]As evening approached, the disciples came to him and said, "This is
a remote place, and it's already getting late. Send the crowds away, so they
can go to the villages and buy themselves some food."
[16]Jesus replied, "They do not need to go away. You give them some-
thing to eat."
[17]"We have here only five loaves of bread and two fish," they answered.
[18]"Bring them here to me," he said. [19]And he directed the people to
sit down on the grass. Taking the five loaves and the two fish and looking
up to heaven, he gave thanks and broke the loaves. Then he gave them
to the disciples, and the disciples gave them to the people. [20]They all ate
and were satisfied, and the disciples picked up twelve basketfuls of broken
pieces that were left over. [21]The number of those who ate was about five
thousand men, besides women and children.

Listening to the Text in the Story: Genesis 40:18–22; Exodus 16:14–18; Leviticus 18:16; 20:21; 1 Samuel 9:13; 1 Kings 17:7–16; 2 Kings 2:9–15; 4:1–7, 42–44; 10:6–8; Esther 1:10–22; Jeremiah 1:1; 11:21–23; 12:6.

Kings of Israel were appointed by God to take care of his people. When they didn't, a prophet would show up to warn them of the devastating consequences—to them as well as to their kingdom (1 Sam 15:10–28; 1 Kgs 22:7–38; Isa 39:1–8). It was the prophet's job to speak to power—often appearing in the biblical narrative without introduction—when the most powerful person in the land was doing something wrong, misleading the people. Whenever the king did evil in the sight of the Lord, the people suffered the consequences. So, these "men of God" (see 1 Kgs 13:1–6) would confront the king, often at their own peril, to tell him what God thinks. One might expect God to speak directly to the king, giving him much-needed advice to rule his kingdom wisely. But that wasn't the case. Kings had to rely upon royal counselors for divine guidance. And when these court-appointed sages kowtowed to the king, tickling his ears with bad advice, God would send a prophet to set them straight. Theirs was a contentious relationship: king versus prophet, God's vicegerent versus God's spokesman. But it didn't have to be that way. By divine design, the separation of powers was supposed to inspire a humble king and a fearless prophet to lead a submissive people like sheep to the Good Shepherd.

But sometimes people don't want a humble king, and most of the time kings don't know how to be humble. So, when God's fearless prophet shows up (right on cue!) and says, "Thus saith the Lord," rather than listen to him, a hard-hearted people prefers to watch the spectacle, and a wicked king does everything in his power to silence the voice. Yet, as Matthew has already made clear (John prepared the way!), the humble king of Israel has appeared to lead God's sheep to the pasture of his keeping despite the royal imposters of the Herodian dynasty. Knowing that a ruthless, illegitimate king-of-Israel wannabe is chasing the crown and that prophets are not honored in their own country—these are ominous signs for a fearless prophet and a humble king—death must be right around the corner. Indeed, the way Matthew has set up this story, it's time for John to meet his fate, forecasting Jesus's destiny as well. In more ways than one, John prophesied Jesus.

EXPLAIN the Story

The parables of chapter thirteen represent a pivotal point in Matthew's narrative, not only summarizing what has been but also forecasting what will be. For just as the mystery of the kingdom of heaven has been revealed and concealed by the parables, so also the identity of Jesus (something greater than Jonah, Solomon, and the temple) will continue to be revealed to some and concealed to others. And, just as Jesus predicted, "whoever has will be given more, and they will have an abundance. Whoever does not have, even what they have will be taken from them" (Matt 13:12). Having eyes to see the kingdom means having ears to hear the king and his prophet. To those who see the king and his kingdom—they are the ones who "[hear] these words of mine and [put] them into practice" (7:24)—more will be revealed. Likewise, the blindness of those who can't see will become even darker (Herod has the crazy idea that Jesus is John "risen from the dead"; 14:2). What is telling for us, as Matthew's readers, isn't seeing who gets it and who doesn't, *but why*. The momentum of this revealing-yet-concealing kingdom seems deterministic—like Newton's cradle, the perpetual motion of ball bearings hanging from a pendulum swinging back and forth, clashing against one another with predictable results (two to the left, two to the right). Because of what we've seen in Matthew's narrative world, we already know who will recognize the king of Israel and who won't. (It's really no surprise that Herod and even Jesus's hometown don't get it.) It's the *reason* some see it and some don't that becomes clearer *the more we read Matthew's Gospel.* "Whoever has will be given more"—Matthew made sure of it. From now on, our Gospel writer will pile on the reasons why many people don't see the kingdom of heaven.

A Prophet Is Never Honored by His Own People

When Jesus went home, probably Nazareth and not Capernaum,[1] things didn't go well. We might have expected a better reception, a homecoming party thrown for the Nazarene who had done so many wonderful things. Yet rather than celebrate his fame, Jesus's hometown was offended by it (Matt 13:57). We sometimes hear it said, "You can never go home," and, "Familiarity breeds contempt." It's because things change, and yet the people back home will act like nothing's changed. That's what happened in Nazareth when Jesus tried to teach his hometown folk about the kingdom of heaven. One wonders whether Jesus simply repeated that day some of the parables he offered to the crowds. Or did he speak plainly to them about his messianic agenda? (Of course, Luke gives us a glimpse of what he said that day [Luke 4:15–27], but Matthew prefers to leave his readers in the dark. Evidently, what Jesus said didn't really matter; it's how the people responded that interests Matthew.) As to be expected (Jesus has been teaching, preaching, and healing for several chapters in Matthew's Gospel), Jesus's fame had already reached the ears of Nazareth. The local boy had impressed outsiders with his wisdom and miracles (Matt 13:54). As he taught in the synagogue, Jesus seemed to make the same favorable impression: "They were amazed" (v. 54). But then things went south fast; it didn't take long for the hometown crowd to take offense. Why? Was it something he said? Was it something he did?

Their question, "Where did this man get this wisdom and these miraculous powers?" is revealing. Their skepticism is fueled by the fact that they know this man and his family (vv. 55–56). To them, he's nothing more than a carpenter who left home and abandoned his family (as well as his community—it took a village to make it in the first-century world). So when they asked one another (in earshot of Jesus, no doubt), "Where then did this man get all these things?" they were implying that he certainly didn't get it from them. What may sound to us like self-incrimination was actually an attempt to shame Jesus. In the first-century Mediterranean world, the social worth of a person—their honor—was the most important resource of any community. Therefore, the social approval of those who know you best—your family, your village, your tribe—would carry more weight than the affirmation of outsiders.[2] You might be able to fool strangers about how important you are. Yet back home your fame would mean nothing. There were no self-made people in Jesus's day; the honor of a person started in their

1. So most scholars (cf. Luke 4:16) and contra Nolland, *Matthew*, 574, who argues that Jesus's entire family had moved with him to Capernaum, which explains why Jesus "withdrew by boat" right after this incident (Matt 14:13).

2. Malina and Rohrbaugh, *Synoptic Gospels*, 106–7.

hometown. A person's identity was embedded in their family name, their father's trade, their village's reputation. Even David had to be recognized first by his family, hometown, and tribe before a nation would coronate him as Israel's king (1 Sam 16:1–13; 2 Sam 2:1–4; 5:1–5). So when the people of Nazareth asked where Jesus got his wisdom and miraculous abilities, they were essentially reminding Jesus from whence he came. He was nothing special. Evidently, growing up in Nazareth, Jesus did nothing to distinguish himself as a wise man with great powers. In their eyes, Jesus had earned no honor beyond that which he had already received. He was "the carpenter's son," his mother's name was Mary, he was the brother of James, Joseph, Simon, and Judas, and his sisters still lived in Nazareth. Nothing more, nothing less. One wonders if word had gotten back to Jesus's hometown about the way he treated his mother and brothers, acting like his disciples were his true family (Matt 12:46–50). That might also help explain why the hometown folk were bent on putting Jesus in his place. It's no wonder they were offended by him (13:57). He was acting as pretentious as a prophet.

At this point, we might expect Jesus to show off a little bit, proving to Nazareth that he was something special. "So, you want to see a miracle, huh? Shazam!" But that didn't happen due to his humility. Instead, Jesus chalked up their response to what typically happened to prophets, who were honored everywhere except in their own town and by their own family (v. 57). Consequently, since the people of Nazareth didn't believe what they had heard about him, Jesus "did not do many miracles there" (v. 58). By contrast, Herod Antipas believed the reports about Jesus having "miraculous powers" (14:1–2). What was ignored in Nazareth was feared by the tetrarch, his worst nightmare coming true: the prophet he murdered had risen from the dead! Herod thought Jesus was the reincarnation of John, a prophet who conquered death and brought back with him secret powers from the netherworld.[3] If they were to hear of it, the people of Nazareth would have felt justified in their judgment. ("See, outsiders will believe anything.") Yet at least Herod took Jesus to be a prophet, albeit a reincarnated one. Nevertheless, what Jesus said to his hometown was still true for both him and John: prophets are without honor in their own country. John's death proved it, and so will Jesus's death.

Scholars have noticed a number of ways that Matthew fashioned the account of John's execution to set it up as a precursor to Jesus's death in Jerusalem. While many of the colorful details that appear in Mark's account have been omitted (Herodias's grudge against John, her part in the plot to have John killed, Herod's fascination with John, mentioning the A-list

3. France, *Matthew*, 553.

attenders at Herod's birthday party; see Mark 6:17–29), several similarities between the martyrdom of John and the execution of Jesus have been highlighted in Matthew's version: 1) both John and Jesus were executed by rulers; 2) Matthew uses the same words to describe their arrest (*krateō*, "seized," 14:3; 21:46, and *deō*, "bound," 14:3; 27:2); 3) both Herod and Pilate were asked by others to execute their victims—which they did reluctantly (14:6–11; 27:11–26); 4) fear of the crowd played a role in both episodes (14:5; 21:46); and 5) both John and Jesus were buried by "disciples" (14:12; 27:57–61).[4]

Once again, then, in Matthew's story John and Jesus appear as fraternal twins of the kingdom of heaven. Although they were very different, both met a similar fate because they did the work of God. When prophets of God challenge the "kings" of the earth, it usually doesn't go well. They know the script. The people won't listen to you, and the rulers will do everything in their power to silence you.[5] Ignored by commoners and killed by kings—that is their fate. Prophets are never honored until long after they're gone (Isa 53:1–12). But that doesn't stop them from doing what they were called to do: prepare all people, in populated areas and deserted places, whether homefolk or outsiders, even tetrarchs and governors, for the coming of the Lord.

"Is Not Life More Than Food?"

At the beginning of his ministry, Jesus taught that there was no reason to worry about having enough food to eat. If God takes care of birds, he will take care of Jesus's disciples (Matt 6:25–26). As long as they seek God's kingdom first, their heavenly Father would take care of all their daily needs (vv. 31–33). But what about the hungry masses? Did Jesus's promise apply to them too? After all, it was Herod's responsibility to manage the region's natural resources. Kings were supposed to provide for the people; if the Galileans didn't have enough to eat, it would be Herod's fault (he certainly had plenty to feast upon during his birthday party; 14:6). So when Jesus and his disciples found themselves among five-thousand men in the middle of nowhere and the day nearly spent, the Twelve acted like the hungry masses were not their problem. One wonders why five-thousand men hung around all day anyway. What were they waiting for? With evening approaching, why didn't they have enough sense to go home or at least head for a village nearby to foray for food? Apparently, these careless fools had made no provisions for the trip, and even the Twelve

4. Davies and Allison, *Matthew*, 2:476.

5. What made John's situation even more perilous was that he was baptizing in southern Perea, Herod's domain, which bordered the Nabatean kingdom, criticizing Herod for divorcing his wife, who happened to be the daughter of the Nabatean king, Aretas. For further discussion of this politically delicate situation, see Keener, *Matthew*, 398–99.

had only a small bit of food to get them through the night. With so many hungry men around, there was no way the disciples could break out their meal and eat it. The only thing left to do, then, was for Jesus to send the crowd away (14:15)—something he would eventually need to do (v. 22). But Jesus had other plans.

It must have startled the disciples when Jesus said, "They do not need to go away. You give them something to eat" (v. 16). In light of what eventually happened, what Jesus should have said was, "*I won't* send them away because *I will* give them something to eat." After all, that would be quite a miracle to pull off, a public-relations coup, feeding all these people in such a deserted place. It might remind the Galileans of their sacred history when Moses fed the Israelites as they wandered through the desert. It might even be taken as a withering indictment of Herod's administration. Where John tended to be more direct, confronting Herod about his illegal marriage to his brother's wife (Matt 14:3–4; Lev 18:16; 20:21), Jesus would be taking a more sanguine approach when critiquing the illegitimate "king"—feeding the people of Herod's kingdom when Herod didn't. Yet, for some reason Jesus put the onus on his disciples, acting as if it was their responsibility to do something about it. (While I was a pastor, I was inspired by Jesus's example when members wanted me to fix problems in the church; problem spotters nominate themselves to be problem solvers.) What is fascinating to me is the way Jesus set up the miracle of feeding five-thousand men. As far as the crowd was concerned, it was the disciples who fed them (Matt 14:19). There is no indication in Matthew's version that anyone knew a miracle had occurred except the Twelve. Sure, "all ate and were satisfied" (v. 20). But it seems as if the miracle was performed for Jesus's disciples as much as to benefit the hungry crowd. Twelve baskets of leftovers—one for each disciple—was the kicker. As long as they were with Jesus, doing the work of the kingdom, they would always have more than enough to eat, even with a wicked ruler like Herod running the place.

Even though it seems Jesus was trying to teach his disciples a lesson when he fed the five-thousand men, I still find it a little odd that the Twelve wanted Jesus to dismiss the crowd to get them to go home. Why was that necessary? Jesus never had to send the crowd away before. A huge crowd showing up looking for a miracle had happened several times. This was nothing new. Whenever that happened, after Jesus healed the people (which always drew a larger crowd), he never had to dismiss the crowd (v. 23), like a traffic cop clearing the scene. ("Alright people. Party's over. There's nothing left to see here. Everyone go home.") Instead, crowds came, crowds went. The Galileans had enough sense to go home when evening came. So, what's different about this situation? Why did they stick around until evening? Were they expecting to see something? Or did the entire group lose track of time, not even paying attention to where they were—what Matthew describes as a "solitary" and "remote place" (vv. 13, 15)? In other words, were the disciples being selfish when they asked Jesus to send the crowd away so that they could eat their food in peace? Or did the Twelve recognize that something else was going on, that these people were there for a reason and wouldn't leave until Jesus told them to go home?

If we knew for sure why Matthew (as well as Mark) numbered the crowd as "five thousand men, *besides* women and children" (v. 21, emphasis added), we would have a clearer picture of the context. If Matthew was implying that women and children were there, then the episode seems to be an impromptu gathering of desperate people, willing to follow Jesus anywhere. The reason Jesus seemed to lead them to the middle of nowhere was that he was trying to leave Herod's jurisdiction and find a solitary place to grieve over John's death. Simply put, he wanted to be left alone, which is why he took a boat to the east side of the Sea of Galilee. But a crowd from several towns followed him anyway, catching up with him on foot (v. 13). Rather than send them away, he had "compassion on them and healed their sick" (v. 14). Evidently, this was one of the largest crowds to gather around Jesus, and so the number was recorded like a census (Num 1:2–3): five thousand men besides all the women and children. But the word translated "besides" (*chōris*) also means "without," so some scholars suggest that Matthew was emphasizing the composition of the crowd and suggest that the number is a census of men for war.[6] Men from the surrounding region had gathered around Jesus for a purpose. But why? Did they follow Jesus into such a deserted place because it was spring (Matt 14:19), believing that they were about to witness the sign of Moses reminiscent of Passover? (That's what happened according to John's version; see John 6:4–15.)[7] Were they hoping to compel Jesus to become their Messiah? If that were the case—something akin to the beginnings of a militia to confront Herod—then women and children would have no place there, and the disciples would have had legitimate concerns. Jesus should send these men away before things get out of hand.[8] But Jesus fed them anyway, a mild critique of Herod's government, and eventually had to dismiss them to send them back home (Matt 14:23).

Because of John's interpretation of the miracle and Matthew's pared down version of it, we may be looking for things that aren't there explicitly. Indeed,

6. France, *Matthew*, 564–65.

7. Davies and Allison, *Matthew*, 2:482–83.

8. A similar situation occurred over twenty years before when a Galilean name Judas stirred up the people and led them in a revolt to confront the rulers of Jerusalem (Josephus, *Ant.* 18.1.1).

Matthew's account can be interpreted a variety of ways: as an allegory for the Eucharist (receiving, blessing, breaking, giving); a proleptic demonstration of the eschatological messianic banquet (Rev 19:9); a prophetic re-creation of the miracles of Elijah and Elisha (1 Kgs 17:7–16; 2 Kgs 4:42–44); another "new Moses" motif (manna in the wilderness); or even a way of promoting the responsibility and authority of the church (disciples serve the people).[9] Nevertheless, even though "Matthew leaves the matter rather open-ended,"[10] however we interpret it the feeding of the five thousand was an *extraordinary* miracle—the only miracle to make it into all four Gospels. After something like this, the only way Jesus would be able to get away from the crowd is to leave the country (Matt 15:21–39). But even in gentile territory, Jesus will have compassion on the people, healing their sick and feeding the hungry. It's who he is, what he does—and of all people, the disciples are going to have to get used to it: "Send them away" isn't an option for him or them (v. 32).

LIVE the Story

Mel Gibson's film *The Passion of the Christ* had a profound impact on many people. What was supposed to be a "tiny, low-budget film" intended for a few Christians turned out to be a blockbuster that shocked Hollywood and provoked controversy.[11] Why did he do it? Some accused Gibson of trying to promote an anti-Semitic agenda, shifting the blame of Christ's death from the Romans to the Jews. Others said his film was penance, a way for him to find forgiveness for his sins (in the film, the hands of the Roman soldier who crucified Jesus were his). Still others argued he wanted to spread the Catholic traditions surrounding the death of Christ to a larger Christian audience. According to Gibson, his purpose in presenting such a graphic film about the violent death of Jesus was to "make it realistic and human. I think the first things that hit you are the human aspects of the story. What we all relate to is a human experience."[12] Yet, by centering on the last week of Jesus's life, staging the excruciatingly long beating and crucifixion of Jesus, utilizing every special effect to make it look so real—Jesus ends up a bloody mess—Gibson left little to the imagination when it comes to wondering what it would have been like to walk in Jesus's sandals. To be sure, the gory execution of Jesus proved he was

9. See Davies and Allison, *Matthew*, 2:480–83; Luz, *Matthew*, 2:312–23; Garland, *Reading Matthew*, 157.

10. Nolland, *Matthew*, 593.

11. See the interview by Paul Fischer, "Gibson Defends His Passion," iofilm, February 13, 2004, http://www.iofilm.co.uk/gibsondefendshispassion.

12. Ibid.

a man. But if Gibson intended for us to "relate" to the "human experience" of Jesus's death, he missed the mark. Instead, most of us walked away from the film shaking our heads in disbelief: "How could *any* man endure such agony?" The only way to explain it, especially for Christians, was to point to the deity of Christ. Indeed, *The Passion of the Christ* held up Jesus as a man to be admired for doing what *only* he could do. His death on the cross was hardly something any of us could relate to. Rather, all we could do was wince, close our eyes, turn away from the grisly spectacle, or perhaps even weep for the man who endured so much. One could hardly imagine Jesus saying at the beginning of Gibson's film, "Follow me."

We should admire Jesus for enduring such torture on our behalf, dying for our sins. Yet, Matthew expects us to admire him (even follow him!) before he was executed in Jerusalem. It's because Jesus experienced a crucified life long before he died. Rejected by his own people, he was a constant threat to powerful rulers. He sacrificed himself for the needs of others, all the while continually teaching his disciples how to carry a cross. That sounds a lot like a summary of the series of episodes we've considered here: rejection at Nazareth, execution of John, compassion for the crowd, lesson for the Twelve. In fact, the way Matthew tells the story, the "passion" of Christ started way before Palm Sunday. Jesus carried the cross of his glorious suffering from the time he was tempted by the devil all the way until the day he was crucified. The invitation "come to me" was issued long before he died on a cross. Therefore, if Mel Gibson wanted to tell the story of Jesus on film that would be "realistic and human," a human drama "we could all relate to," he couldn't have found a better place than in the events leading up to the last week of Christ's life. Most of us can relate to what he went through before he walked the Via Dolorosa.

There are times when we try to minister to people, and they don't want it. And there are times when we don't want to minister to people, yet they expect it. This is not only true for those who earn a living as ministers; it happens to all who follow Christ. Many years ago when I was a seminary student, a friend and classmate, Gerald Bontrager, told me about the time he went home for his father's funeral. Like the rest of his family, he was grieving, hurting over the untimely death of his dad. But in the midst of his grief, he tried to minister to family members, doing what came naturally to him—not because he was preparing to be a minister but because he is a follower of Christ. He tried to offer comforting words. At times, he wanted to pray together with the family. He thought he was doing the right thing until someone made a snide remark, something like "practicing on us, are you Gerald? Look, quit trying to act like a minister and just be yourself." His family took offense at his pretense, acting like he could help them. So, my friend learned the lesson: "A prophet is not without honor except in his own town and in his own home" (Matt 13:57). Other Christ followers have told me similar stories, especially those who are the only believers in their family. A fearful dread comes over them in anticipation of the holidays, knowing that they can't help themselves. They will try to share their faith in Christ, and their family will reject them once again. Sometimes it makes them want to give up, quietly surrendering to the ironclad will of their family. Other times, they want to prove they are right to believe in Jesus. Regardless, the truth of the matter remains the same. Jesus knows what it feels like; prophets are not welcomed by their own families.

A few years later, when I was still in seminary and serving as a youth minister for a church in Texas, I led a group of teenagers on a summer mission trip to the southern tip of the state to help a little Hispanic church minister to the needs of the people. For a week, every day we put on a Bible school for children in the morning, scraped and painted the outside walls of the church building, then held evening worship services for the members and their guests. It was a rigorous schedule. We would get up early every morning, grab a quick breakfast, and then travel to the church building in our bus without air conditioning. I would drop off my group, who would prepare for the morning's activities, while I made two trips throughout the neighborhood, collecting children on the bus for Bible school. After Bible school, I returned the children to their homes—making two trips—and then we would grab a quick lunch before changing into our work clothes for the afternoon chore of scraping and painting in the sweltering, summer heat. Around five o'clock every day, we would return to our lodging (which didn't have air conditioning), shower, put on our church clothes, eat a quick dinner, and return to the church for evening services. Once again, I would make two bus trips into town to bring the people to church—did I mention the bus didn't have air conditioning? We led the worship services, and I preached the sermon. Then, after worship was over I would bus the people back to their homes—two-trips worth—and then return to the church building, pick up my team (by this time it would be around ten o'clock at night), and return to the lodge (no air conditioning!) to crash for the night. I was so proud of my youth group. They never complained. Never fussed about the rigorous schedule. Their only reward was to stop by a convenience store every night to buy some snacks on the way back to the lodge—something they looked forward to with such excitement and great shouts of celebration that you would think we were headed for Six Flags Over Texas.

By the fourth or fifth day, I was spent. I remember driving the local children back home one evening, several of them yelling, laughing—even a few crawling on my back. I was sweating, weary, worn out, a little edgy, and feeling used and abused when the thought occurred to me, "I wonder if this is how Jesus felt—with the crowds always clamoring for attention, his disciples trying to help him, enduring the summer heat, wanting to find refuge in the desert to grieve over John's death?" Then I quickly became embarrassed by the comparison. Tears welled up in my eyes (like most people, when I'm exhausted I tend to get emotional). Maybe I could relate a little to what he went through, when it feels like everyone wants a piece of you. But the truth of the matter was I saw my reflection in the faces of the disciples when they wanted Jesus to "send the crowds away" (Matt 14:15). I was tired. I was ready to go home. And then, as I thought about the weary days ahead, taking the people home for the last time, it felt like Jesus looked right at me and said, "They do not need to go away. You give them something to eat" (v. 16). "But Lord, this is a deserted place. All we have is an old bus, a small group of workers, and a few supplies." Then it was as if he said, "Bring them here to me." And so I kept driving.

When I finally arrived at the church building late that night, the young people were gathered around the piano, singing and laughing and celebrating. Joyously they piled into the bus, we headed for the little convenience store, and all the while I couldn't help but think of the line, "They all ate and were satisfied, and the disciples picked up twelve basketfuls of broken pieces" (v. 20). Indeed, we had more than enough because the King of Israel knows how to take care of his people—even in deserted places.

CHAPTER 20

Matthew 14:22-36

LISTEN to the Story

22 Immediately Jesus made the disciples get into the boat and go on
ahead of him to the other side, while he dismissed the crowd. 23 After
he had dismissed them, he went up on a mountainside by himself to
pray. Later that night, he was there alone, 24 and the boat was already a
considerable distance from land, buffeted by the waves because the wind
was against it.

25 Shortly before dawn Jesus went out to them, walking on the lake.
26 When the disciples saw him walking on the lake, they were terrified. "It's
a ghost," they said, and cried out in fear.

27 But Jesus immediately said to them: "Take courage! It is I. Don't be
afraid."

28 "Lord, if it's you," Peter replied, "tell me to come to you on the water."

29 "Come," he said.

Then Peter got down out of the boat, walked on the water and came
toward Jesus. 30 But when he saw the wind, he was afraid and, beginning
to sink, cried out, "Lord, save me!"

31 Immediately Jesus reached out his hand and caught him. "You of
little faith," he said, "why did you doubt?"

32 And when they climbed into the boat, the wind died down. 33 Then
those who were in the boat worshiped him, saying, "Truly you are the
Son of God."

34 When they had crossed over, they landed at Gennesaret. 35 And when
the men of that place recognized Jesus, they sent word to all the surround-
ing country. People brought all their sick to him 36 and begged him to let
the sick just touch the edge of his cloak, and all who touched it were healed.

Listening to the Text in the Story: Exodus 14:24–31; Job 9:4–12; 26:11–12; 38:16; Psalms 65:7; 69:1–3, 13–18; 77:13–20; 89:8–9; 107:23–32; Wisdom of Solomon 14:2–4; Sirach 24:5–6.

Most miracles make sense. When Jesus heals a paralytic or feeds hundreds of people, we nod our head in approval because we expect nothing less from this man of mercy. "That's just like Jesus," we say to ourselves, knowing that he came to help the helpless. But when Jesus walks on water to get to a boat where his disciples are having difficulty crossing the Sea of Galilee due to stiff winds, well, we can't help but scratch our heads and wonder, "Why?" There seems to be no good reason for Jesus to perform this miracle. It's not like the disciples were in trouble, as in the previous boat story (Matt 8:23–27). At that time, they feared for their lives because the storm was so bad the boat was taking in water. So, when they woke up Jesus and cried to him, "Lord, save us!" we can easily empathize with their plight. Yet that's not what happened here. The disciples were not about to die; their lives weren't in danger. Sure, they were having a hard time sailing their boat against contrary winds in the middle of the night. And boating in the dark of night could be a little intimidating. But, they weren't afraid—that is, *until Jesus shows up* walking on the water (14:26). Then they were scared out of their minds, convinced he was a ghost (*phantasma*), at which point Jesus had to calm them down with reassuring words (v. 27). That's quite a reversal of what we usually read in Matthew's Gospel.

Typically, things get better when Jesus shows up. But not this time. Instead, Jesus's weird miracle tempts Peter to get out of the boat—where he is safe and sound—to "test the waters" literally. Then the fool nearly drowns trying to walk on water too. Of course, the winds die down once Jesus is in the boat with the Twelve, and they finally make it to their destination (vv. 32–34). So, is that the purpose of the story, to show how Jesus can stop contrary winds to ensure smooth sailing? But Jesus didn't have to walk on water to stop the storm. He could have calmed the winds and waves like he did before (8:26). But he didn't do that this time. Instead, it looks like he was trying to set up something else. Notice how he had to convince his disciples to get in a boat without him ("Jesus *made* the disciples get into the boat," 14:22, emphasis added) to cross the sea despite contrary winds. He knew his disciples would have a hard time. So, was this a bit of theatrical staging? Did Jesus set up the scenario so that he could walk on water to them?[1] If there was ever a time when it seems like Jesus was trying to show off, this is it. ("Hey, look at me! I can walk on water.") It certainly had the desired effect: "Then those who were in the boat worshiped him saying, 'Truly you are the Son of God'" (v. 33). After Jesus calmed the wind the first time, the disciples wondered, "What kind of man is this?" (8:27). Once he walked on water, they had no

1. Jesus assumed a role that the Old Testament reserved for God (Keener, *Matthew*, 406; also Turner, *Matthew*, 373).

doubts about his divine nature: this is the first time they confess that Jesus is the Son of God (14:33).

Is that why Jesus walked on water, to finally convince his disciples of his unique identity since God is the only one who can walk on water (Job 9:8; 38:16)?[2] Such an idea certainly shows up in casual conversation today. Talking about a person who is extraordinarily gifted, someone will say sarcastically, "Yeah. But can they walk on water?" Doesn't that tell us something? Of all the miracles Jesus performed, that's the one we speak of dismissively. We don't say, "But can he feed five thousand people?" or "But can he heal the sick?" It's almost as if, revealed by the common vernacular of everyday people, we know this miracle is rather fanciful, even Superman-like. Come to think of it, if Jesus could walk on water, why didn't he fly around like Superman? Since he needed to get somewhere fast when his disciples were having trouble, why didn't Jesus fly to the boat? I realize it sounds irreverent to compare Jesus to Superman (and yet, we do that all the time, treating Jesus as if he were our own, personal superman).[3] But I'm pressing hard to understand why Jesus thought it was necessary to walk on water in the middle of the night when his disciples weren't in danger. There are other ways for Jesus to convince the disciples of his divine identity (resurrection!). It just seems a little embarrassing for him to do it like this.[4] Honestly, I would like the story better if the disciples were drowning so that Jesus could save them.[5] But they weren't going to die; Jesus knew that. Instead, this seems to be a story about tough sailing—that is, until Peter got out of the boat. Then Jesus saves.

EXPLAIN the Story

Matthew has made it clear that as long as the disciples had Jesus with them, everything would be all right. Climb a mountain with him, and he will give rock-solid words to build your life upon. Get in a boat with him, and he will calm the storm when the torrid waves of life's troubles threaten to drown you. When the righteous accuse you of breaking their sacred rules, he will

---

2. Davies and Allison, *Matthew*, 2:504.

3. See David B. Capes, Rodney Reeves, and E. Randolph Richards, *Rediscovering Jesus: An Introduction to Biblical, Religious, and Cultural Perspectives on Christ* (Downers Grove, IL: IVP Academic, 2015), 222–23, 231, 234.

4. Scholars struggle with the relevance of the story as well; for example, see Luz, *Matthew*, 2:322–23; Bruner, *Matthew*, 2:74–75.

5. I marvel over how many times believers conflate the two boat stories when I've asked them to summarize the episode of Jesus walking on the water. Try it sometime. Ask them, "Why did Jesus walk on water?" and most of the time you'll get a response like, "Because their boat was sinking," or, "Because the disciples were about to drown."

defend you. When everyone else is puzzling over his teaching, he will explain it to you. Do what he says, and he'll treat you like family. Follow him into the desert, and you'll never go hungry. It's no wonder, then, that Jesus had to convince his disciples to get in the boat *without* him (Matt 14:22). The only time he had sent them away, he gave them lengthy instructions about how they would face difficulty but that he would eventually come to them and reward them for their faithfulness (10:1–39). This time, he simply told them to "go ahead of him to the other side" of the sea (14:22). Then, after sending the satisfied crowd away from him, Jesus retreated to a mountain to pray (v. 23). Obviously, Jesus wanted to be alone, perhaps to have time finally to grieve over John's death or perhaps to contemplate his own fate. Whatever the reason, Jesus had spent most of the night in prayer when he decided to go looking for his disciples, who had sailed the boat "a considerable distance from land" (vv. 23–25). Both Jesus and the disciples had endured another long day, followed this time by a sleepless night. To say they were tired, perhaps even a little foggy headed due to exhaustion, may help to explain the strange sequence of events that we take for granted because we know the story. No wonder the disciples were scared out of their minds, thinking Jesus was a ghost. We all see strange things at night, especially when we aren't able to sleep. Is that why Peter acted like such a knucklehead? We could certainly attribute his impulsive behavior to a lack of sleep. Speaking of sleep, is that why Jesus went walking on the water to begin with, because he was so tired he wanted to get to the other side of the lake as soon as possible? Sleep deprivation creates all kinds of confusion and can lead to strange behavior. Yet, once this crazy night is over, with the dawning of the morn, everything will become a little clearer in the light of day: "Truly you are the Son of God" (v. 33).

Jesus Is Immanuel

Matthew begins his Gospel with the claim that Jesus is "God with us" (1:23). At the end of the Gospel story, as the resurrected Messiah sends his followers away to make disciples throughout the whole world, the last thing Jesus says—the very last line of Matthew's Gospel—is, "And surely I am with you always, to the very end of the age" (28:20). Even in his absence, Jesus will be present with his disciples. From the beginning to the end, we as readers get to see the story unfold, not only how Jesus became "Immanuel" to his disciples, but also how they came to learn the lesson that even in his absence, Jesus is present with them always, no matter what. And so, smack dab in the middle of his Gospel, Matthew tells this story when Jesus seems to prepare his disciples for this mysterious paradox. In fact, both boat stories appear to function that way, as training exercises in their discipleship development.

The first time, Jesus was present but "absent," asleep while the boat takes in water during a life-threatening storm (8:23–27). In this boat story, Jesus was absent but "present," coming to them on the water during a sleepless night of sailing against contrary winds. After the first boat episode, the Twelve puzzle over Jesus's identity: "What kind of man is this?" (8:27). At the end of this story, they worship him as divine (14:33). Yet, when they first saw him, they thought Jesus was a ghost (v. 26). That's quite a haphazard leap, going from "who is this man?" to "he's a ghost" and ultimately to "truly you are the Son of God." In fact, their confused confessions are very telling: as long as Jesus was *in the boat with them*, the disciples could marvel over the Lord as "Immanuel." But alone, in the middle of a sleepless night, when life is hard, his ghostly presence did more to scare than comfort them. But who could blame them? It's not every day you see a man walk on water.

Let's put ourselves in the boat with the Twelve. It is about eight o'clock in the evening. We've been trying to do what Jesus told us to do: take the boat across the sea. But contrary winds have made obeying this simple command a nightmare. We try to sail our boat, using the force of the wind to push our vessel along, tacking in a zigzag pattern across the lake. Now it is midnight. Not making very good progress, we drop sail and decide to bring out the oars, fighting hard against the waves. Everyone's tired and frustrated. Those not paddling snack on the leftovers we brought along from the miraculous feeding. Now it is two o'clock in the morning. Rowing in shifts, we keep steering the vessel into the wind, knowing that will be our only compass in the pitch-black darkness. We can't see the shoreline—neither where we came from nor where we are headed—so we have no idea how far we have to go. Now it is five o'clock in the morning. Howling winds, arms growing heavy with fatigue, frustrated crew—a one-to-two-hour trip is taking all night. Then, just as the early glimmers of the dawn make it quite evident to everyone that we're in the middle of the lake, someone cries out, "It's a ghost!" Turning to see the phantom, some drop their oars paralyzed with fear; others start paddling like crazy. Malevolent powers are known to traverse the waters, seeking foolish sailors for their eternal keep.[6] Some of us are resigned to the fact that we're going to die. Maybe others wonder, "Where is Jesus?" Then we hear the ghost say in a familiar voice, "Take courage! It is I. Don't be afraid" (v. 27). Are we relieved? Are we confused? Could this be a trick? Is that really Jesus? Who can tell? All we see is a shadowy figure walking on the water. He looks like a ghost, but he sounds like Jesus. What do we do now? Well, like any reasonable person who's had enough sleep to think clearly, we wait until Jesus gets to the boat.

6. France, *Matthew*, 569.

Then we'll know for certain it's him. But Peter can't wait. "Lord, if it's you . . . tell me to come to you on the water" (v. 28). And the phantom says, "Come." Then Peter did the most bizarre, crazy thing he's ever done: he gets out of the boat and walks on the rough waves to see if what we heard is true (v. 29).

We don't know how far Peter walked on water (but I have an idea; see below). Was it only a few steps? Did he make it halfway? Or was he so close to Jesus that from the vantage point of those in the boat, because it was still dark, they looked like two ghosts walking on the water? However far he went, when Peter began to sink it would be easy for those in the boat to think, "The wind spirit got him. It was a trick after all. The voice sounded like Jesus, but everyone knows the only thing that could walk on water is a ghost—something lighter than air. Poor guy, he's crying out for the Lord to save him. How sad is that. We're in the middle of the lake, and Jesus is back there on land where we came from." But then, the unimaginable happens. The ghost saves Peter from drowning. "Wait a minute," they must have thought, "evil powers don't do that!" Then the ghost and Peter start walking toward their boat. At what point did the boated disciples realize it was Jesus? When he saved Peter? Was it the way he walked, his familiar gait? Or, did they finally recognize him when he got close enough to see his face? Whenever it was, we can only imagine the waves of relief that washed over the disciples once Peter *and Jesus* were safe and sound in the boat with them. It's one thing to *hear* him say, "Take courage. It is I. Don't be afraid." It's quite something else to *see* him do what only he can do. Jesus saves because he is Immanuel.

Peter Is a Rock

The purpose of Peter's little stroll on the water is difficult to figure out (it's missing from Mark's version; see Mark 6:45–52). Was it a good or a bad thing that Peter tried to walk on water? Is Peter the model believer, a person who proved he could walk on water while the rest of his shipmates stayed hunkered down in the boat where it was safe and dry? Or should Peter's escapade serve as a cautionary tale, warning doubters what happens to them when they take their eyes off Jesus and focus on the waves of despair that threaten to overwhelm them? Moreover, what about Jesus's role in the story? Since it wasn't Jesus's idea for Peter to walk on the water to begin with, did he grant the absurd request to teach Peter a lesson, that Jesus's word of encouragement ("Take courage! It is I. Don't be afraid") should have been enough? Remember, when they saw Jesus, they cried out in fear, "It's a ghost." Jesus tried to calm them down by reassuring them of his presence, knowing they would believe his word. Sheep are supposed to recognize the voice of their shepherd, but that wasn't enough for Peter. He had to see if what he heard was true.

So, the presumptuous disciple issued a challenge: "If it's really you, I should be able to walk on water too." But then Peter eventually lived up to his name, sank like a rock, and Jesus had to bail him out of danger. That's why the Lord chastised Peter for his "littlefaith" (*oligopiste*), doubting that it really was Jesus. The moral of the story: Peter should have taken Jesus at his word.

But would Jesus really do that, set up Peter for failure? Throughout Matthew's Gospel, Jesus has been teaching his disciples how to follow him. Isn't that what we have here, Peter's attempt to follow Jesus?[7] Let's not forget how it happened. Peter didn't impetuously hop out of the boat and head for Jesus. Rather, he knew the only way he could come to Jesus was if his Lord commanded him to come (Matt 14:28). That's the only reason Peter would get out of the boat; he believed the word of the Lord. Jesus said, "Come," and Peter walked on water—for a while. Sure, Peter nearly drowned when he took his eyes off Jesus. The fierce wind created doubt in his mind. But at least he got out of the boat and tried to walk to Jesus in faith. Furthermore, even when he was about to drown, he knew Jesus was his salvation. In fact, Peter's desperate plea, "Lord, save me!" (v. 29) is the model prayer for all of us who face uncertain times and cry out to Jesus, knowing he's our only hope. How many times have we felt the strong arm of the Lord reaching down to lift us up when we nearly drowned from sorrow or sin? Who doesn't need a helping hand from Jesus? Remember the revivalist hymn so many of us used to sing?

I was sinking deep in sin, far from the peaceful shore,
Very deeply stained within, sinking to rise no more;
But the Master of the sea heard my despairing cry,
From the waters lifted me, now safe am I.
Love lifted me! Love lifted me!
When nothing else could help,
Love lifted me.[8]

To many, then, Peter is a hero. A flawed character to be sure—who isn't?—but a hero nonetheless. The man who skipped on the water like a rock teaches us all that we can walk on troublesome waves as long as we keep our eyes on the Savior.

When we puzzled over the purpose of the first boat story (8:23–27), we noticed how scholarly opinion tended to divide along theological lines. Some saw a christological purpose in Matthew's version of the stilling of the storm. The point of the story was to reveal the divinity of Jesus. Others thought Matthew focused more on the reaction of the disciples than the authority of

7. Keener, *Matthew*, 407.
8. James Rowe and Howard E. Smith, "Love Lifted Me" (1912). Public domain.

Jesus. The entire episode revealed an ecclesiological purpose: the boat (i.e., the church) is the place where Jesus turned fishermen into disciples, teaching them to overcome their little faith *during* the storm. So, here we are again (14:22–33), sitting in a boat with the disciples and wondering, "Is this a story about Jesus or the Twelve? Are we supposed to marvel over Jesus's ability to walk on water? Or should we take a lesson from Peter?" Maybe both. For as Davies and Allison write, "So often the First Evangelist, while addressing christological issues with his right hand, is at the same time delivering teaching on discipleship with his left. And so is it here."[9] Indeed, Matthew's message comes into clearer focus the more we read his Gospel: Jesus's lordship is revealed by our discipleship. The better we see him, the better we understand who we are. Indeed, these two sightlines converge at the climax of this story when Peter "cried out, 'Lord, save me!'" and then "immediately Jesus reached out his hand and caught him. 'You of little faith,' he said, 'why did you doubt?'" (vv. 30–31). That very moment, when Jesus grabbed Peter and asked him, "Why did you doubt?" dramatizes the intersection of Christology and discipleship. Note that Peter never answered the question. Rather, Matthew seems to have left it up to us to infer the answer.

Why did Peter doubt? Or better yet, *what* did Peter doubt? That's what really puzzles me. Did he doubt the voice he heard? Perhaps. Did he doubt that Jesus would save him? Maybe. But I think we can infer conclusively what Peter *didn't* doubt: that he could walk on water.[10] That's what we typically hear. Jesus was berating Peter for doubting that he could walk on water—that the sight of the large waves made him lose faith and sink. But that doesn't make sense. Peter knew the waters were rough. He saw the fierce waves before he got out of the boat. He had already proven he could walk on water. So, what did he doubt? Why did he sink like a rock? I think the key to understanding Peter's doubt is inferred from the line, "immediately Jesus reached out his hand and caught him" (v. 31). That Jesus could reach out "immediately" and grab Peter implies a certain proximity between them. In other words, before Peter went down he was standing right next to Jesus, close enough to see that it really was the Lord walking on water.

Remember, it was still dark when Jesus came to them. The disciples thought the shadowy figure was a ghost because they couldn't see well. Jesus tried to calm their fears by shouting to them, "Take courage! *It is I*" [The Greek text actually reads *egō eimi*, "I am," the covenant name of the God of Israel! See Exod 3:14.] Then Peter tests the waters to see if what he heard is true. The fact that he could walk on water wouldn't settle the issue: evil spirits have magical

9. Davies and Allison, *Matthew*, 2:512–13.
10. Garland, *Reading Matthew*, 159.

powers too. So, as Peter is walking on the water, neither he nor his shipmates would know for certain it was Jesus—that is, until Peter got close enough to Jesus to see that it really was him. That's when Peter doubted, when he could see with his eyes that the ghost was Jesus. Ironically, Peter was able to walk on water because it was dark. But as soon as he could see with his own eyes that it was Jesus, he took his eyes off him and looked around at the waves. Then, I think, it must have dawned on him: now there are *two* men walking on water. And that's when he sank like a rock. I imagine the whole scenario from Jesus's perspective. You see Peter walking out slowly, getting closer and closer to you. You can barely make out the look on his face, perhaps complete astonishment or utter shock. When he finally reaches you, his wide-eyed, openmouthed, awestruck face slowly changes to a look of recognition. You look at him, smiling from ear to ear. He looks at you, then the waves, then to you with a look of horror—as if he had seen a ghost. He sinks. Cries out to you for help. Because he's so close, all you have to do is reach down and grab him. You both know what happened. He didn't doubt he could walk on water until he knew it was you. "Oh, littlefaith. Why did you doubt that it was me?" It reminds me of what the psalmist prayed:

> Save me, O God,
> for the waters have come up to my neck.
> I sink in the miry depths,
> where there is no foothold.
> I have come into the deep waters;
> the floods engulf me.
> I am worn out calling for help;
> my throat is parched.
> *My eyes fail,*
> *looking for my God.* (Ps 69:1–3, emphasis added)

That sounds like an apt description of what happened to Peter: his eyes failed him. Except in this case, it was because he looked at a man and didn't realize he was looking at God—that is, until they all got in the boat: "Truly you are the Son of God" (Matt 14:32). So when the entire village of Gennesaret showed up to welcome Jesus with their sick, it must have dawned on the Twelve that these people had no idea who they were dealing with (v. 35). Sure, they wanted to reach out their hands and touch the hem of his garment to be healed (v. 36)—the disciples had already seen that. But when a man who walks on water reaches out his hand to grab you and pull you from the jaws of death—well, that's an entirely different kind of miracle, one that is hard to explain because it never happened again.

LIVE the Story

Where do we find ourselves in this story? Are we supposed to follow Jesus and walk on water too? Should we want to be like Peter and get out of the boat of our comfort to challenge the stormy waves of life? Or is Peter the poster boy of presumption, pretense, and doubt—a lesson on what not to do? And what about the rest of the disciples? Aren't we supposed to see our reflection in their faces, tirelessly trying to do what the Lord commanded, knowing he promised them that they would see him "on the other side"? Was this a training session for just the Twelve, or are we supposed to take a lesson from this bizarre story? Moreover, what are we to make of Jesus after a story like this? Admire him for his superhuman ability to walk on water? Worship him as the Son of God? Or endlessly puzzle over why he did it, meditating on the mystery of this strange convergence of deity and humanity? Any of these approaches could yield rich insight into how we might "live this story." Yet, rather than direct our attention to the main characters of the story—Jesus, Peter, and the boated disciples—I want to focus on the elements within the story that created tension in the plotline: the wind, water, and darkness.[11]

The wind made it difficult to obey Jesus. For some reason, we often get the impression that doing what Jesus commanded should be easy. After all, he wouldn't tell us to do something unless it could be done. Besides, with God on our side, shouldn't the Lord make our paths straight, put the wind in our sails, make life breezy? And sometimes that happens, when it seems like God removes every hindrance, when circumstances come together so well, when everyone is cheery in their work. He can take a few loaves and fish and feed a multitude. At that point, a peaceful calm hovers over our frenetic activity. Like a well-oiled machine, things get done in a timely manner. Smooth sailing makes for a happy crew. Everyone can see that God is at work among us. He's making this happen. But think about what happens when we're told to sail our boat into the face of contrary winds. Zigzagging our way to where we're trying to go can be incredibly frustrating. "Are we making any progress?" Fighting against the waves of opposition, we can't help but wonder, "Is God for us or against us?" At what point do we drop sails to take another tack and throw our oars in the water to paddle fiercely so we can make *some* headway? Trying to make things happen by trying harder, pushing against the prevailing "wind" (*pneuma*) sometimes feels like we're working against the Spirit (*Pneuma*). "Aren't we wasting time?" Sometimes doing what Jesus commanded is hard

11. "Water, storm, and night are symbols of distress, fear, and death, familiar to the church primarily from the language of the Psalms" (Luz, *Matthew*, 2:318).

work—perhaps the hardest thing you'll ever do. It takes courage to carry on when everyone is tired of rowing—at which point someone in the boat might pray, "I wish he were here with us." Then we hear his reassuring words, "Take courage. It is I. Don't be afraid."

The waves made it difficult to get to Jesus. You've done what he told you to do, but now you find yourself in the middle, navigating the waters when you'd rather find your footing on solid ground. Indeed, life "in between" can be unsettling—between the places of origin and destination, between the times of his presence and his promise. Jesus sent us on this journey of faith with a promise he would meet us on the other side. His absence means he's coming. In the meantime, we can't help but search the shoreline for his return, hoping to catch a glimmer of his presence, our destination. Yet during his absence, sometimes he shows up in unexpected ways. The miracle of his presence inspires us to walk on water, to run to him, to be with him. He bids us to come. Walking on faith, skipping across the waves of doubt and despair, we find ourselves in the middle once again. Only this time we know it's a journey we have to take by ourselves. It can be a lonely feeling, trying to walk on water while others watch from the boat of their reliable habitation. We may falter, our feet failing us when we take our eyes off Jesus. Yet, even then we know he will reach down with his strong arm of salvation when we cry out in desperation for him. Jesus saves because he knows he's our only hope. That's all we want—to cross the great divide and be with him. And, one day *all of us* will be with him, when he comes to us, the captain of our vessel, and boards the ship of our company, bringing us safely to the other side. So we pray in the middle of our journey, in between the times, "Maranatha" ("Come, Lord!").

The night made it difficult to see Jesus. I think about how different things would have been if this episode happened in the middle of the day. "Oh look. I think that's Jesus coming to us, walking on the water. Hey, look guys! It's him. (Laughter and high fives.) Wow, isn't that astonishing? He never ceases to amaze. First, he feeds five-thousand men with five loaves and two fish, and now he tops that miraculous feat by strolling on the water. (More laughter leads to jesting; someone mentions the time Elisha made the ax head float.)[12] Hey Jesus, let's see if a rock can float on water too? Come on Peter, get out there and show us what you've got." What a difference the night makes. It's easy to celebrate Jesus when we see clearly in the light of day. But God made the darkness before there was light. Of course, the best way to get through the night is to close our eyes. Daily troubles, however, often lead to sleepless nights, and with eyes wide open in the darkness we try to make sense of

12. Davies and Allison, *Matthew*, 2:500.

what we can't see. It's especially then when Jesus's ghostly presence is more troubling than reassuring; the cross of his death doesn't look like good news. Why death? Why heartache? Why God? Why does it have to be so hard? But then, Easter's morning light, the dawning of the day, brings clarity after a dark night of the soul. If he could walk on water, if he could still the storm, if he must carry a cross, if he has indeed defeated death, then praise be to God! Praise be to God! Praise be to God! Truly he is the Son of God. Night and day, that's all I need to know. I must see Jesus in the darkness, in the difficulty, in the meantime.

We've just finished chapter fourteen; we're halfway there.

CHAPTER 21

Matthew 15:1–20

LISTEN to the Story

1Then some Pharisees and teachers of the law came to Jesus from Jerusalem and asked, 2"Why do your disciples break the tradition of the elders? They don't wash their hands before they eat!"

3Jesus replied, "And why do you break the command of God for the sake of your tradition? 4For God said, 'Honor your father and mother' and 'Anyone who curses their father or mother is to be put to death.' 5But you say that if anyone declares that what might have been used to help their father or mother is 'devoted to God,' 6they are not to 'honor their father or mother' with it. Thus you nullify the word of God for the sake of your tradition. 7You hypocrites! Isaiah was right when he prophesied about you:

> 8'These people honor me with their lips,
> but their hearts are far from me.
> 9They worship me in vain;
> their teachings are merely human rules.'"

10Jesus called the crowd to him and said, "Listen and understand. 11What goes into someone's mouth does not defile them, but what comes out of their mouth, that is what defiles them."

12Then the disciples came to him and asked, "Do you know that the Pharisees were offended when they heard this?"

13He replied, "Every plant that my heavenly Father has not planted will be pulled up by the roots. 14Leave them; they are blind guides. If the blind lead the blind, both will fall into a pit."

15Peter said, "Explain the parable to us."

16"Are you still so dull?" Jesus asked them. 17"Don't you see that whatever enters the mouth goes into the stomach and then out of the body? 18But the things that come out of a person's mouth come from the heart, and these defile them. 19For out of the heart come evil thoughts—murder, adultery, sexual immorality, theft, false testimony, slander.

20 These are what defile a person; but eating with unwashed hands does not defile them."

Listening to the Text in the Story: Exodus 20:12–16; 30:17–21; Leviticus 15:11; 22:4–16; Numbers 30:2–15; Deuteronomy 21:1–9; 23:21–23; 2 Chronicles 30:17–20; Psalms 7:15; 51:1–18; Ecclesiastes 5:2–7; Isaiah 1:15–18; 5:1–7; 29:13; Jeremiah 31:27–28.

Jesus had spent some time alone—away from the crowds, away from his opponents, even away from his disciples. His prayer time on the mountain was only a brief retreat from the daily demands of life. Indeed, as soon as he returned to the "real world," trouble was waiting on him. The disciples had run into trouble trying to sail their boat against the wind (Matt 14:22–33). Then, crowds had brought their troubles to him as soon as they heard Jesus had returned (vv. 34–36). Now the Pharisees and the scribes have caught up with Jesus to stir up trouble once again (15:1–9). *Everywhere* Jesus turned there was trouble. (It was almost enough to make a guy or a gal want to head back for the mountain.) But this time things were a little different. These Pharisees and scribes were from Jerusalem, evidently on a mission to straighten out this Galilean prophet (v. 2; Paul the Pharisee once did the same thing; see Acts 9:1–2). Apparently, word that Jesus had been encouraging rebellious behavior had reached ears in the holy city. The issue was purity; in particular, Jesus's disciples didn't wash their hands before they ate bread. This was more than a question of hygiene. To wash your hands before you ate was a sign of holiness, a Pharisaical tradition that had been around for a long time. The fact that these Pharisees were obligated to travel all the way to Galilee to correct these miscreants is telling: 1) because they came from Jerusalem, they acted like they had special authority to require Jesus and his disciples to submit to their tradition; 2) because they didn't live near the temple, the Galileans probably held religious leaders coming from Jerusalem in the highest regard—even the disciples tried to "correct" the impertinence of Jesus, knowing he had offended these powerful leaders (Matt 15:12). This was Trouble with a capital "T." But Jesus didn't back down one bit. Instead, he seemed rather annoyed by their presence—brushing them off with a "who do you think you are?" response to their "holy" inquisition. "Leave them," Jesus said to his worried disciples. "They are blind guides" (v. 14).

What surprises me is that these powerful men didn't argue with Jesus. They made no attempt to defend their position or their authority when Jesus attacked them. They asked their question, made their accusation, and then seemed to stand back and watch the fireworks—at least that's the impression Matthew gives to his readers. Did the Pharisees stick around for a while to monitor the situation before reporting back to Jerusalem? ("Oooh, just wait till we get home and tell on you!") Did they retreat from the crowd to plan their counterattack, waiting for the opportune time (16:1)? ("He'll make a serious mistake one day, and we'll be there when it happens.") Or, in light of what the disciples said about them (15:12), did the Pharisees stomp off in protest, shaking the dust off their feet? ("There's nothing left to say. God will judge you.") We don't know, and our Gospel writer doesn't seem to care. These men from Jerusalem appear as marginal characters in Matthew's narrative world, showing up to say their piece, only to fade away from view. Yet, like Matthew we know this can't be the end of it. Jerusalem can never linger for long in the background of Israel's story. Indeed, there is an ominous cloud that hangs over this episode, a forecast of approaching storms. For as Matthew has prepared his readers, we know that Jesus will take his cause to Jerusalem (he has to! He's the King of Israel) and then the *real* fireworks will begin (16:21). They've come to straighten him out? Oh my. Wait till he comes to Jerusalem to straighten them out. We think we see trouble now? Washing hands? Really? This isn't even the half of it.

EXPLAIN the Story

Talk about making a mountain out of a molehill, this hand-washing issue seems ridiculous, especially to us gentile Christ followers. It sounds more like maternal nagging than a serious problem regarding holiness. But we underestimate the severity of the crime because we don't see the world like first-century Jews. First of all, for them purity wasn't a matter of morality like it is for us. When we talk about purity, the great majority of the time we're talking about sexual behavior. To us, to be impure is to be immoral. Yet according to the Old Testament, there were many things that would make an Israelite impure that had nothing to do with morality, like sex between a married couple, childbirth, or a woman's menstrual cycle.[1] These things were common to all people, part of living in a profaned world. To maintain their distinctiveness as a holy people of a holy God (in addition to other rites like circumcision, dietary restrictions, and observing the Sabbath), Israel would submit to purification rites to be holy in his sight, set apart for his purpose. Second, all first-century Mediterraneans (not just Jews) divided the world

1. See the discussion above, 163, 199–200.

into two domains, setting apart sacred space from profaned (common) space. Everyone traversed common space. But temples were erected as sacred spaces where God/gods would dwell on earth, served only by sacred men and/or women (priests). Commoners could draw near to God and enter the sacred precincts around the temple after they had submitted to purification rites. But then, after offering their sacrifices, they would return to the profaned world, having to maintain their holiness by avoiding unclean things (when possible) while routinely submitting to ritual washings. So, there were holy temples and holy people, sacred spaces and sacred rituals. Every God/god had his/her own rules for his/her own people. And, more than any other, Israel's God was emphatic about holiness and purity—especially for his priests (just read Leviticus).

There is some question among scholars as to why the Pharisees pushed purification rites beyond what was required to enter the temple in Jerusalem. Some think they had taken upon themselves the purity code of priests (Exod 30:17–21; Lev 22:4–16). By observing these stricter ritual cleansings, the Pharisees were trying to export temple purity beyond Jerusalem to reclaim the sacred promised land, all the way to Galilee.[2] Other scholars doubt whether the Pharisees subscribed to such an overt campaign. Rather, they argue handwashing was imported by Jews of the Diaspora who adopted certain purification rites to maintain their identity as God's holy people living outside the promised land.[3] Whatever the reason, Matthew feels no need to explain why the Pharisees had a problem with Jews who ate food with "common" hands (unlike Mark 7:1–4), other than the fact that it was "the tradition of the elders" (Matt 15:2). To defy traditions that had been handed down for years was considered incredibly arrogant. We don't know whether Jesus's disciples were "going rogue" or never washed their hands before eating ("who cares?"). Nevertheless, the fact that the Pharisees had come all the way from Jerusalem to call out these Galilean rebels speaks volumes: these purists were drawing a line in the sand, dividing the sacred from the profane. But Jesus had already "crossed the line," and they knew it.[4] That's why they were there. They didn't come all the way to Galilee to debate the question of handwashing, hoping to change Jesus's mind on the matter. Rather, the Pharisees showed up to make sure *nobody*—not even this wonder-working rebel and his band of disciples—blurred the lines.[5]

---

2. Luz, *Matthew*, 2:329–30 (relying heavily upon Neusner).

3. Sanders, *Judaism: Practice and Belief*, 437–40.

4. Jesus was not the first person to reject the tradition of the Pharisees. That distinction belongs to the Sadducees (see Davies and Allison, *Matthew*, 2:520–21).

5. For a good, brief discussion of the purity code, see David A. DeSilva, "Clean and Unclean," *DJG* 142–49.

"Wash Your Hands, You Sinners"

Isaiah has this remarkable image of a priest serving God in the temple. Having offered sacrifices to the Lord, the priest stands in the holy place, bloody hands raised to God in prayer (Isa 1:15). You would think such a picture would please God; it's exactly what he prescribed, a temple filled with sacrifices and a priest doing his job. But the Lord's response to the priest's prayer is jolting; like a bolt of lightning he zaps the priest in judgment. The God of Israel basically says, "Wash your hands! I'm sick of seeing all this blood" (vv. 10–14, 16). The problem was that Israel hoped their sacrifices would cover a multitude of sin, that their bloody sacrifices would remove from their hands the bloody stains of injustice. But God wouldn't tolerate their circumvention of justice, their sacrificial loophole for not doing the right thing. The temple wasn't just a sacred space for holy sacrifices offered by priests with clean hands. The holy place was supposed to inspire a holy people to worship a holy God—to worship him not only with clean hands but pure hearts. But that wasn't happening in Isaiah's day (29:13). Not only that, the indictment of Isaiah's generation became prophecy for future generations: to obey is better than sacrifice. When you "come near to God," "he will come near to you." So, you better wash your hands and purify your heart (Jas 4:8).

That's why, after the Pharisees confronted Jesus about handwashing, the first thing he thought about was Isaiah's prophecy (Matt 15:7–9; Isa 29:13). Even though the Pharisees could claim their hands were as clean as the priests, according to Jesus their hands were stained by the blood of injustice—just like the priests in Isaiah's day. It was a stunning comparison. Just as the priests counted on the holiness of the temple to atone for the sins of injustice against widows and orphans (Isa 1:16–17, 21–23), so also the Pharisees were counting on the sacred temple to cover their sin of ignoring the needs of their own parents. Rather than help their parents in their old age, the Pharisees would make vows to God, dedicating all their possessions to him ("Corban," Mark 7:11), which meant nothing could be sold, no property liquidated, because it all belonged to the temple. The Pharisees could still make use of their possessions and property; they just couldn't sell their stuff for any reason other than to support the temple treasury. Even if their parents were to become destitute—as poor as widows and orphans—the Pharisees couldn't go back on their word because God took vows seriously (Num 30:2–15; Eccl 5:2–7).[6] Of course, the Pharisees were never required to make such a vow.[7]

---

6. For a good summary of the practice of Corban, see Davies and Allison, *Matthew*, 2:523–25; Nolland, *Matthew*, 616–18.

7. France, *Matthew*, 581.

Yet it was part of their tradition of being completely devoted to God—like washing their hands before they ate bread.

Obviously, Jesus and his disciples weren't Pharisees. But rather than state the obvious ("hey, we don't belong to your group") or defend his disciples for not complying ("we think your handwashing rules are ridiculous"), Jesus decided to go straight to the heart of the matter. The Pharisees weren't devoted to God; they were hypocrites who cared more about their tradition than obeying God's word. Proof number one: they violated the sixth of the Ten Commandments (Exod 20:12; cf. 21:17) as well as Levitical law (Lev 20:9) when they made their vow to God (Matt 15:3–6). They didn't honor their parents (which certainly includes taking care of them in their old age). Instead, they actually "cursed" their parents when they said their possessions were dedicated to God. Their words—"what comes out of their mouth"—revealed the evil intentions of their heart. Proof number two: the Pharisees fulfilled Isaiah's prophecy. They appeared to honor God with their lips when they made their vow, but "their hearts were far from" him (Matt 15:7–9). How did Jesus know that? Because, just as Isaiah said, keeping their traditions had become more important to the Pharisees than obeying God's word. Worse than that, Jesus claimed they "*nullify* the word of God" to preserve their tradition (v. 6, emphasis added)—he didn't say *obscure* or *ignore* or even *misunderstand* Scripture. Jesus said the Pharisees *nullified* God's word by holding blindly to their traditions. So, they had no business acting like God's watchdogs, protecting *his* sacred interests; rather, they were only protecting theirs. These men from Jerusalem were nothing more than "blind guides" (v. 14) leading the blind into the pit (of hell?). They didn't see what prophets like Isaiah had warned Israel about long ago. People may sound like they honor the Lord, but God knows when they haven't put their heart into it. Priests may serve God with their purified hands, but the Lord can see their impure heart. The heart of the matter is the matter of the heart. According to Jesus, your heart isn't defiled by the bread you put into your mouth with *common* hands.[8] Rather, it's what comes out of your mouth—*profanity*—that defiles a person's heart (v. 11).

"Purify Your Hearts, You Double-Minded"

When Jesus finally got around to defending his position on handwashing, he addressed his remarks to the crowd (Matt 15:10). He acted like they were the ones who needed to "listen and understand" what he believed—the complete opposite of what the Pharisees taught. Notice that Jesus didn't offer a

8. Luz, *Matthew*, 2:333.

well-reasoned argument in defense of his position. Neither did he offer a parable to make the crowd think about it—something he was known to do (13:1–13). Instead, this time he simply defied the Pharisees' teaching that "you are what you eat." Not so, according to Jesus. It's what comes out of your mouth that reveals who you are. Yet, what about the dietary code? What if you put unclean food in your mouth, like pork or lobster? Wouldn't that defile a person? Did Jesus declare "all foods clean"? (Mark certainly thought so; see Mark 7:19.) Yet, no one from the crowd questioned the implications of his radical reversal of what defiles a person.[9] Not even the Pharisees voiced their objection. It was his own disciples who had a hard time accepting what Jesus said. At first they worried about how the Pharisees took it (Matt 15:12). But Jesus didn't care. God would take care of the Pharisees one day, plucking them like weeds (v. 13; 13:25–30). "Leave them alone," Jesus said. "They can't see a thing." In other words, they have nothing to learn.

Then Peter stepped up and questioned what Jesus said, as if it were a parable that needed further explanation (15:15). But Jesus responded as if what he said was straightforward; only a dimwit wouldn't get it (v. 16). He simply repeated what he said, describing in graphic detail what they should have figured out on their own (vv. 17–19). "Do I need to draw a picture for you guys? Okay. You put food in your piehole, right? Then it goes into your belly—are you with me so far? Then—surprise, surprise—it comes out the other end, and 'plop' into the latrine it goes." (The Greek text is *very* graphic.) Then Jesus speaks just as bluntly about what really defiles a person. "Okay. You know when you lust after a woman or want to kill a man—didn't we already cover this [5:21–30]? Anyway, what's deep inside your heart will eventually come out. You can't hide it. Your mouth is the trapdoor of your heart. People with profaned hearts utter profanities. Dirty-hearted people think dirty. And these evil thoughts will eventually take over your whole body, soil your heart, and trash your soul. That's what you really need to wash—not your hands but your hearts."

The disciples already knew that handwashing didn't matter. They were the ones who ate their bread with "common" hands (one wonders about Jesus). They didn't bother to follow the rules; they weren't disciples of the Pharisees. They were following Jesus. The Pharisees knew that. Jesus knew that. Everyone knew that. It's what sparked this fiery confrontation between Jesus and the leaders from Jerusalem to begin with. The Pharisees had their approach to purity, and Jesus had his. Between the two approaches, it would have been much easier to follow the tradition of the Pharisees. Are you a

9. France, *Matthew*, 575.

pure-hearted person? "Yes I am." How do you know that? "Because I wash my hands before I eat." But to follow Jesus with common hands, to ensure you don't pollute your heart with impure thoughts—how do you do that? Is there a purification ritual for that? If profaned words reveal my dirty heart, how do I clean it up? Since only the pure in heart see God (Matt 5:8), will a sinful man always be blind, consigned to a life of defilement? How does one get a clean heart? Pray, "Create in me a clean heart, O God"? (See Ps 51:10.) Pluck out our eyes and cut off our hands (Matt 5:29–30) or at least shut our mouth? Jesus didn't explain his approach to purity—how to get a pure heart—at least, not in this brief encounter. He made it plain, however, that handwashing had nothing to do with it (15:20). So, what was a person to do? If God is most concerned about a pure heart, and following the Pharisees won't help, then the only thing left to do would be to follow Jesus and look for God. If disciples can see God, then they know that they are blessed with a pure heart. Indeed, this is what Matthew has been trying to show his readers for quite some time: following Jesus will purify your heart because he is Immanuel.

LIVE the Story

Jesus covered a lot of ground in his response to the Pharisaical tradition of handwashing. Therefore, it might be easy to pick one aspect of his teaching and run with it—especially the part where we're convinced that we are on Jesus's side trying to correct our Pharisaical brothers and sisters. Yet I want to try to see this story through the eyes of the disciples to steer away from the pretense that Jesus is always on our side. Think about how quickly they seemed to change sides in this debate. At first, Jesus defends them for their "common" table manners. That must have been very affirming. Then, in the blink of an eye the disciples act like *Jesus* is the one who needs correcting. That puzzles me. After the showdown, I would have expected the disciples to hoop and holler like victors of a sporting event. "Take that, you hypocrites! In your face, you bunch of losers. Jesus told you, didn't he?" Instead, they said, "Do you know that the Pharisees were offended when they heard this?" (Matt 15:12). Really? If the disciples were truly worried about the Pharisees, then why didn't they wash their hands? That's what offended the Pharisees. The fickle behavior of Jesus's disciples is revealing. One minute they're convinced Jesus is on their side as he chastises the Pharisees. The next minute they think Jesus has gone too far. The same thing happens today among Jesus's disciples. We always assume Jesus is with us when we condemn the hypocrisy of others. But when someone takes Jesus's teaching too far, well, all of the sudden we're worried about offending others. Isn't it amazing that we always seem to be on the right side when it comes to these battles of holiness? So, let's not jump to conclusions here, quick to protect our tradition or raise concerns about our latest pet peeve. Instead, I want to try to wrestle with the layers of Jesus's criticism—against the Pharisees and his own disciples. For we certainly don't want Jesus to say about us, "Leave them; they are blinds guides" (v. 14), or even, "Are you still so dull?" (v. 16).

When doctrine exceeds Scripture. "Their teachings are merely human rules" (v. 9). We all believe our doctrine is based on Scripture. (It better be!) Because Scripture is inspired by God, it's easy to presume our doctrine is divine too. But it's not. Therefore, we must always be willing to have Scripture correct our doctrine, which is a hard thing to do because we've organized it, systematized it, explained it, taught it, and defended it.[10] It's taken a lot of time to create this doctrine. It didn't start with us; we inherited most of it from "the elders" who came before us. Therefore, it's up to us to keep, protect, and pass it on. So, it's tempting for all of us to study the Scriptures in service of our doctrine. The parts of Scripture that plainly support what we believe, we celebrate. The verses that seemed to contradict what we believe, we either explain away or ignore. That's a dangerous thing—to prize our human doctrine above any verse of Scripture. When that happens, it should be apparent that we've become more zealous for our doctrine than the inspired word of God. In fact, one of the surest ways that we prize Scripture above our doctrine is to hold up the verses that *don't fit* into our systematized, organized, dogmatized teachings. Here's why: none of us have it *all* figured out. When we act like we have nothing to learn, holding to our infallible doctrine no matter what, even crusading against those who defy our teachings, we reveal that we are blind to the Scriptures. If that happens, how will we be convicted about our impure hearts?

When tradition replaces God's word. "Thus you nullify the word of God for the sake of your tradition" (v. 6). We may have several traditions that have no scriptural basis. Such cultural habits are easy targets of derision. For example, think of all the traditions that inform our worship services—the music we sing, the prayers we offer, the order of service, the sermons we preach. Most of what we do (and especially how we do it) can't be prooftexted by Scripture. Therefore, most of our criticism is culturally informed, often depending upon personal preferences. That becomes evident when we worship with Christians in another country; the cultural baggage we carry is easy to see: West Africans don't worship God like West Coast Americans. The way we worship is as

10. See Bruner, *Matthew*, 2:89–91, who admirably struggles over the subordination of tradition to Scripture.

much an expression of our cultural habits as a reflection of Scripture. What is more difficult to see, ironically, is any tradition that has become more important than Scripture to the extent that it violates the word of God. You wouldn't think that would be the case, but history tells us otherwise. Think of the civil-rights issues we faced in our country fifty years ago. It's hard to believe that a color line divided white from black *even* in the church. The tradition of segregation was so strong back then that Martin Luther King Jr. was slandered, attacked, and killed—all because he held firmly to the Scriptures: *in Christ* there is neither Jew nor gentile, male nor female, slave nor free (see Gal 3:28). After watching the film *Selma*, I shook my head in disbelief: "How could we be so blind? Why couldn't we see that what we white people did to black men, women, and children was so horribly wrong?" More than that, it was evil. I can't help but wonder about the traditions we hold so dear today that fifty years from now will be seen as a clear violation of God's word. Here's a clue: if what we hear in church encourages us to harbor thoughts of murder, adultery, sexual immorality, theft, false testimony, or slander, then we have defiled ourselves. Comments heard at God-and-country rallies such as, "round them all up and drop a bomb on them" and "they're probably pedophiles too," or when people Act Up and say, "My body is my business," and, "If you disagree with me, it's hate speech"—these words come from the mouths of impure hearts. How do I know? When you challenge them, they are *easily* offended—a sign their tradition has become more important than God's word.

When purity is exported. "These people honor me with their lips, but their hearts are far from me" (Matt 15:8). The Pharisees cared about the condition of the heart too.[11] But unlike Jesus, they took an outside-in approach to purity. The temple in Jerusalem operated according to the same pattern: get the details of the sacrifice right (clean animals, pure hands), and God will purify his people with his presence (Mal 1:6–14; 3:1–4). These Pharisees from Jerusalem, living in the shadow of the temple, believed the same about Israel. If we do the right things, our heart will be purified. Get the outside right, and your heart will learn obedience. Rituals and rules were necessary to curb the appetites of a rebellious heart; compliance was key to purity. Therefore, accountability was crucial to ensure everyone played by the rules and observed sacred rituals. The problem with such an approach to purity, however, is that people may conform to the rules to maintain appearances, but their hearts may still be corrupt. Their bodies might be clean, but their minds are filled with evil thoughts. They can say the right words, but their heart is far from

11. Sanders, *Judaism: Practice and Belief*, 444–48.

God. In other words, purity can't be exported by humans; it can only be imported by God. The Pharisees from Jerusalem may have thought they were extending temple purification to the people, but Jesus knew Israel's only hope was to bring the people to God. It's why he said, "Follow me."

This is a sobering thought. Christians can spend a lot of time trying to export our brand of purity, trying to get others to comply with our rules and prize our sacred rituals. We may divide the world into two domains, the sacred and the profane (secular), to mark off territory and marshal forces for our holy cause. We may even win a few battles, getting the impure to adopt our model of compliance, filling our sanctuaries with people who say the right words. And, even more dangerous, all of this may make us feel better about ourselves, better about our cause, better about our faith. But if we aren't following Jesus, none of it really matters. It's because only those who follow Jesus can lead people to him. And, here's the crucial point: he's the *only* one who can purify our heart.

CHAPTER 22

Matthew 15:21-39

LISTEN to the Story

21 Leaving that place, Jesus withdrew to the region of Tyre and Sidon.
22 A Canaanite woman from that vicinity came to him, crying out, "Lord,
Son of David, have mercy on me! My daughter is demon-possessed and
suffering terribly."

23 Jesus did not answer a word. So his disciples came to him and urged
him, "Send her away, for she keeps crying out after us."

24 He answered, "I was sent only to the lost sheep of Israel."

25 The woman came and knelt before him. "Lord, help me!" she said.

26 He replied, "It is not right to take the children's bread and toss it to
the dogs."

27 "Yes it is, Lord," she said. "Even the dogs eat the crumbs that fall
from their master's table."

28 Then Jesus said to her, "Woman, you have great faith! Your request
is granted." And her daughter was healed at that moment.

29 Jesus left there and went along the Sea of Galilee. Then he went up
on a mountainside and sat down. 30 Great crowds came to him, bringing
the lame, the blind, the crippled, the mute and many others, and laid
them at his feet; and he healed them. 31 The people were amazed when
they saw the mute speaking, the crippled made well, the lame walking and
the blind seeing. And they praised the God of Israel.

32 Jesus called his disciples to him and said, "I have compassion for these
people; they have already been with me three days and have nothing to eat.
I do not want to send them away hungry, or they may collapse on the way."

33 His disciples answered, "Where could we get enough bread in this
remote place to feed such a crowd?"

34 "How many loaves do you have?" Jesus asked.

"Seven," they replied, "and a few small fish."

35 He told the crowd to sit down on the ground. 36 Then he took the
seven loaves and the fish, and when he had given thanks, he broke them

and gave them to the disciples, and they in turn to the people. [37]They all ate and were satisfied. Afterward the disciples picked up seven basketfuls of broken pieces that were left over. [38]The number of those who ate was four thousand men, besides women and children. [39]After Jesus had sent the crowd away, he got into the boat and went to the vicinity of Magadan.

Listening to the Text in the Story: Genesis 9:24–27; Joshua 7:9; Judges 1:27–33; 3:1–7; 1 Kings 17:8–24; Isaiah 23:1–18; 35:5–6; 49:5–6; Jeremiah 23:1–8; Ezekiel 26:2–28:24; 34:1–16, 23–24; 37:24–28.

Following Jesus can be tough. He will take you places you least expected to go. "What are we doing *here*?" When he draws near to you, he won't do what you expect. "Why are *you* doing this?" And, when you need him, he expects you to follow him no matter what. "Why do *we* have to do this?" We may be reluctant to admit it, but sometimes it seems like Jesus makes it difficult to follow him. And here's why: he acts like he's the Lord and we are his followers—not his advisors, his planners, or even his assessors. We may try to give him advice: "Send her away, for she keeps crying out after us" (Matt 15:23). We may question his itinerary: "If he were sent only to the lost sheep of Israel, what are we doing in gentile territory?" We might even offer an accurate assessment of the situation: "Where could we get enough bread in this remote place to feed such a crowd?" (v. 33). But if Jesus knows what he's doing (even though we don't), shouldn't that give us enough confidence to believe that we are exactly where we need to be, doing exactly what we should do because we are certainly following him? Given our proclivities to choose the easy way, perhaps a tough road in foreign territory is a strangely comforting sign that we are disciples of Jesus. After all, we're following the one who loved to go to hard places and save difficult people.

There seemed to be no good reason for Jesus to travel to a foreign land. Was he trying to get away from his opponents or seek relief from the crowds? The Pharisees certainly wouldn't dog his trail outside of Israel. There seemed to be no crowds of people waiting for him when he came to the region. But he didn't stay there long—not nearly enough time to let things cool down at home (a huge crowd greeted him when he returned, and the Pharisees weren't far behind either; see 15:29–31; 16:1). So, perhaps this wasn't about "getting away" but "going to"—a missional purpose—having been inspired by Elijah to go to Sidon (1 Kgs 17:9–24). Yet, Jesus didn't go to the region of Tyre and Sidon to save these gentiles. He made that plain when the Canaanite woman asked for help (Matt 15:24). Perhaps he left Galilee to look for "lost sheep of Israel" in foreign lands—reclaiming Jews of the diaspora (Isa 56:3–8). But that doesn't make sense because he didn't visit other gentile cities where there may have been a significant Jewish population. Perhaps Jesus was there to reclaim the territories conquered by King David, presenting himself as the true "Son of David" to both Israelite and non-Israelite subjects of the kingdom.[1] Whatever his purpose, like his previous, brief excursion into gentile territory (Matt 8:28–34), Jesus acted like he didn't go there with much of a plan. Both times he cast out demons, but that's all he did. The first time the locals begged him to leave (v. 34). But this time he finds a woman of great faith (15:28), and yet that wasn't enough to compel him to stay.

After his fight with the Pharisees from Jerusalem, it appears as though Jesus thought, "I've got to get out of here." So he withdraws to gentile country. After healing the daughter of a Canaanite woman, it's as if Jesus decided, "I can't stay here." So he returns home. Truthfully, if I were one of the Twelve, I would have gotten a little perturbed with Jesus. "Are we coming or going? Jesus is walking around aimlessly, and he expects us to follow him." If that were the case, it could explain the disciples' behavior when Jesus wanted to feed the four-thousand men (vv. 32–38). By then they were tired of getting the run around—you can certainly hear it in their response (v. 33). No one suggested, "Hey, why don't you perform another miraculous feeding of the masses?" Most commentators think the Twelve suffered from amnesia. I wonder whether they were dealing with a severe case of apathy. Who could blame them? If Jesus had compassion for these people, why did he wait *three* days to feed them (v. 32)? He didn't seem to care until now, so why should they? I wonder if Jesus's behavior was as confusing to the Twelve as it is to us who are trying to make sense of this story.

EXPLAIN the Story

Scholars puzzle over why Jesus appeared to brush off the Canaanite woman. First, Jesus ignored her (Matt 15:23). Then he said she didn't fit his mission (v. 24). Finally, he acted like it would be foolish for him to help her (v. 26)—living proof of what he had taught the disciples: "Do not give dogs what is sacred" (7:6). Then, he finally gave in and helped her (15:28). But one wonders why, especially since this never happened before—a desperate person having to beg Jesus several times for help. Some think it might have to do with the long, bitter rivalry between Israel and the people of Canaan. Remember, the Canaanites occupied the land long before the Israelites blew in like locusts

1. Willitts, *Matthew's Messianic Shepherd-King*, 210–14.

from the wilderness, claiming their God had promised Canaan to them. After the centuries-long battle over land rights, the Canaanite people were Israel's number one enemy.[2] Or perhaps because Tyre and Sidon were such great trade centers, they had recently posed a significant economic threat to the welfare of the Galileans. So Jesus was determined not to help any of them at all.[3] But if that were the case, why didn't Jesus give the cold shoulder to the Roman centurion—a far more significant threat to Galilee and a more present and oppressive enemy of Israel (8:5–13)? Besides, Jesus taught his disciples to love their enemies, so why wouldn't he help this woman too?

Some commentators think Jesus was testing the faith of the woman (to see if she would be persistent)[4] or her humility (to see if she were willing to admit that she had no claim on Jesus).[5] Some argue Jesus changed his mind—that the woman convinced Jesus to expand his mission beyond Israel.[6] Others maintain that Jesus's behavior wasn't morally offensive for his time; first, Jesus wasn't obliged to heal every person he met,[7] and, second, contending with God for his help was a very common practice (read the Psalms!).[8] Due to our cultural sensitivities, we may have a problem with Jesus's behavior—having to make excuses for him—but neither the disciples nor the woman were offended by Jesus. Besides, this wasn't the first time this had happened. Jesus had ignored two blind men when they cried out for help (9:27–31). As a matter of fact, their plea was very similar to what the Canaanite woman shouted as Jesus walked by: both cried out, "Have mercy," and called Jesus the "Son of David" (9:27; 15:22). Even though Matthew has made this claim from the very beginning of his Gospel (1:1), Jesus ignored the acclamation both times it fell from human lips. Indeed, one might get the impression that Jesus didn't care for the title at all—or at least he was leery of people who used it.

"These People Honor Me with Their Lips"

Was it obvious to Jesus or his disciples that this woman was a Canaanite? Did she dress like one? Did her accent give her away? The reason I bring it up is because she tried to *sound* Jewish when she said, "Lord, Son of David, have mercy on me!" (Matt 15:22). That may explain why Jesus ignored her. People will say all kinds of things they don't mean when they are desperate. Obviously, she had heard reports about Jesus from Syrians who had been

2. Keener, *Matthew*, 414.
3. See the discussion in Garland, *Reading Matthew*, 167.
4. France, *Matthew*, 590–91; Bruner doesn't agree, *Matthew*, 2:100.
5. Chrysostom, *Homilies*, 322–23; Nolland, *Matthew*, 636.
6. Bruner, *Matthew*, 2:103–4; Nolland disagrees, *Matthew*, 636.
7. Garland, *Reading Matthew*, 166–67.
8. Talbert, *Reading Matthew*, 190.

healed (4:24). Moreover, Jesus once said that the people of Tyre and Sidon would be more receptive to the miracles he performed than his own people (11:21). One then wonders why she didn't make the trip to Galilee to find this wonder-working prophet. Possibly her daughter was so demonized that she couldn't find anyone to go with her. Whatever the case, it must have come as a shock to this Canaanite woman when she saw Jesus coming to her country. What was he doing there? Had Jesus come to the region to save the Jewish people who lived there? Or did Jesus come to help gentiles too? It must have felt like a miracle that he came. So, she cried out loudly, using the proper Jewish honorific titles, laying out her case to him: "My daughter is demon-possessed and suffering terribly" (15:22). But Jesus didn't stop for her. And she didn't stop crying out for help—incessant begging that quickly became a nuisance to the Twelve (v. 23).

When the disciples urged Jesus to "send her away," we can't tell if they meant "liberate her" or "get rid of her" (*apolyson* can be translated either way; v. 23). If the former, then it might make better sense of Jesus's oblique response: "I was sent only to the lost sheep of Israel" (v. 24). They knew she was a Canaanite suffering the just consequences of her idolatrous religion: a demonized daughter. But they were sick and tired of her begging. They needed Jesus to grant her request—for their sakes as much as hers.[9] (Obviously, they didn't think they could do it, perhaps because she was a gentile and they only had power to reclaim the lost sheep of Israel; see 10:1, 5–8.) But Jesus wouldn't give in, to her need or his disciples' request, reminding the Twelve of his Jewish mission. On the other hand, if the disciples were asking Jesus to get rid of the woman, then that's exactly what he was trying to do when he told her in essence, "I came here only to help my own kind." Of course, both scenarios assume the disciples had recognized the woman as a Canaanite. But, what if they hadn't? What if her Jewish confession fooled them but not Jesus? In other words, what if Jesus said "I was sent only to the lost sheep of Israel" to expose her duplicity? "You may try to sound Jewish, but I know you're not." I think that helps explain the rest of the story, especially Jesus's calloused remark about bread intended for children and not dogs (15:26). Jesus had already helped gentiles (8:5–13); this was no different—except that here we have a woman trying to talk like someone she's not.[10] A Roman centurion was easily recognized by his appearance and reputation. The centurion who asked Jesus to heal his sick servant even talked like a Roman soldier, giving the analogy of receiving and taking orders. This Canaanite woman, on the

9. Garland, *Reading Matthew*, 165.

10. Bruner thinks the difference could be attributed to Jesus's reluctance to work miracles in gentile territory (*Matthew*, 2:100).

other hand, talked like a Jew,[11] hoping her words would convince Jesus to help her. But I don't think Jesus was going to help her until she confessed her true identity. "These people honor me with their lips, but their hearts are far from me" (15:8). Ironic, isn't it? She had already confessed Jesus's true identity, but that didn't seem to matter—Jesus kept walking. But a genuine confession—admitting who we are because of who he is—will always get his attention.

Saying the right words didn't make Jesus stop. So, the woman knelt down before him and begged for help (v. 25). Was she presenting herself as one of the lost sheep? Or, had she given up the pretense of her proper confession? This time she didn't call him "Son of David"; she simply pleaded, "Lord, help me!" Yet it wasn't until Jesus used the analogy of the children's bread that the woman admitted her station. Everyone knows you don't toss children's bread to dogs. And it was also common knowledge that Jews referred to gentiles as dogs, scavengers of God's grace.[12] Therefore, at that very moment, everyone must have connected the dots: she's the "dog" begging for bread intended for God's children, Israel. What would she do now? She could have persisted with the ruse, keeping up the pretense: "Yes, Lord. Behold, a child at your table!" She could have stomped off in protest, offended by the epithet: "What are you doing *here*, Jesus? To tease us and get our hopes up? Just go back home and help your own kind." She did neither. Instead, she admitted her role in Jesus's little parable (she understood the parable because she saw her reflection!),[13] and then she proposed an "alternate ending." Sometimes housedogs[14] are accidently fed from the master's table (v. 27). Jesus was impressed: "Woman, you have great faith! Your request is granted" (v. 28).

What made her faith great? Was it because she was clever, extending Jesus's parable beyond what even he expected? In other words, did Jesus reward her for her witty response? Or did Jesus grant her request because she was persistent—that never giving up is a sign of great faith? Or was the greatness of her faith revealed by her willingness to humble herself, admitting that she was only a dog hoping for scraps of grace that fall from the Master's table? Probably all these reasons have merit. But one thing is for certain: Jesus was surprised to find great faith among persons like a Roman centurion and a Canaanite woman. These are the *only* people Jesus has praised for having a faith greater than anyone else (8:10; 15:28). Typically, Jesus takes pity on the helpless, attacks his opponents, or corrects his disciples. So far, however, a Roman centurion and

---

11. Davies and Allison, *Matthew*, 2:548; Willitts offers a more gracious assessment: she is exhibiting a Jewish faith (*Matthew's Messianic Shepherd-King*, 215–16).

12. Garland, *Reading Matthew*, 166.

13. See above, 265–66.

14. The word *kynarion* could refer to household pets (Keener, *Matthew*, 416).

a Canaanite woman are the only people who have demonstrated *great* faith in Jesus—something he appreciated and hoped to see in his own disciples.

"But Their Hearts Are Far from Me"

This story, in the words of Yogi Berra, seems that "it's like déjà vu all over again."[15] Jesus and his disciples are faced with the problem of dealing with a hungry mob in the middle of nowhere. The disciples don't know what to do about it. Jesus acts like it's their responsibility to feed the masses. Jesus takes inventory of their food supply, orders the crowd to sit down, blesses God for the meager meal, and has his disciples distribute the food. Miraculously, everyone eats their fill, and the disciples collect the leftovers in several baskets. A head count of several thousand men reveals the magnitude of the miraculous feeding—a large group who had followed Jesus into the deserted place and needed to be sent back home. Afterward, a boat stands ready to take Jesus and his disciples across the lake. Indeed, we have been here before—just a chapter before this episode (Matt 15:29–39), Jesus fed five-thousand men (14:13–21). In fact, the stories are so similar—following the same script—one wonders why there wasn't at least *one* difference: the disciples should have known what to do about the hungry people. But, they didn't (15:33), and that's what makes this story so puzzling.

When Jesus brought up the problem, saying that he had "compassion for these people" and didn't want to send them away hungry (v. 32), the disciples should have said, "Fine. Here are seven loaves of bread and a couple of little fish. That should be more than enough to feed four-thousand men when all it took were fives loaves and two fish for you to feed a thousand more. Here you go. Do that thing you do." Instead, the Twelve act like they've never been in that situation, even though they came to the same conclusion as before: "Where could we get enough bread in this remote place to feed such a crowd?" (15:33; 14:15). That's weird. Surely someone in the group would have remembered the *only miracle* that made it into all four Gospels. "Hey. Wasn't it just a few weeks ago when we were in the same mess, you know—surrounded by thousands of hungry men in the middle of nowhere? Let's see, what happened? Does anyone recall what we did? Wait. I remember: we gave our bread and fish to Jesus, and he performed a miracle. Right? Didn't that happen? Or was I just dreaming?" But they didn't remember; or, at least that's what some scholars think. Matthew is using this story to critique the problem of "Christian amnesia"—when we tend to forget what God has

15. Nate Scott, "The 50 Greatest Yogi Berra Quotes," ForTheWin, September 23, 2015, http://ftw.usatoday.com/2015/09/the-50-greatest-yogi-berra-quotes.

taught us through past experience.[16] Taking the spotlight off the Twelve, other scholars think Matthew had a theological purpose in repeating the story: 1) to highlight Israel's rejection of Jesus;[17] 2) to fulfill Zion eschatology;[18] or 3) to add credibility to his Gospel story via another "doublet"—something Matthew loved to do.[19] All of these explanations assume a Jewish context for the miraculous feeding. But some scholars think the disciples' behavior makes better sense if they were still in gentile territory. In other words, the Twelve weren't suffering from "amnesia" but indifference.

Imagine the scene: Jesus climbing a mountain, followed by his disciples and the large crowd bringing their sick and lame. He keeps ascending, and they keep climbing. To any bystander, it would appear as though Jesus was trying to get away from them. After all, if his intention were to heal the crippled, why would he make them climb the mountain? A level spot would do just fine. I wonder how difficult it was, dragging the lame or leading the blind up the side of the mountain. But that didn't stop them. They kept coming. And, just as we would expect, Jesus healed them—albeit after an arduous hike (15:30–31). Then, all of the sudden, Jesus recognizes how hard it's been on everyone. They've been following him for three days (even hiking up a mountain) without any food (v. 32). He says he has "compassion" on them. Well, if that were the case, why did he make all these lame and blind people hobble up the mountain? Why did he wait three days—approaching starvation ("they may collapse on the way")—to do anything about it? Honestly, if I were one of the Twelve, I would be a little confused and very frustrated. For up to this point it would appear to me that Jesus was trying to get away from the mob, not to help them. Besides, if the crowd was fatigued from walking and hiking for three days without nourishment, wouldn't that be true of the Twelve too? So when the disciples respond with the usual, "Where are we going to get enough food *for them*?" I think they've come to the point where they don't care. Their hearts weren't in it anymore. They're tired, worn out, hungry, and ambivalent, having followed Jesus on a meandering path leading to nowhere.

LIVE the Story

Did anyone ever ask Jesus, "Hey, where are we going?" I'm surprised it never happened—at least no Gospel writer ever recorded such a conversation. I would expect at least one disciple, perhaps Peter, to approach Jesus, wanting

16. Bruner, *Matthew*, 2:109.
17. Luz, *Matthew*, 2:346.
18. Davies and Allison, *Matthew*, 2:566–67.
19. See above in the introduction, 18–20, 28–31.

to know where they were headed. Not only did they walk everywhere they went, but Jesus seemed to have no idea where he was going. Look at the itinerary. Up a mountain, across the lake, some time in Capernaum, back across the lake, brief stop in Gadara, across the lake back to Capernaum, wandering around several Galilean villages, brief stop in Nazareth, across the lake, into the desert, up a mountain, across the lake, traveling through a few Galilean villages, brief trip into gentile territory, back to Galilee, hike up a mountain again. At some point, someone in the crowd (especially one of the Twelve) must have wondered: "Where is he taking us? Does he even know where he's going? What's he looking for? Does he need directions?" Then I imagine one bold soul walking up to Jesus and saying, "Can I help you find something? You seem to be a little lost, wandering around like you really don't have a clue where you're going." Of course, in a few verses Jesus will talk like he has a plan, an itinerary, a destination: "From that time on Jesus began to explain to his disciples that he must go to Jerusalem and suffer many things" (16:21). But up until that point, for his disciples following Jesus meant taking a meandering path without any destination. And, for most of us, if there is no destination there is no purpose.

The most common question I get from ministerial students graduating from college is, "How will I know God's will for my life?" It's a question all Christ followers ask, but for men and women called to gospel ministry it can be a very troubling question to answer. You wouldn't think that would be the case. If God has called you to the ministry, go to it. The problem is that there are so many different kinds of ministry; it's hard to know what you're supposed to do. Sometimes the Lord will put a burning desire in the heart of a young minister to go to a specific place and perform a particular task ("I'm going to plant churches in West Africa"). But most of the time, these men and women have no idea where they are going or what they're supposed to do. Graduation day is fast approaching, so they come to my office seeking some advice about their future. They explain how they are wondering what the next step will be, listening to their friends talk excitedly about their careers, setting up plans, plotting incremental steps to achieve their life goals. Then these young ministers look at me, an old man sitting comfortably in a chair in a nice office, doing everyday what I love to do—teaching students during the week, preaching for pastorless churches on the weekends—and they wonder: "How did you do it? Is this what you planned from the beginning? How did you get here?" When I tell them my story, knowing what it felt like to be a college senior, staring out my dorm window and dreaming about my future, hoping one day that I would be here (teaching New Testament at my alma mater and helping churches), it doesn't seem to help them at all—that is, until I talk about my journey.

I realize, of course, that life works out for some people just as they planned—a straight-line trajectory from point A (origin) to point B (destination). But for most of us, even for those who have dreams of what could be, things don't happen like that.

I believe God called me to preach the gospel when I was sixteen years old. Since I came from a blue-collar family of modest means, I wasn't sure how I would make it to college. But like many others, by God's grace, I graduated from college, attended seminary, and even had the privilege of doing a year of doctoral study at one of the most prestigious universities in the world. All along the way, I served churches in a variety of ways: from youth and music leader, to associate pastor, to pastor, to adjunct professor, to professor, as interim pastor, back to pastor, back to college professor and interim pastor. I want to believe the Lord has led me every step of the way. Even now, looking back, it looks more like a meandering path than a planned itinerary for life—especially when I recall those moments in "the desert" where it felt like I followed Jesus to the middle of nowhere.

One time it got so bad at a church—at the end of a rough day that had been going on for weeks—I assumed a "Charlie Brown posture," bent over in despair, my head face down on my desk, muttering to God, "Get me out of here." The last thing on my mind was trying to help others for the sake of Christ and his kingdom. Like the disciples who plodded along, following Jesus all over Galilee and beyond, one minute headed west, the next east, through familiar neighborhoods and into foreign territory, up the mountain and across the sea, into the city and out to the desert, feasting sometimes and hungry for days—honestly, there have been a few times during the journey when it felt like Jesus was just jerking my chain, seeing how far I would go before I screamed out in frustration: "Where in the [bleep] are you taking me?" There was one moment I will never forget: I had just graduated with my PhD, couldn't find a teaching job, was leading music in a church part-time and working for a temp service, cleaning up computer files at a bank. During break time one afternoon at the bank, I dug around in my pockets, trying to find a dime to buy a lousy cup of coffee when it hit me: I am a desk jockey with a doctorate and no future. At that point, I would have given anything to hear Jesus say, "We're headed for Jerusalem." Going somewhere—*even* a place of crucifixion—would seem more purposeful than heading nowhere.

Recently, I shared my story with a soon-to-graduate ministerial student. He gave me a sympathetic look and said, "I never would have expected that."

"Me neither," I said. Then I told him about the time a seminary professor, Dr. Robert Sloan, offered some invaluable advice. After listening to my sad story he said, "Rodney, where did you get the impression that following Jesus would be easy? At the heart of the gospel we preach is a cross. Sometimes following Christ is the hardest thing you'll ever do." I've never forgotten that moment.

"Yeah," the student said, "that makes a lot of sense. Maybe I already know the answer to my question, 'What is God's will for my life?' It's following Jesus. I just wish I knew where he was headed." We talked a little more, exploring his gifts, desires, and opportunities. (I've discovered that when these three things come together, it may point us in the direction we should go.) Then we prayed together, and I watched him walk out my door and into his future.

As I think about conversations like these, my life's journey, and this story from Matthew's Gospel, I can't help but connect the dots. Maybe all of this "aimless" walking around Galilee had a purpose. Perhaps Jesus was teaching his disciples how to follow him—a meandering path with no particular direction—until it was time to carry the cross to Jerusalem. Then, all things would become clear. Until then, disciples of Jesus have nowhere else to go but follow him. In the meantime, he will continue to look for people with great faith, finding them in the most unusual places.

CHAPTER 23

Matthew 16:1–20

LISTEN to the Story

1The Pharisees and Sadducees came to Jesus and tested him by asking him to show them a sign from heaven.

2He replied, "When evening comes, you say, 'It will be fair weather, for the sky is red,' 3and in the morning, 'Today it will be stormy, for the sky is red and overcast.' You know how to interpret the appearance of the sky, but you cannot interpret the signs of the times. 4A wicked and adulterous generation looks for a sign, but none will be given it except the sign of Jonah." Jesus then left them and went away.

5When they went across the lake, the disciples forgot to take bread. 6"Be careful," Jesus said to them. "Be on your guard against the yeast of the Pharisees and Sadducees."

7They discussed this among themselves and said, "It is because we didn't bring any bread."

8Aware of their discussion, Jesus asked, "You of little faith, why are you talking among yourselves about having no bread? 9Do you still not understand? Don't you remember the five loaves for the five thousand, and how many basketfuls you gathered? 10Or the seven loaves for the four thousand, and how many basketfuls you gathered? 11How is it you don't understand that I was not talking to you about bread? But be on your guard against the yeast of the Pharisees and Sadducees." 12Then they understood that he was not telling them to guard against the yeast used in bread, but against the teaching of the Pharisees and Sadducees.

13When Jesus came to the region of Caesarea Philippi, he asked his disciples, "Who do people say the Son of Man is?"

14They replied, "Some say John the Baptist; others say Elijah; and still others, Jeremiah or one of the prophets."

15"But what about you?" he asked. "Who do you say I am?"

16Simon Peter answered, "You are the Messiah, the Son of the living God."

[17]Jesus replied, "Blessed are you, Simon son of Jonah, for this was not revealed to you by flesh and blood, but by my Father in heaven. [18]And I tell you that you are Peter, and on this rock I will build my church, and the gates of Hades will not overcome it. [19]I will give you the keys of the kingdom of heaven; whatever you bind on earth will be bound in heaven, and whatever you loose on earth will be loosed in heaven." [20]Then he ordered his disciples not to tell anyone that he was the Messiah.

Listening to the Text in the Story: Deuteronomy 13:1–5; 2 Samuel 7:4–16; Job 38:17; Psalm 2:4–7; Isaiah 2:2–4; 22:21–24; 28:15–19; 38:10; 51:1–2; Jeremiah 10:2; 31:31–34; Malachi 4:5–6.

Jesus had one mission: to be the last king of Israel to claim David's throne. What that meant, of course, was that Jesus came to establish the kingdom of heaven on earth—a just reign that would last forever. He knew from the beginning that the leaders in Jerusalem wouldn't take it very well—something that Matthew has emphasized (Matt 2:1–23). But that didn't keep Jesus from doing what he came to do or saying what he came to say. He refused to mince words, telling the people from the start that the scribes and Pharisees weren't even close to entering the kingdom. He told the people that something greater than Solomon and the temple he built was among them. He ignored the traditions of the Pharisees and refused to perform signs to prove his identity. Even when the Pharisaical big guns from Jerusalem showed up to challenge him, he dismissed them as "blind guides." Possibly it was to let things die down a little that he would leave Jewish territory for a spell. But as soon as he returned, even larger crowds would show up looking for help, with the religious leaders not far behind ready to do battle again. Yet, to a certain extent the Pharisees were harmless. They never took matters into their own hands to kill Jesus. Sure, they planned to, but they seemed to be waging a war of public opinion, trying to persuade the crowds to turn on Jesus. But when the Sadducean powerbrokers from Jerusalem came calling, Jesus must have known that time was running out.[1] Offend the Pharisees, and they'll keep coming at you with questions, trying to entrap you. Offend the Sadducees, and your days are numbered. So when the Pharisees *and the Sadducees* came to Jesus and "tested him by asking him to show them a sign from heaven" (16:1), Jesus decided to leave the country again—only this time, he was doing more than buying time,

1. Also France, *Matthew*, 605.

hoping to defuse the situation. Instead, he acted like it was time to ask the big question, the one he had been preparing his disciples all along to answer.

Throughout Matthew's Gospel, even though he came to establish an eternal kingdom, Jesus talked like he wouldn't be with his disciples forever. He said there would come a time when the bridegroom was taken away from them and they would grieve (9:15). He anticipated that his disciples would be persecuted in his absence, and that one day he would return and reward them for their faithfulness (10:17–33). He talked about the "sign of Jonah," explaining that he would spend three days and nights "in the heart of the earth" (12:39–40)—repeating the telltale sign when the Sadducees asked for a "sign from heaven" (16:1–4). Even when he gave little bits of advice along the way, like asking God for gifts or entering the narrow gate or watching out for the leaven of the Pharisees and Sadducees, the assumption behind his words is that he would be gone. They would need to learn to count on God (not Jesus) for food, to find the right path on their own, and to discern for themselves bad teaching. Jesus seemed to be doing two things at once: establishing a kingdom and training his disciples, gathering lost sheep and empowering the Twelve, overcoming evil and purifying hearts. In other words, the way Matthew tells the story, Jesus came not only to set up the kingdom of heaven on earth, but he also needed to prepare his disciples to carry on the work after he was taken from them. Jesus knew the reign of God coming to earth would take more time than he had on earth. The clock was ticking; were the disciples ready?

EXPLAIN the Story

Like an approaching storm in the distance, the arrival of the Sadducees signaled to Jesus that he was running out of time. (He could read the "signs of the times," but the Pharisees and Sadducees were clueless; Matt 16:2–4). There would come a time when Jesus would walk straight into the storm, leading his disciples to Jerusalem to claim David's throne. When he got there, the Sadducees would be waiting for him. They were the ruling aristocracy, the trustees of the temple, the most powerful men in all of Israel. They even made up the majority of the Sanhedrin, the council that would arrest, interrogate, and hand Jesus over to the Romans for execution. Yet, for now Jesus decided to head in the opposite direction, taking the Twelve to the northern tip of Israel, near a city built by Herod and named after Caesar (v. 13).[2] Jesus had

2. According to Chrysostom, Jesus took his disciples to the northern border of Israel so that they could speak their mind in a "safe place," away from the threat of his opponents (*Homilies*, 332).

to test the Twelve to find out if they were ready for what lay ahead (v. 21), to see if they knew the answer to the most important question he had ever asked them. In light of what they discussed during their trip to the north country, it would seem as though they weren't ready at all (vv. 5–12).

Jesus made an offhanded comment about the nefarious ways of the Pharisees and Sadducees, expecting his disciples to understand the simple warning (v. 6). He assumed that what was on his mind was also on the minds of his followers. He was concerned about his disciples dealing with these hostile opponents in his absence; but the Twelve were worried that they hadn't secured provisions for their latest trek to "who knows where" (v. 5). The disciples took Jesus's comment as a criticism of their oversight (v. 7). Overhearing their discussion, Jesus was incredulous that they didn't know what he was talking about *and* that they would even worry about the lack of food (vv. 8–11). After all, if Jesus could feed thousands of men in a deserted place (twice!), then surely he could take care of them during their trip. This one, simple comment revealed two things: that his disciples still had "little faith," and that they still needed Jesus to explain everything he said, especially when he relied upon metaphors, analogies, and parables to make his point. Think about how frustrating that must have been for Jesus. He sees the storms gathering, and his disciples aren't prepared to weather the eschatological forecast. This was a crucial moment. What if they gave the wrong answer? What if they still hadn't figured out whom they were following? Would Jesus need to keep wandering around Galilee, performing miracles and teaching them lessons, hoping everything would sink in one day before things came to a head? Not to overemphasize the risk, but Jesus had put all his eggs into these twelve little baskets. Surely one of them could see what they had been carrying for quite some time.

Jesus Is the Messiah

Jesus didn't "teach to the test," that is, when schoolteachers give their students answers to questions on standardized exams to make sure they score well. He didn't gather his disciples in the beginning and say, "Listen up everyone. I'm going to tell you something very important, and one day I'm going to ask if you remember what I said. [Pause] I'm the Messiah, the Son of God. Now, I know this may come as a surprise; after all, I really haven't done anything to prove it. But, just watch me. You'll see that what I'm telling you is true. Later down the road I'm going to ask you, 'Who am I?' Then you'll say, 'You're the Christ, the Son of God!' Got it? Okay, let's go." Neither did he make his disciples memorize a catechism. "Repeat after me: 'I believe in God the Father Almighty, Maker of heaven and earth. And in Jesus Christ his only Son our

Lord. . . .'" Instead, like he expected for his parables, Jesus anticipated that his disciples would figure out the significance of what he said and did on their own, without explanation. In other words, like a college professor, Jesus was more interested in developing "critical thinking skills" in his students than dumping information into their heads. They needed to know not only *what* they believed but *why* they believed it. This was true for a number of reasons, but particularly it was needed so that they could distinguish the "leaven of the Pharisees and the Sadducees" from the teaching of God. Several Jewish groups had different ideas about the kingdom of God and what it would take for the dream to become reality. But Jesus knew that the reign of God depended upon him—that getting him right would enable his disciples to get the kingdom right.

One wonders why Jesus didn't get straight to the point and ask the Twelve, "Who am I?" Instead, it looks like he's fishing around for information, wanting to hear the scuttlebutt before he drops the big question. When the disciples report what they've heard (16:14), there's really no surprise. Herod thought Jesus was John the Baptist (14:2). Jesus said he was a prophet (13:57). That some believed Jesus was Elijah makes sense in light of all the miracles he performed like the great prophet (9:18–26; 15:21–38; 1 Kgs 17:8–24). Thinking Jesus was Jeremiah is a bit of a mystery, except that Jesus may have sounded like him when he emphasized the purity of one's heart (Matt 15:17–19; Jer 31:31–34).[3] What surprises me is why Jesus didn't discount these crazy ideas. The "leaven" of the people could be just as damaging to his purpose. Yet Jesus didn't use this as a "teachable moment," explaining to his disciples why these answers were so wrong. "Let's take them one at a time. John the Baptist, really? How ridiculous is that? You know that we are two different people; you saw that from the beginning. Elijah, well that's a little flattering, but. . . ." Equally astonishing is that the disciples didn't report *everything* the people said about Jesus, like the blind men and Canaanite woman who called him "Son of David" or the people who dismissed Jesus as a drunk (Matt 11:19). Then again, Jesus already knew these things, so there was no need to repeat them. But there was one opinion that never surfaced; evidently no one ever said that Jesus was "the Messiah." But that was about to change.

It was a pivotal moment, and I wonder if the disciples knew it. Jesus had never talked like this, wanting to know what people thought about him. The subject of his identity seemed off limits. For every time someone challenged him with "who do you think you are?" or wondered out loud about his true identity, Jesus either ignored them or shot back a pithy little response and kept

3. France believes the comparison was made due to Jesus's harsh criticism of the temple that eventually resulted in his death (*Matthew*, 616–17).

moving (8:27; 9:3, 34; 11:3, 19; 12:23–24; 13:54–57; 14:33). But now he wants to know not only what the people think but, more importantly, what his disciples believed (the word order of the Greek text is emphatic: "But *you*, what do *you* say about me?" [16:15]). I wonder how long the question lingered in the air. Did Peter blurt out his answer right away, or was there a moment when the disciples looked at each with a "who's going to tell him?" expression on their faces, a hesitation in their voice? Did they wonder, "Is this a test or an innocuous way of opening up a conversation?" What if they said the wrong thing? Would Jesus be angry with them? I wish we could hear their tone of voice or see their body language, signals that are often telling in critical moments like these. Nevertheless, we know Peter gave the right answer because Jesus fell all over him with praise (16:17). Obviously, "You are the Messiah, the Son of the living God" (16:16) is exactly what Jesus wanted to hear. Hearing them say that he is the Son of God was nothing new (14:33). Having someone call him "the Messiah," on the other hand, was completely novel. And yet, Matthew has been preparing his readers for this moment from the beginning (1:1). Matthew identified Jesus as the Messiah way back at his birth (1:16–18; 2:4). Yet, since then the only time our Gospel writer referred to Jesus as the Messiah was when the Baptizer's disciples showed up questioning whether Jesus was "the one" (11:2–3). So, when Peter said, "You are the Messiah," it must have sounded like a revelation—not only to the disciples but also to Matthew's first-time readers. Since the days of Jesus's birth, no one had talked like this; Peter was the first.

Simon Is Peter

Up to this point in Matthew's Gospel, it's been all about Jesus. But now, because Peter gave the right answer to *the* question, Jesus focuses on Simon, directing our attention to him by pronouncing a blessing on this "rock" (Peter's name means "rock," *petros* in Greek and *kepha* in Aramaic; Gal 2:9, 11, 14). What Jesus says in these few verses is unique to Matthew's Gospel (Matt 16:17–19). Ironically, Jesus's response to Peter's correct answer raises even more questions. What did Jesus mean when he said that he would build his church upon "this rock" (v. 18)? Was he talking about Peter or something else? What are the "gates of Hades," and do they have anything to do with the "keys of the kingdom" that Jesus handed over to Peter (vv. 18–19)?[4] Moreover, why would Jesus hand the keys of the kingdom over to Peter; why wouldn't Jesus keep them? Doesn't that imply Jesus's upcoming departure—that he will need someone to take care of things while he's gone? Speaking of that

4. For a helpful, concise discussion of interpretive options, see Luz, *Matthew*, 2:362–64; also Bruner, *Matthew*, 2:128–35.

power, what exactly is Peter able to "bind and loose" on earth and in heaven (v. 19), and is Peter the only one who can do this?[5] Finally, why did Jesus want his disciples to keep his messianic identity a secret (v. 20)—something that Mark and Luke also record (Mark 8:30; Luke 9:21)? In other words, what is the purpose of this pronouncement that appears only in Matthew's Gospel? Because Peter has revealed the true identity of Jesus as the Messiah, the last king of Israel, are we to suppose that Jesus is now revealing the true identity of Simon as Peter, the first apostle of the church?

A few scholars think this is when Jesus gave Simon his nickname, which explains why up to this point only the narrator has referred to Simon as Peter.[6] But most think Jesus is playing on the meaning of Simon's nickname, one that Jesus gave him much earlier (John 1:42), or perhaps it is a nickname he had before he met Jesus. The more salient question is whether Jesus intended to build his church upon Peter[7] or upon Peter's confession. The reason some argue for the latter is the subtle difference in the wording that can't be seen in English: "You are Peter [*petros*], and on this rock [*petra*] I will build my church" (Matt 16:18). There is some evidence to suggest that *petros* refers to a rock that can be held and *petra* refers to bedrock. So, the argument goes that Jesus was saying, "Well done Peter. God revealed to you that I am the Messiah. You are a 'rock,' and I will build my church upon the bedrock of your confession."[8] The problem with such a nuanced reading is that sometimes *petros* and *petra* are used as synonyms for a "stone," whether large or small. Furthermore, such a distinction is lost in the mother tongue of Jesus and his disciples: the Aramaic version of Simon's nickname, *kepha* ("Cephas"), means "rock" regardless of the size.[9] Finally, if Jesus weren't trying to single out Peter as the "rock" of his church, then what are we to make of the rest of what Jesus said about him—that Simon Peter has been given the keys of the kingdom, able to bind and loose on earth as it is in heaven (v. 19)?[10] It seems more likely, therefore, that Jesus was rewarding Simon Peter for his divine

---

5. Luz makes a helpful comparison to sort out Peter's unique literary role in Matthew by considering parallels with the "beloved disciple" in John's Gospel (*Matthew*, 2:367; for a brief history of interpretation regarding Peter's role in the church, see ibid., 366–68).

6. A new name ("Rock") for a new people of God ("church"). See Davies and Allison, *Matthew*, 2:625–27.

7. For a helpful survey and critique of the Catholic interpretation of Peter as the first pope, see Talbert, *Matthew*, 197–200.

8. Garland, *Reading Matthew*, 173–74.

9. Keener, *Matthew*, 426–27.

10. Some scholars point to the significance of the future, perfect, passive periphrasis (future tense of *eimi* plus perfect, passive participle) to indicate that Peter was to bind on earth what had already been bound in heaven—a kind of divine guidance rather than heavenly endorsement; see France, *Matthew*, 626–27; Bruner, *Matthew*, 2:133–34. Bruner wonders whether Jesus's instructions to the Twelve to "shake the dust off your feet" (10:13–15) was an illustration of binding and loosing (ibid., 133).

insight, a revelation given to him by God. Therefore, Jesus set Peter apart from the rest of his disciples for a divinely appointed task involving keys and binding and loosing. Yet what does that mean?[11]

The truth of the matter is, we don't know. And so, this is where our preunderstanding of Peter comes into play. Since he is a major figure in the gospel story, we can go to other parts of the New Testament—the Acts of the Apostles or the letters of Peter and even Paul—and try to sort out the meaning of Jesus's enigmatic blessing. In Acts, Peter appears as the spokesman of the early church (Acts 1:15; 2:14; 3:6, 12; 4:8), even though James is the one who acts like he's the primary decision maker in Jerusalem (15:13–21). So, when did Peter use the keys of the kingdom to "bind and loose"? Was it when he decided that gentiles could be saved, after he received the vision of the "parachute" and witnessed the salvation of Cornelius and his household (10:1–11:18)? Isn't that a good illustration of what Jesus meant, that he would build his church on Peter? Simon Peter even used the same imagery of rocks and building when referring to the church as a temple of "living stones" built on the foundation of Jesus Christ, the rejected cornerstone that causes people to stumble (1 Pet 2:4–8). Yet, doesn't that reveal the way Peter interpreted Jesus's blessing, that the "rock" upon which the church is built is Jesus Christ and not Peter—that he's just one of the "living stones" of God's temple?[12] Besides, what about Paul? Doesn't he appear as the leading figure in the second half of the story of Acts? Furthermore, Paul recognized John and James (along with Peter) as "pillars" of the early church (Gal 2:6–9), and referred to *all* apostles (and prophets!) as the "foundation" of the church, the temple of God, "with Christ Jesus himself as the chief cornerstone" (Eph 2:20–21). So when we consider the entire New Testament, it's apparent that Jesus built the church using several "rocks," not just Peter.

Since Peter was not the only apostle to have a crucial role in the early church, then why did Jesus single out Peter for special recognition? I think it has a lot to do with the role Peter plays throughout the rest of Matthew's Gospel. From this point forward, Peter will try to use the keys of the kingdom to bind on earth what he thinks should be heaven's purpose (cf. Isa 22:22–24). Right

---

11. Keener's brief summation of Peter's role (*Matthew*, 429–30) is helpful: Was Peter supposed to be the prime minister (first pope), chief rabbi (key interpreter of Jesus's teaching), or premier evangelist (top spokesman; see the book of Acts)?

12. Meyer hears temple language in Jesus's pronouncement, identifying the "cosmic rock" of Zion—the primordial foundation of the world—upon which the church as the temple of God would be built; see Ben F. Meyer, *The Aims of Jesus*, Princeton Theological Monograph Series 48 (London: SCM, 1979), 185–97. The implications of Meyer's approach are fascinating, given the fact that this entire episode is preceded by the demand for a cosmic sign "in heaven." Jesus, on the other hand, will perform a cosmic sign on earth: building the eternal temple of God "made without human hands" on earth via the resurrection.

after receiving the keys, Peter promises that Jesus will not die in Jerusalem (Matt 16:22). On the mount of transfiguration, Peter wants to build three tabernacles for Jesus, Moses, and Elijah—after which the heavenly voice corrects Peter with the admonition, "Listen to [Jesus]!" (17:4–5). Next, Peter tries to limit the number of times forgiveness should be extended (18:21). Later, he wants some assurance from Jesus that he and the rest of the disciples will be rewarded for giving up everything to follow him (19:27). Finally, Peter promises that he will never disown Jesus *even though Jesus had prophesied that Peter would deny him* (26:33–35; cf. Isa 22:25). First prophesied as the rock of the church, now identified as the ultimate traitor in the story of redemption—Peter appears as the embodiment of self-contradiction. So, whatever we make of these paradoxical prophecies, Matthew makes it quite evident that Peter had a lot to learn even though he was the first to confess Jesus as the Messiah. Peter appears as a leader in training, preparing for the time when Jesus will leave his disciples. Then, they would have to contend with the gates of hell in his absence. Indeed, when that day comes, rather than the kingdom of heaven coming to earth, it would surely seem to Peter and the disciples that earth had fallen to hell's purpose.

LIVE the Story

"The gates of hell will not prevail." Of all the things Jesus said that day to Peter and the disciples, nothing would have sounded more incredibly optimistic than that claim. Peter will be the leader of the church? "Yes," the Twelve might have thought, "we can see that, even though he's nothing more than a fisherman." But for Jesus to predict that all the powers of hell—even death—would never defeat his church? Well, imagine how peculiar that would have sounded to the Twelve. Everyone dies; and, as they were about to find out in the very next verse, even Jesus was destined to die (Matt 16:21). So how could it be that the ultimate adversary of all humanity, death itself, would never have its way with Jesus's followers? Of course, two-thousand years later, we see what Jesus meant—not only his resurrection but also the irrepressible presence of the church have proven his words true. We must remember, however, that at this point the Twelve have no idea that Jesus will leave them soon. We see how hard it was for the disciples to accept that their Messiah would die on a cross (not to mention the unfathomable notion of his being raised from the dead). Even though Jesus told them several times about this drastic turn of events that would occur once they arrived in Jerusalem, the disciples refused to believe it. Who can blame them? How could something so horrible happen to someone so divine? Besides, with these words ringing in their ears, "the gates of hell will not prevail," the church was supposed to be an impregnable fortress, a bastion of security against the fallen powers of this world. It's no wonder Peter went about wielding the keys of the kingdom like a sword, promising that no harm would come to Jesus. Peter took Jesus's declaration seriously—his words were supposed to be so reliable you could build your life on them, weathering even the worst storms (7:24–27).

When I think about it now, even with hundreds of years of history between us, it was an incredibly risky move for Jesus to establish the eternal success of the kingdom on Simon Peter due to his simple profession. All he said was, "You are the Messiah, the Son of the living God." That's it. Just a handful of words, and then Jesus starts handing over keys to the kingdom. I would have expected more from Peter, some demonstration of a commitment that went beyond words. How about a sacred ritual where Peter swears allegiance to Jesus to seal their alliance? Or, given their location, perhaps Jesus could have required Peter to build him a temple or a magnificent monument to his kingdom purpose, like the local shrine to the Greek god Pan[13] or the nearby city built by Herod and named after Caesar, Caesarea Philippi. Jesus talked about building his church on a rock, a permanent memorial on earth of his heavenly kingdom. Even to this day, you can travel to the highest mountains around the world or to the most remote corners of the earth and see massive cathedrals or modest tabernacles—all dedicated to the work of Christ and his church. But Jesus never required that. He gave Peter no architectural plans to ensure that his church would stand as an everlasting monument to the end of time (Peter tried to build him a tabernacle! See 17:4). There were no rituals to perform, no vows to swear (of course not! 5:34–37), no pledge of allegiance to recite to preserve the integrity of his church. "Now, everyone place your hand over your heart—you too, Judas—and say, 'I pledge allegiance to the Christ, the Son of the living God, and to the kingdom for which it stands, one church, under God, indivisible, with mercy and justice for all.'" No. All Jesus needed was to hear Peter confess, "You are the Messiah, the Son of the living God." He didn't even make anyone write it down—a document to pass around for everyone to sign. Rather, all that happened that day, the foundation of what would become the church of Jesus Christ, were spoken words. Things said, things heard. And that astounds me.

Yet, then again, words are powerful things. Authors use them to create imaginary worlds. Politicians use them to promise fantasy worlds. God used them to create the world, "'Let there be light,' and there was light" (Gen 1:3).

---

13. See Keener, *Matthew*, 424; Davies and Allison, *Matthew*, 2:616.

So, it shouldn't surprise us that the one who refused to perform a "sign from heaven" would rely on words to create the church on earth—a people who would carry his words in their hearts until the last day—an eternal, living memorial to the kingdom of heaven. "'Let there be the church,' and there was the church. And it was very good." We are the result of his words, the embodiment of his work, because we confess with our mouths and believe in our hearts *words*. Or, to use Paul's words, "We are God's *poem* [*poiēma*] created in Christ Jesus to do good works, which God prepared beforehand in order that we might walk in them" (Eph 2:10, translation mine).

There's a scene from one of my favorite movies, *A River Runs through It*, that reminds me of the reason why Jesus counted on words so much. It's the last line of the movie based on Norman Maclean's autobiography, *A River Runs through It and Other Stories*, that especially reveals what I would call Maclean's "theology of words"—a divine mystery that must be incarnated to be understood.[14] As an old man, Norman has returned to the Blackfoot River, where his father taught him and his brother, Paul, so many lessons about God's grace, life's mysteries, and the beautiful wonders of their homeland, Montana. We see the old version of Norman trying to tie a fly to his line, hands shaking from age. Eventually, he casts his line into the river, hoping a trout will rise, bringing another chance to relive his history. The camera moves in for a close-up; we see deep lines etched on his face, a dark look of sadness reflected in his eyes, the sorrow of loneliness caused by a life of tragedy—the early death of his brother and the most recent passing of his beloved wife. The camera pulls back, allowing us to take in the beauty of the canyon, the sunlight bouncing diamonds on the water that never sleeps. Then, at the very moment when we are caught between the wonder and the heartache of this solitary figure fishing for luck, words fall like leaves into the river that runs through our souls:

> Eventually, all things merge into one and a river runs through it. The river was cut by the world's great flood and runs over the rocks from the basement of time. On some of the rocks are timeless raindrops. Under the rocks are the words, and some of the words are theirs.
>
> I am haunted by waters.[15]

Tragedy and beauty. Mystery and wonder. Rocks and words.

I love the line, "under the rocks are the words, and some of the words are theirs." Indeed, since God created all things with words, then under the

14. Norman Maclean, *A River Runs through It and Other Stories* (Chicago: University of Chicago Press, 1976).

15. Ibid., 104.

"basement of time" are words that hold up all things. Words we say, words we hear; words that are spoken, words that are timeless as rock. For even Jesus chose to build his church upon the rock of words. Words they needed to say, words they needed to hear. Yet, there were still more things to say, more things to be heard: "From that time on Jesus began to explain to his disciples that he must go to Jerusalem and suffer many things" (Matt 16:21).

I am haunted by these words.

CHAPTER 24

Matthew 16:21–17:13

LISTEN to the Story

[21]From that time on Jesus began to explain to his disciples that he must go to Jerusalem and suffer many things at the hands of the elders, the chief priests and the teachers of the law, and that he must be killed and on the third day be raised to life.

[22]Peter took him aside and began to rebuke him. "Never, Lord!" he said. "This shall never happen to you!"

[23]Jesus turned and said to Peter, "Get behind me, Satan! You are a stumbling block to me; you do not have in mind the concerns of God, but merely human concerns."

[24]Then Jesus said to his disciples, "Whoever wants to be my disciple must deny themselves and take up their cross and follow me. [25]For whoever wants to save their life will lose it, but whoever loses their life for me will find it. [26]What good will it be for someone to gain the whole world, yet forfeit their soul? Or what can anyone give in exchange for their soul? [27]For the Son of Man is going to come in his Father's glory with his angels, and then he will reward each person according to what they have done.

[28]"Truly I tell you, some who are standing here will not taste death before they see the Son of Man coming in his kingdom."

[17:1]After six days Jesus took with him Peter, James and John the brother of James, and led them up a high mountain by themselves. [2]There he was transfigured before them. His face shone like the sun, and his clothes became as white as the light. [3]Just then there appeared before them Moses and Elijah, talking with Jesus.

[4]Peter said to Jesus, "Lord, it is good for us to be here. If you wish, I will put up three shelters—one for you, one for Moses and one for Elijah."

[5]While he was still speaking, a bright cloud covered them, and a voice from the cloud said, "This is my Son, whom I love; with him I am well pleased. Listen to him!"

[6]When the disciples heard this, they fell facedown to the ground, terrified. [7]But Jesus came and touched them. "Get up," he said. "Don't be afraid." [8]When they looked up, they saw no one except Jesus.

[9]As they were coming down the mountain, Jesus instructed them, "Don't tell anyone what you have seen, until the Son of Man has been raised from the dead."

[10]The disciples asked him, "Why then do the teachers of the law say that Elijah must come first?"

[11]Jesus replied, "To be sure, Elijah comes and will restore all things.
[12]But I tell you, Elijah has already come, and they did not recognize him, but have done to him everything they wished. In the same way the Son of Man is going to suffer at their hands."
[13]Then the disciples understood that he was talking to them about John the Baptist.

Listening to the Text in the Story: Exodus 24:1–18; 34:29–35; Deuteronomy 18:18–19; 2 Samuel 7:11–16; Job 1:6–12; 2:1–13; Psalms 2:6–7; 49:7–9; 62:11–12; 89:35–51; 104:2–4; Isaiah 42:1–4; 52:13–53:12; 55:8–9; Daniel 7:9–14; Hosea 6:2; Zechariah 3:1–8; 13:7–9; Malachi 4:5–6.

We've finally come to the point of the story. The details of how it all works out are yet to be seen, but here we get a sneak preview of what will be. Like a movie trailer that nearly gives away everything, Matthew teases the reader with excerpts from a script that will be played out in dramatic fashion. All the main characters make a brief appearance: the protagonist, the villains, the confused best friend, the unseen forces of good and evil, and minor characters who help move the plot along by asking questions that are on everyone's mind. Crucial quotes and important taglines help frame the unfolding drama, with all of the expected twists and turns of a roller-coaster ride of exhilarating peaks and precipitous falls: "It is necessary," "Lord, have mercy," "Get behind me, Satan," "This is more like it," "Don't be afraid," "Keep this a secret," and "Is this the end?" The universal conflict, the ultimate challenge of life—overcoming evil and suffering—is the driving force of this compelling story. The only thing missing is the sound of a narrator's booming voice opening with the words, "In a world [pause] where injustice reigns and hope is deferred. . . ." Matthew has quite a story to tell, one that should take everyone by surprise.

Of course, we've heard this story so often that the shock and awe of what happened has worn off. Matthew's sneak preview doesn't hold our attention anymore. Jesus's warning to his disciples about his upcoming death, Peter's devilish rebuttal and Jesus's startling rebuke, his "upping the ante" by expecting his disciples to carry a cross to Jerusalem, and even the mountaintop experience of Jesus talking to Moses and Elijah—all of this is so familiar to us that we aren't arrested by these strange developments. But when you step back and think about it, this is a rather bizarre sequence of events. Not the part about Jesus predicting that he will suffer at the hands of his enemies once he gets to Jerusalem—we've seen that coming for some time. It's what follows—the head-spinning, "what-was-that?" turn of events—that leaves the first-time reader with emotional whiplash. One minute Peter is holding the keys of the kingdom; the next minute he's Satan incarnate. One moment Jesus strikes a melancholy tone, with talk of suffering and death, cross and loss. Then, all of the sudden, the scene shifts to glory on the mountain. We see Jesus morph into an angelic figure—shining face and white-as-light robes—talking to Moses and Elijah, with a heavenly voice chiming in to offer another ringing endorsement. By the time it's all over, we are as disoriented as Peter and as confused as the disciples. It's enough to make even the casual observer question the whole episode: Why did this happen? Was that really necessary? Indeed, the rapid-fire sequence of these episodes ending with the bizarre transfiguration of Jesus is a mystery.

Scholars have puzzled over this unique episode in Matthew's Gospel. Years ago some questioned whether anything actually happened to Jesus[1]—what we have here is a vision experienced by three disciples.[2] The entire vision was for the benefit of the disciples, not Jesus (Luke's version, on the other hand, appears as an encouragement to Jesus; Luke 9:28–36).[3] Still other scholars find a symmetrical arrangement in the details of the transfiguration and the crucifixion—twin stories of God's revelation: a mountain scene, three named onlookers (disciples and women), "Son-of-God" confession, Elijah is mentioned, fear, Jesus's garments are mentioned, the number six appears ("after six days," "from the sixth hour").[4] Some think the transfiguration is a proleptic version of when the resurrected Jesus will appear on the mountain with kingdom authority to send his disciples as missionaries (Matt 28:16–20).[5] Rather than looking ahead to see how the transfiguration functions as a sneak preview of future events in Matthew's narrative world, many scholars look back and

1. David Friedrich Strauss, *The Life of Jesus, Critically Examined*, trans. from the 4th ed. by George Eliot (New York: Macmillan, 1898), 538–40.

2. Talbert, *Matthew*, 207–9. See the discussion in Davies and Allison, *Matthew*, 2:689–93.

3. Luz explores the significance of the transfiguration for disciples via the Feast of Metamorphosis celebrated in the Eastern Church (*Matthew*, 2:400–404).

4. Davies and Allison, *Matthew*, 2:706–7.

5. France, *Matthew*, 640–41; Garland, *Reading Matthew*, 183.

find stories in the Old Testament that share several features: mountaintop meeting, theophanic cloud, shining face, beloved son, Moses and Elijah, erecting booths, numinous awe. Abraham's near sacrifice of his son, Moses's shining face on Mt. Sinai, the feast of Tabernacles, pronouncements in the enthronement scene of Psalm 2, prophecies about the return of Moses and Elijah—these passages bounce around in the echo chamber of the transfiguration of Jesus, inviting all kinds of comparisons.[6]

Here's the bottom line: since this is such a peculiar story, we're all looking for a context to help us make sense of it. Which just goes to show you, perhaps, how much we should identify with the disciples in their confusion. There's so much going on in this story that we're still trying to figure it out. It's a mystery—a marvelous tale that makes us want to lean in, learn more, and wonder.

EXPLAIN the Story

Jesus had taken his disciples to the northern edge of Israel when he asked them, "Who do you say I am?" (Matt 16:15). After Peter gave the right answer, "You are the Messiah, the Son of the living God" (v. 16), Jesus headed south for Jerusalem (v. 21). Jesus expected things to "go south" in a hurry as he anticipated his trip to Jerusalem to claim David's throne. He knew that his arrival in the holy city would incite the "elders, the chief priests and the teachers of the law" to have him killed (v. 21). That explains why, according to Matthew's Gospel, from this point forward Jesus will devote his attention to his disciples, trying to prepare them for the catastrophe of his suffering and death (but also his resurrection).[7] There are no more scenes of large crowds looking for miracles, and only one "public discourse" remains to give to the masses (and it's a humdinger, when Jesus excoriates the Pharisees as hypocrites; see 23:1–39). From now on Jesus will spend much time teaching his disciples about the kind of Messiah he came to be.[8] Indeed, the way Jesus saw it, "it was necessary" (*dei*) for him to go to Jerusalem and die (16:21), a divine destiny not only befitting a prophet (23:37)[9] but also establishing once and for all the radically different way the kingdom of heaven comes to earth—a way that his disciples would be required to follow too.

But Jesus had already warned his disciples that they might have to die for the cause (10:21–23, 34–39). What alarmed Peter (and probably the rest of

6. See the helpful summary in Luz, *Matthew*, 2:395–97. Luz comes to the conclusion that "the transfiguration . . . is a 'polyvalent' story that permits several possibilities of association" (ibid., 397).

7. France, *Matthew*, 628.

8. Luz, *Matthew*, 2:378.

9. Talbert, *Matthew*, 202.

the Twelve) was the part about Jesus having to suffer and die in Jerusalem (16:21). Jesus also predicted that he would be raised from the dead—but one wonders if Peter even heard the tail end of Jesus's dire prediction. In fact, that would have been the part most of us would have seized upon, looking for an explanation. "How exactly are you going to *be raised* from the dead when you are the one so far who's been able to raise people from the dead (9:23–26)? Are you counting on us to do it (10:8)? How about it, Peter? Are you up for this?" Of course, Jesus had already hinted at his upcoming, violent death; one day, the bridegroom would be taken by force (9:15). Yet Peter acted as if that were a brand new idea, something he couldn't wrap his mind around (16:22). That was the troubling part of Jesus's prophecy—his death, not his resurrection. One wonders if that's why Jesus led Peter, James, and John up the mountain, so that they could see his postdeath glory before he died. Perhaps that would help them "see" what he was talking about, enabling them to look past the difficult way of "loss by cross" to the glory of his resurrection. Perhaps Jesus knew that the only way to embrace the cross is to look forward to the resurrection: "Truly I tell you, some who are standing here will not taste death before they see the Son of Man coming in his kingdom. After six days. . ." (16:28–17:1). That must have been a very long week, giving the disciples plenty of time to work through the puzzling prophecy that messianic suffering must precede messianic glory.[10]

Satan Says, "This Shall Never Happen to You"

When the serpent tempted the first couple to disobey God, having misquoted God's command (Gen 3:1), the creature said to Eve, "You will not certainly die" (v. 4). When the devil tempted Jesus in the desert, he quoted Scripture to convince Jesus to "throw yourself down. For it is written: 'He will command his angels concerning you, and they will lift you up in their hands, so that you will not strike your foot against a stone'" (Matt 4:6). So when Peter tries to convince Jesus that "this shall never happen to you" (16:22), Jesus recognized Satan's voice because he was using the same old ploy. In essence he was saying, "God won't let bad things happen to his children."[11] Of course, Satan knew that wasn't true; the story of Job is an insider's look into the heavenly drama played out on earth (Job 1:6–12; 2:1–13). Jesus was wise to the accuser's methods: "It is also written: 'Do not put the Lord your God to the test'" (Matt 4:7). Jesus wasn't going to Jerusalem to throw himself down before the wheels of history to put God to the test to save him.[12] Rather, Jesus knew he

10. See Bruner, *Matthew*, 2:150–54.

11. "Promises of the kingdom without the cross come from the devil" (Keener, *Matthew*, 433).

12. Contra Albert Schweitzer, *The Quest of the Historical Jesus*, ed. John Bowden (Minneapolis: Fortress, 2001), 332–54. For the famous quote that was omitted from later editions, see Dunn, *Jesus*

was going to die when he came to claim David's throne because the only way his kingdom would last forever is if death itself were defeated—something that Peter would eventually figure out as well (Acts 2:23–36). But when Peter heard Jesus predict his imminent suffering and death (and resurrection!) in Jerusalem, it must have sounded like this newly "crowned" Messiah was giving up before he even got there. So, the "Rock" tried to get in Jesus's way to prevent him from pursuing such a doomsday scenario. But Jesus would have none of it; as Satan's mouthpiece, Peter was proving to be the wrong kind of rock—not a foundational stone of the church but a stumbling stone of offense.[13] Therefore, if Peter still wanted to follow Jesus, he'd better get out of the way and get back in line (Matt 16:23).[14] How quickly things can change.

Let's try looking at it from Peter's perspective. Jesus had just showered him with accolades because he answered the question of Jesus's identity correctly (vv. 16–19). What was whispered in the corners was now on the table. Jesus is the Messiah, and it's time for him to reign on earth—at least that's what Jesus seemed to imply, what with all of his talk about defeating Hades and kingdom keys. Indeed, Peter must have wondered what Jesus meant by handing over to him "the keys of the kingdom of heaven." Being told that you can "bind on earth what is bound in heaven" probably encouraged Peter (and the rest of the disciples) to think that they would have an important role in setting up the powerful kingdom of God on earth. After all, they were following a Messiah who had already demonstrated miraculous feats of strength, overcoming even sickness and death. When Jesus told them to keep it a secret (v. 20), thoughts of a clandestine mission to Jerusalem would have made a lot of sense. A surprise attack would leave the rulers of Jerusalem in dismay as they watched the Messiah of God take the holy city by storm. So, when Jesus immediately says, "It's time to go to Jerusalem," visions of victory must have danced in their heads, especially Peter's. After all, he's the one holding the keys to the kingdom.

So when Jesus surprises them with his prophecy (v. 21), Peter can't accept it because it makes no sense. A more literal translation of Peter's "rebuke" is telling: "Be merciful to you [*hileōs soi*], Lord. This shall never happen to you" (v. 22, my translation). Even though our translation reads, "Never, Lord!" what Peter was actually doing is calling upon God (binding on earth what is bound in heaven!) to have mercy on Jesus.[15] In other words Peter was saying, "Our merciful God won't let this happen to you and neither will I!" We'll find

---

Remembered, 47.

13. Davies and Allison, *Matthew*, 2:664.

14. Ibid., 2:663.

15. Nolland, *Matthew*, 688.

out later that this won't be the only time Peter defies Jesus's prophecy, promising what he can't deliver (26:33–35). To be sure, Peter will play a significant part in Jesus's kingdom. But he and the rest of the disciples will need to learn what that means. To follow Jesus to Jerusalem, they will have to deny themselves, even to the point of death, because that's what he's going to do. They need to have God's thoughts on the matter; to think any other way about Jesus's mission is to have "merely human concerns" (16:23). Saving your own skin will eventually fail; everyone dies. Why spend your life for things that don't last (v. 26)? But if you lose your life for the kingdom, you will get it back in the end (vv. 25, 27).

When Jesus warned his disciples that they would need to bring their own cross to Jerusalem (v. 24), it was an ominous sign. The kingdom of heaven coming to earth would threaten all the rulers of Jerusalem—Jewish and Roman. At this time, Judea was an imperial province of the Romans, governed by the Roman procurator, Pontus Pilate. It was his job to protect Roman interests in this volatile region, keeping the peace at all costs. Long before Jesus brought his disciples to Jerusalem, messiah-wannabes would often come to the holy city, trying to incite the masses to rebel against their Roman overlords—typically during one of the Jewish festivals.[16] The larger the crowd, the better the revolution. Of course, the swift, unmerciful sword of Roman "justice" cut any rebellion off at the knees. After a while, Roman procurators like Pilate expected trouble (especially during Passover), having to leave their headquarters at Caesarea and travel to Jerusalem to stop things before they got out of hand. Pilate was notorious for taking a mallet to a fly, slaughtering hundreds of Jewish subjects for any sign of insubordination.[17] And so, "Messiah" Jesus knew he would run into trouble once he came to Jerusalem, not only with Jewish leaders but also the Roman procurator. If his disciples were going to follow him all the way to the end, then they would need to be prepared to die on a cross—the most shameful and excruciating (literally) death of all.

This was a dangerous mission. But to face such a daunting task, Jesus gave them a word of encouragement: "Truly I tell you, some who are standing here will not taste death before they see the Son of Man coming in his kingdom" (v. 28). I imagine some of the disciples looking around at each other, wondering which ones wouldn't make it. Sure, some of them would live to see the day the kingdom comes. But several of his disciples would lose their lives during the conquest—Jesus said so. Yet they had no idea what Jesus meant when he said some of them wouldn't die until they saw "the Son of Man coming in his

16. For a brief and vivid description of the political scene, see Paula Fredriksen, *Jesus of Nazareth, King of the Jews: A Jewish Life and the Emergence of Christianity* (New York: Knopf, 1999), 12–17.

17. Josephus, *Ant.* 18.3.1–2.

kingdom" (v. 28). As a matter of fact, we don't know what Jesus meant either. Some scholars think he's referring to the transfiguration that will occur in six days. Others believe Jesus was talking about his crucifixion,[18] resurrection, the Great Commission, his second coming, or perhaps even the destruction of the Jewish temple in AD 70.[19] When did Jesus "come into his kingdom," and what is the proof of his reign on earth? That's a question theologians have been debating for centuries. The problem is sometimes Jesus talked like the kingdom was present. Other times he acted like the kingdom was yet to come. So, which is it? If Jesus was referring in v. 28 to the imminent, in-breaking kingdom of God, then we could point to several "proofs" of his rule: over sin (on a cross), over death (via the resurrection), over the world (gospel preached to the ends of the earth), and even over Israel (temple veil ripped in half, the eventual destruction of the temple). Some of his apostles witnessed all these things. But if Jesus didn't "come into his kingdom" until the "second coming"—he was referring to a kingdom come—then we have another problem. For Jesus predicted that some of his disciples would live long enough to see the day of his return. But we know that didn't happen, so does that mean Jesus was wrong?

We can't solve the matter until we consider all Jesus had to say on the subject. Suffice it to say that when it comes to answering the question, "Has the kingdom of heaven come to earth, yes or no?" it's not that simple. It's partly because Jewish expectations about the messianic kingdom were not clear-cut. (The fact that Peter had a hard time accepting the notion that the Messiah was supposed to die in Jerusalem proves the point.) Confusion surrounding the timing of Jesus "coming into his kingdom" has much to do with the vague and puzzling prophecies he offered about the matter (not only here but especially during the so-called "Olivet Discourse"; 24:1–25:46). In other words, determining what Jesus meant by his prediction that some of his disciples wouldn't die until they witnessed the kingdom is more complicated than landing on a simple either/or answer; that is, whether the transfiguration or the resurrection fulfills the prophecy. Perhaps it's both because the kingdom of heaven coming to earth takes time—it's always coming—not fully arriving, but still present.

Therefore, maybe it's better to ask, "*Where* does the Son of Man come into his kingdom?" In response to that question Peter, James, and John might say, "We saw it once. On a mountain. The resplendent glory of past, present, and future all rolled up into one moment. Jesus shining like the sun; a bright cloud enveloped all of us. Heaven on earth—something we wouldn't understand until we saw the Son of Man raised from the dead. At least, that's what Jesus

18. Nolland, *Matthew*, 695–96.

19. Turner, *Matthew*, 412–14.

told us [17:9], and God said we'd better listen to him [v. 5]." Indeed, perhaps none of this makes sense until we *all* see Jesus raised from the dead. To quote the apostle Paul, "For now we see only a reflection as in a mirror; then we shall see face to face" (1 Cor 13:12).

God Says, "This Is My Son, Whom I Love"

When the messianic age dawned on Israel, there was supposed to be a war.[20] It would take heavenly forces—the good guys—to overcome evil on earth. The bad guys wouldn't go without a fight, and so Jewish expectations about the end of the world were dark and gloomy because God would show up to vanquish Israel's foes, bringing judgment to the wicked and relief to the righteous. God promised Israel that he would forewarn them by sending Moses and Elijah—two heavenly witnesses—to prepare them for the day of his visitation.[21] Then the Messiah would appear and lead the righteous to victory, defeating all enemies of God (human and angelic) and thus establishing on earth the everlasting rule of God's will. When that happened, there would be peace on earth because justice would reign. The postapocalyptic world would be bright, wonderful, glorious, plentiful, serene, refreshing, and magnificent because God would be present among his people. There would be an everlasting covenant of joyful saints (past and present), reunited to bask in the glow of the Messiah's eternal victory. It would be heaven on earth, forever.

When Peter, James, and John witnessed the transfigured Messiah conversing with Moses and Elijah, it looked like the glory of God had descended upon the mountaintop. Heaven and earth overlapped; the resplendent glory of the messianic age had dawned on them. It must have been a marvelous site to behold, so much so that Peter did what any first-century Jew would want to do: offer the proper acts of hospitality for these three divine visitors. Good news would often come to God's people when angelic visitors came calling (think of the time when three divine messengers visited Abraham and Sarah; the patriarch was quick to compel his visitors to stay in hopes of receiving their blessing; see Gen 18:1–15). There was no fear among the group; overhearing this conversation between these ancient heroes of Israel and their

---

20. One of the Jewish groups who spent a lot of time anticipating the end of the age was the Qumran community, probably a group of Essenes who had withdrawn from the world to prepare themselves for the last war. We even found among the documents they produced, known as the "Dead Sea Scrolls," a book called "The War Scroll." See Florentino García Martínez, ed., *The Dead Sea Scrolls Translated*, trans. Wilfred G. E. Watson (Leiden: Brill, 1994), 95–125.

21. For a good discussion regarding the eschatological roles of Moses and Elijah, see France, *Matthew*, 648; Talbert, *Matthew*, 208–9. Chrysostom (*Homilies*, 346) assumes Jesus summoned Moses and Elijah to appear to his disciples for their benefit, to show why the crowd was wrong about him (Matt 16:14).

Messiah compelled Peter to conclude (to put it in our vernacular): "Now that's what I'm talking about!" (Matt 17:4). I hear a bit of relief in Peter's voice. For six days, they must have pondered Jesus's dire prediction of his execution in Jerusalem. Now, having the "mountaintop experience" of his entire life, Peter was glad to be there, completely uninhibited, reveling in the glory of the moment. Since Jesus is the Messiah, this is the way it's supposed to be: bright lights and celebrities. Peter couldn't have staged a better messianic display. They were having a great time—until God spoke up: "This is my Son, whom I love; with him I am well pleased. Listen to him!" (v. 5).

We don't have to imagine God's tone of voice when he responded to Peter's plan to build the tabernacles—especially when he said, "Listen to him!" The three disciples fell to the ground, terrified when they heard it (v. 6). It appears as though they wouldn't budge from their submissive pose until Jesus came and reassured them everything was all right (v. 7). Of course, this wasn't the first time God said this about Jesus (3:17)—a mash-up of lines from Psalm 2:7 and Isaiah 42:1.[22] But the tagline "listen to him!" was new. I hear a thundering voice of divine displeasure—like a father correcting his child—when God spoke to Peter. Given the infrequency of hearing his voice, one wonders why God decided to speak up at that moment. I can certainly think of other times God should have spoken up to defend his Son. How about during the triumphal entry to Jerusalem? Imagine the scene: Jesus enters the holy city as the Messiah riding on a donkey, and just when the citizens of Jerusalem question the whole affair by asking, "Who is this?" (Matt 21:10), God says, "This is my beloved Son. He pleases me. Listen to him!" Or, consider the moment when the chief priests and elders questioned Jesus's behavior in the temple. They challenged him by asking, "By what authority are you doing these things? . . . And who gave you this authority?" (21:23). Imagine how perfect the timing would have been if God had said in his heavenly, booming voice, "I did! This is my beloved Son. You better listen to him!" Or, what if God had spoken up during the trial of Jesus? What if the living God had answered the high priest, who tried to get Jesus to swear "under oath by the living God: Tell us if you are the Messiah, the Son of God" (26:63)? "Yes, he is!" I would *love* that part of the story if it had happened that way. But, it didn't. In fact, don't we all wish God had said *something* when Jesus was crucified? I couldn't think of a better time. Just as the heavens grow dark and the ground shakes, God booms: "This is my Son! I am well pleased with him!" But heaven was silent. God didn't say a thing. In fact, compared to what they did to his Son, I think Peter's suggestion to set up three tabernacles is rather innocuous.

---

22. Regarding the messianic implications of the heavenly proclamation, see above, 72–73.

But, then again, Jesus wasn't out to prove to his enemies that he was legitimate. His enemies would play a part in his messianic mission. But the future of the kingdom would rest in the hands of his disciples. They had to see what God was doing through their Messiah. They needed to understand what was going on; if building the tabernacles was a bad idea, what else were they confused about? So they asked questions as they headed down the mountain and returned to the "real world." They wanted to know why Elijah appeared on the mountain with Jesus. In the eschatological scheme of things, Elijah was supposed to come before the Messiah to prepare the way of the Lord—at least that's what the scribes taught (17:10). Yet, in light of what just happened it seemed as though his timing was off: Jesus "the Messiah" had appeared before Elijah came to earth.[23] So Jesus had to interpret for his disciples this strange sequence of events.

First of all, the scribes were right: Elijah was supposed to come first to "restore all things," that is, to prepare Israel for the day of divine visitation (v. 11). However, Israel didn't recognize him when he came. John the Baptizer was this "Elijah" forerunner. But rather than submit to his prophetic ministry, they rejected him. Instead of doing what he required, they did to him what they wanted. Therefore, John proved to be a prophetic witness to the Messiah. Ironically, by his suffering "Elijah" prepared the way of the Lord. This is because Jesus will suffer the same destiny (v. 12). If the disciples understood that John was Elijah (v. 13), then they would know the kind of Messiah Jesus came to be: one that would suffer and die at the hands of the leaders of Israel, which is something they had a hard time hearing. This is why God had to speak from heaven: "This is my Son, whom I love; with him I am well pleased. Listen to him!" Messianic suffering isn't evidence of divine displeasure. In fact, it's just the opposite; the cross would prove the love of God. The disciples had to get that right. Building a shelter on the mountain wouldn't bring messianic glory to earth. Rather, it would take a cross.

LIVE the Story

Have you noticed what's missing from this sneak preview of what will happen in the rest of the gospel story? It's the part where Jesus interprets the significance of his death—that he will die for the sins of the people. To be sure, that will come later; Jesus will set up a memorial meal to help his disciples understand that his death will establish a new covenant "for the forgiveness of sins"

23. Bruner, *Matthew*, 2:182.

(Matt 26:28).[24] Jesus will die for the people. Yet here, he makes no mention of his vicarious sacrifice. We might expect it, especially since he's trying to get Peter and the rest of the disciples to understand his messianic mission. I wonder if that would have been easier to take, if Jesus had given a more elaborate theological explanation of his upcoming death. Instead, he simply said, "It is necessary" (16:21). Not only that, he said it was necessary for his disciples to share the same fate, to die with him. That's why he warned them that if they were going to continue to follow him to Jerusalem, they'd better bring their own cross. This wasn't just a matter of dying for them. Jesus expected his disciples to die with him, for that would be the only way they would "save their life"—by losing it (vv. 24–26). Jesus would have no cheerleaders, disciples who would try to encourage him from the sidelines as they watched him die for their sins. "We're praying for you, Jesus. Lord God, please help Jesus carry his cross. God, give him strength to die for our sins. Come on, Jesus. You can do it. Don't give up. We're right here. If you make it to the end, we'll love you forever." No. Jesus will have no spectator disciples. "Whenever Christ calls us, his call leads us to death."[25]

But that's not the gospel we like to sing about. We prefer to sing songs about how Jesus died for us. Now, let me say plainly, that is a *very* good song. We should praise God for the cross of Jesus Christ: how he died for us, how he saved us, how he paid the price for our sins. But I've noticed we don't sing about the rest of the gospel, the part about how we are supposed to die with him and for him. We'll sing about the cross as the gift of God, as something that he has done *for* us. But we rarely sing about the cross as a gift of God done *to* us and *through* us. In fact, the next time you gather with other disciples to worship God, notice how often we praise God for the cross of Jesus as if we were spectators of the divine drama, played out for our benefit. We'll even rehearse the Passion play as a spectacle during Easter, watching the rejection, torture, and execution of Jesus from the comfort of our seats. Yet there's usually something missing from the script of these theatrical performances. As spectators, we never hear Jesus say: "Whoever wants to be my disciples must deny themselves and take up their cross and follow me" (16:24). It's something we don't like to sing about either.

I have these fond memories of growing up in church and attending week-long revival meetings. Typically, we'd have a guest preacher (whom we would

---

24. Davies and Allison overstate the case: "For Matthew, Jesus is not a substitute but a leader" (Matthew, 2:681). See the rebuttal by Bruner, *Matthew*, 2:140.

25. Bonhoeffer, *Discipleship*, 87. (The well-known translation is rather dynamic. Literally, Bonhoeffer wrote, "Jeder Ruf Christi führt in den Tod" ["Every call of Christ leads into death"]; ibid., 87n11.)

call the "evangelist") and a song leader take charge of nightly worship services. There always seemed to be an excitement in the room, a holy anticipation of God's presence. More members would show up for choir; more visitors would attend church. People who hadn't attended worship services in a while would come back. Warm embraces and smiling faces filled the sanctuary—this wasn't "church as usual." The song leader would direct the choir in a rousing number to kick off the service. Revivalist hymns were sung at a faster tempo, a pace that seemed to encourage everyone to sing loud. The song leader would coax even the most reluctant congregants to "make a joyful noise," no matter what it sounded like. We'd sing about heaven, about salvation, about the blood of Christ, about our shared faith. Then, after a solo performance worthy of an audition for *The Voice*, the evangelist would bring down the house with powerful sermons about the atoning death of Jesus. Invitational hymns were the climax of the service; we'd sing "Softly and Tenderly, Jesus is Calling," all the while praying for our friends to go forward and get saved. When that happened, there would be rejoicing like I'd never seen before. Great shouts of joyful celebration, a communion of souls, a nearly palpable sense that God was among us. It would feel like heaven had come to earth, just for a little while. The glory of the Lord would refresh our hearts and resurrect our spirits—so much so that, invariably, a brother or sister would testify to our agreement, "Wouldn't it be great if we could somehow capture this moment, hang on to this feeling? Sometimes, I wish we'd never have to leave." Then, the entire congregation would offer a hearty, "Amen!" We'd all linger for a time before heading home, back to reality.

The glory of those mountaintop experiences never lasted. They were never supposed to—although I didn't realize it at the time. We knew the euphoria wouldn't last; it never does. But we often wondered why the glory of the Lord's presence—lives changed, hearts renewed—always seemed to fade over time. Now I think I see why. We were singing about heaven, preaching about the atoning work of Jesus, celebrating what God has done and will do for us—all very good gifts. But we rarely sang about the necessity of carrying the cross of Jesus, the glory of sharing in his messianic suffering, the importance of losing our lives for the kingdom. We all wanted a glimpse of heaven on earth, trying to capture the glory. Perhaps that's why ministers identify with Peter, wanting to tarry on the mountain and revel in the glory. It's because we prefer the bright lights and celebrity. ("Let's sing one more verse!") Eventually, though, all disciples must follow Jesus down to the valley. Therefore, rather than bask in the glory of his fame, we should learn to sing all the verses about the "old, rugged cross"—not only to cling to it but to carry it, all the way to Jerusalem.

CHAPTER 25

Matthew 17:14–27

LISTEN to the Story

14When they came to the crowd, a man approached Jesus and knelt before him. 15"Lord, have mercy on my son," he said. "He has seizures and is suffering greatly. He often falls into the fire or into the water. 16I brought him to your disciples, but they could not heal him."

17"You unbelieving and perverse generation," Jesus replied, "how long shall I stay with you? How long shall I put up with you? Bring the boy here to me." 18Jesus rebuked the demon, and it came out of the boy, and he was healed at that moment.

19Then the disciples came to Jesus in private and asked, "Why couldn't we drive it out?"

20He replied, "Because you have so little faith. Truly I tell you, if you have faith as small as a mustard seed, you can say to this mountain, 'Move from here to there,' and it will move. Nothing will be impossible for you." [21]

22When they came together in Galilee, he said to them, "The Son of Man is going to be delivered into the hands of men. 23They will kill him, and on the third day he will be raised to life." And the disciples were filled with grief.

24After Jesus and his disciples arrived in Capernaum, the collectors of the two-drachma temple tax came to Peter and asked, "Doesn't your teacher pay the temple tax?"

25"Yes, he does," he replied.

When Peter came into the house, Jesus was the first to speak. "What do you think, Simon?" he asked. "From whom do the kings of the earth collect duty and taxes—from their own children or from others?"

26"From others," Peter answered.

"Then the children are exempt," Jesus said to him. 27"But so that we may not cause offense, go to the lake and throw out your line. Take the first fish you catch; open its mouth and you will find a four-drachma coin. Take it and give it to them for my tax and yours."

Listening to the Text in the Story: Exodus 30:11–16; 32:15–35; 38:26; Deuteronomy 32:5, 20; Psalm 4:2–3; Nehemiah 10:32–33.

Jesus knew his days were numbered and that his disciples had a lot to learn before he left them. Evidently, the end of his life was on his mind quite a bit at this time. He keeps reminding his disciples what will happen when they get to Jerusalem (Matt 17:22–23). He interprets current events in light of his imminent departure (we can certainly hear frustration in his voice as the grains of sand pass quickly through the hour glass): "You unbelieving and perverse generation . . . how long shall I stay with you? How long shall I put up with you?" (v. 17). So much to do, so much for them to learn, so little time. We would almost expect Jesus to lift his eyes to heaven and ask his heavenly Father for more time. That would be a reasonable request, wouldn't it? Don't we all wish we had more time to do what we need to do before the end? Think about Jesus. We certainly could find dozens of reasons why it would have been better for him to live much longer. Instead, his life was cut short. He would soon die in Jerusalem—a young man according to our standards. But if he had lived, say, another twenty years, imagine the lessons he could have taught his disciples (and us)—things that came up long after he was gone, like should the early church have supported the temple before it was destroyed? Speaking of the temple, when it was destroyed by the Romans, was that a sign of the end of the world? Regarding signs, if miracles don't happen, is it due to the lack of faith of the one asking or the one trying to perform the miracle? Since the kingdom of heaven coming to earth is subversive, many people are going to be offended. So, should Christ followers expect to offend others, or are we supposed to try to live at peace in the world? What about taxes? Since we don't belong to the kingdom of this world, should we have to pay taxes? (Oh, I'd like to hear Jesus answer that one! Did he answer? See Matt 22:15–22.)

During his brief life, Jesus taught and did numerous things not recorded in the four Gospels (John 21:25). Therefore, scholars wonder why certain stories made it into the Gospel authors' literary accounts of the life and ministry of Jesus Christ—especially episodes like the miracle of the coin in the fish's mouth and questions about the temple tax (Matt 17:24–27). With only so much papyrus to write on, our authors had to be incredibly selective in what they included in their Gospels. (All four Gospels are about the same length due to the capacity of the papyrus roll. Anything bigger would be difficult to read and too cumbersome to handle. In other words, the size of these "books" were the longest documents written at that time.)[1] When we run across a story like this one—a rather odd tale about temple taxes and fishing for coins—we can't help but question our Gospel writer's decision: Why did Matthew include *this* story—of all stories—and what was he trying to teach his readers?[2] Wasn't he being rather shortsighted, raising an issue that had become moot (most scholars think Matthew's Gospel was written after AD 70)?[3] Besides, in light of the impending tragedy hanging over the heads of Jesus and his disciples in Matthew's narrative world, isn't the question about paying the temple tax rather trivial? Doesn't Jesus have more important lessons to teach his followers, given the little time he has left?

Obviously, Matthew didn't think so. For you can't find a more important lesson to learn when following Jesus than the power of faith and the providence of God.

EXPLAIN the Story

The absence of Jesus is a salient feature of both episodes.[4] When Jesus was on the mountain with Peter, James, and John, the nine disciples were "left behind" and faced the prospect of healing a boy without Jesus being present (Matt 17:14–16). After Jesus and his disciples returned home to Capernaum, tax collectors expected Peter to answer for Jesus regarding the temple tax (v. 24). In both cases, neither the nine nor Peter made the decision to wait for Jesus. Rather, they took matters into their own hands: the nine gave it a go and tried to heal the boy; Peter spoke on Jesus's behalf (v. 25). It's not that they were acting presumptuously, taking liberties while Jesus was gone. Jesus had given all twelve of his disciples the authority to "heal every disease and sickness" as well as to "drive out demons" (10:1–8). Moreover, Jesus had conferred upon Peter a special role as leader of the church (16:17–19). The problem was that the absence of Jesus revealed what they were lacking: for the nine, it was faith; for Peter, it was understanding. In other words, in his absence Jesus would have expected the nine to heal the boy because he had already given them the power to do so (10:1). In the case of Peter, the Messiah would have expected him to understand why they would pay the temple tax because Peter

1. Bruce M. Metzger, *The Text of the New Testament*, 2nd ed. (Oxford: Oxford University Press, 1968), 5–6; also idem, *Manuscripts of the Greek Bible* (Oxford: Oxford University Press, 1981), 16–17.

2. The options seem to include: to serve as an object lesson on how to avoid offense, to confirm Jesus's divine status as God's Son, to confirm Jesus's disciples as his brothers, or to prepare the reader for Jesus's rejection of the temple (see Garland, *Reading Matthew*, 189–90).

3. The temple tax became a compulsory tax collected by the Romans after AD 70 (Keener, *Matthew*, 444).

4. Garland, *Reading Matthew*, 186.

had already shown that he understood the revelation of God (16:16). But neither was the case: in Jesus's absence, the nine exhibited "little faith," and Peter didn't understand—lessons that Matthew thought were important for a church to learn while waiting for the return of Christ.[5]

The Power of Faith

If Jesus never thought he would leave his disciples, then this wouldn't have been much of a problem. So the disciples tried to heal the sick boy and failed—no big deal. Sick people would always have Jesus to count on as the ultimate back-up plan. He was the go-to guy when the chips were down. With a long-term Messiah always waiting in the wings, we would expect Jesus to give an "attaboy" to the nine disciples for trying. "It's all right, guys. At least you did your best. Not to worry, I'm here. I'll take care of everything." But Jesus's impending death exacerbated the situation, making the moment even more stressful—both for Jesus and the disciples. When the father, who pleaded for his son's healing, reported what had happened, Jesus responded with a blistering retort: "You unbelieving and perverse generation!" (Matt 17:17). But, to whom was he speaking? His disciples,[6] the father, or the crowd of onlookers?[7]

At first, it appears Jesus was angry with his disciples. The father of a boy having "seizures" (v. 15; lit., "seized by the moon," *selēniazomai*; a "lunatic")[8] "tattled on" the nine disciples for their inability to cast out the demon—something they should have been able to do (10:1, 8). I wonder if the disciples thought to themselves, "Thanks a lot, fella. Was that really necessary?" In fact, one wonders if Jesus was offended by the comment. After all, their failure to do what Jesus trained them to do reflected poorly on him as well. Later, when the disciples asked him why they were unable to cast out the demon, Jesus said it was because of their "little faith" (v. 20)—his favorite nickname for the Twelve. "Little faith" is not the same as being "faithless," a term used to describe those who hindered Jesus from performing miracles (13:58). In fact, Jesus went on to say that the "little faith" of his disciples—small as a mustard seed—would be enough to move mountains (17:20).[9] Therefore, some think Jesus was criticizing the father for his lack of faith, shifting the blame from the inability of his disciples to the inadequate faith of the boy's father. Yet Jesus seemed to judge his entire generation, not

5. Luz, *Matthew*, 2:410, 418–20.

6. Nolland, *Matthew*, 712.

7. Luz, *Matthew*, 2:408.

8. Ibid., 2:407; different from epilepsy (France, *Matthew*, 659n10).

9. "The reason why 'mustard seed' faith can be so effective has to do not with the adequacy of faith but with the adequacy of God" (Nolland, *Matthew*, 716).

just the boy's father, for their faithlessness and perversity (v. 17).[10] In other words, Jesus acted like the entire situation—the disciples' inability and the father's unmet request—was indicative of a larger problem. The people of his generation, Israel, were "unbelieving and perverse." They should have repented but didn't, even though Jesus performed many miracles (11:20–24). Ironically, their lack of faith would block the miraculous (13:58)—a vicious cycle that was hard to break, even for the Messiah. So it does seem that Jesus blames everyone for the boy's condition, which was a significant problem because he knew he wouldn't be there much longer to say "bring the boy *here* to me" (17:17).

Jesus expected to change Israel, to lead them to repent and believe the good news that the Messiah was here and that it was time for the kingdom of heaven to come to earth. All it would take was a little faith—no bigger than a mustard seed—to move mountains and save the world. So, how would Jesus inspire repentance that leads to faith? By performing miracles. Yet, what happens when miracles are performed and the people don't repent? If the people don't repent, then they won't believe, and if they don't believe, then miracles won't happen, and if miracles don't happen, then they won't repent. How stubborn is the human heart! What was Jesus to do? How would he break the vicious cycle of unbelief?

The last time we came to this roundabout, Jesus challenged anyone who had ears to hear his invitation: "Come to me, all you who are weary and burdened, and I will give you rest" (11:28). Rather than give up and condemn Israel to hell, Jesus was confident that he would break the cycle of unbelief through his death. In veiled terms, he spoke of the cross as his "yoke," summoning his disciples to wear it well (vv. 29–30). Jesus knew the only way he would penetrate the stubborn heart of a "faithless and perverse" generation was to die for them. His yoke would "fit well," his burden would lighten their load. And so, facing the same dilemma, it shouldn't surprise us that Jesus turned to the subject of his death once again (17:22–23). In his absence he knew that all his disciples needed was a little faith (v. 20). Then the people would bring their troubles to his disciples, and the world would be saved because the Messiah was crucified and raised from the dead. To Jesus, that was the reason to have hope for the future. Yet for the Twelve, the idea that their Messiah would be killed only brought grief (v. 23). It is obvious at this stage of things they couldn't see how the cross of Christ would break the cycle of unbelief. But they would, one day. Until then, they still had a lot to learn.

10. France, *Matthew*, 660–61.

The Providence of God

As it is often said, two things are certain in this world: death and taxes. Imagine how Peter's head must have been spinning over the paradox of Jesus's imminent death and the demand to pay the temple tax. He's trying to process the impossible—Jesus is going to be killed—as the tax collectors hit him up for payment (Matt 17:24). Actually, they didn't come looking for Peter to pay the tax (he probably had enough money on him to take care of it—a little more than a day's wage).[11] Rather, they wanted to know if Jesus supported the temple tax. Such a question must have sounded a little ridiculous to Peter. Why worry about taxes when death is right around the door? Some hear a little presumption in Peter's voice when he responds, "Yes, he does" (v. 25), returning to Jesus to see if he was right (vv. 25–27). I wonder if Peter's simple response reveals a bit of appeasement: "Yeah, whatever." As he grieves over the imminent death of Jesus, taxes would have been the least of his concerns. Besides, even though supporting the temple was crucial to Israel's holiness, the legitimacy of a compulsory, annual tax was highly contested—even among the religious leaders. The Pharisees were for it. The Sadducees may have opposed it. The Essenes found the middle, supporting a once-in-a-lifetime payment.[12] What was Jesus's position on the subject? Well, the way they asked their question, the tax collectors assumed Jesus supported their effort.[13] Was it because he had paid it before? Yet, if that was the case, why would they ask the question? There seems to be some question about Jesus's loyalty to the temple, perhaps due to his statement that "something greater than the temple is here" (12:6).[14] Of course, if Jesus paid the temple tax, the issue would be settled. Jesus was for the temple tax. Or, was he?

We're about to discover that Jesus didn't believe in the politics of economic "purity," where money is supposed to indicate one's ideology. The Pharisees will try to put Jesus on the horns of a dilemma to force him to take a position on taxes (22:15–17). But Jesus will expose the hypocrisy of their question when he forces them to produce a Roman coin even as they stand in the sacred precincts of the temple (vv. 18–20). His famous line, "Give to Caesar what is Caesar's and to God what is God's" (v. 21), revealed that he refused to play their political game (a point we will explore later). But suffice it to say at this point that Jesus didn't believe money was a sign of political loyalty—a notion that eats away at the fabric of American politics. "If you are a 'true

11. For details regarding the temple tax—its basis, requirements, purpose, and the controversy surrounding compulsory payment—see Nolland, *Matthew*, 722–25.

12. For further discussion, see Luz, *Matthew*, 2:414–15.

13. The negative particle with the indicative verb expects an affirmative response.

14. France thinks the tax collectors asked because they anticipated Jesus wouldn't pay (*Matthew*, 666).

believer,' you'll give us your money." Instead, when it comes to money, Jesus operated according to a higher standard, one that places a premium on the value of people. Since heavenly power doesn't have a price, loyalty can't be bought. Therefore, how we treat others—even our political enemies—is the true indicator of our devotion to God. Imagine how messy that makes the politics of money when you love your enemies, even with your cash. The reverse is true as well; just because someone supports a "holy cause" doesn't necessarily mean that they share the cause's political ideology.

That's the gist of Jesus's lesson for Peter. Those in power excise taxes from the powerless (17:25).[15] Since they are sons of the kingdom—God's powerful reign on earth—they are exempt (v. 26).[16] Nevertheless, Jesus taught Peter that they were going to go ahead and pay the temple tax so as not to offend the collectors (v. 27). Jesus believed in giving power away—his death on the cross would be the ultimate proof of that. Of course, the tax collectors would interpret monetary payment as endorsement of their cause. But, the *way* a Messiah and a fisherman would "cough up the money" for the tax would tell another story—an inside joke between them and us.

I used to be a little ashamed of this story. It seemed so random, so odd, so unnecessary, even a bit glib. Jesus telling Peter to catch a fish, only to discover a coin in its mouth for the exact amount they owed for the compulsory temple tax (v. 27), sounded weird to my young-adult, sensible, modern ears. Yet now I find it whimsically endearing—perhaps because I no longer have this youthful compulsion to make sense of everything. The older I get, the more I'm drawn to the mysterious. And this is one strange, hard-to-understand story—one that seems to intrigue more than it explains. Why did Jesus choose such an odd way to pay the temple tax? Consider how much it would help if we knew the look on Jesus's face when he gave Peter the directive. Was Jesus smirking when he predicted the miracle? Grinning from ear to ear, eyes dancing with excitement? If he were, then we might think Jesus was being somewhat subversive, refusing to dip into their moneybag to pay the tax. Or, was he annoyed by the whole thing, rolling his eyes in disgust? This was no big deal; just go fishing, and you'll take care of the matter. Moreover, what did Peter do? Did he walk immediately out the door, grab a fishing pole, and head

---

15. Since Jesus used a "secular" analogy, it could be inferred that a Roman tax was being levied; see Carter, *Matthew and Empire*, 135–40, as well as the discussion in Davies and Allison, *Matthew*, 2:738–41.

16. One wonders why Jesus didn't press the issue even further by declaring, "*We* should be the ones collecting taxes!" But that would encourage simony among those who are blind to the power of metaphor. Some people don't recognize a good analogy when they see one—especially when it comes to money. Indeed, we have a hard time thinking clearly about money because it is a very powerful thing.

for the lake? Did Peter catch the fish with the coin in its mouth?[17] And, having done so, would he march right up to the tax collectors and triumphantly place the fishy coin in their hands? "Whew, Peter. I know you're a fisherman, but this coin stinks. Where did you get it?" "You'd never believe me if I told you."

Indeed, this story is hard to believe, but the lesson it teaches is fairly clear. Even Jesus knew we would need to count on the providence of God when it comes to meeting our financial responsibilities. "So, they want their temple tax, huh? Okay, let's count on God to make it happen. It will be serendipitously wonderful!"[18] Indeed, given some of the amazing stories I've heard about how God has supplied money to Christ followers trying to do what is right, catching a fish with a coin in its mouth seems like small potatoes—a simple fishing tale of God's marvelous concern for every little thing, even paying taxes. It takes a big God to pull off such a small miracle. Perhaps we should say, then, that the only thing certain in this world is the providence of God.

LIVE the Story

Time and money are two things we can never get enough of; death and taxes are two certainties we can't escape. Knowing that we only have so much time and so little money, in the last ten years it has become fashionable to speak of a *bucket list*—things people want to do before they die ("kick the bucket"). It sounds like a worthy exercise, trying to seize the day and not waste our lives on things that don't matter. It's easy to get trapped in the routine of life, working for the weekends and paying taxes. Death hangs over all our heads like a prison sentence. Adventuresome types appear to negotiate our common death threat in a more appealing fashion, always ready to throw caution to the wind and take a hike when it strikes them. Planners, on the other hand, will often wring their hands over trivial matters, wondering whether they've managed their time wisely, hoping they've prepared for an uncertain future. Whether it was the thrill seekers living large or the planners sick of the routine, the bucket list became a cultural meme, coaxing everyone to take inventory of our brief lives. The idea of having a Rip-van-Winkle epiphany, awaking on our deathbed from a long, sleepy life, haunted us. Coming to the end of our time on earth, having to face the nightmarish question of regret—"If I had

---

17. France has his doubts, preferring to speak of Jesus's "prediction" as a "playful comment . . . never intended to be taken literally" (*Matthew*, 667). Instead, "[It should be read] as an ironical comment on their lack of resources" (ibid., 671).

18. Carter writes, "The story not only emphasizes God's sovereignty over creation, but also over the tax" (*Matthew and Empire*, 142).

it to do all over again, what would I change?"—scared us to death. Or, more accurately, it scared us to life, making us swear to ourselves that we would try to cram everything we could—every desirable experience, every beautiful scene—into our vapid existence. Indeed, in the midst of our existential angst, it became virtuous to speak openly of our bucket list, comparing notes with one another, swapping ideas on how to live life to the fullest.

Did Jesus have a bucket list? What would be on his list of things to do before he died? See the Seven Wonders of the Ancient World? Visit the glorious city of Rome? Experience the thrill of watching gladiators fight to the death? Or would his bucket list include more sublime goals, like spending more time with family, taking in the beauty of sunsets, or soaking up every moment around a campfire with good food, good friends, and good conversation? More than anyone else, Jesus knew his days were numbered; he only had so much time on earth to live life to the fullest. If there was ever a man who should have had a list of things he wanted to do before he "kicked the bucket," it was Jesus. Yet, somehow we know Jesus would never have a bucket list. In fact, it sounds rather sacrilegious to think that he did—and that should tell us something.

To be sure, Jesus had things to do before he died, like teaching his disciples how to have faith in God. In his absence he knew faith would be the key to living life to the fullest in the kingdom of God. Surprisingly, when his disciples lacked faith, he didn't give them a lengthy sermon, explaining how to keep faith. He simply pointed to a mustard seed and said, "This much faith will do the trick." When the tax collectors came knocking at his door (they always show up, don't they?), he didn't start a theological debate about the politics of money. He simply said to Peter, "Why don't you go fishing and see what God provides?" Regardless of the circumstances, Jesus tried to get his disciples to rest in the assurance that God will take care of us. Whether we are trying to heal the sick or having to pay taxes, all we need to do is have faith in him. It sounds too simple to be true, but it is just that simple. In fact, if Jesus had a bucket list, there would be only one thing on it—what he would expect any of us to do before we die: "Have faith in God."

Besides, why would we try to visit the Seven Wonders of the World—ancient or modern—before we die? We will see it *all* in the resurrection because Jesus died and was raised from the dead.

Today is March 18. Tax day is right around the corner. I think I'll go fishing. There's no telling what I will catch.

CHAPTER 26

Matthew 18:1–35

LISTEN to the Story

[1]At that time the disciples came to Jesus and asked, "Who, then, is the
greatest in the kingdom of heaven?"
[2]He called a little child to him, and placed the child among them.
[3]And he said: "Truly I tell you, unless you change and become like
little children, you will never enter the kingdom of heaven. [4]Therefore,
whoever takes the lowly position of this child is the greatest in the king-
dom of heaven. [5]And whoever welcomes one such child in my name
welcomes me.
[6]"If anyone causes one of these little ones—those who believe in
me—to stumble, it would be better for them to have a large millstone
hung around their neck and to be drowned in the depths of the sea. [7]Woe
to the world because of the things that cause people to stumble! Such
things must come, but woe to the person through whom they come! [8]If
your hand or your foot causes you to stumble, cut it off and throw it
away. It is better for you to enter life maimed or crippled than to have
two hands or two feet and be thrown into eternal fire. [9]And if your eye
causes you to stumble, gouge it out and throw it away. It is better for you
to enter life with one eye than to have two eyes and be thrown into the
fire of hell.
[10]"See that you do not despise one of these little ones. For I tell you
that their angels in heaven always see the face of my Father in heaven. [11]
[12]"What do you think? If a man owns a hundred sheep, and one of
them wanders away, will he not leave the ninety-nine on the hills and go
to look for the one that wandered off? [13]And if he finds it, truly I tell you,
he is happier about that one sheep than about the ninety-nine that did not
wander off. [14]In the same way your Father in heaven is not willing that any
of these little ones should perish.
[15]"If your brother or sister sins, go and point out their fault, just
between the two of you. If they listen to you, you have won them over.

16 But if they will not listen, take one or two others along, so that 'every matter may be established by the testimony of two or three witnesses.' 17 If they still refuse to listen, tell it to the church; and if they refuse to listen even to the church, treat them as you would a pagan or a tax collector.

18 "Truly I tell you, whatever you bind on earth will be bound in heaven, and whatever you loose on earth will be loosed in heaven.

19 "Again, truly I tell you that if two of you on earth agree about anything they ask for, it will be done for them by my Father in heaven. 20 For where two or three gather in my name, there am I with them."

21 Then Peter came to Jesus and asked, "Lord, how many times shall I forgive my brother or sister who sins against me? Up to seven times?"

22 Jesus answered, "I tell you, not seven times, but seventy-seven times.

23 "Therefore, the kingdom of heaven is like a king who wanted to settle accounts with his servants. 24 As he began the settlement, a man who owed him ten thousand bags of gold was brought to him. 25 Since he was not able to pay, the master ordered that he and his wife and his children and all that he had be sold to repay the debt.

26 "At this the servant fell on his knees before him. 'Be patient with me,' he begged, 'and I will pay back everything.' 27 The servant's master took pity on him, canceled the debt and let him go.

28 "But when that servant went out, he found one of his fellow servants who owed him a hundred silver coins. He grabbed him and began to choke him. 'Pay back what you owe me!' he demanded.

29 "His fellow servant fell to his knees and begged him, 'Be patient with me, and I will pay it back.'

30 "But he refused. Instead, he went off and had the man thrown into prison until he could pay the debt. 31 When the other servants saw what had happened, they were outraged and went and told their master everything that had happened.

32 "Then the master called the servant in. 'You wicked servant,' he said, 'I canceled all that debt of yours because you begged me to. 33 Shouldn't you have had mercy on your fellow servant just as I had on you?' 34 In anger his master handed him over to the jailers to be tortured, until he should pay back all he owed.

35 "This is how my heavenly Father will treat each of you unless you forgive your brother or sister from your heart."

Listening to the Text in the Story: Genesis 4:15, 24; 48:16; Leviticus 19:17; 25:39–55; 26:18, 21, 23–24, 27–28; Deuteronomy 19:15–21; 2 Kings 4:1–7; Nehemiah 5:1–12; Psalms 34:7; Ecclesiastes 4:12; Ezekiel 34:1–31; Zechariah 2:10–11.

The disciples had good reasons to ask questions of Jesus. He did so many marvelous things, taught so many challenging lessons that it's no wonder the Twelve kept coming to him, looking for answers. Their questions make a lot of sense; if we had been there, we probably would have asked the same things:

"What kind of man is this?" (Matt 8:27)
"Why do you speak to the people in parables?" (13:10)
"Do you know that the Pharisees were offended when they heard this?" (15:12)
"Where could we get enough bread in this remote place to feed such a crowd?" (15:33)
"Why couldn't we drive it out?" (17:19)
"*Who, then, is the greatest in the kingdom of heaven?*" (18:1, emphasis added)
"Lord, how many times shall I forgive my brother or sister who sins against me? Up to seven times?" (18:21)
"Who then can be saved?" (19:25)
"How did the fig tree wither so quickly?" (21:20)
"When will this happen, and what will be the sign of your coming and of the end of the age?" (24:3)
"Why this waste?" (26:8)
"Where do you want us to make preparations for you to eat the Passover?" (26:17)
"Surely you don't mean me, Lord?" (26:22)
"Surely you don't mean me, Rabbi?" (26:25)[1]

Yet, of the fourteen questions the Twelve disciples asked Jesus, the sixth, "Who, then, is the greatest in the kingdom of heaven?" (18:1), is the most difficult to figure out why they asked it. The immediate context makes sense of all the rest. Jesus calmed the sea, so they ask, "What kind of man is this?" The nine were unable to exorcize the demon, so they wanted to know, "Why couldn't we drive it out?" Jesus predicted the destruction of the temple, so the disciples asked, "When?" Jesus predicted that one of his disciples would

1. For those looking for a sermon series or a Bible-study topic, exploring Matthew's version of "questions disciples ask" (who, what, when, where, why, how) might prove to be very fruitful.

betray him, so they wanted to know, "Who?" Likewise, when they asked, "Who is the greatest in the kingdom of heaven?" the disciples seemed to have been prompted by what Jesus said or did—they introduced their question with an inferential conjunction: "Who, *then*, is the greatest in the kingdom of heaven?" Something triggered their question. Was it Jesus's preferential treatment of Simon Peter? Was it the inability of the nine to cast out the demon? Was it because Jesus took only three disciples to witness the transfiguration?[2] Or, did their question have more to do with Jesus's prediction that he would be executed once they got to Jerusalem?[3] Whatever the reason, the answer should have been obvious (one that commentators seem to overlook[4]). Who is the greatest in the kingdom of heaven? The Messiah, of course. They knew that. So, why did they ask?

It's because their question was informed by the honor game. Honor, the social approval of your group, was the highest good, marking the greatest individuals. Some people automatically received honor due to their position: kings, priests, fathers. Others had to acquire honor by claiming it; if they measured up to their claim, the people would bestow honor on them.[5] Of course, anyone could claim to be the Messiah, the "anointed one" of God. But, could their actions back it up? That's why the Gospels are filled with reactions from the crowd to what Jesus said and did. They're bestowing honor on him, saying they had never seen anything like it—even wondering whether Jesus could be the "Son of David" (Matt 7:28–29; 9:8, 33; 12:23). Of course, Jesus didn't go around claiming he was the Messiah. He only admitted that to his disciples, albeit with a caveat: he would be the kind of Messiah that would be dishonored by Jerusalem, rejected, betrayed, even executed. For the kingdom of heaven to come to earth, messianic suffering (shame) must precede messianic glory (honor). As God's Son, Jesus knew he would be stripped of every privilege and all power—the greatest would become the least—so that the least could become the greatest. As we've already seen, however, the Twelve had a hard time accepting the downward mobility that was required to establish the kingdom of heaven on earth. In fact, the last time Jesus predicted his death in Jerusalem, the disciples "were filled with grief" (17:23).

So, if the Messiah was destined to die when he came to Jerusalem to claim David's throne—and even some of the disciples would die before they witnessed the "Son of Man coming in his kingdom" (16:28)—then the question

2. See Turner, *Matthew*, 434–35.

3. France, *Matthew*, 675.

4. Perhaps due to the influence of Mark and Luke, who couch the question in terms of the Twelve arguing among themselves as to who was the greatest (Mark 9:33–34; Luke 9:46).

5. See Malina, *New Testament World*, 27–48.

remained: Who will be honored as the greatest? It certainly won't be Jesus; he will be humiliated, shunned, shamed, and rejected. I think that's the significance of the inferential conjunction. "Okay, Jesus. In light of everything you've said recently—about your dying and some of us surviving long enough to see the kingdom—we want to know: Who's going to make it? Obviously, whoever it is will be 'greater' than the rest of us. So, who is it? Who is the greatest in the kingdom of heaven?" Jesus seemed to give the answer we would expect because, in the kingdom of heaven, the honor game is turned upside down: "It's me; it could be you. Don't you see? Look at this child. Only by humbling yourself like a child will anyone participate in the kingdom of God. I'll be the first to do it, but you will need to humble yourselves too. Remember what I said about losing your life and bringing your cross? You must follow me to enter the kingdom. You need to change the way you're thinking about this; you need to become like a child again. If you do, you'll already know who is the greatest in the kingdom: it's the one who becomes a child and welcomes a child. Why? Because in my absence, whoever welcomes a child is really welcoming me—the greatest who became the least so that the least could become the greatest" (my paraphrase of 18:2–5).

To be sure, the prospect of becoming a child again wasn't very appealing to Jesus's disciples. After all, they came from the lower ranks of society: fishermen, tax collectors, Galileans. They had spent a lifetime of "humbling themselves" in the presence of the more powerful, honorable people of Israel. They were used to it. But when Jesus came and chose *them* to be his disciples, they finally got a taste of what it felt like to be on top of the world. They probably enjoyed the prestige of following such a popular, powerful man. To lose it all, to start all over again—especially to regress so far as to become a child—must have sounded like punishment to them. Of course, we miss the significance of their dilemma because we idealize childhood, the sweet time of innocence, the perfect picture of a carefree life. To become young again and live out our childhood fantasies is held up in our culture as a good thing. But in the first-century world, children were treated like slaves—the bottom rung of the ladder of honor—completely dependent upon others, having no status of their own, vulnerable. Having to become a child again would be a bad thing, a slavish existence. In fact, the Greek word Matthew uses for the child that Jesus put forward before his disciples as an object lesson, *paidion* (18:2), could also be translated as "slave."[6] You would think that image would be indelibly imprinted on the minds of the disciples, a visual they could always recall when they were tempted to think more highly of themselves than they should: "In the kingdom, we are nothing

6. Luz, *Matthew*, 2:428.

more than childlike slaves—and that's a good thing."[7] Evidently, however, it wasn't enough because Jesus continued to explain to the Twelve what it should look like when disciples treat each other like children.

EXPLAIN the Story

Once again, Jesus compares his mission (and therefore, the mission of his disciples) to a shepherd who's out to reclaim and restore the lost sheep of Israel (Matt 9:36; 10:6; 18:12–13). But this time when he gives advice to his disciples, he focuses not so much on how they will be treated by the world (10:11–31) but on how they should treat each other (18:6–20).[8] As before, Jesus assumes his disciples will need to take extreme measures to deal with the dramatic situations they will face. When it comes to gathering lost sheep, Jesus anticipates a bumpy ride. Therefore, the pendulum of his advice tends to move between two extremes: mercy and judgment. One minute Jesus talks about the relentless pursuit of going after the lost sheep; the next minute he seems to say that they'll need to kick out those who go astray. He tells Peter that true forgiveness doesn't count transgressions; then he seems to teach the church, "Three strikes and you're out." At first he tells his disciples to become like children; then it's as if he says, "Act like an adult and take responsibility for your behavior—cut off your hand if you need to." To put it bluntly, it seems like Jesus can't make up his mind. Mercy or judgment? Are we supposed to welcome tax collectors and sinners or excommunicate them?

Scholars find a structure to this chapter to see how these competing ideas (mercy and judgment) are worked out. To some, the household theme expressed in familial terms helps us see how mercy and judgment relate, distinguishing insiders (children, little ones, brothers, slaves) from outsiders (stumbling blocks, tax collectors/gentiles, the unforgivers).[9] To others, the symmetrical arrangement of the discourse sets Jesus's teaching on parallel tracks (question, teaching, warning, parable) that hold together the mercy and judgment of God.[10] However we outline the material, it seems as though Jesus was relying upon a narrative to undergird his teaching. That is, he's counting on a common story to carry his advice on how to show mercy and require justice at the same time; it is a narrative that functions like prophecy, a this-is-what-you-do-because-this-is-the-way-the-kingdom-overcomes-the-world piece of advice that is timeless and timely. Here are the highlights of the narrative template:

7. Bruner notes that God favors insignificant people (*Matthew*, 2:218).
8. Luz, *Matthew*, 2:478.
9. Turner, *Matthew*, 432.
10. Luz, *Matthew*, 2:422–23.

1. We live in a fallen world filled with scandalous people.
2. The kingdom of heaven overcomes the world when disciples act like children.
3. Kingdom children will be vulnerable to scandalous sinners.
4. Therefore, some kingdom children will be led astray to sin.
5. Scandalous sinners are doomed to hell unless they change their ways.
6. Kingdom children who have been scandalized need to be recovered like lost sheep.
7. Kingdom children must pursue these sheep who have lost their way, and bring them home.
8. The way lost sheep are recovered is to expose sin for what it is: first between the two brothers/sisters/sheep, then at least three brothers/sisters/sheep, and finally the whole family/flock. If the lost sheep listens, they'll come back home.
9. Sometimes lost sheep won't listen.
10. In that case, consider lost sheep who won't listen as if they were tax collectors and gentiles.
11. Always forgive the lost sheep because God always forgives his sheep.
12. God gets angry when sheep don't forgive other sheep. Those who don't show the mercy of forgiveness will be judged by God.

There are many gaps in the narrative, details that are lacking to help us make sense of the whole story. For example, what are the scandalous things that cause people to stumble? Are they really bad sins, or would any sin qualify? Was Jesus's warning about taking drastic measures (cutting off limbs) to correct scandalous behavior directed to his disciples or to unbelievers? What is the proof that the brother or sister listens to correction? Is it an act of contrition, changed behavior, or mental assent? What does it mean to treat the brother or sister who won't listen to the church as if they were a tax collector and a gentile? Excommunication? If so, wasn't Jesus giving his disciples a mixed message since he welcomed tax collectors and gentiles? Was Jesus talking about an official ruling of the church regarding the unrepentant sinner, barring (or "binding"; see Matt 18:18) them from heaven? Furthermore, was Jesus teaching in his parable of the large debt that disciples who don't forgive others will be sent to hell?[11] The more Jesus tried to explain what it would mean for his disciples to become like children, the more questions we have about his teaching. Indeed, answering the question, "Who, then, is the greatest in the kingdom of heaven?" by pointing to a child seems to create more problems than it solves—which says more about us than it does about Jesus.

11. For a history of interpretation, see Luz, *Matthew*, 2:450–51.

We don't know what it means to humble ourselves like children. Furthermore, most of us are very offended when we are treated like children. And there's the rub; becoming a child will mean being treated like one. That's when mercy ("You need help") feels like judgment ("Who do you think you are?"). Here's the problem and why we have a hard time making sense of Jesus's teaching: we really don't know how to treat one another like children.[12]

What God Wants

Jesus makes two comments that may seem ancillary to his main point about recovering lost sheep and always extending forgiveness. Yet these two claims actually anchor the entire discourse. First, God is unwilling that any of "these little ones" perish (Matt 18:14). Second, God will treat us like we treat others—an idea Jesus had already taught his disciples (6:14–15; 7:2). It makes God angry when "little ones" who "believe in" Jesus are harmed (18:6). Those who cause "little ones" to stumble are headed straight for hell. The picture of a person who's thrown into the sea wearing a millstone as a necklace, weighing them down to the bottom, reveals a punishment from which they will not escape (v. 6).[13] Even though the world is filled with people like that (v. 7)—destined for hell because they cause little ones to stumble—God didn't intend for things to be so bad. Hell is the proof and is meant to be a deterrent to evil. So, the scandalous sinner should be alarmed enough to alter their fate; they can take drastic measures to stop what they're doing, thereby averting hell (vv. 8–9).[14] And what about the "little one" who stumbled, led astray by the scandalous sinner? Is he or she equally doomed? Not at all. These "little ones" have angels in heaven who watch over them (v. 10). Not only that, God has shepherds on earth to save the lost sheep who wander from the fold (vv. 12–13). Our "heavenly Father" goes to great lengths to watch over the "little ones" who believe in Jesus (v. 14).

So, how is the one lost sheep recovered? That's what vv. 15–20 are about. Jesus was giving instructions to his disciples on how "little ones" rescue other "little ones," how sheep can act like shepherds, how kingdom children should treat other kingdom children. Notice in his parable of the lost sheep that Jesus didn't anticipate a massive problem, where huge numbers of sheep wander away and need to be saved. I think that's significant; only 1 percent of the sheep may get lost every now and then. So, when he presents the scenario, "If your brother or sister sins," Jesus was anticipating an unusual, highly irregular situation—which should give the watchdogs among us, overzealous with their charge to

12. Luz writes: "Those who are 'low' like a child have the ability to live in community" (*Matthew*, 2:429).

13. Davies and Allison, *Matthew*, 2:763.

14. Keener, *Matthew*, 450.

straighten out their sinful brothers or sisters, pause. What Jesus envisioned was an extreme situation, not a daily occurrence. Furthermore, notice how Jesus shifted terms, from "little ones" and sheep to "brother or sister," dealing with one another as family (vv. 14–15). He didn't use paternal imagery: "Now, the adults among you, confront your children." Nor did he continue with the sheep metaphor: "When you shepherds see one of your flock wander away, go fetch it." No. Jesus put the mutual care for one another in familial terms, a recovery society among equals, children treating one another like children. Therefore, this isn't advice given to those who are "right" correcting those who are "wrong," to those who are "righteous" requiring repentance of the "sinners." Jesus was teaching those who have humbled themselves as "little ones" how to recover others who have humbled themselves as "little ones." This is about a *child* helping another *child*, a brother or sister restoring another brother or sister.

Jesus worked with the assumption that sin is destructive, not only to the individual but to the entire church.[15] Therefore, when a brother or sister has been offended by the world, has lost their way, has wandered from the fold of God, and is continuing in sin, then the rest of the family of God's children must go to the offended and remind them of what sin does to all of us. I think that's why Jesus set up a three-step process for recovering the lost sheep. It's not about one believer confronting another believer about private sin: "I know what you're doing and you better stop it." Then, when the sinner refuses to repent, the crusader finds two or three to gang up on the recalcitrant member to force him or her to change their ways. If that doesn't work, then they take the matter to the church to excommunicate the rebel. That scenario assumes much more than what Jesus actually said. Let's pay careful attention to his well-chosen words.

First, notice how Jesus characterizes the correct response of the sinner. He or she "listens." Jesus didn't say "repents" or "grieves over their sin" or "changes their ways" or "obeys"[16] or even "promises never to do it again." Jesus simply says that the desirable response from the lost sheep is this: he or she "listens." That's it. I find that telling—noticing what Jesus *didn't* say—for we certainly should have expected a more definitive response when exercising what some have called "church discipline." Second, notice how Jesus anticipated a positive response, that is, the brother or sister would listen to what was discussed (v. 15).[17] Why does Jesus assume they will listen? I think it has to do with the context of the conversation. Once again, Jesus is vague about details.

15. Luz, *Matthew*, 2:451.

16. Some commentators suggest that *akouō* here implies obedience (Davies and Allison, *Matthew*, 2:783). However, there were several stronger words that Matthew could have used to express that idea; e.g., *hypakouō* or even *hypotassō*.

17. Turner, *Matthew*, 445.

He didn't prescribe what to say, such as "confront him in his sin" or "show her how wrong she is" or "warn him that if he keeps sinning, he's only hurting himself." Rather, Jesus simply says, "Point out their fault" (v. 15, *elenxon auton*) in *private*. That's the key, especially in an honor/shame culture. The confronter isn't trying to mount a case against their brother or sister, trying to shame them into submission or hoping to convince others of their shameful behavior.[18] Instead, Jesus works with the assumption that the sin is obvious, one that merely needs to be pointed out, brought to light, exposed for what it is. That's why he assumes the brother or sister will listen. Kingdom children know how destructive sin is. Third, it's apparent that this "sin" isn't a matter of interpretation. That is, Jesus assumes the sin is common to all, one that everyone would recognize: first the brother or sister, then two more brothers/sisters, finally the entire church. But more than that, Jesus didn't give this three-step procedure to convince the lost sheep of their sin. Rather, Jesus assumes the corporate reality of sin. Sin affects everyone, the whole body. This isn't a personal matter between two brothers or sisters. Rather, the welfare of the entire church is at stake—which is a hard concept for us to accept today. In our individualistic culture, sin is privatized, a personal matter. We think that what we do with our own lives is only our business. In the first-century world, such an isolated approach to life was hypocritical. No person was an island; everyone knew they needed others to make it in the world—especially one filled with all kinds of evil. Only fools believed their behavior affected no one else.

Yet, of all the places where one should take a minimalist approach to Jesus's words, v. 17 seems to have had the opposite effect, leading many interpreters to go way beyond what Jesus said. I marvel over how many people assume the fourth step in dealing with a brother or sister who doesn't listen to the church is to kick him or her out. That's *not* what Jesus said. Commentators use words like "excommunication" and "discipline," but Jesus didn't.[19] Rather, he simply said, "Let him be to you [singular][20] as a tax collector and a gentile" (v. 17, my translation). Note that first of all, Jesus didn't say, "Let him be to you [plural], the church, as a tax collector and a gentile"—as if the church needed to make some kind of official decision.[21] Rather, throughout his instruction Jesus was telling *one* disciple what to do to reclaim *his* or *her* brother or sister who is sinning.[22] So, what would it mean for a disciple to treat their brother or sister "like a tax collector [I wonder if Matthew winced when he heard it] and a

18. Ibid.

19. Scholars try to mollify the situation and soften the blow: "For Matthew, excommunication, when it comes, will in truth be self-imposed exile" (Davies and Allison, *Matthew*, 2:804).

20. France, *Matthew*, 691.

21. Contra Luz, *Matthew*, 2:452–54.

22. So also France, *Matthew*, 673.

gentile" because they refuse to listen to the church and continue in sin? Let's think about *why* Jesus may have used these two particular groups of people—not prostitutes, thieves, murderers or even hypocrites—to characterize the brother or sister who persists in their sin. (I would have expected Jesus to say, "He's a hypocrite; treat him like one.") There was nothing in the law that made collecting taxes a sin. Nevertheless, tax collectors were considered shameful traitors to the Jews. Gentiles, on the other hand, were born pagans; that's just who they are. Therefore, no amount of "shaming" or "shunning" would lead a tax collector or a gentile to "humble themselves" and change their ways. You can't make a tax collector feel sorry for collecting taxes. You can't make a gentile apologize for being a gentile. And you can't make a brother or sister listen when they refuse to humble themselves like a child. Children take correction; adults don't. So, if a brother or sister won't humble themselves like a child—the very thing it takes to "enter the kingdom of heaven"—then they are acting like a shameless tax collector or gentile.[23]

So, does that mean the brother or sister washes their hands of the situation? After all, they've done their job, pointed out the sin of the brother or sister, took the necessary steps to reclaim them as a lost sheep. You can't force someone to humble themselves like a child so that they may enter the kingdom. Even Jesus knew that. How, then, did Jesus deal with recalcitrant "lost-sheep" tax collectors or pagan gentiles who weren't even in the fold to begin with? He ate with them when he was invited to their table (9:10–13). He helped them when they asked for it (8:5–13; 15:21–28). In other words, he showed them the unending mercy of God.[24] In fact, when the Pharisees objected to his approach when dealing with unrepentant Jewish sinners, Jesus told those self-righteous holiness-enforcers that they needed to learn a lesson from Hosea: "Go and learn what this means: 'I desire mercy, not sacrifice'" (Matt 9:13). We should do the same. To treat lost sheep like tax collectors and gentiles means to show them mercy, no matter what they've done, no matter how many times they stray. This isn't, "Three strikes and you're out." Indeed, according to Jesus mercy never stops to count.

What God Hates

When Jesus told stories about God, he pictured his heavenly Father as a landowner (Matt 13:27; 20:1; 21:33), a farmer (21:28), a shepherd (18:12), a king (18:23; 22:2), or the wealthy head of a household (25:14). In all these stories, God get angry twice. One time he says something harsh: "You wicked,

23. Garland thinks the lost sheep then needs to be evangelized (*Reading Matthew*, 195).

24. According to Chrysostom, this means loving them as our enemies (*Homilies*, 374–75); so also Nolland, *Matthew*, 748.

lazy servant!" (25:26); yet, he's not described as being angry. In fact, most of the time God acts in a fairly cool and calm fashion even though he is the victim of terrible injustices. Only twice does he gets angry, two things that evoke the wrath of God. Interestingly, it happens when God appears as a king. First, the king gets angry when a forgiven slave doesn't forgive a fellow slave (18:32–34). Second, the "king was enraged" when those invited to his banquet table refused to come (22:7). That's it. In the story world of Jesus's parables, the only two things that make God angry are (1) when he extends mercy and we reject it or (2) when we refuse to pass it on to others. Ironically, God's wrath shows up when Jesus was trying to teach lessons about his mercy. The first lesson on God's wrath would be offered later as a warning to the people of Jerusalem (22:1–14). The second lesson was given in response to Peter's question: "Lord, how many times shall I forgive my brother or sister who sins against me? Up to seven times?" (18:21). In these parables, we see how mercy and judgment are inextricably related.

When Jesus responds to Peter by saying, "I tell you, not seven times, but seventy-seven times" (v. 22), we would expect Jesus to tell a parable about forgiving someone many, many times.[25] But, that's not what he does. Instead, Jesus tells the story of forgiveness as a singular act—canceling a huge debt all at once (vv. 23–34). Once again, Jesus speaks of sin and forgiveness in economic terms, like he did during the Sermon on the Mount (6:12–15). The point of the story is the same as the Lord's Prayer: God expects those who have been forgiven much to forgive others. When we don't, we learn here that it makes him angry. In the parable, the "king" takes back what he did, no longer canceling the debt but making the unmerciful person pay what he owes. Of course, what makes that scenario so difficult to comprehend is the size of the debt owed to God, the King. It would take more than a lifetime to pay back "ten thousand bags of gold" (v. 24).[26] Was this supposed to picture an eternal punishment, a debt that could never be repaid?[27] Or, instead of an eschatological lesson about the afterlife, did Jesus offer his fictional story as a cautionary tale—much like his previous warnings about cutting off limbs or plucking out eyes to keep from going to hell (vv. 8–9)? You better forgive or

---

25. According to Augustine, the reason Jesus says we must forgive seventy-seven times is because that is the number of generations listed in Luke's genealogy (Luke 3:23–38), i.e., all the sins of humanity are summed up in seventy-seven generations. "So then if no generation was omitted, there is no exception of any trespass that ought not to be forgiven. For therefore did he reckon up his seventy-seven generations, which number the Lord mentioned as to the forgiveness of sins; since he begins to reckon from the baptism, where all sins are remitted" (Manlio Simonetti, ed., *Matthew 14–28*, ACCS 1B [Downers Grove, IL: InterVarsity Press, 2002], 83).

26. Keener, *Matthew*, 458–59.

27. The highest number (ten thousand) and the heaviest weight (talent) were used to express an immeasurable debt (Davies and Allison, *Matthew*, 2:798).

there's hell to pay.[28] However we read it, the parable makes it clear as to what makes God angry. Surprisingly, it's not the huge amount of debt someone owes. We would think that's when the king should have been enraged, when he discovered how much the slave owed him. But that's not the case. God wasn't angry over the debt. (Think of what that means, for we often assume that God is *angry* with us over our sin.) To be sure, there came a day of reckoning, when it came time to pay back the debt. And when the slave begged the king to give him time to pay it off (a ridiculous request—he could never repay the debt!), the king had mercy on the slave and canceled the massive debt (vv. 26–27). None of that—neither the huge debt nor the slave promising to do what he could never do—made the king angry. Rather, what infuriated the king is when the slave then refused to "do to others what had been done to him"—the Golden Rule in the perfect tense (7:12; 18:28–34).[29]

Mercy is a big deal to God and Jesus. It keeps coming up in Jesus's teaching. It is the motivating factor in his ministry of salvation: "Blessed are the merciful, for they will be shown mercy" (5:7). In fact, it could be said that one of the surest ways a disciple is following Jesus is when they show mercy to another. Therefore, when we refuse to extend mercy, we should give ourselves a warning, perhaps even putting ourselves in "timeout" because we are not following Jesus. Even better, loud alarms should go off in our heads when we exact judgment rather than show mercy: "Warning! Warning! Warning! You've just incited the wrath of our heavenly Father!" It makes God angry for several reasons—not only because he expects us to "pass it on," forgiving others because he has forgiven us. God hates it when we demand judgment because we pretentiously think we're demanding justice. But we're not, because judgment always begins with the house of God. And, if we were to be judged as we judge others, none of us would make it. That's why we cry out for God's mercy (and he *always* forgives us!). To whom much is given, much is required. Besides, judgment belongs to God. Our heavenly Father won't let *anyone* treat his servants mercilessly. Jesus makes that plain—something the faint of heart want to pass over or pretend as if it won't happen. God will judge the merciless. Let's repeat that: *God will judge the merciless*, which will also bring relief to the abused. On *his* terms in *his* time, God will establish justice on earth: "In anger his master handed him over to the jailers to be tortured, until he should pay back all he owed" (18:34). Mercy is serious business—a big deal. The justice of God proves it, not only on the last day but especially on the day when the greatest becomes the least (he will be shown *no* mercy; "oh my Lord") so that the least can become the greatest ("oh my Lord, you have

28. Luz, *Matthew*, 2:474.
29. Davies and Allison, *Matthew*, 2:801.

shown us mercy"). The merciful cross of Jesus will establish justice on earth, forever. What is bound on earth will be bound in heaven (v. 18). Hallelujah.

All this should make a disciple want to humble himself or herself in the presence of an Almighty and merciful God, shouldn't it? Yet I tend to forget to do that—even though the cross of Jesus should be enough to remind me. Perhaps Jesus needs to put someone in front of me, a model of what it looks like to be humble enough to enter the kingdom of heaven on earth. Then, perhaps, I would never forget.

LIVE the Story

I have a hard time humbling myself. Ironically, I think it's because I've been given so much. God's mercy should make us humble. After a while, however, we begin to expect it—as if we've earned it. We forget how much we've been given, not only good gifts but second chances, third chances, and fourth and fifth and sixth and. . . . We have been forgiven so much, we have much to forgive. Why can't we learn that lesson? Why are we so prone to demand what is owed to us? Why do we act like we're privileged, like we're something special, as if we have a right to require more because we think we're better than others? We are *all* slaves, equally indebted to God and to one another. That's the mental picture Jesus drew to help his disciples understand the visual aid he gave them—a child standing before them. I picture in my mind's eye Jesus giving his instruction, telling the whole story, while gesturing to the child as the Twelve take in the full measure of what it looks like to humble ourselves to enter the kingdom of heaven on earth. They're hearing about a merciless "slave" choking another even as they gaze upon the "child," the "little one," the model disciple. I see the child, maybe a little confused, looking around at the Twelve and wondering what he's doing there—having no idea the impact he would make on these men. "And a little child will lead them. . . ." (Isa 11:6).

Since children are objects of undying devotion in our culture, I wonder whom Jesus would put in front of us today to help us see what it means to humble ourselves. It would have to be someone completely vulnerable to a hostile world, someone dismissed as insignificant, perhaps even despised and unwanted, someone completely dependent upon others, someone *none* of us would want to become. I think I know who it is. Jesus would set before us a person with Down syndrome to show us what the model disciple looks like—the one who undoubtedly enters the kingdom of heaven like a child.

They came to lead us during Sunday-morning worship. The Overcomers is a musical group led by Pat Qualls and Joy Williams, two ladies from two different churches in Jonesboro, Arkansas. Members of the group have a variety of disabilities—both physical and mental—including Down syndrome, autism, schizophrenia, multiple sclerosis, cerebral palsy, and blindness, and they range in ages from twenty to eighty years old. Primarily a choral group, several of the Overcomers also play musical instruments and perform sign language. I was serving as the interim preacher at First Baptist Church in Jonesboro, having returned to the city where I once was the pastor of a sister church, Central Baptist, where many of the Overcomers are members. So, having them come to lead the music in our worship services at First Baptist felt like a homecoming to me, getting to visit with many friends I hadn't seen in fifteen years. Even though the group had been invited to perform many times and in many places over the last several years, they had never been asked to fill the choir loft and lead a church in worship. To be sure, there were some unique challenges that the leaders and members of the choir faced that day—special needs, physical challenges, concerns about how certain members would handle the stress and anxiety of sitting in front of such a large crowd, knowing they would be on television. But the service was magnificent. They sang. They played their instruments. They signed for the hearing impaired. They responded respectfully to me as I tried to talk about Paul's vision for the church—many members, much diversity, many gifts, one body. They led us to worship the one, true God. It was a glorious day. Yet it was the last song, the way they ended the service, that left an indelible impression on me.

For the final number, several members of the choir were repositioned to the front steps of the platform to sign the words of the familiar song, "You'll Never Walk Alone." Parents of the choir members as well as several other workers escorted them to their positions. I had noticed that their names had been written on masking tape, evenly placed on the steps, marking where they were to stand. It took several minutes for each member to find his or her spot, some with physical limitations, but others not knowing where they were supposed to go, having to be led by the hand—like children. Sitting on the front row, I had noticed the name of one friend—I'll call him "Freddie"—on a piece of tape on the bottom step in front of me. Freddie is mentally handicapped, but he is able to operate on a higher level than others. He once told me years ago that although he was proud to be a part of the special ministries at Central Baptist, he knew he wasn't as disabled as others. Fumbling for the words, he wanted me to know that he knew he was different—both from me but also from most of his friends. I assured him that I knew that. Then his eyes darted to the floor, and he said, "Thanks." As he walked away, I wondered what that felt like: knowing enough to realize you're not like either the "normal" people or the severely "disabled."

As one of the workers escorted Freddie to his position on the front step, she had a hard time getting him to find his spot. I could see his name. There it was on the floor, written in red: "Freddie." He even looked down at the tape. But, that didn't seem to help. Finally, the escort kept tugging on Freddie's hand—ever so gently—until he found his position and turned to face the congregation. Then the choir sang and signed, "You'll Never Walk Alone." It was spectacular—the musicianship, beautiful hands forming words, the powerful message. The congregation was so moved by the Overcomers that they rose spontaneously to give the choir a standing ovation that lasted for several minutes. At that moment, I saw Freddie. Overcome with emotion, a look of recognition on his face—validation, respect, gratitude—Freddie began to weep. As he took in the spectacle—all these people smiling and clapping and cheering for him and his friends—he discreetly tried to wipe away his tears. It was one of those moments where I felt like I was in the movies—a scene I replay in slow motion. In my mind's eye, I see his teary, joyful face, the congregation cheering with applause, me watching him watch them, all of us standing there, sensing the pleasure of the Lord. "For where two or three gather in my name, there am I with them" (Matt 18:20). One body, many members, *every single one of us* mattering to him, especially the little ones. It was a beautiful model I'll never forget.

At that time, people came to Jesus and asked, "Lord, who is the greatest in your kingdom?" Then Jesus set before them a man with Down syndrome and said, "I'm telling you the truth. Unless you become like him, you won't see the kingdom of heaven on earth."

Have mercy on us, Lord. Open our eyes. We want to see the kingdom.

CHAPTER 27

Matthew 19:1–12

LISTEN to the Story

[1]When Jesus had finished saying these things, he left Galilee and went into the region of Judea to the other side of the Jordan. [2]Large crowds followed him, and he healed them there.

[3]Some Pharisees came to him to test him. They asked, "Is it lawful for a man to divorce his wife for any and every reason?"

[4]"Haven't you read," he replied, "that at the beginning the Creator 'made them male and female,' [5]and said, 'For this reason a man will leave his father and mother and be united to his wife, and the two will become one flesh'? [6]So they are no longer two, but one flesh. Therefore what God has joined together, let no one separate."

[7]"Why then," they asked, "did Moses command that a man give his wife a certificate of divorce and send her away?"

[8]Jesus replied, "Moses permitted you to divorce your wives because your hearts were hard. But it was not this way from the beginning. [9]I tell you that anyone who divorces his wife, except for sexual immorality, and marries another woman commits adultery."

[10]The disciples said to him, "If this is the situation between a husband and wife, it is better not to marry."

[11]Jesus replied, "Not everyone can accept this word, but only those to whom it has been given. [12]For there are eunuchs who were born that way, and there are eunuchs who have been made eunuchs by others—and there are those who choose to live like eunuchs for the sake of the kingdom of heaven. The one who can accept this should accept it."

Listening to the Text in the Story: Genesis 1:26–31; 2:7–25; Leviticus 18:1–30; 21:7, 20; Deuteronomy 22:13–23:2; 24:1–4; Ezra 9:1–10:17; Proverbs 18:22; Isaiah 39:7; 56:3–5; Jeremiah 3:1–10; Ezekiel 44:22; Malachi 2:11–12, 16; Sirach 25:16–26:18.

The last word Jesus gave to his own Galilean people was a dire warning about forgiveness. His heavenly Father would be merciless to those who show no mercy and refuse to forgive others (Matt 18:35). Boom. That's the last thing he said to them. He would never see them again, except for a brief appearance on a mountain with his disciples (28:16–17). His trip to Jerusalem would be his last journey on earth. And so, having offered his parting word to the Galileans, he headed south to Judea, where some Pharisees confronted him with a testy question: "Is it lawful for a man to divorce his wife for any and every reason?" (19:3). That question seems like it comes from nowhere. Why would the Pharisees ask him about divorce, especially since Jesus was already "on the record," having given his position on the subject long ago (5:31–32)? Furthermore, of all the conversations Jesus probably had on his trip to Jerusalem, why would Matthew want to bring up such a random subject? In fact, if we were to skip over this episode, notice how seamless the narrative flow would be—perhaps even improving the story line. Jesus has just given an extended lesson about becoming like children to enter the kingdom, to be humble like the "least of these," even setting before his disciples a child (18:1–5). Then, like bookends to the moral of the story, children come to Jesus to be blessed, prompting him to anchor his point: "The kingdom of heaven belongs to such as these" (19:14). If that weren't enough, a "young man" illustrates how badly he's missed the point, refusing to humble himself because he had *great* wealth (vv. 16–30). Then Jesus tells the parable about the least becoming the greatest (20:1–16). In light of the thematic structure of the episodic narrative, the Pharisees' question about divorce seems out of place, intrusive, disruptive.[1]

But that's not the case at all. In fact, the Pharisees have asked a good question in light of Jesus's teaching about unlimited forgiveness.[2] Think of what it would mean to marriages if husbands and wives forgave each other as God has forgiven them. Or take Jesus's response to Peter's question about the number of times we should forgive someone and apply it to married couples who grow tired of fighting with each other over the same issue. When I was a pastor, counseling sessions over troubled marriages would have ended so much better if just one of the spouses would have said, "I forgive. No debts. No regrets." But, too often forgiveness was the last thing on their minds. Their lazy husband

---

1. According to Garland, themes of the entire Sermon on the Mount are resurfacing here in Matthew 19–20: divorce, low status of the kingdom, law of Moses, command to be perfect, treasure in heaven, danger of mammon, obstacles to entering the kingdom, promise of reward (*Reading Matthew*, 201). Appealing to W. Carter, Talbert thinks Matthew is arranging the material to coincide with the common subjects of household management: advice for husbands/wives, parents/children, masters/slaves, and wealth (*Matthew*, 231).

2. Keener sees a correlation with Jesus's previous teaching about protecting the "weaker ones," in this case wives (*Matthew*, 462).

or contentious wife had built up such a huge debt that the exasperated spouse had come to collect: "Enough is enough. I can't take this anymore. It's time for them to pay for what they've done." Like the unmerciful slave who grabbed his fellow servant by the neck and tried to choke him into submission (18:28), I've seen frustrated wives wish they could do the same to their husbands (or even worse, was told of angry husbands who physically abused their wives). To be sure, marriage is a complex relationship that seems to invite many complicated problems. Divorce often appears to many as the best option to relieve the pressure between two people who hate each other. Nevertheless, one can't help but wonder, "Shouldn't Jesus's teaching about eternal mercy and limitless forgiveness apply to married couples too?" Or are we more likely to stand with the Pharisees and wonder, "Shouldn't a man or woman be able to divorce their spouse for any reason, especially when they've had enough?"

Whether or not the Pharisees tied the issue of divorce to Jesus's teaching about forgiveness is difficult to know, but perhaps Matthew saw the connection. Besides, there may have been political reasons motivating the Pharisees to "test" Jesus with their question about divorce. Although our Gospel writer provides a rather vague location for his trip down south ("the region of Judea to the other side of the Jordan," 19:1), it's very likely that Jesus, his disciples, and the huge crowd following them had come near the same place where John the Baptizer prophesied against Herod's illicit marriage to Herodias (3:1, 13; 14:3–5). Therefore, to bring up such a touchy subject in the same region would put Jesus in danger—a devious tactic. The Pharisees had been plotting for some time "how they might kill Jesus" (12:14). In fact, they had tried three times to get the people on their side to oppose Jesus (12:24; 15:1–2; 16:1). But that only made things worse for them. So, what better way to do away with Jesus than to have Herod do their dirty work? Possibly that's why Matthew says they came to Jesus to "test him," knowing that if he gave the same answer as he did before, Herod would certainly hear of it and execute Jesus too.[3] Nevertheless, Jesus didn't temper his answer. In fact, he expanded on it in ways that may even challenge our ideas about marriage, sexual identity, and commitment to the kingdom.

EXPLAIN the Story

There are two ways to read the Scriptures: one, to look for excuses to live, the other to search for life itself. Jesus and the Pharisees—both taking the Scriptures seriously—approached them differently. The Pharisees were bent

3. Evans, *Matthew*, 340.

on maintaining their tradition, conserving what they had always been taught. Jesus, on the other hand, kept his eye on the singularity, the common thread holding all the pearls of wisdom together on one strand—what we call "God's will." Every time they brought up an issue, Jesus headed straight for the heart of the matter. The supposition, the ancillary, the extrapolated, the implication, the casuistry—the result of a carefully constructed argument built on the foundation of Scripture—only interested him if it held up under the scrutiny of the intentions of God, what would have been known "from the beginning." This was a key hermeneutical move that often put Jesus at odds with the Pharisees, who spent more time maintaining the structure of their traditions than surveying whether the entire edifice of their interpretation was built upon a solid foundation. Again, the major argument between Jesus and the Pharisees had to do with *how* to read the Scriptures.[4] The difference between their approaches shows up here in spades.

The argument between Jesus and the Pharisees looks like a card game. Jesus plays his card, "the intentions of God," going back to Genesis to support his argument that marriage is forever (Matt 19:4–6).[5] Then, the Pharisees "trump" Jesus's play with "the law of Moses" card: divorce is sanctioned in the Scriptures (v. 7). How do we hold these two competing ideas together since God's word is the repository of wisdom? We might call the Pharisees' approach "progressive revelation"—with time more of God's will is revealed. Sure, God established marriage as a covenant between one man and one woman. Yet, over time God revealed a more nuanced position on marriage, one that takes into account the realities of life. Sometimes marriage doesn't work, so exceptions need to be made. Jesus, on the other hand, takes a more "foundational" approach to the revelation of God's will on marriage. Moses allowing the bill of divorce wasn't a more enlightened teaching on marriage, as if Israel was now prepared to handle it. Instead of seeing Israel progressing toward an ever-increasing knowledge of God's will, Jesus saw a downward spiral of rebellion among God's people (a very prophetic worldview). Like Paul claimed, God gave more commandments through Moses to curb Israel's inclination to sin (Gal 3:19). So, Moses gave the bill of divorce as a concession to a hard-hearted people unwilling to obey God's intention for marriage (Matt 19:8). The bill of divorce was supposed to protect women from the capricious behavior of men; when a husband divorces his wife to marry another woman, they are breaking the seventh commandment (v. 9).[6] The only legitimate reason for

4. See above, 25, 113–14, 117, 240–41, 243–44.

5. For discussion of Jesus's view of marriage and divorce, see above, 116–17.

6. "The Jewish divorce bill contained the clause, 'You are free to marry again.' To obtain a divorce was to obtain permission to remarry" (Davies and Allison, *Matthew*, 3:17).

divorce, according to Jesus, was sexual immorality (see Lev 18:1–23)—the result of a hard heart (see Jer 3:1–10 where God gives Israel a bill of divorce due to "adultery," i.e., idolatry).[7] Therefore, if a woman was faithful to her husband, she should never be the victim of divorce.

That idea scared the disciples enough to commit to remaining bachelors for the rest of their lives: "If this is the situation between a husband and wife, it is better not to marry" (Matt 19:10). If there was no "escape clause"[8] for a man to get out of a marriage with a "contentious" wife ("Sure, she may be faithful, but she's driving me crazy!"), then marriage looked more like a prison sentence than a blessed union. But that simply reveals a sexist view informed by a privileged position. Indeed, what Jesus was doing was leveling the playing field of marriage in a male-dominant society, giving husbands a taste of their own medicine. As Nolland states: "The attitude attributed to the disciples here is quite unchivalrous, even rather misogynist. Jewish marriage practice meant that wives had all along experienced marriage more or less on the terms now laid down for men in v. 9."[9] Just as women have to grin and bear it—sticking it out with a man who may have driven *them* crazy—Jesus was requiring the same of his disciples. Marriage was a lifelong commitment, not only arranged by families but instituted by God. "Therefore, what God has joined together, let no one separate" (v. 6)—not even a dissatisfied husband.

When Jesus said, "Not everyone can accept this word" (v. 11), it's difficult to know whether he was referring to his teaching about marriage (vv. 8–9)[10] or the disciples' inference (v. 10).[11] Most commentators think the latter due to the explanation given by Jesus—a cautionary word about resigning oneself to the single life (v. 12).[12] The way the disciples see it, men find themselves between a rock (the prospect of a difficult marriage) and a hard place (Jesus's teaching about marriage). So, why not "jump out of the pan and into the fire" of celibacy? At least, that's the way Jesus takes their comment. To him, if a man isn't going to marry, he's making a commitment to a celibate life—no sex. That's why he immediately brings up the example of eunuchs, men who are unable to have sex. Note that Jesus didn't entertain a "third way": not married, not celibate, yet still single. To him, it's either sex in marriage or no sex. So, if you're going to make a commitment to stay single, then you've decided to live like a eunuch—a decision one needs to make for the right reason. For Jesus, not being able to divorce a wife for any reason isn't the right reason to

7. Ibid., 3:16.
8. Keener, *Matthew*, 471.
9. Nolland, *Matthew*, 775.
10. So Luz, *Matthew*, 2:500.
11. See Davies and Allison, *Matthew*, 3:20–21.
12. See the explanation by France, *Matthew*, 723.

live like a eunuch. Rather, the *only* reason not to marry is to do so "for the sake of the kingdom of heaven" (v. 12). Of course, there are eunuchs who have no choice in the matter, either because they were born with a genital defect or they were disfigured "by others" (due to an accident or, perhaps, because of their vocation; see Acts 8:27). But the decision to remain single—for all intents and purposes, to take the vow of chastity—isn't for everyone: only "the one who can accept this should accept it" (Matt 19:12).

Given the way eunuchs were perceived in the first-century world, it shouldn't surprise us that once again Jesus holds up a person of low esteem as a model disciple for the kingdom.[13] Eunuchs were not allowed to enter the Jewish temple (Deut 23:1). To become a eunuch was the sign of a divine curse, evidence of the punishment of God (Isa 39:7). Furthermore, to be a eunuch "means to be without honor," because the male organ symbolized virility and strength.[14] Therefore, when Jesus encouraged his disciples to consider becoming eunuchs for the kingdom, once again he was inviting them to take the path of downward mobility—a consistent theme in his teaching, but especially emphasized after he predicted his execution in Jerusalem. First a cross (Matt 16:24), then a child (18:2), and now a eunuch. Jesus would be hard pressed to find more humiliating models of discipleship than these three. Yet he never crammed these ideas down the throats of his disciples. Jesus never presumed upon his followers. He always introduced the challenge of entering the kingdom by issuing an open invitation: "Whoever *wants* to be my disciple . . ." (16:24); "Truly I tell you, *unless* you change and become like little children . . ." (18:3); "The one who *can* accept this should accept this" (19:12). It was always up to them whether they would follow Jesus, a single man committed to the kingdom of God who taught that marriage is forever. Even when it came to their sexual life, to be great in the kingdom a disciple had to choose to become one of the *least* of these: either a committed "eunuch" or a forgiving husband. Being a disciple of Jesus affects every aspect of our lives because everyone needs to forgive and be forgiven—even husbands and wives.

LIVE the Story

If a Christian husband considered forgiving his wife as God had forgiven him, then divorce no longer seemed like a good option to him. When a wife would think like a "Christian" about her marriage, then forgiveness sounded more reasonable to her. But that was the hard part, getting them to apply

13. See Nolland, *Matthew*, 777–79.
14. Malina and Rohrbaugh, *Synoptic Gospels*, 122.

such a "religious" idea to their "secular" relationship—at least, that's what they thought I was doing. Often whenever I would bring up our Christian faith in the middle of some intense marital issue, the couple would often give me a dismissive look, a now-your-sounding-like-a-preacher smirk. In fact, once a husband said to me, "Look, preacher. We didn't come here for a sermon. We came to you for help."[15] In their minds, their relationship with the Lord had very little to do with their marriage—a union determined more by the laws of the state than the teachings of Christ. (Sometimes it seemed like the soon-to-be-divorced couple was relying more upon the advice of their attorneys than anything I said. Legal advice tended to trump spiritual advice.) Furthermore, such a distinct separation of church and state has led many couples to divorce spiritual practices (like mercy and forgiveness) from domestic pursuits (like rights and privileges). To say that the "law of Christ" (as Paul called it; Gal 6:2) should take precedence over the laws of the land sounded naive to some and downright silly to others.

A scene from one of my favorite movies, *O Brother, Where Art Thou?* illustrates the point beautifully. Everett, Pete, and Delmar are fugitives running from the law when they come across a baptism.

Streams of men and women wearing white robes are headed for a river, walking like mindless robots through the woods, singing an old gospel song about baptism. As the three fugitives watch the procession of candidates wading into the water to be baptized by a minister wearing a white robe, Everett offers his commentary, dismissing the crowd as "chumps" who can't deal with the hard times. Then, all of the sudden, Delmar rushes into the water, breaking in front of the line of novitiates, insisting the preacher baptize him immediately. Everett and Pete rush to the water's edge, standing slack-jawed as they take in the scene of Delmar's baptism. As Delmar slogs out the water with a big grin on his face, he declares, "Well that's it boys, I been redeemed! The preacher warshed away all my sins and transgressions. It's the straight and narrow from here on out and heaven everlasting's my reward!" When Delmar invites his two partners to join the festivities, Everett dismisses the charade as nonsense.

In the next scene, all three are driving down the road in their stolen vehicle; both Delmar and Pete are dripping wet. Everett is incredulous that Pete got suckered into getting baptized, believing it absolved him of all crimes. Delmar comes to his defense, "But there were witnesses, saw us redeemed!" To which Everett replies, "That's not the issue, Delmar. Even if it put you square with the Lord, the State of Mississippi is more hardnosed." Talking down to

15. Rodney Reeves, *Spirituality according to Paul: Imitating the Apostle of Christ* (Downers Grove, IL: IVP Academic, 2011), 144.

his passengers like they were ignorant children for believing such ridiculous superstition, Everett then shakes his head and exclaims, "You two are just dumber'n a bag of hammers. Well, I guess you're my cross to bear." At which point Delmar encourages Everett to pull over and give a "colored boy a lift."[16]

Perhaps Delmar isn't as dumb as Everett thinks. Everett was the one who tried to manipulate everyone and everything to achieve his purpose to reconcile with his estranged wife and reclaim his children. Yet due to a series of serendipitous events—giving that "colored boy a lift," recording a song at a radio station in the middle of nowhere, the unlikely concert of the Soggy Bottom Boys winning the favor of the opportunistic governor, the timely flooding of the lowlands of Mississippi that saves their lives from the bounty hunter—by the end of the story, the state of Mississippi pardons all three for their crimes, and Everett is reunited with his wife and children. The Lord works in mysterious ways—something Delmar believes with all his heart. Everett counted on his intellectual superiority—even deceiving his jail mates about a nonexistent buried treasure—to ensure a desirable outcome. Ironically, however, Delmar ends up being the voice of reason. By showing mercy to others and forgiving those who wronged him (even Everett), Delmar is the hero of the story—the answer to Cain's age-old question, "Am I my brother's keeper?" (Gen 4:9).

In Christ, a husband is his wife's keeper, and a wife is her husband's keeper because they are brothers and sisters in Jesus's family. "How many times shall I forgive my brother or sister who sins against me?" (Matt 18:21). As many times as it takes to remain brothers and sisters in Christ. For if we refuse to show mercy and to forgive one another—even husbands forgiving wives and wives forgiving husbands—then we incite the wrath of God and his merciless judgment. "This is how my heavenly Father will treat each of you unless you forgive your brother or sister from your heart" (18:35)—especially your husband or your wife. Therefore, we should turn the Pharisees' question around. Rather than ask, "Is it lawful for a man to divorce his wife for any and every reason?" (19:3), we should say, "Is it *unlawful* for a man to *forgive* his wife for any and every reason? Not at all. Moreover, if you can't forgive her, then perhaps you should consider becoming a eunuch instead of marrying. Then you might learn to live for the sake of the kingdom of heaven—just like Jesus."

16. This summary adapted from www.dailyscript.com/scripts/o_brother.html.

CHAPTER 28

Matthew 19:13–20:16

LISTEN to the Story

13Then people brought little children to Jesus for him to place his hands on them and pray for them. But the disciples rebuked them.

14Jesus said, "Let the little children come to me, and do not hinder them, for the kingdom of heaven belongs to such as these." 15When he had placed his hands on them, he went on from there.

16Just then a man came up to Jesus and asked, "Teacher, what good thing must I do to get eternal life?"

17"Why do you ask me about what is good?" Jesus replied. "There is only One who is good. If you want to enter life, keep the commandments."

18"Which ones?" he inquired.

Jesus replied, "'You shall not murder, you shall not commit adultery, you shall not steal, you shall not give false testimony, 19honor your father and mother,' and 'love your neighbor as yourself.'"

20"All these I have kept," the young man said. "What do I still lack?"

21Jesus answered, "If you want to be perfect, go, sell your possessions and give to the poor, and you will have treasure in heaven. Then come, follow me."

22When the young man heard this, he went away sad, because he had great wealth.

23Then Jesus said to his disciples, "Truly I tell you, it is hard for someone who is rich to enter the kingdom of heaven. 24Again I tell you, it is easier for a camel to go through the eye of a needle than for someone who is rich to enter the kingdom of God."

25When the disciples heard this, they were greatly astonished and asked, "Who then can be saved?"

26Jesus looked at them and said, "With man this is impossible, but with God all things are possible."

27Peter answered him, "We have left everything to follow you! What then will there be for us?"

[28]Jesus said to them, "Truly I tell you, at the renewal of all things, when the Son of Man sits on his glorious throne, you who have followed me will also sit on twelve thrones, judging the twelve tribes of Israel. [29]And everyone who has left houses or brothers or sisters or father or mother or wife or children or fields for my sake will receive a hundred times as much and will inherit eternal life. [30]But many who are first will be last, and many who are last will be first.

[20:1]"For the kingdom of heaven is like a landowner who went out early in the morning to hire workers for his vineyard. [2]He agreed to pay them a denarius for the day and sent them into his vineyard.

[3]"About nine in the morning he went out and saw others standing in the marketplace doing nothing. [4]He told them, 'You also go and work in my vineyard, and I will pay you whatever is right.' [5]So they went.

"He went out again about noon and about three in the afternoon and did the same thing. [6]About five in the afternoon he went out and found still others standing around. He asked them, 'Why have you been standing here all day long doing nothing?'

[7]'Because no one has hired us,' they answered.

"He said to them, 'You also go and work in my vineyard.'

[8]"When evening came, the owner of the vineyard said to his foreman, 'Call the workers and pay them their wages, beginning with the last ones hired and going on to the first.'

[9]"The workers who were hired about five in the afternoon came and each received a denarius. [10]So when those came who were hired first, they expected to receive more. But each one of them also received a denarius. [11]When they received it, they began to grumble against the landowner. [12]'These who were hired last worked only one hour,' they said, 'and you have made them equal to us who have borne the burden of the work and the heat of the day.'

[13]"But he answered one of them, 'I am not being unfair to you, friend. Didn't you agree to work for a denarius? [14]Take your pay and go. I want to give the one who was hired last the same as I gave you. [15]Don't I have the right to do what I want with my own money? Or are you envious because I am generous?'

[16]"So the last will be first, and the first will be last."

Listening to the Text in the Story: Exodus 20:12–16; Leviticus 19:13, 18; 25:1–43; Deuteronomy 5:16–20; 7:12–14; 15:1–11; 24:15; 28:1–14; 1 Samuel 30:21–25; Job 1:1–5; 42:10–17; Isaiah 5:1–8; 65:17; Daniel 7:9–14, 22.

Jesus confuses me. If I would have been one of his disciples, I think I would have walked around in a fog most of the time. That's why, perhaps, I identify with the disciples when they appear confused by what Jesus says or does. Of course, from our perspective it's easy to shake our heads in disbelief at the disciples' ignorance, voicing our disapproval with a schoolmarm tone, "Tsk, tsk." Why in the world would the Twelve shoo away the children when desperate parents wanted Jesus to bless them? Didn't Jesus just say that his disciples needed to become like children to enter the kingdom? How could the Twelve be so dense? Everybody knows Jesus loves the little children of the world.

But what if you were one of the Twelve trying to take Jesus's teaching seriously? You've just heard Jesus say that his disciples should consider becoming "eunuchs" for the sake of the kingdom. It's not for everyone, he says. Yet at least you should think about it. As you turn such a strange idea over and over in your head, wondering what that would mean for you—no sex, no children, single for the rest of your days—it would certainly make you look at the world differently. At the end of the day, you might be led to think that Jesus had a negative view of family life.[1] You can almost hear the disciples thinking things through: "Let's add it up. Jesus said, 'Whoever does the will of my Father in heaven is my brother and sister and mother' [Matt 12:50]. He said, 'There are those who choose to live like eunuchs for the sake of the kingdom' [19:12]. He said, 'Everyone who has left houses or brothers or sisters or father or mother or wife or children or fields for my sake will receive a hundred times as much and will inherit eternal life' (v. 29). So, since earthly families don't matter, getting married and having children isn't all that important anymore. I should be focused on kingdom priorities. Be like Jesus. Follow him. Sacrifice all for the kingdom of God. Having a home, working a field—these things don't matter. Children won't preserve my legacy. My family's inheritance is nothing. The only thing that matters is inheriting eternal life. Isn't that what he said to the rich young man? Sell your inheritance and give it to the poor? Family doesn't matter anymore, right? We left our families for the kingdom. Didn't we do the right thing when we told parents not to bother Jesus? They think their children are their future. We know better. The only future worth having is eternal life in the kingdom of God. So, why did Jesus act like *we're* the ones who got it wrong (v. 14)? It just doesn't make any sense."

But that's not all. Throughout these episodes—Jesus's conversation with the rich young man, what he tells the twelve disciples, the parable of the day

1. Davies and Allison, *Matthew*, 3:36.

laborers—practically everything Jesus says is counterintuitive, the opposite of what we would expect. In fact, in light of what we know about Matthew's Gospel, here is a list of what Jesus should have said:

1. To the young man who asked what he should do to get eternal life, Jesus should have said, "Believe in me" or "Follow me" or both. Instead, Jesus said, "If you want to enter life, keep the commandments" (v. 17).
2. When the young man asked, "Which ones?" Jesus should have said, "All of them—you can't set aside even the least of the commandments." Instead, Jesus gave a brief list: five from the Ten Commandments, and the "love your neighbor" commandment from Leviticus (vv. 18–19).
3. After the young man pretentiously claimed he'd kept the commandments and asked, "What do I still lack?" Jesus should have said, "Humility." Instead, Jesus told him to sell his possessions and give them to the poor in order to follow him (v. 21).
4. After the young man walked away, Jesus should have said, "Come back. None of my disciples sold everything and gave it away. They simply left it all behind. So, I won't require more of you than I did of them." Instead, Jesus said it's nearly impossible for rich people to enter the kingdom of God (v. 23).
5. When the disciples asked incredulously, "Who then can be saved?" Jesus should have said, "Only poor people." Instead, Jesus talked about how God makes all things possible (v. 26).
6. After Peter reminded Jesus that they had abandoned their families to follow him, he then asked, "What's in it for us?" Jesus should have said, "Don't follow me for a reward. Follow me because you love me." Instead, Jesus promised Peter and the disciples that they would be rewarded with much more "at the renewal of all things" and that they would "inherit eternal life" (vv. 28–29).
7. After Jesus said to the disciples that the last would be first and the first would be last, he should have told a parable about reversal of fortune—wealthy people losing their riches and poor people gaining wealth.[2] Instead, Jesus told the parable of the day laborers, in which everyone in the kingdom is treated alike, receiving the same reward (20:1–15).

This is a confusing passage. But then again, Jesus has been known to say some unusual things, especially when he's trying to get his disciples to see the kingdom of heaven on earth.

---

2. So also Davies and Allison, *Matthew*, 3:68.

EXPLAIN the Story

In the first-century world, people didn't look at the world as a place of unlimited resources.[3] There was only so much land, so much water, and so much food to go around. If someone had more than what they needed, that meant others had less. Wastefulness, therefore, was considered one of the most egregious sins because it affected everyone. Indeed, in a world of limited goods everyone depended on others to make it. Since a person's prosperity was tied to the land, to their family, and to their community, only fools would leave and try to make it on their own. Villages depended upon every able-bodied man and woman to work to make ends meet. Neighbors were social security. Families were *the* absolute necessity for survival. To turn your back on your family, to leave your hometown, to refuse to pitch in for the benefit of the whole was suicide. There were no success stories of men leaving home to make their fortune. Prodigals always failed. The landless had nowhere to go except the city, hoping to find work for the day. Even the wealthy depended upon others to harvest their fields, to bring goods to the city for purchase, to take care of their dirty work. Of course, the landed rich had more than what they needed, which they considered to be evidence of divine favor. At least that's the way most people saw it—especially in Israel. After all, God had given the promised land to his people, distributed among the twelve tribes, to live, to farm, to share. He even promised to bless them abundantly—long life and bumper crops—if they obeyed him (Deut 28:1–14). So it was easy to infer that God favored the wealthy, while the poor were cursed by God because they had disobeyed him (vv. 15–68).

Jesus had many poor people come to him looking for help. It was to be expected. Time after time this amazing man of God would reverse the curse and bless them—God's favor coming to the least of these. So, it made perfect sense why parents wanted Jesus to "place his hands on" their children and pray for them (Matt 19:13). Children were especially susceptible to disease, sickness, and death. Most of them didn't make it past the age of twelve. Furthermore, these "little ones" were vulnerable to evil spirits; it seems like whenever children appear in Matthew's narrative world, they are either sick, dead, or demonized. If Jesus would pray for them, asking the God who gave him power over disease, death, and demons to protect them, then that certainly would give them a much better chance of living a long life—an undeniable sign of the blessing of God. Needy people needed Jesus. But when

3. See Malina, *New Testament World*, 71–90.

a rich man shows up looking for help, it comes as quite a surprise. Why did he come? What would he need? He had money. He had the blessing of God. What more could he want?

The Greatest Becoming the Least

Every time Jesus talked about the last day—the day that is coming for all of us—he always included the element of surprise. Many who prophesy, exorcize demons, and perform miracles in Jesus's name will be shocked to hear him say on the last day, "I never knew you" (Matt 7:22–23). Outsiders will find a place at Abraham's banquet table, while the "subjects of the kingdom will be thrown outside" (8:11–12). Sodom and Gomorrah will have a better time of it on judgment day than the towns and villages who rejected Jesus's disciples or didn't repent because of his miracles (10:15; 11:23–24). The least will become the greatest (18:2–4). The last will be first (19:30). No one is able to predict when it will happen (24:36). Both "sheep" and "goats" will be surprised as to who makes it and who doesn't (25:37–40, 44–46). It seemed like Jesus was bent on the idea that the last day will hold surprises for *everyone*—pleasant for some, horrible for others. So, when the rich young man approached Jesus with the question, "Teacher, what good thing must I do to get eternal life?" (19:16) no one should have been surprised by Jesus's answer. But they were—not only the rich man but also the Twelve ("Who then can be saved?"; v. 25). Here's why.

The answer to the young man's question isn't a mystery. In fact, Jesus was somewhat incredulous that he asked it (v. 17). God made it plain what it took to live: obey his commandments. So why would the rich man ask, "What good thing must I do to get eternal life?" He already knew the answer; every Jew knew the answer.[4] Obey God and live (Deut 30:15–20).[5] But since he asked, it's almost as if the rich man was saying, "Look. I know what the right answer is. But, I think I should do more"[6]—at least that's the implication of his second question, "Which ones?" (Matt 19:18), to ensure he's covered them all. Either that, or the rich man had come to the conclusion that not all of the commandments were as binding as others—something even the rabbis debated (22:36). No one would contest the Ten Commandments. But other laws didn't seem as important, especially since lesser punishments were required for different violations. Besides, there were certain laws—like what was prescribed during the year of Jubilee (Lev 25:8–55)—that weren't observed as strictly as others. In fact, scholars question whether Israel observed

4. Davies and Allison, *Matthew*, 3:42.
5. Evans, *Matthew*, 346.
6. Bruner, *Matthew*, 2:294.

Jubilee or even the sabbatical year (vv. 1–7) with any regularity.[7] If they had, the prophets wouldn't have had as much to preach against, such as the social injustice resulting from the rich taking advantage of the poor (Isa 5:1–8; Jer 22:13–17). Indeed, if landowners returned purchased property to their ancestral owners every fiftieth year—not to mention the cancelling of all debts and releasing all slaves—such a massive redistribution of wealth would have made it virtually impossible to stay rich. And there's the rub, the very issue the rich *young* man wanted Jesus to deal with.[8] Here's someone who's inherited his wealth, riches that had been passed down probably for generations. If his family never observed the sabbatical year or especially the year of Jubilees, then his question would be especially poignant: "Which commandments do I really need to keep?" So, imagine his relief when Jesus listed five commandments of the Decalogue and the rather vague "love your neighbor" commandment (Matt 19:18–19). He had kept these commandments. But what about his parents and grandparents? Since there were few get-rich-quick schemes available to young men in the first century (13:44), the accumulated wealth of his ancestors would be the *only* reason he was rich. What could he do about that? Honoring father and mother would certainly include taking care of the family fortune, right?

Well, the way Jesus saw it, inherited wealth brought inherited responsibility. To whom much is given much is required (see the parable of the bags of gold; 25:14–30). Therefore, if the young man wanted to be "perfect" in his obedience, leaving no room for doubt, then he would need to follow Jesus (19:21). (Finally, we come to the "right" answer we've expected all along!) And what would that entail? Laying up treasures in heaven rather than storing up wealth on earth (6:19–21). If the young man really wanted to invest in the kingdom of heaven coming to earth—eternal life—then he would need to lose his life and become one of the "*least* of these," just like Jesus.[9] The young man, however, didn't want to go that far because he had "*great* wealth" (19:22). It's one thing to give to the poor; it's quite something else to give your money away to the poor so that you become one of them. Evidently, the young man hoped he could do "good" without losing his life, without giving up his inheritance, without following Jesus. Ironically, the very thing he "lacked" (v. 20) was that he had too much. One of the greatest didn't like the idea of becoming one of the least. In fact, it made him very sad (v. 22),

7. Joel B. Green and Nicholas Perrin, "Jubilee," *DJG* 450–52.

8. Garland, *Reading Matthew*, 206.

9. "The rich man therefore cannot be tested or proved through physical suffering. No one will likely do him violence; rather, he is tested and proved by generosity" (Simonetti, *Matthew 14–28*, 119 [anonymous]).

the living incarnation of the words of Jesus: “For where your treasure is, there your heart will be also” (6:21). What he couldn’t give up revealed what he prized the most. Which should make us wonder: What do I value more than following Jesus? How would I have responded to Jesus if he said to me what he said to the rich young man? Well, perhaps, we might know the answer to the question by filling in the blank: “I can’t live without [fill in the blank].” According to Jesus, we would know we were following him if we didn’t fill the blank with “houses or brothers or sisters or father or mother or wife or children or fields” (19:29) because Jesus left these things behind too.

It probably didn’t seem like it at the time, but Jesus was trying to save the rich young man. To those who have much, the demand to become like Christ—to become one of the least of these—may sound like harsh punishment. But Jesus didn’t see it that way at all. Wealthy people need to be saved too. Besides, there are many things in the world that cause us to stumble. If riches on earth stand in the way of salvation (or even an eye or a hand!), better to live in the world with loss than enter the gates of hell wealthy and healthy (18:7–9). Yet Jesus was realistic about how difficult the challenge was of the greatest becoming the least: “Truly I tell you, it is hard for someone who is rich to enter the kingdom of heaven” (19:23). By way of analogy, he implied it was impossible for some—as unlikely as a camel squeezing through the needle’s eye (v. 24).[10] It’s no wonder, then, that the disciples asked, “Who then can be saved?” (v. 25). At which point Jesus should have said, “Only the poor—have you ever seen someone thread a camel?” But that’s not what he said. As impossible as it sounds to us—those who have much giving up everything for Christ’s sake—Jesus believed it was still possible with God (v. 26). In fact, only *God* can save the rich and the poor. *Anyone* can be a disciple and follow Jesus.

The Last Becoming the First

The chapter division (Matt 20:1) is misleading because it gives the impression that Peter’s question and Jesus’s response (19:27–30) round out the discussion that followed their encounter with the rich young man and that Jesus moved on to a different topic when he told the parable of the day laborers (20:1–15). To be sure, talk about the Twelve leaving everything to follow Jesus sets in sharp relief their discipleship with the young man who “went away sad, because he had great wealth” (19:22). Yet what Jesus said to Peter (and the disciples) really sets up the story of the day laborers (20:1–15). In other words, Jesus told the parable to answer Peter’s question, “What then will

10. For an explanation of the analogy, see Davies and Allison, *Matthew*, 3:51–52.

there be for us?" (19:27). The aphorism, "But many who are first will be last, and many who are last will be first" (v. 30), frames the parable as an *inclusio* (20:16), shedding light on what Jesus meant when he talked of thrones as well as rewards (19:28–29). It's a little confusing.[11] At first, Jesus promises the disciples special rewards for their service, setting them apart from the rest. Then, Jesus tells a parable about how everyone will get the same reward in the kingdom of heaven—a completely different point. The repeated aphorism signals to the reader that Jesus's response to Peter's question (19:28–29) and the parable (20:1–15) go together, explaining what Jesus meant by the first becoming last and the last becoming first (19:30; 20:16).

Some scholars think that Jesus told the parable of the day laborers to bridle Peter's desire for a reward.[12] There's no getting around the idea that Jesus told Peter and the disciples that they would be treated special "at the renewal of all things" (19:28). On the last day, the Twelve will judge the twelve tribes of Israel, reminiscent of the elders who helped Moses render judgments to settle disputes. In the same way, the Twelve will reign with Jesus, sitting on "twelve thrones" when the Son of Man "sits on his glorious throne" (v. 28). Furthermore, Jesus promised anyone who left their homes, family, and lands for his sake would be rewarded a hundredfold on that day and "will inherit eternal life" (v. 29). Peter and the disciples are the many-who-are-last-who-will-be first, and those who are "first"—like the rich young man or the religious leaders in Jerusalem—"will be last" on the last day (v. 30). This answered Peter's question, "What's in it for us?" (v. 27). But to keep Peter's greed in check, Jesus told the parable of the day laborers to inspire humility—a story of everyone getting the same reward. In the parable, this time Peter and the disciples end up representing the "first" workers; they were the first disciples of Jesus. But, those who would come much later in the history of the church—the last to follow Jesus (perhaps a reference to gentile believers)—will still get the same reward as the apostles, eternal life.[13] According to this interpretation, then, the parable of the day laborers should be read as a brief "history" of the Jesus movement, from the earliest apostles to the last followers of Jesus.

Other scholars see the parable operating in a way that confirms the place of the Twelve in the kingdom.[14] Jesus told the story not to offer a mild rebuke but to highlight the significant difference between his disciples and other people of Israel like the rich young ruler, the Pharisees, or even the heroes of

11. See the discussion in Talbert, *Matthew*, 238.

12. For example, Turner, *Matthew*, 476.

13. Nolland, *Matthew*, 813.

14. Keener, *Matthew*, 481.

Israel's past. In this way, the parable reads more like a history of Israel[15] (similar to the parable of the tenants, 21:33–41) with the Twelve (and other followers of Jesus) representing the "last" to work in the vineyard, while the "first" workers represent the religious leaders of Israel (scribes, priests, prophets), who have a long history of doing God's business (the same point as 11:11–13). Jesus may have been inspired by Isaiah, who described Judah as God's vineyard that had been abused by the "caretakers" of Jerusalem (Isa 5:1–8). That Jesus had Jerusalem on his mind—and the events that would transpire once he and the disciples arrived—is evident. Immediately after he tells the parable, Jesus once again warns the Twelve what will happen to him when they get to the holy city (Matt 20:17–19).

Both readings make a lot of sense. In light of the overall message of Matthew, I lean toward the latter: the parable is a critique of Jerusalem (they will be envious of Jesus and his disciples who are "latecomers" to the reign of God in the holy city; 21:10–16). But I wonder if the significance of the parable is broader than that. Perhaps a clue to the wider implications of Jesus's teaching might be found in the way he characterized the reward of those who gave up many things for the kingdom (19:29). They were to receive two things: not only a hundred times more than what they sacrificed but also eternal life. Jesus taught that his disciples would receive both a compensatory reward (some followers will get more because they gave up more) and the same reward (every disciple will inherit "eternal life"). Regarding the first reward, then, those who are "last" (having forsaken homes, family, and land) will become "first" in the kingdom. And, those who are "first" (refusing to forsake homes, family, and land for the kingdom—like the rich young man) will become "last." Regarding the second reward, every disciple of Jesus will receive the same—a point of contention in the parable. Yet if the parable of the day laborers is a critique of Jerusalem, was Jesus implying that *everyone* will receive eternal life, not only the last (his disciples) but also the first (the leaders of Jerusalem)? Not necessarily.

We may think the only point of the parable was to place everyone on the same level when it comes to divine rewards. Rather than set up a hierarchy of recognition—some deserve more than others—Jesus wanted his disciples to know that, in his kingdom, equality reigns because of the grace of God. No matter who you are or what you've done, whoever follows Jesus receives the same reward in the end because God is gracious. We don't earn God's grace. He freely gives it because he's generous (20:15), especially to those who

15. Nolland, *Matthew*, 812; or, it reads like a history of all humanity according to Cyril of Alexandria (Simonetti, *Matthew 14–28*, 108).

know they don't deserve it.[16] There is a presumption within the parable that confirms the same. Those who were hired at five o'clock in the afternoon must have been the least-desirable workers: the old, the sickly, the weak. Certainly, the landowner would have chosen the healthiest, youngest, most virile men at the beginning of the day (vv. 1–2). And, as he kept returning to the marketplace (vv. 3–5), as the crowd thinned out, the quality of workers probably decreased significantly. It's not surprising then, at the end of the workday when daylight was nearly gone, a few men were still standing around "because no one has hired us" (v. 7). No kidding. Who would want them? Yet because the landowner was gracious—even employing these "leftovers" for only an hour—every worker received a day's wage (vv. 9–10).[17] Yet here's where the parable breaks down as a lesson in unearned favor. The workers got *paid* for what they did. Although the least desirable were hired for only an hour, they still *worked* for their reward, which doesn't sound like grace at all. Besides, a denarius for a full day's work wasn't generous pay—it was expected.[18]

To be sure, the parable works with a presumption about the economy of God's kingdom: in the end, all receive the same reward (eternal life?). But I don't think that's the main point of the parable. Instead, the way Jesus told the story—making the first workers stand in line to watch the landowner pay the last workers the same wage—sets up the punch of the parable: a biting critique of the attitude of the first workers who take issue with the generosity of the landowner. Those who worked all day expected to be paid for what they did; what they didn't expect was to be treated the same as everyone else. Their beef with their employer was that "*you have made them equal to us* who have borne the burden of the work and the heat of the day" (v. 12, emphasis added). There's the problem: God makes the last (the least of these—those who followed Jesus) just as important as the first (the greatest—the priests and the scribes) when his kingdom reign comes to earth, even *in Jerusalem*. But that shouldn't surprise us. Like the landowner said, what he does with his land is his business, and the way he conducts his business is his prerogative (vv. 14–15). It's what Jesus has been saying for some time. The way God conducts *his* business in *his* kingdom is this: "The last will be first, and the first will be last" (v. 16). Those who expect to be first in line need to learn to find their place in the back so they can see the justice of God.[19]

16. Luz, *Matthew*, 2:533–34; France, *Matthew*, 748–49.
17. France, *Matthew*, 748–49.
18. Scott, *Hear Then the Parable*, 283–84.
19. Snodgrass, *Stories with Intent*, 378–79.

LIVE the Story

Not everyone will celebrate the justice of God, especially on the last day. In fact, Jesus not only anticipated that "the first" will complain about it, but they will be envious of "the last" when they witness the mercy of God. In Jesus's parable, the landowner sized up the problem quickly. "The first" thought that they were being treated unjustly because they were treated like everyone else (Matt 20:13).[20] To them, justice means getting what you deserve. But God's justice doesn't work like that in the kingdom. In fact, the good news of the gospel of Jesus Christ is that God *doesn't* give us what we deserve. But, to those who think they're first, that sounds only like bad news. Therefore, when they witness the justice of God (mercy!), they will be envious of those who don't get what they deserve (v. 15). Rather than celebrate God's mercy, they cast an "evil eye"—an envious glance—toward the beneficiaries of his goodness.[21] In this way, Jesus identifies the root problem among "the first," the reason some people won't celebrate when God is good to others: envy. Those who are envious always view the world as unfair, a place where the wrong people get the right things, where the nobodies find the favor of God. Indeed, envy is a problem only among those who think they are "first" in God's eyes. They live by the expectation: "I deserve better."[22]

Of course, the question of reward hangs in the balance, not only *who* gets it but *what* it is. In fact, when it comes to the kingdom of God, rewards are a question of timing. That's the problem with most of us who are envious of others. Take the rich young man, for example. We might be tempted to look upon him with envy, believing that he is already receiving his reward—as if we were "the last" watching "the first" get the good stuff. Why should he live so well? He's so young. He didn't work for it. Why does God give him so much? So, we cast an envious eye toward the one who gets more than he deserves, languishing as we watch at the back of the line. But notice that Peter wasn't envious of the rich young man, even when the man couldn't part with his riches. If I were standing there, I might have been tempted to browbeat the young man as he walked away. "Hey you! Think you're better than the rest of us, huh? Okay. Go ahead. Go home. Live it up. You'll regret it one day—the day you have to face God Almighty!" But Peter wasn't envious. Instead, he

20. "The complaint is from the justly paid who cannot tolerate grace" (Bailey, *Jesus through Middle Eastern Eyes*, 361).

21. See Malina and Rohrbaugh for a description of the "evil eye" (*Synoptic Gospels*, 125–26).

22. "The problem with justice as a standard is that it misses the invitation" (Scott, *Hear Then the Parable*, 298).

simply wanted to know if giving up everything to follow Jesus would pay off in the end. Rewards are a matter of timing. So, the question is not only, "Which reward are we living for? Treasure on earth or treasure in heaven?" but also, "When will we receive our reward?" Well, we might confidently say, "Since we stored treasures in heaven, we will receive our reward on the last day." But what happens when God opens his heavenly treasury and starts doling out rewards now, while we watch from the back of the line? We might be able to live in anticipation of God rewarding us all at the same on the last day—we all get to live forever with him. But, what do we do in the meantime, at the end of a day's labor, when God is generous with those who don't deserve it? That's when envy rears its ugly head.

Here are some examples of what the parable of the day laborers might look like today:

When a seasoned pastor has been laboring in a downtown church for many years, and a young, slick, dynamic preacher shows up, starts a church, employs every gimmick known to man, and the new church explodes with dramatic growth.

When an author keeps churning out meaningful books that don't sell, and some young gun hawks his bestseller with a clever title and little substance.

When an irenic blogger offers intelligent posts every day, and an opportunistic poster funnels readers to her new blog, shamelessly tagging every comment with her website.

When a discipleship group of mature believers spends several years helping a new believer, and she joins another Bible study, complaining to the new group that she never was challenged spiritually.

When workers at a food pantry invest many hours gathering staples for the needy only to discover a mobile bakery from a high-powered ministry has invaded the neighborhood for the weekend, handing out sugary treats and invitations to their weeklong, backyard Bible club.

The reason why these scenarios might grate on our nerves (and therefore why we would probably join the chirping of the day-long workers in Jesus's parable) is that we share a worldly presumption that feeds our anger and blinds us to our envy. It's called (innocently enough) "the spirit of competition." It is an insidious impulse, an ingrained compulsion to be better than others, a fire that is stoked by our insatiable desire for recognition. The acquiring of wealth, of influence, of power, of significance—all of it is often cast in the context of competition. We want to be better than the rest. And, we must be rewarded for it. Even churches play the game, trying to outdo each other in the gospel business. So when God seems to reward those who haven't played fair, who don't deserve the success, who have cut into the long line of God's blessing—when we have to stand there and watch them getting what they haven't earned—we can't help but wonder: Where is the justice? Why is God doing this?

But Jesus would have us look at the situation from the perspective of the landowner. He has a vineyard that needs workers. He has a harvest that needs gathering. He hires all kinds of workers at many different times to work in his vineyard. He assumes that all of his hired help know they are working for the same employer to do the same thing. They have one purpose. They have one job. Bring in the harvest. That's all that really matters. If the landowner sees some people who need a higher purpose than just "standing around all day long doing nothing" with their lives,[23] shouldn't the workers be grateful for the extra help? Shouldn't we all celebrate when God rewards those who have worked for the same purpose? Besides, we all have the same calling, invited by the same generous employer. We didn't deserve this job. He gave it to us. He found all of us at the same place. How quickly we forget from whence we came—which is why, I think, he makes us stand in line and wait, watching him reward others. We may be a little confused at first. But then it should eventually dawn on us at the end of the day. It's *his* kingdom, *his* vineyard, *his* business. And we are merely his laborers, for this day until the last.

23. Bailey, *Jesus through Middle Eastern Eyes*, 358–59.

CHAPTER 29

Matthew 20:17–34

LISTEN to the Story

17Now Jesus was going up to Jerusalem. On the way, he took the
Twelve aside and said to them, 18"We are going up to Jerusalem, and the
Son of Man will be delivered over to the chief priests and the teachers of
the law. They will condemn him to death 19and will hand him over to the
Gentiles to be mocked and flogged and crucified. On the third day he
will be raised to life!"

20Then the mother of Zebedee's sons came to Jesus with her sons and,
kneeling down, asked a favor of him.

21"What is it you want?" he asked.

She said, "Grant that one of these two sons of mine may sit at your
right and the other at your left in your kingdom."

22"You don't know what you are asking," Jesus said to them. "Can you
drink the cup I am going to drink?"

"We can," they answered.

23Jesus said to them, "You will indeed drink from my cup, but to sit
at my right or left is not for me to grant. These places belong to those for
whom they have been prepared by my Father."

24When the ten heard about this, they were indignant with the two
brothers. 25Jesus called them together and said, "You know that the rulers
of the Gentiles lord it over them, and their high officials exercise authority
over them. 26Not so with you. Instead, whoever wants to become great
among you must be your servant, 27and whoever wants to be first must
be your slave—28just as the Son of Man did not come to be served, but to
serve, and to give his life as a ransom for many."

29As Jesus and his disciples were leaving Jericho, a large crowd followed
him. 30Two blind men were sitting by the roadside, and when they heard that
Jesus was going by, they shouted, "Lord, Son of David, have mercy on us!"

31The crowd rebuked them and told them to be quiet, but they
shouted all the louder, "Lord, Son of David, have mercy on us!"

[32]Jesus stopped and called them. "What do you want me to do for
you?" he asked.
[33]"Lord," they answered, "we want our sight."
[34]Jesus had compassion on them and touched their eyes. Immediately
they received their sight and followed him.

Listening to the Text in the Story: Exodus 30:12; Psalm 49:7–9; 2 Samuel 7:12–13; 1 Kings 1:15–17; Isaiah 29:18; 35:4–5; 51:17–52:10, 13–15; 53:3–12; Jeremiah 25:15–18, 27–29; 49:12.

The road up to Jerusalem was steep. A fifteen-mile stretch from Jericho in the valley to Jerusalem in the Judean mountains was no easy trek. In fact, to go from one of the lowest places on earth (Jericho was about 846 feet below sea level), climbing a mountainous road, ascending thirty-five hundred feet to Jerusalem[1] would have taken all day. Of course, these pilgrims making the arduous climb to the holy city would have greeted the trip with light-hearted optimism. They were traveling with a man who would be their Messiah, the one who would ascend to David's throne and bring God's justice to Israel and the whole world. A buzz of excitement was running through the crowd—the reports of Jesus's company reached even the ears of two blind men begging by the side of the road.[2] It was an optimum time for begging, what with all the Passover pilgrims heading for Jerusalem to remember the story of Israel's exodus when God redeemed his people from Egyptian slavery. To sit by the road looking for alms from this festive crowd was an opportunistic move. People give more during holidays; celebration inspires generosity among those who give to the less fortunate. (The Salvation Army is equally wise to this impulse.) So, just about everyone that day—the crowd of pilgrims as well as those begging for alms—was hopeful, wistful, anticipating a bright future. This was going to be a good day! Climbing the road to Jerusalem never felt better. Sure, legs would ache and winded pilgrims would have to rest for brief spells along the way. But, their hearts couldn't have been lighter. They were headed to Jerusalem to see all the promises of God come true, when the messianic glory of his kingdom would come to earth, resplendent in power and honor.

It is rather ironic that while Jesus ascended the mountain to claim David's throne, he spoke of a messianic path of descent, of stooping so low that

1. Turner, *Matthew*, 491.
2. Davies and Allison, *Matthew*, 3:107.

he would be "mocked and flogged and crucified" (Matt 20:19). Everyone's going up, while Jesus is anticipating heading down. But no one else saw the precipitous fall coming even though this was the third time Jesus predicted his demise in Jerusalem. Even the disciples expected to rise to dizzying heights when the kingdom of heaven invaded the holy city. Who can blame them? Jesus had recently promised that they would sit on twelve thrones and judge all of Israel once the Messiah took over Jerusalem and ascended to David's throne (19:28). That must have encouraged the mother of James and John to put in a bid for her sons to have the highest places of honor in Jesus's kingdom (20:20–21). Yet I wonder if Jesus was a little disappointed by her request. After all, he had just told his disciples that he's going to be tortured and killed once they get to Jerusalem (vv. 17–19). Then, mom shows up and throws herself down before Jesus, preventing him from going any farther.[3] What does she want (v. 21)? Maybe to try to talk Jesus out of going to Jerusalem, like any concerned mother would. "Please don't go, Jesus. My boys just told me[4] that you said the Romans—God's curse be upon them!—are going to kill you when you get there. Oh, no! What a horrible tragedy. Please don't go. If that's what they're going to do, why would you still want to go? Think of your mother. It will break her heart. Think of my boys—if they kill you, then they'll go after my sons for sure. Please, I beg you, don't go." But that's not what she wanted, even though she looked like she was getting ready to beg for something. Instead, she was hoping to see her boys get the best seats in the house of David (v. 21)—much to the chagrin of the other ten (v. 24).

It's as if everyone was blind to the messianic mission of Jesus. The Twelve didn't see it. The crowd of pilgrims was oblivious to it. For Jesus, that must have made for a lonely climb. Heading up the mountain to Jerusalem, surrounded by people celebrating, and Jesus—alone with his thoughts—knowing that every step brings him closer to his torturous death. We don't know what happened along the way. Matthew gives us no details about the journey, skipping from the healing of the blind men outside Jericho to the story of Jesus entering Jerusalem. Yet I cannot help but wonder if Jesus hoped that someone, *anyone*, would see what lay ahead. A moment of clarity for one of the Twelve. A sullen face or two among the multitude. But no one saw it. Jesus faced his future alone in a crowd of people. It's a holiday, and he's going to die.

---

3. Keener thinks Matthew introduces the mother as the questioner because women in first-century Jewish life could make requests that would be shameful for men to ask (*Matthew*, 485).

4. Garland, *Reading Matthew*, 212.

EXPLAIN the Story

Jesus wasn't looking for sympathy when he predicted his death the third time (Matt 20:17–19). He was trying to prepare his disciples for the way of the kingdom: a cross before a crown, humility leading to glory, not to be served but to serve. This was the road he would take, and all disciples would follow him. It was a hard path to accept, a narrow gate to enter. But it's one that Jesus had been teaching his disciples about from the beginning (7:13–14). He had already warned them about bringing a cross to Jerusalem, to be prepared to lose their life to find it (16:24–25). The closer they got to the holy city, the more he talked about it. Yes, he also spoke of rewards and thrones (16:27; 19:28–29). But the way his disciples would share in the glory of his throne would require a completely different road to power. In fact, ever since he announced their departure for Jerusalem (16:21), Jesus tried to disabuse his disciples of thinking that his kingdom would rely upon conventional methods of ruling the world. He told a parable about the last becoming first (20:1–16). Twice he compared his kingdom to children (18:2–5; 19:13–15), trying to get his disciples to see that "the kingdom of heaven belongs to such as these" (19:14). So, when ten of his disciples were indignant over James and John jockeying for pride of position in Jesus's kingdom (20:24), he had to huddle up the Twelve and tell them once again what it would take to rule the world—for him and for them.

Rule like Slaves

"You don't know what you are asking" (Matt 20:22). If Jesus were to say that to me, it would make me think twice about my request, especially if he followed up with the question, "Can you drink the cup I am going to drink?" If I were James or John, I would have pulled my brother aside to discuss the matter. "What do you think he means by that? What cup is he talking about? It sounds like a setup. Yet we know better than that. Jesus doesn't play mind games with us. So, what do you suppose he means, questioning our ability to drink the cup? Is he talking about raising a toast of victory after the battle for Jerusalem? Is he questioning our resolve to give up our lives for the kingdom?[5] Or, is he wondering whether we will even make it to the end?" But James and John act like they know exactly what Jesus was referring to when he spoke of drinking from his cup. Without flinching they shot back, "We can" (v. 22). And so Jesus didn't hesitate when he said (in a very ominous tone, perhaps),

5. Nolland doesn't think so (*Matthew*, 821).

"You will indeed drink from my cup. . ." (v. 23). For indeed they did. His disciples would drink from the same cup of the new covenant (26:27–28)—a cup of suffering[6]—even though Jesus would pray later for God to take it away from him (v. 39). I imagine James and John thinking to themselves after the Lord's Supper, "See? That wasn't so bad. We knew we could do it. We kept our word." But truly they didn't know what they were asking, especially the part about reigning with Jesus—one on his right, the other at his left—when he comes into his kingdom.[7]

The prophets warned Israel about having to drink the cup of God's wrath.[8] According to Jeremiah, God handed him the cup of his wrath, directing the prophet to force it down the throats of all the nations who disobeyed him—starting with Judah (Jer 25:15–18). Jerusalem too would soon suffer disaster as a result of sin (vv. 27–29). The difference with Jesus, of course, was his willingness to take the cup and drink it himself, not only for Israel's sake but for the whole world. Unlike Jeremiah, Jesus would force it on nobody. He knew he was destined to drink the cup even though he didn't want to (Matt 26:39). So, when James and John agreed (somewhat impetuously) to drink the cup, they should have known what this would mean. They had agreed to suffer the consequences of Israel's sin, to drink the cup of God's wrath down to the dregs. Disaster would fall upon them; like the servant of the Lord (Isa 53:3–12), they would be despised and rejected by mankind—the scapegoat of Israel's disobedience. Jesus would be the first to drink the cup, but he knew his disciples would follow him one day (Matt 20:23). Yet when it came to promising James and John that they would sit at his right and left when he came into his kingdom, Jesus was reticent to say. In fact, Jesus said it wasn't his decision. God had already prepared those who would occupy such significant positions (v. 23). As it turned out, when the time came James and John were nowhere to be found. When Jesus drank from the cup and was hailed the "king of Israel," the disciples proved that they really didn't know what they were asking. Instead, two rebels were at his side—one on the right, the other on his left—when Jesus came into his kingdom, wearing a crown and bearing a cross, just as he predicted (16:21–24; 17:22–23; 20:28; 26:28; 27:28–44).[9]

In light of what happened to Jesus when he "reigned" in Jerusalem as the king of Israel—no one saw it coming except Jesus—the ten probably later came to regret their indignation against James and John (20:24). It was one of those if-only-we-knew-then-what-we-know-now moments, one that the

6. Davies and Allison call it "the cup of eschatological sorrow" (*Matthew*, 3:90).
7. France wonders whether James and John were trying to usurp Peter's position (*Matthew*, 758).
8. See the discussion in Davies and Allison, *Matthew*, 3:89–90.
9. Keener, *Matthew*, 486; Davies and Allison, *Matthew*, 3:100.

Twelve probably recalled with shame as they reflected on what Jesus told them that day (vv. 25–28). The way the gentiles rule the world with irrepressible power and authority is not the way Jesus and his disciples would rule Israel and the nations. Worldly rule is all about power, officials lording it over their subjects. In Jesus's kingdom, it's all about giving power away. It's service; it's slavery. This is an eternal kingdom—the greatest of all rule and authority—because it never fades away. Why? Worldly rulers eventually lose power. Slaves of the kingdom of Jesus, however, will always serve. The world always needs slaves. So, Jesus's disciples will always have a job; we will always reign through service. That's why servants and slaves of Jesus never fear of losing power because we are always giving it away. This is what it means to be great: the first to become a slave rules the world. Jesus proved it. He came not to be served like a king of this world but to rule forever as a slave by paying a king's ransom—his very life (v. 28). This is the way he rules the world, by giving his life away; and so it is with his disciples. But sometimes it's hard to see it.

See like Blind Men

Matthew has paired these stories together, intending for us to draw comparisons and contrasts.[10] Along the way, two disciples asked for seats of honor in his kingdom (Matt 20:21). Beside the way, two blind men begged for mercy from the king (v. 30). Ten disciples stood in silence, indignant over the request (v. 24). The crowd tried to silence the two blind men despite their persistent request (v. 31). Jesus asked his disciples, "What is it you want?" (v. 21). Jesus asked the blind men, "What do you want me to do for you?" (v. 32). What the disciples wanted from Jesus is surprising. No one was surprised by what the blind men wanted. Yet what if we were to switch their responses? What if the blind men sounded like James and John, and these two disciples of Jesus made the same request as the blind men? How strange it would sound to our ears to hear the blind men answer Jesus's question, "What do you want me to do for you?" with, "Grant that we may sit at your right and the other at your left in your kingdom." How audacious! Nothing but a power grab. Think of how refreshing it would have been to hear James and John say to Jesus, "Lord, we want to see," especially in light of Jesus's teaching that his disciples would follow him down the messianic path of suffering. But that's not what happened. James and John asked for what they thought they deserved. The two blind men only asked for what sighted people take for granted every day. And there's the difference between the kingdom of this world and the kingdom of heaven coming to earth. Those who think they see want power; those who know they are blind need Jesus.

10. Davies and Allison, *Matthew*, 3:101, 110.

The annual pilgrimage of Passover visitors must have been a sight to behold for the people of Jericho. Nearly all travelers passed through Jericho on their way to Jerusalem to celebrate the great festival of God's deliverance of his people. The "Jericho Road," as it has come to be known, was one of the most traveled ways to the holy city. The parade of people singing and dancing, wine flowing freely—these joyful pilgrims brought a carnival-like atmosphere to Jericho, the last stop on the road to Jerusalem. Furthermore, knowing that Jesus was among the merry celebrants must have pumped up the crowd of revelers like never before. So when two blind men tried to stop the parade with their incessant begging, crying out loud to get Jesus's attention, several in the crowd took matters into their own hands. They must have thought, "We don't have time for this. We're headed for Jerusalem. We've been walking for miles and we're almost there. The Messiah is going to take care of business when he gets to Jerusalem, and we can't wait to see it! So, let's keep moving. A long day's trip is ahead of us. Somebody shut those fools up." Yet the more the crowd tried to silence the blind men, the more the beggars cried out to Jesus (v. 31). That's just what we would expect from obnoxious people. (I say that sarcastically.) The more you try to put them in their place, the more of a nuisance they become. And yet, it seems like the blind men were the *only* ones on the Jericho road that day who knew this would be their last chance to *see* Jesus. So, they took it. Nothing and no one was going to stop them now.

I'm so glad Jesus decided to stop the parade for these two blind men. If there were ever a time Jesus could have "begged off" serving others, it was then. Alone with his thoughts, knowing what he was about to face when he arrived to Jerusalem—such a singular focus should have compelled him to walk the Jericho road with tunnel vision. But he didn't. Instead, even though his heart could have been heavy with the grief of his upcoming passion, Jesus heard the cries of desperate men, begging at the side of the road. Above the shouts of the disapproving crowd, beyond the noisy celebration of these Passover pilgrims, Jesus always hears those who cry out for his mercy. Indeed, Jesus said he not only came to "give his life as a ransom for many," but he also came to serve (v. 28). This story is a perfect example of what he meant. When he looked into the eyes of these two blind men and asked, "What do you want me to do for you?" his question may have appeared to those standing around as cruel and insensitive. What else would a blind man want except to see? Well, with such an open-ended question coming from such a powerful man, a shrewd beggar might take the opportunity to try to cash the blank check. "Make me wealthy beyond my wildest dreams," or "Give me eternal life," or "Grant that I may sit at your right hand when you come into your kingdom." Yet the only thing a blind man wants is what a blind man needs: to see. That's why Jesus "had compassion on them and touched their eyes" (v. 34).[11] He always had his ears open to the lost sheep who cried for help. It's not surprising, then, that these two who "once were lost but now they are found, who once were blind but now they see" followed Jesus to Jerusalem.[12] For there they would see their shepherd lead his flock to evergreen pastures, the king coming into his eternal kingdom—the "first" to become a slave.

LIVE the Story

As I write these words, the Supreme Court of the United States is hearing a case about the rights of gay people to marry. Many people are anxious about the outcome, not only those hoping to marry regardless of their residence but also those who have been fighting the culture war in America. The politics of this revolutionary decision has turned a complex issue into a black-and-white reality—which is what typically happens in politics. Regardless of the issue—no matter how complicated the matter—political discourse quickly turns into an "us-versus-them" debate. There's no room for nuance, no patience for careful discussion. Everyone is forced to decide. You're either on one side or the other. To pursue a third way, to explore a path where neither side wins, to consider another approach to social issues—these efforts are often dismissed as coming from weak-kneed, spineless cowards. "You need to take a stand!" Shouting down all other voices, each side ratchets up the rhetoric, hoping to win the war of words. Of course, more than public opinion is at stake. The stakes are much higher than that. Indeed, when it comes to power, everyone wants a piece of the action, each side making superior claims of what is right and what is wrong.

When these battles are played out in public, I often listen for the voices that have been silenced, those on the margins who have opinions and stories and ideas that can't be forced into the mold of either/or politics. For example, there are gay Christians who do not believe that homoerotic behavior, under any circumstances, glorifies God. They didn't choose to be gay. It's all they've known. The first time they began to be sexually attracted to others, it was a person of the same sex. Yet their same-sex attraction doesn't define them; there is so much more to life than being gay. They are disciples of Jesus.[13] When it

11. Luz writes: "With the last of many healings of the blind [Matthew] calls attention once again to the great light that 'the people who sat in darkness' saw (4:16)" (*Matthew*, 2:550).

12. Bruner, *Matthew*, 2:349.

13. See the compelling story of Wesley Hill, *Washed and Waiting: Reflections on Christian Faithfulness and Homosexuality* (Grand Rapids: Zondervan, 2010), especially 123–50. (Thank you, Wesley, for your honest reflections and unflinching desire to be faithful to our Lord. You are a rare gift to the church.)

comes to curbing the desires of the flesh, they know they can't "pray the gay away." But, they also believe that a man having sex with a man or a woman having sex with a woman is a sin against God. Yet neither side in the fight over gay marriage wants to hear their story—neither Christians fighting the culture war nor the LGBT community. Why not? It's because their narrative doesn't fit into the mold of either political agenda. The LGBT community patronizes these gay Christians, telling them that they're deceived, that they've been duped by their religious upbringing. How arrogant. Moreover, many Christians who are fighting against marriage equality refuse to admit that there are gay Christians. How ignorant. Here is an important voice that has been marginalized in the politics of marriage. I can't help but wonder what Jesus would think, because there are people on both sides of this issue who are convinced that he would be on their side—one on the right, the other on the left. I'm not so sure. Here's why.

Jesus constantly tried to teach his disciples that following him means giving away your rights. "You know that the rulers of the gentiles lord it over them, and their high officials exercise authority over them. Not so with you" (Matt 20:25–26). Christians who once prized holding the political power of a "moral majority" in America are finally going to learn the significance of Jesus's words. It's about time we admit it. We lost the culture war. (I'm not grieving because I never believed in it.) In fact, I think it may be the best thing that ever happened to Christianity in the United States—to finally be in the minority, to learn a little humility, to learn how to admit we have enemies (we've made *many* during the culture wars), and then learn how to love them as God loves us, to be at the right and left of Jesus in his kingdom (sacrifice!). No more talk of protecting our rights. Why not give away our power for the sake of the king who gave away his power to save us? Furthermore, there are gay Christians who believe the same. They are convinced that following Jesus means giving up their rights, sacrificing themselves for a politic much higher than the kingdom of this world. They've had to suffer the "shame" of belonging to Jesus in a Christian subculture that made same-sex attraction the unpardonable sin. Ostracized like blind men forgotten on the side of the road while the pious sang their song, "Come we that love the Lord, and let our joys be known," they were never invited to "join in the song of sweet accord." For all the years I attended church, I heard many Christians find support and encouragement in their desire to crucify the flesh with all its passions and desires. But *not once* did I see a gay Christian have the freedom to share his burden with the body of Christ. It grieves me now to think about how lonely that must feel. Silenced by the joyous pilgrims "marching for Zion," we left them at the side of the road.

But, thank God, Jesus always hears the voices of those on the margins, persons who have been silenced by the crowd. Moreover, I'm so glad when Jesus asks the same question today, "What do you want me to do for you?" Although dismissed by the crowd as insensitive and foolish, it is still answered the same way by Christ followers, whether gay or straight: "I want to see."

CHAPTER 30

Matthew 21:1–22

LISTEN to the Story

21 As they approached Jerusalem and came to Bethphage on the Mount
of Olives, Jesus sent two disciples, 2 saying to them, “Go to the village
ahead of you, and at once you will find a donkey tied there, with her colt
by her. Untie them and bring them to me. 3 If anyone says anything to you,
say that the Lord needs them, and he will send them right away.”
4 This took place to fulfill what was spoken through the prophet:

> 5 “Say to Daughter Zion,
> ‘See, your king comes to you,
> gentle and riding on a donkey,
> and on a colt, the foal of a donkey.’ ”

6 The disciples went and did as Jesus had instructed them. 7 They
brought the donkey and the colt and placed their cloaks on them for Jesus
to sit on. 8 A very large crowd spread their cloaks on the road, while others
cut branches from the trees and spread them on the road. 9 The crowds
that went ahead of him and those that followed shouted,

> “Hosanna to the Son of David!”
> “Blessed is he who comes in the name of the Lord!”
> “Hosanna in the highest heaven!”

10 When Jesus entered Jerusalem, the whole city was stirred and asked,
“Who is this?”
11 The crowds answered, “This is Jesus, the prophet from Nazareth in
Galilee.”
12 Jesus entered the temple courts and drove out all who were buying
and selling there. He overturned the tables of the money changers and
the benches of those selling doves. 13 “It is written,” he said to them, “ ‘My
house will be called a house of prayer,’ but you are making it ‘a den of
robbers.’ ”

[14]The blind and the lame came to him at the temple, and he healed
them. [15]But when the chief priests and the teachers of the law saw the
wonderful things he did and the children shouting in the temple courts,
"Hosanna to the Son of David," they were indignant.
[16]"Do you hear what these children are saying?" they asked him.

"Yes," replied Jesus, "have you never read,

> 'From the lips of children and infants
> you, Lord, have called forth your praise'?"

[17]And he left them and went out of the city to Bethany, where he spent
the night.
[18]Early in the morning, as Jesus was on his way back to the city, he was
hungry. [19]Seeing a fig tree by the road, he went up to it but found nothing
on it except leaves. Then he said to it, "May you never bear fruit again!"
Immediately the tree withered.
[20]When the disciples saw this, they were amazed. "How did the fig tree
wither so quickly?" they asked.
[21]Jesus replied, "Truly I tell you, if you have faith and do not doubt,
not only can you do what was done to the fig tree, but also you can say
to this mountain, 'Go, throw yourself into the sea,' and it will be done.
[22]If you believe, you will receive whatever you ask for in prayer."

Listening to the Text in the Story: Genesis 49:10–11; Deuteronomy 18:15–19; 2 Samuel 5:6–8; 7:12–13; 1 Kings 1:32–40; 2 Kings 9:12–13; Psalms 8:2; 69:9; 118:22–26; Isaiah 1:3; 34:4; 56:7; 62:11; Jeremiah 7:9–11; 8:13; 24:1–10; 26:11; Hosea 9:10, 16–17; Zechariah 9:9; 14:4; Malachi 3:1–6; 4:1–3.

How would Jesus show Jerusalem that he was the Messiah of Israel? Offer a repeat performance of what he did in Galilee by healing the needy, feeding the hungry, and walking on water? Or, would he find the highest location in Jerusalem and offer "The Sermon on the Mount, part 2"? Would he gather the Twelve and give them special instructions on how they would gather the "lost sheep" in Jerusalem before sending them into the city of David? Or, would he set up shop somewhere inside the city and expect the crowds to show up looking for help? If he did any of these things, it would have made sense, given his track record. But instead Jesus entered Jerusalem according to an ancient script that had been written over the ages—the day the son of

David would claim the throne of his forefather and make all of God's promises come true (1 Kgs 1:32–40).[1] In fact, the way Matthew tells the story of Jesus's royal entrance into Jerusalem, Jesus staged the event according to these messianic expectations (Zech 9:9), sending two of his disciples to find a donkey and her foal to carry him through the eastern gate (Matt 21:1–7). Jesus's entourage picked up on the gesture, deciding to join the performance by gathering branches and laying their garments on the road leading into Jerusalem (v. 8), re-creating the scene of a newly anointed king who would lead a successful military campaign against his enemies (2 Kgs 9:1–13).[2] Up to this point, Jesus had encouraged his followers to keep his messianic identity a secret (Matt 16:20). Now, however, having come to the climax of his story, Jesus knew it was time to let the whole world know—especially the citizens of Jerusalem—that their long-awaited Messiah was here. He had talked a lot about a kingdom. Now it was time to present the king. Finally, Jerusalem would see their king coming to them "gentle and riding on a donkey," just as Zechariah prophesied.

For all the ostentatious display of Jesus's royal introduction to Jerusalem, the citizenry was not impressed. They mused over the spectacle of these rural folk pouring into the big city with their Galilean prophet in tow, hailing him as the new king with shouts of "hosanna to the Son of David!" and "blessed is he who comes in the name of the Lord!" (Ps 118:25–26;[3] Matt 21:9). Taking in the "charade," some citizens muttered contemptuously to no one in particular, "Who is this?" (Matt 21:10).[4] They probably knew who he was. More than likely his reputation had preceded him since their leaders had probably reported what they learned during their reconnaissance mission (15:1). But it was the parade of Galileans marching into town,[5] acting like one of their own was someone special, that must have appeared incredibly pretentious to the ruling class.[6] So, when the city-dwellers harrumphed, "Who does this guy think he is?" the outsiders proudly shouted back, "This is Jesus, the prophet

1. N. T. Wright, *Jesus and the Victory of God*, Christian Origins and the Question of God 2 (Minneapolis: Fortress, 1996), 489–93.

2. "As clothes represent their wearers. . ., their position beneath another's feet means submission" (Davies and Allison, *Matthew*, 3:123).

3. Psalm 118 was often recited during Passover (ibid., 3:126).

4. Is this a deliberate echo of Isaiah 1:3? "The ox knows its master, the donkey its owner's manger, but Israel does not know, my people do not understand." The proposal is especially intriguing in light of the way Matthew phrases Jesus's instructions to the owner of the donkey and her colt: "If anyone says anything to you, say that the Lord needs them." Actually, the phrase *ho kyrios autōn chreian echei* should be translated, "*Their* Lord has a need," referring to Jesus or God as the master of these animals (see Davies and Allison, *Matthew*, 3:117).

5. France, *Matthew*, 773.

6. Malina and Rohrbaugh, *Synoptic Gospels*, 128.

from Nazareth in Galilee" (Matt 21:11). "Nazareth! Can anything good come from there?"—the insiders must have thought (John 1:46). This was more than the age-old contest of rural folk clashing with the big city, farmers and fishermen coming to challenge the retainer class. The Messiah was supposed to be an insider—royal blood coursing through his veins—if not from Jerusalem at least from Judea (Matt 2:6). Everyone knew the one who was destined to inherit David's throne wasn't supposed to come from Galilee. Therefore, the way Jerusalem saw it, these country bumpkins had forgotten their place in society, having come to town to shake up the establishment: "The whole city was stirred" (21:10).

It may seem to us like an unusual place to begin acting like a king, throwing a "temple tantrum" in Herod's massive addition to the holy place, the court of the gentiles (21:12–13). One wonders whether the Galileans who had accompanied Jesus to observe Passover expected him to march straight to the Roman governor's quarters and run the despot out of town. Certainly, if the kingdom of heaven were to come to earth, it would have to begin with the king pushing God's enemies out of Jerusalem. And what better enemy—the first to go!—than the Roman Empire? But Jesus had grander designs, for God had promised king David that one of his descendants would "build a house for my Name," and therefore God promised that "I will establish the throne of his kingdom forever" (2 Sam 7:13). Besides, the temple was the first thing he saw when he entered Jerusalem through the eastern gate. And so, once again conforming to the messianic script,[7] Jesus's first stop in Jerusalem had to be the temple. Acting like the prophesied Son of David who would build a house for God and thereby establish his kingdom forever, Jesus showed all of Jerusalem what he meant when he told the Pharisees, "Something greater than the temple is here" (Matt 12:6).[8]

EXPLAIN the Story

Jesus took Jerusalem by storm. Rather than play it safe and sneak into the Holy City, setting up some clandestine operation to slowly but surely take over the place (like yeast leavening the entire lump), Jesus made his intentions known from the start. Yet he didn't march through the streets shouting, "Your Messiah is here!" He didn't even try to amaze the citizens with miraculous feats of divine power. Come to think of it, Jesus didn't perform many miracles in Jerusalem. (Was it a repeat of Matt 13:58?) Instead, the way Jesus made his

7. See Nicholas Perrin, *Jesus the Temple* (Grand Rapids: Baker Academic, 2010), 101–4.

8. France, *Matthew*, 785.

royal presence known was to employ a more *prophetic* strategy, doing strange things to get people's attention. Like Jeremiah's broken pot (Jer 19:1–15) or Elijah's drought declaration (1 Kgs 17:1), Jesus performed symbolic actions (clearing the temple, cursing the fig tree) to deliver the message of God's judgment against the rulers of Jerusalem.[9] If Jesus came to Jerusalem to reign as God's chosen, that would certainly mean the current leadership was in trouble. They hadn't been taking care of God's house; they weren't running the place rightly. If they had, they would have welcomed God's anointed one, handing over the keys of the city to him. Yet, to their way of thinking Jesus was an intruder, the rogue prophet who was going to take things too far. Therefore, the priests ensured Jesus would suffer a fate worse than Jeremiah or Elijah. Back then, the priest in charge of the temple had Jeremiah beaten and put in stocks (Jer 20:1–2); Elijah escaped from king Ahab by hiding in Zarephath (1 Kgs 17:7–10). But Jesus would find no refuge in Jerusalem, not even in a park outside the city. God wouldn't provide the same protection as he did for Elijah. Instead, Jesus would be hunted down, arrested, beaten, and turned over to the Romans to be impaled on a cross. Treated worse than Jeremiah, Jesus would become the laughingstock of Israel, thrown out of the Holy City like refuse. Enter like a king; exit like a criminal.

But it's not like Jesus was an innocent victim of the sinister ways of the corrupt ruling class, a harmless dove who fell into the hands of these wicked leaders. Jesus didn't come into the city preaching love and forgiveness only to be assaulted by merciless hatemongers. Rather, Jesus got what was coming to him, doing several things that would get anyone killed. Indeed, to any casual observer Jesus's behavior during Passover would have appeared as though this Galilean outsider had a death wish, provoking the Jerusalem insiders—priests and scribes—when he cleared the temple and predicted its demise (Matt 21:12–13; 24:1–2; cf. Jer 26:8–11). It was the high priest's responsibility to keep the peace in Jerusalem so that the Romans wouldn't take their usual mallet-to-a-fly approach, crushing any appearance of unrest by rounding up innocent victims and making them pay for the foolish behavior of a few. Passover during Roman occupation of Judea had a bloody history at times.[10] So, when Jesus created a disturbance in the temple, the very center of all Jewish religious activity, the chief priests were immediately wedged between a rock (pacifying the Roman Empire) and a hard place (placating a rogue prophet). From their perspective, Jesus was asking for trouble. It's one thing to stage a little parade, pretending you're a king. It's quite something else to clear the temple, acting like you own the place.

---

9. Davies and Allison, *Matthew*, 3:136–37.
10. Josephus, *Ant.* 17.9.3; *War* 2.12.1.

"Zeal for Your House Consumes Me" (Ps 69:9)

From the time of Solomon to the destruction of the temple by Nebuchadnezzar (587/6 BC), there were few kings who did what was right in the sight of the Lord. Most rulers, whether of the Northern Kingdom, Israel, or the Southern Kingdom, Judah, did what was evil in the sight of the Lord; that is, they promoted idolatry. Good kings, on the other hand, not only took measures to abolish idolatry, destroying shrines to other gods, they restored the temple by purifying it. At the beginning of his reign, Hezekiah purified the temple by "removing all defilement from the sanctuary" and reconsecrated the priests who served under the wicked king Ahaz (2 Chr 29:1–19). But his efforts didn't last long. When Josiah became king, he found a neglected temple in an awful state of disrepair. Having discovered the lost book of the law during his renovation of the temple, Josiah launched a reformation that was supposed to seal the allegiance of the people in their worship of a holy God (2 Chr 34:1–33).[11] But that didn't last either. After the temple was destroyed by the Babylonians, not even Zerubbabel's efforts to rebuild the temple made Haggai's prophesies come true: "The glory of this present house will be greater than the glory of the former house" (Hag 2:9). The temple built by Zerubbabel was a pitiful site compared to Solomon's magnificent structure. Things were getting worse, not better. That's why Malachi longed for the "coming one"—a divine figure?—to visit God's house and purify the temple, even refining the priests "like gold and silver" (Mal 3:1–4). The day God visited his house would be a fiery ordeal, a purifying presence that would restore his temple to its intended purpose: "Then the LORD will have men who will bring offerings in righteousness, and the offerings of Judah and Jerusalem will be acceptable to the LORD" (vv. 3–4).

But Jesus never made it to the holy place where sacrifices were offered to God. Evidently, the sight of merchants selling animals in the court of the gentiles outside the temple proper was enough to incite his prophetic zeal to purify the place as soon as he entered the complex. By overturning the benches of those selling sacrificial doves to the poor and toppling the tables of those exchanging Roman coins for Jewish currency, Jesus put the trustees of the temple on notice (Matt 21:12–13). They had let the place go, turning sacred space into a marketplace.[12] Animals for sacrifice once sold outside the temple complex were now conveniently available for purchase in the court of the gentiles. Money changers kept corrupt Roman currency—with its graven image of Caesar—out of the temple proper. All of this was to facilitate the pure worship of God. But Jesus found the whole practice detestable. By quoting a mash-up of Isaiah's end-time vision of the temple, "My house will be called a

11. Turner, *Matthew*, 501.

12. Keener, *Matthew*, 497; France, *Matthew*, 783–84.

house of prayer" (Isa 56:7) and a phrase from Jeremiah's temple sermon predicting its destruction, "But you are making it 'a den of robbers'" (Jer 7:11), Jesus justified his efforts of purification. The front porch of the temple (the court of the gentiles), intended to welcome all nations, had become a Jewish agora.[13] Since gentiles weren't allowed in the temple, this massive courtyard was supposed to be a place where all nations could pray to the God of Israel. But Jesus saw the mercantile necessity of money changing hands as prohibitive to prayer.[14] Therefore, it seems the location of buying and selling troubled Jesus (thus the quotation from Isaiah). The gentiles had been doubly marginalized: once by walls, twice by contempt. Not only that, but Jesus implied that the entire business of selling animals and exchanging currency was corrupt (thus the quotation from Jeremiah). They had turned God's house of prayer into a "den of robbers." Yet what does that mean?

Scholars are divided on this issue.[15] Either Jesus was implying that he needed to purify the place where people were getting robbed,[16] or Jesus was pronouncing judgment on a place where robbers hoped to hide from God's righteous indignation.[17] In other words, some infer from Jesus's actions that the merchants were selling sacrificial animals at an exorbitant price, and perhaps even that currency was being exchanged at an unreasonably high rate. One has to pay for convenience (like five-dollar drinks and seven-dollar popcorn at the movies—location, location, location). Either that or Jesus's motivation for clearing the temple was the same as Jeremiah's for delivering his infamous temple sermon: "Will you steal and murder, commit adultery and perjury, burn incense to Baal and follow other gods you have not known, and then come and stand before me in this house, which bears my Name, and say, 'We are safe'—safe to do detestable things?" (Jer 7:9–10). The same was true for Jesus's day: corrupt religious leaders were using the temple as a sanctuary, seeking protection from the wrath of God through animal sacrifice (the prophets *hated* that presumption; "To *obey* is better than sacrifice!"; 1 Sam 15:22, emphasis added). That's why Jesus (and Jeremiah) called the temple a "robber's den." Thievery doesn't happen in the robber's den; it's where robbers go to hide out from their crimes.[18]

Yet if that were the case, why did Jesus pick on the merchants and the money changers since they weren't doing anything unjust? He should have gone straight to the holy place and overturned the tables of incense if the temple needed purification due to wicked priests. But there's another problem, not

13. Keener, *Matthew*, 500.
14. France, *Matthew*, 784.
15. See Talbert for a succinct and helpful summary (*Matthew*, 247–49).
16. Luz, *Matthew*, 3:12.
17. Garland, *Reading Matthew*, 216.
18. Ibid.

only with the temple cleansing as judgment but also as purification. If Jesus intended to "clean up the place" so that sacrifices would be acceptable to God (like Malachi envisioned), then why would he turn right around and predict its destruction (Matt 24:1–2)? Had he so quickly come to the conclusion that the whole thing was hopeless? Cleansing the temple on Sunday, resigned to its destruction on Monday? What's the point of trying to reform the old place (Jer 26:12–13) when Jesus came to build a new temple (Matt 16:18)? That question has led some scholars to suggest that the whole thing was a prophetic act.[19] Jesus wasn't offering a commentary on the righteousness of the priests or the purity of the temple. The place wasn't "dirty," and the priests weren't "corrupt." Rather, like the prophets of old Jesus's "temple tantrum" was symbolic, one that was required to signal the end of the old age and the beginning of the new. In other words, Jesus's temple clearing was not only a sign pointing back to Malachi's prophecy—God visiting his temple—but also a signal ahead of its imminent destruction. Before a new temple can be built, the old one must be destroyed. So, Jesus's actions in the temple—the earthquake of turning over tables, shaking up the place—were a living parable, acting out the prophecy of its destruction. "God has left the building." Without its divine occupant, it would only be a matter of time until the whole thing imploded. No more trying to prop up the old, hoping to clean up the place and reform the priesthood. Rather, the Son of David came to build the eternal house of God, the sanctuary of his kingdom that would last forever. Out with the old, in with the new—a house made without human hands.[20] Indeed, something greater than the temple is here.

However we interpret Jesus's actions and thereby determine his intentions (he left it open to interpretation, like the parables!), what he did in the temple on "Palm Sunday" was climactic to his entire ministry. In fact, it could be said that everything Jesus had done to this point led to this moment. All along, Jesus had defied conventional wisdom and challenged traditional practices through his teaching and wonder-working ministry. Therefore, it isn't surprising that in the aftermath of his tornadic activity that cleared God's house of all the "debris," the blind and the lame were welcomed into the temple, and children seemed to be the only ones praising God for it (Matt 21:14–15).[21] It was more than the chief priests and teachers of the law could take.[22] They were

19. Sanders, *Judaism*, 61–71.

20. See Perrin, *Jesus the Temple*, 106–9.

21. Was this an "anti-Davidic" gesture, reversing David's ban of the lame and blind from his palace after he captured Jerusalem (2 Sam 5:6–8)? Yes, according to Davies and Allison, *Matthew*, 3:140; probably not, according to Luz, *Matthew*, 3:13.

22. The blind and lame were excluded from entering the temple (Davies and Allison, *Matthew*, 3:140; also Garland, *Reading Matthew*, 216). Nolland questions the ban (*Matthew*, 846–47); Luz argues they were not excluded (*Matthew*, 3:13).

indignant: "Do you hear what these children are saying?" (v. 16). A proper sense of shame should have compelled Jesus to shush them up because children often don't know what they are saying. Or perhaps Jesus could have defended them by pointing out the obvious: when the blind and the lame find healing in the temple, shouldn't we all celebrate the miraculous work of God? Instead, Jesus quoted the first part of Psalm 8:2 LXX: "From the lips of children and infants you, Lord, have called forth your praise" (Matt 21:16). He left it to his accusers to finish the rest: "Through the praise of children and infants *you have established a stronghold against your enemies, to silence the foe and the avenger*" (Ps 8:2, emphasis added). But we will learn soon enough that the messianic praise of these children didn't silence Jesus's enemies. When he returned to the temple the next day, the religious leaders would be lying in wait to confront this rogue prophet in hopes of proving that these ignorant children were wrong. And I can't help but hear echoes of Jesus's teaching, "Truly I tell you, unless you change and become like little children, you will never enter the kingdom of heaven. . . . And whoever welcomes one such child in my name welcomes me" (Matt 18:3, 5). Even if we had never read this part of Matthew's Gospel, one could tell where this story is headed.

"May You Never Bear Fruit Again!"

Everyone knows the purpose of a fig tree is to bear figs. But when Jesus inspected a fig tree on his way to Jerusalem the next morning, he didn't find any fruit (Matt 21:18–19). Having spent the night in Bethany (just outside Jerusalem, v. 17), Jesus headed for the city again. (Obviously, none of the city dwellers invited him to stay with them—the honorable thing to do for travelers who were held in high esteem. But Jesus was rejected by Jerusalem; a prophet "without honor" had to find hospitality outside the city.) And so, the next day Jesus wanted to get an early start (v. 18). Having skipped breakfast, he was looking to find fruit on the fig tree. The problem, of course, is that early spring was not the time to find figs on a fig tree (something Mark was obliged to point out; Mark 11:13). Fig trees didn't bear edible fruit until June (Matt 24:32). The fact that this tree was an early bloomer,[23] indicating the possibility that some unripe figs could be found on the tree,[24] may have encouraged Jesus to search its leaves for fruit (ironically, the town Jesus passed through on his way to Jerusalem on "Palm Sunday" was Bethphage, meaning, "House of Unripe Figs";[25] Matt 21:1).

It wasn't a surprise to anyone that Jesus didn't find figs on the tree. What was surprising to his disciples—and to us as well—was the way Jesus handled

23. France, *Matthew*, 792.

24. Keener, *Matthew*, 504.

25. Davies and Allison, *Matthew*, 3:115; Nolland, *Matthew*, 832.

the disappointment. He cursed the fig tree, and it died immediately (v. 19). Jesus had never done anything like that before. Multiply bread and fish to feed a hungry crowd? Check. Rebuke a storm kicking up on the Sea of Galilee? Check. But to curse a fig tree because it hasn't borne any fruit *at the wrong time of the year* appears a little capricious if not impatient. (In fact, this story sounds a lot like one of the apocryphal stories of when Jesus was a little boy with great powers who couldn't control his anger. Not very flattering.) So, what we want to know is, "Why did Jesus do it?" Yet this didn't seem to bother the Twelve. Apparently, all the disciples wanted to know was, "How did the fig tree wither so quickly?" (v. 20). Really? That's their question? Marveling over the effectiveness of Jesus's "curse word" that caused the tree to wither immediately—from the same man who could still a storm and raise the dead with his words—that's what surprised the disciples? We want to know why he did it; the Twelve wanted to know how it happened so quickly—which says more about us than it does about them. Perhaps the reason the disciples didn't ask "Why?" is because they already knew the answer. In fact, that the Twelve knew *why* Jesus cursed the fig tree may explain why they were amazed that it happened so *fast*.

A fruitless fig tree that withers due to divine judgment was a common prophetic symbol of Israel under God's punishment (Jer 8:13; Hos 2:12; 9:10, 16–17; Mic 7:1–8).[26] So, I'm wondering if Jesus's disciples had connected the dots: fig tree = Jerusalem. In light of the previous day's events, they would know why Jesus cursed the fig tree. It was a sign of God's judgment on the city of David. For those who had eyes to see, Jesus was forecasting the destruction of Jerusalem because its citizens did not recognize their king. Jesus had come to the temple and found it full of activity—in full leaf, but he discovered no fruit. This house of prayer that was supposed to draw all nations to Jerusalem to worship God (Isa 56:6–8) had become a den of thieves. So when Jesus cursed the fig tree, he was essentially saying, "The end is near." Although it looked like Jesus was talking to a tree, he was actually prophesying against Jerusalem and the temple: "May *you* never bear fruit again!" (Matt 21:19, emphasis added). What surprised the Twelve was how quickly it would happen.[27] As fast as a leafy fig tree withering right before their eyes, Jerusalem would fall.

If that is the case—if I'm not assuming too much of the disciples' ability to comprehend these things—then Jesus kept talking in apocalyptic terms, teaching his disciples that they would be able to move "this mountain" (v. 21, perhaps the Mount of Olives[28]) just as Zechariah envisioned: "On that

26. Luz, *Matthew*, 3:23–24; France, *Matthew*, 793.
27. Garland, *Reading Matthew*, 217.
28. Keener, *Matthew*, 505; Nolland, *Matthew*, 853.

day his feet will stand on the Mount of Olives, east of Jerusalem, and the Mount of Olives will be split in two from east to west, forming a great valley" (Zech 14:4).[29] Both Isaiah and Micah predicted that mountains would be leveled on the last day: "Look! The LORD is coming from his dwelling place; he comes down and treads on the heights of the earth. The mountains melt beneath him and the valleys split apart. . . . All this is because of Jacob's transgression, because of the sins of the people of Israel" (Mic 1:3–5); "every mountain and hill [will be] made low. . . . And the glory of the LORD will be revealed and all people will see it together" (Isa 40:4–5). On the other hand, if the disciples were simply amazed at the power of Jesus's word, then his lesson on faith that moves mountains was intended to dispel doubt (Matt 21:21). If Jesus could cause a tree to wither and die, then his disciples would be able to do even greater things: to speak to a mountain and toss it into the Dead Sea. Either way, whether forecasting the destruction of Jerusalem or encouraging his disciples to "have faith and do not doubt," Jesus was teaching his disciples that, even without a temple, they would *still* be able to pray so as to move mountains (v. 22). They wouldn't need a house of prayer to have faith in God.

LIVE the Story

This is a difficult story to carry into our world because what Jesus did was unique to his situation. If these actions were symbolic demonstrations of his messianic claims—a once-in-a-lifetime display of prophetic intention—then we would be taking the story too far by trying to re-create a nonrepeatable event. Jesus presented himself as the Messiah of God to Jerusalem once. He cleansed a temple that was eventually destroyed. As followers of Jesus, we already affirm that he is Messiah—not only over Jerusalem but the entire world. There is no need to restage the event of Jesus by taking the Holy City for his messianic purpose. He's already done the job. Besides, there is no temple, no building to cleanse; Christ followers have no official priests offering animal sacrifices as a requirement of worship. Yet that doesn't stop some of us from assuming the role of Jesus when we think it's time to "clean house" and "turn over tables" in righteous indignation. Over the years, many holy crusaders have appeared in our ranks, convinced that Jesus was their model when they decided to create a ruckus and challenge leaders over corruption in the church: from raising a stink over fundraisers setting up tables inside the

29. Some commentators think that Jesus was referring to Zion (the temple mount); see Turner, *Matthew*, 504.

church house to questioning the integrity of all ministers when one has been charged with a serious crime like embezzlement. Many of us like to think that we're acting like Jesus when we get angry over church matters. After all, since the church is the temple of the Lord and *everyone* sees that it's dirty, somebody needs to step up and have the courage to clean the place. Enter the self-appointed prophet with the messiah complex, cracking the whip and running the corrupt people out of the temple. That's when it's easy to "follow Jesus." Pick up a cross and offer yourself as a sacrifice to purify the temple? Not many takers. But to storm the church with holy anger and set everyone straight—that's when some of us are more than willing to "follow the Messiah." However, when we throw a righteous fit to purify the church, I don't think we are acting like Jesus's disciples at all.

I recently saw a church sign that boasted, "We love our church!" That's a nice sentiment, but the sign should read, "We love ourselves!" Sometimes we talk about the church as if it were independent of us, as if the church was an organization that exists outside of us. But that's not the case because we are the church. Whenever we criticize the church, we are criticizing ourselves. Whenever we boast about the church, we are boasting about ourselves. We can't step outside of church and act like an objective observer, pretending that we're talking about someone else. So when we crack the whip and try to purify the church as the temple of the Lord, we'd better realize that we can't do it without submitting to "self-flagellation." That's a crude way of putting it, and I'm certainly not suggesting we should torture ourselves to be purified. But if we're going to "live the story" of Jesus cleansing the temple, we should assume the role of the temple and not the Messiah.[30] Just as the fig tree was supposed to be a living parable of God's people—intended to explain Jesus's prophetic actions in the temple—perhaps we should also ask: "To what extent are we (the church) like the fig tree?"

What would happen if Jesus were to cleanse *our* temple and inspect *our* fig tree?

1. Fig trees are supposed to produce figs. Disciples are supposed to make disciples. If the church isn't making converts, then we are not fulfilling our purpose. We might be full of life, green leaves on every branch, activities galore. But if we are not reaching others with the good news of our king, if we are not bearing fruit, then what's the point of being a fig tree (Luke 13:6–9)?

30. For a helpful critique of our default presumption (that we're always on the side of Jesus), see Mark Allan Powell, *What Do They Hear? Bridging the Gap between Pulpit and Pew* (Nashville: Abingdon, 2007).

2. The temple should be a house of prayer for everyone. But for some people, the church is the last place they come to pray. Prayer at home, prayer outside, prayer alone—many of us pray. Yet to trust the church with our burdens, to share in prayer together, to confess our sins to one another—this is what it means to be a house of prayer. If the church were a people/place where everyone felt comfortable enough (and vulnerable enough) to pray, then we might see our "court of the gentiles" (those on the margins of our community) worshiping God.
3. So, why don't we see the court of gentiles filled with people longing to worship God? Perhaps we have created the same barrier: the opportunism of religious commercialism. Making money at the expense of religious devotion is repulsive. Does it ever seem to you like the church is *always* selling something? There is a lot of money that changes hands in Christian commerce. Every once in a while, I step back and think: "My goodness, the Christian industry is big business." If Jesus were to visit our churches today, one wonders what tables of commerce he would overturn to purify his temple.
4. I wonder if we have the same problem Jerusalem had two thousand years ago: we haven't submitted to Jesus as King. In fact, for those of us in the US, the concept of kingship is an antiquated notion, a throwback to a long-forgotten age. Royalty may fascinate Americans, but we gave up the monarchy a long time ago. That's how we got our start—defying the crown. We shall have no king. So, when I hear songs like "Worship His Majesty" or "All Hail King Jesus," the sentiment is lost on me. The kingship of Jesus is an elusive concept, something I don't relate to. Of course, to switch to a more contemporary metaphor—like referring to Jesus as our "president"—sounds wrong to my reverent ears. So, how are we to make sense of submitting to "King Jesus" when the only examples we have are either royal families who function as national symbols of their countries, or, even worse, fairy tales of kings and kingdoms? We may sing songs about Jesus as King, we may even pay lip service to his monarchy—talk about the "kingdom work"—but have we fully grasped what it should look like to submit to King Jesus? Lost without a context, perhaps a clearer sense of his kingdom will help us understand what it means to honor him as our king.[31] Indeed, we need Matthew's Gospel more than we realize.

"Your Majesty, as we bend our knee to your throne, please refine us with your fiery Spirit so that the nations will gather for prayer as your house, the

31. To recover the context of the kingdom of Jesus, see McKnight, *Kingdom Conspiracy*, 43–63.

lame and blind will find healing in your temple, and children will always be free to praise your name in your courts. Let us be your tree of life that bears fruit to the end of the age. May we always have faith to move mountains. This is our prayer because you are the Messiah, our Immanuel, and we are your temple, a kingdom of priests to our God. All hail King Jesus!"

CHAPTER 31

Matthew 21:23–22:14

LISTEN to the Story

23Jesus entered the temple courts, and, while he was teaching, the chief
priests and the elders of the people came to him. "By what authority are
you doing these things?" they asked. "And who gave you this authority?"
24Jesus replied, "I will also ask you one question. If you answer me, I
will tell you by what authority I am doing these things. 25John's baptism—
where did it come from? Was it from heaven, or of human origin?"
They discussed it among themselves and said, "If we say, 'From heaven,'
he will ask, 'Then why didn't you believe him?' 26But if we say, 'Of human
origin'—we are afraid of the people, for they all hold that John was a prophet."
27So they answered Jesus, "We don't know."
Then he said, "Neither will I tell you by what authority I am doing
these things.
28"What do you think? There was a man who had two sons. He went
to the first and said, 'Son, go and work today in the vineyard.'
29'I will not,' he answered, but later he changed his mind and went.
30"Then the father went to the other son and said the same thing. He
answered, 'I will, sir,' but he did not go.
31"Which of the two did what his father wanted?"
"The first," they answered.
Jesus said to them, "Truly I tell you, the tax collectors and the prosti-
tutes are entering the kingdom of God ahead of you. 32For John came to
you to show you the way of righteousness, and you did not believe him,
but the tax collectors and the prostitutes did. And even after you saw this,
you did not repent and believe him.
33"Listen to another parable: There was a landowner who planted
a vineyard. He put a wall around it, dug a winepress in it and built a
watchtower. Then he rented the vineyard to some farmers and moved to
another place. 34When the harvest time approached, he sent his servants
to the tenants to collect his fruit.

35“The tenants seized his servants; they beat one, killed another, and stoned a third. 36Then he sent other servants to them, more than the first time, and the tenants treated them the same way. 37Last of all, he sent his son to them. ‘They will respect my son,’ he said.

38“But when the tenants saw the son, they said to each other, ‘This is the heir. Come, let’s kill him and take his inheritance.’ 39So they took him and threw him out of the vineyard and killed him.

40“Therefore, when the owner of the vineyard comes, what will he do to those tenants?”

41“He will bring those wretches to a wretched end,” they replied, “and he will rent the vineyard to other tenants, who will give him his share of the crop at harvest time.”

42Jesus said to them, “Have you never read in the Scriptures:

> ‘The stone the builders rejected
>   has become the cornerstone;
> the Lord has done this,
>   and it is marvelous in our eyes’?

43“Therefore I tell you that the kingdom of God will be taken away from you and given to a people who will produce its fruit. 44Anyone who falls on this stone will be broken to pieces; anyone on whom it falls will be crushed.”

45When the chief priests and the Pharisees heard Jesus’s parables, they knew he was talking about them. 46They looked for a way to arrest him, but they were afraid of the crowd because the people held that he was a prophet.

22:1Jesus spoke to them again in parables, saying: 2“The kingdom of heaven is like a king who prepared a wedding banquet for his son. 3He sent his servants to those who had been invited to the banquet to tell them to come, but they refused to come.

4“Then he sent some more servants and said, ‘Tell those who have been invited that I have prepared my dinner: My oxen and fattened cattle have been butchered, and everything is ready. Come to the wedding banquet.’

5“But they paid no attention and went off—one to his field, another to his business. 6The rest seized his servants, mistreated them and killed them. 7The king was enraged. He sent his army and destroyed those murderers and burned their city.

8“Then he said to his servants, ‘The wedding banquet is ready, but those I invited did not deserve to come. 9So go to the street corners and invite to the banquet anyone you find.' [10]So the servants went out into the streets and gathered all the people they could find, the bad as well as the good, and the wedding hall was filled with guests.

[11]"But when the king came in to see the guests, he noticed a man there who was not wearing wedding clothes. [12]He asked, 'How did you get in here without wedding clothes, friend?' The man was speechless.

[13]"Then the king told the attendants, 'Tie him hand and foot, and throw him outside, into the darkness, where there will be weeping and gnashing of teeth.'

[14]"For many are invited, but few are chosen."

Listening to the Text in the Story: Genesis 37:12–20; 1 Samuel 15:28–29; 2 Samuel 10:1–19; 2 Chronicles 24:18–22; Psalms 2:6–8; 80:8–16; 118:22–26; Isaiah 5:1–7; 8:14–15; 27:2–13; Zechariah 3:3–5; Judith 1:7–2:28.

It was an audacious move on Jesus's part—showing up early the next day after he had made such a mess in the temple. One would think he should try to hide out for a while, letting things settle down after his blitzkrieg attack on the temple leadership. These were powerful people, the Sadducees and the high priest. They had tremendous political capital as trustees of the "capitol" of Jerusalem—the temple.[1] Mess with these people, and you could be dead within days. But rather than use a kind of social guerilla warfare, relying upon sneak attacks and quick retreats, Jesus decided to show up early the next day and set up shop in the temple, acting like he was there to stay (in fact, Jesus will remain in the temple for the next two chapters in Matthew's Gospel, finally departing at 24:1). In light of what happened the day before, I wonder if the chief priests and elders were incredulous at the sight of Jesus teaching in their domain. The arrogance of this guy! He may act like he belongs there, but they were card-carrying members of the aristocracy. They had been there a long time, and they would be there long after Jesus was gone. Not only that, God had established their pedigree. God designated Levites as administrators of the sacrificial cult and the high priestly family as guardians of the temple. Prophets may come and go, but the priesthood is forever. So, it's no surprise at all that the temple authorities came to Jesus questioning *his* authority. From

1. There was no division of "religion" and "politics" in Jesus's day. In American parlance, we would say the Jewish temple was the capitol of Jerusalem; see also Malina and Rohrbaugh, *Synoptic Gospels*, 138.

where they were sitting, they were the only ones with unquestioned authority because they were appointed *by God* to take care of his house.

This was the ultimate turf war, a battle over influence and domain. But it's not like this was the first time it happened—a clash between prophets, priests, and kings. Prophets had a reputation for challenging priests and confronting kings. Their authority rested in their claim to speak for God; there was no prophetic office to uphold, no right of succession to pass down. Kings wore royal garments; priests donned holy vestments designed by God. Yet prophets had no uniforms (unless they tried to look like Elijah, Zech 13:4), no divinely prescribed outfit to sanctify them from the rest of Israel. Indeed, it could be said that kings and priests operated in an official capacity, while prophets were the unofficial agents of God. There was always supposed to be a king on the throne of David and a priest serving in the temple of Solomon. But prophets seemed to come and go, called by God at different times and under different circumstances to confront the very priests and kings that God had anointed for his purpose. No matter the time, the same problems persisted, inciting prophets to rail against idolatry and injustice. Kings issued decrees; priests offered sacrifices. But the power of a prophet was the spoken word (although some performed divine wonders, most did not). Of course, the kings and priests of Israel inherited their office. God had chosen two tribes to lead the rest of Israel: kings were to come from Judah (Gen 49:8–12), priests had to be Levites (Num 3:1–13). Prophets, on the other hand, inherited nothing except the destiny that awaited them. It's what always seemed to happen after a man of God would confront such powerful people, these ruling authorities. Prophets were silenced by execution.

In light of this age-old conflict—prophet versus the establishment, outsider versus insider, rebel versus ruler, critic versus official, instigator versus police, charismatic leader versus institutional leadership—Jesus and the rulers of the temple would play out their dramatic confrontation, knowing how it's all going to end (Matt 23:34–37). Everyone knew the answer to the question before the chief priests and elders even asked it: "By what authority are you doing these things?" (21:23). Jesus acted like he received his authority from God; that's why he cleared the temple. He was working with a presumption of divine appointment—not only as a prophet but especially as the rightful heir to David's throne. The trustees of the temple, on the other hand, knew they received their authority from God. They didn't have to do anything to prove it other than to show up and do their duty. That's why they confronted Jesus. The way they saw it, their authority was never in question; they had God on their side, predestined to be priests because they were born Levites. Jesus, on the other hand, was a pretentious intruder, claiming royal rights in God's holy temple—the very place where priests rule by divine design. Therefore, when they asked, "And who gave you this authority?" (v. 23), they were expecting Jesus to claim something like, "God has anointed me to do these things." Then, having fallen into their trap,[2] they would have "the authority" to hand Jesus over to the Romans for treason—something they were eventually able to pull off (Matt 26:63–66; 27:1–2, 11–12), but not now. Instead, Jesus seems to have turned the tables on them, questioning their authority *in the temple,* of all places. Who would have thought? Priests unable to defend their authority—silenced by ignorance—in the very place God gave them to rule. That would almost be as bad as a king unable to convince his subjects in Jerusalem that he has the authority to reign as David's heir because he is God's Son even as he inaugurates the kingdom of heaven on earth. And so, the way Jesus saw it, the question of authority essentially boils down to this: Who is doing God's will? A lot of people claim to speak for God. Yet what they do matters more.

EXPLAIN the Story

The turf war quickly turned into a battle of wits. The chief priests and elders thought they had laid a snare for Jesus, tempting him to step into his own undoing. If Jesus had fallen for their ploy, they would have accomplished two things at once: defended their authority as guardians of the temple and shamed Jesus into submission. In this public contest for honor, the people would side with the victors and condemn the loser. That's the way the honor game worked. The social approval of the group determined who won the contest. Since honor was social capital paid to and collected by the victors—it was the most powerful commodity in the first-century world, even more desirable than wealth—then the shamed would have no recourse but to tuck their tail and run. The embarrassment of losing face[3] in the presence of the people would compel the dishonored to hide from the crowds until he felt he could show his face again in public without ridicule. That's what the chief priests and elders were counting on. Even if Jesus were smart enough to see their trap, refusing to claim the honor of authority at that moment, he would at least be silenced by their clever tactic. There was another option though. The temple rulers could have arrested Jesus on the spot—or at least run him out of the temple just like he did to the merchants and money changers—which would have been a risky move. (What if the people sided with Jesus? See 21:46.) But

2. Davies and Allison, *Matthew*, 3:159.
3. France, *Matthew*, 799.

rather than use the force of their authority (eventually they did, 26:47), they wanted to embarrass Jesus in front of the people by using the skill of their wit. They thought they had Jesus on the horns of a dilemma: speak and get in trouble with the Romans, remain silent and lose face with the people. They had no idea who they were dealing with.

Who Does God's Will? The People Have Already Decided

When Jesus made a deal with the chief priests that he would answer their question if they answered his, I wonder if they were expecting a question about the legitimacy of their authority over the temple—especially the high priest. In earlier times, different Jewish groups had raised questions about the credibility of the high priesthood. Justifying the Maccabean revolt, Jewish literature is replete with examples of how the high priest was corrupted by Hellenistic ways, even describing how the office was purchased by the highest bidder (see 2 Macc 4:7–29). After the Jews regained their sovereignty due to the Maccabean-led rebellion, the Qumran community withdrew from Jewish society because a Hasmonean king (the family name of the Maccabees) had assumed the position of high priest, thereby corrupting the temple and its sacrifices. Two-hundred years later, suspicions were raised in Jesus's day about the integrity of the high priest and his family because they were appointed by the Romans to hold this important office, establishing a dynasty of temple rule.[4] Therefore, in light of the checkered history of the high priesthood and Jesus's actions in the temple, perhaps the chief priests were prepared for the question: "By what authority are you priests doing these things, turning the holy place into a marketplace? And, who gave you this authority? Rome?" Yet that's not what Jesus asked. Much to their surprise, Jesus asked them about the authority of a third party (Matt 21:25)—a subject that must have felt like it came out of nowhere. After all, what did John's baptism have to do with Jesus's behavior in the temple?

We don't know why Jesus asked about John's authority to baptize. Once again, we are left to infer the reasons. Some scholars think Jesus was making a claim about himself by pointing to John.[5] Since the Baptizer had christened Jesus as God's anointed, then Jesus was laying claim to his authority via John. If John was right about Jesus—that he is the Messiah—then Jesus had authority to clear the temple.[6] Other scholars think Jesus brought up the painful subject of John's baptism to the chief priests because the prophet's water

4. Evans, *Matthew*, 366.

5. According to Keener, Jesus claimed that he "shares the same source of authority as John" (*Matthew*, 506).

6. Davies and Allison, *Matthew*, 3:160; France, *Matthew*, 797.

ritual was intended as a critique of the temple leadership. Since John offered a baptism of repentance for sins, and large crowds from Jerusalem flocked to the Jordan River to be baptized (3:5–6), the people were confirming the truth of what John was preaching. Their need of cleansing couldn't be found in the temple because their leaders were corrupt (vv. 7–10).[7] That would put the chief priests on the horns of a dilemma: the people had already "voted" with their feet regarding the questionable dealings of the high priesthood. If the chief priests were to deny the efficacy of John's baptism, their beef would actually be with the people (and not Jesus).[8] Finally, some scholars think Jesus was simply using a diversionary tactic.[9] He referred to John's baptism because both he and the people submitted to it.[10] In that case, Jesus was pressing the people's favorable opinion of John into his service, a kind of an us-versus-them strategy meant to accentuate the great divide between the masses and the elite: "*We* were baptized by John. Why weren't you?"

Whatever the reason, the chief priests sniffed out quickly the implications of their dilemma (21:25–26). However they answered the question, their authority would be questioned *by the people*. The people had already decided John was a prophet of God. If the chief priests weren't perceptive enough to see that, then the people would know that these leaders didn't speak for God.[11] And so, irony of ironies, Jesus's question about John's baptism revealed that the "divine authority" of the chief priests actually came from people—they were worried about what the crowd thought (v. 26). The chief priests tried to make it an either/or question. Either one obtains their authority from God or from people, which is why the chief priests claimed ignorance (v. 27). They couldn't answer the question because they wanted to believe they got their authority *only* from God. But if that were the case, then they should have spoken for God and given their verdict: John's baptism didn't come from God. But their we-don't-know answer proved otherwise.[12] Even they knew the people would have the last word on who does God's will (v. 26).

Silencing his critics should have been enough, but Jesus wouldn't let it go. It was time to hold a mirror up to the chief priests like he did to the Pharisees, the Galilean crowds, and even the twelve disciples. That was the effect of his parables. They functioned like mirrors, reflecting back to the beholder what they saw. Listeners thought they were seeing someone else, offering expert opinions based on their own observations. That's why Jesus started the parable

7. Luz, *Matthew*, 3:29–31.
8. Garland, *Reading Matthew*, 220.
9. Davies and Allison, *Matthew*, 3:160.
10. Luz, *Matthew*, 3:29.
11. Turner, *Matthew*, 507.
12. Blomberg, *Matthew*, 320.

of the two sons with, "What do you think?" (v. 28), deferring to the "wisdom" of the chief priests. Yet what these "experts" ended up doing—without realizing it—was to offer a critique of themselves. Pointing at their mirror image, they accused themselves of their own foolishness. It was a shrewd move, getting those who have an infallible opinion of themselves to point out their obvious flaws to everyone—themselves as well as the people! Jesus couldn't have done it any better himself.

The parable of the two sons is simple (vv. 28–32)—not much of a riddle at all. Perhaps even a child would be able to figure it out (and so, one wonders if the chief priests were a little insulted by the simplicity of the puzzle; in my mind, I hear Jesus use a childlike tone as he tells the story). A man asks his two children (*tekna*) to work in his vineyard (a common symbol for Israel). The first refuses to go, but then changes his[13] mind and does what his father asked him to do (v. 29). The second child agrees to go, but then doesn't do the work (v. 30). It's easy to see which child "did what his father wanted" (v. 31). The second son may have honored his father to his face, even addressing him as "sir" (*kyrie*). But the first son honored his father by doing his will. Of course, Jesus didn't entertain the preferable third option: the child who agrees *and* does his father's will (that's probably the way the chief priests saw themselves). In the binary world of Jesus's parable, the chief priests were forced to choose between these two: "'The first,' they answered" (v. 31). It's ironic, isn't it? Here you have the primary spokesmen for God pointing out those who actually *did* the will of God—and it's not them. But in case they couldn't see it, Jesus made their point for them: tax collectors and prostitutes will enter the kingdom of heaven before the chief priests because the worst sinners in the world believed that John was right (vv. 31–32). Even seeing tax collectors and prostitutes getting right with God didn't convince the chief priests that John's baptism was legitimate.[14] If they had believed that John's authority came from God, Jesus assumes these "sinners" would have repented too (v. 32). (That would have been quite a sight, priests seeking cleansing *outside* the temple.) But they didn't, which proves these priests are the children who *say* they do the will of God but don't—not even in their appointed service to God in the temple. Even a child could see that (vv. 15–16).

What Is God's Will? The Priests Should Already Know

As the old adage goes, "Fool me once, shame on you. Fool me twice, shame on me." In the honor contest between Jesus and the chief priests, the religious leaders were fooled twice, once again falling into the trap of Jesus's

13. The participle, *metamelētheis*, is masculine.
14. Turner, *Matthew*, 509.

self-exposing parables. You would think they would see it coming this time, perhaps even refusing to play the game by remaining silent. But, they didn't, and one has to wonder why. Were they really that imperceptive? As Jesus tells the parable of the tenants (Matt 21:33–39), couldn't they see what he was up to? We see it clearly; connecting the dots of the major players in the parable is rather obvious to us: God = absentee landlord; vineyard = Israel; tenant farmers = priests; servants = prophets; son = Jesus.[15] So when Jesus asked the payoff question (v. 40), why did the chief priests offer their firm but self-incriminating answer? They sound like they think they're talking about someone else when they declare with righteous indignation, "He will bring those wretches to a wretched end"—even offering a solution to the problem of the recalcitrant share croppers: "And he will rent the vineyard to other tenants, who will give him his share of the crop at harvest time" (v. 41). Perhaps they thought Jesus was bringing up a case study in the form of a parable, addressing a problem that landowners faced occasionally.[16] That is to say, perhaps they presumed Jesus was speaking of a situation relevant to the concerns of the retainer class—people like them who owned lands and were absentee landlords, having to deal with sneaky, deceitful share croppers. If Jesus were a prophet, he would stand against injustice wherever he saw it, whether among the elites or peasant farmers. But that would mean they thought Jesus was siding with them, picking up their cause for a change. Given the hostile environment, that seems highly unlikely. But, even if the chief priests had recognized that Jesus was speaking allegorically, doesn't it make better sense to assume they thought the vicious tenant farmers were someone else? For certainly they wouldn't be so blind so as to make the same mistake twice, would they?

Most commentators think the chief priests were that obtuse.[17] They didn't have a clue that Jesus was telling a parable against them until it was too late (v. 45). But that doesn't mean that they didn't see themselves in the parable. In fact, I think they did—but it wasn't in the role of the tenant farmers. Given the politics of imperial provincial rule in Judea, I wonder if the chief priests assigned the role of the tenant farmers to the Romans.[18] That would mean that they saw themselves in the reflection of the servants of the landowner. The fact that Jesus seemed to shift the point of Isaiah's prophecy away from Jerusalem, directed against another enemy, may have given the chief priests the wrong impression. In Isaiah's parable, the problem is that, despite everything the Lord did to produce good wine (planted a choice vine on a

15. For a helpful chart, see Davies and Allison, *Matthew*, 3:176.

16. France, *Matthew*, 808–9.

17. See, e.g., Bruner, *Matthew*, 2:380.

18. Nolland, *Matthew*, 876.

fertile hillside cleared of stones, built a watchtower, carved a winepress), the vineyard only produced bad grapes (Isa 5:1–4). And so, Isaiah predicted that the landowner would tear down the vineyard because he "looked for justice, but saw bloodshed; for righteousness, but heard cries of distress" (vv. 5–7). God was angry with Jerusalem.

In his riff on Isaiah's parable, Jesus seemed to identify a different villain. He used nearly all of the same elements of the story,[19] but made two significant changes: this time the vineyard produced a good harvest, and a new character was causing all the trouble.[20] Some interlopers were doing everything they could to steal what belonged to the landowner—not only killing and torturing the servants he sent to collect what was due to him but even murdering his son outside the vineyard (Matt 21:34–39).[21] To their ears, that probably reminded them of Roman oppression, especially during Passover, when Jerusalem experienced the devastating effects of the procurator's heavy-handed measures of "keeping the peace" (Luke 13:1–2). Indeed, to the people of Jerusalem the story world of Jesus's parable must have sounded like a fit description of their perilous situation: God had "rented the vineyard to some farmers and moved to another place" (Matt 21:33). But they also believed the harvest was coming, the day when God returns to his people and takes back what belongs to him (v. 34). On that day, what will God do to his enemies (v. 40)? The chief priests relished the opportunity to say it: "He will bring those wretches to a wretched end" (v. 41). But they never expected Jesus to pull the same trick as Nathan, holding up the mirror of his parable to their faces and saying, "You are the man!" (2 Sam 12:7). By their own words, they condemned themselves as wretches who would meet a wretched end. Not only that, they predicted what would happen in the aftermath of the long-awaited day of divine visitation: God would rent the vineyard to others who will give him what is owed to him (Matt 21:41). Jesus couldn't agree more (v. 43). What surprised him is that they never saw it coming, even though they had the Scriptures that predicted the same (v. 42)—a line from a psalm that was sung during Passover (Ps 118:22–23).

Jesus worked with the presumption that no one, not even the chief priests and the elders of Jerusalem, could hinder the will of God for Israel and the whole world. That's why he predicted that God would take the kingdom from the leaders of Jerusalem and give it to another "people [*ethnos*] who will

---

19. See Nolland, *Matthew*, 868–71.

20. Turner, *Matthew*, 514.

21. Luz, *Matthew*, 3:40–41, hears echoes of what Joseph's brothers wanted to do to him (Gen 37:20). Bailey points out the necessity of murdering the son outside the vineyard to keep it pure—not cursed by blood—for future profits (*Jesus through Middle Eastern Eyes*, 420).

produce its fruit" (Matt 21:43). Some have thought that Jesus decided right then and there to replace Israel[22] with the gentile church. However, this interpretation doesn't make sense because Jesus had already promised the Twelve[23] that they would rule with him in the kingdom (19:28)—they were "the people,"[24] the tree that would produce figs (21:19), the replacement tenant farmers of the vineyard who will render to God his share of the harvest (v. 34). Acting for God, Jesus replaced the temple leadership[25] with his disciples (then and now), a kingdom of priests to serve in the new temple.[26] And, now we see the problem. The chief priests had served in the temple for so long that they acted like they owned the place—no longer tenants but permanent residents (cf. Jer 7:3–4). So when a prophet like John or an anointed one like Jesus came to do God's will, the temple leadership automatically assumed these rebels were intruders violating their priestly domain, unwelcomed outsiders messing up the place, the last people God would invite to the party (Matt 22:9–10). Therefore, it was up to these guardians of the temple to throw them out, even rejecting the very stone[27] God would use as the cornerstone for his new temple (21:42)—a stone of offense that tripped up the chief priests as well as the Pharisees (v. 45). It's not that the leaders of Jerusalem were excluded from the start. They were invited to join the party—the kingdom of heaven coming to earth—but they refused, some retreating to their work while others resorted to killing the messengers (22:1–6). It was their one shot, and they missed it.

That's the theme of the last of three parables indicting the religious leadership of Jerusalem: the exigency of the moment. The time had come. No more delays. It's either join the feast or not. God had sent earlier invitations (the prophets? the Baptizer? the Galilean ministry of Jesus?) to his guests, giving them a heads up that the time for the messianic banquet was near.[28] But they didn't pay attention (vv. 1–3). So when the time came—the kingdom of heaven coming to Jerusalem—the A-list people refused to join the party (vv. 4–6). Since God wouldn't let the food go to waste (there can only be *one* wedding), he ensured that his house would be full of guests, commoners, even the good and the bad (vv. 8–10; including tax collectors and prostitutes:

22. Luz, *Matthew*, 3:42–43. Although Luz says that *ethnos* here probably doesn't refer to gentiles (but see p. 55 where the second guests are identified as the gentile mission), he claims that Matthew is "one of the fathers of the 'succession theory'" (ibid., 44).

23. Talbert, *Matthew*, 252.

24. Turner, *Matthew*, 516.

25. Nolland, *Matthew*, 870.

26. Davies and Allison, *Matthew*, 3:185–86.

27. Some scholars hear a pun in Hebrew, *ha-eben* ("the stone") and *ha-ben* ("the son"), probably also used by the Baptizer (Matt 3:9); see Evans, *Matthew*, 374–75.

28. Davies and Allison, *Matthew*, 3:197.

21:31–32).[29] But the king was angry, and his wrath had to be placated, his honor defended. Consequently, those who spurned his invitation would be punished; their city would be destroyed (22:7; Jerusalem perhaps? See 23:37–24:2). Moreover, anyone who showed up to the wedding without proper clothing[30] would be banished from the celebration. (See 22:11–13. Is this referring to Judas perhaps? Jesus called him "friend" when he betrayed him [26:50], the same word used by the king [22:12]. Indeed, 22:13 reads like a prophecy fulfilled when Judas hanged himself; see 27:3–5.) All Israel was invited to the messianic banquet, but only a remnant joined the party (22:14)—enough to fill God's house, the new temple.[31]

LIVE the Story

It's easy to be against something. Anyone can be a critic, merely reacting to what is seen. Some even seem to be born for the role, possessing a natural ability to identify the negative. Indeed, given the chance, most of us can find something wrong with anything, voicing what we don't like about this or that. Pointing out the weaknesses of an institution or the undesirable qualities of certain leaders isn't difficult at all. The hard part is to be for something else, to be proactive, to find a better alternative to what we already have. That's when there's trouble. While many may see the same problem, most of us will have different ideas about the remedy. That's because criticism deals with the present—something anyone can see. Creating something new is about the future, having eyes to see what isn't seen. It takes faith to create something new, especially when no one else can see it.

The chief priests thought Jesus was merely criticizing what he saw, overturning tables to clean up the temple. That's why they confronted him with the authority question. Protecting their interests, the temple leadership had to defend themselves against this self-appointed critic. But what they couldn't see is that Jesus had a much higher purpose. Ultimately, this wasn't about them. It was about him. Sure, they were in the way, trying to thwart Jesus's efforts for the kingdom. Yet long before he came to Jerusalem, Jesus already knew God

---

29. Luz hears the part about God's house being filled with outsiders as bad news for Israel; there would be no more room for them (*Matthew*, 3:50).

30. What does the wedding garment represent? Repentance (Keener, *Matthew*, 522), resurrection glory (Davies and Allison, *Matthew*, 3:204), good works (Luz, *Matthew*, 3:56; France, *Matthew*, 827), righteousness (Nolland, *Matthew*, 891; Bruner, *Matthew*, 2:390), or moral worthiness (Garland, *Reading Matthew*, 225)? Whenever we see such polyvalence, we should recognize that we've pushed the allegorical implications of the parable too far; see Snodgrass, *Stories with Intent*, 28.

31. "What is envisaged seems to be more than merely a 'regime change' . . . rather a reconstitution of Israel" (France, *Matthew*, 800).

was going to build a new temple (Matt 16:18) and establish another priesthood (v. 19). He also knew that the current trustees of the temple wouldn't go without a fight (v. 21). And yet, it was the *way* he would battle them—bringing the kingdom of heaven to earth—that seemed to take everyone by surprise. He was creating something completely new, a future that was hard to see—even for his disciples.

Telling stories was an odd way to get the job done. Of course, we're so used to the gospel narrative, Jesus's approach to challenging the temple establishment doesn't appear peculiar to us at all. But imagine how silly Jesus's plan would have sounded if he had told a news reporter what he was going to do once he got to Jerusalem.

"Okay, here's the plan. Sunday's going to be a big day. We're going to stage the whole Messiah-riding-on-a-donkey-entering-Jerusalem parade. Then I'm going to clear the temple of all the merchants, quoting lines from Isaiah and Jeremiah. That should put everyone on notice that I'm ready to do God's business."

"That sounds dangerous," the reporter says, teasing out the repercussions. "That will make the chief priests angry. They'll come after you for sure. Do you plan to stay in Jerusalem? Do you have contacts there?"

"No, I'll probably stay with friends outside the city. But not for long; I plan to show up in the temple the next day and teach the people about the kingdom of God."

"Go back to the temple? Really? What will you do when these powerful men confront you? Perform one of your miracles to prove to them you have the goods? Or do you plan to take a more direct approach, arming your disciples for a counterattack?"

"No, nothing like that. I'm going to tell them stories . . . you know, parables."

"What?" the reporter asks incredulously, "tell them parables? What good is that going to do?"

"Well," Jesus says, smiling with an air of confidence, "everyone loves a good story. Besides, I've discovered that parables are effective weapons in a war of words."

"But, it sounds to me like you'll need more than words to fight your enemies," the reporter says sarcastically.

"Yes, you're right," Jesus quickly affirms. "It's going to take something more powerful than words to turn this thing around—I'll mention that in my parables too. They will see with their own eyes that something greater than Solomon and the temple is here."

It's an amazing strategy when you think about it. Jesus didn't mount a campaign to have the chief priests physically removed from the temple. (If he could cast out demons, surely he could throw his opponents out of the temple.) He didn't try to destroy the temple. (If his words dried up a fig tree, then certainly he could say to Mount Zion, "Go, throw yourself into the sea"; 21:21.) And yet, he eventually created a new temple and established a new priestly nation by telling parables and offering himself as a living sacrifice. That's it. That's how he did it: by telling stories and dying for his enemies. Evidently, when fighting for the kingdom of heaven on earth, it's the *only way* to get your enemies to see the truth. They won't believe it, of course, because most of us are only interested in defending our position. That's why arguments rarely settle anything. You make your point, I'll make mine, and we go our separate ways. Iron may sharpen iron, but then all we have are sharper weapons that cut even deeper the next time we meet. I'll stab you, and you take a swipe at me, and what's the result? Another bloody mess.

When I was young, I relished the opportunity to cross swords with an opponent, fencing for the truth. Now, not so much. The older I get, the less I argue. Some of it has to do with experience. I see now that most of the time those arguments had less to do with the truth and more to do with my pride (just like the chief priests). It could also be that I'm tiring with age. My aversion to "standing up for the truth" in verbal wrestling matches may prove that I'm too old for these battles. Yet I'd like to think that it has more to do with Jesus. I want to learn from him, study his craft, pay closer attention to his deft approach when dealing with people who oppose the kingdom. To be sure, his wit was unmatched. Who could spin such creative stories on the spot to unmask the weakness of the opponent, even making them see it too? Most of us are not as creative as he was. But that doesn't mean we don't have stories to tell. Jesus told several, and they still work today.

His stories change my mind because they stay with me, especially if they reveal something that I had never seen before about me and my world. That's what Jesus's parables do. They invite me not only to see the world like he did, but his parables work like a mirror, reflecting back to me where I stand in the landscape of his kingdom. Kind of like a divine mapping of my heart and soul, with an arrow pointing, "You are here." Most days I feel like the leftovers invited to the messianic feast, the stragglers brought to the table of the king. More times than not, I'd like to think I'm one of the servants sent to God's vineyard to bring back his share of the harvest. In those moments of revelation—seeing the genius of Jesus—I wonder: "Since his parables work on me, then surely they can work on others too, especially enemies of the kingdom." I think about a parable I could use to clobber my latest enemies, make them look foolish. Then, it hits me. In the story world of Jesus's parables, I'll see my reflection in the faces of the tenant farmers who act like they own the place, having "beat one, killed another, and stoned a third" (v. 35)—but I do it with words. At that moment, ironically, it's the *words* of Jesus's enemies that convict me: "He will bring those wretches to a wretched end" (v. 41).

God help my soul. When will I learn to lay down the sword and pick up a cross?

When I have ears to hear his parables.

CHAPTER 32

Matthew 22:15–46

LISTEN to the Story

[15]Then the Pharisees went out and laid plans to trap him in his words.
[16]They sent their disciples to him along with the Herodians. "Teacher,"
they said, "we know that you are a man of integrity and that you teach
the way of God in accordance with the truth. You aren't swayed by others,
because you pay no attention to who they are. [17]Tell us then, what is your
opinion? Is it right to pay the imperial tax to Caesar or not?"

[18]But Jesus, knowing their evil intent, said, "You hypocrites, why are
you trying to trap me? [19]Show me the coin used for paying the tax." They
brought him a denarius, [20]and he asked them, "Whose image is this? And
whose inscription?"

[21]"Caesar's," they replied.

Then he said to them, "So give back to Caesar what is Caesar's, and to God what is God's."

[22]When they heard this, they were amazed. So they left him and went away.

[23]That same day the Sadducees, who say there is no resurrection, came
to him with a question. [24]"Teacher," they said, "Moses told us that if a
man dies without having children, his brother must marry the widow and
raise up offspring for him. [25]Now there were seven brothers among us.
The first one married and died, and since he had no children, he left his
wife to his brother. [26]The same thing happened to the second and third
brother, right on down to the seventh. [27]Finally, the woman died. [28]Now
then, at the resurrection, whose wife will she be of the seven, since all of
them were married to her?"

[29]Jesus replied, "You are in error because you do not know the Scrip-
tures or the power of God. [30]At the resurrection people will neither marry
nor be given in marriage; they will be like the angels in heaven. [31]But
about the resurrection of the dead—have you not read what God said

to you, 32'I am the God of Abraham, the God of Isaac, and the God of Jacob'? He is not the God of the dead but of the living."

33When the crowds heard this, they were astonished at his teaching.

34Hearing that Jesus had silenced the Sadducees, the Pharisees got together. 35One of them, an expert in the law, tested him with this question: 36"Teacher, which is the greatest commandment in the Law?"

37Jesus replied: "'Love the Lord your God with all your heart and with all your soul and with all your mind.' 38This is the first and greatest commandment. 39And the second is like it: 'Love your neighbor as yourself.' 40All the Law and the Prophets hang on these two commandments."

41While the Pharisees were gathered together, Jesus asked them, 42"What do you think about the Messiah? Whose son is he?"

"The son of David," they replied.

43He said to them, "How is it then that David, speaking by the Spirit, calls him 'Lord'? For he says,

> 44'The Lord said to my Lord:
> "Sit at my right hand
> until I put your enemies
> under your feet."'

45If then David calls him 'Lord,' how can he be his son?" 46No one could say a word in reply, and from that day on no one dared to ask him any more questions.

Listening to the Text in the Story: Genesis 38:6–26; Leviticus 19:18; Deuteronomy 6:5; 25:5–10; 1 Kings 4:29–34; 10:1; Psalms 2:1–7; 110:1–2; Isaiah 26:19; Daniel 12:1–3; Tobit 3:7–8; 2 Maccabees 7:23; 4 Maccabees 7:16–19.

We never get to hear what Jesus taught the people the only day he spent in the temple. He had made a rather brief appearance the day before—the end of a long day that included a trip from Jericho to Jerusalem, a staged triumphal entry, and a temple clearing. Was there any time left on Sunday to settle down and do some teaching? Probably not. So, it could be said that this was the only chance he would have to explain the kingdom of heaven to the people of Jerusalem. But hecklers showed up and tried to spoil it all. We may want to see their questions as sincere because, after all, we often say there is no bad question except one that is never asked. Yet first-century debaters didn't take such a charitable approach to inquiry. Instead, all questions asked in public were intended as attacks—challenges to a man's honor.[1] To ask a friendly question for information had to be done in private. (We've seen that several times in Matthew, where the disciples would approach Jesus away from the crowds to ask their questions; see 13:10; 15:12; 17:19; 18:1, 21; 19:25, 27; 21:20.) Therefore, whenever a question was asked in public, the spectators knew the game was on, and it would be up to them to determine the winner of the social contest. If the question stumped the man, evident by his weak response, the crowd would offer their quick condemnation, sneering at the loser with spitballs (Job 17:6), mouths gaped open (16:10), wagging heads (16:4; Matt 27:39), and raspberries (what the psalmist called "separating the lip"; Ps 22:7 NASB). The crowds knew they were the deciding factor in the game of honor.

Just like previous attempts to humiliate Jesus,[2] the Pharisees and Sadducees (now joined by the Herodians)[3] knew they had to get the crowd on their side to dispose of the Galilean. This is why they approached him with brainteasers, riddles, and parables of their own making—confronting him with questions that had no good answer. These were tough issues because they were so divisive (the first was a ringer: "Is it right to pay the imperial tax to Caesar or not?"; Matt 22:17). This wasn't a bunch of theologians kicking around ideas about the Scriptures. This confrontation was a matter of life and death. Answer his opponents wrongly, and Jesus would not only face immediate ridicule from the crowds but also a lynch mob hiding in the shadows. What the leaders of Jerusalem didn't expect, however, was how adept Jesus was at making such clever comebacks. Like a stand-up comic silencing hecklers, Jesus not only successfully protected his honor (confirmed by the crowd's admiration; v. 33) but also shamed his accusers for their inability to make him look bad. Of course, there were more vicious ways to attack a man's honor than simply asking difficult questions in public. Indeed, even though Jesus dispatched his opponents with brilliant responses (v. 46), the war wasn't over. Desperate to win, the losers would turn to more nefarious ways of shaming Jesus into submission—something he saw coming too.

---

1. The honor game was strictly a male-oriented contest; women could only avoid shame; see Malina, *New Testament World*, 42–48.

2. See above, 241–45; 250–57; 301–8; 323–26; 373–76; 422–23.

3. Even though we know very little about the Herodians, some scholars infer from their name that they would have supported the poll tax, being Roman sympathizers. Furthermore, it is inferred that the Pharisees would have opposed the tax on religious grounds (see Turner, *Matthew*, 527–29). Therefore, that these political enemies would join forces to attack Jesus shows how desperate they were to dispose of him.

EXPLAIN the Story

When the Sadducees had confronted Jesus first thing in the morning with the question, "By what authority are you doing these things?" (Matt 21:23), they were referring to his behavior in temple the day before. By clearing out the merchants from the court of the gentiles, Jesus acted like he had done God's business. Continuing in that vein, Jesus had returned to the temple on Monday to teach the people gathered there in preparation for Passover that would begin a few days later (26:2). It was customary for teachers (scribes as well as priests)[4] to teach their disciples in the temple. Some must have drawn larger crowds than others. Apparently, Jesus had attracted mobs of people (note the plural "crowds"; 22:33). So when the Pharisees and Sadducees lobbed their verbal grenades at Jesus—time bombs ready to explode—it was yet another way that they were forcing him to answer the question, "By what authority are you doing these things?" He's there acting like he has something to say, teaching "with authority" *in the temple*. Jesus could have gathered a crowd outside the temple, perhaps even setting up a little tutorial about the kingdom of heaven in the agora that led to the upper city of Jerusalem. He would certainly find large crowds there. But that's not what he did. Indeed, the way the Pharisees and Sadducees probably saw it, Jesus chose to teach in the temple on purpose, trying to rub their noses in the power of his popularity—on their turf, on his terms. They wouldn't stand for it.

Hypocrisy and Ignorance

It didn't take Jesus much time to expose the soft underbelly of his opponents, the weakness in their position. Due to previous meetings, Jesus had already sized them up, fully aware of their deficiencies.[5] The Pharisees were hypocrites (Matt 22:18). They said one thing and did something else (15:1–9). The Sadducees were ignorant (22:29). They could read weather signs but didn't understand the signs of the messianic age prophesied in Scripture (16:1–4). So when the Pharisees sent some of their disciples to ask Jesus about the poll tax (22:16–17), he saw right through them. But that's not surprising. Hypocrisy is easy to see—for everyone except the hypocrites. All you have to do is get hypocrites to reveal what they're hiding (v. 19). When Jesus dealt with the Sadducees, ignorance was even easier to expose. All he had to do was refer to the Scriptures. Of course, if you're dealing with someone who

4. See Sanders, *Judaism*, 176–82.

5. Some scholars find the polemical tone of Jesus's critique a bit too harsh, reflective more of Matthew's context than Jesus's opinion (see Luz, *Matthew*, 3:141–49).

doesn't "know the Scriptures or the power of God" (v. 29), then you have to do a little theology, pointing out the implications of the text (v. 32). Ignorant people are unable to infer answers to their questions of the Scriptures without a little help.

Having learned from their mistake of confronting Jesus to his face (9:11–13; 12:1–8, 24–25; 15:1–12; 16:1–6; 19:1–9; 21:28–45), the Pharisees sent a few of their students (along with the Herodians) to embarrass Jesus in front of the crowds. In a cowardly yet shrewd move, the Pharisees used posers as double agents—students feigning interest—to ensure they wouldn't lose face regardless of what Jesus said. It was the perfect setup. Here are students who show proper respect, honoring Jesus with their words, acting like they want to know what Jesus thinks about an important question. After buttering him up with honorific praise, they asked: "Tell us, what is your opinion? Is it right to pay the imperial tax to Caesar or not?" (22:16–17). But, much like their teachers, the hearts of these Pharisaical students were far from God (15:7–9). In vain they were trying to force Jesus into a no-win situation, a first-century catch-22. Jesus called them on it (22:18). They weren't there to learn; rather, they were trying to trap him, with the Pharisees probably watching the whole thing within earshot (v. 34).

Yet their question was too important to be dismissed simply because they asked it with ulterior motives. Paying the poll tax was one of the hot-button issues at that time.[6] About twenty years earlier, a Galilean by the name of Judas had led a revolt against Rome, inciting many followers to refuse to pay the tax because the money promoted idolatry.[7] Although there were all kinds of currency floating around the first-century world—Greek, Roman, Tyrian, probably even a few Hasmonean coins—Caesar accepted only one coin (a denarius) minted for the purpose of paying the poll tax. This was more than a financial obligation—paying Rome because they ruled the land. By requiring payment via the denarius, Caesar was forcing all subjects to make a statement, to acknowledge symbolically his claims to divinity. His image was stamped on the obverse of the denarius with an abbreviated inscription that read, "The Great Tiberius Caesar son of god Augustus." On the reverse side there was an image of the goddess Roma (or perhaps Tiberias's mother, Livia) with the inscription, "High Priest."[8] Offended by the blasphemous coin, some observant Jews may have avoided carrying the denarius for commerce. Yet when it came time to pay the poll tax, they had to exchange their money for

6. Nolland contrasts two Jewish approaches to foreign domination: submission during the Babylonian and Persian exile, and rebellion incited by the Maccabean revolt (*Matthew*, 896–97).

7. See the brief summary in France, *Matthew*, 829–30.

8. Davies and Allison, *Matthew*, 3:216.

this "portable idol,"[9] handle it with their own hands, and use it to pay back Caesar what belonged to him. They had to do it. There was no choice. For if a rebel decided he'd had enough and refused to pay, then more sensible voices might remind him of what happened to Judas the Galilean and his sons.[10]

So, what was Jesus to do? If he said, "Yes, we should pay it," he would sound like a traitor, accused of condoning idolatry. If he said, "No, we shouldn't pay it," then he would be charged with treason against Rome—the only crime punishable by death according to Roman law. But Jesus refused to entertain the question as an either/or issue typical of politics. To be sure, he would give his answer—one that still baffles us even to this day—but he had to deal first with the hypocrisy of his inquisitors. Indeed, that's what troubled him—not the difficulty of the question but the hypocrisy of those who asked it. Yet how were these students acting like hypocrites? Was it because they were being disingenuous, acting like they were interested in Jesus's opinion but secretly trying to trap him?[11] Or did their hypocrisy have more to do with the coins they carried in their pockets? Jesus certainly acted like he knew what kind of pocket change they were carrying around. He asked *them* to produce the denarius (v. 19), a coin that they shouldn't have been carrying around in the temple to begin with.[12] After all, that's why the money changers were there. When he said in essence, "Show me the money!" and they complied, it revealed two things: Jesus didn't have such an idolatrous coin on him, and they did. Obviously, these men had no qualms carrying around a denarius—even in the temple—to use for everyday transactions.[13] By their actions they proved they had no problem using the coin intended to pay Caesar his tax,[14] so why would they ask? Only one answer: hypocrisy.

It was a brilliant move by Jesus, getting his opponents to expose their own hypocrisy. (He did it again!) Yet he still hadn't answered the question. Having no reservations handling the coin himself, Jesus held up the Pharisees' denarius and asked two simple questions anyone could answer if they had spent any time inspecting the coin: "Whose image is this? And whose inscription?" (v. 20). I imagine a collective gasp coming from the crowd of onlookers, horrified by the sight of this graven image being held up in the temple of God. The fact that they were able to give one answer to both of his questions

---

9. Bruner, *Matthew*, 2:398.

10. Josephus, *Ant.* 18.1.1, 2, 6; 20.5.2.

11. Davies and Allison, *Matthew*, 3:213.

12. France, *Matthew*, 830; Garland, *Reading Matthew*, 227.

13. "The Essenes refused to use the denarius, 'saying that they ought not either to carry, or behold, or fashion an image'" (Davies and Allison, *Matthew*, 3:216, quoting Hippolytus, *Refutation of All Heresies*, 9.26).

14. Luz, *Matthew*, 3:65; Keener, *Matthew*, 526.

revealed the duplicity of their offense. Everyone knew what was on the coin because they all used it. Only the conscientious objector, having never studied the coin, would have been able to respond in ignorance: "I don't know. I've never looked at it." But, in self-incriminating fashion (will the Pharisees ever learn?) they said with one voice, "Caesar's" (v. 21). Some people never forget a face, especially when it's indelibly etched on a coin. Therefore, Jesus was able to say, "So give back to Caesar what is Caesar's, and to God what is God's" (v. 21)—a clever response that served Jesus's purpose of exposing their duplicity. And yet, it still doesn't settle the issue. As long as Caesar only claims what is rightfully his, there's no problem. It's his coin. His image and name are on it. But what should we do when Caesar claims that which belongs to God?[15]

Once again we find ourselves at the crossroads of several interpretive paths because Jesus didn't offer a definitive word—or deed—on the matter.[16] (Think of how helpful it would be to know for certain whether Jesus paid the poll tax, like we do for the temple tax; see 17:24–27.) One group of commentators thinks the key to figuring out what Jesus meant is to parse his words carefully. Therefore, some say Jesus was setting up a clear division of authority, separating the secular from the religious. Let Caesar do his thing, and God will do his. Since Jesus's kingdom is "not of this world," his disciples have higher, eschatological expectations. Therefore, matters of the state are of no concern to him. In fact, the fallen powers of this world are going to hell in a hand basket anyway; why would anyone care about them? Soon there would be no emperor.[17] Other commentators maintain that Jesus encouraged his disciples to pay taxes because all authority comes from God. "Giving to Caesar" is another way to "give to God." Therefore, civil obedience is an act of religious devotion. Paying taxes (no matter how corrupt the government) is the citizen's duty because God has ordained all ruling authority on earth—the same argument made by the apostle Paul (Rom 13:1–7).[18]

Other commentators think the prop Jesus used to make his point is the key that unlocks the mystery of his teaching.[19] When he held up the denarius, some think Jesus was putting Caesar in his place by asking the loaded question, "Whose *image* is this?" (He didn't ask, "Whose coin is this?" or "Who made this?") Therefore, even though they said, "Caesar's," Jesus implied by

---

15. "Since God had created the earth and everything in it, Jesus would have made it perfectly clear by his cryptic statement that nothing could legitimately be owed to Caesar at all" (Richard A. Horsley and Neil Asher Silberman, *The Message and the Kingdom* [Minneapolis: Fortress, 1997], 84).

16. For an excellent, brief summary of the history of interpretation, see Luz, *Matthew*, 3:63–65.

17. See, for example, Albert Schweitzer, *The Mysticism of Paul the Apostle*, trans. William Montgomery (London: Black, 1931), 314.

18. See Blomberg, *Matthew*, 331.

19. Luz, *Matthew*, 3:66–67.

his carefully worded question that they should have said, "God's" because *all* humans are made in God's image—even Caesar! Caesar may think he owns the coin. But since Caesar owes his very life to God—made in God's image to rule, have dominion, and fill the earth just like any other son or daughter of Adam—then Jesus's question was really a warning. Just as Caesar owns the coin bearing his image, God owns Caesar because he bears the image of God.[20] In this light, civil disobedience is the proper response to the "Caesars" of the world who have forgotten their highest responsibility: to reflect the image of God by obeying him. Other commentators think it was the inscription—not the image—that caught Jesus's ire.[21] With this tiny piece of imperial propaganda, Caesar claimed to be a son of God. According to Jesus, however, paying the poll tax only proved that Caesar was a *human* ruler—nothing else.[22] Thus the irony: Jesus held in his hand Caesar's little coin, holding up the token in the massive, ornate temple that was dedicated to worshiping the God of Israel. Context and prop offered a visual lesson that was stunning in its simplicity: give back to Caesar his pittance, but give to God the majesty of what is due him—our worship.[23]

In his brief response, Jesus accomplished several things at once. He exposed the hypocrisy of his questioners. He challenged the claims of Caesar. And he avoided falling into the trap of his opponents by refusing to answer their question on their terms. Once again the strategy of his opponents backfired. They were hoping to expose Jesus as a fraud, but the Pharisees ended up revealing their own duplicity. In fact, even today, much like his parables Jesus's answer to the question of paying taxes has a reflective quality. How we interpret his teaching may say more about us than it does about him—especially our politics. (Ask someone, "What did Jesus mean by rendering to Caesar what is Caesar's and to God what is God's?" and you'll immediately discover their political loyalties.) So when the Sadducees tried to use the same tactic, telling a parable to expose the deficiencies of Jesus (Matt 22:23–28), it ended up being a pitiful attempt at beating him at his own game. They thought they were being clever, using a riddle to silence an ignorant Jesus (just like he had done to them; see 21:23–46). However, it didn't work. Once again Jesus was able to turn the tables on his opponents, making them play the part of the ignorant fool. It didn't take him long to sum up their error: "You do not know the Scriptures or the power of God" (22:29)—a hefty criticism to throw at these religious leaders. He didn't even mention the fact that their parable wasn't very good to begin with. Maybe he was being kind. At least they tried.

---

20. Garland, *Reading Matthew*, 227.
21. Turner, *Matthew*, 528.
22. France, *Matthew*, 830–31.
23. Keener, *Matthew*, 525.

Since the Sadducees didn't believe in the resurrection (and Jesus did—in fact, he was counting on it: 16:21; 17:23; 20:19), they thought the law of levirate marriage proved their point (22:23–24). Levirate marriage was supposed to ensure the immortality of a man who died before producing an heir (Gen 38:6–26; Deut 25:5–10).[24] By requiring his brother to marry his widow and produce a son, the honor of his name would live forever. Therefore, resurrection was unnecessary to achieve immortality. Besides, obedience to the law of Moses made life in the resurrection appear nonsensically foolish, illustrated by the scenario of a "husband-killer" who would have seven husbands in the afterlife—a situation that would have been completely abhorrent to a male-dominant culture (Matt 22:28). But the Sadducees were working with the faulty assumption that the resurrection was merely resuscitation, a continuation of this life after death.[25] Jesus said it wasn't. Resurrected men and women will be different from what they were in this life. For example, like angelic creatures, resurrected humans will neither marry nor give away their daughters in marriage (v. 30). Procreation won't be needed in the resurrection since death is no longer a threat to humanity.[26]

According to Jesus, the Sadducees were also working with a faulty theology. If there is no resurrection, then God ends up being the God of dead people. Yet since God is life, then there must be a resurrection because he identified himself to Moses as God of the living: "I am the God of Abraham, the God of Isaac, and the God of Jacob" (Matt 22:32; Exod 3:6). Without the resurrection the Lord should have said, "*I was* the God of Abraham, Isaac, and Jacob."[27] According to Jesus, then, the fact that God is the God of the living proves that he intends to raise his people from the dead.[28] Evidently, other teachers hadn't relied on such an inferential argument to prove the resurrection, for the crowds "were astonished at his teaching" (Matt 22:33), and the Sadducees had nothing left to say (v. 34) because they were ignorant of the Scriptures—at least the way Jesus read them.

Love and Submission

The next confrontation between Jesus and his opponents appears to be less adversarial, even though the Pharisees asked their question to "test" Jesus (Matt 22:35). To the reader of Matthew's Gospel, the question, "Which is the greatest commandment in the Law?" (v. 36), isn't controversial because Jesus

24. Nolland, *Matthew*, 902.
25. Luz, *Matthew*, 3:70.
26. Garland, *Reading Matthew*, 228.
27. Davies and Allison, *Matthew*, 3:231.
28. Luz, *Matthew*, 3:72; Nolland, *Matthew*, 906.

had already answered it long ago (7:12). The only surprise is that Jesus added a line from the Shema (Deut 6:5) to what he said before (Matt 22:37–39). During his sermon, Jesus had said all the law and the prophets are summed up in one commandment: "Love your neighbor as yourself" (Lev 19:18; Matt 7:12). This time Jesus said loving God completely is the "first and greatest commandment" (22:38). But then he quickly added that the "love your neighbor" commandment was just as important (v. 39). There was really nothing provocative about his answer other than the fact that he didn't quote one of the Ten Commandments as the greatest, of which the first might qualify: "You shall have no other gods before me" (Exod 20:3). Besides, the rabbis were known to debate the question, arguing for this or that commandment as the greatest because some laws were considered weightier than others due to the more severe punishment meted out against the one who violated certain commandments.[29]

Even though scholars think Jesus may have been the first to link these two commandments[30]—loving God, loving neighbors—who could argue with that? Given the fact that the two tablets of the Decalogue are summed up by loving God and loving your neighbor, Jesus had offered a rather safe response to their "testy" question.[31] In the end, the Pharisees' question wasn't difficult to answer at all. It makes you wonder why they asked it. Was this their last attempt to shame Jesus, and was it the best they could do? What were they expecting him to say, something like, "Let us follow other gods and worship them" (Deut 13:2)? Once again, they revealed that they had no idea who they were dealing with—something Jesus had tried to point out several times before (Matt 12:6, 8, 41–42).

It was time to put an end to the fiasco. Rather than poke at the Pharisees with a victor's taunt, Jesus decided to silence his opponents once and for all. They had been throwing riddles at him all day; now it was their turn to answer one. Jesus started them off with an easy question: "What do you think about the Messiah? Whose son is he?" (22:42). The answer was obvious: "The son of David" (v. 42). But this was more than a fill-in-the-blank quiz; the question deserved an essay answer. That's because if the Messiah was David's descendant, then why in the world would David refer to him as his "Lord" (v. 43)? That doesn't make sense if the Messiah was only human (v. 45). Yet since David was inspired by the Spirit of God to call the anointed one "my Lord" (Ps 110:1; Matt 22:44), then the great king of Israel was saying

29. Keener, *Matthew*, 530–31.

30. Ibid., 531.

31. "Love the Lord your God and love your neighbor: all the rest is commentary" (Davies and Allison, *Matthew*, 3:246).

something about the Messiah that the Pharisees had refused to admit. The Messiah was more than a man's son; he had to be God's son[32]—which also explains why the Pharisees left the essay question blank. They wouldn't submit to the idea that Jesus was the answer to the riddle.[33]

LIVE the Story

What would have happened if Jesus had started this entire affair with his riddle? Rather than wait for the Pharisees and the Sadducees to take their shots, wouldn't it have saved some time if Jesus had gotten right to the point? After all, if they had realized that Jesus is the answer to the question, "Who is David's son?" then the rest of their questions would be answered as well. What is the greatest commandment? Following Jesus. He's the only one who has truly loved God and his neighbor, fulfilling the law and the prophets (Matt 5:17–18). What about the resurrection? Jesus is the answer to that question too. Indeed, without Jesus there is no resurrection (1 Cor 15:13). Even the tension surrounding the payment of the imperial tax is somewhat ameliorated in the kingdom of heaven. Since Jesus would eventually give up his *life* to Caesar as an act of obedience to *God*, rendering a coin seems less taxing to those who would follow their king, the Messiah. Indeed, if the Pharisees had believed the words of their own disciples, "We know that you are a man of integrity and that you teach the way of God in accordance with the truth" (Matt 22:16), then they should have followed Jesus along "the way of God." It's not such a far-fetched idea that *even they* would need a righteousness that would exceed their own (5:20). Consider Paul the Pharisee (Phil 3:4–9)! So, imagine how different things would have turned out if the Pharisees had decided right then and there to follow Jesus. Given their zeal to obey God, would they have proven to be more loyal to Jesus than the Twelve who *said* they were willing to die with him (Matt 26:35)? But then again, isn't that what Pharisees are known for, saying one thing but doing something else?

Matthew was hard on the Pharisees; we are too. But a careful reading of Matthew's Gospel won't let us simply dismiss the Pharisees as that group of pesky pests who missed Jesus—an unrepeatable mistake in history. Rather, from the beginning and through the end of his Gospel, it's apparent that Matthew kept holding the Pharisees up to his readers as a cautionary tale, concerned that the church might be guilty of the same hypocrisy. Why else would Matthew—the only Gospel writer who did—include sayings like "the

32. Turner refers to Jesus's "dual paternity" (*Matthew*, 541).

33. Davies and Allison, *Matthew*, 3:254.

teachers of the law and the Pharisees sit in Moses' seat. So you must be careful to *do everything they tell you*. But do not do what they do, *for they do not practice what they preach*" (Matt 23:2–3, emphasis added)? Hypocrisy is saying the right things but not doing them. That sounds like one of the main problems that plagues the church today—especially us gentile Christians. As we read about Jesus's confrontations with the Pharisees and the Sadducees, we may feel better about ourselves because we have answered the last question correctly (22:42). We know what Jesus was driving at. With great conviction, we believe Jesus is more than the son of David—he is the very Son of God. Yet that doesn't necessarily mean we get the rest of the questions right. Consider the following.

What is the greatest commandment? Depends upon which church you attend. Some hold sexual sins above other transgressions. Others act like social sins are the worst. Some concentrate their theological efforts on confronting heretics. Others attack "spineless Christians" who refuse to take a stand on certain political issues. Indeed, most of us aren't satisfied with Jesus's answer (love God and love your neighbor), wanting to add our own taglines to his open-ended response. After all, once we've determined what he meant by loving God and loving our neighbor, then we get to decide who's the hypocrite. And, it's never us. But for those of us who claim to follow him, Jesus won't let us get off that easy. He not only showed us what loving God/loving your neighbor looks like—sacrifice, but he expected his disciples to pick up a cross and follow him. In fact, that's the surest way we know that we're loving God: when we sacrifice ourselves for others, even our enemies (political, social, and theological). Jesus died for Pharisees too.

What about the resurrection? That's a moot point, right? Not necessarily. I've been surprised to discover how many Christians don't believe in the resurrection—that is to say, *our* resurrection. They affirm the resurrection of Christ. They just don't believe that our bodies will be raised from the dead on the last day. Instead, many Christians think that a spiritual place called "heaven" is our final reward. I didn't know that until N. T. Wright's book *Surprised by Hope* was published a few years ago. I received an email from a concerned preacher, wanting to know what I thought about this "heretical book" written by an Anglican priest—a fellow by the name of "Wright." My friend was upset because Wright questioned popular gospel songs like "I'll Fly Away" and "How Great Thou Art" because they encouraged us to sing about the day Christ will return and "take [us] home."[34] A few years earlier, I had read Eugene Peterson's first of his five-volume spiritual-formation

34. N. T. Wright, *Surprised by Hope: Rethinking Heaven, the Resurrection, and the Mission of the Church* (San Francisco: HarperOne, 2008), 22–23.

series, *Christ Plays in Ten Thousand Places*, where he expressed concerns about a gnostic gospel taking root in American Christianity, evidenced by the fact that many Christians think the goal of salvation is to escape from this created world—to shed our mortal coil, as it were.[35] After my email conversation, I decided to do a little case study on my own. I would bring up the resurrection in conversations with members of evangelical churches, and once in a while I was "surprised by ignorance." Nearly everyone believed they would go to heaven when they died. But when I mentioned the rest of the story, what Wright called, "life after life after death,"[36] they said they had never heard it before. To them, the resurrection of dead bodies sounded like the zombie apocalypse—the stuff of horror films. A few times they even raised the objection: "You think our bodies will be raised from the grave? That's impossible according to the laws of physics. How can this be?" What surprised me even more is that when I brought Paul into the conversation (1 Cor 15:12–57), it seemed to make things even worse.

Finally, what about that tax question? Should we pay taxes or not? The fact that no one asks that question for *religious* reasons—we hear plenty of talk from some political corners about "taxation without representation"—may imply that we think such issues are only political. In fact, if Jesus were to visit our world, few of us would even think to ask him about it. (Think how strange it would sound, reporters gathered around Jesus, peppering him with all kinds of questions about the serious issues that plague our world—like terrorism and violence, disease and famine—when someone asks, "Is it lawful to pay taxes?") Seems the burning issue of his day is a nonstarter for us. We don't see how such a political question has anything to do with religion. In fact, we're convinced these two worlds—politics and religion—should be kept apart. Our society has grown weary of religious people trying to impose their beliefs on everyone else (whether it's Christian marriage or Sharia law). The dominant presumption is that believers should keep their faith to themselves, leaving the government (Caesar!) to solve the important issues of our time.

> Since the time of the Reformation, it has been assumed that "religion" is "private," and that matters of the "state" are "public." Or, to put it differently, it begins to be assumed that the church worries about souls, and the state worries about bodies. This "privatization of religion," this move to make religion a "private" matter, results in a profound change of thought: when we ask the "What are we going to do about . . ." question, we of

35. Eugene H. Peterson, *Christ Plays in Ten Thousand Places: A Conversation in Spiritual Theology* (Grand Rapids: Eerdmans, 2005), 59–62.

36. Wright, *Surprised by Hope*, 151.

> course assume that the *we* is the nation or government, because we have long been trained to think of the church as having no social or political significance. To ask, "What are we Christians going to do about terrorism?" sounds ludicrous!—Nothing! That's the government's job.[37]

Seems we have no trouble "rendering to Caesar what is Caesar's." Ironically, the hard part for us religious people is sorting out what it means to "render to God what is God's." Christians may pledge allegiance to a king and his kingdom. But what we say and what we do are sometimes separate things, just like the Pharisees.

---

37. Lee C. Camp, *Mere Discipleship: Radical Christianity in a Rebellious World* (Grand Rapids: Brazos, 2003), 45.

CHAPTER 33

Matthew 23:1–39

LISTEN to the Story

1Then Jesus said to the crowds and to his disciples: 2"The teachers of
the law and the Pharisees sit in Moses' seat. 3So you must be careful to
do everything they tell you. But do not do what they do, for they do not
practice what they preach. 4They tie up heavy, cumbersome loads and put
them on other people's shoulders, but they themselves are not willing to
lift a finger to move them.

5"Everything they do is done for people to see: They make their phy-
lacteries wide and the tassels on their garments long; 6they love the place
of honor at banquets and the most important seats in the synagogues;
7they love to be greeted with respect in the marketplaces and to be called
'Rabbi' by others.

8"But you are not to be called 'Rabbi,' for you have one Teacher, and
you are all brothers. 9And do not call anyone on earth 'father,' for you have
one Father, and he is in heaven. 10Nor are you to be called instructors, for
you have one Instructor, the Messiah. 11The greatest among you will be
your servant. 12For those who exalt themselves will be humbled, and those
who humble themselves will be exalted.

13"Woe to you, teachers of the law and Pharisees, you hypocrites! You
shut the door of the kingdom of heaven in people's faces. You yourselves
do not enter, nor will you let those enter who are trying to. [14]

15"Woe to you, teachers of the law and Pharisees, you hypocrites! You
travel over land and sea to win a single convert, and when you have suc-
ceeded, you make them twice as much a child of hell as you are.

16"Woe to you, blind guides! You say, 'If anyone swears by the temple,
it means nothing; but anyone who swears by the gold of the temple is
bound by that oath.' 17You blind fools! Which is greater: the gold, or the
temple that makes the gold sacred? 18You also say, 'If anyone swears by the
altar, it means nothing; but anyone who swears by the gift on the altar is
bound by that oath.' 19You blind men! Which is greater: the gift, or the

altar that makes the gift sacred? [20]Therefore, anyone who swears by the
altar swears by it and by everything on it. [21]And anyone who swears by the
temple swears by it and by the one who dwells in it. [22]And anyone who
swears by heaven swears by God's throne and by the one who sits on it.

[23]"Woe to you, teachers of the law and Pharisees, you hypocrites! You
give a tenth of your spices—mint, dill and cumin. But you have neglected
the more important matters of the law—justice, mercy and faithfulness.
You should have practiced the latter, without neglecting the former. [24]You
blind guides! You strain out a gnat but swallow a camel.

[25]"Woe to you, teachers of the law and Pharisees, you hypocrites! You
clean the outside of the cup and dish, but inside they are full of greed and
self-indulgence. [26]Blind Pharisee! First clean the inside of the cup and
dish, and then the outside also will be clean.

[27]"Woe to you, teachers of the law and Pharisees, you hypocrites! You
are like whitewashed tombs, which look beautiful on the outside but on
the inside are full of the bones of the dead and everything unclean. [28]In
the same way, on the outside you appear to people as righteous but on the
inside you are full of hypocrisy and wickedness.

[29]"Woe to you, teachers of the law and Pharisees, you hypocrites! You
build tombs for the prophets and decorate the graves of the righteous.
[30]And you say, 'If we had lived in the days of our ancestors, we would
not have taken part with them in shedding the blood of the prophets.'
[31]So you testify against yourselves that you are the descendants of those
who murdered the prophets. [32]Go ahead, then, and complete what your
ancestors started!

[33]"You snakes! You brood of vipers! How will you escape being con-
demned to hell? [34]Therefore I am sending you prophets and sages and
teachers. Some of them you will kill and crucify; others you will flog in
your synagogues and pursue from town to town. [35]And so upon you will
come all the righteous blood that has been shed on earth, from the blood
of righteous Abel to the blood of Zechariah son of Berekiah, whom you
murdered between the temple and the altar. [36]Truly I tell you, all this will
come on this generation.

[37]"Jerusalem, Jerusalem, you who kill the prophets and stone those
sent to you, how often I have longed to gather your children together, as a
hen gathers her chicks under her wings, and you were not willing. [38]Look,
your house is left to you desolate. [39]For I tell you, you will not see me
again until you say, 'Blessed is he who comes in the name of the Lord.'"

Listening to the Text in the Story: Genesis 4:8–10; Leviticus 11:41–45; Numbers 15:38–41; Deuteronomy 6:8; 22:12; 2 Chronicles 24:20–21; Psalm 118:26; Isaiah 5:8–30; Jeremiah 12:7; 22:4–5; Ezekiel 10:18; 21:26; Amos 4:4–5; 5:18; 6:1–7; Micah 6:8; Zechariah 1:1; 11:17; Malachi 1:6; 2:7–9.

Some might say Jesus didn't take his own advice. During the Sermon on the Mount, he warned his listeners not to judge others because it would incite them to return judgment by the same standard (Matt 7:1–2). Yet, before it was all over, Jesus decided to do it anyway, judging the scribes and Pharisees for their hypocrisy, even going so far as to call them "blind guides" and "snakes" (23:16, 24, 33). This isn't the sweet and gentle Jesus we prefer to admire—always patient, never uttering an unkind word. Instead, Jesus acts like he's fed up with his opponents, finally blasting them with such vitriolic words that it makes us cringe. It's not that we couldn't see it coming. From the start Jesus threw down the gauntlet, challenging the righteousness of the scribes and Pharisees—essentially picking a fight with them (5:20). And they didn't take it lying down either; they came after Jesus with their own accusations, trying to make him look bad. Indeed, throughout Matthew's Gospel, Jesus has been at odds with the scribes and Pharisees, a conflict without resolution that eventually led to their climactic battle of wits (22:15–22, 34–45)—a fight Jesus clearly won (v. 46). So, one might be led to think, "Well, he got the best of them. It's over. Now he can move on to tackle more important problems, having exposed the hypocrisy of these pretenders." Yet that's not what happened. Rather, Jesus acted like he couldn't let it go, emptying both barrels of his shotgun sermon against the Pharisees, skewering them one last time with the red-hot poker of his righteous indignation. And, just as Jesus predicted, his judgment provoked them to judge him by the same measure. Convinced that Jesus was the *real* pretender, they mocked him as he hung on the cross, appearing as though they were the ones to have the last word (27:41–43). What goes around comes around.

What makes Jesus's invective against the scribes and the Pharisees even more difficult to appreciate is the subject matter. To be sure, not practicing what you preach is a serious charge (23:3). But the essence of his beef with these religious leaders seems very *Jewish*—something gentiles have a hard time relating to: criticizing certain clothing accessories (phylacteries and tassels), questioning titles (calling someone rabbi or father), nit-picking over certain kinds of oaths (swearing by the gold in/on the temple or the gift on the altar), tithing herbs and straining gnats (but neglecting more important legal matters), washing dishes and white-washing tombs (purity maintenance). Those issues don't interest us today. Talk about weightier issues of justice should take priority—just like Jesus said. And yet, we never hear Jesus critique *specifically* the unjust behavior of the scribes and Pharisees. That is to say, he criticizes them for ignoring the more important matters (v. 23), but he never points out exactly what they were doing wrong. Instead, Jesus spends most of his time questioning their motives (vv. 5–7), delving more into the matters of the heart than what the Pharisees actually did wrong. In other words, Jesus judged them for what no one else could see, claiming to know the condition of their soul. According to him, the scribes and Pharisees were corrupt "on the inside" even though they appeared right "on the outside" (vv. 25–28). Yet who can know the heart of a person except God?

To sum it all up, when we consider the way Jesus attacked his rivals, it looks like he did two things that are unacceptable according to our modern sensibilities: he used "hate speech" to denigrate his opponents in public, and he judged their motives as evil simply because they opposed him.[1] But the fact that Jesus directed his comments to the crowd and his disciples (vv. 1–12) before he turned to pronounce seven "woes" upon the scribes and Pharisees (vv. 13–32) should help us understand why he did it (rather than dismissing it). Those who dismiss it tend to read this discourse in isolation of its context, as if it were an unnecessary addendum—separate from the rest of Jesus's "temple sermon" that started way back in Matthew 21. But it makes better sense to see Matthew 23 as the end of Jesus's attempt to warn the people about the approaching judgment of God. When he first entered Jerusalem and visited the temple, he criticized the trustees of the temple (the high priests and the Sadducees). Before he left the temple, he eventually got around to denouncing the teachers of the law as well (the scribes and the Pharisees). If we take everything Jesus did in the temple as his prophetic warning against the religious leadership of Jerusalem (from the temple clearing to his final pronouncement, "your house is left to you desolate"; 23:38), then it shouldn't surprise us that he wouldn't leave the temple until he gave the scribes and Pharisees a piece of his mind. Indeed, we might consider his critique of both groups as bookends, with the honor contest between him and them (the Sadducees and Pharisees, high priests and scribes) sandwiched in between (21:23–22:46).

That's why Jesus first directed his comments to the crowd and his disciples: it was the last part of the honor contest that started when the Sadducees and Pharisees questioned his behavior. It also explains why Jesus ended his "temple

1. See the critique by Luz, *Matthew*, 3:138, 174–77.

sermon" with woes against the scribes and Pharisees: during his entire time in the temple, Jesus talked and acted like a prophet. Like a prophet of old, Jesus pronounced "woes" against the leaders of Israel (see Isa 5:8–30). In other words, even though Jesus's verbal attack on these religious leaders violates our cultural script, what he said very much conformed to the prophetic script of his day (which is why he sounds like John the Baptizer). Jesus was acting like a prophet, and everyone knew it, especially the part about what usually happens to prophets in the end. Moreover, like a prophet Jesus saw that coming too (Matt 23:30–38).

EXPLAIN the Story

Whether Matthew intended chapter 23 to sound like a "Sermon of Woes"[2] to be contrasted with the Sermon on the Mount, Jesus's oracle against the religious leaders of Jerusalem covers much of the same ground as his prophetic predecessors. In fact, the issues Jesus raised are similar to the *topoi* of polemical attacks that were commonly used against one's enemies in the first-century world: behavior that doesn't match teaching, emphasizing the trivial at the expense of the significant.[3] Essentially, Jesus found the attitudes and behavior of the scribes and Pharisees as dangerously reprehensible due to their influence. The way he saw it, they were not only his enemies but the enemies of the people. Of course, we think it's unfair of someone to paint an entire group of people with a broad brush, condemning all of them. Surely there must have been a good scribe or Pharisee in the bunch (in fact, other Gospels suggest there were; see Mark 12:32–34). But that's not the way the first-century world negotiated social situations. Everyone was either your friend or your enemy. There was no in-between, no benefit of the doubt. In the social world that prized honor above all else, no one could afford ambivalence. Guilt by association ruled the honor game. Therefore, the binary world of friends and enemies made it easier to negotiate a world that *didn't* celebrate diversity as a virtue. Therefore, Jesus had to make it plain: these scribes and Pharisees are not your friends even though they act like it. They are your enemies, and here's why.

The Hypocrisy of Self-Promotion

At the beginning of his ministry, Jesus warned the crowd and his disciples not to "practice your righteousness in front of others to be seen by them"

---

2. Bruner, *Matthew*, 2:430.
3. See Davies and Allison, *Matthew*, 3:259; Talbert, *Matthew*, 256–57.

(Matt 6:1). The reason he issued the warning had to do with rewards. The people may be impressed, but God won't like it. In fact, those who show off their piety lose their reward with God (vv. 2–5). When it comes to righteousness, maintaining your privacy is a matter of self-*interest*, guarding your divine investment. This time, however, when Jesus warned the people about these hypocrites, it had more to do with their deleterious effect on others—why their duplicity ends up being so destructive. The Pharisees eventually lead others to hell, sealing God's judgment against them (23:15, 32–35). So, in this case avoiding hypocrisy is a matter of self-*preservation*, avoiding the wrath of God—which also may explain why Jesus used such a harsh tone.[4] There's a lot more at stake than missing out on divine rewards. Hypocrisy is a deadly problem.[5]

If not practicing what you preach (Matt 23:3) condemns you to hell, then that might encourage all of us to stop preaching. But Jesus doesn't go that far; he expects his disciples to preach the gospel (10:7; 28:19–20). Of course, he also takes "living the gospel" (practicing what we preach) very seriously.[6] Yet he knows his disciples will mess up, sometimes saying one thing but doing something else (26:31–35). So, the problem with hypocrisy seems to be more than deeds not matching words. As scholars have noticed,[7] Jesus seems to be more concerned about *chronic* hypocrisy because it leads to self-deception. After a while, duplicity becomes such an ingrained habit that hypocrisy is no longer recognizable to the hypocrite. In fact, if a person does anything for a long period of time, it will eventually be seen as acceptable behavior in their eyes.[8] That's the problem with the scribes and Pharisees: they have been hypocrites for so long they don't know it. They say the right things (the law) but they're not helping anyone do the right thing (keep the law; 23:3). They *think* they are helping others, trying to get Israel to obey the commandments, strapping the law on the backs of their disciples (v. 4). But they turned the law into a burden rather than a blessing[9]—the same criticism appears in the Sermon on the Mount. They sat in "the seat of Moses," pretending to carry on his tradition as a spokesman for God, but their endgame was to receive the adoration of men (23:5–7). That's why they wore big phylacteries—leather

4. France noticed that when Jesus speaks to the crowd about the scribes and Pharisees, he is polite. But when he talks directly to the scribes and Pharisees, he uses a caustic tone (France, *Matthew*, 867).

5. See above, 112–13, 143–44, 152–54, 436–41, 444 [125–28, 132–33 comments on hypocrisy, Matt 6:1–18].

6. Nolland, *Matthew*, 924.

7. Luz, *Matthew*, 3:103.

8. There have been some interesting neurological studies on how repetitive activity rewires the brain, eventually making any behavior seem acceptable; see Joel B. Green, *Body, Soul, and Human Life: The Nature of Humanity in the Bible* (Grand Rapids: Baker Academic, 2008), 79–105.

9. Garland, *Reading Matthew*, 234.

pouches that held Scripture verses—on their foreheads (Exod 13:9; Deut 6:8; 11:18). That's why they had long tassels dangling from their robes (Num 15:38–41; Deut 22:12). Both clothing accessories were supposed to be visual reminders—for them more than others—to keep the law. According to Jesus, however, these hypocrites wore broad phylacteries and long tassels so that everyone would admire them. How did Jesus know that? When someone called them, "Rabbi," or gave them the best seat in the house, they soaked it up like a dry sponge. They didn't care about others. Everything they did—even teaching others about the law—was to promote themselves.

They were so selfish that when Jesus opened the door of the kingdom to those who needed it the most, the scribes and Pharisees tried to slam it shut. Rather than help Jesus guide sinners to God, they made every effort to block the entrance, refusing to go in and preventing others from entering (Matt 23:13). Yet they would go to great lengths, "travel over land and sea to win a single convert" to their cause (v. 15), trying to get God-fearers circumcised[10] or getting other Jews to join their ranks.[11] Jesus came to save the people; the scribes and Pharisees were out to expand their membership. They also majored on the minor, trivializing the sacred while exaggerating the miniscule. For example, the scribes and the Pharisees valued the gold in the temple more than the temple or its divine resident (vv. 16–17, 21–22). They cared more about the gifts on the altar than the altar's sacred purpose (vv. 18–20). They were fanatical about tithing (Lev 27:30), but ignored injustice (Matt 23:23). They strained their wine for gnats (Lev 11:41–45), but had no problem swallowing the camel of their hypocrisy (Matt 23:24).[12] Like dirty dishes that were clean on the outside (v. 25), like whitewashed tombs that housed unclean corpses (v. 27), the scribes and Pharisees wanted to look good, trying to hide their corrupt, dead hearts (vv. 26, 28). In other words, they were the complete opposite of what Jesus required of his disciples. While the scribes and Pharisees exalted themselves, those who followed Jesus would learn what it meant to humble themselves as slaves (vv. 11–12).

The Hypocrisy of Pretense

There was only one other time in Matthew's Gospel where Jesus quotes the teaching of the scribes and Pharisees (15:5), which reveals, of course, that he had spent some time listening to them. He had heard them give their rulings

---

10. See Scot McKnight, *Light among the Gentiles: Jewish Missionary Activity in the Second Temple Period* (Minneapolis: Fortress, 1991), 106–15.

11. See Nolland, *Matthew*, 934.

12. Jesus may have relied upon a pun, heard only in Aramaic, *qalma* (gnat) and *gamla* (camel); see France, *Matthew*, 874.

about a variety of laws, interpreting for the people what would be a violation of the commandments. Evidently, commoners asked these experts (both the paid professionals, the scribes, and the lay leaders, the Pharisees) about the finer points of the law. After all, the law was vague in certain places, requiring specific interpretations that would ensure compliance. As we mentioned before,[13] not all rabbis agreed, offering different interpretations of the same commandment (the Mishnah is filled with various opinions of more than a hundred rabbis). It's not the differing opinions among the teachers that bothered Jesus but the pretense that they knew *everything*—ferreting out every detail supposedly embedded in the law—even claiming the ability to distinguish between swearing oaths by the temple or by the gold in the temple (23:16). How could *anyone* know that God would hold a man to the latter but not the former? To make such a claim was the height of arrogance—not to mention the fact that they were wrong (vv. 20–22). Furthermore, their microscopic vision blinded them to the more important macroscopic issues of justice, mercy, and faithfulness (v. 23). This is why Jesus had to call them out: they were blind guides (blinded by their pride), who were misleading blind followers (blinded by their ignorance), all headed straight for hell (15:14). To be so wrong, thinking you are so right—self-deception!—was a dangerous situation that had eternal consequences. We may prefer to see Jesus's remarks about hell (23:15, 33), filling up the measure of the sin of their forefathers (v. 32), and the impeding wrath of God on Jerusalem (vv. 37–38) as little more than a rhetorical flourish—his last attempt to dissuade the crowds from following the scribes and Pharisees. (Is that what "hell," "sin," and God's "wrath" have become to us? Words that are used only for rhetorical effect?) But these were not empty threats, intended only to strike fear in the hearts of his listeners. No, when Jesus talked about hell, sin, and the wrath of God, he was deadly serious.

Even though it was somewhat common for one Jew to tell another group of Jews that they were headed for the judgment of God,[14] such damnation was still offensive—as offensive as when one Christian damns other Christians to hell. In certain respects, to damn the Pharisees to hell was inconceivable. For just as most Christians are convinced they are going to heaven when they die, so also the scribes and Pharisees were convinced that they would inherit the kingdom of God. Moreover, these religious leaders were so convinced they were right, they claimed that they wouldn't have made the same mistakes as

13. See above, 112–13; 239–43.

14. The literature produced by the Jewish "monastics" at Qumran are filled with condemnations against the "wicked" in Israel—God will judge them as if they were gentiles; see 1QpHab 2:1–9; 8:8–15; 12:7–13; 1QS 3:20–24; 4:9–19; 5:1–2, 7, 11–15; 1QH 14:29–35.

their ancestors who killed the prophets God had sent to Israel (v. 30). (Don't we all think we're smarter than generations past?) The irony was more than Jesus could take. Here stands the very Son of God, talking like the last prophet of God, and the Pharisees considered him as nothing more than the great pretender. Jesus therefore connected the dots for them: since they claim to be the descendants of prophet killers, they will prove that they belong to their notorious ancestry when Jesus sends his prophets, sages, and teachers to them, and history repeats itself (vv. 31–34). Like a prophet, Jesus predicts the scribes and Pharisees will torture and kill Jesus's disciples just like their ancestors did to the prophets. Therefore, all the injustice of ages past will fall on their heads; this generation of scribes and Pharisees will bear the entire guilt of all prophet killers of all time (past, present, and future). The blood of every biblical martyr, from the first murder victim (Abel) to the last prophet murdered according to 2 Chronicles (Zechariah), will cry out for judgment against these scribes and Pharisees (Matt 23:35–36). And God will make them pay for all of it, for every last drop of righteous blood as if they were the criminals who killed them all. That's quite a reversal. The scribes and Pharisees have gone from expert teachers of the law to the worst criminals in Israel's history.

The patience of God led prophets to assume that even though the Lord was waiting for Israel to repent, her sins were piling up high to the heavens, inciting the day of divine judgment. God couldn't let things go, ignoring past indiscretions. Rather, the prophets worked with the presumption that Israel needed to repent, change her ways, and obey God to avert the day of God's wrath. Yet even if that never happened, the prophets warned the people that a day of reckoning would come. Once Israel had exhausted God's patience, he would judge the people for all their sins—past and present.

That the current generation would have to pay for the sins of their forefathers sounds completely unfair to us.[15] We believe that individuals should be held accountable for their own actions. Furthermore, to make the people pay for the wickedness of their rulers isn't justice according to our standards. Yet we blame politicians for getting us all in a mess, such as bad decisions that lead to war or economic policies that have an adverse effect on the environment. We understand that future generations will suffer the consequences of our sins, our bad decisions. So, when Jesus pronounced judgment upon all of Jerusalem for the sins of their forefathers and religious leaders (vv. 37–39), he not only sounded like an Old Testament prophet but an observant poet. To quote John Donne, "No man is an island."[16] None of us can live only for

15. Luz calls this "the logic of collective guilt" (*Matthew*, 3:156).

16. John Donne, *Devotions upon Emergent Occasions* (Ann Arbor: University of Michigan Press, 1978), 108.

ourselves. What we do affects others. That's especially true for leaders, whose decisions will *always* have consequences—not only for them but also for those who are led. To whom much is given, much is required.

Such influence, such great power, should compel leaders to humility. After all, the way the prophets saw it, God was the one who shared his power with Israel's leaders. He made kings. He established priests. He inspired prophets. So, where did the scribes and Pharisees fit into the divine government of religious life? They weren't "called of God," inspired by the Spirit to say, "Thus saith the Lord." They weren't predestined to serve God, a birthright determined by tribal identity. Instead, they took it upon themselves to be experts in the law. We could even say the scribes and Pharisees were self-appointed teachers of the Scriptures. The only evidence to substantiate their claim that they spoke for God when they interpreted the law was that the people listened to them. According to Jesus, however, those days were over. Jerusalem should have listened to Jesus, but they didn't. Rather, it "kill[s] the prophets and stone[s] those sent to" it (v. 37). Jesus presumed to be their savior, like a hen protecting her chicks ("the day of the Lord is coming! Duck and cover!"), but they refused. Therefore, since judgment begins with the house of God, Jesus declared "your *house* is left to you desolate" (v. 38)—either referring to Jerusalem (*your* house) or more likely the temple (your *house*; 24:2).[17] Like Ezekiel's vision (Ezek 10:18), Jesus declared that the glory of the Lord had departed. And since there was no divine power left to protect the temple, it would be a matter of time until the whole thing would implode, "not one stone left upon another" (Matt 24:2). Jesus was done, and he was leaving. But he would be back. And when that day comes, Jesus predicted Jerusalem will have finally learned to say what they should have said on Palm Sunday: "Blessed is he who comes in the name of the Lord" (23:39).[18]

LIVE the Story

"What's the worse thing you can call another Christian?" I recently asked the question during a Sunday-morning sermon, and the congregation nearly responded with one voice: "Hypocrite!" Isn't that interesting? No one said

17. "Thus Jesus's death is a sign of judgment. That God has abandoned his house means also that 'Immanuel' will no longer be seen" (Luz, *Matthew*, 3:162).

18. Scholars are divided over whether Jesus's pronouncement is a promise or a threat, a reason to hope that Jerusalem will receive her king one day or resignation to the fact that it will be too late for them on the last day. It is as difficult to understand as Paul's claim that one day "every knee will bow . . . and every tongue acknowledge that Jesus is Lord" (Phil 2:10–11). Is it compulsory or voluntary submission? See Garland, *Reading Matthew*, 236–37.

"murderer" or "adulterer." (Nor did anyone shout out the more inflammatory accusations of "cheater" or "liar." Call someone a liar today, and they'll get very angry even though we all lie. When students are caught red-handed, they *always* deny they cheated—what a surprise, cheaters lie). But in Christian subculture, the "chief of sinners" is a hypocrite and a Pharisee. Lay people know that because they've heard countless sermons from preachers warning their parishioners about the dangers of hypocrisy. Yet Jesus wasn't concerned about hypocrisy among the laity of Jerusalem. His sermon of "woes" wasn't directed against the people.[19] When it came to hypocrisy, they weren't the problem. The teachers of the law were the hypocrites, both the professionals (scribes) and the amateurs (Pharisees). One wonders if the same is true today. If Jesus were to preach his sermon of woes in our churches today, would he direct his comments to the laity (like many preachers do)? Or would he instead warn the people about the hypocrisy of the current "scribes and Pharisees"—our preachers and Sunday-school teachers? After all, lay people don't preach and teach. They sit and listen to preachers and teachers every Sunday. They may be guilty of not practicing what they hear—a problem to be sure (Jas 1:22–25). Yet that didn't disturb Jesus as much as those who don't practice what they preach. They are hypocrites bound for hell.

Hypocrisy rooted in self-deception is hard to shake. It's one thing to act like a hypocrite, knowing that your actions don't match your words. Such "actors" are playing politics, feigning sincerity to sway the masses to their own advantage. They still know the difference between right and wrong—their acting proves it. But what about sincere hypocrites, those who don't (can't? won't?) recognize their own duplicity? They can see the hypocrisy of others; they just can't see it in themselves. "What? Me, a hypocrite? You've got to be kidding." Many scholars think that's what Jesus is criticizing here[20]—not teachers who are intentional fakers, trying to pull the wool over everyone's eyes, but hypocrites who were blind to their faults (Matt 23:16–17). In other words, the Pharisees weren't con men playing on the ignorance of the masses, trying to dupe the crowds. Rather, these hypocrites were teachers who believed what they said. The problem, according to Jesus, was that they didn't live up to what they taught, *and it didn't bother them*. They were sincerely wrong, but didn't care. Why not? Because by their own words they were convinced they were right. Having deceived themselves, no one could tell them otherwise.

19. At first, Davies and Allison misplace the emphasis, suggesting that the "contemporary application of Matthew 23 should target the church" (*Matthew*, 3:262). But then they turn their attention more appropriately to the hypocrisy within church leadership (ibid., 3:263).

20. For example, see France, *Matthew*, 869.

I cannot help but wonder if the scribes and Pharisees were more susceptible to hypocrisy due to the role they played in the religious life of Israel. Not the Sadducees, the Herodians, or the Essenes—when it came to obeying the law, the people looked to the *Pharisees* as the voice of reason.[21] The Sadducees and the Herodians played power politics among the elite. The Essenes withdrew from society. But the Pharisees existed for the common person—of the people, for the people. Their scribes copied the Scriptures for the synagogues, and their lawyers interpreted the law for everyday life. Therefore, as local experts the Pharisees were required to talk a lot to the people. Words were their craft. It was their job not only to produce the Scriptures but also explain the Scriptures. And, the people listened to them. Why wouldn't they? So, consider the implications of their influence. The Jewish people attended synagogues to hear Scriptures that were copied by Pharisees, read by Pharisees, interpreted by Pharisees, and then modeled by Pharisees. When people thought about the law, they considered the Pharisees. When the law was lived out before their eyes, they saw the Pharisees. When the people heard the law—the very voice of God—it sounded like the Pharisees.[22] That must be a pretty heady thing: stand before a group of people week after week and speak with the voice of God. After a while, you might begin to believe everything you say is true.

It's easy to believe our own voice. If I say something often enough (especially when I think I'm speaking for God), I'll convince myself that it's true. I may not do what I say. But at least—I think to myself—I'm saying what needs to be said. And yet, when I preach a sermon on James 2:14 (that a genuine faith cannot rely on our words), I begin to feel a little sheepish. How can a *sermon* about the importance of works do any good? "Listen to me. If you have a faith that relies exclusively upon words, that faith won't save you from hell. Let me explain. . . ." The irony is more than I can take sometimes. I'm using words to convince my listeners that words aren't enough. Yet I keep on talking, preaching, writing *words*. But if I've fallen in love with the sound of my own voice, if James is right that an unbridled tongue only leads to self-deception, and I keep talking, who will save me from this body of death? I can't talk myself out of self-deception. My words are the problem. And, if I keep talking, it will only get worse because hypocrisy lives comfortably in the family room of my words. Perhaps it's time to shut my mouth for a change and listen to the hypocrisy of my ways. Then perhaps the words of the prophet might penetrate my heart. Then I might have ears to hear and hands to do what I see in the mirror of God's word (Jas 1:23–25). Then I will have a "religion that God our Father accepts as pure and faultless," which "is this:

21. Josephus, *Ant.* 18.1.3.

22. "The scribes and Pharisees were walking copies of the Law" (Nolland, *Matthew*, 923).

to look after orphans and widows in their distress" (v. 27)—the weightier matters of the law. On the other hand, "those who consider themselves religious and yet do not keep a tight rein on their tongues deceive themselves, and their religion is worthless" (v. 26). Of all things, I don't want to have a worthless religion. I don't want to be deceived by my own words. I don't want to prove once again that the occupational hazard of preachers and teachers is self-deception because we don't know when to stop talking.

But that's not the only problem—knowing when to shut up. If the tree of hypocrisy is rooted in self-deception, then its fertilizer is self-promotion. In Jesus's day, the honor game encouraged self-promotion. In fact, it was required. If you didn't constantly maintain your social standing in the community by boasting, then your honor would be lost to stronger competitors vying for the approval of the same group. That's why the Pharisees loved receiving choice seats and proper greetings (Matt 23:6–7); it proved to everyone they were still important. To be seen in the right places (synagogues), dressed the right way (tassels and phylacteries), called the right things (rabbi) was the primary goal of everyday life. Today, things haven't changed much at all. Social media have fostered a world of self-promotion where everyone seems to compete for attention: "Look at me!" (One wonders how much the Pharisees would have taken social advantage of the "selfie.") Since a picture paints a thousand words, to be seen is more important than being heard. In the old days of social media, blogging was the venue for establishing a voice in the world of self-importance. Now, creating and maintaining a carefully crafted image through pictures is far more crucial to self-worth. You don't have to be a good talker to matter. Consequently, the claim to fame is a game *everyone* is playing—not just for those who think they have something to say.

We recently returned from a trip to Italy, a place I've always wanted to visit. For a New Testament professor, seeing the Colosseum and the Forum in Rome or walking through the ancient streets of Pompeii—well, I couldn't help myself, snapping *hundreds* of pictures. (In the old days one had to be selective, carrying a half-dozen rolls of thirty-six-exposure film. Framing the right picture was crucial in a world of limited snapshots. But these days, digital cameras encourage a lack of restraint.) Even though this was supposed to be a special family trip for our graduating senior, my wife and daughter let me go crazy with the cameras, often leaving them to find that perfect picture. Of course, the place to take that perfect picture was easy to find. Typically, there was a huge crowd of tourists lined up with their cameras at the *punto panoramico* ("viewpoint"). I would stand at the back of the mob, waiting my turn until the others cleared out of the way before I took my picture. But things were different this trip. When we took our oldest daughter on her senior trip to Germany a few years ago, the lines moved fairly quickly. Tourists would snap their picture and move on. This time, it seemed to take forever. Why? Everyone (and I mean nearly *everyone*) would pose for their own camera using a selfie stick. After several minutes of posing (and most of the time, it had to be a dramatic pose), they would take a picture, review their work, then decide to take another, and another, and another until they got that perfect angle of themselves in front of this attraction or that site. I just wanted to take a picture of what I saw. Everyone else was trying to take a picture of themselves. It was maddening. After a while, I lost patience and pushed my way through the "paparazzi" to snap my picture and leave. I was completely shocked by the spectacle. I should have seen it coming, though. Everywhere we went, peddlers were selling selfie sticks, dozens on their arms, pushing them to the hoards of tourists heading for this or that attraction. I thought to myself, "Why are they selling those things? Who needs a selfie stick?" Evidently, I did. When it comes to tourism these days, to be seen is far more important than seeing the sites.

Leaving the Forum, I muttered to my wife and daughter, "I don't understand. They spend so much time trying to take the perfect 'glamor shot' of themselves in front of the arch of Titus that they don't even see the sacking of Jerusalem carved in the side of the monument. Unbelievable. They have no idea what they're missing. Why are they doing that? I just don't get it. Do you see this? They did the same thing at the Colosseum."

At which point my daughter, Grace, said, "Dad, it's bragging rights. They're taking selfies to prove to everyone where they've been. That's far more important these days."

To which I replied, "It's all about image, isn't it?"

Then Grace continued to explain the social dynamics of our foolish world to her out-of-touch father, ending her little tutorial with a wry smile and saying, "To be seen is the only thing that matters." I looked back to see the gang of tourists with their selfie sticks, posing in front of the arch of Titus, ignoring the dramatic scene of the aftermath of the destruction of Jewish temple in AD 70 carved in the wall, wondering what the ancient people of Jerusalem who suffered the tragedy would have thought of the charade. Then, with the words of Jesus echoing in my ears, "For those who exalt themselves will be humbled, and those who humble themselves will be exalted" (Matt 23:12), I couldn't help but connect the dots:

> Jerusalem, Jerusalem, you who kill the prophets and stone those sent to you, how often I have longed to gather your children together, as a hen gathers her chicks under her wings, and you were not willing. Look, your house is left to you desolate. (vv. 37–38)

Indeed, it was. There's even a crowd of people taking pictures of themselves in front of the monument that celebrates the desolation, the victory of an empire that used to rule the world—the remnant of which is little more than a pile of rubble, a tourist attraction for people who want to be seen.

Hypocrisy is a deadly, serious problem. There are even monuments to prove it, surrounded by tourists with selfie sticks and preachers who would rather talk about the vanity of others.

CHAPTER 34

Matthew 24:1–25:46

LISTEN to the Story

1Jesus left the temple and was walking away when his disciples came up to him to call his attention to its buildings. 2"Do you see all these things?" he asked. "Truly I tell you, not one stone here will be left on another; every one will be thrown down."

3As Jesus was sitting on the Mount of Olives, the disciples came to him privately. "Tell us," they said, "when will this happen, and what will be the sign of your coming and of the end of the age?"

4Jesus answered: "Watch out that no one deceives you. 5For many will come in my name, claiming, 'I am the Messiah,' and will deceive many. 6You will hear of wars and rumors of wars, but see to it that you are not alarmed. Such things must happen, but the end is still to come. 7Nation will rise against nation, and kingdom against kingdom. There will be famines and earthquakes in various places. 8All these are the beginning of birth pains.

9"Then you will be handed over to be persecuted and put to death, and you will be hated by all nations because of me. 10At that time many will turn away from the faith and will betray and hate each other, 11and many false prophets will appear and deceive many people. 12Because of the increase of wickedness, the love of most will grow cold, 13but the one who stands firm to the end will be saved. 14And this gospel of the kingdom will be preached in the whole world as a testimony to all nations, and then the end will come.

15"So when you see standing in the holy place 'the abomination that causes desolation,' spoken of through the prophet Daniel—let the reader understand—16then let those who are in Judea flee to the mountains. 17Let no one on the housetop go down to take anything out of the house. 18Let no one in the field go back to get their cloak. 19How dreadful it will be in those days for pregnant women and nursing mothers! 20Pray that your flight will not take place in winter or on the Sabbath. 21For then there will be great distress, unequaled from the beginning of the world until now—and never to be equaled again.

22“If those days had not been cut short, no one would survive, but for the sake of the elect those days will be shortened. 23At that time if anyone says to you, ‘Look, here is the Messiah!’ or, ‘There he is!’ do not believe it. 24For false messiahs and false prophets will appear and perform great signs and wonders to deceive, if possible, even the elect. 25See, I have told you ahead of time.

26“So if anyone tells you, ‘There he is, out in the wilderness,’ do not go out; or, ‘Here he is, in the inner rooms,’ do not believe it. 27For as lightning that comes from the east is visible even in the west, so will be the coming of the Son of Man. 28Wherever there is a carcass, there the vultures will gather.

29“Immediately after the distress of those days

> ‘the sun will be darkened,
>   and the moon will not give its light;
> the stars will fall from the sky,
>   and the heavenly bodies will be shaken.’

30“Then will appear the sign of the Son of Man in heaven. And then all the peoples of the earth will mourn when they see the Son of Man coming on the clouds of heaven, with power and great glory. 31And he will send his angels with a loud trumpet call, and they will gather his elect from the four winds, from one end of the heavens to the other.

32“Now learn this lesson from the fig tree: As soon as its twigs get tender and its leaves come out, you know that summer is near. 33Even so, when you see all these things, you know that it is near, right at the door. 34Truly I tell you, this generation will certainly not pass away until all these things have happened. 35Heaven and earth will pass away, but my words will never pass away.

36“But about that day or hour no one knows, not even the angels in heaven, nor the Son, but only the Father. 37As it was in the days of Noah, so it will be at the coming of the Son of Man. 38For in the days before the flood, people were eating and drinking, marrying and giving in marriage, up to the day Noah entered the ark; 39and they knew nothing about what would happen until the flood came and took them all away. That is how it will be at the coming of the Son of Man. 40Two men will be in the field; one will be taken and the other left. 41Two women will be grinding with a hand mill; one will be taken and the other left.

42“Therefore keep watch, because you do not know on what day your Lord will come. 43But understand this: If the owner of the house had known at what time of night the thief was coming, he would have kept watch and would not have let his house be broken into. 44So you also must be ready, because the Son of Man will come at an hour when you do not expect him.

45“Who then is the faithful and wise servant, whom the master has put in charge of the servants in his household to give them their food at the proper time? 46It will be good for that servant whose master finds him doing so when he returns. 47Truly I tell you, he will put him in charge of all his possessions. 48But suppose that servant is wicked and says to himself, ‘My master is staying away a long time,’ 49and he then begins to beat his fellow servants and to eat and drink with drunkards. 50The master of that servant will come on a day when he does not expect him and at an hour he is not aware of. 51He will cut him to pieces and assign him a place with the hypocrites, where there will be weeping and gnashing of teeth.

25:1“At that time the kingdom of heaven will be like ten virgins who took their lamps and went out to meet the bridegroom. 2Five of them were foolish and five were wise. 3The foolish ones took their lamps but did not take any oil with them. 4The wise ones, however, took oil in jars along with their lamps. 5The bridegroom was a long time in coming, and they all became drowsy and fell asleep.

6“At midnight the cry rang out: ‘Here’s the bridegroom! Come out to meet him!’

7“Then all the virgins woke up and trimmed their lamps. 8The foolish ones said to the wise, ‘Give us some of your oil; our lamps are going out.’

9‘No,’ they replied, ‘there may not be enough for both us and you. Instead, go to those who sell oil and buy some for yourselves.’

10“But while they were on their way to buy the oil, the bridegroom arrived. The virgins who were ready went in with him to the wedding banquet. And the door was shut.

11“Later the others also came. ‘Lord, Lord,’ they said, ‘open the door for us!’

12“But he replied, ‘Truly I tell you, I don’t know you.’

13“Therefore keep watch, because you do not know the day or the hour.

14“Again, it will be like a man going on a journey, who called his servants and entrusted his wealth to them. 15To one he gave five bags of

gold, to another two bags, and to another one bag, each according to his
ability. Then he went on his journey. [16]The man who had received five
bags of gold went at once and put his money to work and gained five bags
more. [17]So also, the one with two bags of gold gained two more. [18]But the
man who had received one bag went off, dug a hole in the ground and
hid his master's money.

[19]"After a long time the master of those servants returned and settled
accounts with them. [20]The man who had received five bags of gold
brought the other five. 'Master,' he said, 'you entrusted me with five bags
of gold. See, I have gained five more.'

[21]"His master replied, 'Well done, good and faithful servant! You have
been faithful with a few things; I will put you in charge of many things.
Come and share your master's happiness!'

[22]"The man with two bags of gold also came. 'Master,' he said, 'you
entrusted me with two bags of gold; see, I have gained two more.'

[23]"His master replied, 'Well done, good and faithful servant! You have
been faithful with a few things; I will put you in charge of many things.
Come and share your master's happiness!'

[24]"Then the man who had received one bag of gold came. 'Master,' he
said, 'I knew that you are a hard man, harvesting where you have not sown
and gathering where you have not scattered seed. [25]So I was afraid and went
out and hid your gold in the ground. See, here is what belongs to you.'

[26]"His master replied, 'You wicked, lazy servant! So you knew that I
harvest where I have not sown and gather where I have not scattered seed?
[27]Well then, you should have put my money on deposit with the bankers,
so that when I returned I would have received it back with interest.

[28]'So take the bag of gold from him and give it to the one who has
ten bags. [29]For whoever has will be given more, and they will have an
abundance. Whoever does not have, even what they have will be taken
from them. [30]And throw that worthless servant outside, into the darkness,
where there will be weeping and gnashing of teeth.'

[31]"When the Son of Man comes in his glory, and all the angels with
him, he will sit on his glorious throne. [32]All the nations will be gathered
before him, and he will separate the people one from another as a shep-
herd separates the sheep from the goats. [33]He will put the sheep on his
right and the goats on his left.

[34]"Then the King will say to those on his right, 'Come, you who are
blessed by my Father; take your inheritance, the kingdom prepared for

you since the creation of the world. [35]For I was hungry and you gave me something to eat, I was thirsty and you gave me something to drink, I was a stranger and you invited me in, [36]I needed clothes and you clothed me, I was sick and you looked after me, I was in prison and you came to visit me.'

[37]"Then the righteous will answer him, 'Lord, when did we see you hungry and feed you, or thirsty and give you something to drink? [38]When did we see you a stranger and invite you in, or needing clothes and clothe you? [39]When did we see you sick or in prison and go to visit you?'

[40]"The King will reply, 'Truly I tell you, whatever you did for one of the least of these brothers and sisters of mine, you did for me.'

[41]"Then he will say to those on his left, 'Depart from me, you who are cursed, into the eternal fire prepared for the devil and his angels. [42]For I was hungry and you gave me nothing to eat, I was thirsty and you gave me nothing to drink, [43]I was a stranger and you did not invite me in, I needed clothes and you did not clothe me, I was sick and in prison and you did not look after me.'

[44]"They also will answer, 'Lord, when did we see you hungry or thirsty or a stranger or needing clothes or sick or in prison, and did not help you?'

[45]"He will reply, 'Truly I tell you, whatever you did not do for one of the least of these, you did not do for me.'

[46]"Then they will go away to eternal punishment, but the righteous to eternal life."

Listening to the Text in the Story: Genesis 6:5–7:23; Exodus 12:39; Deuteronomy 30:3–5; Proverbs 14:31; Isaiah 13:6–13; 27:12–13; 34:1–4; 56:4–8; 58:7; 66:15–24; Jeremiah 7:8–15; 9:10–11; Ezekiel 32:3–10; 34:1–31; Daniel 7:9–14; 9:25–27; 11:31–35; 12:1–3, 11; Joel 2:1–11; 2:30–3:2; Haggai 2:6–7; Zechariah 2:6–13; 9:14–17; 12:10–14; 14:1–9; 1 Maccabees 1:20–24, 39; 2:28–38.

When Jesus left the temple, he said three things that seemed to puzzle his disciples: because Jerusalem refused to accept him as their Savior/Protector/Messiah, 1) the temple would become desolate, 2) the temple leadership wouldn't see him for a while, and 3) when he returned to the temple, they would recognize him as the Messiah (Matt 23:37–39). The last two statements probably didn't alarm them. Since things hadn't gone well while Jesus was in the temple, it would make perfect sense to them that he wouldn't want to go back there for a while. Since they weren't even staying in Jerusalem during their Passover visit, the odds were slim that Jesus would see them again when he celebrated the meal with his disciples. So, perhaps they wondered: "What would Jesus do to convince them that he was the Messiah? For he said that when he returned to the temple—sometime after Passover?—the temple leadership would welcome him with messianic praise. Would he perform a sign to prove to them he was the Messiah? Would that be the sign that the kingdom had come, when Jerusalem accepted Jesus as king?" The disciples eventually got around to asking him that question (24:3), but it wasn't their first concern. Evidently, what really bothered them was what Jesus said about the temple becoming desolate, which is why they pointed out Herod's impressive building project (v. 1)—a structure that must have seemed indestructible to the average person due to its massive stones (Mark 13:1).[1]

If the disciples had any doubts about what Jesus meant by the prophecy, "Look, your house is left to you desolate" (Matt 23:38), they were dispelled after he told them plainly, "Truly I tell you, not one stone here will be left on another; every one will be thrown down" (24:2). Was Jesus subtly suggesting to his disciples that *he* would be the one to destroy the temple (something his opponents accused him of later; 26:61)? Or was he predicting that God would do what he did before, that is, use a pagan nation to destroy his temple (last time, the Babylonians; this time, the Romans)? Imagine the power it would take to throw down *every* stone—especially the massive ones. Would it require the strength of a powerful army like the Romans or the kind of divine power that could also move mountains (21:21)? So many questions must have been buzzing around in their heads.

After leaving the temple, having headed down the Kidron Valley and up the side of the Mount of Olives, the disciples would have had enough time to cobble together Jesus's words, trying to sew the scraps of what he said and did during his momentous visit to the temple into a coherent whole. Things certainly hadn't gone like they expected even though Jesus had spent a lot of time preparing them for the shocking turn of events that would transpire in Jerusalem. Yet how did it all fit together? If Jesus were the long-awaited Messiah of Israel, and yet the leaders of Jerusalem had rejected him to this point, what would it take for him to establish his messianic rule on earth? Run the Jewish leaders out of town along with the Romans? Is that why he

1. Describing the excavation of the Western Wall, Evans points out that "one stone has gained attention owing to its enormous dimensions. It is more than fifteen meters in length and 2.5 meters in height. Because its width is unknown, estimations of its weight vary from 420 to 600 tons. What is especially remarkable is that this stone is not set at the base of the wall but has been set on the second tier above the pavement" (*Matthew*, 401).

predicted the destruction of the temple? Was he about to abolish the old priesthood to establish a new temple?[2] If so, would that be the sign to end all signs, signaling not only the end of the age but also the dawning of the messianic age, the *parousia* of his reign as the king of Israel? Is this what he meant by the kingdom of heaven coming to earth—out with the old, in with the new? That his disciples would join him in the new order, sitting on twelve thrones, to rule over Israel and the whole world from Jerusalem? And, just as important, when would all these things happen? Before Passover? After Passover? Sooner or later?

When the disciples approached Jesus with their queries, "When will this happen, and what will be the sign of your coming and of the end of the age?" (24:3), it sounds to us like they were asking three separate questions: When will the temple be destroyed? What is the sign of the second coming? And what is the sign of the end of the world?[3] But, given their context, the Twelve were actually asking one question three different ways. For them the destruction of the temple would not only signal the end of the world[4] but would also mark the beginning of the messianic age—something they had already experienced in part for quite some time: "The kingdom of heaven has come near" (4:17). They weren't asking questions about three events that would happen several years, decades, or even centuries apart (something we assume given our perspective). Furthermore, we also know that when they asked about the "sign of your coming," they *weren't* inquiring about the *second* coming of Christ. How do we know that? Because the disciples refused to accept the idea that Jesus would ever leave them (16:22; 20:21; 26:8–11, 56). There can't be a second coming without a "first departure." To their way of thinking, when the disciples asked Jesus about the "sign of his coming," they were actually referring to his first coming. That is to say, since the Twelve never believed Jesus would leave them, they must have been asking Jesus as to when he would "appear" as king of Israel. Would there be a sign to help them anticipate the day? Is that what the destruction of the temple was supposed to be, a sign of his *parousia*—the appearance of his kingly reign? Indeed, in light of Jesus's talk about the kingdom of heaven coming to earth and everything that happened in Jerusalem, the disciples were basically asking, "Are we there yet? And if not, how will we know it when we get there?"

---

2. Davies and Allison, *Matthew*, 3:330.

3. Actually, the Greek text indicates only two questions, since the last phrase [literally, "the sign of your coming and end of the age"] is governed by one definite article.

4. Nolland, *Matthew*, 963.

EXPLAIN the Story

The reason the disciples came to Jesus "privately" (Matt 24:3) is that their questions were not a test, a way of challenging his audacious claim about the temple. Rather, when friends asked questions in private, it was a way to gain insider knowledge.[5] That's exactly what Jesus was doing: giving insider knowledge as to what was about to happen. Of course, many read Jesus's teaching about the end of the world as if it were a blueprint for the future to help his disciples see the sign of his second coming. Yet if that were the case, if the disciples were truly asking about the second coming of Christ, then the Olivet Discourse comes at the wrong place in the narrative. Jesus should have told them about the eschatological future at the end of the Gospel, after the "Great Commission." That would make better sense. First of all, the disciples would have already experienced the absence of Jesus—something they couldn't see happening—asking about his "second coming" in light of his "first departure." Having been commissioned to make disciples of all the nations, the eleven disciples would still have that nagging question hanging over their heads: "When are you coming back to finish what you started?" (That's the way Luke sets it up; see Acts 1:6.) Given that scenario, it would make perfect sense to read their question, "What will be the sign of your coming?" as their curiosity about the second coming of Christ. Furthermore, having witnessed Jesus defeat the enemies of sin and death through the cross and resurrection, the disciples would be in a much better position to make sense of his teaching about the end of the world: "First, the temple will be destroyed in your lifetime. Then there will be long period of time before my second coming—that's why I'm telling you several parables about being faithful until I return (but, they're really not for you—by then you'll be dead and gone). That will give plenty of time for the gospel to reach the ends of the earth. Then, after many, many years, I will return and bring about the end of the world." But such a reading assumes too much—not only for the disciples but also for Jesus. They didn't ask him about his second coming (they asked about his *parousia*),[6] and Jesus didn't know when the end of the world would happen (Matt 24:36).

Parousia is a loaded word, primarily because Paul used it to describe the second coming of Christ (1 Cor 15:23; 1 Thess 2:19; 3:13; 4:15; 5:23; 2 Thess 2:1). Yet Paul also used the term to refer to the "appearance" of

5. See above, 434–35.

6. "A deliberate anachronism is involved in having the disciples ask about Jesus's coming" (Nolland, *Matthew*, 961).

himself, other friends, and even "the lawless one" (1 Cor 16:17; 2 Cor 7:6–7; 10:10; Phil 1:26; 2:12; 2 Thess 2:8–9). So, obviously, *parousia* wasn't a technical term reserved for the second coming of Christ. Outside of Christian literature, *parousia* referred to the appearing of a ruler or a deity.[7] During the Olivet Discourse, Jesus refers to the *parousia* of the Son of Man three times (Matt 24:27, 37, 39). Therefore, "in Matthew it means public 'arrival' (not 'return') and refers to the eschatological coming of the Son of Man (which was foreshadowed by the entry into Jerusalem. . .)."[8] When the disciples inquired about the *single* sign pointing to the *parousia* of Jesus and the end of the age (with Jesus's prediction about the destruction of the temple still ringing in their ears), they were trying to figure out whether the end of the temple would be the public sign revealing the beginning of Jesus's reign as king of Israel when he would take the throne of David. One would think the orchestrated royal entry into Jerusalem on "Palm Sunday" would have been the sign that marked the beginning of his claim to David's throne, or perhaps even his temple clearing, when Jesus re-created Malachi's prophecy of God visiting his temple. *Parousia* would have been a fitting word to describe both: the sudden appearance of their king and God[9]—the one whom David called "Lord" (Matt 22:43–45). But, Jerusalem did not welcome her king; the temple leadership rejected Jesus's authority. So, the Twelve inferred that the *parousia* of Jesus's rule over Jerusalem hadn't happened yet. Given Jesus's prediction about the soon-to-be-destroyed temple, they had to wonder: "When will that happen? And, will that be the sign of your kingdom come, the end of the old age and the beginning of your messianic reign?" This is what they had been waiting for their whole lives, the reason they followed Jesus in the first place: to see the Messiah reign over Israel and the whole world.

"When Will This Happen?"

The closest Jesus came to answering their question, "When?" was when he said, "Truly I tell you, this generation will certainly not pass away until all these things have happened" (Matt 24:34). Without giving a specific date, Jesus promised that some of them would still be alive when the temple was destroyed. Throughout Matthew's Gospel, whenever Jesus spoke of "this generation," he was always referring to present company (11:6; 12:41–42, 45; 23:36). Furthermore, one of the "things" that Jesus describes in 24:4–33 is the "abomination that caused desolation" in "the holy place" (v. 15)—a reference to Daniel's prediction regarding the desolation of the temple (Dan 9:27;

7. Davies and Allison, *Matthew*, 3:337–38.
8. Ibid., 3:338.
9. *Parousia* is "the traditional language of the OT theophany" (ibid., 3:357).

11:31; 12:11). Jesus warned his disciples that when they saw that,[10] they were supposed to head for the hills because the "great distress" surrounding the destruction of the temple was imminent (Matt 24:15–21).[11] Therefore, it is apparent that Jesus predicted the temple would be destroyed within the lifetime of his/their generation. Indeed, it was; forty years later, the Romans ended the first Jewish war by sacking Jerusalem and destroying the temple. Moreover, much of what Jesus predicted came true prior to, during, and after the first Jewish war: the "appearance" of false messiahs, false prophets, wars, famine, and earthquakes, the persecution of the church, the worldwide expansion of the gospel, and the horrible atrocities of the first Jewish war (vv. 4–28).[12] Yet Jesus didn't stop there.

Jesus predicted other things would happen right after the temple was destroyed. Strange, cosmic events would occur "immediately after the distress of those days," like solar and lunar eclipses, a shower of comets racing across the sky, even that "heavenly bodies will be shaken" (v. 29). That's when the "sign of the Son of Man in heaven" would appear, signaling his *parousia* (v. 30). The implication seems obvious: the way Jesus saw it, right after the destruction of the temple, a sign that the Son of Man's appearance was imminent would appear in heaven. That would also mean that some of his disciples would be alive to witness the *parousia* of his messianic reign (see also 16:28).[13] Indeed, Jesus even promised, "Truly I tell you, this generation will certainly not pass away until *all these things* have happened"—which appears to include the "appearance" of Christ as the Son of Man (24:30–34). Jesus was so sure he was right, he claimed that "heaven and earth will pass away, but my words will never pass away" (v. 35). Indeed, we can't get away from what he said, even though some might wish he'd never spoken those words. This is because to some it appears as though Jesus was wrong: his *parousia* didn't occur after the destruction of the temple in AD 70. In fact, several scholars think that's one of the purposes of Matthew's Gospel: to account for the delay of the *parousia*.[14] Matthew's "generation" needed an explanation: "the temple is a pile of rubble and Jesus hasn't returned. Where is he? Did we miss something?" So, Matthew tried to separate the two events,[15] showing how Jesus gave specific details about the destruction of the temple (vv. 4–28) but only made vague references to the *parousia* (vv. 29–41). That's also why Matthew has so many parables about the

10. Echoes of the exodus, or Lot? See Davies and Allison, *Matthew*, 3:347–48.

11. Finding refuge in the hills of Judea had become sage advice built on tradition, e.g., during the Maccabean war (see Davies and Allison, *Matthew*, 3:347; Luz, *Matthew*, 3:196).

12. Blomberg, *Matthew*, 356.

13. See above, 337–38, 359–60.

14. See above, 30, 34.

15. France, *Matthew*, 918.

delay of a king or a bridegroom or a master returning home (24:42–25:30). So, the point of the Olivet Discourse wasn't to settle the question "when?" Instead, Jesus gave vague answers about the timing of the temple's destruction and his *parousia*—even admitting he didn't know when "all these things" would happen (v. 36)—to encourage his disciples to be faithful in his absence. His teaching may sound eschatological, but it was supposed to be taken as a pastoral warning:[16] "No one knows when I'll come back, so watch and pray."

If Matthew was trying to put some distance between the destruction of the temple and the *parousia* of Christ, he didn't do a very good job of it. Seamlessly, Jesus moved from talk about the days surrounding the "abomination that caused desolation" to the time when the "sign of the Son of Man" would appear in heaven, apparently linking the two events. Obviously, Jesus didn't return after the destruction of the temple, and "this generation" did "pass away" before "all these things" happened (v. 34). Therefore, some scholars aren't reticent at all to say that Jesus was wrong about the timing of the *parousia*,[17] pointing out even he confessed that he didn't know when "these things" would occur. And yet, it's one thing for Jesus to admit ignorance on the subject; it's quite something else for him to make a prediction that proved to be wrong. That would mean his accusers were right; Jesus was a false prophet (26:61–62; 27:40)—something Matthew tried to disprove (he characterized their testimony as "false evidence"; see 26:59–60). Besides, claiming "Jesus was wrong" isn't the only way to explain his enigmatic teaching. Indeed, it should come as no surprise that such prophetic talk informed by apocalyptic thinking is hard to nail down, defying a "this-was-fulfilled-at-this-time" historical explanation. Perhaps Jesus's warning that no one can predict when "these things" will happen is because history cannot contain apocalyptic events. These kinds of revelations are unpredictable because they are ahistorical, spiritual realities. Therefore, we've misunderstood Jesus's teaching because apocalyptic language cannot be taken literally.

Taking into account the nature of apocalyptic language, scholars have put forward two approaches to Jesus's teaching about the destruction of the temple, the sign of his *parousia*, and the end of the age that don't lead to the inference, "Jesus was wrong." First, some scholars have suggested the reason Jesus relied upon apocalyptic language (quoting heavily from Daniel) to describe the *parousia* of the Son of Man is because such an event couldn't be seen on earth; it was a spiritual revelation—a sign located "in heaven." These "heavenly" signs—the sun and moon "darkened" and stars falling from the sky—were never meant to be read as historical depictions but rather symbolic representations of a spiritual

16. Turner, *Matthew*, 565.

17. Dale C. Allison, *Jesus of Nazareth, Millenarian Prophet* (Minneapolis: Fortress, 1998), 218.

reality.[18] Accordingly, the *parousia* of Jesus—an apocalyptic reality expressed as a vivid metaphor—has already occurred: when Jesus ascended to the throne of David at the right of God in heaven. But how does the *parousia* relate to the destruction of the temple? It was the event "on earth" that corresponded to the "Son-of-Man-in-heaven" sign. According to France, then, "the time of the temple's destruction will also be the time when it will become clear that the Son of Man, rejected by the leaders of his people, has been vindicated and enthroned at the right hand of God."[19] Second, some scholars suggest that Jesus anticipated these ahistorical, apocalyptic signs would be fulfilled over and over again. For example, Davies and Allison think the main lesson of the Olivet Discourse is that the destruction of the temple in AD 70 would not "exhaust" the messianic woes yet to come.[20] Therefore, what happened to Jerusalem in AD 70 was a proleptic event[21] that not only signaled the end of the age but also taught two important lessons for every generation: there will always be more hell to pay until Jesus comes back, and the faithful should always be prepared for the ever-imminent return of Christ.[22] Another way of putting it would be that with every generation God keeps hitting the eschatological "reset button" until it is time for the Son of Man to return—a date God only knows.

Challenging the first approach, even though Jesus used apocalyptic language to describe the *parousia* of the Son of Man, some scholars aren't satisfied that his "appearance in heaven" is a cosmic symbol meant to describe a spiritual reality. According to Jesus his appearance as Daniel's heavenly "Son of Man" will be public, visible, even ostentatious—as prominent as lightning flashing across the heavens (Matt 24:27). This isn't a spiritual truth only to be "seen" by the faithful who can contemplate heavenly things.[23] When Jesus appears at the end of the age, *everyone will see it. "All the peoples of the earth* will mourn when they see the Son of Man coming on the clouds of heaven with power and great glory" (v. 30, emphasis added). His appearance will be as obvious as vultures gathered around a carcass (v. 28). According to Luz, then, "Matthew 24:29–31 speaks not of a human parousia within history and also not symbolically of a suprahistorical parousia. Instead, it makes real statements about the descent from heaven of the deified Christ for the purpose

---

18. Wright, *Jesus and the Victory of God*, 513–19.

19. France, *Matthew*, 924. He writes further that "in that case the 'sign' is not a preliminary warning of an event still to come, but the visible manifestation of a heavenly reality already established, that the Son of Man is in heaven sitting at the right hand of Power" (ibid., 926).

20. Davies and Allison, *Matthew*, 3:331.

21. Bruner, *Matthew*, 2:474.

22. Keener, *Matthew*, 578–83.

23. Wright pokes fun at those who believe in the physical return of Christ, "that a transcendent figure is about to come floating, cloudborne, towards earth" (*Jesus and the Victory of God*, 516).

of judging the world. It is a descent that takes place at the end of history *in time* and *in space*."[24] Ultimately, there will be no "secret coming" of Christ for the faithful few, whether in the desert (appearing in the desert like Moses *redivivus*) or the inner rooms of a building (like a priest in the temple). One day the *parousia* of Jesus's reign on earth will be evident to everyone. Every knee will bow on the last day. Until then, only those who follow him will recognize him as king. Therefore, like the kingdom of God his *parousia* as *king* is already/not yet.

Perhaps that's the key. Even though Jesus presumed his absence when answering his disciples' questions—"don't go looking for me here or there; you'll know it when you see me"—he didn't speak *explicitly* about a *second* coming because the *parousia* of his kingdom would not happen suddenly. There was only *one* coming of the messianic age, and it wouldn't happen overnight. Therefore, I think the second approach makes better sense. Indeed, Jesus's "appearance" as king of Israel would take time, just like the kingdom of heaven coming to earth—a mystery to be revealed—starting out one way (crowned with thorns) and ending another way (crowned with glory). Since the temple functioned as a symbolic microcosm of earth,[25] then its destruction would be a proleptic demonstration of the end of the world (already/not yet). Consequently, at the beginning of his *parousia* as the king of Israel (27:31–50), it would appear as though nothing had changed—which is why Jesus was especially concerned about his disciples falling prey to deception. Hearing the disciples ask about the future, the first words out of his mouth were, "Watch out that no one deceives you" (24:4). Why would they be fooled? Because the *way* Jesus would become the king of Israel (a cross!) would appear as defeat, not victory; as loss, not gain; as death, not life; as weakness, not strength—something he had been trying to teach the disciples for some time.

Who could say that Jesus had ascended to the throne of David when wars and rumors of wars persist? Who would claim that Jesus reigns when nations continue to rise up against nations? Famine and earthquakes would give every appearance that the kingdom of heaven hadn't come to earth. And without a kingdom, there is no king. Persecution, death, hatred, false prophets, and messiah wannabes (vv. 9–12, 22–24)—even the upcoming destruction of the temple (vv. 15–21)—this is the evidence of his *parousia*, that Jesus reigns as the Christ? Enter the scoffers: "Where is this 'coming' he promised? Ever since our ancestors died, everything goes on as it has since the beginning of creation" (2 Pet 3:4). Yet Jesus was convinced his disciples wouldn't be fooled by these

---

24. Luz, *Matthew*, 3:205 (emphasis his).

25. John H. Walton, *The Lost World of Genesis One: Ancient Cosmology and the Origins Debate* (Downers Grove, IL: IVP Academic, 2009), 81–85.

things (Matt 24:24). Why? Because they had insider knowledge that this was the way it was supposed to be: "See, I have told you ahead of time" (v. 25).[26] These things were only "the beginning of birth pains" of the messianic age (v. 8), but that didn't mean his disciples would retreat in despair. They would continue to preach the gospel, taking his message to the whole world; then the end would come (v. 14). Jesus might not know "when" (v. 36). But he knew enough to warn his disciples that things won't turn out like anyone expected.

"Therefore Keep Watch"

When Jesus's enemies asked for a "sign from heaven," he dismissed them with a curt reply: "A wicked and adulterous generation asks for a sign, but none will be given it except the sign of Jonah" (Matt 16:4). Why? Because even if they saw the sign, they wouldn't recognize it (vv. 2–3).[27] Of course, the presumption behind their request implies that God owed it to his people to give them a "heads up" before the great and terrible day of the Lord. (That's why God always sent prophets to "prepare the way of the Lord.") Israel shouldn't be caught flat-footed, surprised by the judgment day. So when Jesus's disciples asked about "the sign" that signaled the beginning of the messianic age (24:3), the Messiah told them everything he knew. They should be able to read "the signs of the times." He told them that the sign that the end was near was when the gospel reached the ends of the earth (v. 14). Moreover, the sign that he was about to appear before the end of the world as the heavenly Son of Man ready to judge all nations would occur "in heaven" (v. 30). He never said *when* the gospel would reach the ends of earth.[28] Nor did he describe what the sign in heaven would look like. Some think the expression, "the sign of the Son of Man" should be interpreted appositionally: the sign is the Son of Man appearing in heaven.[29] Other scholars read it as an objective genitive, the heavenly sign pointing to the Son of Man—which could be anything from the cross[30]

26. Chrysostom wrote, "Then lest on hearing of the showers of evils, they should suppose the gospel to be broken through, He added, 'See, be not troubled, for all things must come to pass,' i.e. which I foretold, and the approach of the temptations will set aside none of the things which I have said; but there shall indeed be tumults and confusion, but nothing shall shake my predictions" (*Homilies*, 451).

27. According to Luz, no more signs would be given to warn the people because Jesus appearing as the Son of Man is the sign of the end of the world (*Matthew*, 3:202).

28. According to Jerome, this "sign" had already been fulfilled in his generation: "The sign of the Lord's coming is that the gospel will be preached throughout the entire world, leaving no one any excuse. We believe that this has already been accomplished or is about to be accomplished, since it appears to me that there remains no nation that does not know the name of Christ" (Simonetti, *Matthew 14–28*, 191).

29. Bruner, *Matthew*, 2:510.

30. Chrysostom, *Homilies*, 459. Davies and Allison write: "The eschatological ensign is the cross" (*Matthew*, 3:360).

to a cosmic omen.[31] Whatever the case, Jesus made it plain that at the end of history when he appears as the Daniel-prophesied Son of Man, he would come with "great power and glory," accompanied by angels, announced by "a loud trumpet call" (v. 31). Like fig leaves that indicate summer is near, the disciples would know "the end is near" when they saw the sign (vv. 32–33). They won't be fooled like the rest of humanity, surprised by the judgment day like Noah's generation (vv. 37–41). Instead (ironically), because they *don't know* "on what day your Lord will come" (v. 42), the disciples will be ready.

When Jesus talked about the end of the world, he always included the element of surprise. Some people will be surprised that he returned; they carried on with the daily affairs of life as if nothing else mattered (vv. 38–41).[32] Others will be surprised when he returns; they thought he would never come (24:42–25:13). Some will be surprised by the verdict against them on the judgment day; they thought they had done the right thing (25:14–30, 41–46). Others will be surprised to learn that they had done the right thing; they will be welcomed by Jesus because they unknowingly welcomed him (vv. 31–40). Certainty is the casualty of eschatology. No one knows for sure what will happen on the last day. Therefore, Jesus warned his disciples twice to "keep watch" (24:42; 25:13). The only way to be prepared for the judgment day is to always be faithful, doing what they are supposed to be doing (24:44–47). What are they supposed to be doing? Feeding their fellow slaves "at the proper time" rather than abusing them and carousing around with the wrong kind of people (24:45–49); waiting expectedly for the return of Christ rather than being caught off guard when he appears (25:1–13); advancing his cause while he's away rather than hiding to avoid responsibility[33] (vv. 14–30); taking care of the needy rather than ignoring them (vv. 31–46). Ignorance is no excuse for laziness. Vigilance is required to face an uncertain future. Only the foolish will be unprepared for the last day. Fidelity is evident among the wise because they know that "the one who stands firm to the end will be saved" (24:13).

Once again, Jesus relied upon parables to change people's minds about God and the way his kingdom works. We can tell by the way the disciples asked their question(s) that they held to the common expectation that the old

31. Perhaps as the fulfillment of Isaiah 13:10. Nolland writes: "The sun, moon, and stars are glorious heavenly bodies, frequently identified as gods and worshipped, but they must humble themselves when God acts; when God's glory is revealed, their glory must be veiled" (*Matthew*, 982). When the Son of Man comes to earth, the powers in the sky must fall in submission because there can be no power above him.

32. "The crime indicted by Jesus in this verse is not *gross* sin (the people of Noah's generation are not doing vicious things in Jesus's description); it is *secular indifference*" (Bruner, *Matthew*, 2:524 [emphasis his]).

33. According to rabbinical tradition, "anyone who buried a pledge or a deposit immediately upon receipt of it was free from liability" (Davies and Allison, *Matthew*, 3:406).

age would come to an end with a bang—that the messianic age would begin with cosmic fireworks that would put everyone on notice that the Messiah is large and in charge. But that's not how it would happen. Yes, the temple would be destroyed. Yes, Jesus would descend from heaven one day as the powerful Son of Man, just as Daniel 7 predicted. Yet these things wouldn't happen all at once, which is why Jesus kept warning his disciples not to be alarmed because the "end is still to come" (Matt 24:6). Others might be fooled because nothing seemed to change after Jesus left them. But Jesus's disciples know better. Even though it will look like the world is going to hell in a hand basket, these persecuted disciples will continue to preach the gospel of the kingdom: Jesus reigns (vv. 9–14). Even in the wake of the destruction of the temple, they won't be fooled by false messiahs and prophets who promise a better world because they are able to perform "signs and wonders" (vv. 15–24).[34] Disciples of Christ won't let their love grow cold, abusing each other because Jesus is gone (vv. 12, 48–49). Instead, faithful followers of Jesus will take care of each other (vv. 45–47), watching and waiting together like a bridal party ready to welcome the groom (25:1–10) or faithful servants prepared to give an account to their master when he comes home (vv. 14–16, 19–23). The fact that the master and groom would be gone a long time won't deter them in their devotion to him (24:48; 25:5, 19). They know that when Jesus returns there will be rewards for those who were faithful to the end—not only a big party but also more responsibility (24:47; 25:10, 21, 23). But the fools who ignored Jesus's warning, who didn't have ears to hear his parables, will all get the same thing: eternal punishment "where there will be weeping and gnashing of teeth" (24:51; 25:30, 46). There is no "in-between," no middle of the road, no purgatorial chance of redemption.[35] When the end comes, you're either in or your out, wise or a fool, faithful or lazy, rewarded or punished.

It is noteworthy that the absence of Jesus "appears" in all these parables; it is the defining problem that informs every story. Even though the characters and circumstances change with each parable, the message is the same: true disciples must be faithful to Jesus while he is away. Yet in the parable of the sheep and the goats (25:31–46)—the last parable in Matthew's Gospel,[36]

34. France writes that catastrophe is a "fertile breeding-ground for the sort of messianic claimants already predicted in vv. 5 and 11. . . . Anyone who offered new hope of divine intervention would be eagerly listened to" (*Matthew*, 916). For a list of the false messiahs who appeared between AD 30–70, see Keener, *Matthew*, 569; Talbert, *Matthew*, 266–67.

35. Davies and Allison, *Matthew*, 3:431.

36. Some scholars question whether it qualifies as a parable since the shepherd/sheep/goat imagery doesn't run throughout the story. Instead, the scene pictured at the last judgment comes closer to an apocalyptic vision than a parable; see France, *Matthew*, 960.

which also happens to deal with the last day—the absence of Jesus presents another problem. Even though Jesus was enthroned in heaven as the Son of Man, both the sheep and the goats discover on the last day that he wasn't totally absent on earth. Instead, Jesus was present among them *incognito*.[37] And, here's the real shocker: no one recognized him because he didn't appear on earth as a king (vv. 37–39, 44). His *parousia* was more like a pauper than a prince. Standing before the heavenly Son of Man on judgment day, both the sheep and the goats are incredulous that someone so regal, so mighty, so powerful could ever become someone so lowly, so helpless, so needy. "Lord, when did we see *you*. . . ?" They can't believe it, and who can blame them? The man who fed thousands is hungry? Jesus the healer gets sick? The Lord of heaven and earth is thrown into jail? What prison could hold the man who walked on water and calmed the storm? What disease could make sick the man who raised the dead? Jesus, the Messiah, a stranger? Jesus, the Lord, stripped naked? And yet, even though the sheep and the goats can't believe their ears, Matthew will tell the story of how it all came true, why the disciples won't believe their eyes. Jesus, the Christ, will become one of "the least of these"—hungry, thirsty, estranged, stripped naked, abused, killed, and entombed like a prisoner guarded by soldiers (26:17–27:66)—and they didn't see it coming.

LIVE the Story

Even though Matthew seems to be very concerned about the delay of Christ's appearance as the heavenly Son of Man, we find the repeated refrain a bit monotonous. Do we really need three parables (reckless slave, shortsighted virgins, lazy slave) to get the message across? Jesus isn't coming back for a while. After two-thousand years of church history, we say, "no surprise." The threat of Jesus coming back to find us unfaithful doesn't hold much purchase for us. It's the other scenario—the one described in the parable of the sheep and the goats—that gets our attention: one day we will stand before him and give an account of our lives. We may not be anxious about him coming to us, but we know that one day we must go to him. That's why the last parable about the last day packs a punch. When it's all over and there's nothing left to do, all humanity will be judged by Christ; the blessed will be separated from the cursed, the righteous from the wicked. There will be surprises for everyone—not only who makes it, but why. And what will be the dividing line, that which separates the sheep from the goats (cf. Ezek 34:17)? It's not what we would expect. In light of Matthew's presentation of Jesus as the king

37. One can experience Immanuel even in this dark, apocalyptic world (Luz, *Matthew*, 3:206).

of Israel, we would expect the enthroned Son of Man to say to the sheep, "Well done, good and faithful servants. For you accepted me as your king and followed me all the days of your life. Here is your heavenly reward." Likewise, Christ should say to the goats, "Cursed are you, unbelieving slaves. For you rejected me as your king and ignored my teachings. Here is your everlasting punishment." But that's not what he said.[38] As a matter of fact, his answer—what separates the sheep from the goats—comes as a surprise to all humanity, even Christians.[39] It's not what the sheep or the goats expected him to say on the last day. Furthermore, in light of what I heard growing up in a Southern Baptist Church—what's supposed to separate the sheep from the goats—Jesus seems to get it all wrong.

I was standing in the Sistine Chapel, staring at Michelangelo's painting of the last judgment on the western wall behind the altar, and it felt like the end of the world.

Packed into the little chapel as if we had just boarded a crowded bus, I stood with hundreds of tourists, slack-jawed, mouths gaping open, looking up, trying to take in with our eyes the awe and splendor of what we had heard about. The room was stuffy, dark, and a bit foreboding. Pushing my way through the crowd, I squeezed into the bench seat on the south wall. From there I was able to strain my neck, lean my head against the wall and gaze up at the ceiling, marveling over the scenes of the first three chapters of Genesis. Then, after surveying paintings about the life of Christ on the northern wall, I decided to give up my coveted seat and weave my way through the packed crowd to feast upon the pictures of the southern wall. By then I was separated from my family. I quickly scanned the crowd to see if I could spot them—there they were, in the corner, also trying to absorb the ineffable. Occasionally, the rumblings of the crowd would rise to the level of a mild roar, inciting officers by the altar to chide the crowd, "Silenzio! Silence, please." For a moment, there would be complete silence. A quiet room was supposed to help us focus our attention on the sacred. Yet, ironically, it was at that moment when I would become more aware of my surroundings—all these people shoved together, pushing up against me, from every walk of life and ethnic group, all muttering

---

38. Some scholars suggest that the nations gathered for judgment do not include Christians. Therefore, that which separates the sheep from the goats is how they treated all Christians ("the least of these" is a cipher for all disciples, Matt 18:2–10) or a particular group of Christians ("least of these" = missionaries, 10:40–42, or persecuted Christians, 10:16–31). See Keener, *Matthew*, 605; Talbert, *Matthew*, 275–76; Garland, *Reading Matthew*, 248.

39. Luz writes: "Matthew believed that the Christian church has no special position at the judgment" (*Matthew*, 3:284). Therefore, the parable pictures the judgment of all people and the "least of these" refers to all needy people (not just Christians); see Davies and Allison, *Matthew*, 3:429. France writes that "as far as they [sheep] were concerned, it was simply an act of kindness to a fellow human being in need, not an expression of their attitude toward Jesus" or Christians (*Matthew*, 959).

commentary in their own language, and me standing in the middle of this incredibly diverse sea of humanity. Eventually, my eyes would go back to the walls, to the ceilings, then back to the walls, but then I took notice of Michelangelo's depiction of the last judgment and I couldn't take my eyes off it. For all the beauty of the paintings on the ceilings, the frescos on the walls, and the tapestries that hung like curtains around the edges, I was completely arrested by Michelangelo's last contribution to the Sistene Chapel—a dreadfully wonderful picture of the last day.

As I stared at the painting, Rick Steves was providing audio commentary through one earbud, and the buzz of the crowd was getting louder in my other ear, provoking the officers to warn the forgetful mob once again, sternly correcting with ever-increasing paternal contempt, "Silenzio!" Then it hit me. It seemed like I was living a scene straight from the Revelation of John. A massive crowd sandwiched into a dark room, people from every "tribe and language and people and nation" (Rev 5:9) all around me, whispering anxiously, discretely pointing up at what they saw, the firm, authoritative voice warning the crowd, "Silenzio!" and me gazing at the last judgment, with Christ dealing out rewards for the righteous and eternal damnation to the wicked. It was easy to identify the sheep from the goats. The righteous were at the right hand of Christ, corpses rising from the grave, skeletons putting on new flesh as they ascend into heaven. The goats were at the left of Christ, whose right hand was raised, ready to consign their souls to demonic hoards who drag them down to the pit—all of them trying to resist the inevitable—demons yanking on their legs, pulling at their hair, forcing them down to eternal damnation. Taking in the dark spectacle—some going up, others pulled down—Rick Steves giggles in my ear, pointing out the peculiar site of Michelangelo's self-portrait. Having painted himself into the horrific scene, an angel holds the elder Michelangelo by the nape of the neck, dangling his withered body over the pit of hell. He is a shell of a man, looking like a worn-out sack of skin without bones. His face is gaunt, appearing more like the ghost of a haunted past than the incarnation of sheer genius. The brilliant painter and sculptor, who will draw *millions* of admirers to pay *millions* of dollars to see his work, appears at the last judgment as a huge question mark. Will the angel drop him into hell? Or will he join the parade of skeletons resurrected to the glory of heaven? No one knows. His eternal life hangs in the balance. As I stand there and wonder about him—along with hundreds of tourists from all over the world taking in the beauty of his work—I can't help but wonder about me. Standing there at the last judgment, I am overwhelmed by the question: What does it take to be found among the resurrected righteous and not the damned wicked?

The parable of the sheep and the goats answers that question. Yet, according to what I heard growing up in church, the parable should have gone something like this: "Then the King will say to those on his right, 'Come, you who are blessed by my Father; enter your heavenly reward. For you confessed Christ as your personal Lord and Savior, and you were baptized. You attended worship services every Sunday. You studied your Bible. You tithed ten percent of your income. You even shared your faith with lost people. You were a good church member.'" The fact that Jesus didn't emphasize being a good church member to indicate what separates the sheep from the goats is what gave me pause as I stood and stared at Michelangelo's depiction of the last judgment. Since the great artist didn't paint himself into the picture of the resurrected or the damned, was he saying that we can't know the difference between the righteous and the wicked, that there's no way to avoid surprises on the last day?

Richard and Connie Cummins found themselves following Christ to the other side of the world. Richard's new job as a logistics coordinator led them to Thailand, and quickly they began to set up their life together there, with four children in tow. After a while, Connie began to wonder: "Lord, what would you have me to do? My children are in school. I'm happy to support Richard in his work. But, do you have anything else for me?" Looking around, she soon discovered an orphanage run by the government and decided to volunteer her time. On her first day there, she noticed a very sick baby girl lying on a mat all alone, no one taking care of her. Expressing a desire to hold the baby, the nannies at the orphanage discouraged her from taking an interest. They explained that the baby was cursed, the result of a failed abortion attempt, and they were waiting to see if the child died. Connie refused, deciding to pick up the little girl, rocking her gently, trying to feed her even though the baby suffered from horrible dysentery. The locals were convinced the baby was a lost cause, but Connie persisted. She showed up every day, repeating the routine, trying to nurse the little one to health. After several days, Connie wanted to take the little girl home with her. At first the orphanage was hesitant. But after they saw that the baby girl was getting stronger, they agreed. Connie and Richard not only asked to adopt the little girl, but also wanted more children, babies that were "cursed" and considered lost causes. The orphanage gave them five more chronically ill children. Having outgrown their home, the Cummins moved to a larger home and hired nannies to help them nurse these orphans to health. Children that were "cursed" were being "blessed" by God; even the government was amazed at their success. Consequently, more babies were sent to Connie, and more, and more. Nearly all of them were eventually restored to health, playing, learning, waiting to be adopted by loving families. Then, one ministry led to another, to something neither Richard nor Connie planned for, but the Lord provided. Here's their daughter, Bethany, describing what happened:

> Not only is the family caring for the Thai orphans but they also provide second chances for young women in a juvenile detention center who were arrested for illegal trafficking of drugs. Richard and Connie have arranged a work-release program with the center so that the women can work as live-in nannies while receiving a monthly salary. While working in the home the women learn how to make an honest living so that when they are released they don't return to the unending cycle of illegal drug trafficking. Every Sunday volunteers come to watch the children so that the nannies have the opportunity to fellowship together, learn about Jesus, the life He lived, and the sacrifices He made for all people including drug traffickers and abandoned children. The women may not always be thankful for the opportunity they have been given or take full advantage of it, and the children may never come back to thank Connie for helping them survive infancy; yet, Connie and Richard remain faithful to those they know God loves and has called them to love.[40]

"[They] learn about Jesus, the life He lived, and the sacrifices He made for all people including drug traffickers and abandoned children"—the least of these finding the love of Christ because a woman from Arkansas moved to Thailand with her husband and asked the Lord, "What would you have me do?" That's what separates the sheep from the goats, which is why I'm convinced on the last day, I'll hear the Lord say to Richard and Connie:

> "Come, you who are blessed by my Father; take your inheritance, the kingdom prepared for you since the creation of the world. For I was hungry and you gave me something to eat, I was thirsty and you gave me something to drink, I was a stranger and you invited me in, I needed clothes and you clothed me, I was sick and you looked after me, I was in prison and you came to visit me."

Then Richard and Connie will say to him, "Lord, when did we see you hungry and feed you, or thirsty and give you something to drink? When did we see you a stranger and invite you in, or needing clothes and clothe you? When did we see you sick or in prison and go to visit you?" And the Lord will reply, "Truly I tell you, whatever you did for one of the least of these brothers and sisters of mine, you did for me."

Amen. Come, Lord Jesus.

---

40. From personal correspondence, 26 June 2015.

CHAPTER 35

Matthew 26:1–30

LISTEN to the Story

1When Jesus had finished saying all these things, he said to his dis-
ciples, 2"As you know, the Passover is two days away—and the Son of Man
will be handed over to be crucified."

3Then the chief priests and the elders of the people assembled in the
palace of the high priest, whose name was Caiaphas, 4and they schemed to
arrest Jesus secretly and kill him. 5"But not during the festival," they said,
"or there may be a riot among the people."

6While Jesus was in Bethany in the home of Simon the Leper, 7a woman
came to him with an alabaster jar of very expensive perfume, which she
poured on his head as he was reclining at the table.

8When the disciples saw this, they were indignant. "Why this waste?"
they asked. 9"This perfume could have been sold at a high price and the
money given to the poor."

10Aware of this, Jesus said to them, "Why are you bothering this
woman? She has done a beautiful thing to me. 11The poor you will always
have with you, but you will not always have me. 12When she poured this
perfume on my body, she did it to prepare me for burial. 13Truly I tell you,
wherever this gospel is preached throughout the world, what she has done
will also be told, in memory of her."

14Then one of the Twelve—the one called Judas Iscariot—went to the
chief priests 15and asked, "What are you willing to give me if I deliver him
over to you?" So they counted out for him thirty pieces of silver. 16From
then on Judas watched for an opportunity to hand him over.

17On the first day of the Festival of Unleavened Bread, the disciples
came to Jesus and asked, "Where do you want us to make preparations
for you to eat the Passover?"

18He replied, "Go into the city to a certain man and tell him, 'The
Teacher says: My appointed time is near. I am going to celebrate the

Passover with my disciples at your house.'" [19]So the disciples did as Jesus had directed them and prepared the Passover.

[20]When evening came, Jesus was reclining at the table with the Twelve.
[21]And while they were eating, he said, "Truly I tell you, one of you will betray me."

[22]They were very sad and began to say to him one after the other, "Surely you don't mean me, Lord?"

[23]Jesus replied, "The one who has dipped his hand into the bowl with
me will betray me. [24]The Son of Man will go just as it is written about
him. But woe to that man who betrays the Son of Man! It would be better for him if he had not been born."

[25]Then Judas, the one who would betray him, said, "Surely you don't mean me, Rabbi?"

Jesus answered, "You have said so."

[26]While they were eating, Jesus took bread, and when he had given thanks, he broke it and gave it to his disciples, saying, "Take and eat; this is my body."

[27]Then he took a cup, and when he had given thanks, he gave it to
them, saying, "Drink from it, all of you. [28]This is my blood of the cov-
enant, which is poured out for many for the forgiveness of sins. [29]I tell
you, I will not drink from this fruit of the vine from now on until that day when I drink it new with you in my Father's kingdom."

[30]When they had sung a hymn, they went out to the Mount of Olives.

Listening to the Text in the Story: Exodus 12:1–28; 21:32; 24:6–8; 29:7; Deuteronomy 15:11; 32:45–47; 1 Samuel 10:1; 2 Kings 9:3; Psalms 2:2; 22:1–24; 41:7–9; 133:2; Isaiah 25:6–9; 52:13–53:12; Jeremiah 31:31–34; Daniel 9:26; Zechariah 9:11; 11:10–13.

Jesus may not have known exactly when he would fulfill Daniel's prophecy, appearing as the Son of Man reigning in heaven, ready to judge the nations (Matt 24:29–36). But he knew what it would take to get there: a cross before a crown, death before resurrection. He had told his disciples that many times before, warning them he would be killed in Jerusalem (16:21; 17:22–23; 20:18–19). Up to this point, he had never indicated precisely *when* he would die—only where. He also knew what would happen afterwards: he would be raised from the dead and one day "come in his Father's glory with his angels" (16:21, 27). So, when the disciples asked, "When will this happen [the destruction of the temple], and what will be the sign of your coming and of the end of the age?" (24:3), Jesus could only give them a vague answer—one without a temporal referent—until now. For the first time, Jesus gave his disciples a timetable, linking his death—the event that would set in motion his *parousia*[1] as the king of Israel—to the Passover (26:2). Such information probably surprised the Twelve, for Jesus had just finished his lengthy remarks about all these things and never really answered their question "when?" (24:4–26:1). But now, with the holiday fast approaching, Jesus must have inferred that the timing of his death would coincide with Passover, even though his enemies were planning—at that very moment—*not* to kill him during the festival (26:3–5).

Their plan wasn't complicated: "Arrest Jesus secretly and kill him" (v. 4). They knew it would be nearly impossible to seize Jesus by stealth during the Passover. There were a lot of people surrounding him all the time. Moreover, even if they tried to get him at night when there wasn't a huge crowd around him, they would risk inciting a riot because he was so popular among the Galilean visitors (v. 5). Waiting until the weeklong festival was over was risky too: What if Jesus returned home after the holiday? Would they still be able to nab him before he left town? But then again, if Jesus were to leave Jerusalem, then their problems would be solved—at least until he came back. So, the chief priests and elders must have assumed Jesus was there to stay. After all, a man trying to claim David's throne would need to stick around. Once his support system (the Galileans) left Jerusalem, the leaders would arrest Jesus and kill him, perhaps inciting fellow Jerusalemites to rise up and stone him (cf. Acts 7:54–58). He was their problem, and they were going to take care of him.

But Jesus knew better. He predicted that he would be "handed over to be crucified" during Passover (Matt 26:2). In other words, Jesus knew the Jewish leaders wouldn't kill him by stealth.[2] Rather, they would "hand him over" to the Romans who would crucify him—a very public death, certainly not something that could be done "in secret."[3] Furthermore, Jesus knew the Romans would execute him during Passover. So, the chief priests and elders were wrong on both counts. How did he know that? According to Matthew, Jesus knew that Judas was about to make a deal to betray him (vv. 14–16, 21–25)—something the chief priests and elders hadn't counted on. All Judas needed was an "opportunity to hand him over" (v. 16), which happened that very evening. Alone in the middle of the night in the garden of Gethsemane, Jesus put himself in a vulnerable position. With his disciples

1. Luz writes that "Jesus's suffering is the beginning of his victory" (*Matthew*, 3:332–33).

2. Luz notes that murder committed by deceit (the word Matthew used was *dolos*, 26:4) was unpardonable according to rabbinical law (Exod 21:14); see *Matthew*, 3:332.

3. Keener, *Matthew*, 617.

asleep (vv. 40, 43, 45), Jesus would be defenseless, praying by himself (vv. 39, 42, 44). Consequently, Judas would find the perfect opportunity to alert Jesus's enemies, probably sneaking away while the disciples slept. Once the temple police showed up, everyone would wake up to see Judas innocuously greet Jesus like he probably had done many times before. Nobody would suspect that he was the betrayer—no one except Jesus (v. 46).

By the time it was over, Jesus was "handed over" several times "into the hands of sinners" (v. 45): once by Judas, once by the chief priests and the elders (27:2), and twice by the Roman procurator (vv. 26–27, 58).[4] This invincible man appears more like a pawn in the hands of powerful men than the king destined to rule the world. Like any other commoner, Jesus will have fallen prey to tactics employed exclusively by elites: secrecy, bribery, betrayal, deceit, arrest, false witnesses, false charges, and execution.[5] And yet, Matthew tells another story: Jesus knew what was going down. No one caught him by surprise. He wasn't a victim of power politics. Instead, he was a willing sacrifice, laying down his life for the forgiveness of sins (26:28). He was following a script that had been written long ago, a narrative that would play out as a surprise to everyone but him. "The Son of Man will go just as it is written about him" (v. 24). Passover was the perfect time for God's deliverer to save his people from their sins (1:21). And nobody saw it coming except Jesus.

EXPLAIN the Story

God had saved his people many times, from the desert, from enemy nations in and around the promised land (Canaanites, Jebusites, Edomites, Moabites, Midianites, and Philistines), and from threatening powers outside the land (Assyrians, Babylonians, Persians, Greeks, and Romans). But the high-water mark of God's salvation, the ultimate act of deliverance of his people, happened when Israel was miraculously released from Egyptian slavery (Exod 3:1–14:31). Every year, there were several holidays to mark the occasion of God's deliverance: from surviving the desert (Tabernacles) to entering the land (Pentecost). But the greatest holiday, the festival that commemorated the supreme act of salvation in the history of Israel, was Passover. It was also the most popular. The people might not make the trek to Jerusalem for the other two pilgrimage festivals. But they wouldn't miss Passover and the Feast of Unleavened Bread—a weeklong celebration of the exodus that began with eating the paschal lamb and continued every night by consuming unleavened bread dipped in herbs.

4. Bruner, *Matthew*, 2:594.
5. Malina and Rohrbaugh, *Synoptic Gospels*, 152.

Just as Israel was required to participate in the tenth plague that resulted in their deliverance from the Egyptians—slathering their doorposts with the paschal lamb's blood so that the death angel would "pass over" their home and not kill their firstborn son—so also later generations were commanded to participate in the Lord's deliverance by reenacting the scene of the memorial meal (Exod 12:14–27).[6] For a man whose name meant "The LORD Delivers," it's no wonder Jesus inferred that he would die during Passover in an act of God that would bring about an even greater salvation for Israel and the whole world. The death angel may pass over the homes of those who celebrate the feast on that holy night, but all firstborn sons eventually die. Therefore, Jesus knew that the approaching holiday meant one thing: "My appointed time is near" (Matt 26:18). To prepare for Passover was to prepare for his death.[7]

The chief priests and elders wanted him dead. To the disciple who betrayed him, Jesus was as good as dead. The disciples couldn't imagine him dead. To the woman who anointed him, Jesus was already dead. The death of Jesus hangs like a pall over the entire story. From now on, the death of Jesus will be the focal point of Matthew's Gospel. Jesus has been hinting at it for quite some time, even outright predicting it now and then. But now the time has come for Jesus to die. Everyone in Matthew's narrative world will react differently to the death of Jesus. Some will weep, others will mock. Some will mourn, others will be shocked. Some will turn their heads, others will wash their hands. Some will help bury him, others will help kill him. All through the passion of the Christ, the reader can't help but wonder: Does anyone see it? Does anyone get it? Is this just another senseless death, coming at the hands of despotic rulers? Did Jesus die in vain? Or will his death mean more than our predestined mortality—the fact that we're all going to die? Since Jesus knew he was supposed to die, will anyone have eyes to see and ears to hear what it means—that his death will be the only one that really matters? Did he die alone, no one understanding why? Was there someone—*anyone*—who knew why Jesus would see it through?

The Woman Who Prepared Jesus for Burial

We don't know her name. She came to Jesus while he was staying at Simon the Leper's house in Bethany (Matt 26:6–7),[8] a little village just outside of Jerusalem. We don't even know why she did it. Even though it was customary

---

6. Davies and Allison, *Matthew*, 3:470.

7. For parallels between the Last Supper and the exodus narrative, see Davies and Allison, *Matthew*, 3:477–78.

8. Turner infers that Jesus's willingness to eat at Simon's home reveals that he had already healed the leper (*Matthew*, 619; so also France, *Matthew*, 974). Yet in light of the fact that he's still known as "Simon the Leper," could Matthew be pointing out another example of Jesus's revolutionary ideas about purity and mercy, i.e., that Jesus would eat with a leper? See Bruner, *Matthew*, 2:599–600.

to anoint the heads of guests before a meal,[9] it must have been somewhat unusual (and perhaps a little difficult) to dump an entire vial of myrrh on someone's head while they were eating. For special meals, guests would normally recline on pillows around a u-shaped table (called a *triclinium*), leaning on one arm as they ate and drank with the other. To get to Jesus's head, the anonymous woman would have to intrude upon the group, squeezing between Jesus and one of his disciples, then kneel down on the pillow and pour the perfume on his head. A powerful aroma must have filled the room, perhaps even spoiling the taste of their meal. Who knows if the woman had interrupted conversation between Jesus and his disciples? They certainly had a lot to discuss, what with all of Jesus's talk about his upcoming death by crucifixion. So, I wonder if Jesus was a little surprised along with the others. There he is with oil streaming down his face, the perfume perhaps dripping on the table and pillows, the woman still kneeling beside him, the room silent and filled with fragrance. The disciples eventually break the silence, indignant over the foolish behavior of this woman: "Why this waste?" (v. 8).

It could be inferred that the disciples were upset over the woman's lavish gesture because she used too much myrrh for one guest.[10] This is certainly implied by the first part of their criticism: "This perfume *could have been sold at a high price* and the money given to the poor" (v. 9, emphasis added). Other scholars think the disciples were upset over the wastefulness of such a luxurious act. Given Jesus's concern for the poor, surely he would rather have used the proceeds as alms for the destitute—a common sentiment during Passover.[11] Yet I'm wondering if there's more to it than that—especially in light of the way Jesus interpreted the ritual. He didn't take it as the typical act of hospitality extended to a dinner guest. If that were her purpose, her foolishness would be evident in the volume of the perfume or the timing of the gesture: she poured too much on his head at the wrong time. Yet nowhere does Matthew say that the woman's wastefulness had to do with an excessive amount of perfume (we import that detail from Mark's account; see Mark 14:5). It was the act itself, pouring myrrh on Jesus's head, that got the disciples riled up. In light of the way Jesus interpreted the woman's gesture—she was preparing him for burial (Matt 26:12)—the "anointed one" knew why his disciples objected. Yes, she had anointed Jesus at the wrong time, but it had little to do with table customs. Yes, her luxurious act seemed to be wasted on Jesus, but

9. Davies and Allison, *Matthew*, 3:445.

10. See Bruner, *Matthew*, 2:602; by combining John's version (12:1–8) with Matthew's account, Blomberg pictures the woman pouring a large amount of perfume—anointing his entire body—from his head to his feet (*Matthew*, 384).

11. Keener, *Matthew*, 618–20.

it had little to do with the poor ("The poor you will always have with you," v. 11; cf. Deut 15:11). Rather, by pouring myrrh (a perfume used on corpses before interment) on him, she was acting as if Jesus was already dead. That would certainly be wasteful, using burial spices on a man who was still very much alive—not to mention the fact that such an improper gesture would be incredibly offensive, especially to the disciples who had a hard time accepting the idea that Jesus was going to die. (It would be like a stranger asking your loved one who just found out they had cancer, "Have you picked out your casket?") Perhaps it would seem to them like she had given up, resigned to the fact that Jesus's enemies would win and that his disciples would just let it happen, unwilling to lay down their lives and fight for him (Matt 26:35, 51). Or perhaps they took it as her questioning their loyalty to Jesus, that even if he died they wouldn't be around to bury him properly,[12] which is exactly what happened (27:57–61). Usually, victims of crucifixion didn't receive proper burial, either because they were abandoned by the family or it was denied by Roman officials. Therefore, it would seem to the Twelve that the woman was following the advice, "Better to do what you can when you can. Besides, you can never count on a man to do a woman's job."[13]

Whether the woman had any of these intentions or not, her gesture makes perfect sense in Matthew's narrative world.[14] Jesus had just told the parable of the sheep and the goats where he describes how the royal Son of Man would become "the least of these" (25:37–40). Jesus also included this little wrinkle in the story: no one saw it coming, not the righteous or the wicked. Everyone was incredulous to the notion that the prince would become a pauper. Nevertheless, the parable came true. Jesus became the "least of these," and no one could see how he would still be the king of Israel—not his disciples or his enemies. The Twelve ran like cowards; the rulers dismissed him as a fraud. The placard affixed above his head on the cross sarcastically proved the point (27:37): this is *Jesus*, the *King* of the Jews. Who would believe that? Well, there was one person who believed it, one woman who had ears to hear the parable and eyes to see Jesus coming into his kingdom. By preparing him for burial, she anointed him "king."[15] And, our Lord loved her for it (26:10–13).

---

12. According to Jewish piety, burial was the greatest act of benevolence; see Davies and Allison, *Matthew*, 3:446.

13. Most of the preparations associated with burial and funerals were performed by women; therefore, "the unknown woman in Bethany does precisely what the women at the tomb no longer need to do: she anoints the body of Jesus" (Luz, *Matthew*, 3:329).

14. So also Bruner, *Matthew*, 2:386; contra Luz, who sees the story of the woman anointing Jesus as having "no connection to its context" (*Matthew*, 3:329). Therefore, he dismisses those who interpret the story as an insightful gesture—preparing Jesus for burial—as "superficial" (ibid., 342).

15. "Jesus is the messianic King whose throne is a cross" (Davies and Allison, *Matthew*, 3:448).

She was the first person to get it: messianic suffering must precede messianic glory.[16] What she did revealed the heart of the gospel, and it was beautiful. For that reason alone, Jesus said everyone would remember her.[17] Wherever we preach the gospel, we'll thank God for her memorial. And yet, we don't even know her name.

Thank you, lady, for being there for him. What you did was beautiful. We will never forget you, for you were the first to see his kingdom. "The King is dead. Long live the King."

The Man Who Betrayed Jesus for Money

It comes as no surprise that Judas betrayed Jesus; Matthew already let us in on that secret a long time ago (Matt 10:4). As a reader, however, we've been waiting to see when it would happen. To this point, Judas hasn't stood out at all; he's been lurking in the background of Matthew's Gospel. But here, all of the sudden, Judas appears front and center, having made a deal with Jesus's enemies to betray him (26:14–16). We really don't know why he did it other than the fact that he made a small profit from his betrayal. Thirty pieces of silver is a paltry sum[18] compared to the value of the perfume poured on Jesus (echoes of Zech 11:10–13?).[19] This makes us wonder. If all Judas wanted out of life was a little cash, why would he follow Jesus at all? Sure, Jesus excited the crowds with his power. But he was also the kind of Messiah who talked about giving up everything for the kingdom, especially money. In fact, Jesus was fairly hard on wealthy people; they didn't have much of a chance of entering the kingdom (Matt 19:21–24). If Judas was money hungry, why would he stick around this long? Shouldn't he have left Jesus long before they got to Jerusalem?

Perhaps Judas hoped following Jesus would pay off in the end. He counted on Jesus's words coming true, that he and the other disciples would eventually sit on twelve thrones, receiving hundred times more in the kingdom come (19:28–29). Yet once they arrived to Jerusalem, everything changed. Jesus started acting like he had a death wish. A dead Messiah would hardly be able to deliver on the promise of the kingdom coming to earth. So perhaps that's why Judas bailed. After Jesus made it clear that he was resigned to his own fate—that he would die in Jerusalem—Judas gave up on the dream of the

---

16. According to Stagg (referenced by Blomberg, *Matthew*, 385), both the woman and Judas were the first two persons to believe Jesus was going to die.

17. "Her act will be viewed as meritorious because she is involved in the burial of a king" (Talbert, *Matthew*, 286–87).

18. Depending upon the denomination, worth perhaps four months' wages; see Davies and Allison, *Matthew* 3:452–53.

19. Turner, *Matthew*, 621.

poor realizing kingdom riches on earth.[20] Indeed, Jesus seemed to confirm the same: "The poor you will always have with you, but you will not always have me" (26:11). Affirming the woman's wasteful gesture was the last straw. That surprised the disciples. But what must have been even more astonishing to them was when Jesus chided them for their lack of vision. Jesus didn't think it was a good idea to sell the perfume to help the poor? "Really?" I imagine Judas (and the rest of the disciples) thinking, "Who's lost perspective now? If the poor will always be around, then what's the point of the kingdom come—especially when the one man powerful enough to make it happen is resigned to die?"

We'll never know whether Judas was disillusioned with Jesus in light of recent events. But the way Matthew tells the story, moving quickly from the woman's "wasteful" gesture to Judas's bargain with the chief priests, readers can't help but connect the dots. One thing led to the other. It looks like Judas was fed up and took matters into his own hands. But that's not the whole story according to Matthew. Evidently, we're supposed to learn a lesson by comparing the two, contrasting the woman's generosity with Judas's opportunistic move to score a little money. Judas sold out, and the woman poured out, both apparently motivated by the imminent death of Jesus. Jesus's plan to follow the divine script—to make a covenant with his own blood for the forgiveness of sins—provoked different reactions. One wanted to help out, the other was determined to cash out. Caught in between these polar opposites were the eleven disciples, confused by both the woman's strange behavior and Jesus's troubling announcement: "Truly I tell you, one of you will betray me" (26:21). The disciples were not only convinced the woman was wrong (vv. 8–9), but they even questioned whether Jesus was right: "Surely you don't mean me, Lord?" (v. 22). Rather than point out the betrayer ("It's Judas, isn't it?"), the disciples couldn't believe that a member of their group would do such a dastardly deed. The chief priests? Yes. The elders of the people? Probably. Perhaps even one of the crowd who followed along with Jesus and the Twelve. But surely not one of them—somebody who walked with them, ate with them, bedded down at night with them. But Jesus stated the matter plainly: "The one who has dipped his hand into the bowl with me will betray me" (v. 23).[21] Of all people, one of the twelve men whom Jesus

---

20. So also Keener, *Matthew*, 621; France, *Matthew*, 978.

21. The phrase "*the one who has dipped* his hand into the bowl with me" (an aorist participle) can be interpreted in at least three ways: 1) the one who is currently dipping his hand in the bowl with me (Luz, *Matthew*, 3:359); 2) the one who dipped his hand in the bowl at the same time as I—a past event recalled by Jesus that only he and Judas noticed but was lost on the Twelve (Nolland, *Matthew*, 1067); or 3) a general remark implicating all the disciples (Davies and Allison, *Matthew*, 3:461–62).

chose to follow him would betray him, having given up on the dream of the kingdom of heaven coming to earth.

Their Last Meal Together (For a While)

There is nothing in Matthew's version of the Last Supper that indicates Jesus intended for his followers to continue to observe the meal as a memorial. That idea shows up in Luke's Gospel, where Jesus counted on his disciples to "do this in remembrance of me" (Luke 22:19)—an expectation promoted by Paul as well (1 Cor 11:24). In fact, Paul interpreted our observance of the memorial as a proclamation of the gospel (v. 26). Every time we eat the bread and drink the cup we not only preach what Christ has done (his death) but also what he will do (come again). In that light, the Last Supper becomes the Lord's Supper, a meal hosted by the absent-but-still-present-and-coming Christ. Yet, here, that doesn't seem to be Matthew's intent. Instead, the purpose of the meal was for Jesus to reveal the betrayer (Matt 26:20–25), to reinterpret parts of the Passover meal (vv. 26–28), and to help his disciples realize that this would be their last meal together (v. 29)—but it wouldn't be the end. Jesus promised his disciples that the kingdom of God would come to earth one day, and then they would celebrate together once again. In the meantime, a lot would happen, and Jesus used the occasion of the Passover to help his disciples make sense of the inexplicable: how a disciple's betrayal and the death of the Son of Man would accomplish the will of God. Up to this point, Jesus had relied exclusively upon words to prepare his disciples for his upcoming death. But this night Jesus used food to make his point. The disciples would not only need ears to hear and eyes to see the reign of God; they would use hands to hold and mouths to eat and drink their way into the kingdom.

It is a stunning fact that Jesus would share his last meal on earth with a traitor. Why would he do it? Wouldn't it have made better sense to get rid of the bum before Jesus reclined at table with his disciples? Since he already knew Judas was the one who would betray him, why didn't Jesus expose the rat earlier that evening? Take care of the matter before it spoiled the holiday meal—that would have been my approach. The last thing I would want to do is eat with him. Indeed, when I think about it now, I can't stand the idea of sharing a meal with an enemy pretending to be my friend. Just looking at the scoundrel would make me so angry I'd lose my appetite. "Look at him! This man acts like we're friends, all cozied up to the table and chomping on bread—like he doesn't have a care in the world. The hypocrite! Sure, guzzle down the wine, you parasitic leech. Go ahead! Stuff your face like it's your last meal, you heartless animal. You make me sick. How could you eat at a time like this?" At that point, nauseated by the whole thing, I would have exposed the traitor, humiliating him in front of everyone. "Do you see this guy? He's already made a deal with the devil, prepared to hand me over to my enemies like a coward." Or, if I were as clever as Jesus, I would tell a parable about a wolf in sheep's clothing. Then, like Nathan did to king David, I would expose the fraud, pointing my finger at him with righteous indignation while exclaiming, "You're the man!" But Jesus did none of those things. Instead, rather discreetly he let everyone know there was a traitor among them.[22] Each disciple persisted in protesting his innocence, but Jesus didn't identify the guilty party. Even when Judas joined the chorus of "surely you don't mean me," Jesus enigmatically replied, "You have said so" (v. 25).[23] That's it. No dramatic confrontation. No climactic revelation. Jesus left it to them to figure out who would make his words come true:[24] "Woe to that man who betrays the Son of Man! It would be better for him if he had not been born" (v. 24)—words that must have echoed in Judas's ears when he hung himself (27:5), a prophecy coming true. For a cursed death was interpreted as God's final indictment of a wasted life.

Rather than celebrate Passover with his family according to custom, Jesus had arranged with a "certain man" to eat the memorial meal with his disciples, his new family (26:17–19).[25] It is unclear whether the meal included the paschal lamb; Matthew never mentions it.[26] Other elements of the meal, unleavened bread and wine, were consumed every night throughout the weeklong festival. Evidently, the bread and the cup were the only things Jesus needed to reinterpret the significance of this holiday. (Paul could imagine a better correlation had Jesus wanted to compare himself to the paschal lamb! See 1 Cor 5:7). Treating his disciples like family, Jesus played the role of the host and explained the meaning of the meal. But no one had ever interpreted the bread and the wine like he did that night. The unleavened bread—also known as the "bread of affliction"—was supposed to remind Israel of their hasty exit from Egypt (Exod 12:39; Deut 16:3). Jesus claimed the bread, broken into pieces for them to eat as their last meal together, was his body (Matt 26:26). A usually joyful celebration of God's deliverance of his people

---

22. Chrysostom thinks that Jesus concealed the matter to give Judas a chance to repent (*Homilies*, 486).

23. The phrase can be taken a couple of ways, either as a qualified "yes" or a coy "that's what you say"; see Bruner, *Matthew*, 2:618–19. "Jesus had to find a reply that was not a yes, a no, or a no comment. . . . The reply manages at once to tell Judas 'yes' and to tell the disciples, if they should overhear it, nothing clear at all" (ibid., 2:619).

24. Some scholars suggest Judas tipped his hand by calling Jesus "Rabbi" (a title that is only used by Jesus's enemies in Matthew), or because he dipped his hand in the bowl at the same time as Jesus, or because Jesus responded to no one but him—the last disciple to protest his innocence; for a summary of the discussion, see Luz, *Matthew*, 3:360–63.

25. Davies and Allison, *Matthew*, 3:458; Malina and Rohrbaugh, *Synoptic Gospels*, 155.

26. See the discussion in Keener, *Matthew*, 622–23.

suddenly turned into a morbidly strange ritual. Why would Jesus make his disciples eat "his body"—an odd and surely offensive analogy?[27] To be sure, bread was often associated with death; the bread of consolation was usually given to grieving families *after* the funeral, to encourage them to carry on with their lives (Jer 16:7; Ezek 24:17). But Jesus took the "bread of affliction" and turned it into the bread of consolation, making his disciples eat it *before* his death. He also gave new meaning to a cup of wine used during Passover and offered it along with the bread of consolation, saying, "This is my blood of the covenant, which is poured out for many for the forgiveness of sins" (Matt 26:28)—a bizarre idea to the Jewish mind given all the legal prohibitions of drinking blood (Lev 17:10–14). Eating his body, drinking his blood—the only thing more offensive would be for the Messiah, the king of Israel, to die a cursed death. How could anyone find consolation in that?

It is one of the great ironies of the gospel story: both Jesus and his betrayer would die a cursed death: "Anyone who is hung on a pole is under God's curse" (Deut 21:23). Moreover, Jesus predicted both: he would be crucified and Judas's destiny would be filled with such woe that it would have been better if he had never lived (a sad inference often made by those who intend to commit suicide). The difference, of course, is that Jesus's death was according to God's will, a sacrifice that would effect a new covenant for the forgiveness of sins (Matt 26:28).[28] Judas, on the other hand, experienced such remorse he couldn't imagine finding forgiveness for his sin (27:3–4) even though his betrayal was revealed at the table of forgiveness (26:20–28). But Judas wasn't the only sinner at the table. In fact, Jesus predicted that all of his disciples would "fall away on account of me" (v. 31) and that Peter would deny him three times that very night (v. 34). When Jesus passed around the cup of forgiveness and said, "Drink from it, all of you" (even Judas?), he knew they needed it. They all needed to drink. They all needed God's forgiveness. They all needed Jesus's blood to be "poured out for many." Indeed, their last supper together would be the one meal they would always need until the last day: the bread of consolation, the wine of forgiveness. Eat, drink, and be forgiven, for tomorrow he dies.

LIVE the Story

Death always ruins the holidays. Families reunite, but no one is celebrating. A feast is prepared, but no one is hungry. Laughter usually associated with the

27. So also Keener, *Matthew*, 632.

28. "Why can it have been that He ordained this sacrament then, at the time of the passover? . . . The evening is a sure sign of the fullness of times, and that the things were now come to the very end. . . . And thus the very chief of the feasts He brings to an end" (Chrysostom, *Homilies*, 491).

holidays is tempered with unspeakable grief. When the family gathers around the table for the holiday meal, the empty chair reminds everyone things will never be the same again. People pick at their plates. Everyone has their head down, trying to push through the ritual. The conversation wanders aimlessly until someone says what everyone is thinking: "I sure miss. . . ." Tears, memories, heartache, loss. It looks like Thanksgiving, but gratitude is hard to come by. Carolers come to the door to sing about Christmas joy, but the grieving family would rather hide away in sorrow. The whole world may be feasting, but who can eat at a time like this? No one should have to bury their loved one during the holidays. But death is irrepressibly intrusive, even during the most sacred times.

But then there's Easter. It's the one holiday where celebrating life in the face of death doesn't seem cold or hard-hearted. It's the only time when talk about death around the holiday meal doesn't sound morbid. It's because Jesus died during Passover. His disciples were obliged to eat unleavened bread because his body would be broken for them. They all drank from the same cup of wine because they needed his sacrifice for the forgiveness of sins. They couldn't see it at the time, but this somber occasion would become a festival of joy because Jesus, the Messiah, would die for the sins of the whole world—even betrayers. Yet more than that, Jesus told them that this wouldn't be the end. Even with a traitor at the table and talk of his imminent death dominating the conversation, Jesus tried to lighten their heavy hearts: "I tell you, I will not drink from this fruit of the vine from now on until that day when I drink it new with you in my Father's kingdom" (Matt 26:29). Death would not have the last word. Jesus would drink with them again, in the kingdom, when sin and death are no more. That should be reason enough not only to keep eating and drinking but also to keep singing. Having heard once again that death would not win, that his crucifixion wouldn't be the end of the story, they all sang hymns (probably Psalms 113–118)[29] before they walked out together into the darkness of that fateful night (Matt 26:30). Yes, Jesus would be betrayed. Yes, Jesus would be handed over to his enemies. Yes, the Romans would humiliate him and kill him mercilessly. His body would be broken, his blood poured out for many. The shepherd would be struck down, and the sheep would be scattered. But Jesus promised them he would see them again in Galilee, a shepherd gathering his sheep (vv. 31–32). Death may try to ruin the holidays, but this would be the holiday that marks the ruin of death *once and for all.*

When the disciples gathered to celebrate Passover the next year, did they notice the empty place at the table and remember the night Jesus was

29. Evans, *Matthew*, 432.

betrayed, took bread, broke it, and gave it to them to eat? When they gathered for Passover in Jerusalem every year, did memories of that fateful night flood their minds, inspiring them to recall Jesus's reinterpretation of the Passover meal? When a child came up to them during the meal and asked, "What does this ceremony mean to you?" (Exod 12:26), did the disciples add to the story of the exodus of Israel from Egyptian slavery the good news of the deliverance of God's people from sin and death through Jesus Christ? When they preached the good news during Passover, did they also remember her—the woman who prepared Jesus for burial before he died? Evidently so, because here we are, two-thousand years later, gathering around a table of bread and wine, celebrating the new covenant, preaching the good news of Jesus Christ, remembering him *and* her—all because we have eyes to read the Gospel of Matthew, ears to hear the stories of the faithful who have gone before us, hands to hold one another in communion, and mouths to eat and drink our way into the kingdom.

When we celebrated communion in my childhood Baptist church, it felt like someone had died. Even though we observed the Lord's Supper every three months—I knew the routine well—in my mind it seemed like we were conducting a funeral. The organ played somber music, the kind we often hear looping through the sound system of funeral homes. The elements on the communion table, covered with a crisply ironed white sheet, looked like a draped coffin situated front and center. Everyone sitting quietly in the pews whispering to each other, waiting for the minister to appear and start the service, reading the same passages of Scripture associated with the occasion—all of these things reminded me of our sacred rituals dealing with death. Then I would think about him—the deceased. My mind would rush to the crowded streets of Jerusalem, reliving what it must have felt like to carry his cross through the mob gathered to watch the spectacle. I would see him, exhausted from the beating, stumbling toward his destiny. I would see the people, some gasping in horror, others cursing at him in disgust. Then I would look at my hands, holding the little, pill-shaped piece of unleavened bread, hearing the preacher quote Jesus, "Take and eat; this is my body," wincing at the thought of nail-pierced hands. I was only a child, but I couldn't help but feel sorry for my sin, having heard many times in church that Jesus died because of us. Having lost my appetite, I didn't feel like eating at all.

Then, all of the sudden, the mood would change dramatically. Once we finished eating and drinking, the minister would invite us to stand and sing a congregational hymn, usually a peppy number, always reminding us that Jesus ended the first Lord's Supper by having the disciples sing a hymn. The organist would hit the keys with staccato-like rhythm—sounding like the rousing music heard during professional baseball games. Soft tones and hushed songs would give way to hearty voices gladly belting out the melodic notes of the cheery hymn: "I will sing the wondrous story, of the Christ who died for me. . . ." Then, it was over. Kids would run through the pews during the unofficial contest to see who could collect the most cups. Adults would gather in little groups to make plans for their "after-church fellowship." And I would stand there a little dazed, suffering from slight emotional whiplash, wondering how we could move so quickly from grief to celebration. Of course, I knew the resurrection of Jesus made it all better. Yet I never felt like I had enough time to deal with the grief of my sin and his death—especially when I became a teenager. Now, as an adult, our time of lamentation flies by far too fast for a man who knows too well the heartache of his sin and the necessity of a covenant sealed by blood.

Since those days, I've celebrated communion with several different denominations of Christians, being introduced to new traditions and meaningful rituals. We never "passed the peace" in my Baptist church, but I've come to appreciate the significance of that moment even more. And whenever I'm with brothers and sisters who offer the bread with the words, "This is his body broken for you," then they pass the cup and say, "The blood of the new covenant shed for you," I drink it up like fresh hope. For some reason, those words pierce my heart with joy as the taste of bread and wine lingers in my mouth. Yet, despite all these new experiences around the Lord's table, regardless of how the congregation is led to observe communion—whether joyful or reflective—I repeat the childhood habit of reimagining the sacrifice of Jesus. Joy mingles with sorrow, and I can barely sing the hymn.

He was broken for us. His blood was poured out for the forgiveness of sins. Until the day we drink the cup with him in our Father's kingdom, we shall sing of the wondrous story of the Christ who died and was raised for every single one of us—even as we go together into the darkness of the night.

CHAPTER 36

Matthew 26:31–56

LISTEN to the Story

31 Then Jesus told them, "This very night you will all fall away on
account of me, for it is written:

> 'I will strike the shepherd,
> and the sheep of the flock will be scattered.'

32 But after I have risen, I will go ahead of you into Galilee."
33 Peter replied, "Even if all fall away on account of you, I never will."
34 "Truly I tell you," Jesus answered, "this very night, before the rooster
crows, you will disown me three times."
35 But Peter declared, "Even if I have to die with you, I will never
disown you." And all the other disciples said the same.
36 Then Jesus went with his disciples to a place called Gethsemane,
and he said to them, "Sit here while I go over there and pray." 37 He took
Peter and the two sons of Zebedee along with him, and he began to be
sorrowful and troubled. 38 Then he said to them, "My soul is overwhelmed
with sorrow to the point of death. Stay here and keep watch with me."
39 Going a little farther, he fell with his face to the ground and prayed,
"My Father, if it is possible, may this cup be taken from me. Yet not as I
will, but as you will."
40 Then he returned to his disciples and found them sleeping. "Couldn't
you men keep watch with me for one hour?" he asked Peter. 41 "Watch and
pray so that you will not fall into temptation. The spirit is willing, but
the flesh is weak."
42 He went away a second time and prayed, "My Father, if it is not
possible for this cup to be taken away unless I drink it, may your will be
done."
43 When he came back, he again found them sleeping, because their
eyes were heavy. 44 So he left them and went away once more and prayed
the third time, saying the same thing.

45Then he returned to the disciples and said to them, "Are you still
sleeping and resting? Look, the hour has come, and the Son of Man is
delivered into the hands of sinners. 46Rise! Let us go! Here comes my
betrayer!"
47While he was still speaking, Judas, one of the Twelve, arrived. With
him was a large crowd armed with swords and clubs, sent from the chief
priests and the elders of the people. 48Now the betrayer had arranged a
signal with them: "The one I kiss is the man; arrest him." 49Going at once
to Jesus, Judas said, "Greetings, Rabbi!" and kissed him.
50Jesus replied, "Do what you came for, friend."
Then the men stepped forward, seized Jesus and arrested him. 51With
that, one of Jesus's companions reached for his sword, drew it out and
struck the servant of the high priest, cutting off his ear.
52"Put your sword back in its place," Jesus said to him, "for all who
draw the sword will die by the sword. 53Do you think I cannot call on my
Father, and he will at once put at my disposal more than twelve legions of
angels? 54But how then would the Scriptures be fulfilled that say it must
happen in this way?"
55In that hour Jesus said to the crowd, "Am I leading a rebellion, that
you have come out with swords and clubs to capture me? Every day I sat
in the temple courts teaching, and you did not arrest me. 56But this has
all taken place that the writings of the prophets might be fulfilled." Then
all the disciples deserted him and fled.

Listening to the Text in the Story: Genesis 9:6; Exodus 12:42; 2 Samuel 15:1–31; 2 Kings 6:17; 19:35; Psalms 40:6–8; 42:5–11; 55:1–5; Isaiah 50:4–11; 51:17–23; 52:3; Jeremiah 25:15–29; Daniel 7:9–10; Zechariah 13:7–9.

Kings are not supposed to surrender to their enemy without a fight. They may retreat for a time when outnumbered or overmatched by their foes. But they eventually return to battle having rallied the troops and marshaled reinforcements. They may lose the war, leading their army into certain death. But they don't give themselves up without exacting a toll on their opponents. If a king is going to lose his kingdom in battle, at least he will have died trying to save it. Better to die fighting as a king than to give into a pagan nation and become its slave.

But what happens when a king is opposed by his own subjects, the very people he's supposed to rule? What does the king do when he is betrayed by his people, when his kinsmen are his enemies, when treason comes from his own house? When his opponents come to do battle, does he stand and fight with those who are faithful to his cause? Or does he vacate the palace and run away, hoping to find safe haven outside the city he once ruled? That's the very predicament King David faced when his own son, Absalom, led a rebellion against his father (2 Sam 15:1–13).[1] When David got wind of Absalom's betrayal, what did he do? He retreated, leading his people and the priests out of Jerusalem, down the Kidron Valley, up the side of the Mount of Olives, weeping as they went (vv. 14–30). When David was told that one of his advisors betrayed him by joining the conspiracy, the king prayed to God, "LORD, turn Ahithophel's counsel into foolishness" (v. 31)—a prayer that was answered when the traitor hung himself (17:23). And, as the story goes, although David waited as long as he could, he was finally compelled to lead an army to retake Jerusalem, which resulted in the cursed death of Absalom, hung from a tree (18:9–15). During the mini-exodus, when David convinced the priests to take the ark of the covenant back to the temple, he said, "If I find favor in the LORD's eyes, he will bring me back and let me see it and his dwelling place again. But if he says, 'I am not pleased with you,' then I am ready; let him do to me whatever seems good to him" (15:25–26)—almost a "not-my-will-but-yours-be-done" prayer.

As the son of David, we might think history was repeating itself in the life and times of Jesus, especially at a time like this. Similarities between these two stories are too obvious to ignore: betrayed by a family member; followers take the same trip out of Jerusalem, ascending the Mount of Olives; weeping and praying on the mountain; traitor commits suicide by hanging himself; son of David dies a cursed death; the king promises to return to the holy city; a "Gethsemane-like" prayer. All of it reads like a Davidic script meant to be played out in the messianic drama of Jesus's last days. However, like the rest of the story of "Jesus the Messiah the son of David" (Matt 1:1), this king will follow a divine script to establish the eternal kingdom of heaven on our troubled earth. Rather than retreat from his opponents, Jesus goes out to meet them.[2] Rather than rally his supporters, Jesus expects his disciples will betray him. Rather than have his faithful men fight the battle as he waits anxiously for good news, safe and secure, this son of David gives himself up to be good news, condemned and crucified. Rather than wonder whether the Lord was "pleased with him," this king prayed to the Lord with confidence, "My Father." Rather than launch a counterattack, this son of David surrenders. Rather than kill his enemies, this anointed one dies for them. Yes, Jesus is

1. Davies and Allison, *Matthew*, 3:484.
2. Ibid., 3:483.

the son of David destined to ascend his Father's throne. Yet the way he will conquer his enemies and rule the world is like no other king of Israel.

EXPLAIN the Story

Jesus knew that when his disciples saw the gospel of the kingdom coming true, they would be scandalized. It's one thing to talk about the way of the kingdom; it's quite something else to incarnate the way of the kingdom. The disciples had a hard time accepting his words; Peter even tried to talk Jesus out of going through with it (Matt 16:22). And yet, as difficult as it was to hear about the cross as the way of the kingdom, they were never offended by it. Certainly, they didn't like it. They even tried to ignore it. But since it was only talk up to this point, the disciples weren't scandalized by the cross. Although Jesus kept mentioning it—even saying they would need to bear a cross too—they stuck it out. Even though they ate a meal that symbolized his broken body and spilled blood—Passover would never be the same again—they stayed with him. But Jesus knew the time had come for his disciples to *see* the good news of the cross. When that happened, Jesus predicted his followers would be tripped up by him, the rock of offense: "This very night you will all fall away [*skandalisthēsesthe*, "scandalized"] on account of me" (26:31). Death by crucifixion was scandalous, an offense to the Jewish people, and hardly the way the Christ is supposed to reign over sin and death—something the apostle Paul knew all too well: "Jews demand signs and Greeks look for wisdom, but we preach Christ crucified: a stumbling block [*skandalon*] to Jews and foolishness to Gentiles" (1 Cor 1:22–23). The cross wasn't a "sign" that anyone was looking for as proof that the Messiah reigns (the cross proved that Rome reigned supreme, not the king of Israel). God striking down the shepherd with a Roman cross would have been hard to see (Zech 13:7). Jesus would offend them all; the gathered sheep would be scattered once again (Matt 26:31).[3]

The disciples couldn't believe their ears. Jesus predicted that he would offend them so badly that they would eventually abandon him that very night (vv. 31–35). Peter couldn't take it. How could Jesus say such a thing about him? The rest of the disciples, perhaps, but not Peter.[4] Had Jesus forgotten? Jesus called him "the rock" (16:18). Jesus gave him the keys to the kingdom (v. 19). Jesus ensured that Peter was one of three disciples to see the glory of his kingdom (16:28; 17:1–4). There may have been a traitor among them,

3. Evans, *Matthew*, 433.

4. According to Brown, Peter didn't refute the prophecy. He was only trying to get Jesus to make an exception (*Death of the Messiah*, 2:133).

but it couldn't be Peter. Earlier that evening Jesus announced that one of the Twelve would betray him, even as Peter and the rest of the disciples protested, "Surely you don't mean me, Lord?" (26:21–22). But Jesus never specifically pointed out the traitor, leaving it to the Twelve to identify him. This time Peter couldn't let the accusation hang in the air without making it clear to everyone—especially Jesus—that *he* wouldn't be the one to let him down (v. 33). But then, in what must have sounded to the disciples like the unveiling of the traitor ("now we know who it is!"), Jesus predicted that *Peter* would deny him three times that very night (v. 34). What!? Peter? How could that be? Peter was convinced that he would be the *only one* not to betray Jesus. Now Jesus has singled him out as the very one who would deny him not once, not twice, but three times, which incited "the Rock" to up the ante: he would rather die with Jesus than deny him (v. 35). Before, he couldn't stomach the idea that Jesus would be crucified (16:22).[5] Now he is ready to die with him, resigned to the fact that Jesus's enemies were powerful enough to get him. Not to be outdone by Peter's pledge of undying allegiance to Jesus, the rest of the disciples (even Judas?) "said the same" (26:35). But Jesus wasn't going to argue with them. He said what he said, knowing that Zechariah's prophecy would come true. When God strikes the shepherd, the whole world will be offended—even the ones who claim to follow him. The Twelve may follow him to Gethsemane. But not a single disciple will deny himself and follow the Lord all the way to the cross.

Is This the Only Way?

Something happened between the first and second times Jesus prayed in Gethsemane. At first he asked God to take away the cup of suffering, knowing that it was possible[6] (Matt 26:39). The second time Jesus prayed, he was resigned to the fact that he had to drink the cup—that it wasn't possible to remove the cup until he drank it (v. 42). The difference is staggering.[7] At first, Jesus considered the possibility that he wouldn't have to go through with it. He wondered if there was another option, a way out, a different course, an alternative, a "plan B" for the inauguration of his kingdom, the salvation of the world. Clearly Jesus believed that it was possible for him to escape death, for the Father to take away the cup of suffering. Indeed, later that very night Jesus

5. Brown, *Death of the Messiah*, 1:138.

6. A first-class conditional clause, the protasis could be translated, "*Since it is possible*, let this cup be taken away from me." Was Jesus asking God to change his mind? See Davies and Allison, *Matthew*, 3:497; Luz, *Matthew*, 2:396. "In the biblical outlook, it is not irreverent to ask God for a change of mind" (Brown, *Death of the Messiah*, 1:166).

7. So also Luz, *Matthew*, 3:397. Davies and Allison deny there's a difference: "But it does not represent an advance over Mt 26:39, as if Jesus is now more resigned than he was then" (*Matthew*, 3:500).

claimed he could "call on my Father, and he will at once put at my disposal more than twelve legions of angels" to protect him from his enemies (v. 53). And so, knowing all this, with the cross before him Jesus was essentially asking God, "Is there any other *way* for the kingdom of heaven to come to earth?" But then, the second time he prayed, he knew there was no other way. He had to drink the cup of suffering to do his Father's will. What changed his mind?

Perhaps it was the disciples' behavior that changed Jesus's request from "if it is possible," to "if it is not possible." Once Jesus and the disciples came to Gethsemane in the middle of the night, he took three disciples from the group (Peter and the two sons of Zebedee) to keep him company as he prayed (vv. 36–37).[8] After Jesus prayed the first time "if it is possible," he returned to find the disciples fast asleep (v. 40). A little indignant (I hear an exasperated tone in his voice), Jesus chastised them for their lack of support: "Couldn't you men keep watch with me for one hour?" (v. 40). Just a couple of hours before, Peter and the rest of the disciples had promised Jesus that they would stick with him to the end, even if it meant death (v. 35). Now they're sleeping like children. So, Jesus woke them up with the warning: "Watch and pray so that you will not fall into temptation" (v. 41). This wasn't only a matter of helping Jesus get through a difficult night. The disciples should have been concerned about their own soul, whether they would "fall into temptation" (*peirasmon*, which also can mean "test"[9]). Jesus had taught them to pray, "Lead us not into temptation [*peirasmon*], but deliver us from the evil one" (6:13).[10] Now it was time to live the prayer, for this very night Peter and the disciples would be tested/tempted like never before.[11] How would they fare? Jesus already knew what would happen. As he took in the sight of his bleary-eyed disciples, he summed up the entire evening very well: "The spirit is willing, but the flesh is weak" (26:41). With great bravado, these men claimed they were willing to die with Jesus. But the way of the cross is more than words; it is incarnation.

"The spirit is willing, but the flesh is weak" sounds like an accurate assessment of Jesus's first prayer.[12] He was willing to do his Father's will, but he also knew crucifixion takes more than a pound of flesh. Seeing that his disciples couldn't even stay awake for an hour in the middle of the night may have

8. Nolland, *Matthew*, 1096, thinks Jesus brought these three along to give them an opportunity to live up to their words: Peter, willing to die with Jesus (Matt 26:35), and James and John, willing to drink the cup of suffering (20:22)—to be at "the right hand and the left" when Jesus comes into his kingdom (the cross!).

9. See above, 79–88.

10. Davies and Allison, *Matthew*, 3:497. In Gethsemane, Jesus modeled the "Lord's prayer" (Matt 6:9–13); see Garland, *Reading Matthew*, 256.

11. France, *Matthew*, 1006.

12. For a brief history of interpretation regarding the christological implications of Jesus's prayer, see Luz, *Matthew*, 3:399–409.

provided a visual lesson for Jesus. Before he saw them sleeping like babies, he prayed, "*If it is possible*, may this cup be taken from me" (v. 39). Now, as he returns to pray with his own words still hanging in the air, "the spirit is willing, but the flesh is weak," Jesus understands that it is *not* possible for this cup to be taken away. Why? It's because our mortal flesh gets tired, hungry, weary, worn out—even for the Son of God, who took upon himself "the likeness of sinful flesh to be a sin offering," doing "what the law was powerless to do because it was weakened by the flesh" (Rom 8:3). Resolved to overcome the weakness of his flesh (and ours! Hallelujah!), Jesus prayed, "*If it is not possible* for this cup to be taken away unless I drink it, may your will be done" (Matt 26:42). The *only* way Jesus could save us—every bit of us, not only our willing spirit but also our weak, mortal flesh—was to bear the cross. Indeed, Jesus is *the only way* the kingdom of heaven comes to earth. Enfleshment. Incarnation. He knew it would take a special man, a unique man, the Son of Man, the Son of God, to save us from our sins, especially sleepy disciples who fall into temptation. And so, thank God, he ended his prayer with, "May your will be done" (v. 42)—only to return once again to find his disciples sound asleep "because their eyes were heavy" (v. 43), the weakness of their flesh.

Rather than wake them up again, Jesus let his disciples sleep as he returned to his prayer for a third time, "saying the same thing" (v. 44). Once he was finished praying, Jesus came back to his disciples to rouse them for the last time. Why did he stop praying? Did something happen to alert him it was time to go? Since his disciples fell asleep and didn't keep watch, there was no one to warn him that his captors were coming. So, one wonders if Jesus could see the mob coming for him given his vantage point on the side of the mountain.[13] We don't know for certain where Gethsemane was located back then,[14] but if the current garden is anywhere close to where Jesus prayed that night, he would be able to look across the Kidron Valley at the eastern gate of Jerusalem and see the line of torches coming from the high priest's quarters near the temple. That makes the episode of his threefold prayer even more compelling.

At first Jesus prays, "Let this cup pass from me," hoping there was another way. Wondering about his disciples, he returns to check on them, only to find them sleeping, perhaps noticing that Judas is gone.[15] Guards sleeping at their post wouldn't be much help to him now. Returning to his prayer, he eventually looks across the valley and sees the parade of torches. Resigned to his fate, this time he prays, "May your will be done," after which he returns to find his disciples bedded down for the night. With very little time left, he prays and

13. So also France, *Matthew*, 1007.
14. See the discussion in Keener, *Matthew*, 634.
15. So also Nolland, *Matthew*, 1109.

waits, having to keep watch all by himself in the middle of the night (that image pains me). Then, as light from the torches pierces the darkness, and the rumble of the rabble draws near, Jesus knows his hour has come. Perhaps any other king would retreat. Surprised by the sneak attack (what happened to the sentinels?), most rulers would quickly fall back one more time, hoping to rally his troops to fight another day. But not this king. Having prayed to his Father, Jesus was ready to die. His enemies wouldn't take him by stealth, and his betrayer wouldn't surprise him even though Judas tried to conceal his treachery with a kiss. No! Jesus saw it coming. But his disciples didn't; they were sound asleep: "Are you still sleeping and resting? Look, the hour has come, and the Son of Man is delivered into the hands of sinners. Rise! Let us go! Here comes my betrayer!" (vv. 45–46).

"Come on, get up. Look who's here! My betrayer." These are, in essence, the last words he said to them before he died. Not, "thanks for waiting up with me," or "I'm grateful for all the times we had together," or "don't forget what I told you." One of the last things he said to his sleepy disciples before he died was, "Here comes my betrayer." How sad is that? Yet, sadder words are still to come—among which are one of the saddest lines in the entire Gospel: "Then all the disciples deserted him and fled" (v. 56).

"But How Then Would the Scriptures Be Fulfilled That Say It Must Happen in This Way?"

It was a terrible night. Sleeping-on-their-watch disciples, a mob armed with swords and clubs, the Son of Man handed over to sinners, a traitor's kiss, a man's ear cut off, Jesus giving up without a fight, the disciples deserting him. Yet Jesus didn't shrink from the horror. Instead, he tried to get his disciples to wake up enough to go with him to meet the posse sent by the high priests and elders. But while he was trying to rustle the deadheads from their slumber, another disciple greeted him with a salutation and a kiss (Matt 26:47–49). Even though they were suddenly surrounded by a large mob with weapons, the disciples wouldn't have been alarmed by Judas's behavior. To their eyes, he was simply greeting Jesus as he'd done probably many times before. Of course, as readers we know that Judas's kiss wasn't sincere because Matthew has told us what happened behind the scenes—not only that Judas made a deal with Jesus's enemies to betray him but also that he had arranged a secret way to identify Jesus for his captors (v. 48). Judas tried to make it look like he was completely innocent,[16] but Jesus wouldn't let him get away with it. That's why he said, "Do what you came for, friend" (v. 50)—a curious phrase that

16. Nolland, *Matthew*, 1109.

could be interpreted as a question ("is *that* why you are here?") or an exclamation ("*that's* why you are here!"), with "that" referring either to the kiss or the betrayal.[17] Whatever the case, Jesus wouldn't let Judas's hypocrisy pass without an "I know what you're doing" comment. Judas may have tried to act like he didn't share the mob's intentions, but we know better. Even though Americans refer to a traitor as a "Benedict Arnold" rather than a "Judas Iscariot," in our minds Judas's notorious gesture—to betray someone with a kiss—has become one of the most ironic[18] and, therefore, iconic expressions of betrayal (even more dastardly than stabbing someone in the back). Using a kiss to kill is the ultimate act of duplicity, intended to conceal the cold-hearted soul of an evil man. Yet Jesus is well aware of the one who betrays him with a kiss.

Very few things surprised Jesus that night. He did marvel, however, over his enemies' effort to take him by force as if they would need an army to arrest him (26:55). What did their precautions imply? That Jesus wouldn't go peacefully? That he would resist them like any other king, calling upon his disciples to take up arms and fight for his life? That he was leading a rebellion like other revolutionary bandits, willing to use violence to achieve his kingdom agenda? Of course, the slave standing there with only one ear, blood streaming down his neck, could ask sarcastically, "What was your first clue?" It's hard to believe that all these swords were really unnecessary when it was one of Jesus's company who struck first (v. 51). Obviously, Jesus's enemies weren't surprised at all that one of his disciples carried and used his weapon even though Jesus had preached to "love your enemies." They didn't take him at his word, and neither did his disciples.[19] Nevertheless, for several reasons, Jesus dismissed the whole affair as a farce.

First, they *all* should have known (both his enemies and his disciples) that Jesus wouldn't countenance violence on his behalf because "all who draw the sword will die by the sword" (v. 52)—a lesson the Romans taught the Jews all the time. Second, if Jesus really wanted to fight to save his life, he had a heavenly host, an irrepressible army of angels ready at his command (v. 53). This pitiful mob with their little weapons would have been no match for the King of men and angels. Third, Jesus lived by the Scriptures. The prophets predicted this would happen; Jesus had told his disciples the same thing,

---

17. There are at least nine ways to translate the phrase; see Davies and Allison, *Matthew*, 3:509–10.

18. Davies and Allison, *Matthew*, 3:506. Luz, quoting Crossan, writes: "For if, in that ancient Mediterranean world, to betray *after* a kiss was shameful, to betray *with* a kiss was infamous" (*Matthew*, 3:417n42 [emphasis his]).

19. Luz, *Matthew*, 3:419, infers that since Jesus commanded his disciples not to carry a stick, then they shouldn't have carried a sword (Matt 10:10). Besides, Jesus had taught them not to resist an evildoer (5:39).

quoting Zechariah, earlier that evening. Had they forgotten? What happened to Jesus that night—everything from the betrayal to his arrest to his disciples forsaking him like scattered sheep—fulfilled the Scriptures (Matt 26:54, 56). So, why would he resist? He came to do his Father's will, clearly revealed in God's word. Finally, if the chief priests and elders truly believed Jesus was so dangerous that they needed a lynch mob to take him by force as quickly as possible ("no time for sleep, boys; let's get the vermin now"), why didn't they take care of the matter when he was in the temple, right under their noses, in their domain? That would have been their prime opportunity, after Jesus had "defiled" the temple, but they did nothing. He even returned to them the next day, daring them to do something, and all they did was try to trap him with a riddle (v. 55). Really? A war of words? That's all they could do? Please. Everyone knew the priests had a temple guard at their command, ready to do their dirty work.[20] So, why the big show of force now, in the middle of the night, when all of Jerusalem sleeps? The answer is obvious: the chief priests may have lost the war of words in the temple with all the people watching, but this time they would take matters into their own hands under the cover of darkness. They were the ones trying to enforce the kingdom of God with human weapons. But Jesus came to bring an entirely different kingdom to earth, one that relies upon the power of God and not the weapons of men,[21] which also explains why "all the disciples deserted him and fled" (v. 56). There was nothing left for them to do but scatter like sheep.

LIVE the Story

Like the parables of Jesus, this story has a reflective quality that says a lot about us, often revealing where we are in the journey of following Christ. Our eyes are drawn to the two main characters, identifying with Jesus or Judas, depending on what we are experiencing at the time. Sometimes we see ourselves in the passion of Jesus, experiencing our own "Gethsemane," praying our hearts out, hoping God will find another way as we face a torturous future. At other times, we identify with Judas, having betrayed Jesus with the kiss of our lip service, pretending like he's our Lord even though we've already forsaken him for a little cash. Certainly, there are lessons to be learned when we wear the existential clothes of either Jesus or Judas. For example, it's the hardest prayer to pray, "Not my will but yours be done," when all we can see is a cross before us—a cursed death. "If he really loves me, why would he make me go through this?"

20. Evans, *Matthew*, 437–38.

21. "The pacifistic Messiah eschews holy war" (Davies and Allison, *Matthew*, 3:513).

All alone in the darkness of the night, evil and suffering show up in spades. Fear and anxiety pump through your body like blood rushing through your veins. Headaches. Night sweats. Where is the hope? Where is the comfort? Where is God? Having spent a sleepless night despairing over troubles that wait for you like a greedy serpent ready to swallow you whole (while the rest of the world lies comfortable in their beds), you wonder, "How did he do it? How did he face down the giant, the hellish torment of unyielding despair? All I can see in the darkness is pain. Why does it have to be this way? Why does it hurt so bad? Why doesn't God do something?" Then you remember. God did do something. He made a way through the dark night because his Son not only prayed the hardest prayer, "Not my will but yours be done," but he lived it.

Then there's Judas. How many times have we heard the unfaithfulness of a Christian compared to betraying Jesus with a kiss? It's because sin can be cold and calculating, requiring the hard heart of a traitor. We know it's wrong. We even know the Lord already knows of our intent to betray him. But, we'll go through with it anyway, turning our back on him for an immediate payoff. Afterward, when we come to him in prayer, we try to cover our betrayal with the kiss of affectionate words, "Greetings, Lord!"—pretending like we are not as bad as other sinners, trying to distance ourselves from the nefarious mob and their wicked intentions. But then, like Judas, remorse eventually kicks in. The truth of our selfish ways comes to roost in our wayward soul, weighing upon us with heavy regret. Connecting the dots, we cannot deny our sin has led to his death. Ashamed, we see our reflection in the face of the one who betrayed Jesus with a kiss. And yet, for all the emotional connection we may find in the story of Judas's betrayal, there is a huge difference between our inclination and his resignation: damnation. Jesus said of him, "It would be better for him if he had not been born!" (Matt 26:24). But Jesus said of the rest of his disciples—everyone who would deny him that very night—"But after I have risen, I will go ahead of you into Galilee" (v. 32).[22] Jesus knew that, unlike Judas, his disciples would learn to follow him again. Even though they had given up on him as their king because of the way of his kingdom, scandalized by the cross, he would never give up on them. His resurrection would result in their restoration.[23]

So maybe our eyes should be drawn to the rest of the disciples to consider how we live that part of the story too. It seems to me that in the everyday experience of trying to follow Jesus, we come closer to the behavior of the eleven disciples that night than the worst traitor of all time or the most obedient man who ever lived. Consider the similarities.

22. This is the *only* statement Peter didn't dispute that night (Davies and Allison, *Matthew*, 3:486).
23. Ibid., 3:517.

"The Spirit Is Willing, but the Flesh Is Weak"

We've heard this many times, but it doesn't make it any less true. The things that trouble Jesus don't keep us awake at night. Sure, when I'm in trouble or when the people I love are in trouble, I can't sleep. Tossing and turning, my mind won't turn off as I endlessly contemplate worst-case scenarios that could lead to disastrous results. So, I pray, and pray, and pray. But when I hear of other people's problems, I may say a quick prayer but then I easily drift off to sleep for a good night's rest. I'd like to think, after seeing Jesus "overwhelmed with sorrow to the point of death" (Matt 26:38), that I would pray for him through the night, keeping him company as he faced his destiny. But since I have never done that for the "least of these," then it's more likely that I would have bedded down for the night along with Peter and the rest of the disciples. It's not that I don't care. It's just that my comfort means more to me than the kingdom of heaven coming to earth.

"Couldn't you men keep watch with me for one hour?" Wake us up, Lord.

"Put Your Sword Back in Its Place"

I've seen this happen many times too. There's usually a lot of damage done when disciples try to save Jesus from his enemies. We act like we're his bodyguards, appointed to protect him from those who oppose God. Awakened from our slumber—what's going on here?—we decide the best course of action is to start hacking away with our weapons. After all, could there be a more righteous cause than to protect our king from those who would attack his kingdom? But Jesus would rebuff our pretentious attempts to fight his battle with our human weapons. Have we forgotten that he could marshal a force so terrible, so powerful, so irrepressible that no human army could oppose it—that the King could call upon legions of angels at a moment's notice to protect him and destroy the enemy if he wanted to?[24] But he has chosen a better way, the will of God. Rather than kill his enemies, Jesus chose to die for them. The cross is the only weapon Jesus would use against the enemies of God. So, what he said about the kingdom of men is also true of the kingdom of God, "for all who live by the cross will die by the cross."

"Do you think I cannot call on my Father?" Help us, Lord.

"Then All the Disciples Deserted Him and Fled"

"That's no way to win the war! Surrender to the enemy? What good will that do?" The disciples' heads must have been spinning. They tried to live up to their oath. They were willing to fight to the end, prepared to die for the cause

---

24. So, was Satan telling the truth (Matt 4:5–7)?

of Christ. But Jesus made them stop. He gave up without a fight. He said it had to be this way. Of course, they hadn't come to the same realization that it was God's will for Jesus to drink the cup of suffering. They were asleep when Jesus prayed, not knowing how he went from "if it is possible" to "if it is not possible." To their way of thinking, it was still possible to avoid the cross. Evidently, they couldn't believe Jesus meant what he said: "For whoever wants to save their life will lose it, but whoever loses their life for me will find it" (Matt 16:25). They were willing to lose their lives, on their terms, with their weapons. But Jesus came to bring the kingdom of heaven (not the kingdom of men) to earth. So, when Jesus's words became reality—the way of the cross fleshed out right before their eyes—they couldn't stand to watch, much less follow him. What a strange way for the King to rule the world! Who would believe it?

"But this has all taken place that the writings of the prophets might be fulfilled." Restore us, Lord.

CHAPTER 37

Matthew 26:57–75

LISTEN to the Story

57 Those who had arrested Jesus took him to Caiaphas the high priest,
where the teachers of the law and the elders had assembled. 58 But Peter
followed him at a distance, right up to the courtyard of the high priest. He
entered and sat down with the guards to see the outcome.

59 The chief priests and the whole Sanhedrin were looking for false
evidence against Jesus so that they could put him to death. 60 But they did
not find any, though many false witnesses came forward.

Finally two came forward 61 and declared, "This fellow said, 'I am able
to destroy the temple of God and rebuild it in three days.'"

62 Then the high priest stood up and said to Jesus, "Are you not going
to answer? What is this testimony that these men are bringing against
you?" 63 But Jesus remained silent.

The high priest said to him, "I charge you under oath by the living
God: Tell us if you are the Messiah, the Son of God."

64 "You have said so," Jesus replied. "But I say to all of you: From now
on you will see the Son of Man sitting at the right hand of the Mighty
One and coming on the clouds of heaven."

65 Then the high priest tore his clothes and said, "He has spoken blas-
phemy! Why do we need any more witnesses? Look, now you have heard
the blasphemy. 66 What do you think?"

"He is worthy of death," they answered.

67 Then they spit in his face and struck him with their fists. Others
slapped him 68 and said, "Prophesy to us, Messiah. Who hit you?"

69 Now Peter was sitting out in the courtyard, and a servant girl came
to him. "You also were with Jesus of Galilee," she said.

70 But he denied it before them all. "I don't know what you're talking
about," he said.

71 Then he went out to the gateway, where another servant girl saw him
and said to the people there, "This fellow was with Jesus of Nazareth."

[72]He denied it again, with an oath: "I don't know the man!"

[73]After a little while, those standing there went up to Peter and said, "Surely you are one of them; your accent gives you away."

[74]Then he began to call down curses, and he swore to them, "I don't know the man!"

Immediately a rooster crowed. [75]Then Peter remembered the word Jesus had spoken: "Before the rooster crows, you will disown me three times." And he went outside and wept bitterly.

Listening to the Text in the Story: Exodus 20:16; Leviticus 5:1; 21:10; 24:10–16; Numbers 14:6; Deuteronomy 13:1–5; 19:15–19; 2 Samuel 7:13–14; Ezra 9:3; Job 30:10; Psalms 27:12–14; 37:12; 110:1–2; Isaiah 50:5–9; 53:5–8; Jeremiah 26:8–11; Daniel 7:9–14; Zechariah 6:12–13.

It's a sad reality in Matthew's Gospel. Even though Jesus knew it would happen, not a single disciple would follow him to the cross. From this point on, the disciples fade from the story as quickly as they appeared. We're so used to that part of the story—the failure of Jesus's disciples—that it doesn't shock us anymore. Perhaps the fact that Jesus predicted it would be this way softens the blow for the reader. We aren't disappointed in them because Jesus saw it coming. But then again, when we think about it, the failure of the disciples doesn't reflect very well on Jesus either. After having spent so much time with these twelve men, teaching them the way of the kingdom—intensive training that makes up much of Matthew's Gospel—Jesus's inability to produce faithful disciples is evidenced by the unfavorable outcome. He had already told them, a long time ago, what it would take to follow him (Matt 16:24–27), but they didn't do it. He repeated the lesson many times, but they didn't get it. (Few things are more frustrating to a teacher than when your students don't perform well even though you've poured your heart out, giving them everything they need to succeed. It's hard to take when they fail.) When it was crunch time, the final exam—pick up a cross and follow Jesus—the disciples failed. They had the most innovative, most inspiring, most creative and committed teacher in the history of education, and they still didn't understand. *Jesus* teaching a class on discipleship, where the instruction is delivered 24–7—could it get any better than that?

In higher education, we talk a lot about *outcome assessment*, methods of determining whether we've done what we claim to do: teach our students to master their subject. Students giving right answers to test questions isn't enough. There has to be other evidence of competency—behavior!—to determine whether students have learned their lesson. Biblical-studies students learn about hermeneutics in the classroom. Yet unless they read the Scriptures with integrity—applying consistently the principles of interpretation—what's the point? Behavior reveals competency. The same would be true for a class on discipleship. Giving the right answers to important questions wouldn't suffice. There had to be other levels of learning, of actually following Jesus, that make for being a disciple—a lesson Peter had to learn the hard way.

Although we can't see it in our translation, there's an ominous tone to Peter's intention to follow Jesus "from a distance" in order "to see the end" (*idein to telos*, Matt 26:58). Before it all fell apart, Peter had promised Jesus to see it through to the end, even willing to die with him if necessary (v. 35). Perhaps prompted by his special status as the one who held the keys of the kingdom, Peter was convinced he was different from the rest: he would never fall away even though all else might forsake Jesus (v. 33). But at this point in the story, Peter has already "fallen away" along with the other disciples. Yet, unlike them he seems to be the only one who tried to keep following Jesus at a safe distance so that he could see with his own eyes "the end." Nevertheless, for all his intentions to witness the end of Jesus, Peter only made it as far as Caiaphas's house. Once he was there, the man who held the keys to the kingdom realized that trying to follow the Crucified One without having anything happen to you is quite impossible.

EXPLAIN the Story

Like other Gospel writers, Matthew sets these two scenes on parallel tracks, giving the impression to the reader that while Jesus was being interrogated by the high priest, Peter was avoiding interrogation outside Caiaphas's palace (Matt 26:57–58). We can't help but allow our eyes to dance back and forth between the two, drawn to the proceedings inside the house, all the while glancing outside to catch a glimpse of Peter squirming around and slinking away. It's as if the narrator wants us to hold these two episodes in tandem, side by side, daring us to compare Jesus and Peter.[1] Of course, at first glance we know there is no comparison. Jesus is God's Son, and Peter is supposed to be his disciple. And yet, there are curious similarities that invite us to puzzle over the ironies of their shared experience. For example, both men find themselves in a dangerous situation. Both are quizzed over their identity.

1. Luz, *Matthew*, 3:455.

Both are recognized as Galilean outsiders. Both have witnesses pitted against them. Both evade answering questions put to them. Both are victims of guilt by association. Both are the subjects of fulfilled prophecy. And finally, there's a lot of oath swearing and cursing in both stories. Yet for all the comparisons we may find, the stark contrast between Jesus and Peter couldn't be more evident. Jesus is the faithful witness, rejected and abused. Peter is the false witness, spared and ashamed.

While Jesus spoke the truth to the most powerful Jewish man in Jerusalem who wanted him dead, Peter lied to a female slave who simply claimed she recognized him. While Jesus remained silent in the face of false testimony, Peter swears an oath and pronounces a curse to deny what is true. While Jesus stands to face his accusers in open defiance, Peter sits with the guards, trying to hide in obscurity. While Jesus's enemies crow that he's worthy of death due to blasphemy, Peter hears the rooster crow and remembers that Jesus spoke the truth. While Jesus is abused as a false prophet, Peter's denial fulfills the prophecy of Jesus. While Jesus has spit running down his face because his enemies have tried to shame him, Peter has tears flowing down his cheeks because he was ashamed of Jesus. While Jesus was held captive inside the enemies' lair because he owned his fate, Peter ran away like a coward because he was trying to escape his. Finally, while Jesus lived up to his name, Peter seemed to forget his. Simon was hardly a rock upon which Jesus could build his church.

So, the question for any reader is this: Was Jesus wrong about Peter? Even though Jesus was right about Peter's denial, was he ultimately wrong about Simon being the rock? If Peter received the keys of the kingdom because he professed Jesus as the Christ, did he lose the keys because he denied him? That is to say, even though Peter's denial revealed that Jesus's prediction came true, did Peter end up fulfilling another prophecy of Jesus that would disqualify both of them? "Whoever acknowledges me before others, I will also acknowledge before my Father in heaven. But whoever disowns me before others, I will disown before my Father in heaven" (10:32–33).[2] If Jesus warned that he would disown people who disowned him (26:75), does it mean that Peter wasn't the rock after all? Since Peter left the building, did he take the keys of the kingdom with him?

Jesus Is the Rock

If the chief priests and elders wanted Jesus dead, why didn't they send a lynch mob to kill him?[3] The posse they sent was certainly armed like one, what with

2. Luz, *Matthew*, 3:456.

3. For discussion regarding the limits of the political power of the Sanhedrin, see Luz, *Matthew*, 3:438–46. For full treatment of the historical question regarding the composition and jurisprudence

all the clubs and swords (Matt 26:47). Maybe they were counting on a blood bath; provoked by Jesus or his followers, the mob would cross swords with the rebel and kill him on the spot. But that didn't happen. Jesus surrendered to them without a fight. Besides, Matthew gives the impression that it was the intention of the ruling class to do things properly and not violate the law—especially the sixth commandment (Exod 20:13). Of all people, the chief priests should be the very ones who did things "by the book." At the same time, that doesn't mean that they brought Jesus before them to determine whether he was guilty—as if they were conducting a fact-finding mission free of prejudice. On the contrary, led by the high priest, Caiaphas, the chief priests and elders were already convinced that Jesus was a false prophet and pseudo-Messiah who desecrated the temple of God and deserved death (Matt 26:3–4).[4] But when the ruling council began to hear testimony against Jesus, they couldn't find two witnesses who agreed on what Jesus said or did (v. 60). Even though they were trying to trap Jesus with his own words to prove he was a false prophet (Deut 13:1–5; 18:20–22), they wouldn't break the ninth commandment in the process: "You shall not give false testimony against your neighbor" (Exod 20:16).[5] According to the law, there had to be at least two credible witnesses to establish the guilt of the accused (Deut 19:15–19). Yet, in light of Matthew's account it's difficult to determine whether the high priest eventually gave up on the requirement. According to our Gospel, the Sanhedrin was looking for "false evidence" against Jesus when two witnesses finally came forward who agreed on *one* thing Jesus said: "I am able to destroy the temple of God and rebuild it in three days" (Matt 26:61)—something Jesus *didn't* say according to Matthew.[6]

Did Jesus refuse to answer his accusers because they misquoted him (vv. 62–63; compare with 24:2)? Or was he simply keeping his own advice, refusing to give these dogs his sacred words so that they wouldn't turn on him and "tear" him "to pieces" (7:6)? But, then again, that's exactly what they did, convinced he was a false prophet (26:66–68). Ironically, in their effort to shame Jesus the Sanhedrin ended up treating him like the prophesied suffering servant (Isa 50:5–9; 53:5–8). Is that why Matthew highlighted Jesus's silence, because he wanted to link Jesus to the suffering servant—a man who refused to talk to save his life?[7] Or did Jesus keep silent because a righteous

---

of the Sanhedrin, see Brown, *Death of the Messiah*, 2:340–48.

4. How else do we explain the gathering of so many witnesses in the middle of the night? See Nolland, *Matthew*, 1125.

5. Davies and Allison, *Matthew*, 3:524.

6. Though it is closer to what Jesus said according to John 2:19.

7. Nolland, *Matthew*, 1129.

man is only accountable to God and not his enemies?[8] Whatever the reason, what eventually got Jesus in trouble wasn't what the two witnesses claimed Jesus said. Rather, it's what Jesus actually said to the high priest that convinced the Sanhedrin that he was a blasphemer worthy of death.[9]

It may seem to us like a leap in logic, the high priest moving so quickly from talk about the temple's destruction to questioning Jesus about his identity as "the Messiah, the Son of God" (Matt 26:62–63). Was the high priest working with the assumption that no Messiah would predict the temple's destruction? No, according to Davies and Allison—just the opposite. The true son of David would say such a thing in light of two messianic prophecies that were paired together: one day "the Branch" would rebuild the temple because God made a promise to David that his descendant would build the house of God as God's son (Zech 6:12; see 2 Sam 7:13–14).[10] That's why the high priest tried to get Jesus to swear an oath whether he was this messianic Son of God, knowing that Jesus couldn't keep quiet. "Silence would be the same thing as denial."[11] This is what got Jesus in trouble with the high priest: "Claiming to be God's Son, to have a heavenly throne, and to be the exalted figure of Daniel 7.13" because such a claim "insults the majesty of God."[12] According to Luz, the high priest connected Jesus's temple prediction to his ability to perform miracles—a correlation that is made throughout Matthew's Gospel, where "the Son of God title is frequently associated with Jesus's supernatural power."[13] Therefore, "in light of Jesus's temple saying the high priest is thinking: 'this one could be the Messiah, the Son of God,' and he challenges Jesus to declare his colors under oath."[14] At first, Jesus seemed to avert the challenge by offering his usual, vague response: "You have said so"—the same thing he said to Judas and will later say to Pontius Pilate (Matt 26:25; 27:11). But then, for some unexplained reason, this time Jesus kept talking, giving the appearance that he had fallen into the high priest's trap. Yet, to Matthew's readers both the high priest's question and Jesus's response comprise a true confession, which ironically incites the charge of blasphemy (26:65).[15] Thus the conundrum, something Matthew's readers must have

8. Luz, *Matthew*, 3:428.

9. What exactly was blasphemous about Jesus's words? See Luz, *Matthew*, 3:431–32, for a range of interpretive possibilities.

10. Davies and Allison, *Matthew*, 3:528. So also France: "To purify and restore the temple was a prerogative of the Messiah" (*Matthew*, 1024).

11. Davies and Allison, *Matthew*, 3:528 (quoting Gehardsson).

12. Ibid., 3:533.

13. Luz, *Matthew*, 3:428.

14. Ibid.

15. "By declaring that the Son of God, who has spoken the truth, has blasphemed, is not the high priest himself ironically guilty of blasphemy?" (Davies and Allison, *Matthew*, 3:532).

faced in their confession of Christ: speaking the truth about Jesus will get you in trouble with the authorities.

In what looks to us like a bit of theatrics, the high priest ripped his clothes when Jesus "spoke blasphemy" (v. 65). It's possible that the high priest broke the law when he tore his priestly garments (Lev 21:10).[16] But it's more likely he wasn't wearing his priestly vestments in the middle of the night. By tearing his clothes in open disgust, the high priest was performing what Malina and Rohrbaugh call a "status degradation ritual."[17] In the honor/shame culture of the New Testament world, maintaining or degrading someone's status was crucial to the community upholding the standard of "truth." Status degradation was a way of "publicly recasting, relabeling, humiliating, and thus recategorizing a person as a social deviant. Such rituals express the moral indignation of the denouncers and often mock or denounce a person's former identity in such a way as to destroy it totally."[18] So, when members of the Sanhedrin spit in Jesus's face, they weren't simply being mean (Matt 26:67). They were performing an important ritual intended to shame Jesus—for all intents and purposes, putting him in his place—for claiming divine status (Job 30:10; Isa 50:6). By spitting on him and hitting him with their fists, they were proving to him that he wasn't who he claimed to be. The one who sits at the right hand of God, worthy of honor, would hardly put up with such dishonorable treatment. Even those who played the "who-hit-you?" game were following the same script (Matt 26:68): a false prophet is worthy of derision—an age-old conviction going back to the days of Zechariah (Zech 13:2–6). No wonder Jesus took courage from the very next lines in Zechariah's prophecy: "'Awake, sword, against my shepherd, against the man who is close to me!' declares the LORD Almighty. 'Strike the shepherd, and the sheep will be scattered, and I will turn my hand against the little ones'" (Zech 13:7; Matt 26:31). For, even though his enemies couldn't see it, his suffering as a "false prophet" would lead to his exaltation as the Messiah of God.[19]

The Sanhedrin was already convinced Jesus was a false prophet because he supposedly predicted that the temple's destruction and restoration would happen in three days. If his temple clearing on Monday was interpreted as a prophetic sign enacting the destruction of the temple (Matt 21:12–13;

16. Was this gesture an ironic foreshadowing of the temple veil that was about to be ripped in half? See Davies and Allison, *Matthew*, 3:533.

17. Malina and Rohrbaugh, *Synoptic Gospels*, 159.

18. Ibid.

19. Keener writes: "The trial scene, heavily laden with ironies, exemplifies Jesus's teaching about the hiddenness of the kingdom (13:31–33). Apart from those who share the correct suppositions, the kingdom's presence remains ambiguous to those it confronts" (*Matthew*, 644).

24:2),[20] then more than three days had passed and nothing had happened (26:17)—neither destruction nor restoration. What further proof did they need that Jesus was a false Messiah other than the fact that he persisted in his claim that "from now on" they would see him ascend to the right hand of the very throne of God (v. 64)? Another prophecy. Really? From their perspective, it must have seemed like another desperate attempt made by Jesus—a false prophet trying to keep up the charade. Shamelessly, this pretender wouldn't give up making outlandish predictions. Ironically, however, by condemning Jesus to death the religious leaders would be the very ones to help make this prophecy come true. For when they tried to prove to the world that Jesus was *not* the prophesied king of Israel—what anointed king dies a cursed death on a cross?—they unknowingly lifted him up to the right hand of God (1 Cor 2:6–8). The rock of offense would become the cornerstone of the new temple of God, just as Jesus told them (Matt 21:42), and it would only take three days.[21] So, when members of the Sanhedrin slapped Jesus and said, "Prophesy to us, Messiah. Who hit you?" (26:68), I wished Jesus would have said, "The ones who will help make my prophecies come true."

Peter Needs Salvation

This story doesn't require much comment, does it? Peter's behavior speaks for itself. We all can relate to the tension within the narrative. It's a plot played out in the lives of all kinds of people, regardless of context. Lying to get out of trouble is the modus operandi of all humans—from childhood to retirement. Maybe that's why we're a little sympathetic to Peter. Who wouldn't do the same, given these circumstances? All he did was tell a little fib to save his skin. Who could blame him for that? Besides, his white lie didn't hurt anyone. It's not like the chief priests called on Peter to testify on Jesus's behalf, to bear witness that Jesus was a true prophet, to save him from death. In fact, it could be said that Peter didn't let Jesus down at all. Since Jesus had predicted that Peter would deny him three times before sunrise, *and* that he would meet up again with Peter and the rest of the disciples in Galilee (Matt 26:32–34), one could say that Peter was "predestined" to betray Jesus and then be restored. So, what's a little denial every now and then? It doesn't hurt anyone, does it? At least Peter didn't betray Jesus like Judas did. It's one thing to say, "I don't know the man" (v. 72). It's quite something else to lead enemies to Jesus *because* you know him.[22] It's no surprise Judas hung himself. Even he knew his dastardly deed was unforgivable. But all Peter had to do was to show a little

20. See above, 411–12; 467–75.
21. Davies and Allison, *Matthew*, 3:525.
22. Brown, *Death of the Messiah*, 1:641.

remorse—have a good cry—to get over his regret. Lie, cry, feel better in the morning—that's the way we deal with our sin.

But we know that's not the whole story. Something far more sinister is going on here. Even though some may want to interpret Peter's regret as an act of repentance, Matthew doesn't describe it that way. In fact, there is no indication in Matthew's Gospel that Peter ever "repented" of his sin. Peter isn't even mentioned by name among those who received the Great Commission—the reader is led to infer that Peter is just one of "the eleven disciples" gathered on the mountain (28:16). There is no scene of Jesus restoring Peter like we read in John's Gospel (John 21:15–19). In fact, after Peter remembers Jesus's fateful words (that he would deny him three times before the rooster crows), Peter is never heard from again. He leaves the Gospel narrative when he leaves the high priest's courtyard. By the end of the story, Peter is no longer identified as the special disciple appointed to hold the keys of the kingdom. He's just one of the eleven. Nothing more, nothing less. Why? I think the progressive "downfall" of Peter, tracked both verbally and geographically,[23] make it evident that he did more than simply deny Jesus. Matthew gives the impression that Peter lost the keys to the kingdom—no longer the leader of the group—because he cursed Jesus.

Peter's fall began with an evasive response to a simple observation. The slave girl didn't accuse him of much; she simply recognized Peter as someone who had been with Jesus (Matt 26:69). She didn't say, "You are one of his disciples, aren't you?" or even "What are *you* doing *here*?" She only recognized Peter as one who had been with Jesus. Peter's response didn't amount to much either. He neither affirmed nor denied that he knew Jesus. Instead, he simply feigned ignorance, "I don't know what you're talking about"—which could be passed off as, "Silly slave girl. She thinks she sees things in the dark." Obviously, the mob that seized Jesus was still hanging around the courtyard. Perhaps those who lived next to the high priest were awakened by the racket and joined the crowd to see what was going on. Apparently, Peter wanted to hide anonymously among those gathered outside the high priest's house. But he got too close to the action. He therefore decided to leave the courtyard to keep a safe distance. And yet, no sooner had he walked through the gate when another slave girl repeated the same thing: "This fellow was with Jesus of Nazareth" (v. 71). The timing of Peter trying to slink away unnoticed, along with the way Jesus was identified by the slave—he's an *outsider* from Nazareth[24]—convinced Simon that he was in trouble. No more feigning

23. France, *Matthew*, 1032.

24. France, *Matthew*, 1033. What's a Galilean doing in the high priest's courtyard in the middle of the night (Nolland, *Matthew*, 1142)?

ignorance. To save his skin, Peter denies him outright: "I don't know the man," swearing an oath to prove that he means what he says (v. 72)—another indication that Peter wasn't behaving like a disciple of Jesus, who taught his followers not to swear oaths (5:33–37).

But Peter swearing an oath wasn't enough to convince the crowd that he didn't know Jesus. One of them inferred that Peter had to be a disciple of Jesus because he talked like an outsider (26:73). The Galileans were known to slur certain consonants,[25] making them sound inarticulate and perhaps even lazy (the same prejudice Yankees have against Southerners). In other words, it was Peter's *words* that convinced the company that he had been lying about his identity—not to mention the fact that oaths were commonly used to mask a lie against one's enemies. Now Peter must take his case to the next level. In addition to repeating the same sworn oath ("I don't know the man"), Peter "began to call down curses [*katathematizein*]" (v. 74). We may misread Peter's cursing as profanity, what we call "cussing." But that's not what he did. Rather, when Peter "began to call down curses," he was calling upon God to curse someone. But who? Did Peter issue a self-inflicted curse, as in, "May God strike me down if I'm lying"?[26] Or did Peter call upon God to curse Jesus—similar to what Paul refers to in 1 Corinthians 12:3: "Jesus be cursed"? To use our vernacular, Peter basically said something like "God damn it"—the "it" referring to himself or Jesus. Therefore, in certain respects Peter's curse would have sounded like "cussing" to our ears because we use this curse so often. (When some of us say, "God damn it," are we *truly* calling upon God to damn certain people or things to hell?) Is that what Peter did? Did he call upon God to damn himself or Jesus to hell?

We can't tell whether Peter cursed himself, Jesus, or perhaps even those confronting him. There is no direct object of the verb. In light of the way Christians were later called upon to curse Christ as a sign of loyalty to the Roman Empire, however, several scholars think Matthew presumes his readers would know that Peter cursed Jesus to prove he wasn't his disciple.[27] If that were the case, then Peter's intention to "see the end" of Jesus has been aborted by his own words. By pronouncing God's curse upon Jesus, Peter has already declared "the end of Jesus"—a shameful death that will reveal (and confirm?) the curse of God. No need to "see" it; Peter has declared by his curse that Jesus is "dead" to him, which may also explain why the keys-of-the-kingdom disciple "wept bitterly" when he heard the rooster crow. For Jesus had

25. See Evans, *Matthew*, 444.

26. Keener, *Matthew*, 655.

27. See Davies and Allison, *Matthew*, 3:548–49; Luz, *Matthew*, 3:456; France, *Matthew*, 1034; Brown, *Death of the Messiah*, 1:624–26.

predicted that whatever Peter would "bind on earth will be bound in heaven" (Matt 16:19). And so, irony upon irony, Peter used his keys to condemn Jesus to a cursed death—"and the gates of Hades will not overcome it" (v. 18). This is not the way Peter expected to be the rock upon which Jesus would build his church. He said he would die with Jesus to bring the kingdom of heaven to earth (26:35). But that didn't happen. Just as Jesus predicted, Peter denied him three times, finally using a curse to prove he wasn't a disciple. Yet "in the end" Peter's denial only proved—being a disciple of Jesus—how much he needed Jesus to die a cursed death on a cross to save him from his sin. "The end" that Peter pronounced by way of his curse was the very way Jesus took for our salvation.

LIVE the Story

Jesus promised his disciples that they would still be forgiven when they "blasphemed" the Son of Man (Matt 12:32). The truth of that promise ended up being fleshed out in living color, not only in the lives of all Jesus's disciples but especially in the downfall of Peter. Peter not only blasphemed Jesus with his words but also his deeds. He not only denied Jesus by saying, "I don't know the man"—probably even cursing him—he also denied him by not following him. By denying Jesus, Peter also denied himself—a double blasphemy—for Jesus's lordship was supposed to be revealed by his discipleship. But at this point of the gospel story, it didn't look like Jesus had made *any* disciples, much less one he nicknamed "the Rock." Not even Peter followed him to the end. When Peter left the courtyard and "wept bitterly," he left Jesus.

Even though Jesus had already forgiven Peter by not only predicting his downfall but also his recovery, I wonder how long it took Peter to forgive himself. I think the shame of his betrayal must have stayed with him for a long time. Since he failed to live up to his name—having used the keys Jesus gave him to call down God's curse upon his Lord—who could blame Peter if he preferred his given name for a while? Every time one of the disciples called him by the nickname Jesus gave to him, I wonder if he cringed. Every morning when he heard a rooster crow, I wonder if he remembered what he did to Jesus that fateful night.[28] His shame would have been hard to hide. His indiscretion was public knowledge. Jesus had told *everyone* that Peter would let him down—a rock offended by the rock of offense—a story that made it into all four Gospels. "Hey, Peter, tell us again what it felt like when you betrayed Jesus."

28. Also Bruner, *Matthew*, 2:699.

"Don't call me that. I'm no rock. I'm simply Simon, the black sheep of the family."

In her memoir *Little Black Sheep*, recording artist Ashley Cleveland tells the story of her betrayal.[29] It's a stunningly honest account of how she consistently betrayed her family, herself, and her Lord. Sometimes she blames her dysfunctional family for her addictions. The daughter of a closeted, gay father and perfectionist mother—both alcoholics whose marriage ended in divorce when Ashley was still a little girl—Cleveland was surrounded by hypocrisy her whole life. To appear to be one thing while doing the opposite was her family's unspoken mantra, the only way to negotiate the repressive social expectations embedded in the honor culture of the South. As I read her story, sometimes I thought to myself, "No wonder she was so messed up," as if her addiction was predictable—predestined to disappoint. But then, just as I was ready to condemn her family for her addictions, Ashley would put the blame of her betrayal squarely on her own shoulders. After recounting the advantages of being loved by her kindhearted, handsome father or resilient, hardworking mother, this Grammy Award-winning musician would hold her foibles up to me, a reader, with disdain and disgust. As she described yet another screwup—the result of foolish decisions fostered by a self-absorbed myopia—Ashley would quickly admit that the bed she was forced to sleep in was of her own making. Holding up the mirror of her own disgust, she seemed to cry out to the reader, "What's wrong with me?" Wanting so desperately to fix herself or be fixed, she wondered why things couldn't be different, why God didn't "zap" her to make her better, why she always seemed to struggle with addictions in many forms. She wanted to be the victory story, the girl who could speak confidently of salvation from her past as if it were a faded memory. But that didn't happen.

> The path I have taken is the low road of the gospel where I live as a broken person among the broken and where repeated failures have provided the Ebenezer stones for the things that I most cherish. I assumed that in coming to faith, my cracks and splits would be sewn together again in a seamless, saint-like fabric, but such is not the case. Much like the Velveteen Rabbit, I am a series of threadbare patches, irregular stiches with the stuffing poking out, and one button eye displaced and down cast.
>
> I have serious issues with this.
>
> I have despised my brokenness and cry out to God regularly and petulantly, particularly after a public display of contempt, shame, greed, gluttony,

29. Ashley Cleveland, *Little Black Sheep: A Memoir* (Colorado Springs: David C. Cook, 2013).

grandiosity, or insensitivity: "Would it be such a big deal to relieve me of some of this? Could You make me just a little less broken?"

The answer that I perceive is always the same: "No. More broken."[30]

Of course, for those of us who have been following Jesus for a while, we recognize Ashley's story as a victory story. Because, like all good stories, victory takes time. With time Ashley has experienced victories in her life every now and then.[31] Her weakness has become a testimony to God's strength—the bedrock of grace upon which we all have built our Ebenezer. Indeed, she's not the first to add a stone to the monument of God's salvation. For the memorial is not only made up of Ashley's stones or our stones, but way down at the bottom of the tower—one of the first rocks placed upon the cornerstone of our faith—is the rock that was put there by a man named Peter. He was a disciple of Jesus who knew a lot about rejection and restoration, shame and forgiveness:

> As you come to him, the living Stone—rejected by humans but chosen by God and precious to him—you also, like living stones, are being built into a spiritual house to be a holy priesthood, offering spiritual sacrifices acceptable to God through Jesus Christ. For in Scripture it says:
>
> "See, I lay a stone in Zion,
> a chosen and precious cornerstone,
> and the one who trusts in him
> *will never be put to shame*." (1 Pet 2:4–6, emphasis added)

This is why Christ followers shouldn't throw stones. Rather, we must use them to build a memorial to the grace of our God: the church of Jesus Christ, the rock.

Yet, the fact that Ashley has been made to feel like "the black sheep of the family"—as if she were an oddball in the game of Christianity—proves that we'd rather pelt one another with humiliating words than build up the temple of God as living stones of the one who was humiliated for us. It's because we've been made to believe our weaknesses, our failures, our mistakes—despite the fact that *we all sin and fall short of the glory of God*—are a source of shame, things which are to be tucked away in the privacy of our disappointment. On the other hand our strengths, successes, and achievements—things which are worthy of boasting—have been heralded by the church, meant to be put on display for the entire world to see. It's our concerted effort at public relations,

30. Cleveland, *Little Black Sheep*, 22–23.

31. "Henry and Lily [her children] do not remember me as a drinker. They think of Kenny [her husband] and I as boring parents who get excited over a good night's sleep. When we make vague references to our former wild nights, they roll their eyes and look at us with something like good-natured pity, as if. I cannot even begin to articulate how much this thrills me" (ibid., 182).

putting on our collective brave face for pagans who need to be converted from their pitiful, messed-up lives to our glorious, upstanding life worthy of imitation. Of course, when the "Simon Peters" among us mess up, we're ashamed of their shortcomings, knowing the church will suffer another black eye of abusive critique from the world. Which is why those of us who sit comfortably at the table of our Lord are compelled to say, "Even if all fall away on account of you, I never will. . . . Even if I have to die with you, I will never disown you" (Matt 26:33, 35). Eventually, ironically, all the disciples end up saying "the same" (v. 35).

But rather than boast in our loyalty, our faithfulness, and our strength and success, perhaps it's time we learn to imitate the apostle Paul and boast in our weakness. After all, if we've joined Paul to preach "Jesus Christ and him crucified" as the hope of the world (1 Cor 2:2), then maybe it's time to imitate him and embody the message we proclaim. That's why Paul boasted in the cross of Jesus Christ. Boasting was one way of getting your community to confirm your words. Of course, the quest for honor—social worth—compelled first-century people to boast about their accomplishments. But Paul decided to boast in his weaknesses and failures—that he was "the least of the apostles," a nobody (1 Cor 15:9; 2 Cor 12:11). Ironically, his converts (especially in Corinth) confirmed the same. Paul's foolish boast was on target: in their eyes, Paul was the poorest excuse for an apostle. He was a lousy preacher (1 Cor 2:3–4; 2 Cor 10:10). He was the personification of weakness, the embodiment of foolishness, the incarnation of the cross (1 Cor 4:9–13; 2 Cor 4:7–10)—which Paul, of course, took as the highest compliment. For it was only in weakness where Paul experienced the power of the cross. And that kind of grace was enough for him (2 Cor 12:9–10).[32]

Paul was the black sheep of the family, always getting into trouble (2 Cor 11:23–27), and he was proud of it. However, it was not the kind of pride that exults in rebellion; rather, Paul boasted in the foolishness of his weakness because he found resurrection power in the cross of Jesus Christ—the good news of experiencing life in death, honor in shame, strength in weakness—the reason we should all boast in our failures. Our God can use the least of the apostles to write a fourth of the New Testament. He can turn a betrayer into a disciple named "Peter." He can lead a black sheep into the fold of God (along with all the other black sheep—like me!) and wash her clean. See? When we boast in the weakness of the church, we find ourselves boasting in people named Simon, Paul, and Ashley. Therefore, we might as well boast in our own weaknesses too, for then we will find that his grace is enough for all of us.

---

32. See Reeves, *Spirituality according to Paul*, 41–53.

CHAPTER 38

Matthew 27:1–26

LISTEN to the Story

Early in the morning, all the chief priests and the elders of the people
made their plans how to have Jesus executed. 2So they bound him, led him
away and handed him over to Pilate the governor.
3When Judas, who had betrayed him, saw that Jesus was condemned,
he was seized with remorse and returned the thirty pieces of silver to the
chief priests and the elders. 4"I have sinned," he said, "for I have betrayed
innocent blood."
"What is that to us?" they replied. "That's your responsibility."
5So Judas threw the money into the temple and left. Then he went
away and hanged himself.
6The chief priests picked up the coins and said, "It is against the law to
put this into the treasury, since it is blood money." 7So they decided to use
the money to buy the potter's field as a burial place for foreigners. 8That
is why it has been called the Field of Blood to this day. 9Then what was
spoken by Jeremiah the prophet was fulfilled: "They took the thirty pieces
of silver, the price set on him by the people of Israel, 10and they used them
to buy the potter's field, as the Lord commanded me."
11Meanwhile Jesus stood before the governor, and the governor asked
him, "Are you the king of the Jews?"
"You have said so," Jesus replied.
12When he was accused by the chief priests and the elders, he gave
no answer. 13Then Pilate asked him, "Don't you hear the testimony they
are bringing against you?" 14But Jesus made no reply, not even to a single
charge—to the great amazement of the governor.
15Now it was the governor's custom at the festival to release a prisoner
chosen by the crowd. 16At that time they had a well-known prisoner whose
name was Jesus Barabbas. 17So when the crowd had gathered, Pilate asked
them, "Which one do you want me to release to you: Jesus Barabbas, or

Jesus who is called the Messiah?" [18]For he knew it was out of self-interest that they had handed Jesus over to him.

[19]While Pilate was sitting on the judge's seat, his wife sent him this message: "Don't have anything to do with that innocent man, for I have suffered a great deal today in a dream because of him."

[20]But the chief priests and the elders persuaded the crowd to ask for Barabbas and to have Jesus executed.

[21]"Which of the two do you want me to release to you?" asked the governor.

"Barabbas," they answered.

[22]"What shall I do, then, with Jesus who is called the Messiah?" Pilate asked.

They all answered, "Crucify him!"

[23]"Why? What crime has he committed?" asked Pilate.

But they shouted all the louder, "Crucify him!"

[24]When Pilate saw that he was getting nowhere, but that instead an uproar was starting, he took water and washed his hands in front of the crowd. "I am innocent of this man's blood," he said. "It is your responsibility!"

[25]All the people answered, "His blood is on us and on our children!"

[26]Then he released Barabbas to them. But he had Jesus flogged, and handed him over to be crucified.

Listening to the Text in the Story: Exodus 6:6–7; Leviticus 24:17, 21; Numbers 12:6; Deuteronomy 21:1–9; 23:18; 27:25; Joshua 2:19; 1 Samuel 19:5; 2 Samuel 16:15, 20–17:4, 14–16, 21–23; Job 33:14–18; Psalm 26:6; Isaiah 53:4–8; Jeremiah 19:1–15; 32:6–9; Lamentations 4:1–2; Ezekiel 33:1–5; Zechariah 11:12–13.

"Cursed is anyone who accepts a bribe to kill an innocent person" (Deut 27:25). Those responsible for the death of Jesus refused to accept responsibility for it. Judas took drastic measures to absolve himself of his terrible betrayal; he first returned the money he took from the chief priests for handing Jesus over to them. But then the traitor took his own life because he realized he had "betrayed innocent blood" (Matt 27:3–5). The chief priests refused to take the money back—the small price they paid to carry out their plan—because it was "blood money" that would defile the holy temple (v. 6). The procurator literally tried to wash his hands of the matter because he was convinced that

Jesus was "innocent" (vv. 23–24). And yet, the protests of all three actors—the betrayer, the chief priests, and the procurator—are puzzling to the reader because they all got what they wanted. Judas traded Jesus for money. The priests paid to have Jesus executed. Pilate placated an angry mob by handing Jesus over to the executioners. All three actors should have been pleased by the outcome. They all used Jesus as currency to buy what they desired—a small price to pay in the dog-eat-dog world of power politics. Indeed, after Jesus was crucified, all of them should have gathered at Pilate's place for a toast—Judas with his money, the high priest with a satisfied grin on his face, and Pilate relishing in his unabated power. Raising their glasses, each one would acknowledge their newly formed triumvirate: "I couldn't have done it without you."

But these unlikely partners in crime all shared in one nasty little problem. God cursed the person who shed innocent blood. For the most part, the Romans believed this as much as the Jews (although some would question whether Pilate ever operated with a such a conscience).[1] Therefore, to accept responsibility for the death of Jesus was the same as calling down God's curse upon themselves, the guilty party. And so, the constant refrain, the common theme that runs throughout this narrative, is the dilemma of being stained by Jesus's innocent blood (vv. 4, 6, 19, 24–25). Who will take responsibility for the curse of God because innocent blood was shed? That's the question that hangs over the entire episode, like the blade of a guillotine ready to drop on the offender. Although Judas tried to accept responsibility, the chief priests refused to do their job by offering a pardon. The chief priests couldn't accept responsibility because they didn't have the power to execute Jesus, having to stir up the mob to call for Jesus's crucifixion. Therefore, technically, they could say, "Our hands did not shed innocent blood" (Deut 21:7). And the one who carried out the sentence, Pilate, tried to act like none of this was his fault, pretending as if the crucifixion of Jesus wasn't his doing.

The only actor in the story prepared to accept full responsibility for shedding innocent blood are the very people the Christ was supposed to rule as "king of the Jews": the people of Jerusalem (see Matt 2:2; 27:11, 29, 37). Rather defiantly, they were more than willing to take the curse upon themselves and their children (27:25). Matthew seems to work with the presumption that if the blood of Abel cried out to God from the ground resulting in the curse of Cain (Gen 4:10–11), how much more does the blood of Jesus his Son cry out for vindication? For those who have ears to hear or eyes to read Matthew's Gospel, we already know the answer (Matt 23:33–38). God's curse will result in the desolation of their house. "And so upon you will come all

1. For an excellent description of Pilate's reputation in the first-century world, see Brown, *Death of the Messiah*, 2.693–705.

the righteous blood that has been shed on earth, from the blood of righteous Abel to the blood of Zechariah son of Berekiah, whom you murdered between the temple and the altar. Truly I tell you, all this will come on this generation. Jerusalem, Jerusalem, you who kill the prophets and stone those sent to you. . ." (vv. 35–37). Ironically, this "city of peace" would be destroyed one day for shedding innocent blood. According to several scholars, Matthew writes with a presumption that his readers would know when that happened: AD 70.[2]

EXPLAIN the Story

Even though Jesus is the main subject of this episode, he isn't the main character, which is rather surprising. As readers, we are used to seeing Jesus do amazing works and say provocative things. He dominates Matthew's Gospel story. Yet, as we watch his fate unfold before our eyes, Jesus doesn't say much. He doesn't do anything. Furthermore, Matthew doesn't spend any time trying to explain things from Jesus's perspective. We don't get to see his reaction to anything that happens to him. We don't know what he thinks about this travesty of justice. By contrast, Matthew clues the readers into much of what the other actors think, prying into their minds, sorting out their motivation for the part they played in "shedding innocent blood." For example, we are privy to what Pilate thinks (Matt 27:14, 18, 24), what was going through Judas's mind as he dealt with his regret (vv. 3–4), why the chief priests refused to accept Judas's "blood money" and how they dealt with the dilemma (vv. 4–7)—we even know what Pilate's wife thought about the whole affair (v. 19). Yet we don't hear much from Jesus at all. He is a flat character in this episode. Even though he's the focal point of the story, Jesus functions more like a necessary prop handed from one actor to another to help draw the reader's attention to the dramatic twists and turns of the all-too-familiar story of how an innocent man was condemned to death.

Jesus's silence speaks as loudly as the absence of God. For where injustice prevails, God is not present. That's what the prophets tried to teach Israel over and over again (Isa 1:7–23; 5:7; Amos 5:21–24; Mic 6:6–8). For unless Israel repented of their wicked ways, God would leave them, no longer hearing their prayers or accepting their sacrifices in the temple. If his children persisted in disobedience, perpetuating injustice against the most vulnerable—the defenseless—he would hand them over to their enemies to teach them a lesson: God will not be placated with scapegoat sacrifices and feigned sincerity. The prophets didn't believe in trickle-down economics when it came to justice.

2. For example, see Luz, *Matthew*, 2:503.

As long as the weak are not experiencing the justice of God, then no one will—especially the strong, those who were supposed to lead the people to serve God. According to Isaiah, their priestly hands were bloody with the sacrifice of innocent victims, the silent voices of those who had no one to defend them but God. As far as the prophet was concerned, the only way they would be able to wash and cleanse their priestly robes white as snow was to "stop doing wrong. Learn to do right; seek justice. Defend the oppressed" (Isa 1:16–17).

But when the leaders of Jerusalem persisted in being agents of oppression, doing wrong and promoting injustice, then the prophet predicted that they would be devoured by the sword. Isaiah wasn't optimistic about their repentance, however; he didn't believe the rulers of Jerusalem would learn their lesson. "See how the faithful city has become a prostitute! She once was full of justice; righteousness used to dwell in her—but now murderers! . . . Your rulers are rebels, partners with thieves; they all love bribes" (vv. 21, 23). Isaiah makes it plain that Jerusalem, a city of rulers and priests as well as the retainer class (those who owned the property, the aristocracy), was the problem. When they did what was evil in the sight of the Lord, the rest of Israel would suffer the consequences (vv. 24–25), after which God would restore Israel with righteous leaders: Immanuel (7:14), Prince of Peace (9:6), Righteous Branch (11:1), Servant of the Lord (52:13–15), Silent Lamb (53:7–12). Therefore, the way Matthew saw it, the story of Jesus not only reveals *how* it all came true but also *why* it had to happen like this.[3]

Looking for Forgiveness in the Wrong Place

It's a pitiful sight, Judas seeking absolution for his sin. We don't know why he suddenly experienced pangs of regret for betraying Jesus (Matt 27:3). Didn't he see that it might turn out like this, that the chief priests would hand Jesus over to the Romans? Was he that shortsighted, thinking the priests would only give Jesus a good tongue lashing for his temple tantrum or, at worst, put him through their infamous forty-minus-one whipping (a corporal punishment for Jewish rebels)? That seems to be the impression given by Matthew, for it's only after the chief priests turned Jesus over to Pilate to carry our their plans of having him executed that Judas "saw that Jesus was condemned" and thereby was "seized with remorse" (vv. 1–3). Maybe it was the strange sight of seeing Jesus bound like a common criminal—this powerful man doing nothing to break free—that caused the reality of the situation to sink in for

3. There are several similarities between the trial of Jesus (Matt 27:11–26) and the circumstances surrounding his birth (2:1–18): called "king of the Jews," role of the chief priests, reference to the "Christ," all Jerusalem/all the people, warning to gentiles in a dream, plot to kill Jesus, suffering of Jewish children (See Davies and Allison, *Matthew*, 3:594).

Judas (v. 2). An accused man handed over to Pilate to do as he pleased, like a neatly wrapped gift for the taking, would spell certain doom for Jesus. So, perhaps, Judas didn't expect the chief priests to hand Jesus over to the Romans, a betrayal of Jew against Jew. Others think Judas wasn't that dimwitted. They want to give him credit for arranging the whole thing. Judas was either counting on a meeting of the minds between Jesus and the temple leadership, or he was trying to force Jesus to take matters into his own hands by conquering his enemies with his supernatural power.[4] But the way Matthew tells the story, it appears as though Judas was surprised by the outcome. Cashing in on Jesus wasn't supposed to go this far. Consequently, once he saw "the end" of Jesus, Judas returned the bribe to the chief priests to get them to call off the deal. Or perhaps the traitor was trying to make restitution for his sin.

There's a double irony that shows up here as Judas tries to find absolution in the temple. First, the chief priests act like it's not their job to pardon a sinner.[5] Judas comes to the priests, confessing his sin, ready to make restitution,[6] and the chief priests respond rather unexpectedly, "What does that have to do with us?" We might expect Judas to say, "What do you mean, 'What does that have to do with us'? You're priests. Absolution is your job, for goodness sake!" I imagine the shocked look on Judas's face when the priests respond to his desperate condition—a sinner needing God's forgiveness—by saying, "That's your responsibility" (v. 4). Without a priest to broker remission of sin, what's a man to do? But the irony runs even deeper. That the priests act like there's nothing they can do in the temple to help Judas deal with his sin appears to confirm Jesus's indictment of the chief priests.[7] Because of their wickedness, the temple was no longer serving the purposes of God. An impure temple guaranteed that their sacrifices would mean nothing to God. Even worse, when the anointed showed up to clean up God's house, those in charge decided he had to be killed. Therefore, Jesus predicted the temple would be destroyed (24:2); their house would be left desolate (23:38). God had left the building. So, ironically, Judas hadn't learned the lesson[8] that the chief priests unknowingly seemed to confirm: the temple was no longer a place where a sinner could be reconciled to God. The veil would be ripped in half (27:51). The abomination of desolation would confirm the absence of God (24:14–16). Not one stone would be left upon another (v. 2). Without a temple, where would Israel find Immanuel?

---

4. For a brief history of interpretation of Judas, see Luz, *Matthew*, 2:478–90.

5. Garland, *Reading Matthew*, 259.

6. Brown, *Death of the Messiah*, 1:641.

7. "By sentencing Judas to take care of his own guilt, they have unconsciously sentenced themselves before God" (Keener, *Matthew*, 661).

8. Garland, *Reading Matthew*, 260.

Judas took matters into his own hands. Since the chief priests refused to help, evidently Judas thought the only way he could deal with the treachery of his sin was to return the bribe and kill himself (27:5).[9] Eye for an eye, tooth for tooth, life for life—that's what was required by the law to make restitution (Exod 21:23–25; Lev 24:19–20; Deut 19:21). Some scholars think Judas committed suicide because it was his only chance at redemption, to take the curse upon himself as a last resort (Deut 27:25). Consequently, some even suggest Judas's death was efficacious; he modeled true repentance, taking responsibility for his actions.[10] According to Matthew, however, Judas died a cursed death because Jesus said he would (Matt 26:24).[11] The dye was cast. The one who betrayed the Son of Man would be filled with such woe that he would come to the realization that he never should have been born. By his betrayal and his death, Judas proved life meant nothing to him. He had already given up on the kingdom Jesus came to establish. What was left? The fact that he threw away the money signaled his resignation: What good is a little money when you have nothing to live for?

No one wants this money, not Judas or the chief priests; it's not even fit for the temple. Like Jesus—passed around from one person to the next, no one willing to take responsibility for his death—the bribe that bought him was handled like a prickly pear that no one wanted in their hands. Even though it came from the temple treasury, resources dedicated to God, everyone acted like the money was anything but sacred. Judas tried to return the thirty pieces of silver to its source, handing the money back to the ones who gave it to him. He didn't want it anymore, but the chief priests wouldn't take it either. Since he couldn't get the "owners" (those who represent God in the temple) to take it off his hands, Judas threw the coins into the temple—the returned bribe would be their problem. Having coins lying around on the floor wasn't an option. ("Whose money is this?") Returning the money to the temple treasury wasn't acceptable either (evidently, using the money to purchase Jesus's death rendered it unclean).[12] The chief priests therefore decided to use the "blood money" to purchase some land to bury visitors who died in Jerusalem. Funds from the temple treasury were often used for projects to improve the community.[13] What better way to use "unclean" money than to buy a field for "unclean" (dead) people (Matt 27:6–8)?[14]

9. Davies and Allison, *Matthew*, 3:565; Garland, *Reading Matthew*, 260. Are there here echoes of 2 Sam 17:23?

10. Nolland, *Matthew*, 1153.

11. So also Garland, *Reading Matthew*, 259; Brown, *Death of the Messiah*, 1:641.

12. Davies and Allison, *Matthew*, 3:566; Evans, *Matthew*, 449.

13. Keener, *Matthew*, 660.

14. Davies and Allison, *Matthew*, 3:567.

What the chief priests did to keep the temple pure was a stroke of genius, but Matthew wasn't impressed. He sees through their charade, quoting a mash-up of Jeremiah and Zechariah to expose their hypocrisy (Matt 27:9–10).[15] In Jeremiah 19:1–15, the prophet rails against Jerusalem for shedding innocent blood, pronouncing the impending judgment of God. Jerusalem will become a burial ground, defiled by their own uncleanness: "I will smash this nation and this city just as this potter's jar is smashed and cannot be repaired. They will bury the dead in Topheth until there is no room. . . . The houses in Jerusalem and those of the kings of Judah will be defiled like this place, Topheth" (vv. 11–13). Jeremiah's invective, linked with Zechariah's prophecy ("'Throw it to the potter'—the handsome price at which they valued me! So I took the thirty pieces of silver and threw them to the potter at the house of the Lord"; Zech 11:13), explained everything: Judas's behavior, the chief priests' hypocrisy, and the ominous threat that would hang over the house of Jerusalem because they willingly shed innocent blood. According to Matthew, this was the last prophecy fulfilled in the story of Jesus the Messiah, the Son of God.

Looking for Salvation in the Wrong Jesus

At times I wished we knew the tone of voice used by certain characters in the story. For example, did Pilate use a sarcastic tone when he asked Jesus, "Are you the king of the Jews?" (Matt 27:11). Or did he use a somber tone, like an FBI agent trying to get to the bottom of things? Furthermore, one wonders which word he emphasized, for that would change the implications of his question. Did he ask, "Are *you* the king of the Jews?" making fun of Jesus's pitiful condition—a man who was hardly a threat to the Roman Empire? Or did he emphasize the word "king," which would certainly belie Roman interests? Pontius Pilate was the ruler of Jerusalem, not some messianic pretender. Treason against Rome was the only crime punishable by death. So, such a question would put Jesus in peril. Answer yes, and the Romans will kill you. Or maybe Pilate emphasized the last word of his question, "Are you the king of the *Jews*?"[16] as if to imply, "This is what the Jews do to their kings?" Then again, perhaps Matthew has already given us the answer. In Greek, word order does not reveal grammatical function but emphasis. The subject of the sentence could be the last word. In this case, the first word of the question is "you." Therefore, the way Matthew frames the question, Pilate seems to challenge the idea that this man standing before him presented any threat to the Roman Empire.

15. Brown, *Death of the Messiah*, 2:647–52.

16. Perhaps a better translation might be: "Are you the king of the *Judeans* [*Ioudaiōn*]," referring to the southern kingdom/Roman province. See France, *Matthew*, 1051.

We are not told how Pilate came to ask the question. Did the leaders of Jerusalem accuse Jesus of claiming to be king? We know that after Jesus gave his somewhat evasive response, "You have said so" (the same answer he gave when Judas asked if he were the betrayer, 26:25), the chief priests and elders piled on the accusations (27:12). Again, whatever they said, we don't know. Did they bring up his behavior in the temple? Did they quote him, using the testimony they gained from him during their trial against him that one day he would sit beside God's throne and judge the world? Did they bring up his threats against the temple that he would destroy the temple and raise it in three days? Whatever they said, Jesus refused to defend himself, which surprised Pilate (vv. 13–14). Perhaps the governor was used to hearing the accused vehemently deny all charges, even begging for their lives. (Is that what Barabbas did?) Regardless, Pilate came to the conclusion that Jesus was no threat to him or Roman interests. So, he decided to release him—at least that's what it looks like he was trying to do, according to the "governor's custom at the festival to release a prisoner chosen by the crowd" (v. 15).

The problem, however, was that Pilate underestimated either the crowd's negative opinion of Jesus or the influence the chief priests and the elders had on the citizens of Jerusalem. Pilate assumed his position as judge, taking the bema seat (v. 19).[17] He had already called for a notorious criminal, Jesus[18] Barabbas, to be brought from prison. Having heard of Jesus's popularity, Pilate assumed the crowd was there to ask for the release of Jesus of Nazareth[19] per the governor's custom of liberating one Jew during Passover—a symbolic gesture meant not only to reflect a Roman attempt at goodwill but also to provide a not-so-subtle reminder that Israel was presently subservient to a different kind of "pharaoh." Several times before and after Jesus, Jewish rebels would appear, trying to play the role of Moses, claiming to have performed dramatic signs indicating that God's deliverer was prepared to confront Israel's Roman overlords with the historic demand: "Let my people go!" But, of course, what always happened was the current Roman governor would seize the Jewish insurgent, round up his followers, and have them all crucified.[20] Nevertheless,

---

17. "Things are upside-down, and words have unintended meaning. The judge of the world, instead of sitting upon his judgment seat, stands before the *bema* of a lesser" (Davies and Allison, *Matthew*, 3:593).

18. The earliest Greek manuscripts and versions (old Latin and Coptic) of the New Testament omit the name "Jesus." However, some scholars contend that scribes probably omitted the name from their copies since Jesus was a sacred name. See the discussion in Bruce M. Metzger, *A Textual Commentary on the Greek New Testament*, 2nd ed. (Stuttgart: United Bible Societies, 1994), 56.

19. Or, as some suggest, the Jerusalem crowd gathered, anticipating the amnesty gesture in hopes of asking for the release of Barabbas (see France, *Matthew*, 1053; Nolland, *Matthew*, 1167).

20. See Richard A. Horsley, with John S. Hanson, *Bandits, Prophets, and Messiahs: Popular Movements at the Time of Jesus* (New York: Harper & Row, 1985), 161–72.

in honor of Passover, evidently it was the governor's habit to release one prisoner to the Jewish people.[21] Taking his seat as judge to render his decision, Pilate put the question to the crowd: Did they want Jesus Barabbas or Jesus of Nazareth (v. 17)?

Pilate thought the people would side with Jesus of Nazareth because the chief priests were jealous of him. The way Pilate sized it up, the leaders of Jerusalem must have wanted Jesus dead because he was so popular with the crowd (v. 18). At this point, it's quite apparent that Pilate was more suspicious of the leaders of Jerusalem than Jesus. He thought he would use the crowd's opinion against the chief priests and elders, the very people who were supposed to represent Israel. But Matthew gives the impression that Pilate was distracted for a moment, considering the message passed to him from his wife (v. 19). The governor seems unaware of the chief priests and elders working the crowd to make sure the people asked for the "right" Jesus (v. 20). So, as he turns to the crowd and asks for their decision—expecting them to shout out, "Jesus the Messiah"—Pilate appears a bit confused when the people of Jerusalem call for the release of Barabbas. It could be that Pilate didn't consider the makeup of the crowd, which probably consisted primarily of Jerusalemites and not sympathetic Galileans.[22] Whatever the cause of his miscalculation, Pilate had a big problem on his hands. If Barabbas was released, then what was he supposed to do with "Jesus who is called the Messiah" (v. 22)? Send him to jail to take the place of Barabbas? Flog him and let him go? For a governor who is supposed to have a firm hand in running the place, Pilate sure looks like a weakling—hardly the impression gained from Luke's Gospel (Luke 13:1) or Josephus (*Ant.* 18.3.1–2, 4.1–2.). The governor thought he could play the chief priests and elders for fools, making them look bad in front of the people. But he's the one who ends up being manipulated by the religious leaders. Jesus was their problem, but now he's Pilate's problem. Once a ruler has taken his seat on the bema, there must be judgment.[23]

Matthew assumes his readers will appreciate the irony, the people of Jerusalem having to choose between two Jesuses: the one who called himself "the Son of the Father" (Matt 11:27) and the one whose name meant, "son of the father" (*bar abba*).[24] The contrast is even more compelling when we remember that the name Jesus means "Yahweh saves." So, which "savior"

---

21. There is no corroborating evidence that this was standard practice in Jerusalem. Nevertheless, Roman rulers were known to do things like this; see Davies and Allison, *Matthew*, 3:583. According to Brown, the paschal release was a secondary development; see *Death of the Messiah*, 1:815–19.

22. France, *Matthew*, 1055.

23. Brown, *Death of the Messiah*, 1:803, 854.

24. Another possibility is that the name Barabbas could derive from the Aramaic *bar rabban*, meaning "son of the teacher." See Brown, *Death of the Messiah*, 1:799.

does Jerusalem ask for? Which "son of the Father" do they prefer?[25] A notorious criminal who was probably a zealot (why else would he be in Pilate's prison?), dedicated to overthrowing the Roman government by force? Or the Messiah who took the opposite approach as one willing to die for his enemies rather than kill them? No surprise, the people of Jerusalem chose Jesus Barabbas,[26] released from prison to fight another day. And, what to do with Jesus? Jerusalem had already decided. Treat him like a man who is guilty of treason against Rome: "Crucify him!" (27:22). Pilate, whose head was probably spinning, asked the obvious question: When did Jesus commit treason against Rome (v. 23)? At this point, the crowd should have said, "He claimed to be king!" But no rationale was forthcoming. Why would it matter? Did Pilate really need a reason? He was notorious for killing Jewish subjects capriciously. So, as the bloodthirsty mob was about to get out of hand, Pilate feigned innocence by washing his hands of the matter, claiming the death of Jesus would be their "responsibility" (v. 24). He gave the crowd what they wanted, which was a rare tactic employed by Roman governors yet something the Jerusalem mob relished. It didn't happen very often that *they* got to choose whom Rome would crucify: "His blood is on us and our children" (v. 25). And so, having just washed up, Pilate got his hands dirty when he ordered the beating and execution of Jesus (v. 26).[27]

LIVE the Story

Jesus saves. That's the message of Matthew's Gospel, from beginning to end. Therefore, if anyone tries to find salvation anywhere else, then they will have missed the whole point. Jesus is the deliverer who will save his people from their sins (Matt 1:21). He is the narrow gate that leads to life (7:13). His cross is the yoke that makes life bearable because we find Sabbath rest in him (11:28–30). His sacrifice is the only way the kingdom of heaven comes to earth (16:24–25). His innocent blood was shed to establish the new covenant "for the forgiveness of sin" (26:28). Therefore, ironically, those who cry out, "Let his blood be upon us and our children" (27:25), have modeled the sinner's prayer, for only the blood of Jesus can atone for our sin.[28]

25. Bruner, *Matthew*, 2:718.

26. Hilary of Poiters wrote: "They preferred this 'son of the father' to Christ. At the instigation of their leaders, they chose the Antichrist, a man of sin and son of the devil. They chose the one elected for damnation over the author of life" (Simonetti, *Matthew 14–28*, 280).

27. Davies and Allison write: "Washing the hands does not make them clean" (*Matthew*, 3:555).

28. Blomberg, *Matthew*, 414. John Nolland writes: "If complicity in the death of Jesus is a barrier to benefiting from the ransom paid (20:28) and from the blood poured out for the forgiveness of sins (26:28), then the giving of the bread and wine at the Last Supper (26:26–29) is an empty

What Matthew can't understand is why anyone would try to find salvation anywhere else. But they do, and it *always* leads to destruction. Whether it's the Pharisees or the Sadducees, the chief priests or the elders, the Galileans or the citizens of Jerusalem, if they reject Jesus then they will have missed the way of salvation. Even if they try to find salvation in the law or the temple, the people will have failed to realize that something greater than the temple and someone wiser than Solomon was here. All that the law required, everything the prophets predicted, what the temple stood for was to be found in Jesus the Messiah, the Son of God. The Law and the Prophets would be fulfilled; the temple would be destroyed. Therefore, the only way Israel would have Immanuel, "God with us"—the one whose sacrifice would effect the everlasting presence, peace, forgiveness, and justice of God—is Jesus. Period. No one else. No where else. That's the way Matthew saw it, which makes the story of Judas's suicide and Jerusalem's rejection so tragic. Judas tried to find forgiveness in the wrong place. Jerusalem looked for salvation in the wrong Jesus. The result? Death and destruction.

Same thing happens today. Many people refuse to enter the narrow way of Jesus's mercy. They would rather find salvation somewhere else. Some, like the Pharisees, look for salvation in the law, believing the only way we can establish justice is to get people to obey the rules. Listening to these scribal lawyers, you'll hear a lot of talk about law and order, the constitution, and proper interpretation of the law. What is written is supreme. Words are eternal. Others, like the Sadducees, find sanctuary in powerful institutions, especially those that claim a divine purpose. To these priestly aristocrats, propping up their political allies is their chief cause, making sure money and influence fall into the "right" hands to sustain their position in government, medicine, education, religion, or business. What is accomplished is success. Office equals power. Yet, even though justice can be found in the law at times and powerful offices can be used for the common good, one question remains: What are we going to do about our sin? Sin creeps into the courts of justice and institutions of power, perverting what is right and corrupting what is good. Since sinners are prone to shed innocent blood, where are we going to find deliverance from our selfish, destructive, wicked ways? "O wretched man that I am! Who will set me free from this body of death?" (Rom 7:24, my translation). Only one: "Thanks be to God, who delivers me through Jesus Christ our Lord" (v. 25). Jesus saves us from our sin.

And yet, even though we have found forgiveness in Jesus Christ ("his blood be upon us and our children"), sometimes we cry out for Barabbas, the

gesture" ("The Gospel of Matthew and Anti-Semitism," in *Built upon the Rock: Studies in the Gospel of Matthew* [Grand Rapids: Eerdmans, 2008], 168).

one who would kill our enemies rather than die for them. Like the capital city of Jerusalem, we ask for the wrong savior—the "sons of our fathers" who might live to fight another day, risking their lives, willing to offer the ultimate sacrifice. But, the truth of the matter is, dying while trying to kill your enemy isn't the *ultimate* sacrifice. Instead, Jesus taught us that the cross, dying to *save* your enemies, is the ultimate sacrifice—a lesson we too easily forget.

I used to teach a college course, "The Bible and American Culture," where we explored how cultural "scripts" influence the way we read Scripture. The purpose of the class was to help students develop what could be called a "hermeneutic for living"—thinking through principles that govern the way we interpret "cultural texts" (music, plays, films, novels.).[29] In one of the assignments, students were to study a film where the main character is scripted to appear like a Christ figure. Sometimes the contrasts between the movie version of a messianic hero and the Gospels were readily apparent (e.g., the obvious differences between Superman of *Man of Steel* and Jesus Christ—even though both are saviors, one is a superhero, while the other is divine). At other times, the differences between our cultural "messiahs" and the Messiah of the Gospels were so subtle, some students were alarmed by how easily American convictions trumped gospel truth. The American version of the Messiah ended up being far more appealing to us than the Christ of our faith—a lesson we all learned when a student made his presentation on his favorite film *Braveheart.*

He dressed up for the part, wearing a kilt, face painted to look like William Wallace. He even had a sword, using it as a prop to punctuate the comparisons he made between the messianic hero from Scotland and the story of Jesus Christ. To him Wallace was a hero worth emulating, bringing hope to the poor and fighting the injustice of evil rulers. He played a clip from the film—the betrayal, trial, imprisonment, and execution of Wallace—showing how this Scottish messiah died a martyr's death trying to bring freedom to his people. He finished his talk with a rhetorical flourish, raising his sword and encouraging us to "raise the sword of the Spirit and carry on the battle of bringing freedom in Christ to all." The class loved the analogy—especially some of the male students, who offered a military version of the "amen": "Whooo ahhhh!"

Once things settled down, I asked him why he thought Wallace was a martyr. He recounted the events leading up to and including Wallace's death: betrayed by a close friend, beaten by soldiers, imprisoned by rulers, a woman offering a drink to ease his pain, strapped to a cross, mocked by a crowd, lifted

29. Kevin J. Vanhoozer, Charles A. Anderson, Michael J. Sleasman, eds., *Everyday Theology: How to Read Cultural Texts and Interpret Trends* (Grand Rapids: Baker Academic, 2007).

up with arms stretched wide, spear thrust in his side, death-defying scream. Then I said:

> "Yes, his death portrayed in this film looks like a sacrifice. . . . But we all know it wasn't. All who live by the sword, die by the sword, right? Wallace got what was coming to him. He was a murderer, and the law finally caught up with him. History does not give us the details of Wallace's execution. So why do you suppose Mel Gibson wanted Wallace's death to look like the death of Christ?"
>
> At this point, some of the presenter's male compatriots rushed to his defense. Talk of "making the ultimate sacrifice," and "dying for freedom while fighting your enemies," and a "soldier's noble sacrifice" filled the room. Then I said bluntly, "Wallace didn't follow Jesus, did he? He didn't respond to injustice like Jesus did." Silence. "What if he did? How would the film be different if Wallace had followed the ways of Christ?"
>
> What happened next took everyone by surprise. A student said sarcastically, "Well, I suppose he would have visited all the villages, preaching peace and telling them to love their enemies. But we all know *that* doesn't work." An audible gasp could be heard from several students, followed by a pensive silence.
>
> The presenter's face fell, his eyes looking down, as if he were inspecting the floor. He sheathed his sword, looked up at the class and said, "Why didn't I see that before? I claim to be a disciple of Christ, and yet I would rather have a Messiah who kills his enemies than one who loves them." The irony of the moment hit us all like a ton of bricks: there stood a young man dressed like William Wallace talking about loving his enemies.
>
> After his presentation, several students thanked the presenter with a common confession, "You said what we were all were thinking, but we didn't have the guts to admit it. We all want a Messiah who kills his enemies."[30]

Indeed, even in countries that say they want "justice for all" sometimes cry out for the wrong Savior. And so, when that happens, who will save us from our sins?

30. Reeves, *Spirituality according to Paul*, 30.

CHAPTER 39

Matthew 27:27–66

LISTEN to the Story

27Then the governor's soldiers took Jesus into the Praetorium and gathered the whole company of soldiers around him. 28They stripped him and put a scarlet robe on him, 29and then twisted together a crown of thorns and set it on his head. They put a staff in his right hand. Then they knelt in front of him and mocked him. "Hail, king of the Jews!" they said. 30They spit on him, and took the staff and struck him on the head again and again. 31After they had mocked him, they took off the robe and put his own clothes on him. Then they led him away to crucify him.

32As they were going out, they met a man from Cyrene, named Simon, and they forced him to carry the cross. 33They came to a place called Golgotha (which means "the place of the skull"). 34There they offered Jesus wine to drink, mixed with gall; but after tasting it, he refused to drink it. 35When they had crucified him, they divided up his clothes by casting lots. 36And sitting down, they kept watch over him there. 37Above his head they placed the written charge against him: THIS IS JESUS, THE KING OF THE JEWS.

38Two rebels were crucified with him, one on his right and one on his left. 39Those who passed by hurled insults at him, shaking their heads 40and saying, "You who are going to destroy the temple and build it in three days, save yourself! Come down from the cross, if you are the Son of God!" 41In the same way the chief priests, the teachers of the law and the elders mocked him. 42"He saved others," they said, "but he can't save himself! He's the king of Israel! Let him come down now from the cross, and we will believe in him. 43He trusts in God. Let God rescue him now if he wants him, for he said, 'I am the Son of God.'" 44In the same way the rebels who were crucified with him also heaped insults on him.

45From noon until three in the afternoon darkness came over all the land. 46About three in the afternoon Jesus cried out in a loud voice, *"Eli, Eli, lema sabachthani?"* (which means "My God, my God, why have you forsaken me?").

47When some of those standing there heard this, they said, "He's calling Elijah."

48Immediately one of them ran and got a sponge. He filled it with wine vinegar, put it on a staff, and offered it to Jesus to drink. 49The rest said, "Now leave him alone. Let's see if Elijah comes to save him."

50And when Jesus had cried out again in a loud voice, he gave up his spirit.

51At that moment the curtain of the temple was torn in two from top to bottom. The earth shook, the rocks split 52and the tombs broke open. The bodies of many holy people who had died were raised to life. 53They came out of the tombs after Jesus's resurrection and went into the holy city and appeared to many people.

54When the centurion and those with him who were guarding Jesus saw the earthquake and all that had happened, they were terrified, and exclaimed, "Surely he was the Son of God!"

55Many women were there, watching from a distance. They had followed Jesus from Galilee to care for his needs. 56Among them were Mary Magdalene, Mary the mother of James and Joseph, and the mother of Zebedee's sons.

57As evening approached, there came a rich man from Arimathea, named Joseph, who had himself become a disciple of Jesus. 58Going to Pilate, he asked for Jesus's body, and Pilate ordered that it be given to him. 59Joseph took the body, wrapped it in a clean linen cloth, 60and placed it in his own new tomb that he had cut out of the rock. He rolled a big stone in front of the entrance to the tomb and went away. 61Mary Magdalene and the other Mary were sitting there opposite the tomb.

62The next day, the one after Preparation Day, the chief priests and the Pharisees went to Pilate. 63"Sir," they said, "we remember that while he was still alive that deceiver said, 'After three days I will rise again.' 64So give the order for the tomb to be made secure until the third day. Otherwise, his disciples may come and steal the body and tell the people that he has been raised from the dead. This last deception will be worse than the first."

65"Take a guard," Pilate answered. "Go, make the tomb as secure as you know how." 66So they went and made the tomb secure by putting a seal on the stone and posting the guard.

Listening to the Text in the Story: Exodus 10:21–22; 26:31–33; Leviticus 24:14–16; Deuteronomy 21:22–23; Psalms 22; 69:16–21; 109:14–29; Isaiah 50:6–8; 53:3–12; Jeremiah 19:11–15; Lamentations 1:12–14, 21; 2:15; Ezekiel 37:11–14; Daniel 6:16–17; Amos 8:8–9; Zechariah 14:3–9; Wisdom of Solomon 2:17–20.

It was the end of a very bad day. Twenty-four hours earlier, even though it was supposed to have been a joyous occasion, Jesus had gathered his disciples during Passover to eat their last meal together, using the occasion to unmask the betrayer and predict the end of his life. From that moment on, things only got worse. Betrayed by Judas, denied by Peter, abandoned by the disciples, accused and abused by the chief priests, rejected by Jerusalem, condemned by Pilate, tortured by soldiers—and now, this. Mockery, humiliation, crucifixion, and death. It couldn't get any worse; all creation above the earth, on the earth, and under the earth proved it.[1] The sky grew dark in the middle of the day. The God-forsaken king left this earth with a blood-curdling scream. The veil of the temple was ripped in half when God left the building. The earth shook, the rocks crumbled, the grave spewed its keep, and corpses walked into the holy city. This ancient horror story reads like a scene taken directly from the script of a modern-day zombie-apocalypse movie. When Jesus died, it was scary.

Why shouldn't it have been? God was angry, and everyone was terrified—even hardened Roman soldiers—due to the strange, eerie happenings on that dreadful and terrible day of the Lord (Matt 27:54). Indeed, it was a very dark day, with very little light breaking through. To make matters worse, even when "the truth" pierced the darkness of evil and suffering, it was offered in jest.[2] "Hail, king of the Jews." "He saved others, but he can't save himself." "He's the king of Israel." "He trusts in God. Let God rescue him now if he wants him." In the midst of these taunts, I wished someone would have had the guts to shout out, "Oh, God wants him all right, just not the way you wanted him. You'll see! One day he'll rise from the dead and prove you all wrong as hell itself!" But, no one was there to defend him. Not his disciples, not his friends, not his family, and—some might say—not even God. When Jesus died, he died all alone.[3] It was a very bad day.

Once it was all over, however, there were a few bright spots. The terrified Roman soldier—the one who crucified Jesus and gambled for his robe—changed his mind about the criminal and said, "Surely he was the Son of God!" (v. 54). Probably motivated by the horrible thought of Jesus's body hanging on a cross for days—picked over by birds and scavengers—a rich man, Joseph of Arimathea, risked guilt by association to have the corpse interred in his new family tomb (vv. 57–60). A few of Jesus's female disciples stayed with the Lord until the end, watching the whole affair "from a distance"

1. Bruner writes: "In the darkness the natural world puts on, as it were, widow's weeds, dresses in dark clothing, and goes into mourning, for here the world has committed its most heinous crime" (*Matthew*, 2:745).

2. "The mockers are unwitting evangelists" (Turner, *Matthew*, 664).

3. Brown, *Death of the Messiah*, 2:999.

(vv. 55–56, 61).[4] But other than that, there's not much here that would inspire any of us to hold our heads up high. This is humanity at its worst, evil run amok. It was a bad Friday, especially for those of us who love him. Taking in the ugly scene, all we can do is shake our heads in disgust while the world looks on and, even to this day, continues to hurl insults at the crucified: "Is this any way to save the world?"

Yes, it is.

EXPLAIN the Story

Matthew doesn't describe the act itself. Instead, he merely sums up the horrific, barbaric crucifixion of Jesus with only two words: *staurōsantes* … *auton* ("after they crucified him," Matt 27:35). Even though classical works of art and modern films try to picture every gory detail of the execution of Jesus, Matthew's reticence to give a blow-by-blow account of the crucifixion is telling. No mention of the hammer, nails, or agonizing sounds of a tortured man. No hoisting the body above the crowd. No crown of thorns left on his head. No blood. No gaping wounds. Not even a loincloth. All of these imaginative details, so fixed in our minds as gospel truth, are missing from Matthew's Gospel. It's not that Matthew was numb to the agony of Jesus's execution. Rather, it appears as though what was more painful to our author was the way Jesus was mocked throughout the entire ordeal. Matthew spends a lot of time writing about how they humiliated him.

It really bothers me, too. Even though Matthew directs our attention to the humiliation of Jesus, I can't bear to watch. I tend to rush through these verses, not allowing my mind to re-create the scene in my head. When I think about the way they treated him, dressing him like a faux king, kneeling before him sarcastically, repeatedly striking his head with the fake scepter, daring him to come down from the cross and act like a *real* king—it all makes me angry. I can't dwell on those details. But Matthew won't let me look away. To him, seeing the social, emotional, and spiritual suffering of Jesus—adding insult to horrific physical injury—is what makes the crucifixion even more unbearable, something we should *never* forget. In his crucifixion Jesus was humiliated, completely stripped of all dignity. It wasn't enough to kill the man. His enemies had to prove to everyone—to the crowd, to his disciples, even to themselves—that this cursed man was no king of Israel. For no true king would reign like this (Phil 2:5–11).

4. "Let us men imitate the women; let us not forsake Jesus in temptations. For they for Him even dead spent so much and exposed their lives, but we (for again I say the same things) neither feed Him when hungry, nor clothe Him when naked, but seeing Him begging, we pass Him by" (Chrysostom, *Homilies*, 522).

"Hail, King of the Jews!"

After Pilate handed Jesus over to the Roman soldiers to crucify him, they decided to make sport of the Jewish "rebel."[5] Imitating the children's game of dress up and make believe, these coarse men played pretend with Jesus.[6] But this was no tea party. Already nearly beaten to death, Jesus stood before them hardly looking like the crime of which he was accused: king of the Jews. So they decided to dress him up for the part. Stripping him of his robe, the soldiers crowned him with thorns, threw a scarlet robe around his shoulders, and put a stick in his hand. Then, in utter contempt these hardened men bowed before their human-sized doll and mocked him with royal acclamation (Matt 27:28–29). But the charade didn't last long. For as soon as they rose to their feet, instead of greeting him with a kiss they spat on him. Instead of taking orders from the one who rules with a scepter in his hand, they snatched the stick out of his hand and began to beat him over the head, "again and again" (v. 30). Of all the things they did to him, for some reason that image—soldiers whipping Jesus like a dog—bothers me the most. It's not that the blows may have driven his crown of thorns deeper into his skull, making it more painful. It's seeing with my mind's eye the looks on their faces—their gleeful disgust—and Jesus enduring the shame of being beaten like a slave. These brutes had already taken a pound of flesh when they beat him to a pulp (v. 26). Now, they rap his head with a stick (hardly painful in comparison to the beating he received earlier), proving they can do *anything they want to him*. They have all the power, and they know it. He is completely powerless in their hands, and they flaunt it. But we know better, for there is a difference between being powerless and giving up power. He may look like a pitiful excuse for a king—is there any doubt Rome is in power now? But appearances deceive, especially when it comes to the kingdom of heaven on earth.

In moments like these, when evil moves in and takes over, we can't help but look for any act of kindness, wanting to believe that humans are not utterly depraved. Any gesture, the simplest act of mercy can often soften the edges of such a harsh picture of human cruelty. Is that what's happening in verses 31–36? Most victims of crucifixion were made to carry the wooden beam of their own cross, often led to the place of execution completely naked and exposed.[7] But these soldiers put Jesus's clothes on him before they led him through the city and impressed another man to carry his cross the rest of the way, outside Jerusalem (vv. 31–32). Just before they crucified him, the soldiers offered Jesus a mixed drink

5. Jesus was crucified with two bandits executed for the same charge: treason (Keener, *Matthew*, 681).

6. Philo tells the story of the mocking of a delusional man, Carabbas (Philo, *Flaccus* 6.36–38), which has many of the same details: crowned with a fake diadem, clothed with a pseudo-royal robe, a papyrus reed put in his hands like a scepter, mock salutations. See Evans, *Matthew*, 456, for the comparisons. For other examples of mockery, see Davies and Allison, *Matthew*, 3:599.

7. Davies and Allison, *Matthew*, 3:605.

of wine and gall, perhaps to dull the pain (v. 34).[8] Then, the soldiers stayed with Jesus till the end, keeping him company during his last hours on earth (v. 36). But such an optimistic view of things is probably unjustified in light of other details.

For example, the soldiers were required to guard their victims in case one of their friends or family members tried to free them from the cross. (Was it really necessary for Roman soldiers to guard Jesus?[9] His disciples certainly posed no threat; they ran like cowards when Jesus was arrested. Besides, Jesus wasn't going anywhere. His death was an act of obedience to God. If Jesus wanted to come down from the cross, he wouldn't need the help of his disciples, and the Roman soldiers wouldn't be able to stop him.) Furthermore, that the soldiers gambled for his clothing reveals Jesus was naked when they crucified him (v. 35).[10] Why they offered him the mixed drink before they nailed him to the cross could be seen as an act of cruelty, hoping to keep him alive as long as possible. The Romans crucified their victims along major roads leading in and out of the city. They wanted as many subjects of the empire to witness the long, agonizing death of those who committed treason against Rome to serve as an unforgettable deterrent. That they had to find someone else to carry the crossbeam for Jesus demonstrates how badly they beat him. Even though he was scourged within an inch of his life, Jesus probably could have carried the cross all the way to Golgotha, but it would have taken a long time. So, what better way to speed up the affair than to find a healthy man to carry the beaten man's cross? Of course, that these soldiers picked a man named "Simon" to do it is ironic since another "Simon" had promised that he would do that very thing: "Even if I have to die with you, I will never disown you" (26:35).[11] The final indignity was the placard affixed above his head: "THIS IS JESUS, THE KING OF THE JEWS" (27:37). In light of the fact that his name means "Yahweh Saves," the sarcastic sign implied the crucified man didn't live up to his name or office—he neither saves nor reigns.

That feature runs throughout the story of Jesus's crucifixion. It's called "dramatic irony" when actors say and do things that are true even though they may not believe it or are completely unaware of the truth.[12] Irony is built on insider language. Outsiders miss the point because the only way to recognize irony is to realize that what you see *isn't* what you get. Only those who have eyes to see what's *really* happening—the truth embedded in what is ironic—can appreciate what is true.[13] For example, obviously Pilate didn't believe that

8. Bruner, *Matthew*, 2:751.

9. Ibid., 2:735.

10. Davies and Allison, *Matthew*, 3:614.

11. France, *Matthew*, 1065.

12. For a helpful summary of the different kinds of irony (dramatic, situational, verbal), see Paul D. Duke, *Irony in the Fourth Gospel* (Atlanta: John Knox, 1985), 21–27.

13. What Keener calls "tragicomic irony" (*Matthew*, 673–74).

Jesus was king even though the placard said so. And those who passed by decided to hurl "insults at him" because in their eyes Jesus was obviously not a king (v. 39). A crucified man is in no position to reign or offer a kingdom. Yet, even their taunts and accusations—meant to prove to everyone that Jesus wasn't "king of the Jews"—end up being ironic acclamations of his kingdom. In other words, like the placard fixed above his head, even Jesus's enemies unintentionally said what is true even though their words were meant to discredit Jesus and his claims.[14] When they taunted him, "You who are going to destroy the temple and build it in three days, save yourself! Come down from the cross, if you are the Son of God!" (v. 40), we recognize the irony. Since Jesus didn't save himself by coming down from the cross, he not only lived up to his name, "Yahweh Saves," but he also proved that he was God's Son because his death on the cross was an act of obedience to his heavenly Father (26:42). Indeed, the very reason "he saved others" was because "he can't save himself" (27:42)—the essence of his kingdom.[15] Ironically, then, even the chief priests and elders, beholding Jesus on the cross, end up saying what is true even though they don't mean it: "He's the king of Israel" (v. 42).

"He Trusts in God"

When the chief priests, teachers of the law, and elders said that it would be up to God to rescue Jesus, they based their conclusion on a simple inference. Since Jesus "trusts in God" like a son trusts his father, then Jesus would be saved *only if God wanted him* (Matt 27:43, emphasis added). Of course, any member of Israel was considered a "child of God." Yet, according to the religious leaders Jesus had set himself above everyone else "for he said, 'I am the Son of God'" (v. 43)[16]—even though Jesus never said such a thing according to Matthew. Nevertheless, the religious leaders were convinced that Jesus was a fraud.[17] Emboldened by his horrible situation, the chief priests and company knew that the only recourse left to Jesus was for God to rescue him. If God didn't come through—if Jesus died a cursed death on the cross—their righteous indignation would be vindicated:

> Let us see if his words are true,
> and let us test what will happen at the end of his life;
> for if the righteous man is God's child, he will help him,

---

14. Davies and Allison, *Matthew*, 3:619.

15. Ibid.

16. Perhaps echoing the voice of the devil during the temptations, "If you are the Son of God" (see Davies and Allison, *Matthew*, 3:618).

17. Their mocking echoes the charges leveled against Jesus during his trial before the Sanhedrin (Nolland, *Matthew*, 1196).

> and will deliver him from the hand of his adversaries.
> Let us test him with insult and torture,
> so that we may find out how gentle he is,
> and make trial of his forbearance.
> Let us condemn him to a shameful death,
> for, according to what he says, he will be protected. (Wis 2:17–20 NRSV)

They trusted in God to punish this rebel, and that's what was happening right before their eyes—the curse of God so evident that even the rebels who were crucified with Christ joined the chorus and "heaped insults on him" (Matt 27:44). The fact that God didn't *do anything* to "save" Jesus from death or *say anything* to vindicate him proved that Jesus got what was coming to him.[18] Indeed, the silence of God spoke volumes.

But then, something strange happened. In the middle of the day, when the sun is supposed to shine the brightest, "darkness came over all the land" for three hours, "from noon until three in the afternoon" (v. 45). The way Matthew tells the story, during those three hours no one said a word—not Jesus, not his enemies, not the executioners. Since darkness in the middle of the day was often interpreted as a theophanic sign of divine presence or an omen of approaching judgment (or both!),[19] it comes as no surprise that everyone shut their mouths as if they were waiting for God to speak. But the heavens were silent. Jesus hung there, suspended between heaven and earth, and not a sound came from heaven. For three hours, there was no voice on earth or in heaven—just darkness. I wonder why. If there were ever a time for God to speak up, to let everyone know that this was *his* plan, *his* idea—that Jesus was completely obedient to his Father's will—it was now. *This was the time* for God to say, "This is my Son, whom I love; with him I am well pleased." He said it at the beginning (3:17) and in the middle (17:5) of Matthew's Gospel. Why not at the end, when everyone needed to hear it? But God didn't say a word. For three hours, heaven was silent. And just about the time the darkness lifted and the first rays of light broke through,[20] Jesus broke the silence and screamed, "'*Eli, Eli, lema sabachthani*?' (which means 'My God, my God, why have you forsaken me?')" (27:46). Even though God didn't say anything in the midst of the darkness, Jesus decided it was time to speak up when the sun began to shine again. But why did he quote the first line of Psalm 22?

Psalm 22 reads like a script of the crucifixion of Jesus. Because he was "despised by the people," the mockers show up and "hurl insults, shaking their

18. "His present helpless situation is the proof of the falsity of his claims" (France, *Matthew*, 1070).
19. Are there echoes here of the ninth plague against Egypt? See France, *Matthew*, 1075.
20. Contra Nolland, who insists the sky was still dark when Jesus cried out (*Matthew*, 1205).

heads" (Ps 22:6–7) when Jesus was crucified (Matt 27:39). Jesus's enemies even end up saying the same thing, as if they were reading lines from the script: "'He trusts in the LORD,' they say, 'let the LORD rescue him. Let him deliver him since he delights in him'" (Ps 22:8; Matt 27:43). Dry mouth, pierced hands and feet, clothes divided by casting lots (Ps 22:15–18)—all of these details show up here too (Matt 27:34–36), which is why Jesus quoted the first verse of Psalm 22. He connected the dots, watching Scripture be fulfilled before his eyes. To his enemies Jesus appeared to be abandoned by God. Yet the way Jesus saw it, all of this happened by divine design. Psalm 22 proved it. Therefore, quoting the first verse of the divine script seemed *apropos*, not only because all the details of the crucifixion were on display for anyone who had eyes to see, but also because Jesus may have been pointing to the end of the psalm where the victim knows that God will rescue him: "For he has not despised or scorned the suffering of the afflicted one; *he has not hidden his face from him* but has listened to his cry for help" (Ps 22:24, emphasis added).[21]

The problem, however, is that many interpret the darkness that overshadowed the crucifixion as God turning his back on his Son, hiding his face from the dreadful scene. The psalmist, on the other hand, knew that God wouldn't hide his face in the midst of *his* affliction. Rather, because he prayed, "Deliver me from the sword," he trusted that God would "come quickly to help me" (vv. 19–20). Because God came through in the end to save the afflicted (vv. 22–31), it's apparent that the one who cried out, "My God, My God, why have you forsaken me?" in the first verse changed his tune by the end of the psalm. He trusted that God wouldn't just stand by silently and watch his righteous one suffer. Instead, having "listened to his cry for help," God would save the psalmist before the song was over—a salvation so apparent that all the "assembly," even "all the families of the nations," would praise the Lord, knowing "he has done it!" (vv. 25, 27, 31). Yet unlike the psalmist, God didn't save Jesus from his affliction. God didn't deliver him from the cross.

I wonder if that's why Jesus finally cried out, "My God, my God, why have you forsaken me?" When darkness fell upon the place, Jesus expected God to say something,[22] like the psalmist who cried out: "Answer me, LORD, out of the goodness of your love; in your great mercy turn to me. Do not hide your face from your servant; answer me quickly, for I am in trouble" (Ps 69:16–17). In fact, Psalm 69 reads like another script for the crucifixion narrative, with references

21. Davies and Allison, however, are against this interpretation (*Matthew*, 3:625; cf. Luz, *Matthew*, 3:553).

22. Brown writes that "Jesus is not questioning the existence of God or the power of God to do something about what is happening; he is questioning the silence of the one whom he calls 'My God'" (*Death of the Messiah*, 2:1046).

to the temple ("zeal for your house consumes me"), the mockers ("those who sit at the gate mock me"), the disgrace ("you know how I am scorned, disgraced and shamed; all my enemies are before you"), and especially the wine offered to Jesus ("I looked for sympathy, but there was none, for comforters, but I found none. They put gall in my food and gave me vinegar for my thirst") (vv. 9, 12, 19, 20–21).[23] Several times the psalmist expects God to do something—to pour out his wrath on his enemies (vv. 22–28)—or to say something to vindicate him in the presence of his enemies (vv. 13–18). Of course, unlike the psalmist Jesus knew he was going to die. Yet I think he expected God to do or say something in the presence of his enemies, especially when the sky turned black. But then once the darkness lifted, it became apparent to everyone that the heavens would remain silent. At that moment—even as the sun breaks through the darkness—Jesus expressed his disappointment: God had forsaken him. "Jeered as one who trusts in God, he promptly displays that trust in a lament."[24]

In light of the dissipating, legendary, ominous, theophanic darkness, Jesus's enemies mistook his lament for a last-ditch effort, turning to Elijah for help (Matt 27:47). That's why Matthew includes the detail of someone offering Jesus "wine vinegar" in what is a deliberate echo of Psalm 69:21. Since God wouldn't save him now, his enemies relished the irony of this false prophet calling out to the end-time prophet to deliver him: "Let's see if Elijah comes to save him" (Matt 27:49).[25] Of course, nothing happened this time either. Neither God nor Elijah saved Jesus. And so, this God-forsaken man, mocked as a false prophet and crucified as a fake king, died.[26] Leaving this world with a death-defying scream, Matthew says Jesus "gave up his spirit," suggesting that he died when he was ready (v. 50).[27] With nothing left to say or do, Jesus completed his Father's will. When Jesus "gave up his spirit"—his last act of faith—he ironically proved the mockers right: "He trusts in God. Let God rescue him now if he wants him" (v. 43).

"Go, Make the Tomb as Secure as You Know How"

It's a pretty silly idea, needing Roman soldiers to guard a dead man in his tomb. But that's exactly what the chief priests and Pharisees wanted the day after Jesus died (Matt 27:62–64). Of course, their rationale made some sense: perhaps

---

23. Luz, *Matthew*, 3:552. Chromatius wrote: "Take note of the mystery revealed. Long ago, Adam tasted the sweetness of the apple and obtained the bitterness of death for the whole human race. In contrast to this, the Lord tasted the bitterness of gall and obtained our restoration from death's sting to the sweetness of life" (Simonetti, *Matthew 14–28*, 287–88).

24. Garland, *Reading Matthew*, 264.

25. Keener, *Matthew*, 684.

26. For a great summary of the "failure of Jesus," see Luz, *Matthew*, 3:537.

27. France, *Matthew*, 1078.

Jesus's disciples wouldn't give up on their Messiah, rigging a faux resurrection by stealing his body from the tomb. Yet, where would they get such a preposterous idea, especially when Jesus's disciples showed no courage or resourcefulness to counter or contest his arrest, trial, and execution? Maybe it was the strange turn of events that happened the day before. Not only were there earthquakes that caused rocks to split in two, but tombs outside of Jerusalem "broke open" right after Jesus died (vv. 51–52), which got them to thinking. Jesus's disciples might steal the body and claim the same for him. Opportunistically, at that point Jesus's disciples would be able to say with some credibility, "God broke open the tomb of Jesus too. Just like Jesus said, 'After three days I will rise again.' He's alive!" (v. 63). Such a worst-case scenario would be the chief priests' never-ending nightmare because the people might believe it, and "this last deception will be worse than the first" (v. 64). So, Jesus's enemies were going to ensure that didn't happen, which is why they needed Pilate's help. If the disciples previously acted like cowards in the face of Roman power, surely they wouldn't make any effort to overtake Roman soldiers guarding the tomb of Jesus.[28] Other tombs around Jerusalem might have "mysteriously" broken open, but not this one.[29]

The chief priests knew something else happened that day—perhaps something no one else knew, something just as mysterious and earth shattering as unsealed tombs. "At that moment [when Jesus died] the curtain of the temple was torn in two from top to bottom" (v. 51). We can't tell which curtain was ripped in half, the one separating the holy of holies from the rest of the holy place (something only priests would notice), or the curtain that hung as the "front door" of the temple, which just about any Jewish man could see from the court of Israel. If the inner curtain was ripped, that would signify not only God's judgment against the priests but also that Jesus's death created direct access to God.[30] Others infer it had to be the outer curtain since the catastrophe would have been visible to many and the priests wouldn't want the story spread all over town about the ripped inner curtain—that which veiled the presence of God from the priests. If that was the case, then the torn outer curtain would symbolize the approaching destruction of the temple.[31] Others think it doesn't matter which curtain was torn since it was the result of the earthquake—the common theophanic sign of the approaching judgment of God[32] and salvation of Israel.[33] In other words, it's

28. Keener, *Matthew*, 713.

29. "In accordance with divine providence the tomb was sealed so that the resurrection would be verified all the more" (Luz, *Matthew*, 3:589 [quoting Ishodad of Merv]).

30. Bruner, *Matthew*, 2:757.

31. "It is most appropriate that, immediately after people mock Jesus for his prophecy about the temple (v. 40), his words should be vindicated" (Davies and Allison, *Matthew*, 3:630).

32. Chrysostom, *Homilies*, 520–21.

33. See Garland, *Reading Matthew*, 264–65; Luz, *Matthew*, 3:566.

the earthquake that shook people up; the ripped curtain (along with the opened tombs) was consequential. "The chain reaction of events that occurs immediately after his death" was God's answer to Jesus's prayer of lament.[34]

However we interpret the significance of these cosmic events, Matthew wants his readers to know one thing: this was God's doing. The earth was shaken by God.[35] The curtain was ripped by God—only God could tear it from top to bottom. The rocks were split by God, and the tombs were opened by God, apparently fulfilling the prophecy that when he set his feet on the Mount of Olives, rocks would split in two and God would bring "all the holy ones with him" (Zech 14:4–5).[36] In other words, Matthew is picturing for his readers what happened when God left his temple,[37] which is why the order of sequence is important.[38] The earthquake didn't cause the curtain to rip in half. Rather, the temple curtain was ripped from top to bottom *first* to indicate God had left the building.[39] What happened next—"the earth shook, the rocks split and the tombs broke open" (Matt 27:51–52)—was a picture of God "throwing his weight around."[40] When Jesus died, God stormed out of the temple; having ripped the curtain in half, he stomped around the earth, splitting rocks with every step. Then, he raided the tombs, taking his holy ones with him.[41] All these things were ominous signs of the judgment of God, including the appearance of "zombies" in Jerusalem after the resurrection of Jesus (Matt 27:52–53). What could be more scandalous to the Jews than a bunch of corpses walking around Jerusalem? Since graves were marked during Jewish festivals to keep pilgrims from being defiled by the unclean, imagine the horror of hearing that these dead bodies walked into Jerusalem during the week-long feast of unleavened bread![42] Jerusalem had Jesus taken outside the city to execute him, keeping the unclean a safe distance from the holy confines of a sacred people.[43] Now, the dead are invading the holy city during a holy season. One wonders if the people heard echoes of the prophecy of Jeremiah

34. Garland, *Reading Matthew*, 264.

35. The verb is passive (Luz, *Matthew*, 3:566).

36. Davies and Allison, *Matthew*, 3:629.

37. Keener, *Matthew*, 686; Talbert, *Matthew*, 305–6; Brown, *Death of the Messiah*, 2:1101.

38. Nolland, *Matthew*, 1212–14.

39. Since the temple was a symbolic representation of all creation, Daniel Gurtner suggests that the torn veil (= firmament) pictures heaven split open—an eschatological sign of the presence of God on earth (*The Torn Veil: Matthew's Exposition of the Death of Jesus*, SNTSMS 139 [Cambridge: Cambridge University Press, 2007], 200–201).

40. Nolland, *Matthew*, 1213.

41. Though perhaps not king David, for Peter claimed "his tomb is with us to this day" (Acts 2:29).

42. According to Talbert (quoting Schnackenburg), the story of the zombies "is to be understood only as a theological concept portrayed as an event" (*Matthew*, 307).

43. Brown, *Death of the Messiah*, 2:912.

(Jer 19:10–13) or Ezekiel (Ezek 37:11–14)?[44] Was this a sign of judgment or hope? According to the centurion and the Roman soldiers who crucified Jesus, it was both. They were not only terrified by these cosmic signs but were also inspired to draw a shocking inference: this Jewish man they crucified was surely "the Son of God" (Matt 27:54).

All this makes Pilate's response to the request of the chief priests even more ironic: "Take a guard. . . . Go, make the tomb as *secure as you know how*" (v. 65, emphasis added).[45] If this God—the one who tore out of the temple, stomped around Jerusalem, and busted open the tombs of the righteous—wanted his Son (v. 43), then no Roman guard or sealed tomb with a "big stone in front of the entrance" (v. 60) would be able to stop him (v. 66). The way Matthew sees it, God is a grave robber, and his greatest heist is yet to come. Not even death can stop him. So, making things "as secure as you know how" won't matter in the end.

LIVE the Story

In the parable of the sheep and the goats (Matt 25:31–46), when Jesus compared himself to a king who would become a pauper, the sheep are incredulous to the whole idea. How could such a horrible thing happen to him? Now we see why it wasn't so far-fetched: the greatest did in fact become the "least of these." Jesus came to the table hungry, but the only bread offered would be his own body. He went to the cross thirsty, but he refused to drink the wine. He was run out of town like a stranger. Jerusalem did not take him in. Naked and exposed, no one was there to clothe him except the soldiers who made sport of him. When he was about to die, only mockers visited him. Guarded by Roman soldiers like a prisoner, Jesus was interred in a tomb by a stranger. Only a few women disciples were there with him in the end, keeping company by the tomb. It was the pitiful end to a magnificent life. Who would have thought it would come to this? A mighty king who single-handedly brought the kingdom of heaven to earth is dead. For a brief moment in time as he walked the earth and reclaimed the glory of God's creation, evil lost its grip. But then every enemy of God (seen and unseen) came roaring back with all of their pent-up vengeance against this beautiful man, the beloved Son of

---

44. Perhaps it was even reminiscent of the time corpses were strewn all over the temple during Passover by the Samaritans; see Josephus, *Ant.* 18.2.2.

45. Another translation is possible: "You have a guard. Go and secure the tomb as you know how," indicating that Pilate refused their request since they had the Jewish guards of the temple police. Yet Matthew refers later to these guards as *stratiōtai* (Matt 28:12), a term used for Roman soldiers (Matt 27:27); see Davies and Allison, *Matthew*, 3:655.

God, the prophesied Son of David, the king of Israel. By the time they were finished with him, after all the physical and emotional abuse, the ugliest side of humanity—our sin!—was clearly revealed for all to see. This is what we do to love. This is how we treat mercy. This is why we need a Savior.

When it's all said and done, Jesus shows us who we are and what we need. We are a messed-up, broken-down, easily deceived, quick-to-judge, spitefully motivated, self-consumed, desperately lost people who need to be saved—from our sin, from ourselves, from evil powers, from the vices of the world. Even though we might turn away in disgust, hoping to shield our eyes from the cruel violence, God forces us to see what we did to his Son. Indeed, his death on the cross not only reveals the ugly reality of our sin. The crucified one shows us all why evil is such a nefarious problem. We can't fix this on our own. We can't save one another from ourselves. We need help. We need hope. We need a merciful, quick-to-forgive, and slow-to-wrath God to save us. That's exactly why he sent his Son to endure this wicked death. The only way the God of Israel would defeat the worst enemies of humanity—evil, sin, and death—was to allow evil, sin, and death to be spent on the *one and only king* sent to redeem Israel and the whole world. Jesus saw it too, which explains why he endured the pain and humiliation of the cross. He knew the *only* way to bring the kingdom of heaven to earth, the *only* way to forgive our sins, and the *only* way to save his life was to lose it. The greatest had to become the least. The first will be last. The king must die. This is the way it had to be. Therefore, he drank the cup of suffering to the dregs (Matt 20:22). When he came into his kingdom, he was cursed by two thieves—one on his right and the other on his left (20:23; 27:38). When he was lifted up as the "king of the Jews," he was forsaken by God. He saved others, but he couldn't save himself. For "the Son of Man did not come to be served, but to serve, and to *give his life as a ransom for many*" (20:28, emphasis added). He knew that, so did the prophets, and now, so do we.

> Surely he took up our pain
> and bore our suffering,
> yet we considered him punished by God,
> stricken by him, and afflicted.
> But he was pierced for our transgressions,
> he was crushed for our iniquities;
> the punishment that brought us peace was on him,
> and by his wounds we are healed. (Isa 53:4–5)

But not everyone sees it. There are always mockers. For while we point to a crucified man and call him our king—because we have eyes to see the kingdom—they are quick to point out what is "clearly seen" by everyone. "This is the king of Israel? This is his crown? This is how he reigns over evil? This is how he makes the world a better place? Looks to me like the devil won this one. Even Jesus admitted he was forsaken by God." But we believe his death wasn't in vain. Strange things happened when he died, "acts of God" prove that his death mattered: earthquakes, ripped veil, violated graves. Nevertheless, scoffers will say there's nothing new here, reciting the catastrophic calamities that mar our earth. Like two crucified thieves suffering the same torturous fate, they join the chorus of mockers: "You think that's bad? What about the 'acts of God' like earthquakes that kill thousands of innocent people? Or consider how our sacred temples, the veils of our bodies, are ravaged by horrible diseases, ripped apart by cancer and neurological disorders. What about war? Mass graves hold the victims of evil regimes, tossed like rag dolls into a pit that is covered by dirt-pushing bulldozers. Where could you find a more desecrated grave than that?" Indeed, mockers like these have been around for a long time: "For they reasoned unsoundly, saying to themselves, 'Short and sorrowful is our life, and there is no remedy when a life comes to its end, and *no one has been known to return from Hades*'" (Wis 2:1 NRSV, emphasis added).

Of course, just as it happened to Jesus, we recognize that mockers can tell the truth. But they don't mean it. They think they're alerting us to things we've ignored, trying to rub our noses in the disappointment of "things are not the way they're supposed to be." But nothing could be further from the truth. We know it as well as anyone. The cross of Jesus proves it: evil, sin, and death will always raise their ugly, triumvirate head against the sacred work of God, marring all creation and trying to destroy his best work, temples that bear his image. So we are not surprised when we who pick up the cross and follow Jesus receive the same treatment. On cue, mockers appear and rail against the crucified ones: "They save others! They cannot even save themselves! Look at their pitiful state. They are hungry. They are lonely. They get sick and die. There is no justice for them or anyone else. They trust in God, and he abandons them! They praise God, and he forsakes them. Fine. Let this God rescue them if he wants them." Even as the mockers have their say, we know things may get dark. Heaven remains silent. God doesn't vindicate us in the presence of our enemies. This is what often happens. In response, some of us may even be inclined to join in Jesus's lament: "Our God, our God, why have you forsaken us?" But in the end, even though mockers wag their collective heads at the death of Jesus, railing against the folly of the cross in our lives, we still declare, "This is Jesus, our Savior and our king." Why? It's because only those who have eyes to see the king and his kingdom understand the irony.[46] Because Jesus died his God-forsaken death, God didn't forsake him in the end. Therefore, we believe he won't forsake us either. Death may guard our graves like a soldier holding post over a prison. But one day the grave robber will come for us too.

> Then Jesus said to his disciples, "Whoever wants to be my disciple must deny themselves and take up their cross and follow me. For whoever wants to save their life will lose it, but whoever loses their life for me will find it. What good will it be for someone to gain the whole world, yet forfeit their soul? Or what can anyone give in exchange for their soul? For the Son of Man is going to come in his Father's glory with his angels, and then he will reward each person according to what they have done." (Matt 16:24–27)

So, what are we to do in the meantime as we wait for the resurrection? I've often wondered why the Gospel writers didn't tell us what happened between "Good Friday" and "Resurrection Sunday." Jesus had promised his disciples that his cross would bring them Sabbath rest (11:28–30).[47] Did it? While they observed the Sabbath—the day between the two most significant events in human history—did they rest confidently in the promises of Jesus, anticipating the victory of Easter Sunday? Or did they hide away in fear and doubt, haunted by the cross, puzzling over why evil can ruin even the best of us? Matthew doesn't say.[48] But I wish he had given us a little peak into the happenings of that Sabbath, because I identify with the eleven disciples—stuck between a cross and resurrection—trying to find Sabbath rest. Like the eleven disciples, we are Saturday's children, looking back at the cross while looking forward to resurrection Sunday when our faith will become sight. That's what happened for the eleven—their faith did become sight the day after the Sabbath. They got to see what resurrection looks like, what a cross conquering evil feels like, what death swallowed up by victory sounds like. Following Jesus after Resurrection Sunday must have turned the cross into a Sabbath's rest, knowing that God can turn the most atrocious event of all time into the greatest hope of all humanity. Looking back must have helped them look forward, their faith having become sight. But not for us. We haven't seen the resurrected Lord. We don't know what death swallowed up by life looks like. Rather, all we have are words—promises of a cross bringing rest and a resurrection hope conquering death in the end. Indeed, in more ways

46. Luz, *Matthew*, 3:540.

47. See the discussion above, 232–33.

48. But does John? He says that the disciples were holed up in Jerusalem on Sunday night, "with the doors locked for fear of the Jewish leaders" (20:19)—probably the same thing they did during the Sabbath.

than one we are children of the Sabbath, trying to find rest in a cross between "Good Friday" and "Resurrection Sunday."

Some days I find rest. Other days not so much. Which is why I've always appreciated the Pauline notion that our faith is a fight, a struggle to believe. For even though I know "our struggle is not against flesh and blood . . . but against the powers of this dark world and against the spiritual forces of evil in the heavenly realms" (Eph 6:12), sometimes the darkness of this world makes me struggle with my own flesh. When I pick up the cross of my doubt, that's when the mockers show up on cue, heckling me for the weakness of my faith. That's when it gets bad. The sky grows dark. The earth shifts beneath my feet. The heavens remain silent. Indeed, when evil overwhelms me—when it looks like our enemy is winning, when death hangs over my head like a Roman verdict, when I cry out, "My God, my God, why have your forsaken me?"—I remember him. The one who, "for the joy set before him . . . endured the cross, scorning its shame, and sat down at the right hand of God" (Heb 12:2) and promised us a Sabbath's rest. Since I claim to follow him, all the way to the end, I will fix my eyes on Jesus, "the pioneer and perfecter of faith." He started it back then; he will finish it in the end: "Resurrection Sunday."

Amen. Come, Lord Jesus.

So I wrestle with you,
   swing my fists just like Jacob
   at angel or demon
   until both my hands are broken.
God, my Father,
   you found me like Adam,
   so cursed and useless,
   crying out from these ashes.
Don't leave me here—
   take my bones in your mercy
   and create something beautiful
   or just crush me back into this
   dirt that I came from,
   the clay you used to make me.
I wait for you now.
   There's nothing left for you
   to take from me at all.[49]

49. Andrew Reeves, from "Lay Me Down," unpublished, used by permission.

CHAPTER 40

Matthew 28:1–20

LISTEN to the Story

[1]After the Sabbath, at dawn on the first day of the week, Mary Magdalene and the other Mary went to look at the tomb.

[2]There was a violent earthquake, for an angel of the Lord came down from heaven and, going to the tomb, rolled back the stone and sat on it. [3]His appearance was like lightning, and his clothes were white as snow. [4]The guards were so afraid of him that they shook and became like dead men.

[5]The angel said to the women, “Do not be afraid, for I know that you are looking for Jesus, who was crucified. [6]He is not here; he has risen, just as he said. Come and see the place where he lay. [7]Then go quickly and tell his disciples: ‘He has risen from the dead and is going ahead of you into Galilee. There you will see him.’ Now I have told you.”

[8]So the women hurried away from the tomb, afraid yet filled with joy, and ran to tell his disciples. [9]Suddenly Jesus met them. “Greetings,” he said. They came to him, clasped his feet and worshiped him. [10]Then Jesus said to them, “Do not be afraid. Go and tell my brothers to go to Galilee; there they will see me.”

[11]While the women were on their way, some of the guards went into the city and reported to the chief priests everything that had happened. [12]When the chief priests had met with the elders and devised a plan, they gave the soldiers a large sum of money, [13]telling them, “You are to say, ‘His disciples came during the night and stole him away while we were asleep.’ [14]If this report gets to the governor, we will satisfy him and keep you out of trouble.” [15]So the soldiers took the money and did as they were instructed. And this story has been widely circulated among the Jews to this very day.

[16]Then the eleven disciples went to Galilee, to the mountain where Jesus had told them to go. [17]When they saw him, they worshiped him; but some doubted. [18]Then Jesus came to them and said, “All authority

in heaven and on earth has been given to me. [19]Therefore go and make disciples of all nations, baptizing them in the name of the Father and of the Son and of the Holy Spirit, [20]and teaching them to obey everything I have commanded you. And surely I am with you always, to the very end of the age."

Listening to the Text in the Story: Genesis 12:1–3; 17:1–7; Isaiah 54:1–6; Daniel 7:9, 13–14; 10:4–9; Haggai 1:13.

Death, be not proud, though some have called thee
Mighty and dreadful, for thou art not so;
For those whom thou think'st thou dost overthrow
Die not, poor Death, nor yet canst thou kill me.
From rest and sleep, which but thy pictures be,
Much pleasure; then from thee much more must flow,
And soonest our best men with thee do go,
Rest of their bones, and soul's delivery.
Thou art slave to fate, chance, kings, and desperate men,
And dost with poison, war, and sickness dwell,
And poppy or charms can make us sleep as well
And better than thy stroke; why swell'st thou then?
One short sleep past, we wake eternally
And death shall be no more; Death, thou shalt die.[1]

Even though Jesus told his disciples three times this would happen (Matt 16:21; 17:23; 20:19), nearly everyone was surprised by his resurrection. Moreover, even though three of his disciples got a sneak peak of a glorified Messiah on a mountain (17:1–8), some of the disciples doubted when they saw him on a mountain on another occasion (28:17). It's rather surprising how surprised they were. We should expect someone within the group to have remembered what he said: "Hey, isn't this Sunday morning? Didn't he say, 'After three days I will rise again'? Today would be the day, wouldn't it? Let's go to the tomb and see if it's true." But that didn't happen. Although two women disciples went to the tomb early Sunday morning (28:1), it wasn't out of curiosity. According to other Gospel writers, the women returned to Jesus's tomb to finish the job of interring his body for the grave (Mark 16:1;

1. John Donne, "Holy Sonnets: Death, be not proud," poetryfoundation.org, https://www.poetryfoundation.org/poems-and-poets/poems/detail/44107.

Luke 24:1). But Matthew leaves it to the reader to infer the reason for their visit. Perhaps they returned to his tomb to grieve over his death—a common practice among the Jewish people, who would return several times to the grave during their weeklong mourning. Whatever their motivation—since they followed him to the end (Matt 27:61), where else would they go?—these two women seem just as surprised as anyone by what happened that day, arriving just after an angel had "rolled back the stone and sat on it" (28:2). Ironically, the *only* people who weren't surprised by these things were Jesus's enemies, which included the chief priests who *denied* the resurrection (22:23). They remembered his prediction that he would rise from the dead (27:63). Even more astonishing, the *only* people who actually "witnessed" what happened at the tomb were Roman soldiers sent there to guard a dead man. But these tough guys were so shook up by what they saw and heard that they became like the dead man they were guarding (28:4)[2]—becoming unlikely witnesses to the very people who believed this sort of thing couldn't happen (v. 11). So this day, the first day of the week, the beginning of a new age, was a day filled with surprises for *everyone.*

But then again, maybe we should be surprised too. Even though we've heard this story many, many times, we are also fully aware of this one, undeniable reality: death is permanent. Dead people don't come back from the grave. We may read in Matthew's Gospel about an earthquake that broke open a few tombs, with zombies walking around Jerusalem (27:52–53). But today that sounds more like the plotline of the television series *The Walking Dead.* We are more likely to recognize this stuff as "make believe," horror stories meant to *entertain*—not to inspire faith. Indeed, to our way of thinking, fear belongs to the movies, not religion. It is welcomed as a good friend in the world of entertainment but scorned as a villain in the house of faith. Therefore, when we read these fantastic stories of soldiers dropping dead from fear, corpses walking out of their tombs, violent earthquakes, an angel's dazzling appearance, women greeted by a once-crucified-but-now-very-much-alive Jesus, we can see why the chief priests and elders would conspire with the guards to offer a "reasonable" explanation for these strange happenings (28:11–15).[3] This sort of thing doesn't happen today except in the movies.

But then again, the story concocted by the chief priests wasn't a "reasonable explanation" of what happened, intended to assuage the fears of these ignorant men. Rather, it was a conspiracy to cover up their inability to keep

---

2. Davies and Allison, *Matthew,* 3:666; France, *Matthew,* 1100.

3. Ironically, the chief priests ended up getting their sign from heaven (Matt 16:1, 4), but dismissed it; see Luz, *Matthew,* 3:610.

Jesus's prediction from coming true.[4] The chief priests and elders weren't surprised by what the guards told them; they knew something like this might happen but were unable to stop it (27:63–64)—did the cracked-open tombs give them a clue? Therefore, the only thing left for them to do was damage control. The story they once tried to prevent they will now invent: by their own authority (and with a "large sum of money" to buy their disciples), they "devised a plan" and launched their own mission to preach another version of the gospel story—one that persisted among the Jews even in Matthew's day (Matthew 28:12–15). But such an effort paled in comparison to Jesus's kingdom work:[5] his disciples would be sent to "all nations" with a mission—unaided by bribery—that would last to the end of the world because "all authority in heaven and on earth" had been given to him (vv. 18–20). His enemies had a plan. Jesus had a resurrected body. The difference is both expected (this is what Jesus's enemies always did) and completely surprising (even though Jesus said it would be this way). They had Jesus crucified, but God raised him from the dead—something only God could do. Therefore, Jesus would be with his disciples to the end of the world because no enemy could stop him now—not even death. For Matthew, then, there's nothing left to say: the end of the gospel story pronounces the end of the world because Jesus is Immanuel.[6]

EXPLAIN the Story

Matthew's marvelous account of the resurrection of Jesus is remarkable for its brevity,[7] especially when compared to the Gospels of Luke and John. In fact, there are many details from their stories that we might be tempted to import, given all the gaps in Matthew's version. For example, Matthew doesn't tell us why the women visited the tomb (Matt 28:1; Luke 24:1), or why it was necessary for an angel to roll away the stone door (Matt 28:2; Mark 16:3), or why Jesus needed to make an appearance to repeat instructions the angel had already given to the women (Matt 28:7–10; John 20:11–18). Furthermore, there are other parts of Matthew's version that are left to the imagination of the reader. For example, without knowing how Jesus moved from one place to the next, one might get the impression that Jesus walked to Galilee to meet his

4. "Having failed to prevent the resurrection, they are reduced to trying to render it unbelievable" (Davies and Allison, *Matthew*, 3:671).

5. France writes: "The women have a message of hope and victory for the disciples, the guards one of confusion and failure for the priests" (*Matthew*, 1104).

6. "He [Jesus] has experienced the end of history" (Davies and Allison, *Matthew*, 3:667).

7. Luz, *Matthew*, 3:596.

disciples there (Matt 28:10, 16–17). (According to the other Gospel writers, the resurrected Jesus mysteriously appeared and disappeared inside houses as if he could walk through walls even though he had a physical body; see Luke 24:28–31; John 20:19–29.) That's why he told the women, "Go and tell my brothers to go to Galilee; there they will see me"—he needed a head start (Matt 28:10).[8] Yet if that was the case, why didn't he go directly to the eleven disciples and walk with them to Galilee (like he did on the road to Emmaus; Luke 24:13–35)? It's because in Matthew's Gospel, Jesus didn't go to his disciples (as in Luke and John). Rather, they were supposed to come to him, to the "mountain where Jesus had told them to go" (Matt 28:16).[9]

But when did he tell them that? And what mountain was it? The place where he delivered the Sermon on the Mount?[10] Or was it the Mount of Transfiguration?[11] Furthermore, once the disciples got there, notice how Matthew doesn't end his Gospel with the ascension of Christ. That certainly would have been a mixed message. Imagine their confusion: as Jesus is carried into the heavens he shouts down to them, "I will never leave you!"—a puzzling situation that Luke felt obliged to explain (Acts 1:9–11). So, if all we had was Matthew's Gospel, one wonders how we would interpret Jesus's promise, "Surely I am with you always" (Matt 28:20). Even though we might think Jesus was referring to the Holy Spirit (as in Luke 24:49 or John 20:22), Matthew doesn't say that.[12] So, given the way Matthew ends his Gospel, what did Jesus mean when he said that he would always be with his disciples? Would some readers infer that since Jesus never "left" the eleven, he must have remained there on the mountain? Then Jesus would truly be "Immanuel" (God with us).[13] Perhaps they would even be inspired to make the pilgrimage to the same place (a carefully guarded secret) to "be with Jesus." Indeed, this is the time Peter should have said, "Lord, it is good for us to be here. If you wish, I will put up" a shelter for you (Matt 17:4).[14]

---

8. Bruner, *Matthew*, 2:787, 793. Jesus called them brothers because "their unfaithfulness has not abolished his faithfulness" (Luz, *Matthew*, 3:607).

9. "'Come to Galilee' is Jesus's call to the walk of discipleship" (Bruner, *Matthew*, 2:799).

10. Bruner, *Matthew*, 2:807; Evans, *Matthew*, 482.

11. See the suggestion by Luz, *Matthew*, 3:622.

12. So also Garland, *Reading Matthew*, 271.

13. According to Terrence L. Donaldson, *Jesus on the Mountain: A Study in Matthean Theology*, JSNTSup 8 (Sheffield: JSOT Press, 1985), Jesus summoning his disciples to the mountain is the eschatological fulfillment/replacement of Mt. Zion as the end-time centripetal force that gathers all the nations to God (Isa 56:3–8).

14. "Theophanic presence requires sacred space for God's people to remain his" (David D. Kupp, *Matthew's Emmanuel: Divine Presence and God's People in the First Gospel*, SNTSMS 90 [Cambridge: Cambridge University Press, 1996], 217). Kupp hears echoes of Sinai, where Jesus (the new Moses) summons his disciples to the mountain for them to become the new tabernacle of God's presence, having gathered in his name (ibid., 203–19).

Of course, we find such a scenario to be ridiculous for a variety of reasons but most of all because we fill in the blanks of Matthew's Gospel with information we gained from the other Gospels. But I'd like for us to read Matthew's account of the resurrection of Jesus with blinkers blocking from our view information we might want to import from Mark, Luke, or John. Then we might be able to appreciate Matthew's message and why he decided to tell the most important part of the gospel story like this.

"Come and See"

When the angel said to the women, "Come and see" (Matt 28:6), we might expect the object of interest to be the resurrected Jesus. After all, the fact that Jesus conquered death is the most important part of the story. Plus, who wouldn't be curious about what a resurrected body looks like, feels like, sounds like? So it would make more sense to me if Jesus had appeared outside the tomb (or even better, walked out of the tomb having knocked over the stone door with his superhuman power) and presented his resurrected self to all people. Imagine how fantastic that would have been! After the women see him, they would spread the news, "Come and see Jesus! He's alive! God raised him from the dead just like he said he would!" His disciples would run to the tomb and find Jesus standing there in all his resurrection glory. He would say, "Touch me and see. I'm real!" Then the disciples would bow down to him and worship him in complete surrender. Jesus would then come to each one and put his hand on their shoulder, helping them to their feet, and then he would forgive them for abandoning him—especially Peter. After spending some time talking—perhaps even gathered around a fire to eat—one of the disciples might say, "I'd love to see the look on Pilate's face if he saw you now, Jesus." Then another pipes in, "Oh, even better. What do you say we go pay Caiaphas a visit? He'd probably keel over like a dead man if you walked right up to him in the temple! You might even say, 'Hey. What happened to the curtain?'" at which point the disciples would burst into uncontrolled, giddy laughter. Then, after everyone quiets down, a more sensitive soul (perhaps John?) might say, "I think the first person he needs to see again is his mother. Mary would love to see you, Lord. When you died, it broke her heart. Should we go to her?"

That's the story I would like to read, filled with spectacular details, astonishment, hilarity, reverence, and a much deserved "I told you so." With so many witnesses—both friends and enemies—the resurrection would be an incontrovertible fact, a huge exclamation mark planted in the middle of history. Or, even better, what if Jesus had remained on the mountain? Then all doubters and naysayers would receive the same invitation to "come and see" and could be led to the sacred place where the glory of Jesus's reign would be undeniably present. But that's not what the angel said to the women. Instead, the women were invited to see the empty tomb: "Come and see the place where he lay" (v. 6). Furthermore, the resurrected Jesus doesn't show up much in Matthew's account, making only two brief appearances: first to the two women (vv. 8–10) and then to the eleven disciples (vv. 16–20). That's it. Come to think of it, the resurrected Jesus doesn't do much either, and he says only a few words. But for Matthew, that should be enough. In fact, telling the story of an angelic visitor sitting on the opened stone door, inviting the women to come and see the empty tomb, was more than enough to frame what is arguably the most important verse in the entire Gospel: "He is not here; he has risen, just as he said. Come and see the place where he lay" (v. 6).[15]

But there's more to the story than an empty tomb, more to see than an angel. For when the two women "hurried away from the tomb" to deliver the second part of the angel's message to the disciples (v. 8), for some reason the resurrected Jesus appeared to them and repeated his instructions (vv. 9–10). Curiously, when he met them, all he said was, "Greetings" (*chairete*)—the Hellenistic version of our casual "hello." Of course, Jesus probably spoke to them in Aramaic and thereby used the typical Jewish greeting, "shalom" (peace), which would have more theological significance. His resurrected body embodies our peace. Yet the fact that Matthew used the standard Hellenistic greeting conveys purposely the somewhat casual tone of the encounter. Jesus didn't talk like an angel, offering at first the standard, "Do not be afraid" (v. 5). He didn't try to identify himself ("Take courage! It is I"; cf. 14:27) or explain what had happened (17:9–13). He simply said, "Hello," and the women immediately recognized him, fell down before him, wrapped their arms around his feet, and worshiped him.[16] They didn't say anything, didn't ask any questions, and didn't even break out in jubilant praise or sob tears of joyful relief. They simply held on to him, faces to the ground, arms wrapped around his ankles. In the silence of their brief embrace, the beauty of this worshipful moment speaks volumes—something we all long to do. For one day, after God empties our graves when he raises us from the dead, we will see Jesus. When that happens, there won't be much to say at first. Instead, we'll probably want to do the same as these faithful women: fall on our faces, wrap our arms around his blessed feet, and worship him, knowing that our ultimate enemy, death, has been defeated forever. On that day, the last day, we will hear the invitation, "Come and see."

When the eleven disciples were told to "come and see," they knew they were going to see Jesus and not an empty tomb. Unlike the two women who

15. Bruner writes: "So much depends on the truthfulness of this one word. Yet there is no way Christians can prove it" (*Matthew*, 2:789).

16. "Grasping of feet indicates that Jesus is not a spirit" (Davies and Allison, *Matthew*, 3:669).

were surprised by a visit from Jesus, the disciples were told they would see him on a mountain in Galilee (28:10, 16), returning to the region where they first met and followed him.[17] It is noteworthy that even though they worshiped him as soon as they saw him, their response to their resurrected Lord was different from the women. Matthew says that "some doubted" (v. 17), which provokes all kinds of questions. First of all, the Greek text is somewhat ambiguous (*hoi de edistasan*), a phrase that could be translated several ways: 1) "and they doubted" (meaning all eleven doubted); 2) "but others doubted" (meaning other people were there; the eleven disciples didn't doubt); or 3) as our translation has it, "but some doubted" (meaning some of the eleven doubted).[18] Second, the word "doubted" (from *distazō*) can mean to "waiver" or "have doubts" about oneself or others, and it can refer to someone who is hesitant about taking a certain course of action.[19] Third, Matthew doesn't explain what the doubters doubted. Did they question their eyes? ("Is this really Jesus?") Did they question their purpose? ("What does he want with us?") Did they question everything? ("What's going on here?") Finally, why didn't Jesus do something about their doubt? This is where we might expect a story about Jesus inviting his disciples to "put your finger here; see my hands," like he did for doubting Thomas (John 20:27).[20] Isn't that telling? We've hung the moniker "doubting" on one disciple but not the rest of them (or at least only *some* of them). Indeed, if Matthew had named names, we might refer to several disciples as doubters: "doubting Simon" or "doubting John" or even (dare I say?) "doubting Matthew." (Ah, maybe now we know why our writer didn't identify the doubters.)

Yet, in certain respects I don't blame them for doubting. Unlike the two women, the eleven disciples had plenty of time to think about what they heard before they saw with their own eyes the resurrected Jesus. It was at least a two-day journey (if the eleven hurried) from Jerusalem to Galilee. The women had obviously reported to them what both the angel and Jesus had told them; that's why the eleven were headed for some mountain in the north country. They had to wonder, "Why did Jesus appear to them and not to us? Are we in trouble for abandoning him? Why weren't we visited by an angel? Is it because the women went to the tomb and we didn't? Is that why Jesus is making us travel all the way to Galilee to see him?" Two to three days is plenty of time for doubts to have a life of their own. "Is he really alive? How could he come back

17. France, *Matthew*, 1107.

18. See the discussion in Davies and Allison, *Matthew*, 3:681–82.

19. BDAG 252. For further discussion, see Nolland, *Matthew*, 1262–63; Bruner, *Matthew*, 2:809–11.

20. Garland, *Reading Matthew*, 271.

from the dead? Did he really die? We weren't there in the end, so how would we know? Is this all a big hoax, the hysterical hopes of silly women? They said the angel told them, 'He is not here; he is risen.' We know the tomb is empty; rumor has it we stole the body. How ridiculous is that idea—a bunch of cowards overtaking Roman soldiers to take the corpse. So, what really happened? And what does it mean, 'He is risen'? What is resurrection?" Indeed, I think by the time they saw Jesus, the eleven had *many* questions buzzing around their heads and doubts about what actually happened. Several days of doubt were supposed to be dispelled by one moment of clarity? It was too much to take in all at once. Moreover, Jesus didn't take time to explain anything. All he said was, "All authority in heaven and on earth has been given to me" (Matt 28:18). Evidently, that's all they needed to know to fulfill the mission that would take the rest of their lives: to make disciples of all nations (v. 19).

"Go and Tell"

The two women were the first evangelists commissioned by Jesus to "go and tell" the good news (Matt 28:10).[21] Not the eleven disciples. Not Joseph of Arimathea. Rather, Jesus gave the good news *first* to the disciples who were the *last* ones to follow him all the way to the end (27:61; 28:1). That's fitting because he had promised, "The last will be first, and the first will be last" in his kingdom (20:16)—which also explains why the eleven were the "last" to see Jesus. They were the first to follow him. Of course, the only reason they were the last ones to see the resurrected Jesus was because the two women—the last ones to follow him—were faithful evangelists. The women did exactly as they were commanded: go and tell. That's why the eleven disciples gathered on the mountain to see Jesus, so that they could hear him give them the same charge. In fact, it could be said that without these two women, there would have been no Great Commission. We know the two women were faithful to the mission Jesus gave. What about the eleven?

It is interesting to me how quickly we assume the commission that Jesus gave to the eleven applies to us. We act as if we were there, standing among the eleven, pretending like Jesus was speaking to us too. Yet we don't do the same in other cases. For example, how many Christians take to heart Jesus's saying about becoming a eunuch for the kingdom (19:12)? Or notice how quickly we assume Jesus wasn't speaking to us, like the time when he told the rich young man to "sell your possessions and give to the poor, and you will have treasure in heaven. Then come, follow me" (19:21). Of course, we could argue that in both cases, Jesus was either addressing a particular situation or

21. Hardly a good choice according to first-century standards of credibility; see Keener, *Matthew*, 698–99.

an individual person. These teachings don't apply directly to all of us like the Great Commission. Yet we'll read the other "commission" Jesus gave to his disciples somewhat selectively too (10:1–42). We'll ignore the part about going only to the lost sheep of Israel (v. 6), but then read the rest of Jesus's instructions to the Twelve as if they apply to us—except the part about taking no money or provisions with us wherever we go (vv. 9–10). So why do we assume that when Jesus commissioned the eleven disciples to "make disciples of all nations" that every word applies to us as well?

We could think of several reasons, but one seems to be the most obvious: we believe we can fulfill the Great Commission because we have ears to hear and eyes to read Matthew's Gospel.[22] Even though we didn't follow Jesus like the eleven, we believe we are able to make disciples, "teaching them to obey everything" Jesus commanded (28:20), because Matthew wrote it all down for us. Therefore, we heard Jesus preach the Sermon on the Mount. We saw him heal the leper, the centurion's slave, and the paralytic. We watched as Jesus calmed the storm, cast out demons, and raised a dead girl. We are witnesses of how Matthew became a disciple, how Judas betrayed Jesus, and how the chief priests and elders handed Jesus over to the Roman governor. When we join the table of the Last Supper, we take his words to heart: "Take and eat; this is my body" (26:26). While the disciples slept, we heard him pray, "My Father, if it is possible, may this cup be taken from me" (26:39). We winced when the disciples betrayed him. We were ashamed when his enemies mocked him. We wept when the soldiers crucified him. Most of all, we marvel over the fact that God raised him from the dead. It's no wonder we act like Jesus was talking to us when he gave the Great Commission. We are witnesses of these things because the eleven disciples of Jesus *were faithful to our resurrected Lord*. When he said, "Make disciples of all the nations," we know they were obedient. We are living proof. We are disciples from all nations, reading the Gospel according to Matthew, ready to give what we received, disciples making disciples, knowing that what Jesus promised the eleven applies to us too: he will be with us "always, to the very end of the age" (28:20).

Therefore, it's easy to infer that the eleven disciples were faithful to the charge Jesus gave to them, just like the women before them. Mary and Mary "evangelized" them, and the eleven "evangelized" others, and so on and so on, until today. Because Jesus stood before them as the resurrected Messiah—the embodiment of all power "in heaven and on earth"—the disciples saw with their own eyes and heard with their own ears the reason their mission would

22. Luz writes: "With his understanding of missionary preaching the evangelist makes his book indispensable. One might speak of a 'self-canonization' *in nuce*" (*Matthew*, 3:634).

last till the "end of the age."[23] The irrepressible authority of his resurrection would empower the eleven to make disciples of all nations because the kingdom of heaven has come to earth, and not even death will stop them.[24] When these disciples make disciples of all peoples, then the reign of Christ is present. And when those disciples make other disciples, then the unstoppable kingdom of heaven will continue to extend all the way to the ends of the earth.

At this point, we might expect Matthew to speak of the Holy Spirit as the abiding power that would enable the eleven to fulfill their holy mission (Luke and John!). But that's not Matthew's emphasis. Rather, the way Matthew ends his Gospel, these eleven men would be able to make disciples of others because they knew everything Jesus commanded (v. 20). Therefore, the way disciples make disciples is to teach the baptized what Jesus taught. Consequently, when disciples disciple, Jesus is present—our Immanuel—"to the very end of the age" (v. 20).[25]

LIVE the Story

I grew up in church, hearing many sermons based on the Great Commission. Often the preacher would emphasize what sounded like the first of two commands, "*Go* and make disciples of all nations," imploring us to evangelize the whole world. Evangelism was about "winning people to Christ," and the primary challenge was to get the message out: go and tell. The problem, of course, was that we weren't "going" like we should. And if we weren't going, then we weren't telling the good news. And if we weren't telling the good news, then we weren't making disciples for Christ. Making disciples, then, was about getting people saved. And the only way people would get saved is if we obeyed Christ when he said, "Go!"

When I began to study Greek in college, I was surprised to learn that the first word of the Great Commission wasn't an imperative. Instead, Matthew used an aorist passive participle (*poreuthentes*, meaning "after going") to set up the *only* command Jesus gave the eleven in the Great Commission: make disciples (*mathēteusate*). More literally, then, the Great Commission should read: "Therefore, after you go, make disciples of all the nations." In other words,

23. A new day, the first day of the week, Sunday, marks a new history; see Davies and Allison, *Matthew*, 3:663.

24. France, *Matthew*, 1119.

25. So also Luz: "The evangelist does not need to have the Risen One who has appeared to the disciples disappear, because he remains there, in his word, in his commandments and in the experience of the presence of God among those who hear and do his word" (*Matthew*, 3:635; cf. France, *Matthew*, 1119).

Jesus didn't command his disciples to "go."[26] Rather, he commanded them to "make disciples of all nations," knowing they would go—from that place (they wouldn't stay on the mountain), from Galilee (they wouldn't be able to make disciples of *all* nations there)—from Israel to the whole world.[27] It was a radical departure from their previous mission. Before, they were instructed to "go" (the imperative *poreuesthe*) only to "the lost sheep of Israel" (10:6), which could have resulted in a worldwide mission due to the diaspora. Now, they are commanded to make disciples of all nations—not just of Israel but of all people.

It's a rather audacious mission to give to those who live in such a multi-religious, multicultural world—both theirs and ours. Some might say, "How dare Jesus command his followers to make disciples among people who already worship their god(s). What makes him so special? Why should he presume that his way is better than the way of other religions? Was he looking only for the malcontents, counting on his disciples to find those who were already dissatisfied, looking for another religion? Or was he claiming his way is the only way?"

Even though Jesus doesn't give (or even anticipate having to give) an answer to the scoffer at this point, we can say he built his worldwide mission on this singular claim: "*All* authority in heaven and on earth has been given to me" (28:18).[28] What is the proof of such a claim? His resurrection. Setting aside all the prophecies that Matthew has pointed out that Jesus fulfilled—how he is the Messiah that makes good on every promise God ever made to Israel[29]—one could infer that the reason Jesus believed his mission applied to all people is because he conquered the ultimate enemy of all humanity: death. Everyone dies. Furthermore, we recognize that death is always an intrusion because everyone wants to live. Sickness and suffering may pound the life out of us, perhaps even making some of us desire our own death to end the pain. Yet since we have eternity in our hearts—Woody Allen has famously said, "I don't want to achieve immortality through my work, I want to achieve it through not dying"[30]—we can't help but desire life after death. To a world sick

26. Donaldson, *Jesus on the Mountain*, 184–85. Yet Blomberg rightly cautions: "Too much and too little have often been made of this observation. Too much is made of it when the disciples' 'going' is overly subordinated, so that Jesus's charge is to proselytize merely where one is" (*Matthew*, 431).

27. So also Keener, *Matthew*, 718. Often Matthew uses the circumstantial participle as presumed within the imperative (2:8; 9:13; 11:4; 17:27; 28:7); see Davies and Allison, *Matthew*, 3:683–84; Blomberg, *Matthew*, 431.

28. Countering Satan, who claimed that he had authority over "all the kingdoms of the world" (4:8–9); see Davies and Allison, *Matthew*, 3:682. That the Great Commission is predicated upon two christological claims (all authority and always present), see Turner, *Matthew*, 687.

29. "The prophecy that in Abraham all the families of the earth will be blessed (Gen 12.3) comes to fulfillment in the mission of the church" (Davies and Allison, *Matthew*, 3:683).

30. Linda Sunshine, ed., *The Illustrated Woody Allen Reader* (New York: Alfred A. Knopf, 1993), 250.

of dying, Jesus sends his followers to make disciples of *all* people because "the end of Jesus is the end of the world in miniature."[31] "Death, thou shalt die."

This isn't about getting your ticket punched to live forever. No. Making a disciple involves far more than making a convert, "getting people saved." For if that were the case, then Matthew spent a lot of time giving many unnecessary details about what Jesus said and did. In fact, if the Great Commission was only a matter of "go and tell" the good news to unbelievers, if that's all it would take to "make disciples" of all nations, then the only gospel we would need is a simple explanation as to how someone "gets saved."[32] But that's not what Matthew did. Instead, he acted like we would need to know the Gospel according to Matthew 1:1–28:18 before we could obey the last two verses. Indeed, embedded in the Great Commission is the explanation as to how we are to "make disciples of all nations," contained in two explanatory participles: baptizing and teaching. Not just teaching for the sake of instruction but "teaching them to obey everything I have commanded you" (28:20). There it is again. The way of the kingdom, the way disciples are made, the way we follow Jesus is to obey him. We obey not only the instruction he gave in his sermons and parables but also *the way he taught us about "the way" of the kingdom by the way he lived as our king.* And since he is our king and we are his brothers and sisters (v. 10), to be a disciple is to follow Jesus in word and deed. That's what disciples are supposed to do, and that's how disciples make disciples. Ironically, when we do that, the way of the kingdom of heaven comes to earth. The reign of Christ our king—his resurrection power found in the cross—is evident on earth. Immanuel is present, here and now, with us always until the last day because disciples always need to be taught the way of the kingdom.[33] The gospel isn't just for unbelievers. Disciples need the gospel everyday too. Indeed, when disciples make disciples—something that never stops happening because we always need to be "discipled"—then Jesus is Immanuel until the end of the age, a story that began with a genealogy and ended in resurrection.

Surprise! The gospel is a story. The story of God. The story of Israel. The story of Jesus the Messiah, the Son of God. The story of twelve disciples. The story of faithful women disciples. The story of our lives.

I love the way Matthew tells the story. Makes me want to not only **Listen to the Story** and **Explain the Story** but also **Live the Story**—from the first verse to the last.

"Death be not proud." For "he has risen, just as he said."

---

31. Davies and Allison, *Matthew*, 3:673.

32. What McKnight pejoratively calls a "soterian gospel"; see Scot McKnight, *The King Jesus Gospel: The Original Good News Revisited* (Grand Rapids: Zondervan, 2011), 28–44.

33. So also Keener, *Matthew*, 720–21.

Scripture Index

Genesis

1:1–5:2. 40
1:2 73
1:3 331
1:26–31 372
1:29 136
2:2–3 239
2:4 . . . . .32, 42
2:7–25 372
3:1 338
3:4 338
4:3–16 116
4:3–24 110
4:8–10 449
4:9 379
4:10–11 527
4:15 358
4:24 358
5:1 . . . . .32, 42
6:5–7:23. 466
6:9 42
8:8–12 73
9:6 . . . . .110, 499
9:24–27 312
10:1 42
10:32 42
11:10 42
11:27 42
12:1–3 . . . . .40, 557
12:2 80
12:3 567
15:1–6 40
17:1–19 40
17:5–6 80
18:1–15 342
18:16–19:29. 223
19:1–29 210
22:13–14 85
25:12 42
25:19 42
25:21–34 53
25:23 54
26:12 . . . . .264, 269
26:34–27:41. 53
36:1 42
37:2 42
37:12–20 420
37:20 427
38:6–26 .40, 434, 441
40:18–22 277
48:16 358
49:8–12 421
49:9–12 40
49:10–11 405

Exodus

1:15–2:10. 53
3:1–14:31. 486
3:6 441
3:14 295
4:1–9 . . . . .250, 255
4:12 211
4:29–31 . . . . .250, 255
6:6–7 526
7:8–13 255
10:21–22 540
12:1–28 484
12:13 515
12:14–27 487
12:15–20 264
12:26 496
12:39 . . . . .466, 493
12:42 499
13:9 453
14:16 244
14:24–31 288
15:27–16:36. 136
16:1–17:7. 79
16:14–18 277

16:22–30 . . . 239
17:2 . . . 85
17:3 . . . 85
17:5–6 . . . 85
17:7 . . . 85
18:14–26 . . . 136
19:3–4 . . . 98
19:3–6 . . . 96
20:3 . . . 442
20:7 . . . 110
20:8–11 . . . 113, 239
20:12 . . . 172, 177, 305
20:12–16 . . . 301, 381
20:13–17 . . . 110
20:16 . . . 512, 515
21:14 . . . 485
21:17 . . . 305
21:23–25 . . . 110, 531
21:32 . . . 484
21:33–34 . . . 239
22:25–27 . . . 110
22:26–27 . . . 119
24:1–18 . . . 335
24:6–8 . . . 484
24:12–13 . . . 96
26:31–33 . . . 540
29:7 . . . 484
30:11–16 . . . 348
30:12 . . . 395
30:17–21 . . . 301, 303
31:13–17 . . . 239
32:1–33:4 . . . 79
32:15–35 . . . 348
33:12 . . . 231
34:21 . . . 239
34:27–28 . . . 79
34:28 . . . 82
34:29–35 . . . 335
35:2 . . . 239
35:3 . . . 240
38:26 . . . 348

Leviticus

4:1–5:19 . . . 186
5:1 . . . 512
5:14–6:7 . . . 56
10:1–2 . . . 185
11:1–15:33 . . . 162
11:7 . . . 136, 142
11:9–12 . . . 264
11:20–23 . . . 68
11:41–45 . . . 449, 453
12:1–5 . . . 70
12:1–8 . . . 163
13:1–14:32 . . . 161
13:45–46 . . . 163
14:2–32 . . . 165
14:3–32 . . . 163
15:1–12 . . . 163
15:11 . . . 301
15:16–18 . . . 163
15:16–33 . . . 70
15:19–27 . . . 200
15:19–31 . . . 198
15:33 . . . 199
17:1–26:46 . . . 136
17:10–14 . . . 494
18:1–23 . . . 376
18:1–30 . . . 110, 372
18:16 . . . 277, 282
18:20 . . . 185
18:29 . . . 185
19:2–34 . . . 110
19:9–10 . . . 239
19:12 . . . 114
19:13 . . . 381
19:17 . . . 358
19:18 . . . 114, 381, 434, 442
19:20–22 . . . 185
20:9 . . . 305
20:10–26 . . . 110
20:21 . . . 277, 282
21:1–4 . . . 163, 172
21:7 . . . 372
21:10 . . . 512, 517
21:11 . . . 179
21:11–12 . . . 172
21:20 . . . 372
22:4–16 . . . 301, 303
24:5–9 . . . 239, 242

24:10–16 . . . 512
24:14–16 . . . 540
24:17 . . . 526
24:17–23 . . . 110
24:19–20 . . . 114, 118, 531
24:21 . . . 526
25:1–43 . . . 381
25:8–55 . . . 385
25:39–55 . . . 358
26:14–33 . . . 185, 187
26:18 . . . 358
26:21 . . . 358
26:23–24 . . . 358
26:27–28 . . . 358
27:30 . . . 453

Numbers

1:2–3 . . . 283
3:1–13 . . . 421
5:19–22 . . . 115
6:2–12 . . . 115
6:6 . . . 179
12:6 . . . 526
14:6 . . . 512
14:26–35 . . . 80
15:32–36 . . . 239–240, 244
15:38–39 . . . 201
15:38–41 . . . 198, 449, 453
19:11–22 . . . 198
20:14–21 . . . 53
24:17–18a . . . 54
24:17–19 . . . 53
25:1–5 . . . 48
27:15–17 . . . 210
28:9–10 . . . 242
30:1–15 . . . 115
30:2–15 . . . 301, 304
30:2–16 . . . 110
35:16–34 . . . 110

Deuteronomy

5:1–28:68 . . . 150
5:14–15 . . . 242
5:16–20 . . . 381
5:17 . . . 114
5:18 . . . 114
6 . . . 84
6–8 . . . 82, 90
6:1–8:20 . . . 79
6:3–9 . . . 124
6:5 . . . 434, 442
6:8 . . . 449, 453
6:13 . . . 82
6:16 . . . 82, 85
7:12–14 . . . 381
8:1–3 . . . 80
8:3 . . . 82
9:7–25 . . . 79
11:13–21 . . . 124
11:14 . . . 271
11:18 . . . 453
11:26–28 . . . 96, 151
13:1–4 . . . 256
13:1–5 . . . 150, 153, 250, 323, 512, 515
13:2 . . . 442
13:5 . . . 251
13:10 . . . 251
15:1–11 . . . 381
15:7–11 . . . 110, 124
15:11 . . . 484, 489
16:3 . . . 493
18:15–19 . . . 96, 98, 405
18:15–22 . . . 150
18:18–19 . . . 335
18:20–22 . . . 515
18:21–22 . . . 153, 188
19:4–20:18 . . . 110
19:15–19 . . . 512, 515
19:15–21 . . . 358
19:21 . . . 531
21:1–9 . . . 301, 526
21:7 . . . 527
21:18–21 . . . 229
21:18–23 . . . 223
21:22–23 . . . 540
21:23 . . . 494
22:4 . . . 229
22:12 . . . 198, 449, 453
22:13–21 . . . 53, 57
22:13–23:2 . . . 372

22:21 . . . 57
22:23–27 . . . 53
23:1 . . . 377
23:18 . . . 526
23:21–23 . . . 301
23:24–25 . . . 239
24:1 . . . 53, 57, 114, 117
24:1–4 . . . 116, 372
24:1–18 . . . 110
24:12–13 . . . 119
24:15 . . . 381
25:5–10 . . . 434, 441
27:25 . . . 526, 531
28:1–14 . . . 381, 384
28:15–68 . . . 185, 187, 384
28:20–52 . . . 100
28:58–68 . . . 100
29:2–4 . . . 264
30:1–20 . . . 96, 100
30:2–10 . . . 161
30:3–5 . . . 466
30:11–31:2. . . . 150
30:15–20 . . . 385
30:19 . . . 150
32:5 . . . 348
32:20 . . . 348
32:45–47 . . . 484

Joshua

2:1–21 . . . 40
2:19 . . . 526
6:22–25 . . . 40
7:9 . . . 312
24:2–28 . . . 150

Judges

1:27–33 . . . 312
3:1–7 . . . 312
9:7–15 . . . 265
21:25 . . . 241

Ruth

1:22–4:22. . . . 40
2:2–3 . . . 239

1 Samuel

9:13 . . . 277
10:1 . . . 484
14:45 . . . 210
15:10–28 . . . 277
15:22 . . . 186, 410
15:28–29 . . . 420
16:1–13 . . . 40, 280
16:14–23 . . . 251
19:5 . . . 526
21:1–6 . . . 239, 242
30:21–25 . . .

2 Samuel

2:1–4 . . . 40, 280
5:1–5 . . . 40, 280
5:6–8 . . . 405, 411
7:1–16 . . . 40
7:4–16 . . . 323
7:11–16 . . . 335
7:12–13 . . . 395, 405
7:13 . . . 407
7:13–14 . . . 512, 516
8:11–14 . . . 53
8:13–14 . . . 54
10:1–19 . . . 420
11:2–12:25. . . . 40
12:1–4 . . . 265
12:1–5 . . . 136
12:1–14 . . . 264
12:7 . . . 265, 427
12:11–23 . . . 185
12:15–23 . . . 128
12:16–23 . . . 124
14:1–20 . . . 265
15:1–13 . . . 500
15:1–31 . . . 499
15:14–30 . . . 500
15:25–26 . . . 500
15:31 . . . 500
16:15 . . . 526
16:20–17:4. . . . 526
17:14–16 . . . 526
17:21–23 . . . 526
17:23 . . . 500
18:9–15 . . . 500

1 Kings

1:15–17 395
1:32–40 405–406
4:29–34 434
9:3 153
9:3–9 151
10:1 434
10:1–13 250
10:4–29 136
13:1–6 . . . . 239, 277
17:1 . . . . 66, 408
17:1–6 65
17:5 68
17:7–10 408
17:7–16 . . . . 277, 284
17:8–24 . . . . 312, 326
17:9–24 312
17:17–24 198
18:16–40 255
18:21 136
18:26–29 124
19:1–8 79
19:8 82
19:19–21 . . . . 79, 172, 179
20:29 256
22:7–38 277
22:17 210

2 Kings

1:3–10 65
1:8 65
2:9–15 277
4:1–7 . . . . 277, 358
4:42–44 . . . . 277, 284
5:1–27 161
6:17 499
8:12 59
9:1–13 406
9:3 484
9:12–13 405
10:6–8 277
14:9–10 265
19:35 499
24:10–25:26. 40

1 Chronicles

1:32 47
1:34 40
1:39 47
1:50 47
2:1–15 40
2:3 47
2:4 47
2:16 47
2:18–19 47
2:21 47
2:24 47
2:26 47
2:29 47
2:35 47
2:46 47
2:48 47
2:49 47
3:1–19 40
3:11–12 46

2 Chronicles

6:18–21 239
21:12–19 . . . . 185, 187
24:18–22 420
24:20–21 449
29:1–19 409
30:17–20 301
34:1–33 409
35:25 198
36:15–16 96

Ezra

9:1–10:17. 372
9:3 512
10:9–12 48

Nehemiah

5:1–12 358
5:13 210
9:5–10:39. 150
10:32–33 348
13:15–18 . . . .
241. . . . .
13:15–22 239
13:19 240

Esther

1:10–22 277
4:16–5:1 256

Job

1:1–5 381
1:6–12 . . . . 335, 338
1:6–2:10 79
1:20–22 128
2:1–13 . . . . 335, 338
2:8–13 128
3:8 176
9:4–12 288
9:8 290
14:7 224
16:4 435
16:10 435
17:6 435
26:10–12 172–173
26:11–12 288
28:12–28 223
30:10 . . . . 512, 517
31:1 110
33:14–18 526
38:8–11 173
38:16 . . . . 288, 290
38:17 323
41:1 176
41:25 176
42:10–17 381

Psalms

1 150
2 . . . . 65, 337
2:1–7 . . . . 72, 434
2:2 484
2:4–7 323
2:6–7 335
2:6–8 420
2:7 . . . . 73, 343
4:2–3 348
7:15 301
8:2 . . . . 223, 405, 412
18:2–36 150
19:7–14 110
22 . . . . 540, 546–547
22:1–24 484
22:7 435
22:8 547
22:15–18 547
22:19–20 547
22:22–31 547
22:24 547
22:25 547
22:27 547
22:31 547
24:3–6 96
24:4–5 100
26:4–6 185
26:6 526
27:12–14 512
32:1–7 124
34:7 358
34:14 100
35:12–14 124
37 136
37:7–11 96
37:11 100
37:12 512
37:22–34 96
37:37–40 96
39:5 136
40:6–8 499
41:7–9 484
42:5–11 499
45 55
46:1 85
47 55
49:7–9 . . . . 335, 395
51:1–13 124
51:1–18 301
51:10 307
55:1–5 499
62:11–12 335
65:5–8 172–173
65:7 288
69 547
69:1–3 . . . . 288, 296
69:9 . . . . 405, 408, 548
69:12 548

69:13–18 . . . 288, 548
69:16–17 . . . 547
69:16–19 . . . 124
69:16–21 . . . 540
69:19 . . . 548
69:20–21 . . . 548
69:21 . . . 548
69:22–28 . . . 548
77:13–20 . . . 288
78:1–8 . . . 264
78:2 . . . 274
80:8–16 . . . 420
84:11–12 . . . 136
89:8–9 . . . 288
89:9–10 . . . 172–173
89:35–51 . . . 335
91. . . . 79, 85–86
91:9 . . . 85
91:11–12 . . . 85
91:14 . . . 85
91:14–16 . . . 84
104:2–4 . . . 335
104:25–26 . . . 176
104:27–28 . . . 136
107. . . . 161
107:23–30 . . . 172–173
107:23–32 . . . 288
109:14–29 . . . 540
110:1 . . . 442
110:1–2 . . . 434, 512
113–118. . . . 495
118. . . . 406
118:22–23 . . . 427
118:22–26 . . . 405, 420
118:25–26 . . . 406
118:26 . . . 449
119. . . . 110
119:29–35 . . . 150
120:7 . . . 96
122:7–9 . . . 210
126:1–6 . . . 96
133:2 . . . 484
137:4 . . . 42
137:7 . . . 53–54
137:8–9 . . . 110
137:9 . . . 59
139:1–18 . . . 124–125
139:19–22 . . . 117
139:23–24 . . . 124, 125

Proverbs

1:20–22 . . . 231
1:20–33 . . . 172, 175, 223
1:26 . . . 231
1:28–29 . . . 231
1:30–33 . . . 231
2:1–5 . . . 264
3:5–8 . . . 136
3:13–18 . . . 264
3:27–28 . . . 110
8:1–21 . . . 223
8:32–36 . . . 223
10:18–21 . . . 250
11:17 . . . 96, 100
12:25 . . . 136
14:31 . . . 466
16:18 . . . 133
18:22 . . . 372
20:14 . . . 110
23:4–5 . . . 136

Ecclesiastes

4:12 . . . 358
5:2–7 . . . 301, 304

Song of Solomon

4:1–9 . . . 110

Isaiah

1:3 . . . 405–406
1:4–18 . . . 185
1:7–23 . . . 528
1:9 . . . 215
1:10–14 . . . 304
1:10–15 . . . 186
1:10–25 . . . 56
1:15 . . . 304
1:15–18 . . . 301
1:16 . . . 304
1:16–17 . . . 304, 529

1:21 . . . . 56, 529
1:21–23 . . . . 55, 304
1:23 529
1:24–25 529
2:2–4 323
3:13–15 55
5:1–4 427
5:1–7 . . . . 265, 301, 420
5:1–8 . . . . 381, 386, 389
5:5–7 427
5:7 528
5:8–30 . . . . 449, 451
6:5 230
6:8–13 264
6:9–10 269
6:13 . . . . 61, 224
7:10–15 53
7:14 529
7:14–25 55
8:7–15 55
8:8–10 53
8:14–15 420
9:1 89
9:1–7 . . . . 79, 96
9:2 89
9:6 529
9:6–7 53
10:20–23 215
10:22–23 . . . . 71, 168
11:1 . . . . 61, 529
11:1–2 224
11:1–5 53
11:6 369
13:6–13 466
13:10 476
13:16 59
14:13–15 223
19:18–25 . . . . 161, 166–167
22:21–24 323
22:22–24 329
22:25 330
23:1–18 . . . . 223, 312
25:4–9 161
25:6–9 . . . . 166, 484
26:16 124
26:19 . . . . 226, 434
26:20 124
27:1 176
27:2–13 420
27:12–13 466
28:15–19 323
29:13 . . . . 186, 301, 304
29:13–15 124
29:14 223
29:18 395
32:6–7 250
34:1–4 466
34:4 405
35:1–10 . . . . 223, 226
35:3–6 . . . . 198, 202
35:4–5 395
35:5–6 312
35:10 198
38:10 323
39:1–8 277
39:7 . . . . 372, 377
40:1–11 67
40:1–14 65
40:4–5 414
40:11 250
41:1–42:2. 177
42:1 . . . . 73, 343
42:1–2 198
42:1–4 . . . . 65, 239, 244, 335
42:1–7 . . . . 72, 223, 226
42:5–9 96
42:6 105
42:6–7 202
42:6–9 198
42:16 . . . . 198, 202
42:18–20 264
43:5–13 . . . . 161, 167
43:25 185
49:1–25 . . . . 161, 167
49:5–6 . . . . 210, 312
49:6 . . . . 172, 215
50:1 110
50:4–11 499
50:5–9 . . . . 512, 515
50:6 517

50:6–8 540
50:6–9 110
51:1–2 323
51:1–8 96
51:9–11 172
51:13–15 395
51:15 172
51:17–23 499
51:17–52:10. 395
52:3 499
52:13–15 529
52:13–53:12. . . . . 72, 335, 484
53:1–12 281
53:3–4 104
53:3–12 . . . . . 74, 398, 540
53:4 . . . . . 161, 166
53:4–5 552
53:4–8 526
53:5–6 166
53:5–8 . . . . . 512, 515
53:7–12 529
54:1–6 557
55:1–2 100
55:1–3 96
55:6–8 166
55:8–9 335
55:10–11 264
56:1–8 88
56:3–5 372
56:3–8 . . . . . 161, 313, 560
56:4–8 466
56:6–8 413
56:7 . . . . . 405, 410
57:3 250
58:2–12 124
58:3–7 185
58:7 466
60:1–4 96
60:1–7 . . . . . 53, 58
60:15–22 96
61. 101
61:1 . . . . . 100–101, 250
61:1–2 101
61:1–3 . . . . . 223, 226
61:1–11 96
61:2 100
62:4–5 185
62:11 405
63:10 59
63:11–12 59
64:1 67
65:17 381
66:1–2 239
66:15–24 466

Jeremiah

1:1 277
3:1–10 . . . . . 372, 376
3:6–8 110
3:14–15 210
6:16 223
7:1–15 153
7:3–4 428
7:3–15 55
7:8–15 466
7:9–10 410
7:9–11 405
7:11 410
7:14 153
8:13 . . . . . 405, 413
9:10–11 466
9:17–20 201
9:17–21 198
9:24 201
10:2 323
11:21–23 277
12:6 277
12:7 449
16:5 179
16:5–7 . . . . . 172, 179
16:7 494
16:10–15 60
17:9–10 124
19:1–5 . . . . . 408, 532
19:1–15 526
19:10–13 551
19:11–13 532
19:11–15 540
20:1–2 408
22:4–5 449

22:13–17 . . . 386
23:1–2 . . . 211
23:1–4 . . . 59
23:1–8 . . . 210, 312
23:3–6 . . . 210
23:5 . . . 60–61
23:7–12 . . . 60
23:9–15 . . . 153
23:16–21 . . . 153
23:22 . . . 153
24:1–10 . . . 405
25:15–18 . . . 395, 398
25:15–29 . . . 499
25:27–29 . . . 395, 398
26:8–11 . . . 408, 512
26:11 . . . 405
26:12–13 . . . 411
29:12–14 . . . 136
31:15–18 . . . 61
31:27–28 . . . 301
31:31–34 . . . 110, 323, 326, 484
32:6–9 . . . 526
33:15 . . . 61
49:7–22 . . . 53
49:12 . . . 395
50:6 . . . 210

Lamentations

1:12–14 . . . 540
1:21 . . . 540
2:15 . . . 540
4:1–2 . . . 526
4:20–22 . . . 53
5:4–5 . . . 223

Ezekiel

10:18 . . . 449, 456
12:1–6 . . . 264
13:9–17 . . . 150
16:49–50 . . . 210
17:22–23 . . . 264
20:33–44 . . . 79–80
21:26 . . . 449
22:23–29 . . . 150
23:1–49 . . . 250
24:15–24 . . . 172, 179
24:15–27 . . . 179
24:17 . . . 198, 494
26:2–28:24. . . . 223, 230, 312
31:2–14 . . . 264
32:3–10 . . . 466
33:1–5 . . . 526
34:1–10 . . . 211
34:1–16 . . . 312
34:1–24 . . . 210
34:1–31 . . . 466
34:11–16 . . . 210, 250
34:17 . . . 478
34:23–24 . . . 312
37:11–14 . . . 540, 551
37:24–28 . . . 210, 312
44:22 . . . 372

Daniel

6:16–17 . . . 540
7. . . . 477
7:9 . . . 557
7:9–10 . . . 499
7:9–14 . . . 335, 381, 466, 512
7:13 . . . 516
7:13–14 . . . 174, 185, 215, 557
7:14 . . . 215
7:22 . . . 381
9:25–27 . . . 466
9:26 . . . 484
9:27 . . . 470
10:4–9 . . . 557
10:13 . . . 87
11:31 . . . 471
11:31–35 . . . 466
12:1–3 . . . 434, 466
12:11 . . . 466, 471

Hosea

1:2–4:1. . . . 250
2:12 . . . 413
2:14 . . . 59
2:14–15 . . . 80
2:14–23 . . . 67, 79
2:21–23 . . . 96
2:23 . . . 168
5:3–4 . . . 250

6:1–6 . . . 185, 191
6:2 . . . 335
6:6 . . . 35, 239, 242
8:4 . . . 59
9:10 . . . 405, 413
9:16–17 . . . 405, 413
11:1–11 . . . 60
12:9 . . . 59
13:9–11 . . . 59
13:16 . . . 59

Joel

2:1–11 . . . 466
2:18–19 . . . 211
2:18–24 . . . 210
2:21–22 . . . 69
2:23 . . . 271
2:24 . . . 69, 211
2:25–27 . . . 69
2:25–32 . . . 65
2:28 . . . 69
2:30–3:2. . . . 466

Amos

4:1–3 . . . 100
4:4–5 . . . 449
4:4–13 . . . 187
5:2 . . . 198
5:14–24 . . . 55
5:16–17 . . . 198
5:18 . . . 449
5:21–24 . . . 528
5:21–27 . . . 185
6:1–7 . . . 449
8:8–9 . . . 540

Obadiah

1–7. . . . 53–54
10–13. . . . 54
10–18. . . . 53

Jonah

1:4–16 . . . 172, 176
1:4–17 . . . 256
1:12–3:10. . . . 250

Micah

1:3–5 . . . 414
6:6–8 . . . 185, 239, 528
6:8 . . . 55, 449
7:1–7 . . . 210
7:1–8 . . . 413

Zephaniah

1:2–6 . . . 264

Haggai

1:13 . . . 557
2:6–7 . . . 466
2:9 . . . 409

Zechariah

1:1 . . . 449
2:6–13 . . . 466
2:10–11 . . . 358
3:1–8 . . . 335
3:3–5 . . . 420
3:8 . . . 61
6:12 . . . 61, 516
6:12–13 . . . 512
7:11–14 . . . 264
9:9 . . . 405–406
9:11 . . . 484
9:14–17 . . . 466
10:2–3 . . . 210–211
11:10–13 . . . 484, 490
11:12–13 . . . 526
11:13 . . . 532
11:17 . . . 449
12:10–14 . . . 466
13:2–5 . . . 150
13:2–6 . . . 66, 517
13:4 . . . 421
13:7 . . . 501, 517
13:7–9 . . . 250, 335, 4998
14:1–9 . . . 466
14:3–9 . . . 540
14:4 . . . 405, 414
14:4–5 . . . 550

Malachi

1:2–3 151
1:2–5 53
1:6 449
1:6–14 309
1:8 186
1:11 161
1:12–14 186
2:1–9 186
2:7–9 449
2:11–12 372
2:16 372
3–4 225
3:1–4 . . . . 56, 186, 309, 409
3:1–5 . . . . 65, 223
3:1–6 405
3:3–4 409
4:1–3 405
4:1–6 . . . . 65, 223
4:5 66
4:5–6 . . . . 65, 323, 335

Matthew

1–10 229
1–11 229
1:1 . . . . 19, 31–32, 42, 50, 202, 314, 327, 500
1:1–17 39
1:1–4:16 33
1:1–28:18 568
1:6 47
1:8–9 46
1:11 47
1:11–17 40
1:16–18 327
1:17 28
1:18 . . . . 42–43, 56, 254
1:18–2:23 51
1:19 57
1:20 . . . . 56, 254
1:21 . . . . 35, 190, 486, 535
1:22–23 35
1:23 291
1:24 57
2:1–18 529
2:1–23 323
2:2 527
2:3 59
2:4 327
2:5 32
2:6 407
2:7 57
2:7–2:22 52
2:8 . . . . 57, 567
2:9–10 58
2:11 58
2:14 172
2:16 59
2:17 32
2:19–23 60
2:23 . . . . 32, 53, 60–61
3:1 . . . . 66, 374
3:1–17 64
3:2 67
3:2–6 187
3:3 . . . . 32, 66
3:5 67
3:5–6 424
3:7 71
3:7–10 424
3:8 68
3:9 . . . . 71, 168, 428
3:10 . . . . 67, 153, 224
3:11 . . . . 66, 72, 224, 254
3:12 . . . . 68, 211, 224
3:13 374
3:14 . . . . 72, 224
3:15 72
3:16–17 65
3:17 . . . . 73, 224, 343, 546
4:1 254
4:1–22 78
4:2 81
4:4 . . . . 82, 102
4:5–7 509
4:6 . . . . 85, 338
4:7 . . . . 82, 338
4:10 . . . . 82, 88
4:11 88
4:12 . . . . 88, 224
4:13–17 88

4:14–17 88
4:15 89
4:16 . . . . . 89, 97, 105
4:17 . . . . . 29, 33, 89, 191, 468
4:17–16:20 33
4:17–22 79
4:18–22 89
4:19 90
4:20 90
4:21 178
4:22 90
4:23 . . . . . 96, 102, 210
4:23–5:16 95
4:23–9:35 98
4:24 . . . . . 25, 187, 315
4:24–25 97
4:24–5:2 210
4:25 97
5–7 32
5–8 25
5:1 . . . . . 97, 102, 172
5:1–2 264
5:1–20 180
5:3 . . . . . 29, 102
5:3–6 102
5:3–7:27 98
5:4 102
5:5 102
5:6 101–102
5:7 . . . . . 101, 142, 368
5:7–10 102
5:8 . . . . . 101–102, 307
5:8–9 102
5:9 102
5:10 . . . . . 29, 98, 102
5:10–12 . . . . . 152, 217
5:11 102
5:11–12 103
5:12 104
5:13 104
5:13–16 96
5:14 105
5:15 105
5:16 125
5:17 112
5:17–18 443
5:17–19 112
5:17–20 72
5:17–48 109
5:18 112
5:20 . . . . . 98–99, 112, 152, 443, 449
5:21 114
5:21–22 113
5:21–30 306
5:21–32 114–115
5:22 115
5:22–26 131
5:23–24 . . . . . 24, 116, 186
5:25 116
5:26 116
5:27–28 113
5:27–48 20
5:28–30 50
5:29–30 . . . . . 117, 307
5:30–48 110
5:31 116
5:31–32 . . . . . 113, 373
5:32 117
5:33 . . . . . 114, 118
5:33–34 113
5:33–37 . . . . . 115, 520
5:33–48 114–115
5:34 . . . . . 115, 118
5:34–36 118
5:34–37 331
5:37 117–118
5:38–39 113
5:38–41 142
5:38–48 217
5:39 . . . . . 117, 145, 506
5:39–41 119
5:39–45 111
5:42 . . . . . 119, 142, 145
5:43–44 . . . . . 113, 119
5:44 . . . . . 34, 118
5:45 . . . . . 117, 119
5:46–47 . . . . . 111, 119
5:48 . . . . . 112, 118–119, 125
6 113
6:1 . . . . . 98, 125–126, 452

6:1–2 125
6:1–6 113
6:1–18 . . . . . 72, 123
6:2 125–127
6:2–5 452
6:3 127
6:3–4 128
6:4 125
6:5 126–127
6:6 . . . . . 125, 128
6:7 . . . . . 129, 142
6:7–15 129
6:8 129
6:8–9 367
6:9–13 129
6:12 . . . . . 130, 137
6:12–15 367
6:13 . . . . . 79, 503
6:14 142
6:14–15 . . . . . 116, 130, 137, 363
6:14–18 124
6:16 127
6:16–18 113
6:17–18 128
6:18 . . . . . 125, 141
6:19 . . . . . 137, 139
6:19–20 141
6:19–21 . . . . . 137–138, 386
6:19–24 138
6:19–34 . . . . . 139, 145
6:19–7:12. . . . . 135, 137
6:20 . . . . . 140–141, 274
6:21 . . . . . 141, 387
6:22 139
6:22–23 138–139
6:23 139
6:24 . . . . . 138, 140, 367
6:24–25 137
6:25 . . . . . 50, 139
6:25–26 . . . . . 130, 281
6:25–31 140
6:25–34 138–139,
175. . . . .
6:26 139
6:26–27 368
6:28 139
6:31–33 281
6:32 . . . . . 140, 142
6:33 . . . . . 98, 137, 140, 142
6:34 . . . . . 50, 130, 141
7:1 . . . . . 139, 142
7:1–2 . . . . . 138, 449
7:1–5 142
7:1–6 138
7:1–11 139
7:1–12 . . . . . 136, 141, 145
7:2 . . . . . 137, 142, 363
7:3–5 . . . . . 138–139, 143
7:6 . . . . . 138–139, 142–143, 515
7:6–7 137
7:7–8 145
7:7–11 138
7:9–11 145
7:11 . . . . . 137, 145
7:12 . . . . . 102, 114, 138, 145, 152, 368, 442
7:13 . . . . . 102, 177, 535
7:13–14 . . . . . 150, 397
7:13–27 99
7:13–8:1. 149
7:14 . . . . . 152–153, 177
7:15 150
7:15–20 153–154
7:15–23 154
7:16 153
7:16–18 153
7:19 153
7:20 153
7:21 154
7:21–22 154
7:21–23 . . . . . 132, 154
7:22–23 . . . . . 154, 385
7:23 154
7:24 . . . . . 30, 150, 155, 278
7:24–27 . . . . . 36, 155, 331
7:26 313
7:26–27 155
7:27 156
7:28 156
7:28–29 . . . . . 216, 264, 267, 359
7:29 156

8:1 . . . . . 150, 156
8:1–9:34. 98
8:2 164–165
8:2–17 160
8:2–9:34. 162
8:3 164
8:4 165
8:5 166
8:5–6 166
8:5–13 . . . . . 143, 165–166, 314–315, 366
8:7 166
8:8 167–168
8:9 166–167
8:10 . . . . . 167, 201, 316
8:10–17 72
8:11–12 . . . . . 167, 385
8:12 167–168
8:13 168
8:14 165
8:15 165
8:16 . . . . . 165–166, 172
8:17 166
8:18 172
8:18–22 172
8:18–34 171
8:19 174
8:20 . . . . . 173, 175
8:21 178
8:22 . . . . . 173, 178, 180
8:23–27 . . . . . 289, 292, 294
8:24 173
8:25 176–177
8:26 . . . . . 34, 173, 175, 289
8:27 . . . . . 176–177, 289, 292, 327, 358
8:28 172–173
8:28–34 . . . . . 173, 180, 313
8:29 180
8:30–33 180
8:32 174
8:34 . . . . . 174, 181, 313
9:1 . . . . . 165, 174, 181
9:1–2 189
9:1–17 184
9:2 . . . . . 188, 201
9:2–3 107
9:2–8 187
9:3 . . . . . 188, 192, 251, 327
9:5 188
9:6 188
9:6–7 188
9:7 202
9:8 . . . . . 188, 190, 216, 225, 359
9:9 . . . . . 19, 36, 190, 195, 264
9:9–13 190
9:10 192
9:10–11 . . . . . 36, 107, 190
9:10–13 366
9:11 241
9:11–13 437
9:12 190
9:13 . . . . . 35, 190–191, 193, 242, 366, 567
9:14 . . . . . 107, 191
9:14–11:30. 242
9:14–12:6. 36
9:15 . . . . . 187, 189, 191, 324, 338
9:16–17 191
9:18 198–199
9:18–26 . . . . . 199, 326
9:18–34 197
9:18–11:30. 172
9:20 200
9:21 200
9:22 201
9:23 201
9:23–26 338
9:25 202
9:26 . . . . . 202, 206
9:27 . . . . . 188, 314
9:27–31 314
9:28 203
9:28–29 201
9:29 207
9:29–31 252
9:30 203
9:31 . . . . . 203, 207
9:32–34 204
9:33 . . . . . 188, 204, 206, 216, 225, 359
9:34 . . . . . 187, 204, 216, 253, 327
9:35 98
9:35–11 208

9:36 . . . . . 210, 214, 219, 361
9:36–10:8 264
9:37 210
9:37–38 221
9:37–10:42 239
9:38 218
10 . . . . . 32, 214
10:1 . . . . . 218, 255, 315, 349–350
10:1–8 349
10:1–23 213
10:1–39 291
10:1–42 565
10:2–3 19
10:2–4 213
10:4 490
10:5–6 . . . . . 28, 166, 211, 213
10:5–8 315
10:5–23 213
10:6 . . . . . 27, 215, 361, 565
10:7 . . . . . 216, 218, 452
10:7–8 . . . . . 213, 216
10:8 . . . . . 193, 211, 218, 338, 350
10:9 567
10:9–10 . . . . . 213, 565
10:9–14 215
10:10 . . . . . 211, 506
10:11 211
10:11–13 215
10:11–31 361
10:12–13 218
10:12–15 213
10:14 211
10:14–15 215
10:15 385
10:16 . . . . . 215, 221
10:16–17 214
10:16–20 216
10:16–31 479
10:17–20 213
10:17–33 324
10:18 . . . . . 30, 212
10:18–19 221
10:18–38 209
10:19–20 211
10:20 . . . . . 255, 350
10:21–23 . . . . . 211, 216, 337
10:22 . . . . . 216, 221
10:23 . . . . . 211–213, 216
10:24–25 216
10:25 221
10:26–27 217
10:26–42 . . . . . 213–214, 217
10:28 . . . . . 211, 217
10:28–31 217
10:29 213
10:32 217
10:32–33 . . . . . 212, 514
10:34 217
10:34–36 221
10:34–37 216
10:34–39 . . . . . 211, 337
10:35–37 217
10:37 217
10:38 216–217
10:39 . . . . . 216, 217
10:39–11:1 210
10:40 216–217
10:40–41 104
10:40–42 . . . . . 30, 212, 217, 479
10:41 . . . . . 75, 218
10:41–42 212
10:42 218
10:56 20
11:2–3 327
11:2–30 222
11:3 . . . . . 225, 327
11:4 567
11:4–5 226
11:4–15 229
11:6 . . . . . 225–226, 470
11:7 227
11:7–9 228
11:7–14 226
11:7–19 . . . . . 226, 252
11:7–24 269
11:7–30 226
11:11–13 389
11:12 227
11:13 227
11:14 226

11:16 228
11:16–19 228
11:17 228
11:17–19 229
11:18 191
11:18–19 224
11:18–30 223
11:19 . . . . 228–229, 326–327
11:20–24 . . . 20, 216, 229–231, 255, 264, 351
11:21 . . . . 230, 315
11:21–24 252
11:23–24 . . . . 230, 385
11:25 . . . . 231, 269, 274
11:25–27 254
11:26 231
11:27 . . . . 231, 534
11:28 . . . . 232, 351
11:28–30 . . . . 175, 535, 554
11:29–30 . . . . 232, 351
11:30 . . . . 232, 240
12–27. 229
12–28. 229
12:1 . . . . 216, 239, 241
12:1–2 107
12:1–8 437
12:1–13 253
12:1–21 . . . . 72, 238
12:2 . . . . 188, 239, 241
12:3 239
12:3–4 242
12:3–8 . . . . 239, 241
12:4 242
12:5 . . . . 239, 242
12:6 . . . . 242–243, 245, 352, 407, 442
12:7 36
12:8 . . . . 243, 245, 442
12:9 243
12:10 . . . . 188, 243
12:10–14 188
12:11–13 251
12:12 244
12:13 251
12:14 . . . . 244, 250, 252, 374
12:15 244
12:15–21 73
12:16 244
12:18–21 . . . . 244, 254
12:20–21 239
12:21 245
12:22 252
12:22–24 187
12:22–50 249
12:23 . . . . 251, 359
12:23–24 327
12:24 . . . . 188, 216, 253, 374
12:24–25 437
12:25 253
12:25–26 253
12:25–29 188
12:27 253
12:28 . . . . 29, 180, 188, 254–255
12:29 . . . . 88, 254
12:30 257
12:31 254
12:31–32 254
12:32 521
12:33–35 255
12:34 259
12:36 . . . . 255, 260
12:37 . . . . 255, 259
12:38 255
12:38–50 250
12:39 . . . . 252, 255–256
12:39–40 324
12:40 256
12:40–45 255
12:41 255–256
12:41–42 . . . . 255, 442, 470
12:42 256
12:43–45 257
12:45 470
12:46 200
12:46–50 . . . . 179, 280
12:47–50 258
12:50 382
13. 32
13:1–13 306
13:1–15 268
13:1–46 254
13:1–52 261

13:3 265
13:3–8 268
13:3–9 269
13:4 272
13:5 156
13:6 271
13:8 269–270
13:9 265
13:10 . . . . . 264, 358, 435
13:11 . . . . . 264, 266
13:11–15 269
13:11–17 265
13:12 . . . . . 264, 278
13:14–15 . . . . . 264, 266
13:16–17 266
13:16–33 262
13:18–23 265–266
13:23 266
13:24 267
13:24–26 268
13:25–30 306
13:27 366
13:28 271
13:29 272
13:30 . . . . . 269, 272, 274
13:31 267–268
13:31–33 29
13:32 . . . . . 268–269, 272
13:33 . . . . . 267–269, 272
13:34–52 263
13:35 274
13:36 266
13:36–43 265
13:36–50 265
13:37–43 266
13:38 272
13:40–42 268
13:41 272
13:41–42 273
13:43 273
13:44 . . . . . 267–268, 272, 386
13:44–46 266
13:45 267
13:45–46 268
13:46 272
13:47 267–268
13:48–50 269
13:49–50 . . . . . 265, 274
13:51 266
13:51–52 273
13:52 . . . . . 266–268, 273
13:53–14:21 276
13:54 279
13:54–57 327
13:55–56 279
13:57 . . . . . 74, 217, 279–280, 286, 326
13:58 . . . . . 280, 350–351, 407
14:1–2 280
14:2 . . . . . 278, 326
14:3 281–282
14:3–5 374
14:5 281
14:6 281
14:6–11 281
14:9 271
14:12 281
14:13 . . . . . 279, 283
14:13–21 . . . . . 83, 317
14:14 283
14:15 . . . . . 282–283, 287, 317
14:15–21 277
14:16 . . . . . 282, 287
14:19 282–283
14:20 . . . . . 282, 287
14:21 283
14:22 . . . . . 282, 289, 291
14:22–23 173
14:22–33 . . . . . 177, 295, 301
14:22–36 288
14:23 . . . . . 282–283, 291
14:23–25 291
14:26 . . . . . 289, 292
14:27 . . . . . 289, 292, 562
14:28 293–294
14:28–31 175
14:29 293–294
14:30–31 295
14:31 295
14:32 296
14:32–34 289

14:33 . . . . . 289–292, 327
14:34–36 301
14:35 296
14:36 . . . . . 201, 296
15–21. 29
15:1 406
15:1–2 . . . . . 107, 188, 374
15:1–9 . . . . . 301, 436
15:1–12 437
15:1–20 . . . . . 72, 300
15:2 . . . . . 301, 303
15:3–6 305
15:3–9 177
15:5 453
15:6 . . . . . 305, 308
15:7–9 . . . . . 186, 304–305, 437
15:8 . . . . . 309, 316
15:9 308
15:10 305
15:11 305
15:12 . . . . . 301–302, 306–307, 358, 435
15:12–14 107
15:13 306
15:14 . . . . . 301, 305, 308, 454
15:15 306
15:16 . . . . . 306, 308
15:17–19 . . . . . 306, 326
15:20 . . . . . 301, 307
15:21–24 27
15:21–28 366
15:21–38 326
15:21–39 . . . . . 284, 311
15:22 314–315
15:23 . . . . . 312–313, 315
15:24 . . . . . 27, 312–313, 315
15:25 316
15:26 . . . . . 313, 315
15:27 316
15:28 . . . . . 201, 313, 316
15:29–31 312
15:29–38 83
15:29–39 317
15:30–31 318
15:32 . . . . . 284, 313, 317–318
15:32–38 313
15:33 . . . . . 312–313, 317, 358
15:37–39 312
16:1 . . . . . 256, 302, 312, 323, 558
16:1–4 . . . . . 324, 436
16:1–6 437
16:1–12 71
16:1–20 322
16:2–3 475
16:2–4 324
16:4 . . . . . 29, 475
16:5 325
16:5–12 325
16:6 325
16:7 325
16:8–11 325
16:13 324
16:14 . . . . . 326, 558
16:15 . . . . . 327, 337
16:16 . . . . . 36, 327, 337, 350
16:16–19 339
16:17 327
16:17–19 . . . . . 327, 349
16:17–20 323
16:18 . . . . . 327–328, 411, 430, 501, 521
16:18–19 327
16:19 . . . . . 328, 430, 501, 521
16:20 . . . . . 328, 339, 406
16:21 . . . . . 33, 302, 319, 325, 330, 333, 337–339, 345, 397, 430, 441, 484, 557
16:21–24 398
16:21–17:13. 334
16:21–28:20. 33
16:22 . . . . . 330, 338–339, 468, 501–502
16:23 339–340
16:23–36 339
16:24 . . . . . 340, 345, 377
16:24–25 . . . . . 36, 397, 535
16:24–26 345
16:24–27 . . . . . 512, 554
16:25 . . . . . 340, 510
16:26 . . . . . 88, 340
16:27 . . . . . 340, 397, 484
16:28 . . . . . 340–341, 359, 471, 501
16:28–17:1. 338
17:1–4 501

17:1–8 . . . 557
17:4 . . . 331, 343, 560
17:4–5 . . . 330
17:5 . . . 73, 342–343, 546
17:6 . . . 343
17:6–13 . . . 335
17:7 . . . 343
17:9 . . . 342
17:9–13 . . . 562
17:10 . . . 344
17:10–13 . . . 226
17:11 . . . 344
17:11–12 . . . 75
17:12 . . . 344
17:13 . . . 344
17:14–16 . . . 349
17:14–27 . . . 347
17:15 . . . 350
17:16 . . . 218
17:17 . . . 348, 350–351
17:18 . . . 177
17:19 . . . 358, 435
17:20 . . . 350–351
17:22–23 . . . 348, 351, 398, 484
17:23 . . . 351, 359, 441, 557
17:24 . . . 349, 352
17:24–27 . . . 20, 24, 331, 248, 439
17:25 . . . 349, 352–353
17:25–27 . . . 352
17:26 . . . 353
17:27 . . . 353, 567
18. . . . 32
18:1 . . . 358, 435
18:1–5 . . . 373
18:1–35 . . . 356
18:2 . . . 360, 377
18:2–4 . . . 385
18:2–5 . . . 360, 397
18:2–10 . . . 479
18:3 . . . 377, 412
18:5 . . . 412
18:6 . . . 363
18:6–20 . . . 361
18:7 . . . 363
18:7–9 . . . 387
18:8–9 . . . 363
18:10 . . . 363
18:12 . . . 366
18:12–13 . . . 361, 363
18:14 . . . 363
18:14–15 . . . 364
18:15 . . . 364–365
18:15–20 . . . 30, 363
18:16–35 . . . 357
18:17 . . . 365
18:18 . . . 362, 369
18:20 . . . 34, 371
18:21 . . . 330, 358, 367, 379, 435
18:21–35 . . . 131
18:22 . . . 367
18:23 . . . 366
18:23–24 . . . 367
18:28 . . . 374
18:28–34 . . . 368
18:32–34 . . . 367
18:34 . . . 368
18:35 . . . 373, 379
19:1 . . . 374
19:1–7 . . . 386
19:1–9 . . . 437
19:1–12 . . . 372
19:3 . . . 117, 188, 373, 379
19:3–9 . . . 20
19:4–6 . . . 375
19:6 . . . 376
19:7 . . . 375
19:8 . . . 375
19:8–9 . . . 376
19:9 . . . 375–376
19:10 . . . 117, 376
19:11 . . . 376
19:11–12 . . . 117
19:12 . . . 376–377, 382, 564
19:13 . . . 384
19:13–15 . . . 397
19:13–20:16. . . . 380
19:14 . . . 373, 382, 397
19:16 . . . 385
19:16–30 . . . 373
19:17 . . . 383, 385

19:18 . . . 385
19:18–19 . . . 383, 386
19:20 . . . 386
19:21 . . . 383, 386, 564
19:21–24 . . . 490
19:21–30 . . . 274
19:22 . . . 386–387
19:23 . . . 383, 387
19:24 . . . 387
19:25 . . . 358, 385, 387, 435
19:26 . . . 383, 387
19:27 . . . 330, 388, 435
19:27–30 . . . 387
19:28 . . . 388, 396, 428
19:28–29 . . . 383, 388, 397, 490
19:28–20:16. . . . 381
19:29 . . . 382, 387–389
19:30 . . . 388
20:1 . . . 366, 387
20:1–2 . . . 390
20:1–5 . . . 387
20:1–15 . . . 383, 387–388
20:1–16 . . . 373, 397
20:3–5 . . . 390
20:7 . . . 390
20:9–10 . . . 390
20:12 . . . 390
20:13 . . . 391
20:14–15 . . . 390
20:15 . . . 140, 389, 391
20:16 . . . 388, 390, 564
20:17–19 . . . 389, 396–397
20:17–34 . . . 394
20:18 . . . 214
20:18–19 . . . 484
20:19 . . . 396, 441, 554, 557
20:20–21 . . . 396
20:21 . . . 396, 399, 468
20:22 . . . 397, 503, 552
20:23 . . . 398, 552
20:24 . . . 396–399
20:25–26 . . . 402
20:25–28 . . . 399
20:28 . . . 189, 398–400, 535, 552
20:29–34 . . . 203
20:30 . . . 50, 399
20:31 . . . 399–400
20:32 . . . 399
20:32–34 . . . 395
20:34 . . . 401
21. . . . 450
21:1 . . . 412
21:1–7 . . . 406
21:1–22 . . . 404
21:8 . . . 406
21:9 . . . 50, 406
21:10 . . . 343, 406–407, 435
21:10–16 . . . 389
21:11 . . . 407
21:12 . . . 251
21:12–13 . . . 407–409, 517
21:12–46 . . . 83, 245
21:14–15 . . . 411
21:14–22 . . . 405
21:15–16 . . . 425
21:16 . . . 412
21:17 . . . 412
21:18 . . . 412
21:18–19 . . . 412
21:19 . . . 413, 428
21:20 . . . 358, 413
21:21 . . . 413–414, 431, 467
21:22 . . . 414
21:23 . . . 245, 343, 421–422, 436
21:23–27 . . . 66
21:23–46 . . . 440
21:23–22:14. . . . 418
21:23–22:46. . . . 450
21:25 . . . 423
21:25–26 . . . 424
21:26 . . . 226, 424
21:27 . . . 424
21:28 . . . 366, 425
21:28–32 . . . 425
21:28–45 . . . 437
21:28–46 . . . 72
21:29 . . . 425
21:30 . . . 425
21:31 . . . 425
21:31–32 . . . 425, 429

21:32 425
21:33 . . . . 366, 427
21:33–39 . . . . 245, 426
21:33–41 389
21:34 427–428
21:34–39 427
21:35 432
21:35–22:9 419
21:40 426–427
21:41 . . . . 426–427, 432
21:42 . . . . 427–428, 518
21:43 . . . . 214, 427–428
21:45 . . . . 426, 428
21:45–46 251
21:46 . . . . 281, 422
22:1–3 428
22:1–6 428
22:1–14 . . . . 24, 367
22:2 366
22:4–6 428
22:7 . . . . 24, 367, 429
22:8–10 428
22:9–10 428
22:10–22:14. . . .
22:11–13 429
22:12 429
22:13 429
22:14 . . . . 192, 429
22:15–17 . . . . 107, 188, 352
22:15–22 . . . . 348, 449
22:15–46 433
22:15–23:36 71
22:16 443
22:16–17 436–437
22:17 435
22:18 436–437
22:18–20 352
22:19 . . . . 436, 438
22:20 438
22:21 . . . . 352, 439
22:23 . . . . 436, 558
22:23–24 441
22:23–28 440
22:28 441
22:29 . . . . 86, 436–437, 440
22:30 441
22:32 . . . . 437, 441
22:32–46 434
22:33 . . . . 435, 441
22:34 . . . . 437, 441
22:34–36 188
22:34–45 449
22:35 441
22:36 . . . . 385, 441
22:37–38 442
22:38 442
22:39 442
22:42 . . . . 442, 444
22:43 442
22:43–45 470
22:44 442
22:45 442
22:46 . . . . 435, 449
23. . . . . 25, 112, 450–451
23:1–12 450
23:1–36 . . . . 27, 72
23:1–39 . . . . 337, 447
23:2 . . . . 97, 107, 114
23:2–3 . . . . 20, 193, 444
23:3 . . . . 103, 126, 449, 452
23:4 240
23:5–7 . . . . 113, 450, 452
23:6–7 . . . . 107, 459
23:11–12 453
23:12 460
23:13 453
23:13–32 450
23:15 . . . . 452, 453–454
23:16 . . . . 449, 454
23:16–17 . . . . 453, 457
23:18–20 453
23:20–22 454
23:20–39 448
23:21–22 453
23:23 . . . . 115, 450, 453–454
23:24 . . . . 449, 453
23:25 453
23:25–28 450
23:26 453
23:27 453

23:27–28 . . . 113
23:28 . . . 453
23:30 . . . 455
23:30–38 . . . 451
23:31–34 . . . 455
23:32 . . . 454
23:32–35 . . . 452
23:33 . . . 449, 454
23:33–38 . . . 527
23:34 . . . 217
23:34–36 . . . 217
23:34–37 . . . 421
23:35–36 . . . 455
23:35–37 . . . 528
23:36 . . . 470
23:37 . . . 252, 337, 456
23:37–38 . . . 454, 460
23:37–39 . . . 455, 466
23:37–24:2 . . . 429
23:38 . . . 450, 456, 467, 530
23:38–24:2 . . . 29
23:39 . . . 456
24–25 . . . 32
24:1 . . . 420
24:1–2 . . . 24, 408, 411
24:1–25:46 . . . 341, 462
24:2 . . . 456, 467, 515, 518, 530
24:3 . . . 29, 358, 467–469, 475, 485
24:4 . . . 474
24:4–28 . . . 471
24:4–33 . . . 470
24:4–26:1 . . . 485
24:6 . . . 477
24:6–13 . . . 130
24:8 . . . 475
24:9–12 . . . 474
24:9–14 . . . 477
24:11 . . . 75
24:12 . . . 477
24:13 . . . 155, 476
24:14 . . . 475
24:14–16 . . . 530
24:15 . . . 470
24:15–21 . . . 24, 471, 474
24:15–24 . . . 477
24:20 . . . 20
24:22–24 . . . 474
24:22–41 . . . 463
24:24 . . . 475
24:25 . . . 475
24:26–31 . . . 212
24:27 . . . 470, 473
24:28 . . . 473
24:29 . . . 471
24:29–30 . . . 29
24:29–31 . . . 29, 473
24:29–36 . . . 484
24:29–41 . . . 471
24:30 . . . 471, 473, 475
24:30–34 . . . 471
24:31 . . . 476
24:32 . . . 412
24:32–33 . . . 476
24:34 . . . 470, 472
24:35 . . . 471
24:36 . . . 385, 469, 472, 475
24:37 . . . 470
24:37–41 . . . 476
24:38–41 . . . 476
24:39 . . . 470
24:42 . . . 30, 476
24:42–25:13 . . . 476
24:42–25:15 . . . 464
24:42–25:30 . . . 472
24:44–47 . . . 476
24:45–47 . . . 477
24:45–49 . . . 476
24:45–51 . . . 27
24:47 . . . 477
24:48 . . . 477
24:48–49 . . . 477
24:51 . . . 477
25:1–10 . . . 477
25:1–13 . . . 476
25:1–46 . . . 27
25:5 . . . 477
25:10 . . . 477
25:13 . . . 30, 476
25:14 . . . 366
25:14–16 . . . 477

25:14–30 . . . 386, 476
25:16–34 . . . 465
25:19 . . . 477
25:19–23 . . . 477
25:21 . . . 477
25:23 . . . 477
25:26 . . . 367
25:30 . . . 477
25:31–40 . . . 476
25:31–46 . . . 133, 476–477, 551
25:34–40 . . . 215
25:35–46 . . . 466
25:37–39 . . . 478
25:37–40 . . . 385, 489
25:41–46 . . . 476
25:44 . . . 478
25:44–46 . . . 385
25:46 . . . 477
26:1–30 . . . 483
26:2 . . . 436, 485
26:3–4 . . . 515
26:3–5 . . . 485
26:4 . . . 485
26:5 . . . 485
26:6–7 . . . 487
26:6–13 . . . 50
26:8 . . . 358, 488
26:8–9 . . . 491
26:8–11 . . . 468
26:9 . . . 488
26:10–13 . . . 489
26:11 . . . 489, 491
26:12 . . . 488
26:14–16 . . . 485, 490
26:14–27:50. . . . 216
26:16 . . . 485
26:17 . . . 358, 518
26:17–19 . . . 493
26:17–27:66. . . . 478
26:18 . . . 487
26:19–30
26:20–25 . . . 492
26:20–28 . . . 494
26:21 . . . 491, 502
26:21–25 . . . 485
26:22 . . . 358, 491
26:23 . . . 491
26:24 . . . 486, 493, 508, 531
26:25 . . . 358, 493, 516, 533
26:26 . . . 493, 565
26:26–28 . . . 492
26:26–29 . . . 535
26:27–28 . . . 398
26:28 . . . 398, 486, 494, 535
26:29 . . . 492, 495
26:30 . . . 495
26:31 . . . 494, 501, 517
26:31–32 . . . 495
26:31–35 . . . 452, 501
26:31–56 . . . 498
26:32 . . . 508
26:32–34 . . . 518
26:33 . . . 502, 513, 524
26:33–35 . . . 330, 340
26:34 . . . 494, 502
26:35 . . . 443, 489, 502–503, 513, 521, 524, 544
26:36–37 . . . 503
26:38 . . . 50, 509
26:39 . . . 398, 486, 502, 504, 565
26:40 . . . 486, 503
26:40–41 . . . 93
26:41 . . . 503
26:42 . . . 502, 504, 545
26:43 . . . 486, 504
26:44 . . . 504
26:45 . . . 486
26:45–46 . . . 505
26:45–56 . . . 499
26:46 . . . 486
26:47 . . . 423, 515
26:47–49 . . . 505
26:48 . . . 505
26:50 . . . 429, 505
26:51 . . . 489, 506
26:52 . . . 506
26:53 . . . 503, 506
26:54 . . . 507
26:55 . . . 506–507
26:56 . . . 468, 505, 507

26:57–58 513
26:57–75 511
26:58 513
26:59–60 472
26:60 515
26:61 . . . . . 466, 515
26:61–62 472
26:62–63 515–516
26:63 343
26:63–66 422
26:64 518
26:65 516–517
26:66–68 515
26:67 517
26:68 . . . . . 345, 517–518
26:69 519
26:71 519
26:72 . . . . . 518, 520
26:72–75 512
26:73 520
26:74 520
26:75 514
27:1–2 422
27:1–3 529
27:1–26 525
27:2 . . . . . 281, 486, 530
27:3 529
27:3–4 . . . . . 494, 528
27:3–5 . . . . . 429, 526
27:4 . . . . . 527, 530
27:4–7 528
27:5 . . . . . 493, 531
27:6 526–527
27:6–8 531
27:9–10 532
27:11 . . . . . 516, 527, 532
27:11–12 422
27:11–26 . . . . . 281, 529
27:12 533
27:13–14 533
27:14 528
27:15 533
27:17 534
27:18 528
27:18–26 526
27:19 . . . . . 527–528, 533–534
27:20 534
27:22 534–535
27:23 535
27:23–24 527
27:24 . . . . . 528, 535
27:24–25 527
27:25 . . . . . 527, 535
27:26 . . . . . 535, 543
27:26–27 486
27:27 551
27:27–66 539
27:28–29 543
27:28–44 398
27:29 527
27:30 543
27:31–32 543
27:31–36 543
27:31–50 474
27:34 544
27:34–36 547
27:35 . . . . . 542, 544
27:36 544
27:37 . . . . . 55, 489, 527, 544
27:38 552
27:39 . . . . . 435, 545, 547
27:40 . . . . . 472, 545
27:41–43 449
27:42 545
27:43 . . . . . 545, 547–548, 551
27:44 546
27:45 546
27:45–28:7 212
27:46 . . . . . 50, 93, 546
27:47 548
27:47–66 540
27:49 548
27:50 . . . . . 252, 548
27:51 . . . . . 530, 549
27:51–52 . . . . . 549, 550
27:52–53 . . . . . 550, 558
27:54 . . . . . 541, 551
27:55–61 542
27:57–60 541
27:57–61 . . . . . 281, 489

27:58 486
27:60 551
27:61 . . . . . 542, 558, 564
27:62–64 548
27:63 . . . . . 549, 558
27:63–64 559
27:64 549
27:65 551
27:66 551
28:1 . . . . . 557, 559, 564
28:1–20 556
28:2 558–559
28:4 558
28:5 562
28:6 561–562
28:7 567
28:7–10 559
28:8 562
28:8–10 562
28:9–10 562
28:10 . . . . . 560, 563–564, 568
28:11 558
28:11–15 558
28:12 551
28:12–15 559
28:15 23
28:16 . . . . . 519, 560, 563
28:16–17 . . . . . 373, 560
28:16–20 . . . . . 181, 336, 562
28:17 . . . . . 557, 563
28:18 . . . . . 215, 564, 567
28:18–20 . . . . . 83, 559
28:19 . . . . . 214, 255, 564
28:19–20 . . . . . 28, 213, 215, 452, 557
28:20 . . . . . 30, 34–35, 93, 97, 217, 291, 560, 565–566, 568

Mark

1:1 . . . . . 21, 42
1:11 73
3:4 243
4:1–34 267
4:35–5:20 172
4:39–40 173
5:1 172
5:1–20 173
5:20 172
5:22–43 199
6:12–13 216
6:17–29 281
6:30 216
6:45–52 293
7:1–4 303
7:11 304
7:19 306
8:29–30 27
8:30 328
9:33–34 359
11:13 412
12:32–34 451
13:1 467
13:33–37 27
14:5 488
16:1 557
16:3 559

Luke

1:1–4 17
3:22 73
3:23–38 367
3:31 46
4:6 87
4:15–27 279
4:16 279
4:16–21 101
4:28–30 101
5:29 192
6:9 243
6:20–49 98
7:3–5 200
8:4–18 267
8:22–39 172
8:24–25 173
8:41–56 199
9:21 328
9:28–36 336
9:46 359
9:57–60 172
11:2–4 98
11:9–13 98
11:33–36 98

12:14 . . . 166
12:22–34 . . . 98
13:1 . . . 534
13:1–2 . . . 427
13:6–9 . . . 415
13:18–21 . . . 267
13:23–30 . . . 98
14:16–24 . . . 24
14:34–35 . . . 98
16:13 . . . 98
18:9–14 . . . 174
18:12 . . . 128
18:18–24 . . . 174
19:1–10 . . . 174
21:5–36 . . . 30
22:19 . . . 492
24:1 . . . 558–559
24:13–35 . . . 560
24:28–31 . . . 560
24:49 . . . 560

John

1:42 . . . 328
1:46 . . . 407
6:1–69 . . . 90
6:4–15 . . . 283
10:10 . . . 260
16:7–13 . . . 254
20:11–18 . . . 559
20:19–29 . . . 560
20:22 . . . 560
20:27 . . . 563
21:15–19 . . . 519
21:24–25 . . . 17
21:25 . . . 348

Acts

1:6 . . . 469
1:6–7 . . . 30
1:9–11 . . . 560
1:15 . . . 329
2:14 . . . 329
2:23–36 . . . 339
3:6 . . . 329
3:12 . . . 329
4:8 . . . 329
6:9–7:58 . . . 251
7:54–58 . . . 485
8:27 . . . 377
9:1–2 . . . 301
10:1–11:18 . . . 329
15:13–21 . . . 329
19:3–4 . . . 66
23:6–10 . . . 71

Romans

1:16 . . . 215
2:9 . . . 215
5:10 . . . 121
6:19–23 . . . 151
7:24 . . . 536
7:25 . . . 536
8:3 . . . 504
9:4–7 . . . 215
9:6 . . . 168
9:6–7 . . . 71
9:23–29 . . . 215
9:27–29 . . . 71
11:1–5 . . . 215
11:7–36 . . . 168
11:11–12 . . . 215
11:25–29 . . . 215
13:1–7 . . . 439

1 Corinthians

1:18–2:16 . . . 233
1:22–23 . . . 501
2:1–5 . . . 237
2:2 . . . 524
2:3–4 . . . 524
4:9–13 . . . 524
5:7 . . . 493
10:13 . . . 94
11:24 . . . 492
11:26 . . . 492
12:3 . . . 520
12:31–13:13 . . . 275
13:12 . . . 342
14:1 . . . 75
15:9 . . . 524
15:12–57 . . . 445
15:13 . . . 443

15:23 469
16:17 470

2 Corinthians

1:6 152
4:7–10 524
7:6–7 470
10:10 . . . . 470, 524
11:4–15 151
11:23–27 524
12:9–10 524
12:11 524

Galatians

1:6–9 21
2:6–9 329
2:9 327
2:11 327
2:14 327
3:19 375
3:28 309
4:6 129
5:22–23 260
6:2 378

Ephesians

2:10 332
2:20–21 329
6:12 555

Philippians

1:26 470
2:5–11 542
2:10–11 . . . . 63, 456
2:12 470
3:4–9 443

1 Thessalonians

2:19 469
3:4 152
3:13 469
4:15 469
5:20–21 75
5:23 469

2 Thessalonians

1:7 152
2:1 469
2:8–9 470

Titus

3:10 260

Hebrews

12:2 555

James

1:13 79
1:22–25 457
1:22–27 254
1:23–25 458
1:25 101
1:26 459
1:27 459
2:12–13 241
2:13 142
4:8 304

1 Peter

2:4–6 523
2:4–8 329

2 Peter

3:4 474

Revelation

5:9 480
16:17 75
19:9 284
21:6 75

Subject Index

Abraham, 31, 35, 39, 40–43, 46, 64, 71–72, 80, 82, 85, 91, 160, 167, 194, 337, 342, 385, 434, 441, 567
Adam, 82, 91, 440, 548, 555
adultery, 47, 109–110, 113, 115, 116–117, 119–120, 152, 185, 300, 309, 372, 376, 380, 410
age, 35, 59, 65, 75, 179, 181, 227–228, 233–234, 248–249, 263, 291, 304–305, 332, 342, 358, 379, 384, 407, 411, 416–417, 421, 431, 436, 462, 468, 470, 472–475, 477, 485, 517, 557–558, 565–566, 568
alms, 126–128, 395, 488
amen, 100, 129, 346, 482, 537, 555
angel, 51–52, 55, 57, 60–61, 78, 81–82, 85–88, 151, 190, 263, 274, 334, 338, 356, 363, 433, 463, 465–466, 476, 480, 484, 487, 499, 503, 506, 509, 554–556, 558–559, 561–564
anger, 122, 175, 357, 368, 392, 413, 415
Antipas, 88, 166, 172, 227, 251, 280
antithesis, 28, 114
anxiety, 50, 111, 139, 141, 145, 146, 370, 508
apostle, 18, 22–23, 75, 151, 208, 216–217, 219, 275, 328–329, 341–342, 378, 388, 439, 501, 524
Aramaic, 18, 129, 175, 327–328, 453, 534, 562
Archelaus, 52
atonement, 191
author, 17–19, 20–21, 23–25, 35, 234, 331, 348, 392, 535, 542, 571
authority, 34, 36, 66, 83, 87, 90, 149, 160, 170, 172–173, 184, 188, 190, 208, 215, 217–218, 225, 240–241, 243, 245, 253, 284, 294, 301, 336, 343, 349, 394, 399, 402, 418, 420, 421–425, 429, 436, 439, 470, 556, 559, 564, 566–567
authorship, 18–19
bank, 137,171, 320
baptism, 45, 65–66, 68–73, 172–173, 224, 227, 367, 378, 418, 423–425
Barabbas, 525–526, 533–536
beatitude, 100–104, 106–108, 112, 133, 155, 226
Beelzebul, 87, 187, 209, 216, 249, 253, 256–257
Bethany, 405, 412, 482–483, 487, 489
Bethlehem, 51–52, 57–60, 62–63
Bethsaida, 216, 223, 230, 233, 252
betray, betrayal, 24, 209, 359, 462, 484–486, 490–492, 494, 500, 502, 505–508, 518, 521–522, 526, 530, 531, 537
Bible, 16, 42, 47, 57, 61, 86, 100, 106, 111–113, 129, 158, 168–169, 183, 235, 274, 286, 349, 358, 392, 452, 481, 533, 537
blasphemy, 249, 251, 254, 511, 514, 516–517, 521
blessed, 44, 95, 98–108, 112–113, 145, 148, 151, 156, 158–159, 161–162, 164, 225–226, 236, 252, 262, 307, 323, 368, 373, 376, 404, 406, 448, 456, 465, 478, 481–482, 562, 567
blessing, 44, 54, 59, 60, 65, 100–101, 107, 112, 179, 235, 258, 284, 327, 329, 342, 384–385, 393
blind, 36, 138, 143, 197–198, 202–204, 206, 222, 226, 234, 242, 249, 252, 254, 266, 300–301, 305, 307– 309, 311, 314, 318, 323, 326, 353, 394–395, 396, 399–402, 405, 411–412, 417, 426, 447–449, 454, 457
boat, 33, 79, 171–177, 182–184, 256, 261, 265, 276, 279, 283, 288, 289, 290–298, 301, 312, 317
bread, 75, 78, 81–87, 90–91, 102, 123, 130, 131, 136, 141, 145, 147, 238, 242, 269,

277, 301, 305–306, 311–312, 315–317, 322, 358, 413, 483–484, 486, 492–497, 535, 550–551

brother, 24, 39–40, 47, 53–54, 74, 79, 109, 114, 116, 120, 131, 136, 141, 143, 147, 153, 174, 176, 208–209, 219, 250, 258, 276, 280, 307, 332, 349, 361–362, 364–365, 379, 381–382, 387, 394, 427, 433, 447, 466, 482, 497, 556, 560, 568

burial, 50, 70, 177–179, 181, 201, 256, 483, 487–490, 496, 525, 532

Caesar, 53, 57, 195, 324, 331, 352, 409, 433, 435, 437–440, 443, 445–446

Caesarea Philippi, 322, 331

Caiaphas, 483, 511, 515, 561

Canaanite, 27, 198, 253, 311–317, 326

Capernaum, 78, 88–89, 160, 165–166, 187, 192, 200, 216, 223, 230, 233, 243, 252, 279, 319, 347, 349,

capital punishment, 251

celibacy, 376

charismatic, 89, 179, 258, 421

children, 41–42, 44, 52–53, 57–59, 61–64, 67, 71–72, 76, 79–82, 85, 91, 93, 95, 98–99, 102–103, 105, 110, 113, 118, 128–129, 136, 141, 144–145, 148, 150–151, 158, 167, 169, 175, 194, 209, 219, 221–223, 228–231, 252, 269, 274, 277, 283, 286, 309, 312, 315–316, 338, 347, 356, 357, 360–366, 369–370, 373, 377, 379, 380–382, 384, 387, 397, 405, 411–412, 417, 425, 433, 448, 460, 481–482, 503, 523, 526–529, 535–536, 554–555

Christ, 16–17, 18, 21, 26, 28–31, 33–35, 42, 46, 57, 74–75, 82, 90–94, 103, 105, 108, 115, 122, 133, 141, 158–159, 170, 173, 183, 194, 198, 212, 219, 233, 235–237, 248, 256, 260, 275, 284–285, 286, 290, 302, 309, 319–321, 325, 329, 331–332, 345–346, 348, 350–351, 354, 378–379, 387, 391, 402–403, 414, 444–445, 468–482, 487, 492, 496–497, 501, 507, 510, 514, 517, 520, 523–524, 527, 529, 535–538, 546, 560, 566, 568

Christians, 20, 22, 25–26, 28, 30–31, 62, 70, 75–76, 105, 107, 113, 126, 129–133, 147, 151, 157–159, 195, 198, 212, 218–220, 246–248, 258, 275, 284–285, 308, 310, 317, 377–378, 401–402, 406, 416, 444–446, 454, 456–457, 470, 479, 497, 508, 520, 562, 564

church, 16, 18–26, 28, 30–31, 57, 70, 74–76, 90, 121, 158, 172–173, 195, 212, 215, 217, 219–220, 235–236, 247–248, 258–259, 266, 272, 282, 284, 286–287, 295, 297, 309, 319–320, 323, 327–333, 336, 339, 345–346, 348–350, 357, 361–362, 364–366, 370, 378, 388, 392, 401–402, 414–416, 428, 443–446, 457, 471, 478–480, 496–497, 514, 521, 523–524, 566–567

clean, 68, 160, 162–165, 169–170, 200, 250, 257, 303–304, 306–307, 309, 411, 414–415, 429, 448, 453, 524, 530, 535, 540

coming, 26, 29–30, 32–35, 41, 44, 52, 54, 56, 64, 66–69, 72, 82, 103, 114, 119–120, 130, 133, 138, 141, 155, 163, 166, 168, 171, 174, 180, 195, 210–212, 215, 219–220, 224–229, 233–234, 272, 274, 280–281, 292, 298, 301, 313, 315, 318, 323–324, 330, 334–336, 338, 340–341, 348, 354, 358–359, 368, 384–386, 396, 398–401, 406–409, 414, 426–428, 435, 438, 449, 451, 456, 460, 462–464, 468–470, 473–475, 478, 485–487, 489–490, 492–493, 501, 504–505, 509, 511–512, 522, 538, 545–546, 559

commandment, 28, 30–31, 35, 84–85, 87, 97, 100, 112–118, 152, 177, 185–186, 240–241, 246, 256, 305, 375, 380, 383, 385–386, 434, 441–444, 452, 454, 515, 566

community, 19–21, 24–26, 28, 63, 68, 71, 105, 119, 131, 139, 173, 177, 185, 194–195, 200, 220, 279, 342, 363, 384, 402, 416, 423, 459, 517, 524, 531

compassion, 208, 210, 219, 276, 283–285, 311, 313, 317–318, 395, 401

condemnation, 435
confession, 27, 36, 70, 76, 194–195, 292, 315–316, 328, 336, 516–517, 538
context, 20, 45, 66, 71, 86–87, 92, 102, 114–115, 142, 150, 213, 218, 220, 229, 268, 283, 318, 337, 358, 364, 392, 416, 436, 440, 450, 468, 489, 518
Corban, 304
court, 109, 115–116, 118–119, 121, 277, 401, 404–405, 407, 409–410, 416–418, 436, 499, 536, 549
covenant, 35, 41, 44, 54, 59–60, 71, 80–81, 85–86, 105, 112–114, 124, 185, 194, 220, 295, 342, 344, 375, 398, 484, 491, 494, 496–497, 500, 535
cross, 28, 36, 55, 58, 91, 93–94, 97, 99–100, 119, 171–172, 189, 194, 196, 209, 212, 216–217, 233–234, 236–237, 285, 289, 298–299, 321, 330, 334, 336, 338, 340–341, 344–346, 351, 353, 360, 369, 377, 379, 397–398, 408, 415, 431–432, 444, 449, 469, 474–475, 484, 489, 496, 501–504, 507–510, 512, 515, 518, 521, 524, 535, 537, 539, 541–545, 547, 551–555, 568
crucifixion, 194, 233, 284, 320, 336, 341, 488–489, 495, 501, 503, 527, 541–544, 546–547
culture, 77, 107, 131, 164, 360, 365, 369, 401–402, 441, 517, 522, 537
cup, 210, 218, 320, 394, 397–398, 448, 484, 492–495, 497–498, 502–504, 510, 552, 565
cursed, 67, 99, 100, 102–104, 107, 112, 127, 151, 161–162, 164, 169, 189, 198, 219, 251–252, 305, 384, 413, 427, 466, 478–479, 481, 493–494, 500, 507, 518–521, 526–527, 531, 542, 545, 552, 555
custom, 20, 62, 488, 493, 525, 533

date, 24–25, 29, 228, 271, 470, 473
David, 31, 33, 36, 39–44, 46–51, 54, 56, 60–61, 72, 188, 197, 202–204, 207, 238–239, 242, 249, 251, 265, 280, 311, 313–314, 316, 326, 359, 394, 396, 404–407, 411, 413, 421, 434, 442, 444, 470, 473–474, 493, 500–501, 516, 550, 552
day, 19, 21, 23, 29, 43, 50, 55–56, 63, 65–70, 72, 74, 75–76, 79, 85, 89, 92, 100–101, 105–106, 112–113, 116, 126–135, 137, 140–141, 145, 147, 149, 151, 154–156, 158, 161–162, 165, 167–168, 175, 177, 180, 185–190, 192, 195–196, 199, 202, 204, 206, 208, 211, 215, 223–226, 230, 233–236, 239–240, 242–244, 246–247, 249, 251, 255–256, 260–261, 268–269, 272–273, 279, 281, 285–286, 291–292, 298–299, 302, 304, 306, 319–320, 324–325, 330–332, 334, 338, 340–342, 344, 347, 351, 354–355, 368, 370, 381–385, 387–395, 398–400, 405, 409–410, 412, 414, 420, 423, 427, 430, 433–434, 436, 438, 442, 444–445, 451, 455–456, 459, 463–464, 468, 474–484, 492, 494–495, 497, 499, 505, 507, 516, 525, 528, 533, 535, 537, 540–542, 546, 548, 549–550, 554, 556–559, 562–563, 566, 568
Day of Atonement, 191
Dead Sea Scrolls, 151, 342
deaf, 222, 226, 234
death, 22, 33, 35–36, 41, 52, 55, 57, 66–67, 79, 82–84, 89, 91, 93, 97, 119–121, 128, 150–152, 162, 178–181, 187, 189, 192, 199, 201–202, 209, 225, 233, 244, 251–252, 256, 278, 280, 283–285, 287, 291, 296–297, 299–300, 326, 330, 332, 334, 336–341, 344–346, 350–355, 359, 384, 394, 396–397, 408, 435, 438, 441, 445, 456, 458, 462, 469, 474, 484–485, 487–488, 490–503, 507–509, 511, 514–516, 518, 520–521, 524, 526–528, 530–532, 534–538, 541, 543–555, 557–559, 561–562, 566–568
debts, 123, 130–131, 133, 137, 141, 145, 357, 362, 367–368, 373–374, 386
Decalogue, 113, 386, 442
Decapolis, 95, 180
deceived/deceiver, 93, 153–154, 205, 258, 402, 457, 459, 540, 552

delay, 30, 201, 428, 471–472, 478
demon, 29, 81, 95, 149, 160, 166, 171, 173, 177, 180, 188, 197–198, 202, 204, 208, 211, 216, 218, 223, 228, 230, 249, 251–254, 257, 259, 311, 313, 315, 347, 349–350, 358–359, 384–385, 431, 480, 555, 565
denial, 69, 128, 514, 516, 518, 521
desert, 28, 46, 65–69, 71, 74–77, 79–88, 90–94, 224, 226–227, 230, 281–283, 287, 291, 317, 319–320, 325, 338, 474, 486, 499, 505, 507, 509
desire, 35–36, 57, 63, 119, 125–126, 128–129, 141–142, 180, 184, 190, 193, 203, 223, 238, 241–242, 274, 289, 319, 321, 366, 388, 392, 401–402, 481, 527, 567
destroy, destruction, 24–25, 29–30, 41, 54, 59, 63, 99, 133, 135, 149–153, 155, 157, 177, 180, 185, 191, 209, 250, 253, 258–260, 341, 348, 358, 409–411, 413–414, 419, 429, 431, 460, 467–474, 477, 485, 509, 511, 515–518, 528, 530, 533, 536, 539, 545, 549, 553
devil, 78–81, 83–84, 87–88, 90, 92–93, 180, 253–254, 258, 263, 273, 285, 336, 338, 466, 493, 535, 545, 553
Didache, 25, 75, 151, 212
discernment, 33, 88, 118, 150, 153, 168, 324
disciple(s), 16, 18–20, 22–25, 27, 30–36, 45, 50, 79, 83, 89–91, 93–97, 99, 101–105, 113, 115, 117, 119, 121, 125, 129–130, 136, 138–143, 145, 150, 153, 155–157, 159, 167, 171–184, 190–193, 197–201, 206, 208, 210–211, 213–222, 224–226, 228, 230, 232–233, 237–239, 241–242, 245–247, 250, 254, 258, 261, 263–267, 269, 271, 273–277, 280–285, 287–297, 300–303, 305–308, 311–330, 333–351, 355–356, 358–363, 365, 368–369, 372–374, 376–377, 380, 382–383, 385, 387–389, 394, 396–399, 401–402, 404–406, 412–415, 424, 428, 430, 433, 435–436, 439, 443–444, 447, 450–453, 455, 462, 466–472, 474–479, 483–496, 498–509, 512–513, 518–521, 523–524, 538, 540–542, 544, 549, 551, 554, 556–557, 559–568
discipleship, 22, 30, 82–83, 99, 103, 117, 143, 172–174, 203, 212, 291, 295, 345, 377, 387, 392, 446, 512–513, 521, 560
discipline, 186, 191, 205, 364–365
discourse, 27, 30, 217, 337, 341, 361, 363, 401, 450, 469–470, 472–473
divorce, 48, 51, 57, 110, 113, 115–117, 120–121, 152, 372–379, 522
dog, 136, 139, 141–145, 154, 311–313, 315–316, 515, 527, 543
donkey, 343, 404, 406, 430
doubt, 87, 124, 183, 225–226, 253, 269, 288, 290, 293–298, 303, 354, 386, 405, 414, 467, 554–557, 561, 563–564
dove, 65, 73, 208, 220, 404, 408, 409
dream, 41, 51–53, 57–58, 60, 100, 161, 317, 319–320, 326, 490, 492, 526, 529

earth, 22, 28–30, 33, 35, 41–42, 54, 56, 63, 65–68, 73, 76, 79, 81, 83–84, 88, 91, 95–96, 107–110, 113, 115, 118–120, 123, 129–130, 135, 137–138, 140–141, 145–148, 156, 158–159, 161–162, 167, 174–175, 180, 184, 188, 190, 202, 209, 211–212, 215, 219–220, 223, 227, 230, 241, 247, 250, 254, 256, 266–268, 270, 272–275, 281, 303, 323–325, 328–332, 337–342, 344, 346, 348, 351, 353–355, 357, 359, 363, 368–369, 371, 373, 382–383, 386–387, 390, 392, 395, 399, 407, 414, 422, 428, 430–431, 439–440, 447–448, 463, 467–469, 471–476, 478, 490–492, 500, 503–504, 507, 509–510, 521, 528, 535, 540–541, 543–544, 546, 549–553, 555, 557, 559, 564–568
Egypt, 22, 25–26, 33, 41, 52, 60–61, 63, 74, 91, 167, 244, 395, 486–487, 493, 496, 546
Elijah, 65–66, 68, 72, 74–75, 82, 88, 90, 153, 179, 212, 222, 224, 226–228, 255, 284, 312, 322, 326, 330, 334–337, 342, 344, 408, 421, 540, 548
encouragement, 11, 125, 138, 139, 259, 293, 336, 340, 402

enemy, 53, 91–93, 110, 113, 116, 118–121, 133, 140, 158, 166–168, 170, 259, 262–263, 314, 407, 426, 451, 486, 492, 499, 509, 537, 551, 555, 559, 562, 567
epilepsy, 350
eschatology, 20, 103, 168, 318, 476
Essenes, 124, 163, 186, 243, 342, 352, 438, 458
eternal, 133, 137, 141, 230, 254, 267, 273–274, 292, 324, 329, 331–332, 342, 356, 367, 374, 380–383, 385–386, 388–390, 399–401, 411, 454, 466, 477, 480, 500, 536, 557
Eucharist, 143, 218, 284
eunuch, 372, 376–377, 379, 382, 564
evangelism, 566
Eve, 338
evil, 36, 57, 59, 79, 86, 88, 93, 95, 97, 110, 117–119, 121–123, 130, 136, 138–143, 145–146, 154, 180, 184, 220, 229–230, 244, 249, 251, 253, 255–256, 259, 262–263, 267–268, 272–273, 275, 277, 293, 295, 300, 305–306, 309, 324, 335, 342, 363, 365, 384, 391, 409, 433, 450, 503, 506, 508, 529, 537, 541–543, 551–555
exhortation 138
Exodus, 42
exorcism, 173, 206, 236, 253
eye, 22, 29, 32, 34, 36, 40, 43, 62, 77, 82, 92, 109–110, 113, 117, 120, 128, 133, 135–136, 138–148, 154, 156–157, 159, 161, 164, 174–175, 182, 197, 204–206, 212, 225, 229, 231–234, 236, 239, 241, 251, 255, 261–262, 264, 268–269, 274, 278, 280, 285, 287, 293–294, 296, 298, 307, 332, 348, 353, 356, 367, 369–371, 375, 380, 387, 391, 395, 400–401, 413, 419, 429–430, 452, 457–458, 478–480, 487, 489, 492, 496, 498, 500, 504–505, 507–508, 510, 513, 522–524, 527–528, 531, 538, 543–547, 552–553, 555, 563, 565

faith, 22, 29, 34, 36, 47, 80, 84, 113, 120, 135, 140, 151, 157, 160, 167–168, 170–177, 183–184, 195, 197, 201, 203, 205–207, 216, 218, 220, 237, 247–248, 257, 275–276, 286, 288, 294–295, 298, 310–311, 313–314, 316–317, 321–322, 325, 346–351, 355, 378, 405, 414, 417, 429, 445, 458, 462, 481, 522–523, 537, 548, 554–555, 558
faithfulness, 80, 91, 115, 217, 223, 234, 257, 291, 324, 401, 448, 454, 524, 560
false prophet, 66, 75, 99, 149–150, 153–154, 157, 188, 251–252, 256–257, 462–463, 471–472, 474, 514–515, 517–518, 548
family, 43–44, 46–50, 58, 60, 62, 76, 90, 105, 116, 136, 140, 144, 146–147, 158, 169, 177–179, 201, 206, 212, 216–217, 220–221, 253, 257–258, 279–280, 285–286, 291, 320, 355, 362, 364, 376, 379, 382–384, 386, 388–389, 416, 420, 423, 458–459, 479, 481–482, 489, 493–495, 500, 522–524, 541, 544, 547, 567
farmer, 131, 156, 195, 210, 218, 261, 269–272, 366, 407, 418, 426–428, 431
fasting, 78, 124–128, 131, 187, 189, 191, 193–195, 198–199, 228–230, 242
father, 18, 20, 39–41, 43–44, 47, 49–50, 53, 55, 56, 64, 71, 73, 79–80, 84, 91, 96, 105, 110, 112, 116, 118, 123–126, 129–131, 133, 135–137, 139–141, 149, 171, 175, 177–179, 182, 199, 201–202, 209, 217, 223, 231, 250, 258, 260, 263, 281, 300, 323, 325, 332, 343, 348, 350–351, 356–357, 359, 363, 366, 368, 372–373, 379–382, 386–387, 394, 418, 425, 428, 447, 449, 458, 460, 463, 465, 481–482, 498–500, 502–503, 505, 509, 514, 522, 534–535, 537, 545, 555, 557, 565
fear, 26, 33, 55, 82, 85, 118, 141, 145, 155, 176, 182, 212, 217, 231, 237, 266, 280–281, 286, 288–289, 292–293, 295, 297, 336, 342, 399, 453, 454, 508, 554, 558
fellowship, 192, 248, 258, 482, 497
female, 199, 309, 372, 514, 541
fig, 149, 153, 358, 405, 408, 412–413, 415, 428, 431, 463, 476

fish, 79, 90, 96–97, 136, 250, 256, 263, 268–269, 274–275, 277, 297–298, 311, 317, 347, 353–354, 413
flesh, 17, 178, 323, 372, 402, 480, 498, 503–504, 509, 543, 555
flowers, 135, 139
food, 62, 64, 68, 75, 77, 81–82, 86, 125, 128–129, 135, 138, 140, 142–146, 153, 162, 177, 192, 242, 277, 281–283, 303, 306, 317–318, 324–325, 355, 384, 392, 428, 464 492, 548
fool, foolish, 50, 58, 66, 71, 104–105, 109, 115, 120, 122, 131, 137, 141–142, 146, 149–151, 154–156, 193, 198–199, 202, 206–207, 230–233, 235, 243, 269–271, 273, 275, 279, 281, 289, 292, 313, 315, 365, 384, 400, 403, 408, 425, 431, 440–441, 447, 460, 464, 474, 476–477, 488, 500–501, 522, 524, 534
forgive, forgiveness, 57, 107, 123–124, 129–131, 133, 136–137, 141–142, 145, 148, 152, 156, 184–196, 198, 230, 234, 249, 254, 258, 260, 284, 330, 344, 357–358, 361–363, 367–369, 373–374, 377–379, 408, 484, 486, 491, 494–495, 497, 521, 523, 529–530, 535–536, 552, 561
fornication, 185
fruit, 64, 67–69, 71, 75, 99, 149–151, 153–155, 157, 224, 239, 249–250, 255, 257, 259–260, 262, 268, 270–271, 273, 275, 358, 405, 412–413, 415, 417–419, 428, 484, 495
fulfill, fulfillment, 19–20, 23, 28, 31–32, 34–35, 44, 50–53, 56, 60, 64, 72–73, 75, 78, 83, 88–89, 103, 109–110, 112, 115, 160, 185, 202, 226, 228, 238, 247, 261, 263–264, 268, 305, 318, 341, 404, 415, 429, 443, 472–473, 475–476, 484, 499, 505, 507, 510, 514, 525, 532, 536, 547, 550, 560, 564, 567
future, 34–35, 50, 83, 100–102, 140–141, 145–146, 150, 166, 181, 212, 217–218, 232–234, 241, 256, 304, 319–321, 328, 336, 341, 344, 351, 354, 382, 395–396, 427, 429–430, 455, 469, 474, 476, 507
Galilee, 28, 33, 53, 60–01, 64, 78–79, 88–89, 95, 156, 172, 180, 210, 212–215, 236, 247, 251, 270–271, 289, 301, 303, 311–312, 314–315, 319–321, 325, 347, 372, 404–405, 407, 413, 495, 498, 508, 511, 518, 540, 556, 559–560, 563, 567
gate, 99, 102, 149–154, 156, 159, 177, 180, 231, 240, 323–324, 327, 330–331, 387, 397, 406–407, 504, 519, 521, 535, 548
gay, 169, 195–196, 401–403, 522
Gehenna, 162
gematria, 20, 46
genealogy, 19, 27–28, 32, 39–40, 42–50, 202, 367–368
generation, 28, 31–32, 40, 42–44, 46, 60, 66, 74, 186, 217, 222, 228–229, 241, 250, 252, 255–257, 304, 322, 347–348, 350–351, 367, 386, 448, 455, 463, 470–473, 475–476, 487, 528
generosity, 63, 127, 144, 272,, 386, 390, 395, 491
gentile(s), 20–21, 26–31, 34, 48, 70–71, 78, 88–89, 97, 105, 113, 142–143, 166–168, 172, 180, 208–209, 211, 213–214, 218, 240–241, 245–246, 284, 302, 309, 312–313, 315–316, 318–319, 329, 361–362, 365–366, 388, 394, 399, 402, 407, 409–410, 416, 428, 436, 444, 449, 453–454, 501, 529
Gethsemane, 233, 485, 498, 500, 502–504, 507
gift, 24, 52, 58–59, 62–63, 75, 91, 101, 109, 111, 120–121, 127, 136–137, 139, 141, 145, 148, 160, 175, 182, 185, 203, 205–206, 212, 272, 290, 321, 324, 345–346, 369–370, 401, 447–449, 453, 530
giving, 47, 62, 85, 115, 119, 123, 126–127, 132, 140–142, 145, 158, 163, 177, 180, 182, 198, 202, 205, 212, 219, 242, 277, 284, 315–316, 330, 338–339, 353, 362–363, 369, 376, 379, 386–387, 392, 399, 402, 428, 439, 463, 469–470, 490, 505, 512–513, 516, 535, 543, 568
glory, 62, 65, 83, 87, 125, 129, 161, 195, 215, 230, 235–237, 334, 336, 338, 341–344, 346, 359, 395, 397, 409, 414, 429, 456,

463, 465, 473–474, 476, 480, 484, 490, 501, 523, 551, 554, 561
Golden Rule, 138, 368
Golgotha, 539, 544
good news, 21, 41–42, 55, 68, 95, 101–102, 147, 158, 204, 208, 222, 226, 235, 244, 273, 275, 299, 342, 351, 391, 415, 496, 500–501, 524, 564, 566, 568
grace, 102, 106, 143, 145, 170, 193, 251, 316, 320, 332, 389–391, 460, 523–524
Greek, 18, 25, 42, 80, 98, 126, 175–176, 295, 306, 327, 331, 360, 437, 486, 501, 532, 563, 566
grief, 128, 141, 178, 189, 285, 347, 351, 359, 400, 495, 497

habit, 77, 117, 145, 255, 308–309, 452, 497, 534
Hades, 223, 323, 327, 339, 521, 553
happy, 32, 101, 106–107, 297, 481
harvest, 68–69, 75, 208, 210–211, 215–219, 221, 224, 239, 241–242, 262–263, 270–274, 384, 393, 418–419, 426–428, 431, 465
hate, 103, 110, 114, 116–119, 122, 131, 135, 151–152, 157, 170, 183, 195–196, 209, 221, 231, 259, 309, 366, 368, 374, 408, 410, 450, 462
heal, 36, 95–98, 100, 121, 159–160, 164–170, 172, 187–190, 197, 199–206, 208, 210–211, 218–220, 227, 230, 234, 236, 238, 242–244, 249, 251–253, 260, 262, 276, 279, 282–284, 288–290, 296, 311, 313–315, 318, 347, 349–350, 355, 378, 396, 401, 405, 412, 417, 478, 487, 552, 565
hear, 17, 20, 22–23, 29, 32, 34, 36, 42–43, 48–49, 51–53, 57, 61–62, 73–74, 76–78, 83, 87, 97, 99–100, 102, 106, 109–111, 113, 123, 125, 127, 129, 131, 133, 136, 139, 145, 149–150, 153–154, 157–162, 175–176, 184, 189–190, 201–202, 206, 212, 218–219, 222, 225–236, 239, 248–249, 255–256, 258–266, 268, 274–276, 278–280, 292–295, 298, 300–301, 307, 309, 313–314, 320, 325–327, 329, 331, 335, 338–339, 342–345, 348, 351–352, 354, 358, 365, 369–370, 374, 380, 382, 385, 394, 399–403, 405, 412, 415–416, 419, 425, 427–429, 432–434, 445, 450, 453, 457–459, 468, 474–475, 477, 479, 481–482, 487, 489, 492, 495–496, 501, 503, 508–509, 511, 514–515, 519–521, 525, 527–528, 533, 536, 538, 540, 546, 550, 558, 560, 562–566
heart, 34, 57, 65, 80, 86, 95, 101–103, 109, 114, 117, 119, 122, 125, 128, 134–135, 141, 157, 159, 169–170, 174, 184, 186–187, 189, 195, 197, 201, 205, 212, 223, 232, 234, 236, 249–250, 255–257, 259–262, 264, 268, 278, 299–300, 304–310, 316–319, 321, 324, 326, 331–332, 346, 351, 357, 368, 372, 375–376, 379, 387, 395–396, 400, 431, 434, 437, 450, 453–454, 458, 490, 495, 497, 506–508, 512, 522, 561, 564–565, 567
Hebrew, 18–20, 42, 46–47, 60, 85, 111, 113, 265
hell, 63, 109–110, 119, 122, 175, 180, 209, 220, 230, 234, 252, 305, 330–351, 356, 362–363, 367–368, 387, 439, 447–448, 452, 454, 457–458, 473, 477, 480, 508, 520, 541
Hellenistic, 423, 562
Herod the Great, 227
high priest, 245, 343, 408, 420, 423–424, 437, 450, 483, 499, 504–505, 511, 513, 515–517, 519, 527
history, 20–21, 40, 43–44, 46–50, 60, 70, 74, 83, 121, 172, 205, 219, 228, 282, 309, 328, 331–332, 338, 362, 388–389, 408, 423, 439, 443, 455, 472–474, 476, 478, 486, 500, 503, 512, 530, 538, 554, 559, 561, 566
holy, holiness, 61–62, 78, 85, 113, 118, 129, 141–142, 151, 161–166, 169, 174, 201, 214, 219, 240–244, 246–248, 301–304, 310, 337, 339–340, 343, 346, 353, 389, 395–397, 400, 407–410, 414–415, 421, 423, 462, 470, 487, 500, 507, 523, 526, 540–541, 549–550, 557, 566

Holy Spirit, 51, 56, 64, 72–73, 91, 158, 249, 254–255, 258–260, 557, 560, 566
homoerotic, 401
homosexuality, 401
honor, 19, 84, 116, 118, 123, 124–127, 132, 158, 177–179, 186, 192, 200, 203–204, 251, 276, 278–281, 286, 300, 305, 309, 314–316, 359–360, 365, 377, 380, 386, 395–396, 399, 412, 416, 422, 425, 429, 435, 437, 441, 447, 450, 451, 459, 517, 522, 524, 534
hospitality, 30, 104, 175, 213, 215, 342, 412, 488
human, 54, 63, 91–93, 115, 119, 126, 128, 137, 143, 146, 185–186, 192, 195–196, 233, 237, 242, 267, 284–285, 300, 308, 310, 314, 329, 334, 340, 342, 351, 411, 418, 440–442, 452, 473, 479, 507, 509, 518, 523, 543, 548, 554
humanity, 36, 50, 91–92, 112, 128, 147, 156, 164, 166, 246, 267, 297, 330, 367, 389, 441, 452, 476, 478–480, 542, 552, 554, 567
humble, humility, 72, 101–102, 133, 144, 156–157, 159, 174, 199–200, 223, 232, 260, 268, 277–278, 280, 314, 316, 360, 363–364, 366, 369, 373, 383, 388, 397, 402, 447, 453, 456, 460, 476
hypocrite, hypocrisy, 27, 112–113, 123–129, 131–133, 136, 139, 143–144, 152–153, 157, 177, 300, 305, 307, 337, 352, 366, 433, 436, 438, 440, 443–444, 447–449, 451–453, 456–459, 461, 464, 492, 506, 522, 532

idolatry, 87, 91, 185, 376, 409, 421, 437–438
idols, 258, 438
image, 61, 69, 113, 131–132, 169, 172, 211, 259, 304, 360, 409, 425, 433, 437–440, 459–460, 477, 505, 543, 553
Immanuel, 31, 35–36, 51, 55–56, 93–94, 231, 291–293, 307, 417, 456, 478, 529–530, 536, 559–560, 566, 568
immorality, 441, 567
incest, 41
individual, 22, 41, 98, 105, 130–131, 162, 359, 364–365, 455, 565
interpretation, 21, 23, 25, 82–83, 105, 111, 113–115, 117, 143, 172–173, 180, 212, 229, 239–241, 243, 266, 273, 283, 328, 362, 365, 375, 388, 411, 428, 439, 454, 496, 503, 513, 530, 536, 547
Isaiah, 56, 60, 64, 67–68, 71–72, 73, 88–89, 101, 160, 166–167, 186, 202, 214–215, 224, 226, 230, 235, 238, 244, 261, 264, 269, 300, 304–305, 389, 406, 409–410, 414, 426–427, 430, 529

James, 21, 79, 96, 157, 178, 182, 208, 276, 280, 329, 334, 338, 341–342, 349, 396–399, 458, 503, 540
Jeremiah, 52, 60, 68, 104, 153, 179, 322, 326, 398, 408, 410, 430, 525, 532, 550
Jericho, 48, 394–396, 400, 434
Jerusalem, 20, 24, 29, 33, 51, 53–54, 58–59, 61, 64, 67, 71, 79, 84, 88, 94–95, 105, 110–111, 120, 127, 162, 165, 167, 211, 214, 229, 233, 240, 247, 251–252, 280, 283, 285, 300–303, 305–306, 309–310, 313, 319–321, 323–324, 329–330, 333–334, 336–341, 343, 345–346, 348, 359, 367, 373, 377, 388–390, 394–398, 400–401, 404–409, 411–414, 416, 420, 422, 424, 426–430, 434–436, 448, 450–451, 454–457, 460, 466–468, 470–471, 473, 484–487, 490, 496, 500, 504, 507, 514, 527–529, 531–537, 541, 543, 549–551, 554, 558, 563
Jews, 21, 23, 27, 46, 51, 53, 55, 57–59, 70–71, 89, 97, 118, 127, 129, 142, 151, 165–166, 177, 214, 243, 284, 302–303, 313, 316, 340, 366, 423, 437, 453–454, 489, 501, 506, 525, 527, 529, 532, 539, 541, 543–545, 550, 552, 556, 559
John the Baptist/Baptizer, 36, 64, 66, 75, 77, 153, 168, 222–223, 227, 276, 322, 326, 335, 344, 374, 451
Jonah, 29, 176, 250, 255–257, 278, 322–324
Joseph, 40, 44, 46, 51–52, 54–57, 60–61, 66
Joseph of Arimathea, 540–541, 564

Judas Iscariot, 208, 331, 429, 483–486, 490–494, 499, 502, 504–508, 516, 518, 525–533, 536, 541, 565
Judea, 33, 51–52, 60, 64, 67, 69, 89–90, 95, 214, 251, 340, 372, 373, 374, 407, 426, 462, 471
Judeans, 20, 25, 57, 65–66, 68–69, 395, 532
Judaism, 20, 54, 70, 116
judge, 20, 103, 107, 109, 116, 136, 138–139, 142–143, 145, 152, 154, 156–157, 159, 161–162, 192–193, 196, 241, 247, 249, 257, 260, 302, 350, 362, 368, 388, 396, 449–450, 454–455, 475, 478, 484, 526, 533–534, 552
judgment, 49, 55, 61, 65, 68–69, 71, 77, 109, 115, 133, 138–139, 142–144, 147, 151–154, 156–157, 162, 164, 169, 180, 191, 194, 196, 204, 208, 211, 223–225, 230, 235, 241, 249–250, 255–256, 260, 265, 267, 280, 304, 342, 361, 363, 367–368, 379, 385, 388, 408, 410–411, 413, 449–450, 452, 454–456, 475–481, 532–534, 546, 549–551
justice, 41–42, 55–56, 74–75, 100, 102, 115–116, 118–119, 142, 167, 185–186, 188, 194, 238–239, 245, 260, 272–273, 331, 340, 342, 361, 368–369, 390–391, 393, 395, 427, 448, 450, 454–455, 528–529, 536, 538, 553
justification, 62

Kaddish, 127
kill, 48, 52–53, 66, 115, 170, 181, 185, 209, 212, 217, 229, 234, 238, 244–245, 250–252, 256–257, 260, 276, 280–281, 306, 309, 323, 326, 334, 337, 347, 351–352, 374, 396, 408, 419, 427–428, 432, 448, 455–456, 460, 478, 483–485, 487, 495, 500, 506, 509, 514–515, 526, 528–532, 535, 537–538, 542, 553, 557
king, 22, 24, 28–31, 39, 41–42, 44, 47–48, 50–61, 63, 72–74, 103, 110, 119, 158, 188, 193, 209, 212, 214, 222, 224, 230, 241–242, 247, 253, 257, 264, 266, 275–278, 280–282, 287, 302, 313, 323, 328, 347, 357, 359, 366–368, 398–399, 401–402, 404, 406–409, 413, 415–416, 419–423, 429, 431, 442–443, 446, 456, 465–468, 470, 472, 474, 478–479, 481, 485–486, 489–490, 493–494, 499–501, 505–506, 508–510, 518, 525, 527, 529, 532–533, 539, 541–545, 548, 550–553, 557, 568
knowledge, 201, 231, 261, 264, 266, 316, 375, 469, 475, 521

labor, 135, 232, 246, 250, 268–269, 392
lamp, 96, 105, 135, 136, 138, 140, 154, 464
Last Supper, 487, 492, 494, 535, 565
law(s), 20, 23, 25, 27–28, 36, 42, 47, 51, 56–58, 97, 99–100, 109, 111–115, 117–120, 124–125, 136, 138, 145, 149, 160, 163–165, 169, 171, 174, 177–179, 184–185, 187, 209, 222, 227–228, 232–233, 239–242, 244–245, 247–248, 250–251, 253, 255, 263, 273, 300, 305, 334–335, 337, 366, 373, 375, 378, 385, 394, 405, 409, 411, 434, 438, 441–445, 447–448, 450, 452–459, 485, 504, 511, 515, 517, 525, 531, 536, 538–539, 545
leaders, 17, 71, 85, 112, 151, 197–203, 214, 251, 256, 301, 306, 320, 323, 330, 340, 344–346, 349, 352, 370, 388–389, 406, 408, 410, 412, 414, 421, 424–425, 427–429, 435, 440, 449, 451, 454–456, 467, 473, 485, 518–519, 529, 533–535, 545, 554
least, 22, 65, 109, 112, 162, 179, 226, 231, 273, 352, 359–360, 368, 373, 377, 383–387, 390, 466, 478–479, 482, 489, 524, 552
leaven, 29, 268, 272–273, 275, 324, 326, 407
legalism, 248
leprosy, 160, 162–165, 208, 211, 222
lex talionis, 142
light, 36, 58, 65, 79, 82, 89–90, 96, 98–99, 102–103, 105, 108, 112, 125, 132, 134–135, 137–141, 151–153, 162, 214, 223, 232–234, 237, 240, 245–246, 268, 291, 298–299, 331, 334, 336, 365, 388, 395, 401, 440, 463, 492, 505, 541, 546

love, 16, 20, 26, 34, 48–49, 63, 65, 73, 80, 88, 103, 110–111, 113, 115–116, 118–123, 127, 135, 140–141, 143, 145, 152, 156–159, 161–162, 165–166, 169, 179, 181, 183, 198, 205, 218, 238, 247–248, 274–275, 294, 314, 319, 332, 334, 342–345, 353, 380, 383, 386, 402, 408, 415, 434, 441–442, 444, 447, 458, 462, 477, 482, 506, 509, 529, 538, 542, 546–547, 552, 561, 568

lust, 50, 114, 116, 119–120, 152, 185, 306

magi, 28, 51–53, 55, 57–59, 62–63

male, 19, 116, 309, 372, 376–377, 435, 441, 537–538

mammon, 140–141, 145, 373

margin, marginalized, 34, 43, 54, 99, 107, 127, 214, 302, 401–403, 410, 416

marriage, 46, 51, 57, 80, 116–117, 119–120, 282, 373–378, 402, 433, 441, 445, 463, 522

martyr, 23, 36, 251, 281, 455, 537

Mary, 40, 46–48, 51–52, 55–57, 61, 63, 258, 276, 280, 540, 556, 561, 565

master, 27, 30, 89, 140, 146, 209, 234, 246–247, 294, 357, 368, 406, 464–465, 472, 477, 513

meek, 28, 67, 81, 84, 91, 95, 100, 102–105, 108, 119, 152, 157, 159, 162, 174

mercy, merciful, 35–36, 50, 95, 101, 103, 108, 115–116, 127, 142, 148, 152, 154, 156–159, 161–165, 167–170, 184, 187, 189–193, 195–197, 202–203, 207, 224, 230, 238, 241–243, 253, 289, 311, 314, 331, 335, 339–340, 347, 357, 361–363, 366–369, 371, 373–374, 378–379, 391, 394, 399–400, 448, 454, 487, 536, 546, 547, 552, 555

Messiah, 19–20, 28, 31, 33, 35–36, 39–45, 47–48, 50–51, 54–60, 65–66, 72–73, 79–80, 82–84, 88, 90, 93, 167, 173, 181, 183, 202, 204, 222, 225–226, 228, 231, 233, 253, 255, 275, 283, 291, 322–323, 325–328, 330–331, 337, 339–344, 349–351, 353, 359, 395–396, 400, 405–407, 414–415, 417, 423, 430, 434, 442–443, 447, 462–463, 466, 467, 470–471, 474–475, 477–478, 490, 494–495, 500–502, 507, 511, 515–518, 520, 526–527, 530–538, 541, 547, 549–550, 557, 565, 567–568

messianic, 20, 44, 55, 58, 61, 65, 82–83, 89–90, 103, 115, 129–130, 155–156, 167, 172, 202–203, 211, 214, 220, 227, 235, 279, 284, 313, 316, 328, 338, 341–346, 359, 395–369, 399, 406–407, 412, 414, 428–429, 431, 436, 467–468, 470–471, 473–475, 477, 489–490, 500, 516, 532, 537

military, 118–119, 406, 537

ministry, 27, 33–35, 69, 72–73, 75, 88–89, 96, 158, 165, 187, 216, 227–229, 236, 244–245, 252, 257, 275, 281, 319, 344, 348, 368, 392, 411, 428, 451, 481

miracles, 29, 34, 61, 65, 90, 96, 102, 149, 162, 164–166, 173, 187–188, 195, 203–207, 210, 223, 230, 234–236, 252–253, 255–256, 264, 266, 268, 271, 276, 279–280, 282–284, 289–290, 296, 298, 315, 317, 325–326, 348, 350–351, 353–354, 385, 407, 430, 516

Mishnah, 113–114, 177, 240–241, 454

mission, 17, 20–21, 27–31, 35, 83, 105, 143, 172, 180, 195, 210–212, 214–220, 226, 235, 266, 286, 301, 313–315, 323, 339–340, 344–345, 361, 396, 406, 428, 444, 515, 559, 564–567

mock, 50, 229, 231, 235, 252, 394, 396, 449, 487, 517, 537, 539, 541–543, 545–546, 548–549, 551–553, 555, 565

money, 53, 75, 116, 118, 133, 135, 137–138, 212–213, 234, 352–355, 381, 385–386, 404, 409–410, 416, 422, 437–438, 465, 483, 488, 490–491, 525–528, 531, 536, 556, 559, 565

morality, 302

Moses, 20, 28, 31, 33, 48, 59–60, 67, 80, 82, 84–86, 90, 97–98, 100, 114, 117, 150, 160, 163, 211, 231, 240, 244, 255, 282–284, 330, 334, 336–337, 342,

372–373, 375, 388, 433, 441, 444, 447, 452, 474, 533, 560
Mount of Olives, 404, 414, 462, 467, 484, 500, 550
mountain, 28, 30, 34, 78, 84–85, 87, 94–95, 97, 100, 105, 137, 149–150, 155–157, 161–162, 164, 170, 172, 176, 181, 288, 290–291, 301–302, 311, 318–320, 331, 334–338, 341–344, 346–347, 349–351, 373, 395–396, 405, 413–414, 417, 462, 467, 500, 504, 519, 556–557, 560–561, 563–564, 567
mourn, 52, 63, 95, 100, 102, 104, 128, 177–179, 184, 191, 201–202, 222, 228–229, 463, 473, 487, 541, 558
murder, 41, 59, 62, 109, 113, 115, 152, 170, 185, 233, 251, 280, 300, 309, 366, 380, 410, 419, 427, 448, 455, 457, 485, 528–529, 538
mute, 36, 197, 204, 242, 249, 252, 311

name, 17, 19, 34, 36, 42–47, 51, 56, 69, 74, 76, 85, 87, 92, 118, 123, 129, 149, 153–154, 176, 184, 190, 195, 208, 213, 218, 221, 239, 245, 248, 253, 276, 280, 283, 294–295, 324, 327–328, 331, 336, 350, 356–357, 370–371, 385, 404, 406–407, 410, 412, 417, 423, 435, 437, 439, 441, 444, 448, 456, 462, 475, 483, 487, 490, 519, 521, 523–525, 533–534, 539–540, 544–545, 557, 560, 563
narrative, 18–19, 21–22, 26, 31–36, 43, 45, 48, 54, 66, 82–83, 89–92, 168–169, 173–174, 181–182, 189, 202, 217, 225, 244–245, 269, 277–278, 302, 336, 349, 361–362, 373, 384, 402, 430, 469, 486–487, 489, 518–519, 527, 547
narrator, 61, 328, 335, 513
natural, nature, 43, 72, 74, 173, 176, 203, 247, 281, 285, 290, 429, 452, 472, 516, 530, 541
Nazareth/Nazarene, 18, 21, 23, 26–27, 53, 60–61, 78, 251, 279–280, 285, 319, 340, 404, 407, 472, 511, 519, 533–534
neighbor, 54, 97, 110, 113–117, 133, 138, 140–141, 145, 147–148, 152, 156, 164–166, 169–170, 185, 286, 320, 380, 383–384, 386, 392, 434, 442–444, 515

oath, 110–111, 115, 117–120, 276, 343, 447, 449, 454, 509, 511–512, 514, 516, 520
obedience, 20, 56, 80, 83, 100, 112, 124, 186, 195, 232, 248, 273, 309, 364, 386, 398, 439–441, 443, 528, 544–545
Old Testament, 42, 73, 83, 100, 265, 289, 302, 337, 455

pagan, 57–58, 62–63, 107, 110, 123, 128–129, 133, 135, 140, 142, 151, 219–220, 230, 357, 366–367, 499, 524
parousia, 30, 34, 130, 468–474, 478, 485
Passover, 60, 191, 283, 340, 358, 395, 400, 406–408, 427, 436, 467–468, 483–488, 492–496, 501, 533, 534, 541, 551
pastor, 16, 61, 157, 183, 206, 219–220, 235–236, 258, 275, 282, 319–320, 370, 373, 392, 472
Paul, 21, 71, 75, 121, 151, 168, 215, 237, 260, 275, 284, 301, 329, 332, 340, 342, 370, 375, 378, 439, 443, 445, 456, 469, 492–493, 501, 520, 524, 538, 544, 555
peace, 41, 102–103, 108, 208–209, 216–218, 260, 283, 340, 342, 348, 408, 427, 497, 528–529, 536, 538, 552, 562
pearl, 101, 136–138, 141–146, 263, 267–268, 272, 274–275, 375
perfect, 23, 46, 67, 76, 80, 92, 97, 110, 112, 117, 119, 121, 125, 133, 163–164, 200, 219, 229, 247, 328, 343, 360, 368, 373, 380, 384, 386, 400, 437, 439, 459–460, 466, 469, 486, 489, 522, 555
persecution, 23, 102, 155–156, 214, 239, 262, 471, 474
perspective, 21, 89, 155, 259, 290, 296, 339, 382, 393, 408, 468, 491, 518, 528
Peter, 18–19, 23, 27, 36, 79, 96, 160, 165, 169, 175–176, 192, 208, 288–291, 293–298, 300, 306, 318, 322–323, 327–331, 334, 336–343, 345–347, 349–350, 352–355, 357, 359, 361, 367, 373, 380, 383, 387–388, 391, 398, 444–445, 494, 498,

501–503, 508–509, 511–514, 518–521, 523–524, 541, 550, 560–561
Pharisees, 20, 25, 27, 35–36, 64, 70–72, 98–100, 103, 105, 107, 109, 111–115, 117, 120, 124–125, 127–128, 132, 152–153, 156, 162–165, 170, 174, 177, 184, 187–193, 197–200, 204–205, 207, 216, 238–246, 248–257, 259–310, 312–313, 322–326, 337, 352, 358, 366, 372–375, 379, 388, 407, 419, 424, 428, 433–444, 446–459, 536, 540, 548
pig, 136–139, 141–145, 154, 171, 180–181
pious, piety, 68–69, 81, 86, 111, 113, 124–128, 130–132, 153, 194, 205, 402, 452, 489
Pontius Pilate, 281, 340, 516, 525–530, 532–535, 540–541, 543–544, 549, 551, 561
poor, 29, 49, 55, 74, 95, 98–105, 112, 125–128, 133, 158, 161, 164, 177, 212, 214, 222, 226, 230, 235, 239, 242, 252, 265, 293, 304, 350, 380, 382–384, 386–387, 409, 483, 488–489, 491, 524, 537, 557, 564
possessions, 74, 88, 116, 127, 140, 163, 249, 272, 304–305, 380, 383, 464, 564
poverty, 99–101, 127
power, 25, 29, 42, 50, 53, 55–56, 59–60, 63, 65, 86–88, 90–92, 118, 129, 139–140, 151, 157, 164, 167–170, 173, 180–181, 187, 190, 201, 205, 215, 220, 227–228, 234, 236–237, 251–255, 258–259, 275, 277–278, 281, 315, 328, 349–350, 353, 359, 384, 392, 395, 397, 399, 401–402, 407, 414, 421, 433, 436–437, 440, 456, 458, 463, 467, 473, 476, 486, 490, 507, 514, 516, 524, 527, 530, 536, 543, 547, 549, 561, 565–566, 568
prayer, 79, 83, 93, 111, 125, 127–131, 136–137, 158, 173, 183, 190, 193, 196, 200, 210, 218, 221, 236, 253, 291, 294, 301, 304, 308, 367, 404–405, 410, 413–414, 416–417, 500, 503–504, 507–509, 528, 535, 550
preach, preacher, preaching, 16–17, 22, 37, 64–68, 75, 79, 86, 88–89, 96–98, 103–104, 111, 132, 134, 151, 153, 157, 161, 186–187, 191, 210, 216, 218–219, 224, 231, 236–237, 250, 255, 264, 279, 286, 308, 319, 320–321, 341, 345–346, 370, 378, 386, 392, 408, 424, 444, 447, 449, 452, 457–459, 461–462, 475, 477, 483, 490, 492, 496, 501, 506, 524, 538, 559, 565–566
priest, 28, 51, 56–57, 59, 105, 113–114, 160, 162–165, 179, 185–186, 238, 242–243, 245–246, 303–305, 334, 337, 343, 359, 389–390, 394, 405, 408–411, 414, 417–431, 436–437, 444, 450, 456, 474, 483, 485–487, 491, 499–500, 504–505, 507, 511, 513–519, 525–536, 539–541, 545, 548–549, 551, 556, 558–559, 565
priesthood, 411, 420, 423–424, 430, 468, 523
procurator, 251, 340, 427, 486, 526–527
prophecy, 19, 20, 31–32, 53–54, 60–61, 75, 88–89, 153, 166, 202, 225–226, 229, 261, 264, 304–305, 338–341, 361, 411, 426, 429, 467, 470, 484, 493, 501–502, 514, 517–518, 532, 549–550, 567
providence, 43, 141, 349, 352, 354, 549
public, 27, 51, 76, 92, 125–128, 131–132, 136, 152, 165, 198, 200–201, 206, 231, 248, 251–252, 273, 282, 294, 323, 337, 401, 422, 435, 445, 450, 470, 473, 485, 517, 521–523
punishment, 55, 57, 120, 251, 360, 363, 367, 377, 385, 387, 413, 442, 466, 477, 479, 529, 552
pure, purity, 70, 95, 101–103, 107, 114, 126, 157, 159, 162–164, 241, 301–304, 306–307, 309–310, 326, 352, 409, 411, 427, 450, 458, 487, 532

Qumran, 68, 70–71, 342, 423, 454

rabbi, 23, 48, 90, 97, 172, 232–233, 240, 246–248, 268, 329, 358, 385, 442, 447, 449, 453–454, 459, 484, 493, 499
Rachel, 52, 61, 63
ready, 30, 66–67, 71, 73, 77, 88, 93, 142–143, 174, 221, 287, 317, 323, 324–325, 354,

396, 419, 430, 436, 464, 475–477, 480, 484, 500, 502, 505, 506–508, 522, 527, 530, 548, 565
reconcile, reconciliation, 24, 109, 114, 116, 120–121, 186, 194, 379, 530
redeem, redemption, 60–61, 189, 194, 330, 378, 395, 477, 531, 552
relation, 143, 121, 198, 251, 282, 523
repent, repentance, 29, 36, 64–68, 70–72, 75, 79, 88, 101, 107, 186–187, 189, 191, 193–195, 219, 223–224, 229–230, 235–236, 250, 255, 264, 351, 364, 385, 418, 424–425, 429, 455, 493, 519, 528–529, 531
resource, 37, 63, 116, 140–141, 200, 272–273, 279, 281, 354, 384, 531
resurrection, 18, 24, 28, 33, 35–36, 40, 62, 70, 73, 83, 90, 194, 212, 233, 256, 290, 329–330, 337–339, 341, 355, 429, 433, 441, 443–445, 469, 484, 497, 508, 524, 540, 549–550, 554–555, 557–559, 561, 564, 566–568
retainer class, 407, 426, 529
retaliation, 118–119
revelation, 115, 231, 327, 329, 336, 350, 375, 431, 472, 480, 493
reward, 96, 104, 110, 119, 123–128, 132–134, 137–138, 141–142, 151, 156, 168, 179, 210–212, 214, 218, 257, 269, 286, 291, 316, 324, 328, 330, 334, 373, 378, 383, 388–393, 397, 444, 452, 477, 479–481, 554
rich, 50, 92, 100, 107, 121, 125, 174, 189, 203, 244, 265, 274, 297, 380, 382–389, 391, 540–541, 564
rights, 74, 119, 309, 314, 378, 401–402, 421, 460
righteous, righteousness, 23, 28–29, 31, 35–36, 55–58, 60–61, 64, 72–73, 95, 98–105, 107, 109–115, 117, 120–121, 123–125, 127–128, 132–133, 135, 138, 140, 142, 145, 152, 154, 156, 169, 184, 186–187, 190–194, 198–199, 202, 204, 210, 212, 218, 245, 253, 262–263, 273, 290, 342, 364, 366, 409–411, 414–415, 418, 426–427, 429, 443, 448–449, 451–452, 455, 466, 478, 480–481, 489, 493, 509, 515, 528–529, 545, 547, 551
rock, 65, 85, 106, 132, 149, 155–156, 178, 248, 290, 293–296, 298, 323, 327–333, 339, 376, 408, 501–502, 514, 518, 521–523, 536, 540–541, 549–550
Rome, Roman, 22–26, 29, 34, 53, 87, 97, 100, 118, 120–121, 129, 162, 165–168, 170, 177, 186, 195, 198, 213, 245, 251, 284, 314–316, 324, 340, 348–349, 352–353, 355, 396, 407–409, 422–423, 426–427, 435, 437–438, 459, 467, 471, 485–486, 489, 495, 501, 506, 520, 527, 529–530, 532–535, 541, 543–544, 548–549, 551, 555, 558, 564–565

Sabbath, 20, 36, 113, 200, 219, 233, 238–248, 251–253, 302, 462, 535, 554–556
sacrament, 494
sacred, 35, 43, 58, 118, 136, 142–145, 161, 185, 246, 282, 290, 303–305, 309–310, 313, 331, 352, 409, 447–448, 453, 479, 495–496, 515, 531, 533, 550, 553, 560–561
sacrifice, 35–36, 56, 70, 85–86, 91, 116, 137, 156, 175, 184–191, 193, 198, 238, 242, 271, 285, 303–304, 309, 337, 345, 366, 382, 389, 402, 409–411, 414–415, 421, 423, 431, 444, 482, 486, 494–495, 497, 523, 528–530, 535–538
Sadducees, 25, 64, 71, 86, 105, 124–125, 153, 187, 198, 243, 245, 303, 322–326, 352, 420, 433–436, 440–441, 443–444, 450, 458, 536
sage, 155, 231, 277, 448, 455, 471
saint, 228, 342, 522
salt, 96, 104–105, 108, 154
salvation, 21, 28, 43, 56, 82, 84, 130, 180, 191, 201, 274, 294, 298, 329, 346, 368, 387, 395, 445, 486–487, 502, 518, 521–523, 532, 535–536, 547, 549
Samaritans, 20, 27, 208, 211, 213, 551
sanctify, sanctification, 74, 246, 421
Sanhedrin, 71, 245, 324, 511, 514–518, 545

Satan, 78–79, 82–88, 90–91, 97, 151, 188, 249, 253–254, 256, 259–260, 268, 270, 334–336, 338–339, 509, 567
scribe, 57, 90, 98–99, 105, 111, 113–114, 125, 129, 152, 156, 165, 174–178, 182–183, 187–188, 190, 216, 240, 273, 301, 323, 344, 389–390, 408, 436, 449–458, 533
secret, secrecy, 52, 57, 80, 86, 123–125, 128–129, 132, 134, 137, 141, 200–201, 203, 205, 250, 261, 264, 266, 269, 273, 280, 328, 335, 339, 406, 438, 474, 483, 485–486, 490, 505, 560
secular, 245, 310, 353, 378, 439, 476
seed, 29, 54, 158, 261–263, 267–271, 273, 275, 347, 350–351, 355, 465
sermon, 18–19, 21–23, 27, 34, 37–38, 56–57, 65, 76, 90, 96–99, 101–103, 105, 107, 111–114, 118, 126–130, 133, 137–138, 140–143, 150, 152–155, 157, 159, 161–162, 165, 172, 174, 210–212, 214, 217–219, 231, 236, 248, 258, 264, 266–268, 308, 346, 355, 358, 367, 373, 378, 405, 410, 442, 449–452, 456–458, 560, 565–566, 568
serpent, 259, 338, 508
servant, 72–73, 121, 133, 160, 165–168, 209, 238, 244–245, 255, 262, 271, 315, 357, 367–368, 374, 394, 398–399, 418–420, 426–427, 431, 447, 464–465, 477, 479, 499, 511, 515, 529, 547
sex, 47, 70, 195, 302, 376, 382, 401–402
sexual immorality, 110, 300, 309, 372, 376
sexuality, 195–196
shame, 121, 201, 279, 359, 365, 399, 402, 412, 425, 465, 442, 514–515, 517, 521–524, 543, 555
sheep, 20, 27–28, 30, 34, 36, 48, 59, 61, 104, 153–154, 166–167, 208, 210–211, 213–221, 230, 238, 242, 244, 251–252, 257, 265, 277–278, 293, 311–312, 315–316, 324, 356, 361–366, 385, 401, 405, 465, 477–482, 489, 495, 498, 501, 507, 517, 522–524, 551, 565, 567
Shema, 442
shepherd, 28, 52, 54, 58–61, 68, 208, 210–211, 214, 219, 221, 244, 252, 277, 293, 313, 316, 361, 363–364, 366, 401, 465, 477, 495, 498, 501–502, 517
sign, 28–30, 32, 55, 58, 61, 65–66, 69, 71–72, 74, 89–90, 153–154, 187, 202, 211, 217, 230, 236, 241, 250, 254–257, 278, 283, 301, 309, 312, 316, 322–324, 329, 331–332, 340, 348, 352, 358, 370, 377, 384, 411, 413, 415, 436, 456, 462–463, 467–473, 475–477, 485, 494, 501, 517, 520, 533, 544, 546, 549–551, 558
simple, 21, 27, 54, 58, 67, 112, 118, 128, 132, 147, 154, 164, 204, 220, 231, 246, 266, 292, 325, 331, 341, 352, 354–355, 425, 438, 519, 545, 568
sin, sinner, 21, 30, 35, 51, 56, 59, 64, 67, 70, 75, 80, 83, 86, 91, 107, 122, 124, 128–131, 137, 151, 166, 179, 184–196, 198 207, 219, 228–230, 235–236, 249, 252, 254, 263–264, 272, 284–285, 294, 304, 341, 344–345, 356–358, 362–368, 375, 378–379, 384, 398, 402, 414, 416, 424, 444, 454–455, 469, 476, 484, 486, 491, 494–497, 501, 504, 508, 519, 521, 523, 525, 529–531, 535–536, 538, 552–553
sister, 41, 47–48, 74, 109, 116, 122, 219, 234, 250, 258, 276, 280, 307, 346, 356–358, 362–367, 370, 379, 381–382, 387, 466, 482, 497, 568
slave, 75, 80, 91, 97, 122, 145–146, 151, 185, 242, 309, 360–361, 367–369, 373–374, 386, 394, 397, 399, 401, 453, 476, 478–479, 499, 506, 514, 519, 543, 557, 565
snake, 136, 208, 259, 448–449
social, 55, 65, 74, 92, 102, 116, 124–126, 131–134, 192, 199, 203, 213, 242, 251, 279, 359, 384, 386, 401, 420, 422, 435, 444, 446, 451, 459–460, 517, 522, 524, 542
Sodom and Gomorrah, 208, 215, 223, 230, 235, 255, 385
Son of David, 36, 50, 56, 188, 197, 202–204, 207, 249, 251, 311, 313–314, 316, 326, 359, 394, 404–407, 411, 552

Son of God, 17, 28, 31, 42, 56, 78, 82–83, 86, 91, 93, 171, 173, 288–292, 296–297, 299, 325, 327, 336, 343, 444, 455, 504, 511, 516, 532, 536, 539–541, 545, 551, 568
Son of Man, 34, 50, 171, 173–175, 184, 190, 209, 211–213, 215, 223–224, 229, 238, 241, 243, 245, 249–250, 256, 263, 322, 334–335, 338, 340–341, 347, 359, 381, 388, 394, 463–465, 470–473, 475–479, 483–484, 486, 489, 492–493, 499, 504–505, 511, 521, 531, 552, 554
spirit, 11, 29, 95, 98, 100, 102–104, 107, 140, 159, 160–161, 164, 208, 218, 250–251, 253, 293, 295, 346, 384, 392, 498, 503–504, 540, 548, 562
spouse, 373–374
star, 41, 48, 51–52, 54–55, 57–58, 61, 106, 132, 463, 472, 476
stone, 57, 64, 70–71, 74, 77–78, 82, 84–86, 96, 106, 136, 177–178, 205, 251, 328–329, 338–339, 419, 427–428, 432, 448, 456, 460, 462, 467, 485, 522–523, 528, 530, 540, 551, 556, 558–559, 561–562
structure, 31–33, 43, 268, 361, 373, 375, 409, 467
student, 16, 21, 89–90, 147, 195–196, 209, 232, 285, 319–321, 325–326, 437–438, 457, 512–513, 537–538
stumble, 93, 109–110, 222, 225–226, 329, 356, 362–363, 387
suffer, suffering, 33, 59, 63, 80, 83, 95, 100, 103–104, 122, 131, 160, 162, 166, 217, 231, 233–234, 275, 277, 285, 311, 313, 315, 318–319, 333–339, 344, 346–347, 359, 386, 398–399, 402, 408, 455, 460, 481, 485, 490, 497, 502–503, 508, 510, 515, 517, 524, 526, 529, 541–542, 547, 552–553, 567
swear, 110–111, 115, 118–120, 331, 343, 355, 447–449, 454, 514, 516, 520
symbol, 20, 46, 68–69, 73, 126, 272, 297, 377, 408, 411, 413–414, 416, 425, 437, 472–474, 501, 533, 549–550
synagogue, 20, 25, 28, 95–96, 113, 123, 126–127, 129, 197–203, 208–209, 212, 219, 238, 243, 251, 276, 279, 447–448, 458–459
synoptic, 19, 172, 243
Syria, 25–26, 95, 97, 314

talent, 77, 367
tax, 24, 347–349, 352–355, 433, 435–440, 443, 445
tax collector/farmer, 36, 43, 110, 174, 184, 187, 190, 192, 194–196, 208, 223, 228, 349, 352–355, 357, 360–362, 365–366, 418, 425, 428
teacher, teaching, 16–18, 24, 27, 30–32, 34–37, 51, 70, 75, 79, 90, 95–101, 109, 111–115, 117–120, 125–126, 130, 134, 142–143, 145, 149, 151–153, 155, 158–159, 164–165, 171, 173–174, 184, 190, 199–200, 208–210, 212–213, 215, 241–242, 247–248, 250–251, 255, 263–267, 270, 273, 276, 279, 285, 291, 294–295, 300, 306–308, 319–322, 324–326, 329, 334–335, 337, 347, 355, 361–364, 368, 373–380, 382, 385, 389, 394, 397, 399, 405, 411–414, 418, 420, 433–434, 436–437, 439–441, 444, 447–448, 450–451, 453–457, 459, 469, 472, 479, 483, 499, 511–512, 517, 534, 539, 545, 557, 565, 568
Tefillah, 127
tempt, temptation, 45–46, 50, 78–84, 86–87, 90–94, 102, 117, 123, 130–131, 133, 159, 190, 254, 256, 259, 285, 289, 338, 360, 391, 475, 498, 503–504, 542, 545, 559
Ten Commandments, 113, 177, 246, 305, 383, 385, 442
test, 55, 78, 80–81, 83–88, 91, 93, 130, 164, 206, 256, 289, 295, 322–323, 325, 327, 338, 372, 374, 386, 434, 441, 469, 503, 513, 545–546
theology, 22, 42, 71, 129, 332, 437, 441, 445
tithe, 236, 450, 453, 481
Torah, 23, 31–32, 84, 90, 107, 115, 185, 200, 247, 273
tradition, 18–20, 22–23, 25, 47, 89, 107, 114, 124, 127, 151, 191, 195, 219, 229–230,

241, 248, 258, 284, 301, 303, 305–309, 323, 375, 411, 452, 470–471, 476, 497
transfiguration, 330, 336–337, 341, 359, 560
transform, 33
treasure, 52, 58, 125, 135–137, 139–141, 144–148, 255, 263, 266–268, 272–275, 373, 379–380, 386–387, 392, 564
trial, 121, 129, 155, 343, 517, 529, 533, 537, 545–546, 549
tribulation, 130
trinity, 43
truth, 19, 62, 118, 157, 168, 198, 266, 286–287, 329, 365, 371, 424, 431, 433, 443, 473, 508–509, 514, 516–517, 521, 537, 541–542, 544, 553
twelve, 16, 30, 34, 36, 45–46, 59, 90–91, 104, 197, 200, 208, 210–220, 225, 239, 242, 265, 267, 277, 281–283, 285, 287, 289, 292, 295–297, 313, 315, 317–319, 324–326, 328, 330, 338, 349–351, 358–359, 361, 369, 381–382, 384–385, 387–389, 394, 396–397, 399, 405, 413, 424, 443, 468, 470, 483–485, 489–491, 499, 502–503, 512, 565, 568
typology, 20, 31, 98
Tyre and Sidon, 223, 230, 255, 311–312, 314–315

unclean, 36, 68, 70, 124, 142, 151, 162–165, 169, 177, 199–201, 230, 242, 253, 303, 306, 448, 453, 531, 550
understand, 23, 30, 86, 113–115, 142, 158, 168, 182, 190, 196, 206, 224, 231, 246, 261–262, 265–267, 272–275, 290, 295, 300, 305, 322, 325, 329, 341, 344–345, 349–350, 353, 369, 406, 416, 436, 450, 455–456, 460, 462, 464, 487, 504, 512, 536, 553, 565
universal, 335

vineyard, 381, 389, 393, 418–419, 425–428, 431
violence, 118–119, 185, 194, 222, 227, 386, 445, 506, 552
virgin, 47, 51, 56, 464, 478
virtue, 98, 101, 175, 451
vow, 110, 113–115, 117–118, 152, 182, 304–305, 331, 377

war, 41–42, 54, 62, 86, 90–92, 113, 119, 163, 220, 234, 251, 253, 270, 283, 323, 342, 401–402, 421–422, 430, 435, 455, 462, 471, 474, 499, 507, 509, 553, 557
wealth, 74, 262, 373, 380, 383, 386–387, 392, 422, 464
wedding, 24, 419–420, 428–429, 464
wilderness, 28, 46, 59, 64, 66–69, 76–78, 80–85, 87–88, 91, 222, 224, 284, 314, 463
wine, 185, 187, 191, 199, 400, 426, 453, 492–497, 535, 539–540, 544, 548, 551
wisdom, wise, 31, 58, 61–62, 81, 99, 101, 107, 118, 142, 147, 149–151, 154–157, 164, 175, 223–224, 229, 231–235, 237, 244, 250, 256, 259, 269, 271–276, 279–280, 288, 338, 375, 395, 411, 425, 464, 476–477, 501, 536, 540
witness, 30, 68, 85, 180, 206–207, 209, 212, 235, 283, 329, 341–342, 344, 357, 359, 378, 391, 469, 471, 486, 511, 513–516, 518, 544, 558, 561, 565
woe, 223, 230, 356, 447–448, 484, 493–494, 531
woman, women, 17, 27, 36, 43–44, 47–48, 50, 63, 74, 96, 108–110, 116–117, 120–122, 128, 163, 165–166, 169–170, 178, 195–201, 222, 231, 234, 241–242, 259, 262, 272, 277, 283, 303, 306, 309, 311–317, 319, 326, 336, 372, 374–376, 378, 384, 396, 402, 433, 435, 441, 462–463, 482–483, 487–491, 496, 537, 540, 542, 551, 556–565, 568
word, 17, 21, 23, 37, 42, 57–58, 63, 75–76, 78, 80, 82, 84–86, 88, 90, 97–98, 101–102, 106–107, 111–114, 120, 125–126, 130, 140, 147, 152, 154, 160–161, 165, 167, 170, 175–177, 179, 188, 190, 201–202, 221, 234–235, 244, 249, 251–252, 257–260, 262, 264–265, 267, 280, 283, 288, 293–294, 300–301, 304–305, 308–309, 311, 316, 327, 340, 360, 372–373, 375–376, 398, 413–414,

421, 424, 429, 434, 439, 449, 458, 469–470, 485, 495, 506–507, 512, 532, 546, 562–563, 565–566, 568
work, works, 16–19, 21–27, 30–32, 34–35, 42, 45–47, 55, 62, 70, 79, 87, 89, 91, 97, 101–103, 105, 113, 117, 125, 139–140, 143, 145, 147–148, 158, 166, 168, 170, 179, 181, 194, 204–206, 210–213, 220–221, 223, 225, 230–231, 234–236, 239–240, 242–244, 248, 252–254, 257–260, 264–265, 267, 270–273, 275–276, 280–282, 286, 297–298, 315, 320, 324, 331–332, 335, 338, 346, 364–365, 374–375, 379, 381, 384, 389–391, 393, 412, 416, 418, 425, 428–429, 431, 440, 458, 460, 465, 476, 480–482, 507, 527–428, 538, 542, 553, 559, 567
worry, 50, 130, 135, 137–138, 145–147, 209, 214, 226, 281, 325, 350, 352
worship, 20, 51–52, 56–57, 63, 74, 76, 78, 84, 87–88, 91–92, 116, 121, 137, 161, 167, 186, 219, 236, 248, 286, 292, 297, 300, 304, 308, 345–346, 369–370, 409, 413–414, 416, 440, 442, 476, 481, 561–562, 567

Yahweh (YHWH), 31, 36, 56, 73, 84, 534, 544, 545
Yom Kippur, 191
yoke, 223, 232–234, 237, 239–240, 246, 351, 535

zeal, 174, 409, 443, 548
Zechariah, 66, 406, 413, 448, 455, 507, 528, 532
Zealot, 25, 208, 227, 535

Author Index

Allison, D. C., 18, 20, 23–25, 37, 42, 44, 46, 57–58, 60, 68, 71–73, 81, 83, 87–90, 98, 100–101, 103–105, 114, 119–120, 127–130, 138–140, 143, 150, 152, 154–155, 162, 165–167, 172, 174, 176, 179, 187–188, 191–192, 194, 203, 211–213, 217, 228–229, 231–233, 239–240, 242, 244–245, 254, 265, 268, 270, 273, 281, 283–284, 290, 295, 298, 303–304, 316, 318, 328, 331, 336, 339, 345, 353, 363–365, 367–368, 375–376, 382–383, 385, 387, 395, 398–399, 406, 408, 411–412, 422–424, 426, 428–429, 437–438, 441–443, 451, 457, 468, 470–473, 475–477, 479, 487–491, 493, 500, 502–503, 506–508, 515–518, 520, 529, 531, 533–535, 543–545, 547, 549–551, 558–559, 562–563, 566–568
Anderson, C. A., 537
Augustine, 46, 131, 155, 233, 367

Bauckham, R., 23, 26, 34
Bailey, K. E., 58, 156, 267, 391, 393, 427
Barth, G., 172
Betz, H. D., 98, 128
Blomberg, C. L., 18–19, 37, 173, 270, 424, 439, 471, 488, 490, 535, 567
Bock, D. L., 1, 174
Boda, M. J., 73
Bonhoeffer, D., 117, 143, 345
Borg, M. J., 165
Bornkamm, G., 172–173
Brown, J. K., 15, 21, 31, 35, 37
Brown, R. E., 43, 45, 47, 58–59, 233, 501, 502, 515, 518, 520, 527, 530–532, 534, 541, 547, 550
Bruner, F. D., 195, 202, 214, 217, 227–228, 235, 245, 270, 272, 290, 308, 314–315, 318, 327–328, 338, 344–345, 361, 385, 401, 426, 429, 438, 451, 473, 475–476, 486–489, 493, 521, 535, 541, 544, 549, 560, 562–563
Burridge, R. A., 21–22, 26

Capes, D. B., 21, 69, 290
Camp, L. C., 446
Campbell, K. M., 116
Carter, W., 87, 353–354, 373
Chapman, D. W., 116
Chilton, B. D., 113–114, 172
Chrysologus, P., 192
Chrysostom, J., 49, 103, 112, 220, 225, 228, 241, 314, 324, 342, 366, 475, 493–494, 542, 549
Clement of Alexandria, 177
Cleveland, A., 522–523
Cyril of Alexandria, 389
Cohick, L., 14, 162
Cullmann, O., 129

Dauermann, S., 220
Davies, W. D., 18, 20, 23–25, 37, 42, 44, 46, 57–58, 60, 68, 71–73, 81, 83, 87–90, 98, 100–101, 103–105, 114, 119–120, 127–130, 138–140, 143, 152, 154–155, 162, 165–167, 172, 174, 176, 179, 187–188, 191–192, 194, 203, 211–213, 217, 228–229, 231–233, 239–240, 242, 244–245, 254, 265, 268, 270, 273, 281, 283–284, 290, 295, 298, 303–304, 316, 318, 328, 331, 336, 339, 345, 353, 363–365, 367–368, 375–376, 382–383, 385, 387, 395, 398–399, 406, 408, 411–412, 422–424, 426, 428–429, 437–438, 441–443, 451, 457, 468, 470–471, 473, 475–477, 479, 487–491, 493, 500,

502–503, 506–508, 515–518, 520, 529, 531, 533–535, 543–545, 547, 549–551, 558–559, 562–563, 566–568
Denton, M. L., 247
DeSilva, D. A., 303
Dodd, C. H., 168
Donaldson, T. L., 560, 567
Donne, J., 455, 557
Duke, P. D., 544
Dunn, J. D. G., 27, 30, 89, 162, 224, 235–236, 338

Evans, C. A., 18–19, 24–25, 191, 215, 228, 374, 385, 423, 428, 467, 495, 501, 507, 520, 531, 543, 560

Ferguson, E., 70
Fischer, P., 284
Foreman, J., 106
Foster, R., 67
France, R. T., 16, 24, 33, 38, 60, 66, 83, 89–90, 97, 102, 104, 114, 119, 127, 130, 153–155, 162–163, 165–166, 172, 180, 191, 215, 229, 232–233, 243, 253, 255, 266, 270, 280, 283, 292, 304, 306, 314, 323, 326, 328, 336–337, 342, 350–352, 354, 359, 365, 376, 390, 398, 406–407, 409–410, 412–413, 422–423, 426, 429, 437–438, 440, 452–453, 457, 471, 473, 477, 479, 487, 491, 503–504, 516, 519–520, 532–534, 544, 546, 548, 558–559, 563, 566
Fredriksen, P., 340

Garland, D. E., 17, 37, 48, 56, 72, 83, 97, 101–103, 105, 115, 117–118, 126, 156, 166, 174–175, 188–189, 212, 214, 231, 233, 244, 246, 251, 256, 268, 272, 284, 295, 314–316, 328, 336, 349, 366, 373, 386, 396, 410–411, 413, 424, 429, 438, 440–441, 452, 456, 479, 503, 530–531, 548–550, 560, 563
Gilmore, M., 106
Goldingay, J., 73
Green, J. B., 15, 37, 386, 452
Gregory the Great, 83, 90
Guelich, R. A., 114
Gurtner, D. M., 21, 550
Gushee, D. P., 114

Hagner, D. A., 47
Hanson, J. S., 533
Hays, R. B., 37, 119
Hedrick, C. W., 268
Held, H. J., 172
Hengel, M., 89, 179
Hill, W., 401
Hippolytus, 438
Holmes, M. W., 151–152
Horsley, R. A., 439, 533
Howell, D. B., 34

Jeremias, J., 129
Jerome, 89, 475
Josephus, 54, 66, 71, 125, 163–164, 283, 340, 408, 438, 458, 534, 551

Keener, C. S., 18, 23–25, 30, 38, 48, 57–58, 68, 71, 73, 82–83, 87–88, 90, 101, 115–116, 118, 129, 131, 143, 153, 155, 163, 166–167, 173, 175–176, 188, 195, 201–202, 205–207, 214, 217, 227–228, 232–233, 244, 254, 270–271, 281, 289, 294, 314, 316, 328, 331, 338, 349, 363, 367, 373, 376, 388, 396, 398, 409–410, 412–413, 423, 429, 438, 440, 442, 473, 477, 479, 485, 488, 491, 493–494, 504, 517, 520, 530–531, 543–544, 548–550, 564, 567–568
Kingsbury, J. D., 33, 37
Kupp, D. D., 560

Levine, A-J., 268
Lewis, C. S., 91–93
Lofaro, M. A., 49
Louth, A., 274
Luz, U., 21, 28, 34, 37, 40, 42, 82–83, 88–90, 97, 100–101, 105, 111, 114–115, 129, 139, 142, 152–155, 167–168, 172, 174, 180, 187, 191, 202, 212–214, 231,

242–243, 245, 253–254, 256–257, 266, 268, 272–275, 284, 290, 297, 303, 305, 318, 327–328, 336–337, 350, 352, 360–365, 368, 376, 390, 401, 410–411, 413, 424, 427–429, 436, 438–439, 441, 450, 452, 455–456, 471, 473–475, 478–479, 485, 489, 491, 493, 502–503, 506, 513–514, 516, 520, 528, 530, 547–550, 554, 558–560, 565–566

Maclean, N., 332
Magness, J., 70, 178
Malina, B. J., 116, 124, 128, 140, 164, 181, 279, 359, 377, 384, 391, 406, 420, 435, 486, 493, 517
Martinez, F. G., 342
McConville, J. G., 73
McKnight, S., 11, 14, 19, 21, 90, 98–99, 102–103, 105, 107, 111, 118, 126–127, 129–130, 140–141, 143, 150, 152, 154, 157, 213, 266, 416, 453, 568
Metzger, B. M., 129, 349, 533
Meyer, B. F., 329

Neusner, J., 113–114, 240, 246–247, 303
Nolland, J., 22, 24, 30, 33, 72, 83, 87–88, 100, 105, 119, 129, 131, 142, 144, 152–153, 155, 162, 198–199, 232, 239, 242, 245, 253–254, 265–266, 270, 273, 279, 284, 304, 314, 339, 341, 350, 352, 366, 376–377, 388–389, 397, 411–413, 426–429, 437, 441, 452–453, 458, 468–469, 476, 491, 503–505, 515, 519, 531, 533, 535, 545–546, 550, 563

O'Brien, B. J., 274

Pennington, J. T., 67
Perrin, N., 15, 37, 386, 407, 411
Peterson, E. H., 445
Philo, 543
Pickup, M., 113
Powell, M. A., 157, 415

Reed, J. L., 89
Reeves, A., 11, 555
Reeves, R., 21, 174, 290, 378, 524, 538
Richards. E. R., 21, 274, 290
Rohrbaugh, R. L., 116, 128, 164, 181, 279, 377, 391, 406, 420, 486, 493, 517
Rowe, J., 294
Rudolph, D., 220
Runesson, A., 200, 243

Sanders, E. P., 125, 162–163, 189, 214, 303, 309, 411, 436
Schaff, P., 49
Schweitzer, A., 338, 439
Scott, B. B., 270–271, 390–391
Scott, N., 317
Silberman, N. A., 439
Simonetti, M., 46, 83, 90, 115, 131, 177, 192, 216, 367, 386, 389, 475, 535, 548
Sleasman, M. J., 537
Smith, C., 113, 247, 274
Smith, H. E., 294
Snodgrass, K. R., 267, 390, 429
Song, C–S., 8, 275
Stanton, G. N., 21–22
Stassen, G. H., 114
Strauss, F. S., 336
Sunshine, L., 567

Talbert, C. H., 56, 83, 102, 141, 233, 267, 314, 328, 336–337, 342, 373, 388, 410, 428, 451, 477, 479, 490, 550
ten Boom, Corrie, 234
Tertullian, 172
Theodore of Mopsuestia, 82
Twelftree, G. H., 188
Turner, D. L., 68, 71, 101–102, 115, 126, 143, 151–152, 180, 212, 227, 229, 254, 256–257, 268, 270, 289, 341, 359, 361, 364, 388, 395, 409, 414, 424–425, 427–428, 435, 440, 443, 472, 487, 490, 541, 567

Vanhoozer, K. J., 537
Vinson, R. B., 126
Volf, M., 193–194

Walton, J. H., 474
White, K. D., 270
Willard, D., 119
Willitts, J., 11, 21, 61, 214, 220, 313, 316
Wilson, A. N., 8, 92
Woodley, M., 83
Wright, N. T., 406, 444–445, 473